THE HISTORY OF
WISCONSIN

THE HISTORY OF
WISCONSIN

VOLUME II
The Civil War Era, 1848–1873

RICHARD N. CURRENT

WILLIAM FLETCHER THOMPSON
General Editor

1976
STATE HISTORICAL SOCIETY OF WISCONSIN
MADISON

THE HISTORY OF WISCONSIN
is a contribution of the State Historical
Society of Wisconsin to the American Revolution
Bicentennial celebration.

Smith, Alice Elizabeth, 1896–
    The history of Wisconsin.
    Vol. 2 by R. N. Current.
Bibliography: v. 1, p. 685–731; v. 2, p. 601–632
CONTENTS: v. 1. From exploration to statehood.—
v. 2. The Civil War era, 1848–1873.
1. Wisconsin—History. I. Current, Richard Nelson,
joint author.
F581.S64   977.5   72-12941
ISBN 0-87020-122-0

To the memory of my mother's mother
INDIANA CHRISTIANSEN, *nee* OLSEN (1864–1922)
Who was brought from Norway in 1865
And who lies buried in Bruce, Wisconsin.
Her given name reflects the America-dreaming that led
her parents to emigrate the year after she was born.

And to the future of my daughter's daughter
MARIA RINTZ
Who was born in Milwaukee in 1965
And who is very much alive in Racine.
She inherits the aspirations of her Norwegian, English,
Scottish, Irish, German, and Polish ancestors.

PREFACE

THOSE WHO KNOW Wisconsin and its history can hardly avoid having both a respectful and an affectionate regard for the state. They are not likely to be put off by an account that undertakes to tell the story *wie es eigentlich gewesen ist*—as it actually happened. Wisconsin during the period this volume covers, the first generation of statehood, was still largely in a frontier stage of development. More than almost any other state at the time, it had an ethnically diverse and divided society. The central theme of the book, insofar as it has one, must be the struggle to subdue and civilize the wilderness, with the bad as well as the good implications of the civilizing process. A related theme is that of antagonism and adjustment among the various elements of the population. In telling the story, it has been necessary to touch upon scandals in business and politics (even a sex scandal), prejudice and discrimination, unpatriotic acts, instances of mob violence resulting from social tensions, and other such unedifying matters. But it has also been a pleasant duty to record the much more numerous cases of public spirit, of heroism and sacrifice, of hard work and achievement. The emphasis is on the positive, the constructive, simply because that is the essential truth of the story.

A fairly thick volume such as this one might seem like more than enough paper and ink for only a quarter-century of the history of but a single state. Yet in writing it I have been acutely conscious all along that I have been relating merely a small part of the rich and varied life of the people of Wisconsin during the period. For lack of space, I have had to forgo even so much as a reference to many men and women and many events that are interesting and important in themselves. The frequency of mention of names is not necessarily a measure of their intrinsic importance in my sight; often a person is cited or quoted because the person well represents the point of view or the activity of a large number of others.

When referring to members of foreign nationality groups I use the terms "German," "Irish," "Norwegian," and the like— rather than "German-American," "Irish-American," "Norwegian-American," etc.—and reserve the term "American" for the people of older native stock. There are two reasons for this: it is less cumbersome, and it conforms to the actual usage of the time. It is not intended to be invidious. When I deal with ethnic groups, I consider the settlers from New England, New York, and other states as constituting one of the groups, no less than the immigrants from any of the European countries. I am aware of my own biases of birth and upbringing, and I have certainly tried to counteract them.

To some extent the book is derived from original sources, and it contains information not to be found in other writings on Wisconsin history. For the most part, however, it is based upon the previous studies of a large number of scholars, as the footnotes and the bibliographical essay indicate. I am beholden to all those writers. More immediately, I am deeply obligated to those who served at one time or another as my research assistants and who made it feasible to exploit the vast array of primary and secondary materials—Margaret Walsh, David McLeod, and especially John O. Holzhueter. Above all, I am indebted to the general editor of the series, William Fletcher Thompson, for his overall encouragement and guidance and for the rigorous standards of historical scholarship that he imposed. I join him in thanking the members of his staff—Dale Treleven, Jeanne Delgado, and George Roeder—who assisted him in the meticulous checking of every quotation and every fact. Without his and their prodigious efforts to rid the manuscript of error, the book would have contained misstatements too numerous and too horrendous to contemplate.

RICHARD N. CURRENT

Lake Delton, Wisconsin

CONTRIBUTORS

THE STATE HISTORICAL SOCIETY OF WISCONSIN

THE UNIVERSITY OF WISCONSIN

WESTERN PUBLISHING COMPANY, INC.

FIRST WISCONSIN FOUNDATION, INC.

THE JOURNAL COMPANY

THE NORTHWESTERN MUTUAL LIFE INSURANCE COMPANY

PABST BREWERIES FOUNDATION

SCHLITZ FOUNDATION, INC.

APPLETON COATED FOUNDATION, INC.

APPLETON WIRE WORKS CORP.

BANTA COMPANY FOUNDATION, INC.

BERGSTROM FOUNDATION

THE FALK CORPORATION

FOX RIVER PAPER CO.

KIMBERLY-CLARK FOUNDATION, INC.

THE MARINE FOUNDATION, INC.

MARSHALL & ILSLEY BANK FOUNDATION, INC.

THILMANY PULP AND PAPER COMPANY

WISCONSIN ELECTRIC POWER COMPANY

THE JOHNSON'S WAX FUND, INC.

MILLER HIGH LIFE FOUNDATION, INC.

NEKOOSA-EDWARDS FOUNDATION INCORPORATED

WISCONSIN MICHIGAN POWER COMPANY

WISCONSIN NATURAL GAS COMPANY

WISCONSIN PUBLIC SERVICE CORPORATION

CHARLES W. WRIGHT FOUNDATION OF BADGER METER, INC.

CONTENTS

ILLUSTRATIONS

Following pages 128, 304, and 432 are selections of
pictures from the third quarter of the nineteenth
century. Unless otherwise noted, the illustrations
are from the Iconographic Collection of the State
Historical Society of Wisconsin.

MAPS

Designed by
NANCY STROVER

Prepared by
The University of Wisconsin Cartographic Laboratory

Note on the Maps

All statistics for the maps are from the federal census reports for 1850 and 1870, with the exception of the four election maps. Data for these maps are from the following record series in the WSA: Election Return Statements of the County and State Boards of Canvassers, 1847–1914, Series 140, Records of the Executive Department; Election Return Statements of the County Boards of Canvassers, 1836——, Series 211, Records of the Secretary of State; Certificates of the State Board of Canvassers, 1848——, Series 213, Records of the Secretary of State; and Election Return Statements of the County Boards of Canvassers, 1848——, Series 214, Records of the Secretary of State. When vote totals differed among presidential electors for the same candidate, the largest total was used. The map on page 18 showing the proposed Milwaukee harbor straight cut, 1854, is adapted from a map, "Plan and Section of the North Cut at Milwaukee," in *Senate Documents,* 33 Cong., 2 sess., no. 1 (serial 748).

THE HISTORY OF
WISCONSIN

Note on Citations

DWB	*Dictionary of Wisconsin Biography.* Madison, 1960.
SHSW	State Historical Society of Wisconsin.
Wis. Hist. Colls.	*Collections of the State Historical Society of Wisconsin.* 21 vols., Madison, 1855–1915.
WMH	*Wisconsin Magazine of History.*
WSA	Wisconsin State Archives.

Unless otherwise indicated, all manuscripts, broadsides, and pamphlets cited are in the collections of the State Historical Society of Wisconsin.

1

Opening the Way

W ISCONSIN had been a state for less than a week when, on June 5, 1848, Governor Nelson Dewey delivered his first message to the new legislature. The governor, a rather short man with a colorless personality, had no gift for public speaking, yet he grew almost eloquent as he turned to the state's present condition and future prospects. "Wisconsin possesses the natural elements, fostered by the judicious system of legislation," the governor said, "to become one of the most populous and prosperous States of the American Union." Among the natural elements, he mentioned not only the fertile soil, the mineral wealth, and the manufacturing facilities but also the "commercial advantages," which he said were as good as or better than any other inland state could boast. He concluded: "It is under the most favorable auspices that the State of Wisconsin has taken her position among the families of States."[1]

The governor had touched upon a familiar theme—that Wis-

[1] Dewey is quoted in C. W. Butterfield, "History of Wisconsin," in Western Historical Company, *The History of Sauk County, Wisconsin* . . . (Chicago, 1880), 54. On Dewey, see Alexander M. Thomson, *A Political History of Wisconsin* (Milwaukee, 1900), 69–72.

consin possessed a unique geographical destiny. This could be
seen, boosters said, from a mere glance at the map. The new
state lay right between the country's two great natural systems
of transportation, the one leading eastward to the Atlantic
Ocean by way of the Great Lakes, and the other southward to
the Gulf of Mexico by way of the mighty Mississippi and its
tributaries. One of these tributaries, the Wisconsin, ran close
by the headwaters of the Fox, which flowed in the opposite
direction, emptying into Lake Michigan. To an enthusiastic
map viewer, the Fox–Wisconsin alignment seemed like a bonus
added to nature's already bounteous gifts, promising as it did
a waterway that would go diagonally across the state and connect the two great transportation systems. Before the promised
connection could be made, however, much work would have
to be done. And lake-port harbors would have to be improved
before full advantage could be taken of the Great Lakes route.

To realize her destiny, Wisconsin could not depend on waterways alone. She needed improved means of land transportation to supplement them. For some twenty years, railroads had
been under construction in the older states. Originally the
lines were rather short, mere links between water routes, but
the time was approaching when the segments might be joined
so as to make a continuous line from the Atlantic to the Mississippi, and there was beginning to be talk of building railroads from the Mississippi and from Lake Superior all the
way to the Pacific Coast. Surely these transcontinental lines
would contribute to Wisconsin's greatness if the state itself
were traversed by rails that would bring through it the produce of the developing trans-Mississippi West.

There was no time to be lost. "If we are not early in the
field, others will be in possession," one Wisconsin booster
warned. "The streams of industry, trade, and commerce are
passing into Chicago, like mountain torrents. The sagacity and
enterprising spirit of her citizens have commenced to draw
some of these streams from our state, and they will inevitably
succeed in injuring our best interests, if we neglect to tap
them at their source, and convey them through the legitimate

channels of the state." This danger aroused the particular concern of Milwaukeeans.[2]

No doubt Wisconsin needed "internal improvements" of various kinds, but these would be expensive, and capital was scarce in the new state. Its constitution prohibited state expenditures for such improvements and prevented the creation of a public debt of more than $100,000 for any purpose. These restrictions appeared sensible enough in view of the earlier experience of some other states, notably Illinois and Indiana, which had borrowed and spent for extravagant canal and railroad schemes and then suffered financial disaster in consequence of the Panic of 1837. Still, the Wisconsin fundamental law stood as an obstacle to those who sought easy funds for improving transportation.

Unless the state somehow found means for improvements, its amazing development might slacken. Growth had been rapid indeed between 1842 and 1848—from fewer than 45,000 people to nearly 250,000 in only six years. When admitted to the Union, Wisconsin already was ahead of a half-dozen of the other twenty-nine states in population. The newest state presented a variegated scene, ranging from well-tilled fields and budding cities to primeval wilderness.[3]

[2]

Approaching Wisconsin by way of the Straits of Mackinac and Lake Michigan, a steamship passenger in 1848 could make out the edge of a dense forest. As the ship proceeded southward,

[2] John Gregory, *Industrial Resources of Wisconsin* (Milwaukee, 1855), 18, 26–28. The quotation is on p. 26. See also Gunnar J. Malmin, ed. and trans., *America in the Forties: The Letters of Ole Munch Raeder* (Minneapolis, 1929), 90; and Balthasar H. Meyer, "A History of Early Railroad Legislation in Wisconsin," in *Collections of the State Historical Society of Wisconsin* (21 vols., Madison, 1855–1915), 14: 256, hereinafter cited as *Wis. Hist. Colls.*

[3] Horace A. Tenney, "Census of Wisconsin from the Year 1836 to August 1860, Inclusive," a broadside compiled for the *Wisconsin State Journal*, certified by the Assistant Secretary of State, and bound in a collection of broadsides and pamphlets entitled *Census of Wisconsin, 1836–1880*, in the SHSW; *Seventh Census of the United States, 1850: Compendium*, 97.

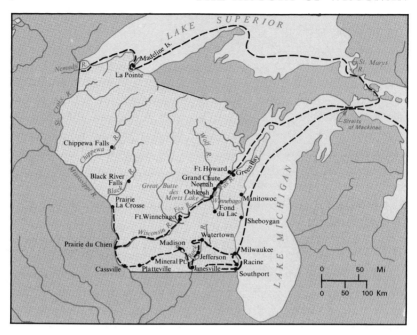

WISCONSIN JOURNEY, 1848

from time to time a stump-filled clearing and a cozy-looking
log cabin came into view, and then the raw village of Manitowoc with its five to six hundred people. Farther down the
coast, the ship put in at Sheboygan, a larger and more developed port, though still primitive enough that Indians wearing blankets stood on the dock to stare at the arrivals.[4]

Between four and six days after setting out from Buffalo,
the ship arrived at Milwaukee, ninety miles short of its final
destination, Chicago. Disembarking at Milwaukee, the main
gateway to Wisconsin, the traveler could find handsome stores

    [4] See Raeder's account of his 1847 trip to Wisconsin in Malmin, ed., *Letters
of Ole Raeder*, 1–5, 10–11. On Manitowoc, see also Samuel Freeman, *The Emigrant's Hand Book and Guide to Wisconsin, Comprising Information Respecting
Agricultural and Manufacturing Employment, Wages, Climate, Population &c.;
Sketch of Milwaukee, The Queen of the Lakes; Its Rise and Progress; Business
and Population; List of Public Officers; With a Full and Accurate Table of
Statistical Information of That and Other Ports on Lake Michigan; Also Table
of Routes from New-York, Boston, &c., to Milwaukee, Racine, and Kenosha;
And Other General Information to Emigrants* (Milwaukee, 1851), 85–86.

and houses, many of them built of cream-colored brick, as well as newly graded and graveled streets, limestone-slab sidewalks, a spacious theater, and many of the other amenities of urban life. The population, over 40 per cent of it German, already numbered over 14,000 and was growing fast.[5]

From Milwaukee a voyage of twenty-five miles to the south would take the traveler to Racine, another wheat port and manufacturing center, a fast-growing city of about 4,000, the second largest in the state. Ten miles farther south was Southport (to be incorporated in 1850 as the city of Kenosha), the third largest at nearly 3,000.[6]

A journey on horseback forty or fifty miles inland would reveal a fairly well settled farming country to the west of Racine and Southport. This undulating land, at the time white settlers first saw it, had not been thickly forested but, like most of the southern half of Wisconsin, had been covered partly by prairies with tall grass and partly by groves of scattered oaks. By 1848, the area that lay within easy hauling distance of the lake ports was mostly under cultivation, except for swamps and meadows that served for pasture. Farmhouses, about a half-mile apart, were nearly all frame buildings, painted white, the original log dwellings having been converted into stables or toolsheds. Here and there, at intervals of several miles, houses clustered to form a village, usually around a milldam. The recently made millponds supplemented the numerous small lakes that the glacier had long ago deposited. All in all, this

---

[5] Fredrika Bremer, *The Homes of the New World: Impressions of America* (2 vols., New York, 1864, 1868), 1: 615–616; Bayrd Still, *Milwaukee: The History of a City* (Madison, 1965), 72, 75, 97–98, 197, 206–207; Kathleen N. Conzen, "'The German Athens': Milwaukee and the Accommodation of Its Immigrants" (doctoral dissertation, University of Wisconsin, 1972), 45–46. Still indicates that the Germans constituted one-third of the total population by 1850, while Conzen, on the basis of a 25 per cent head-of-household sample, concludes that the Germans in 1850 comprised 41 per cent of the total population in Milwaukee and 52 per cent in 1860.

[6] Freeman, *Emigrant's Hand Book,* 81–84. Estimates of mid-1848 population for Racine, Southport, and other places are based in part on the census figures for December 1, 1847, as given in Tenney, "Census of Wisconsin from the Year 1836 to August 1860," and in part on the *Seventh Census of the United States, 1850,* pp. 918–924.

southeastern corner of Wisconsin, though less hilly, looked much like western New York, from which many of the settlers had come and which they were trying to re-create.

Heading northward from Racine, the traveler would enter a very different region, a thick forest of maple, basswood, beech, elm, and oak. At first, in the vicinity of Milwaukee, the clearings were extensive and the farms numerous and highly productive under the careful tillage of their owners, especially the Germans. Only a few miles north, the fields became smaller, the farming methods cruder, and the frame houses fewer. Here agriculture was still in the pioneering stage.[7]

The main route west from Milwaukee, going up and down over moraines and cuestas, passed through heavily wooded country on the way to Watertown. Taking this trip by stage, the traveler would be "shaken, or rather hurled, unmercifully hither and thither upon the new-born roads of Wisconsin," which were "no roads at all, but a succession of hills, and holes, and water-pools, in which first one wheel sank and then the other, while the opposite one stood high up in the air." Watertown, on the Rock River, was a "newly sprung-up, infant town" of about 2,000.[8]

Several miles beyond Watertown the forest began to thin out, and at last the traveler (leaving the stage route and proceeding northwest on horseback) could get a view of "oak openings" still uncut and unplowed. These were "great open spaces set with trees, orchard-like," almost free of underbrush, and covered with "lovely turf." Finally, the openings gave way to a virgin prairie, its tall grass undulating like a sea fringed by a wooded shore. This was the edge of Sun Prairie, ten or more miles wide at the widest, and stretching twenty-five or thirty miles to the west. Much of this prairie had already been turned into farms; the same was true of the prairie-and-oak-openings country that extended to the north, as far as

[7] John T. Curtis, *The Vegetation of Wisconsin: An Ordination of Plant Communities* (Madison, 1959), 103–104; Joseph Schafer, *A History of Agriculture in Wisconsin* (Madison, 1922), 77–80.

[8] Bremer, *Homes of the New World*, 1: 613–614, 628.

the upper Fox River and Lake Winnebago. In that whole area, frame buildings were beginning to replace log structures.[9]

A trip to the south of Watertown, down the valley of the Rock River, would present a similar picture. At Aztalan the traveler might pause to puzzle over the mysterious mounds, and reflect upon the people who built them, and in nearby Jefferson he might catch a glimpse of an Indian or at least a wigwam. Some forty miles below Watertown he would come to Janesville, which with nearly 3,000 people was almost as large as Southport. To the east of Janesville lay Rock Prairie, more than twenty miles long and almost as wide, not yet very thickly populated.[10]

Going back up the Rock River and then turning northwestward, toward Madison, the traveler would encounter "mostly wild, uncultivated land" and "no inhabitants scarcely but Norwegians," some of them living in rude log cabins and others in still ruder "mud houses," partially dug into the ground. He would cross Liberty Prairie, make his way around marshes, and pass First, Second, and Third Lake (Kegonsa, Waubesa, and Monona) before reaching Madison, the state capital, a "pretty little town" of more than a thousand "most beautifully situated" on the narrow isthmus between Third Lake and Fourth (Mendota).[11]

Westward from Madison the stage took the old military road along the prairie-covered Military Ridge. The traveler now entered upon a more rugged terrain than what he had been

[9] These oak openings and prairies still existed in 1855, when Carl Schurz described them in a letter to his wife. Joseph Schafer, ed. and trans., *Intimate Letters of Carl Schurz, 1841–1869* (Madison, 1928), 149–150. Wisconsin oak openings and prairies were also described by many other early visitors, among them Raeder in Malmin, ed., *Letters of Ole Raeder,* 137–138; and Bremer, *Homes of the New World,* 1: 631–633. See also Gregory, *Industrial Resources of Wisconsin,* 150–151.

[10] Schafer, *Agriculture in Wisconsin,* 77–80; Malmin, ed., *Letters of Ole Raeder,* 137–138, 141–142; Tenney, "Census of Wisconsin from the Year 1836 to August 1860."

[11] Bremer, *Homes of the New World,* 1: 628–629, 631–633, described the area as it was in 1850. Charles I. Linsley to his father, May 30, 1852, in Alice E. Smith, ed., "Wisconsin's First Railroad, Linsley Letters, 1852," in the *Wisconsin Magazine of History,* 30 (March, 1947), 348, described the area as it was in 1852; hereinafter cited as *WMH.*

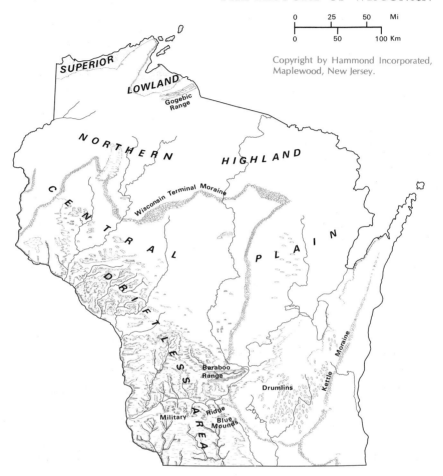

TOPOGRAPHY OF WISCONSIN

going through. The valleys, falling away on either side of the ridge, were steeper. The hills, dominated by Blue Mound, were less softly rounded. Rock outcroppings were more frequent, but boulders scarcer—indeed, nonexistent. Lakes, seldom out of sight before, were no longer to be seen at all. This was a part of what geologists were later to call the Driftless Area, the land which the last glacier had left untouched.

This—the southwestern corner of Wisconsin—was also the mining country. Its settlers had arrived earlier than those of the southeast and until recently had outnumbered them. Lead continued to be mined and smelted in considerable quantities, but production had already passed its peak and was declining. Abandoned mines looked like giant gopher holes. Among them were farms that provided food for the local market. Mineral Point, about fifty miles from Madison, and Platteville, some twenty miles farther, fairly close to the Mississippi, were the most important towns in this part of Wisconsin. Both had been in existence for twenty years or more. Mineral Point, with its stone houses on Shake Rag Street, was nearly twice as populous as Madison. Platteville, recently booming, had grown from 400 to 2,700 in eight years, a figure that would practically tie the town with Janesville as the fourth largest place in the state; Platteville, however, would soon begin to lose population.[12]

From Cassville, on the Mississippi, the traveler could take a luxurious steamboat upriver, observing on the way a steady stream of lumber rafts, many composed of more than forty cribs. Landing at Prairie du Chien, near the mouth of the Wisconsin, he would find a sleepy village of less than 1,000, with a military post near by. Compared to most towns in the new state, Prairie du Chien was an ancient settlement, dating back to the days of the French fur trade. Farther up the Mississippi was Prairie La Crosse, a crude frontier provisioning center for Indians and loggers, inhabited by fewer than 100 persons. Within five years settlers would be streaming into the area, and existing shanties would be replaced by substantial frame buildings.

Choosing instead to go up the Wisconsin, the traveler might be told that a small steamboat could navigate the river for a long distance, at least in seasons of high water; but if the water were low he would probably have to take a canoe. On the journey he would discover that the land bordering the river on the north, most of it prairies and oak openings, was in

[12] Joseph Schafer, *The Wisconsin Lead Region* (Madison, 1932), 12–20, 92–109; Tenney, "Census of Wisconsin from the Year 1836 to August 1860." For a general description of the state's geography, see Lawrence Martin, *The Physical Geography of Wisconsin* (Madison, 1965).

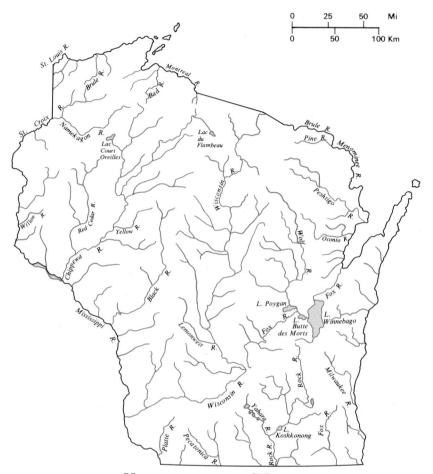

HYDROGRAPHY OF WISCONSIN

the log-cabin stage of pioneering. Portaging from the Wisconsin to the upper Fox, passing Fort Winnebago, and continuing down the sluggish, meandering stream, he could observe some stretches of land without a wheel-track or cattle-track and traversed only by Indian trails. More and more pioneer homesteads would come into view as he neared Great Butte des Morts Lake and Lake Winnebago.

Along the Fox between the two large lakes, the sawmill village of Oshkosh was just springing into life, and at the south end of Lake Winnebago was another milltown, Fond du Lac. At the north end, two rival villages, Neenah and Menasha, were just being platted at the two channels through which the lake emptied into the lower Fox. Proceeding past Grand Chute (Appleton), the canoeist would have to run a series of rocky rapids or portage around them before reaching Fort Howard and the village of Green Bay. This, with about 1,500 inhabitants, many of them French-speaking, was somewhat larger than Madison and very much older. Some thought that this would yet become the state's metropolis, rivaling or even surpassing Milwaukee.[13]

The Fox–Wisconsin diagonal, from Green Bay to Prairie du Chien, corresponded roughly to the frontier line as of 1848. It divided the relatively settled from the almost completely unsettled portion of the state. The area below that line, roughly a fourth of the total area, contained almost all the population. To the north lay even more prairie-and-oak-opening land than in the south, but much the greater part of the north was covered by a thick, unbroken forest (a continuation of the hardwood stands found in eastern Wisconsin almost to the southern boundary, together with species unique to the north). The great north woods consisted of vast tracts of red and white pine and even larger tracts of pine mixed with maple, beech, birch, and hemlock.

The traveler making his way up any of the rivers draining the north woods—the St. Croix, Black, Chippewa, Wisconsin,

[13] Freeman, *Emigrant's Hand Book,* 17, 20–26. Schafer, *Agriculture in Wisconsin,* 130–131; Benjamin F. Bryant, ed., *Memoirs of La Crosse County From the Earliest Historical Times Down to the Present With Special Chapters on Various Subjects, Including Each of the Different Towns, and a Genealogical and Biographical Record of Representative Families in the County, Prepared From Data Obtained From Original Sources of Information* (Madison, 1907), 33–34; Robert F. Fries, *Empire in Pine: The Story of Lumbering in Wisconsin, 1830–1900* (Madison, 1951), 17–67; John Muir, *The Story of My Boyhood and Youth* (Madison, 1965), 166–167; Alice E. Smith, *Millstone and Saw: The Origins of Neenah-Menasha* (Madison, 1966), 8–14; John O. Holzhueter, *Madeline Island and the Chequamegon Region* (Madison, 1974), 43–45. The word *town* as used here (and in the same context hereinafter) means a village or small city. Elsewhere the word *town*—and sometimes *township*—is used to indicate a unit of government which is a subdivision of a county. The reader will recognize which meaning applies by the context in which the word *town* appears.

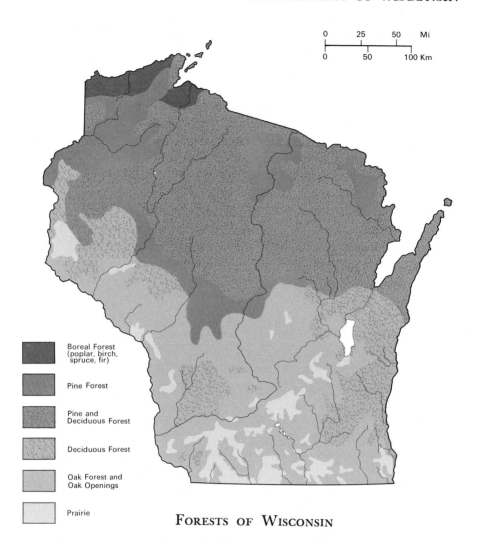

Boreal Forest
(poplar, birch,
spruce, fir)

Pine Forest

Pine and
Deciduous Forest

Deciduous Forest

Oak Forest and
Oak Openings

Prairie

FORESTS OF WISCONSIN

Wolf, or one of the streams emptying into Green Bay—would come upon dozens of busy lumber camps and sawmills. As yet, however, only a tiny fraction of the tremendous forest had even been touched. The north land was still the hunting ground of the Chippewa and the Menominee.

If the traveler wished to visit the northernmost reaches of the state, he would find the going hard through the virtually trackless forest. The distance itself was discouraging—at least 250 miles from any point below the Fox–Wisconsin line to the nearest point on the state's Lake Superior shore. Even from the lumbering outpost at Chippewa Falls, well up the Chippewa River, the distance was 150 miles. In winter the trip from Chippewa Falls, with a small load of freight, took ten days by a single horse or by dog team.

From a Lake Michigan port it would be possible, in summer, to take a roundabout water route, voyaging through the Straits of Mackinac, portaging around the Saint Marys River rapids, and then traversing the length of Lake Superior. The traveler could stop at La Pointe, on Madeline Island, where the French had set up trading posts as early as 1680. There he would find a thriving fishing village of about 400 people, many of them French Canadian traders and Indian or half-breed trappers and women. Cruising on westward along the shore he could see occasional clusters of Chippewa lodges and Chippewa fishermen. Venturing up the Nemadji River (past the site of the future city of Superior) he could gaze upon the American Fur Company's old warehouse, now deserted, a relic of the great fur-trading past.[14]

[3]

During the early years of statehood, lake shipping had to meet the competition of rail transport as tracks were extended farther and farther inland from the Atlantic seaboard. Still, the Great Lakes remained the principal thoroughfare between Wisconsin and the East.

[14] Fries, *Empire in Pine*, 13–20; Curtis, *Vegetation in Wisconsin*, 184–185; James S. Ritchie, *Wisconsin and Its Resources; With Lake Superior, Its Commerce and Navigation. Including a Trip Up the Mississippi, and a Canoe Voyage on the St. Croix and Brule Rivers to Lake Superior. To Which are Appended, The Constitution of the State, With the Routes of the Principal Railroads, List of Post-Offices, etc.* (3d revised edition, Philadelphia, 1858), 249–250, 254, 259–261; Western Historical Company, *History of Northern Wisconsin, Containing An Account of its Settlement, Growth, Development and Resources; An Extensive Sketch of its Counties, Cities, Towns and Villages, Their Improvements, Industries, Manufactories; Biographical Sketches, Portraits of Prominent Men and Early Settlers; Views of County Seats, etc.* (Chicago, 1881), 194.

Eight or nine of every ten vessels on the lakes were sailing craft—schooners of a few hundred tons burden—and they carried most of the freight leaving Lake Michigan (grain and flour) as well as most of that returning (coal, iron, and barreled merchandise). Small schooners of less than 100 tons burden took produce and camp supplies from Milwaukee to Sheboygan, Manitowoc, Manistee (Michigan), and Green Bay and brought back lumber, shingles, and logs. Much more impressive were the palatial steamships, the sidewheelers, some as large as 1,000 tons or more. As early as 1849 twelve sidewheelers were operating on regular schedules between Buffalo and Chicago, with stops at Milwaukee, and a number of others were offering local service between Milwaukee and various Lake Michigan ports. Captains of such queenly vessels as the *Lady Elgin* and the *Sultana* scorned the freight business and preferred the passenger traffic. Competing for both freight and steerage passengers were screw-driven "propellers" of a new-fangled, primitive kind. "They are large-sized Schooners," a contemporary explained, "with a small steam engine in the after-part of their hold, to use in head-winds and in calms, using their sails at other times."[15]

Steamships on the lakes faced the threat of locomotives on the land after 1849, when trains first crossed the state of Michigan from Detroit to New Buffalo, an improvised port on the lower lakeshore opposite Chicago. The Michigan Central Railroad Company acquired its own lake boats and operated them between Buffalo and Detroit to connect with its trains to and from New Buffalo. Another line of steamers plied between New Buffalo and Chicago (fifty miles), Racine, and Milwaukee. The lake-and-land trip was nearly 300 miles shorter than the voyage all the way around the Michigan peninsula to Milwaukee, and it took only three and a half days instead of four to six days.

[15] William E. Derby, "A History of the Port of Milwaukee, 1835–1910" (doctoral dissertation, University of Wisconsin, 1963), 143–144, 192–193. The quotation is from Freeman, *Emigrant's Hand Book*, 89–90.

After three years New Buffalo lost what little importance it had, and Chicago gained a great deal, when the railroad was completed around the lower end of Lake Michigan, giving Chicago a direct rail connection with Detroit. The next year Chicago became the terminus of a line reaching all the way to New York and Boston, though the line was not quite continuous and several changes had to be made from one segment to another. In 1855 the Green Bay, Milwaukee and Chicago railroad connected Chicago with Milwaukee.

The coming of the railroad from the East—to New Buffalo, then to Chicago, and finally to Milwaukee—brought the prospect of loss as well as gain for the main Wisconsin lake ports. Milwaukee, Racine, and Kenosha now had the benefit of rail as well as lake shipping, but to the extent that the rail route should predominate in the future, these cities would lose one advantage they formerly had held over Chicago. By water, they were nearer (Milwaukee ninety miles nearer) to eastern markets; by rail, they were correspondingly farther away. They therefore had a stake in the outcome of the struggle between shipowners and railroad companies.

Railroad companies, following the example of the Michigan Central, bought competing steamboat lines and consolidated and controlled them. Small, independent shipowners combined in self-defense. Milwaukee businessmen had long desired a steamer line that would make Milwaukee its western terminus rather than merely a stop on the Chicago route, and with the approach of the railroad they renewed their efforts to get such a line. They appealed to one of the boat owners' combinations, the American Transportation Company, promising to patronize the company's boats, and by 1855 its line of propellers was operating between Milwaukee and Buffalo. Though not locally owned, the line enhanced Milwaukee's prestige as a major lake port. In 1856 the Clements Steamship Company, Milwaukee-based and Milwaukee-owned, began to serve Lake Michigan ports between Chicago and Green Bay. The next step, Milwaukeeans hoped, would be the completion of a Michigan railroad to Grand Haven, directly opposite Milwaukee, and the establishment of a connecting cross-lake steamer line that would completely bypass Chicago.

In 1858, lake shipping seemed to be holding up well. More than 1,500 ships with a total tonnage of more than 400,000 plied the northern Great Lakes. Small schooners, becoming more numerous with the growth of the lumber trade, comprised 80 per cent of the ships in service. Steamships, especially propellers, were also multiplying, and steamers of all sorts now totaled nearly 250. It was not yet apparent that the magnificent side-wheelers, having lost much of their first-class passenger business, were doomed, and that during the next two decades they would gradually disappear. On the whole, steamboats and sail-boats were losing little if any of their eastbound freight traffic to the railroads. All the wheat and nearly all the flour leaving Milwaukee continued to go by water.[16]

While lake travel and transportation held the advantage of cheapness in comparison with rail transport, there were also disadvantages. Trains were faster, and capable of moving passengers and freight the year around. All navigation between the lakes ceased each winter for four or five months, the Straits of Mackinac remaining blocked by ice until some time in April, though Lake Michigan opened earlier for local traffic.[17]

Lake shipping might better compete with rail hauling—and Milwaukee might better compete with Chicago—if channels and harbors along the Great Lakes route were improved. In 1855 the Sault Ste. Marie canal opened, giving ships from the lower lakes access to Lake Superior. Traffic between Lake Erie and Lake Huron had been delayed by the bottleneck of the St. Clair flats, where the channel was so narrow and uncertain that many captains refused to risk it except in broad daylight. In 1855 the Buffalo Board of Trade used private

[16] Derby, "History of the Port of Milwaukee," 139–147, 183–189; Frederick Merk, *Economic History of Wisconsin During the Civil War Decade* (Madison, 1916), 372–381.

[17] Gregory, *Industrial Resources of Wisconsin,* 215–216, 218–220.

funds to dredge the channel, and a year later the combined Great Lakes shipping interests (estimated to be worth $260 million) finally obtained a congressional appropriation for further widening, deepening, and straightening.

Milwaukee leaders gave their support to the St. Clair River project, but understandably they were much more interested in the improvement of the Milwaukee harbor. Unfortunately they differed among themselves on the question where the improvement ought to be made. Within the city the Milwaukee River received the Menomonee and, separated from the lake only by a narrow sandspit, flowed south for a mile and a half before being joined by the Kinnickinnic and finally emptying into the lake. Docks had been built at the river's mouth, other docks upriver, and still others north of the mouth along the lakeshore. Large vessels had difficulty entering the river, which was partially silted up, and once inside they had trouble turning around in the tight channel. Property owners to the south insisted that the natural harbor ought to be developed. Those farther north called for a new channel—a "straight cut" —to be dug through the sandspit to the lake, a mile north of the river's mouth.

The dispute between the two factions delayed Milwaukee's attainment of harbor facilities. Supporters of the new channel gained a point when, in 1848, the state authorized the city to levy a tax for making the straight cut. In doing so, the legislature interpreted the constitution (which empowered it to restrict taxing and borrowing on the part of villages and cities) to mean that local governments could aid internal improvements even though the state government could not. For the time being, however, Milwaukee refrained from imposing the tax, and the supporters of the natural harbor scored when they persuaded the legislature to let individual wards provide for dredging the existing channel. In 1852 Congress appropriated $15,000 and specified that the money be spent for the "north cut." But the sum was much too small, and the army engineers refused to go ahead until, in 1854, the city, with permis-

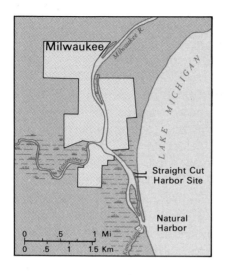

PROPOSED STRAIGHT CUT,
MILWAUKEE HARBOR,
1854

sion from the legislature, issued $50,000 in bonds. The city
then hired a private contractor, who completed the job in 1857.[18]

Other lakeshore cities, competing with Milwaukee for steamer traffic, undertook dredging work, built bridge piers, and extended makeshift wharves and piers into Lake Michigan. In
1850, Kenosha used municipal funds to purchase a harbor
dredge, while the nearby rival lake port of Racine already had
added $17,500 in local funds to a $12,500 congressional grant
to develop its harbor. Sheboygan, after hosting a county-wide
convention on its harbor, received permission from the state
legislature in January 1852 to borrow $30,000 on the credit of
the county and city for improvements. A new $6,500 steam
dredge began straightening the harbor entrance. Manitowoc,
like Sheboygan the recipient of a small congressional grant,
in 1852 also raised money locally to begin dredging its harbor.[19]

[18] Derby, "History of the Port of Milwaukee," 108–114, 125–126, 149–160, 178–
183; Still, *Milwaukee*, 178–181.
[19] Ralph G. Plumb, "Early Harbor History of Wisconsin," in the *Proceedings
of the Mississippi Valley Historical Association for the Year 1910–1911* (Cedar
Rapids, Iowa, 1917), 189–198; *Senate Miscellaneous Documents*, 31 Cong., 1 sess.,
no. 60 (serial 563), 12; Gustave W. Buchen, *Historic Sheboygan County* [Sheboy-
gan, Wisconsin, 1944], 198–201; Ralph G. Plumb, *Lake Michigan* (Manitowoc,
Wisconsin, 1941), 73.

[4]

Far more ambitious than the Milwaukee harbor cut or improvements in the other lake ports was the Fox–Wisconsin improvement, which supposedly would complete a through waterway from the Great Lakes to the Mississippi and incidentally would make Green Bay rather than Milwaukee the state's leading lake port. Money to pay for this grand scheme would presumably be forthcoming from a special land grant that Congress had bestowed upon the infant state as a kind of birthday gift. The grant consisted of alternate sections, in a checkerboard pattern, within a strip three miles wide on each side of the upper and lower Fox River. The land was to be sold at a minimum price of $1.25 an acre. Promptly accepting the grant, the first state legislature set up a board of public works, which in turn appointed an engineer to take charge of the project.

The undertaking looked simple enough on the map, but difficult engineering problems emerged upon inspection of the actual ground. North of Lake Winnebago the lower Fox River in a course of thirty-eight miles dropped 170 feet over eight falls and cascades. Canoes and shallow-draft Durham boats (which were poled) could pass in high water all except the Grand Kaukauna, a mile of violent rapids, and the Grand Chute, a four-foot perpendicular drop. Larger boats would require dams and locks not only at these two places but also at several others in order to get through under any conditions. West of Lake Winnebago the upper Fox was very different, a sluggish, meandering stream that took 104 miles to cover fifty-four compass miles. From its headwaters the portage to the Wisconsin was only a little over a mile, and the land was low, so that digging a canal ought to be easy; but the channel walls would be unstable in the soggy mixture of mud and sand. The remaining 120-mile stretch on the Wisconsin River presented problems of its own, with its shallows and its shifting sand bars, especially during late summer and early autumn, when traffic on the waterway could be expected to be at its heaviest.

Leaving the Wisconsin to take care of itself, the state board of public works began in 1849 to let contracts for digging the Portage canal, dredging the upper Fox, and building a complex on the lower Fox. For this complex the engineer proposed six dams, sixteen locks, and several miles of canal. The contractors soon ran into trouble. When water was let into the Portage cut, some of the planks lining the walls floated to the surface, and later a part of the walls caved in. On the upper Fox the dredge repeatedly got stuck. On the lower Fox the dams leaked, and one was washed away. Before long, some of the contractors quit for want of funds.

The work had to be done on a pay-as-you-go basis, both because of the fiscal limitations in the state constitution and because of the terms of the federal land grant. According to the act of Congress, the state could sell no more than $20,000 worth of the land (16,000 acres at $1.25) at a time. The state would have to use up these proceeds before disposing of additional land. According to an act of the legislature, in keeping with the constitutional provisions regarding state aid and the public debt, no contract could be let until there were "available means devisable from the lands" to pay for it. The laws meant that, even if the lands sold well, the procedure for financing construction would have to be cumbersome and slow. And land sales were falling off.

It looked as if the Fox–Wisconsin improvement was almost hopeless when, in 1851, a would-be savior came forward in the person of Morgan L. Martin, Green Bay lawyer, Democratic politician, veteran land speculator, and a champion of the project from the very beginning. Martin proposed a way of getting around the financial technicalities. He himself would take over the work and would see that it was completed in two years. He was willing to wait for his profit, which presumably was to come from future land sales and waterway tolls, the balance due him gathering interest meanwhile at 12 per cent. Governor Dewey, a Democrat, urged the legislature to accept Martin's offer, and the legislature did so. But Governor Leonard J. Farwell, a Whig who took office in 1852, viewed the arrangement with Martin as violating the spirit if not the letter of both the state constitution and the land-grant act. Farwell thereupon held up the work so long that Martin could not complete it within the specified time.[20]

Farwell favored removing the state from the project and turning it over entirely to private enterprise. In 1853 he approved a bill incorporating the Fox and Wisconsin Improvement Company and transferring to the company all of the state's interest in the works, tolls, water powers, and lands. The company undertook, for its part, to complete the waterway within three years "in a substantial and durable manner, and so as to enable boats with a draft of two feet and a breadth of thirty feet, during ordinary stages of low water, to pass with facility from Green Bay into the Wisconsin River." The organizers of the company, among them Morgan L. Martin and other local men, counted upon a profitable future. They estimated that the lands alone were worth at least $1,000,000. And these—together with the works, tolls, and water powers— were to be theirs in return for an estimated expenditure of $600,000 to complete construction.

Lacking ready capital, the company approached Horatio Seymour, Erastus Corning, and other New York land speculators and bankers to inquire about the possibility of floating a $500,000 bond issue. The bankers sent their own engineer to look into the value of the company's assets. This engineer reported that the Portage canal was complete, though an "imperfect and perishable structure"; that the upper Fox had one steamboat plying regularly between Lake Winnebago and Berlin and a number of horse-drawn scows carrying lumber from the Wolf to the Wisconsin; and that navigation on the lower

[20] Joseph Schafer, *The Winnebago-Horicon Basin: A Type Study in Western History* (Madison, 1937), 99–106; Robert W. McCluggage, "The Fox-Wisconsin Waterway, 1836–1872: Land Speculation and Regional Rivalries, Politics and Private Enterprise" (doctoral dissertation, University of Wisconsin, 1954), 1–22, 191–217, quoting from the *Laws of Wisconsin*, 1848, pp. 58–68. For detailed examination of legal-economic aspects of the Fox-Wisconsin project, see Samuel Mermin, *The Fox-Wisconsin Rivers Improvement: An Historical Study in Legal Institutions and Political Economy* (Madison, 1968).

Fox extended from Green Bay through the canal and lock at
De Pere as far as the Grand Kaukauna. He concluded that the
existing improvements, together with the unsold lands, amounted to adequate security for the desired loan. The New Yorkers
undertook to dispose of the bonds, but the market was poor,
and the company grew desperate for money. Seymour and
Corning finally agreed to put up the necessary cash themselves
—on condition that they be given control of the company. "The
big imported fish swallowed up the little natives," as Martin
later said.

In an oft-repeated lecture, Seymour revealed a shining vision
of a waterway that eventually would stretch 4,000 miles from
the Atlantic to the Pacific. It would go by way of the Erie
Canal, the Fox–Wisconsin route, the Missouri River, and the
Columbia. Seymour declared that "but a single mile separates
the head waters of the Missouri from those of the Columbia
River"—as if joining those two rivers were a task no harder
than joining the Fox and the Wisconsin. But he was appealing
to prospective investors. In truth, he and the other owners
of the Fox and Wisconsin Improvement Company were much
more interested in land speculation than in long-distance water
transport.[21]

The company was carrying on an all-out campaign to get
more land from Congress. An earlier grant to Indiana for
the Wabash and Erie canal had given alternate sections within
a zone as long as the canal itself, with all its sinuosities, but the
grant to Wisconsin was based on the distance covered by the
Fox River in a straight line. So the company lobbied for an
act to "clarify" the Wisconsin grant in accordance with the
Indiana rule. Succeeding in this in 1854, the company immediately sought a further reinterpretation. Indiana's zone
had a width of five miles on each side of the project, not three.

[21] Schafer, *Winnebago-Horicon Basin*, 106–110; McCluggage, "Fox–Wisconsin
Waterway," 217–220, 235–248, 269–273. The Seymour quotation on p. 247 is
from Horatio Seymour, *A Lecture on the Topography and History of New York*
(Utica, New York, 1856), 7–8. The Martin quotation is from Reuben Gold
Thwaites, ed., "Narrative of Morgan L. Martin," in *Wis. Hist. Colls.*, 11: 413.

A joint resolution of 1855 gave Wisconsin the additional width, and the state conferred all the land upon the company, on condition that the company enlarge and complete the project. The original grant had now been more than doubled (to a total exceeding 700,000 acres) at an expense to the company of $1,000 in cash and 100,000 acres of land, which it had used to bribe congressmen and government officials.[22]

The state of Wisconsin no longer owned the land, the works, or the water-power rights. Neither did the state have the benefit of a dependable through water route. Small steamboats (when the water was high) as well as lumber rafts and other vessels were traveling the Wisconsin River. In 1856 the steamer *Aquila*, drawing thirty inches of water, made its way from the Mississippi to Green Bay but remained thereafter on the lower Fox. Later the owners of an Oshkosh-built steamboat attempted to open a regular freight line between Oshkosh and St. Paul, Minnesota. The vessel made one round trip, with a full load each way, but the trip took six weeks and did not pay expenses. Several small steamers were plying the waters of Lake Winnebago, and some of them ventured a short distance up the Fox and Wolf rivers. Local traffic on the lower Fox was fairly heavy, but Green Bay still lacked a regular ship connection with Buffalo or any other eastern lake port.[23]

As of 1857, the dream of a great waterway across the state remained little more than a dream. Indeed, the Fox-Wisconsin route, important though it had been in the day of the fur trade and the canoe, was already something of an anachronism. Improved wagon roads and, more important, newly built railroads were drawing traffic away from that route and leading it in quite other directions.

[22] Schafer, *Winnebago-Horicon Basin*, 111–128; McCluggage, "Fox-Wisconsin Waterway," 250–268; Robert R. Flatley, "The Wisconsin Congressional Delegation from Statehood to Secession, 1848–1861" (bachelor's thesis, University of Wisconsin, 1951), 38–44.

[23] McCluggage, "Fox-Wisconsin Waterway," 273–291; W. A. Titus, "Early Navigation on the Fox and Wolf Rivers and Lake Winnebago," in *WMH*, 25 (September, 1941), 23, 28; Smith, *Millstone and Saw*, 44–53.

[5]

A campaign for highway betterment was gaining momentum
in Wisconsin at the very time that statehood was achieved.
According to a report to the late territorial legislature, capital
was lacking for the building of railroads, and therefore "a class
of improved public thoroughfares, less costly in their construction and more practical for *everyday's use,*" was called for.
The ideal highways for Wisconsin, the report went on, would
be plank roads, which had been tried with great success in
Canada and in some of the eastern states. Smooth, all-weather
roads would benefit the farmer in particular; they would "give
him a choice of time in carrying his products to market," and
they would "enable him to accomplish twice the distance in
the same time, and haul double the load with less effort," than
would common roads. Ten miles of wood-surfaced highway,
it was said, could be built for the cost of one mile of iron railway. Businessmen in rival lake ports looked hopefully to the
laying of plank roads as a practicable means of expediting
trade with the hinterland. Some civic leaders advocated both
planks and rails, as Mayor Byron Kilbourn did for Milwaukee.
"With a good system of plank roads extending in all directions
into the interior, and a railroad to the Mississippi, the founda-
tions of the prosperity of our city would be laid deep and
strong," the mayor declared in his 1848 inaugural address.[24]

The territorial legislature had already chartered a corporation for building a plank road a short distance westward from
Milwaukee. In 1848, while rechartering this corporation and
allowing it to extend its road to Watertown, the state legislature created fifteen additional plank-road companies, among
them the Milwaukee and Janesville, the Racine and Rock River,
and the Southport and Beloit. During the next several years,
dozens of additional companies appeared, thirty-two of them

[24] Patricia J. Pommer, "Plank Roads: A Chapter in the Early History of
Wisconsin Transportation (1836–1871)" (master's thesis, University of Wisconsin, 1950), 28–33. The quotations on the utility of plank roads are from
the *Wisconsin Council Journal, Appendix,* 1848, pp. 306, 311.

in 1852, the peak year of the plank-road craze. The acts of incorporation authorized the taking of private land, with compensation to the owner, and the charging of tolls after the construction of a specified number of miles (usually ranging from two to five). Toll rates varied, a typical charge being two cents per mile for a vehicle drawn by one or two animals.

The preferred wood for building the roads was oak, which was expected to last as long as fifteen years or more before needing replacement, and which fortunately was abundant in Wisconsin. In heavily wooded areas a movable steam saw produced the necessary lumber from giant oaks that were felled on or near the right of way as the work progressed. The road was laid out along as level a route as possible, usually going around hills rather than over them. After the roadbed had been graded, long beams or stringers were embedded in two parallel trenches, as far apart as a wagon's wheels, and across these stringers were nailed eight-foot planks. On one side of this single wooden roadway, and flush with it, the earth was rolled and packed to a width of ten or twelve feet, so as to form a continuous turnout track for passing.

"There are seven plank roads issuing out of Milwaukee; and indeed," wrote an enthusiast as construction was getting well under way, "every town and village in the State either has its plank roads already constructed, or is preparing to do so." Before the end of 1852 Milwaukee had 150 miles of the new roads radiating from it. Five years later the total mileage for the state as a whole was over 1,000. But not every town or village had its plank road, by any means. Most of the construction lay well within fifty miles of one or another of the lake ports. It fell far short of constituting a statewide network.[25]

The mileage of common roads was far greater. Some of these—the old military roads such as the one from Green Bay to Prairie du Chien—the federal government had provided. It had done little more, however, than hew a swath through

[25] Derby, "History of the Port of Milwaukee," 132–135; Pommer, "Plank Roads," 18–26, 37–46, 58; Gregory, *Industrial Resources of Wisconsin* (the quoted "enthusiast"), 239–244.

the woods and stake out a route across the prairies. The state government possessed the constitutional power to "lay out" state roads but not to finance or build them. This was left to local governments, which were responsible also for laying out, building, and maintaining town and county roads.

An act of 1849 spelled out the responsibility of town (civil township) supervisors. They were to divide the town into road districts and appoint or provide for the election of an overseer of highways to take charge of the road work within each district. The supervisors were also to impose a seventy-five-cent poll tax and a three-to-seven-mill property tax for highway purposes. Any man who wanted to could pay his highway tax in labor. He would be credited seventy-five cents a day for eight hours of actual work and another seventy-five cents a day for "every cart, wagon, plow, scraper, yoke of oxen or span of horses" he furnished.[26]

County boards of supervisors had the authority to plan roads for the county as a whole, as town boards did for the towns, but the district overseers and their crews did the actual construction and maintenance, neighborhood by neighborhood. The crews consisted of the local citizens themselves, for only the wealthiest residents or the absentee landlords paid their road taxes in cash. At the call of the overseer the men would meet, and "if there was a mudhole to be filled up, they would cut some green brush, throw it into the hole, and scatter over it a few shovels of earth and lo! the road was fixed." They would corduroy a marshy stretch with logs and would bridge a small stream—if it were not easily fordable—by dragging a couple of tree trunks across it and spiking planks to them.[27]

[26] Wisconsin State Highway Commission and United States Public Roads Administration, *A History of Wisconsin Highway Development, 1835–1945* (Madison, 1947), 14, 16.

[27] The quotation is from the reminiscences of C. A. Verwyst in Henry S. Lucas, ed., *Dutch Immigrant Memoirs and Related Writings* (2 vols., Assen, Netherlands, 1955), 2: 183. For other accounts of local road making, see Joseph Schafer, ed. and trans., "Christian Traugott Ficker's Advice to Emigrants," in *WMH*, 25 (December, 1914–June, 1942), 331; and Merle Curti, *The Making of an American Community: A Case Study of Democracy in a Frontier County* (Stanford, 1959), 37–39, 49, 51, 310.

Rivers too broad for easy bridging and too deep for easy fording were generally left to private enterprise. The state legislature granted charters to individuals or companies for the construction and operation of toll bridges or ferries. The first bridge to span the Wisconsin—and for several years the only one—was chartered in 1849 and opened in 1852, at Prairie du Sac. Its wooden superstructure, a quarter of a mile long with a draw, was designed to rest on wooden piles, but before its completion some of these were torn away by a winter freeze and a spring freshet, and stone piers had to be put in. Regular ferry service was being offered at an increasing number of points on the Wisconsin and other rivers. Old-fashionel ferry-boats were poled across or were powered by horses on a tread-mill connected to paddlewheels. Some of the newer ones were steam-powered. A few, where the water ran swiftly enough, were propelled by the current. At Matt's Ferry, which operated at Merrimac under an 1848 charter, a cable was stretched over the Wisconsin, and a rope was run from each end of the boat to a pulley on the cable. The rope on the end heading into the river was wound up so as to draw that end closer to the cable and hold the boat at an oblique angle. The current did the rest.[28]

Over the roads moved an unrehearsed and unself-conscious pageant: freight wagons hauling supplies or produce; Concord coaches carrying passengers, mail, baggage, and parcels; private vehicles of various kinds; horsemen and pedestrians; drovers following cattle or hogs. Stage lines served the main population centers, at least in the southern third of the state. By 1850, for example, stages were running three times a week from Milwaukee to La Crosse, Green Bay, and Chicago, and every weekday from Milwaukee to Madison, Fond du Lac, and

[28] *Wisconsin Highway Development,* 96; Western Historical Company, *History of Sauk County,* 588, 605, 678–679; Harry E. Cole, ed., *A Standard History of Sauk County, Wisconsin: An Authentic Narrative of the Past, with Particular Attention to the Modern Era in the Commercial, Industrial, Educational, Civic and Social Development* (2 vols., Chicago, 1918), 1: 517–521; Schafer, *Agriculture in Wisconsin,* 74n; Joseph Schafer, "Ferries and Ferryboats," in *WMH,* 21 (June, 1938), 432–436.

Sheboygan. The telegraph, which reached Wisconsin in 1849, was an occasional help to stagecoach travelers, as it was to the Swedish novelist Fredrika Bremer while she was journeying from Watertown to Madison in October 1850. "My portmanteau had been sent on by mistake from Watertown, by some diligence, I knew not how or whither, but thanks to the electric telegraphs, which sent telegraphic messages in three directions, I received again the next day my lost effects safe and sound," she reported. "It is remarkable that in all directions throughout this young country, along these rough roads, which are no roads at all, run these electric wires from tree to tree, from post to post, along the prairie-land, and bring towns and villages into communication."

Travel on such roads, slow and difficult at best, was nearly or quite impossible in certain seasons. During the spring thaw, horses and vehicles could hardly move through the deep mud. Winter had its advantages, when sleighs were brought out and coaches were placed upon runners, and—at least in retrospect— the going became most pleasant as passengers glided noiselessly, except for the jingling of bells, down snowy aisles that were free from mud and dust. Yet winter also had its terrors (as in 1855–1856 and again in 1856–1857) when heavy drifts with a thick crust hid the roads and hobbled the horses, and a traveler risked losing his way or even his life. At river crossings the winter freeze usually halted the ferries; traffic could proceed over the ice when it was solid but not when it was in the process of congealing or thawing.[29]

The plank roads, so far as they reached, made possible much faster and much more nearly year-around traffic than did the

[29] Louise P. Kellogg, "The Story of Wisconsin, 1634–1848," in *WMH,* 3 (March, 1919–June, 1920), 199–200; *Wisconsin Highway Development,* 17; Bremer, *Homes of the New World,* I: 628–629; Harry E. Cole, *Stagecoach and Tavern Days in the Baraboo Region* (Baraboo, Wisconsin, 1923), 12, 19–22, 37–38; Alfred Brunson, *A Western Pioneer: or, Incidents of the Life and Times of Rev. Alfred Brunson, Embracing a Period of Over Seventy Years* (2 vols., Cincinnati, 1872, 1879), 2: 252–256, 262–265. Off the stagecoach routes, individual contractors carried the mail on foot, horseback, or by wagon. For some details on postal service, see K. L. Hatch, "An Early Rural Mail Carrier in Wisconsin," in *WMH,* 27 (March, 1944), 344–347; Publius V. Lawson, ed., *History of Winnebago County, Wisconsin: Its Cities, Towns, Resources, People* (2 vols., Chicago, 1908), 1: 669; Freeman, *Emigrant's Hand Book,* 71–73.

ordinary roads. On the Sheboygan and Fond du Lac plank road a British tourist covered sixteen miles in two hours; after leaving it, only twenty-four miles in two days. Still, the wooden highways on the whole quickly proved a disappointment. Only a few of the routes, notably the Sheboygan and Fond du Lac and the Milwaukee and Watertown, paid a satisfactory return to investors. The oak planks rotted much sooner, and hence upkeep costs were much higher, than had been anticipated.

The heyday of the plank roads was over by 1853, though old ones continued to be used and new ones to be laid for many years thereafter. The enduring plank roads served mainly as feeders to the railroads, which were fast becoming the predominant means of long-distance travel and transport within the state.[30]

[6]

Rival groups from Milwaukee and other places were keeping the state legislature busy as they logrolled for special acts of incorporation creating, altering, or combining railroad companies and giving them rights of eminent domain. More than forty-five such bills were introduced during the legislative session of 1853 alone. "Our young State," the Milwaukee *Sentinel* commented, "thanks to the railroad mania encouraged by our Legislature, which charters improbable and impossible routes ad libitum," has authorized "some 15,000 miles of Railroad, involving a capital of $300,000,000 in their construction—all to be completed immediately of course." Some of the companies projected lines to California or Puget Sound, and one laid out a grandiose route from Port Ulao (a village north of Milwaukee) by way of Lake Superior to Bering Strait. All together, the legislature chartered more than 100 railroad companies during the 1850's. Only a few of these actually laid any track.[31]

[30] Pommer, "Plank Roads," 68–86; W. A. Titus, "Three Pioneer Taverns," in *WMH,* 17 (December, 1933), 180–181; John F. Kienitz, "Wilderness Travelogue and Doty's Loggery," in *WMH,* 31 (June, 1948), 397–409.

[31] Herbert W. Rice, "Early History of the Chicago, Milwaukee and St. Paul Railway Company" (doctoral dissertation, State University of Iowa, 1938), 120.

The first to begin construction was the Milwaukee and Waukesha, which the territorial legislature had incorporated in 1847, and which was formally organized two years later. Its president and chief engineer was Byron Kilbourn, a Connecticut-born and Ohio-reared surveyor, land speculator, canal promoter, and (with Solomon Juneau) co-founder of Milwaukee. Kilbourn promptly took charge of the survey, laying out a twenty-one-and-a-half-mile route of "almost unrivalled excellence," as he reported, "without a deep cut or high embankment, without a yard of rock excavation, and with only a few bridges of small dimensions." On September 12, 1850, after grubbing and grading, workmen spiked down the first rails, and that same day a crowd of Milwaukeeans gathered on the banks of the Menomonee to watch as a schooner from Buffalo unloaded the first locomotive to arrive in Wisconsin. About five months later, on February 25, 1851, other crowds at Waukesha and along the way cheered as the "brave little engine," pulling four passenger cars and one freight car, "panted up the grades or flashed around the numerous curves," and the special excursion train "went tearing over its new road bed at ten miles an hour all the way to Waukesha" for the opening ceremonies.[32]

Meanwhile Kilbourn and his fellow promoters had had their corporate name changed to the Milwaukee and Mississippi Rail Road Company so as to reflect an authorized extension of their line. From Waukesha the workmen went on laying track in the direction of Whitewater. As they did so, Kilbourn schemed to get personal control of the company. Secretly he issued to a Waukesha henchman an "immense amount" of stock, receiving only "one mill on the dollar in return," so that he could use the new shares to vote in his own board of directors. He was forestalled by the directors already on the board. On January 7, 1852, they removed Kilbourn from the corporation's presidency, and thereafter he had no connection with the Milwaukee and Mississippi.

[32] *Ibid.*, 49–51, quoting from the Milwaukee *Sentinel*, February 26, 1851.

Construction proceeded from Whitewater to Milton, Stoughton, and Madison, ninety-six miles from Milwaukee by the roundabout route. On May 23, 1854, farmers and townspeople waited impatiently on the shore of Lake Monona for a glimpse of the iron horse. They were doubly rewarded when two locomotives came into sight, drawing a long train of thirty-two cars. More than 2,000 passengers got off the train and, with several thousand spectators, marched to the capitol grounds for speeches, music, and food.[33]

From Madison the surveyors staked out a line down the valley of Black Earth Creek and then down the valley of the Wisconsin River. Tracks were laid through Mazomanie and Lone Rock to Boscobel in 1856 and on to Prairie du Chien in 1857. At Prairie du Chien, on April 15, 1857, hundreds of people awaited the arrival of the first passenger train, "and when the smoke of the engine became visible in the distance there was such an expression of anxiety as we have seen when a new and great actor is expected on the stage," one of the onlookers reported. "As the train came in view, and the flags with which it was decorated were seen waving in the breeze, a shout of welcome broke forth from the gazers"—who seemed well aware that they were attending an historic event. "The shriek of the Lake Michigan locomotive was echoed by the bluffs and responded to by a shrill whistle of welcome from a Mississippi steamer just coming into port."[34]

Already the Milwaukee and Mississippi Rail Road Company was planning a second line to the Mississippi River, this one to branch off the main line from Milwaukee at Milton and proceed southwestward via Janesville, Monroe, and Shullsburg to a point opposite Dubuque. The directors of the Milwaukee and Mississippi had set up a separate corporation, the Southern Wisconsin Railroad Company, which the M & M soon absorbed,

[33] *Ibid.*, 51–54, quoting from the Milwaukee *Sentinel*, January 15, 1852. Descriptions of the Madison celebration appear in a letter from Minerva Stone to Elizabeth Gordon, June 9, 1854, in the Elizabeth Gordon Correspondence, and in the *Wisconsin State Journal*, May 24, 1854.

[34] Rice, "Chicago, Milwaukee and St. Paul Railway," 57–58, quoting the *North Iowa Times* of McGregor [April, 1857].

| 0 | 25 | 50 | Mi |
| 0 | 50 | 100 Km |

Superior

Green Bay

Berlin
Ripon
Tomah
New Lisbon
La Crosse
Fond du Lac

Portage
Horicon
Beaver Dam
Minnesota Jct.
Columbus
Watertown
Sun Prairie
Madison
Milwaukee
Prairie du Chien
Stoughton
Mineral Point
Milton
Janesville
Elkhorn
Racine
Monroe
Kenosha
Beloit

La Crosse and
Milwaukee Railroad
Company

Milwaukee and
Mississippi Railroad
Company

All Other   *R.R.V.U.*   Rock River Valley Union Railroad Company
          R.&M.   Racine and Mississippi Rail Road Company
          GB,M.&C.   Green Bay, Milwaukee and Chicago Rail Road Company

RAILROADS IN WISCONSIN, 1858

to build the new road. Construction got no farther than Monroe.

But a competitor, the La Crosse and Milwaukee Railroad Company, was successfully laying tracks to the Mississippi by a more northerly route. This company had originated from the secret maneuverings of Byron Kilbourn after his ouster from the M & M. Kilbourn and his new associates boasted that, at La Crosse, their railroad would be eighty-six miles nearer St. Paul (by steamboat channel) than "any road south of it"; that at St. Paul it would connect with the "northern route" for a Pacific railroad; and that it therefore "must become and ever remain an indispensable link without a competitor in the great chain of travel and trade between the East and the West." The tracks of the La Crosse and Milwaukee reached Horicon in 1855, Portage in 1856, New Lisbon in 1857, and La Crosse (approximately 200 miles from Milwaukee) in 1858.

While pushing construction of its main line, Kilbourn's company acquired a couple of branches. In 1856 it took over the Milwaukee and Watertown, which had built to Watertown from Brookfield Junction, where the tracks connected with those of the Milwaukee and Mississippi. The La Crosse and Milwaukee extended the tracks from Watertown to Sun Prairie in 1857. Meanwhile the La Crosse company made a traffic arrangement with the Milwaukee and Horicon, which built from Horicon to Berlin, on the Fox River (1855–1858). The Horicon road, using the La Crosse tracks from Milwaukee to Horicon, was in effect a branch line to Berlin, though constructed and operated by a separate company.[35]

The La Crosse road and the Prairie du Chien road competed for the Mississippi River traffic, yet both served the interests of Milwaukee. The rival lake ports of Racine and Kenosha aspired to tap the western trade for themselves. The Racine, Janesville and Mississippi Railroad Company, chartered in 1852, received insufficient aid from Janesville and laid out its

[35] Rice, "Chicago, Milwaukee and St. Paul Railway," 54–57, 59–73, quoting from the *Annual Report* of the La Crosse and Milwaukee Railroad Company, 1855, pp. 11–14.

line to Beloit and from there to Freeport, Illinois, in 1858, where the line joined the Illinois Central and thus had access to Dunleith, on the Mississippi. The Kenosha, Rockton and Rock Island, which originally had planned a railroad to Beloit, routed it to Rockford instead and there connected with the Galena and Chicago Union Railway.[36]

Reaching out to the Mississippi by way of these same Illinois railroads, Chicago was of course a much more serious commercial threat to Milwaukee than either Racine or Kenosha. Milwaukee merchants opposed the construction of a north–south line, the Rock River Valley Union Railroad, which would give Chicago a direct route to Janesville, Watertown, and Fond du Lac. The Milwaukeeans protested that this railroad would drain off Wisconsin's wealth to the enrichment of a foreign state. But townspeople and farmers along the route, eager for access to an alternative market, were quite unconvinced by the argument that what was good for Milwaukee was good for Wisconsin. Some contended that Milwaukeeans themselves must not be much impressed by the argument, since they planned a Milwaukee-Chicago railroad. In fact, completion of the Green Bay, Milwaukee and Chicago in 1855 did not really hurt Milwaukee's wheat trade, for it failed to secure a track connection with the other lines entering the city. In 1859 the Chicago, St. Paul and Fond du Lac Rail Road Company (successor to the Rock River Valley Union) was completed between Janesville and Fond du Lac.[37]

By 1858, Wisconsin had more than 750 miles of railroad track, and most of it contributed to the prosperity of Milwaukee. Freight cars were bringing in six times as much wheat as were teams and wagons. The east–west lines reached beyond their termini for trade, the Milwaukee and Mississippi operating a steam ferry that crossed the river at Prairie du Chien,

[36] Derby, "History of the Port of Milwaukee," 173–174; Carrie Cropley, "When the Railroads Came to Kenosha," in *WMH*, 33 (December, 1949), 188–196.
[37] Frank N. Elliott, "The Causes and the Growth of Railroad Regulation in Wisconsin, 1848–1876" (doctoral dissertation, University of Wisconsin, 1956), 111–112, 146–151; Derby, "History of the Port of Milwaukee," 174. The quotation is from the Milwaukee *Daily American*, August 30, 1856.

and both lines maintaining connections with steamboat companies that provided upriver service as far as St. Paul. But the north–south line from Fond du Lac to Chicago also was altering the course of traffic. Soon after that road's opening, a Menasha manufacturer sent one shipment of wooden pails and tubs to Chicago by way of the Fox–Wisconsin improvement and Green Bay, and another shipment by way of Lake Winnebago, Fond du Lac, and the railroad. The goods that went by the second route cost less to ship, took half the time, and arrived in better condition.

For passengers as well as freight, however, older methods and routes continued to be used as supplements or alternatives to the new. A single journey could require a miscellany of vehicles and vessels. For example, the traveler might go from Prairie du Chien to Chicago by train and then make the kind of roundabout return that the Reverend Alfred Brunson did in 1856. "From Chicago I took a steamer to Sheboygan, thence the stage to Fond du Lac, and then a steamer on Lake Winnebago to Menasha and a stage to Appleton, to attend the commencement of the Lawrence University," Brunson recalled. "This interesting season over, I took stage to Menasha, steamers to Berlin, stage to Portage City, and a steamer down the Wisconsin, home, having traveled about eight hundred miles."[38]

[7]

Railroads were generally welcomed as the prime means of making available the natural resources and realizing the potential wealth of Wisconsin. They were indeed to affect the state's economic growth far more than was any other mechanical innovation of the period. Yet they were also to have unhappy consequences. For they had been expensive to build, much more expensive than anyone had foreseen, and they had been financed in precarious ways.

Construction costs were higher than they might have been

[38] Derby, "History of the Port of Milwaukee," 174–177; Smith, *Millstone and Saw,* 44–53; Brunson, *Western Pioneer,* 2: 257.

because, especially at the beginning, many of the contractors and their engineers had never seen track laid. Some of the contractors were company officials and, as such, were in a position to pad their own pay. Even when experienced construction firms were brought in from the East, expenses continued to be forced up by the railroad companies' insistence on deviating so as to "hit some small village or somebody's saw mill" (and thus get stock subscriptions) instead of following the straightest and most economical route. Cost estimates kept going up. For instance, Kilbourn on his La Crosse road at first allowed $7,000 per mile and later raised the figure to $21,875.[39]

A number of the contractors were financially irresponsible in dealing with their employees, most of whom were either newly arrived immigrants or farmers living along the right of way. Common laborers were hired for seventy-five cents a day but sometimes were not paid at all. They occasionally struck, calling upon the contractor to raise their wages to a dollar a day, or demanding that the railroad company itself hand over the back pay he owed them. A state law of 1855 made railroad companies responsible for all labor on their construction projects and required contractors to put up bonds sufficient to guarantee the payment of wages.[40]

Some companies added to their financial obligations by taking over other companies that had charters for the construction of competing lines. Thus the Milwaukee and Mississippi consolidated with the Madison and Prairie du Chien, and the La Crosse and Milwaukee with the Milwaukee, Fond du Lac, and Green Bay. These and other companies that were taken over

[39] Rice, "Chicago, Milwaukee and St. Paul Railway," 54; Elliott, "Railroad Regulation in Wisconsin," 121–122; Charles I. Linsley is quoted from a letter to his father, May 14, 1852, in Smith, ed., "Linsley Letters," in *WMH*, 30: 347. For an important interpretive study of the impact of railroads on national and regional economic growth, see Albert Fishlow, *American Railroads and the Transformation of the Ante-Bellum Economy* (Cambridge, 1965), especially Chapters 4 and 5.

[40] On wages, back pay, and strikes, see for example the Milwaukee *Sentinel*, July 19, 1851; July 12, 13, 1853; February 8, 10, 11, March 9, 1854. On the state law of 1855, see Donald J. Berthrong, "Social Legislation in Wisconsin, 1836–1900" (doctoral dissertation, University of Wisconsin, 1951), 162–163.

possessed little or no physical assets and few if any stockholders who had actually paid in more than a small fraction of the book value of their shares. Yet the acquiring companies assumed the burden of paying dividends on all the watered stock.

Railroad promoters early turned to municipalities in the search for ready funds. In 1849 the Milwaukee council empowered the city to subscribe $100,000 for stock in the Milwaukee and Waukesha. The money was to be raised by a special real-estate tax, and the taxpayers were to become stockholders of the railroad. Later the city aided the Milwaukee and Mississippi, the La Crosse and Milwaukee, and three other companies. These corporations exchanged their stock for municipal bonds, which they could sell more readily to eastern capitalists (though only at a discount) than they could their own securities. By 1857 Milwaukee, with a population of about 40,000 and an assessed valuation of less than $6,000,000, was shouldering a total debt of $1,802,000, of which $1,384,000 represented aid to railroads. Other cities and towns along the various routes had lent their credit in the same way, though in lesser amounts. Milwaukee and many of the others had also donated property for depot sites or rights of way.[41]

Despite the generosity of local governments, the railroad companies remained desperate for construction money. The promoters of the Milwaukee and Mississippi repeatedly tried to get assistance from the state government as well. The state held lands that the federal government had granted it, the proceeds to be used for the support of public schools. True, the Wisconsin constitution prohibited the state from giving or lending aid for internal improvements, but that same constitution also provided that the school fund commissioners should "invest all moneys arising from the sale of the school lands" in whatever manner the legislature might direct. Why not invest the moneys in railroad stocks? Surely no investment could be safer, and none could bring a more handsome return. The legislature resisted these importunities, though it encouraged

[41] Rice, "Chicago, Milwaukee and St. Paul Railway," 57, 66–67, 103–108; Still, *Milwaukee,* 169–177; Elliott, "Railroad Regulation in Wisconsin," 105–107.

rail construction by an act of 1854 exempting railroad companies from all taxes except a 1 per cent levy on gross earnings.[42]

Rebuffed in their attempts to get their hands on the school fund, the directors of the Milwaukee and Mississippi looked for other means of financial support. From the beginning they had sought the help of men who owned farms along the prospective route. Surely the farmers would have much to gain from the coming of the railroad, for it promised to enlarge the market for their wheat and other crops, lower the price of the manufactured goods they had to buy, and increase the value of their property, perhaps even doubling it.

Eager though they were to realize these benefits, many farmers harbored an old suspicion of all corporations, capitalists, and monopolies—including those that owned and operated railroads. The railroad promoters recognized this prejudice and skillfully played upon it. "The interests of farmers have always been subject to a ruinous monopoly; which monopoly, as used by the capitalists, has always been diametrically opposed to the ultimate success of the farmer," a Milwaukee and Mississippi director conceded in an appeal for stock subscriptions. He then explained to the farmers how they could escape the clutches of the monopolizing capitalist. Buy railroad stock! Make yourselves the owners of the tracks, depots, locomotives, cars. "The railroad must be built, and it remains for you to say whether the stock-holders shall consist of enterprising farmers or eastern capitalists," the railroad director urged. "If you refuse to take stock there is no alternative—eastern capital will step in *and we shall forever be cursed with monopolies.*"[43]

This image of "the farmers' railroad," an image that appeared again and again in the promotional literature, undoubtedly exerted on some farmers a good deal of persuasive charm. But no enchantment could draw much money out of people who were chronically short of cash. The Milwaukee and Mis-

[42] Rice, "Chicago, Milwaukee and St. Paul Railway," 94–97; Elliott, "Railroad Regulation in Wisconsin," 1–7.

[43] E. D. Clinton letter in the Milwaukee *Sentinel,* June 8, 1849, quoted by Meyer, "Early Railroad Legislation," in *Wis. Hist. Colls.,* 14: 222–223.

sissippi offered stock on easy terms, as little as 5 per cent down, the balance to be called for in occasional installments. Even so, the promoters were disappointed in their hopes of raising capital through stock sales.

In 1850, at a moment when the company's funds were nearing exhaustion, its directors hit upon a magical scheme by which farm owners could become stockholders without spending a cent—and the company could obtain a large part of the funds it needed. Instead of paying cash for shares, the farmer would give his personal note, secured by a mortgage on his farm. The company would attach the note and the mortgage to its own bond and would then sell the package on the money market. Eastern investors, who hesitated to buy such a bond on its own merits, would be glad to take it with the added security. Thus the railroad would gain and, by virtue of the financial magic, the farmer could not lose. Though he would owe interest at 8 per cent on his mortgage, he was promised dividends of 10 per cent on his stock. These dividends would leave a balance of 2 per cent a year, which would accumulate to his credit on the books of the company over a ten-year period. Meanwhile the image of the farmers' railroad would presumably become a reality.

The farm-mortgage idea quickly took hold and spread. Soon the agents of sixteen different railroad companies were roaming Wisconsin, calling at farmhouses to solicit mortgages in exchange for stock. By 1857, nearly 6,000 people owned railroad stock for which their farms were mortgaged. The largest beneficiaries of the stock-for-mortgages swap were the La Crosse and Milwaukee ($1,100,000), the Milwaukee and Mississippi ($900,000), and the Milwaukee and Horicon ($375,000). The farmers' mortgage debt totaled almost $5,000,000.[44]

From the beginning, railroad promoters had hoped to benefit from a federal land grant. The expectation seemed reason-

[44] Rice, "Chicago, Milwaukee and St. Paul Railway," 116–125; Elliott, "Railroad Regulation in Wisconsin," 30–38, 45–48; Philip A. Schilling, "Farmers and Railroads: A Case Study of Farmer Attitudes in the Promotion of the Milwaukee and Mississippi Railroad Company" (master's thesis, University of Wisconsin, 1964), 5–55.

able enough. After all, Congress had given Wisconsin, among other states, a gift from the public domain to be used for waterway improvements, and in 1850 Congress granted land to Illinois for the construction of the Illinois Central Railroad. Wisconsin railroaders kept agitating for a similar favor, but made no headway for several years, their cause being weakened by their own rivalries and jealousies. Byron Kilbourn, after launching the La Crosse and Milwaukee, clamored the loudest for a land grant and resisted the claims of the Rock River Valley Union, which had an active and almost successful lobby in Washington. The Milwaukee and Mississippi, once it had moved its own construction well along without federal aid, strongly opposed the granting of such aid to any Wisconsin line.

Finally Congress passed and on June 3, 1856, President Franklin Pierce signed a bill giving the state a total of about 2,000,000 acres. A part of this, the "northwest grant," was to be used for a railroad from Madison, or Columbus, by way of Portage to the St. Croix River and thence to Lake Superior; the rest of the land, the "northeast grant," for a railroad from Fond du Lac north to the state boundary. It was up to the state legislature to dispose of the gift. The foremost claimants were Kilbourn's La Crosse company and the Rock River Valley Union's successor, the Chicago, St. Paul and Fond du Lac. To enhance its claim, the La Crosse company absorbed two other petitioners (the Milwaukee and Watertown and the St. Croix and Lake Superior), and it finally obtained the northwest grant. The Chicago company arranged for the incorporation of a new firm, the Wisconsin and Superior, which it controlled; this new firm received the northeast grant.

Successful though it had been, the La Crosse and Milwaukee found itself weakened rather than strengthened by the contest over federal largess. The company had greatly increased its indebtedness, issuing a million dollars in bonds for the purchase of one of the rival land petitioners, and making other extravagant commitments. Rumors began to circulate hinting at bribery on a grand scale. Yet, for all its costly expedients, the Kilbourn company was never to qualify for a single acre of the land it supposedly had won.[45]

After seven years of building—during which Kilbourn and others had constantly presented railroading as a democratic, community enterprise—the railroads of Wisconsin were indeed owned largely by the people of the state: the municipalities, the farm mortgagers, and others. But these stockholders could exert little or no influence on the management of the corporations, which were not democracies at all but oligarchies controlled by underhanded schemers such as Kilbourn. And the stockholders had only an uncertain grasp upon the property itself. They had put up little actual money. Most of the money had come from Eastern capitalists, who had demanded bonds instead of stocks. As bondholders, these outsiders held liens on the property, and the property could become theirs if payments on the debt were not kept up. The debt was vast and growing. "The thing is being overdone," a writer who signed himself "A Badger" cautioned in the Milwaukee *Sentinel* of February 14, 1857, "and the moment confidence begins to fall, the whole fabric of our Rail Road system collapses."[46]

[45] Rice, "Chicago, Milwaukee and St. Paul Railway," 149–158; Elliott, "Railroad Regulation in Wisconsin," 151–156; Gordon O. Greiner, "Wisconsin National Railroad Land Grants" (master's thesis, University of Wisconsin, 1935), 8–16.
[46] Quoted in Rice, "Chicago, Milwaukee and St. Paul Railway," 124.

2

Peopling the Land

[1]

"THE MORE RAPID our growth in population, the sooner will all our industrial resources be fully developed," declared John Gregory in his book *Industrial Resources of Wisconsin,* which Starr's Book and Job Printing Office of Milwaukee published in 1855. "Therefore it is to the interest of all, to induce foreigners to settle among us; notwithstanding the opinion of a few, possessing strong Native American feelings, to the contrary." Certainly it was to the interest of Gregory himself to encourage settlement from abroad. Born in County Kerry, he had arrived in Milwaukee in 1849 as secretary of the Irish National Emigration Society, and in addition to working for the society he was running his own real-estate business.[1]

If some Wisconsinites differed with Gregory on the desirability of attracting foreigners, particularly Irish Roman Catholics, few if any disputed the idea that rapid population growth would be a good thing for the new state and hence for themselves. Just as Gregory gave a special welcome to his own countrymen, so did other immigrants to theirs, and American-born settlers to their old neighbors from the East. Most of the people already living in Wisconsin shared the promoter spirit in

---

[1] John Gregory, *Industrial Resources of Wisconsin* (Milwaukee, 1855), 12; M. Justille McDonald, *History of the Irish in Wisconsin in the Nineteenth Century* (Washington, D.C., 1954), 25–26.

some degree and wished to divert in their direction a large part of the vast population movement, European and American, then under way.

For Europeans considering emigration, no advertisements of Wisconsin were more persuasive than "America letters," that is, the letters from friends or relatives who had already made the move. Whatever their disappointments and difficulties, these correspondents often enough put the best possible light on their new life and their new home. "Here ten-year-old children can earn more than adults in Norway," Sjur and Nils Eidsvaag of Cambridge (Dane County) assured the members of their family who had remained in the old country (1849). "We can't thank God enough that we are in America," Jakob Buehler of Sauk Prairie told his brother in Switzerland (1855). "America has supported me so richly. . . . I give God honor and thanks," Joseph Krings of Jefferson wrote to his sister-in-law in the German village of Ripsdorf (1857). Every year, thousands of such letters beckoned from Wisconsin.[2]

Thousands of copies of immigrant guidebooks and pamphlets supplemented the personal correspondence. A basic work, from which other writers derived many of their facts, was Increase A. Lapham's *A Geographical and Topographical Description of Wisconsin,* the first sizable book ever published in Wisconsin (1844). Its author, a New York native who had come to Milwaukee as a canal engineer, also drew maps of the area, including the first one published in the territory (1845). A number of foreign-born promoters of immigration, besides Gregory, produced books and pamphlets that were directed to particular nationalities. The Dane L. J. Fribert, for example, appealed to Danes and Norwegians in *Haandbog for Emigranter til Amerikas Vest* (Christiania, 1847). Among

[2] The quotations are from Sjur and Nils Eidsvaag to relatives, September 23, 1849, in Beulah Folkedahl, ed. and trans., "Norwegians Become Americans," *Norwegian-American Studies,* 21 (1962), 98; Jakob Bühler to his brother, March 9, 1855, in Lowell J. Ragatz, ed. and trans., "A Swiss Family in the New World: Letters of Jakob and Ulrich Bühler, 1847–1877," in *WMH,* 6 (March, 1923), 327; Joseph Krings to Margareta, June 18, 1857, translation by Joseph Schafer included in correspondence, December 3, 1931, in the Halbert L. Hoard Papers.

the many German writers, Dr. Carl de Haas addressed his countrymen in *Nordamerika, Wisconsin, Calumet: Winke für Auswanderer* (Elberfeld, 1848), and Theodore Wettstein in *Der Nordamerikanische Friestaat Wisconsin* (Elberfeld, 1851). Samuel Freeman hoped to attract well-to-do Englishmen with *The Emigrant's Hand Book and Guide to Wisconsin . . .* (Milwaukee, 1851).[3]

To the literary appeal was added the personal touch. Foreigners visiting or residing in Wisconsin returned to their homelands to bring back groups of immigrants. Agents of emigration companies or societies, located in New York or abroad, directed emigrants toward Wisconsin. Representatives of churches sought additional communicants. Members of the principally German Roman Catholic hierarchy, from the bishop of Milwaukee to parish priests and missionaries, were especially active in attracting settlers of their faith. Churchmen voyaged overseas to recruit in person, or enlisted the co-operation of their fellow clergymen already on foreign ground.[4]

For a few years, the government of Wisconsin joined in the effort to entice settlers, thus setting an example for other states of the Northwest. A law of 1852 provided for a commissioner of emigration with an office in New York, and a law of 1853 added a traveling agent who was "to see that correct representations be made in eastern newspapers of our Wisconsin's great natural resources, advantages, and privileges, and brilliant prospects for the future; and to use every honorable means in his power to induce emigrants to come to this state." The commissioner—at first a Dutchman, then a German, and then another German—hired German, Irish, Nor-

[3] Increase Allen Lapham in *DWB*; Peter T. Harstad, "Health in the Upper Mississippi River Valley, 1820 to 1861" (doctoral dissertation, University of Wisconsin, 1963), 38–40; Thomas P. Christensen, "Danish Settlement in Wisconsin," in *WMH*, 12 (September, 1928), 19–26; Kate Everest Levi, "Geographical Origin of German Immigration to Wisconsin," in *Wis. Hist. Colls.*, 14: 371–373.
[4] See, for example, Christensen, "Danish Settlement," in *WMH*, 12: 19–26; Levi, "German Immigration," in *Wis. Hist. Colls.*, 14: 371–374; John Martin Henni in *DWB*; M. Hedwigis Overmoehle, "The Anti-Clerical Activities of the Forty-Eighters in Wisconsin, 1848–1860: A Study in German-American Liberalism" (doctoral dissertation, St. Louis University, 1941), 265–268.

wegian, English, and American assistants. They annually distributed about 30,000 copies of a pamphlet especially prepared
by John Lathrop, the chancellor of the state university, and
issued in German, Norwegian, and Dutch versions as well as
an English one. Half of these they sent to Europe; the rest
they placed on ships and in hotels in New York. They also
advertised in American and European newspapers, answered
letters from Europe, gave personal advice to callers, and kept
in touch with emigration societies, foreign consuls, shipping
lines, railroad companies, and freight handlers. The commissioner found shippers and forwarders co-operative, since these
men stood to gain from sending immigrants to a far-off place
like Wisconsin. Meanwhile the state's traveling agent visited
northeastern and Canadian cities and even New York and New
England villages, inserting notices in more than 900 papers.
In 1854 the commissioner expanded his operations by opening a branch office in Quebec. The next year the Wisconsin
legislature, under pressure from nativists, abolished the entire
emigrant agency, and was not to revive it for more than a
decade.[5]

In fact, through its newspaper advertising, the agency had
reached native New Yorkers and New Englanders as well as
Europeans. Settlers from the East sent enticing letters to
friends and relatives back home, just as settlers from Europe

---

[5] Theodore C. Blegen, "The Competition of the Northwestern States for Immigrants," in *WMH*, 3 (September, 1919), 3–29; McDonald, *Irish in Wisconsin,*
20–22; the quotation is on p. 22 and is taken from the Wisconsin Emigration Commissioner, *Annual Report,* 1853, p. 6. See also Ira J. Kligora, "The
German Element in Wisconsin, 1840–1880" (master's thesis, University of Wisconsin, 1937), 52–57; and Harstad, "Health in the Upper Mississippi River Valley," 41. The sixteen-page pamphlet distributed by the Wisconsin State Emigration Agency is simply entitled *Wisconsin.* Authorship has been attributed to
both Increase Lapham and John H. Lathrop. Most probably Lathrop is the
author, since the pamphlet was filed in the Library of Congress under his
name. Lapham's daughter Julia Lapham, in her thorough Bibliography of Dr.
Increase Lapham (Increase Allen Lapham Papers, Box 23), makes no mention
of it. Furthermore, the first Commissioner of Emigration, in his *Annual Report,*
1853 (bound in *Wisconsin Senate and Assembly Journals Appendix,* 1852–1853),
14–15, urges that Lapham be engaged to write an updated version of his large
1844 work, and in his discussion implies that Lapham is not the author of
the commission's small pamphlet.

did. Typical of many a cautious Yankee was the recent arrival
whose farm in Fond du Lac County suited him "to a charm"
and who reported to a cousin in Vermont: "My idea of Wisconsin was not formed too high, there is more advantages here
than I expected." And a number of the promotional pamphlets,
including the one written by John Lathrop, were intended as
much for American as for European readers.[6]

The attractions of Wisconsin, according to its eulogists,
depended on the work of both God and man. The climate,
Lathrop averred, was much the same as that of New York and
New England, but milder and more beautiful. "The atmosphere is drier, more transparent and salubrious, and the whole
area of the State is remarkably free from those causes of endem-
ic diseases which were by no means unknown in the settlement of western New York, which have been the misfortune of
large portions of Michigan, and the scourge of Indiana, Illinois,
Missouri, and, in part, of Iowa." Indeed, Wisconsin was the
most healthful state in the Union, some boosters claimed. They
cited the death rate as evidence (only 1 to 105.82 in comparison with 1 to 51.23 for Massachusetts), without bothering to
point out that the rate might have reflected, in part, the comparative youthfulness of the new state's population. Supposedly Wisconsin also had other natural advantages. "Among her
ten thousand undulations," Lathrop rhapsodized, "there is
scarcely one which lifts its crown above its fellows, which does
not disclose to the prophetic eye of taste a possible Eden, a
vision of loveliness, which time and the hand of cultivation
will not fail to realize and to verify." The hand of cultivation
would have an easier time and Eden would be faster realized
here than elsewhere in the West. Nature had blessed Wisconsin with an ideal combination of prairie land, oak openings,
and timber—much better for farm-making than the vast and

---

[6] Clinton Matteson to James T. Matteson, August 2, 1846, in the Clinton
Matteson Letters; "Wisconsin: Population, Resources and Statistics," in *De
Bow's Review*, 14 (January, 1853), 24–28. Lathrop, *Wisconsin*, was reprinted
in its entirety as "Wisconsin and the Growth of the Northwest," in *De Bow's
Review*, 14 (March, 1853), 230–238.

timberless prairies of Illinois, Missouri, Iowa, or Minnesota, or the thick and difficult woods that once had cumbered Ohio.[7]

The lawmakers of Wisconsin had increased the state's attractiveness, its promoters pointed out. During its first decade it was the only state (except for Indiana after 1851) that gave the franchise to the foreign-born after only one year's residence. Since the constitution prohibited state borrowing for internal improvements and strictly limited the public debt, taxes could be expected to remain comparatively low. And if by some rare mischance a settler should fall into overwhelming debt, the law would protect him and his family from creditors by sparing not only a house and forty acres of land but also all clothing and a good deal of furniture, livestock, and farm or shop equipment. "These are exemptions," Gregory said, "which place us here beyond the reach of abject poverty, or absolute want."[8]

The basic attraction of Wisconsin was the land itself. This was of course available elsewhere in the West, but nowhere else was good farming land so abundant or so cheap, if the enthusiasts were to be believed. They pointed to the state's vast acreage that was still in the public domain, waiting for squatters to occupy and make their own. This "gives to Wisconsin an advantage over other Western States, for it precludes entirely the possibility of its becoming, as are the States of Illinois and Iowa, a country of speculators," one writer proclaimed. "Here are golden opportunities opening every day to emigrants," he went on. "Immense tracts of the finest land in the

[7] Wisconsin's atmosphere is discussed in Lathrop, *Wisconsin*, 3; the "ten thousand undulations" are described on p. 5. See also Gregory, *Industrial Resources of Wisconsin*, 276–280; and Freeman, *Emigrant's Hand Book*, 46. Freeman doubted whether the "western climate of America" was "favorable to health and longevity," but thought there were "other circumstances, and particularly that of the diet and mode of life among the Americans," which might "sufficiently account for their inferior health."

[8] Kate A. Everest, "How Wisconsin Came By Its Large German Element," in *Wis. Hist. Colls.*, 12: 314; Albert B. Faust, *The German Element in the United States, with Special Reference to Its Political, Moral, Social, and Educational Influence* (2 vols., Boston, 1909), 1: 469–476; Gregory, *Industrial Resources of Wisconsin*, 11.

country are still open to pre-emption, and let no man say 'I am too late,' while he has land inviting. . . ."[9]

[2]

Originally, in the view of the United States government, the land belonged to the Indians. Before the settlers could become its owners, the government had to acquire the Indian title. It did so by compelling the chiefs to designate tribal boundaries (a concept of ownership alien to them), then to sign treaties giving up the tribal lands in exchange for money, supplies, and a place to live—a place ostensibly reserved against the further encroachment of the whites and preferably located on the far frontier, to the west of the Mississippi River.

Two Wisconsin tribes, the Winnebago and the Potawatomi, had already been moved to reservations west of the Mississippi by the time the state was formed. Some of the Potawatomi had refused to leave, however, and many of the Winnebago kept filtering back. In 1850 it was reported that several hundred Winnebago were wandering around in the western part of the state as far south as Prarie du Chien and as far east as Baraboo. "They are constantly on the alert, and on the look-out for the arrival of soldiers, and continue in small encampments, and as much scattered as possible, and hope, by so doing, to succeed in remaining where they are. . . ." That year the federal government contracted with a trader, Henry M. Rice, who had the confidence of the Winnebago, to persuade them to return to their Minnesota reservation. He was to be paid $70 a head. Though he succeeded with more than three hundred, the number of Winnebago in Wisconsin was soon larger than it had been before his effort.[10]

The Chippewa, the most numerous tribe in Wisconsin, wide-

[9] James S. Ritchie, *Wisconsin and Its Resources* . . . (3d revised edition, Philadelphia, 1858), 164–167, 255–266.

[10] George W. Thatcher, "The Winnebago Indians, 1827–1932" (master's thesis, University of Wisconsin, 1935), 143–145, 148–150; p. 143 quotes a letter from W. H. Bruce, Green Bay Subagency, to Orlando Brown, Commissioner of Indian Affairs, March 22, 1850, printed in *House Reports,* 30 Cong., 1 sess., no. 501 (serial 585), 24.

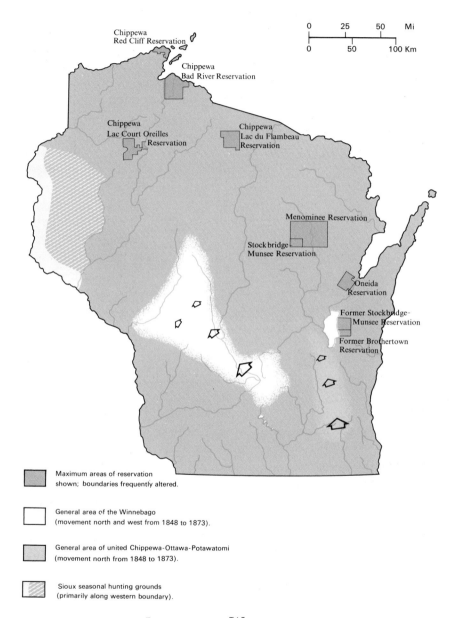

Chippewa
Red Cliff Reservation

Chippewa
Bad River Reservation

Chippewa
Lac Court Oreilles
Reservation

Chippewa
Lac du Flambeau
Reservation

Menominee Reservation

Stockbridge
Munsee Reservation

Oneida
Reservation

Former Stockbridge–
Munsee Reservation

Former Brothertown
Reservation

Maximum areas of reservation
shown; boundaries frequently altered.

General area of the Winnebago
(movement north and west from 1848 to 1873).

General area of united Chippewa-Ottawa-Potawatomi
(movement north from 1848 to 1873).

Sioux seasonal hunting grounds
(primarily along western boundary).

INDIANS OF WISCONSIN

ly dispersed through the pineries of the far north and north-west, had agreed in 1842 to a treaty ceding the last of their Wisconsin lands in title but giving them occupancy, with removal possible only "at the Pleasure of the President." In return, the government was to give them annuities at La Pointe, on Madeline Island in Lake Superior, for a period of twenty-five years. But the Indians had not anticipated the effects of the treaty's terms. They said that they were led to believe that they really were disposing of only timber and mineral rights, since the President was unlikely to ask them to leave. So they were shocked when, in 1849, they were told to move on to Minnesota, and the order was emphasized by relocation of their annuity payments from La Pointe to a new agency at Sandy Lake. After a protracted council, the chiefs in 1851 sent a delegation of about 500 to collect the annuities at the new site and to look into the possibilities of living there. More than a hundred of them died in Minnesota—as a result of being fed rotten provisions, the Indians believed—and the survivors returned to Wisconsin with an unshakable determination to stay there.

The Chippewa had a white friend in Benjamin G. Armstrong, an Alabaman who had joined the tribe, learned its language, and married one of its women. In 1852 Armstrong guided Chief Buffalo (who was over ninety years old), Chief Oshoga, and four braves to Washington. The "great father" himself, President Millard Fillmore, cordially received them in the White House and promised to countermand the removal order and to restore the annuity payments at La Pointe. In 1854 federal commissioners arrived at La Pointe to negotiate a new treaty. With Armstrong interpreting for them, the Chippewa managed to get four reservations in the areas they preferred—at Lac Court Oreilles, Red Cliff, Bad River, and Lac du Flambeau.[11]

The only other tribe continuing to occupy a portion of its ancestral domain in Wisconsin, at the time of Wisconsin's state-

[11] Benjamin G. Armstrong, "Reminiscences of Life among the Chippewa," in *WMH*, 55–56 (Spring, 1972–Winter, 1972–1973), 55: 287–304; Richard F. Morse, "The Chippewas of Lake Superior," in *Wis. Hist. Colls.*, 3: 338–369.

hood, was the Menominee. They still claimed an expanse of several million acres lying to the north of the upper Fox River and consisting largely of prairies and oak openings—the kind of land that white farmers prized the most. Settlers were already moving into the area. Reluctant though the Menominee were to leave this beautiful country, the chiefs saw little choice but to yield all of it at the demand of the government, which they did in a treaty of October 18, 1848, in return for $350,000 and a reservation in northwestern Minnesota.

Soon the chiefs regretted their agreement to move to Minnesota where they would be near an unfriendly people, the Eastern Sioux. They had good reason to suspect that the new land was lacking in game and fish and was poor for raising corn. They confirmed their doubts when, in the summer of 1850, they made a trip to the Crow Wing River site and looked over the land reserved for them. Appealing to the President of the United States, they were invited to present their case in Washington. There, in September 1850, Chief Oshkosh, at the head of the chiefs of the nine Menominee bands, told President Fillmore that their people preferred "a home somewhere in Wisconsin, for even the poorest region in Wisconsin was better than that of the Crow Wing." The upshot was that the Menominee were allowed to stay where they were for the time being. In 1852, some 2,000 Menominee were resettled on a 400-square-mile tract of timberland, a comparatively small and remote portion of the territory they had lately ceded, on the upper Wolf and Oconto rivers. In 1854 a treaty confirmed this as their permanent reservation, although many were slow to give up hunting and food-gathering and stay within its boundaries to take up the white man's type of family farming. In 1857, the local agent reported that of 358 adult males on the reservation, fifty-eight still made livings by "the chase" (which may also have included ranging for wild foods), and 150 were "employed in farming."[12]

---

[12] See the editor's synopsis and epilogue in "A Mission to the Menominee: Alfred Cope's Green Bay Diary," in *WMH*, 49–50 (Summer, 1966–Spring, 1967), 49: 302–303, 50: 239–240. See also "William Powell's Recollections: In an Interview with Lyman C. Draper," in *SHSW Proceedings*, 1912, pp. 173–175; the

In addition to the tribes that had inhabited Wisconsin for many generations, the state contained a number of Indians who had but recently (in the late 1820's and early 1830's) arrived from New York, having left their old reservations for new ones at the persuasion of the federal government. These recent arrivals belonged to the following groups: the Oneida, once a member of the Iroquois confederation; the Brothertown (or Brotherton), a collection of survivors of various New England tribes, including the Pequot; the Stockbridge, the former Housatonic, a part of the Mahican confederacy; and the Munsee, a Delaware remnant whom the Stockbridge had incorporated. The Oneida occupied the 65,000 acres near Green Bay designated as their reservation in an 1838 treaty. They continued to have a tribal organization and a tribal system of land tenure. The Brothertown were settled on the eastern shore of Lake Winnebago. They, unlike the Oneida, no longer lived as tribesmen but owned individual farms, having voted to become citizens. The Stockbridge had a reservation along the lake north of the original Brothertown reservation. Some of the Stockbridge had accepted citizenship and allotments of land; others insisted on maintaining tribal government and ownership.[13]

All these "civilized" New York tribes ran the risk of expropriation as white land-seekers arrived in larger and larger numbers. The Stockbridge especially were endangered, both because of their division between a "citizens" party and an "Indian" party and because of the attractiveness of the terrain they occupied. Responding to clamors for their removal, the federal government persuaded the Stockbridge to accept a treaty, signed on November 24, 1848, according to which the citizens could

quotation, from p. 175, is Powell's rendition of Chief Oshkosh's plea to the President. On the establishment of the Menominee reservation, see Patricia K. Ourada, "The Menominee Indians: A History" (doctoral dissertation, University of Oklahoma, 1973), 190–198; and the U.S. Commissioner of Indian Affairs, *Annual Report*, 1857, p. 42.

[13] Frederick W. Hodge, ed., *Handbook of American Indians North of Mexico* (2 vols., Washington, D.C., 1907, 1910), 1: 166, 957; 2: 123–125, 637–638; Nancy O. Lurie, "Wisconsin: A Natural Laboratory for North American Indian Studies," in *WMH*, 53 (Autumn, 1969), 11–12, 15.

remain and keep their land. The others, including the great majority, would be relocated on a new reservation beyond the Mississippi. The next spring, before the relocation was scheduled to begin, a sympathetic white Easterner visiting the Stockbridge wrote: "We found ourselves in a fine country on the borders of Lake Winnebago among good farms and comfortable houses all these all belong to Indians but Alas! shame on the government for allowing such evil—these fields have attracted the covetous gaze of some greedy speculators and for this, forsooth, they [the Indians] are to be driven from their homes to make new ones in the wilderness until some adventurer is again desirous of the comforts their toil has gathered around them." But when the time came the Stockbridge all refused to go.

Several years later, in February 1856, most of the Stockbridge agreed to a new treaty, which confirmed a small number in their claims to land ownership and offered the rest a new reservation in Wisconsin. This was taken from the southwestern part of the Menominee reservation and consisted of barren, sandy pineland. Some of the Stockbridge again resisted and stayed on for a while in the hope of keeping their excellent farm land. Because of earlier grants and cancellations and regrants, the titles to much of the land were tangled and unclear. Yet white newcomers were eagerly buying, and within a few years only a few Brothertown and Stockbridge homesteads remained in the midst of a prosperous white settlement.[14]

[3]

The federal government's usual procedure, after acquiring land from the Indians, was to survey it and put it up for sale. Some of it, however, the government donated to the state or granted to canal or railroad companies for them to dispose of.

[14] J. N. Davidson, *Muh-he-ka-ne-ok: A History of the Stockbridge Nation* (Milwaukee, 1893), 38–45; Joseph Schafer, *The Winnebago-Horicon Basin: A Type Study in Western History* (Madison, 1937), 56–57, 64–66; the quotation, p. 56n, is from a letter by Robert B. Haines, Green Bay, to his sister, June 11, 1849, in the Robert B. Haines Letters (typed copies).

Settlers, then, could buy land from the federal or the state government or from companies that had received grants. They could also buy it from speculators who had accumulated tracts, or from previous settlers who wanted to sell out and move on.

When the Indians made their last cessions, the federal surveyors were already working their way northward. By 1856 the survey covered the state up to a new base line six miles north of the Forty-fifth parallel (on a level with Marinette). The survey above that line, covering more than a third of the state's entire area, was not to be completed until 1865.[15]

As fresh lands were surveyed, new federal land offices were set up in the newly created districts, while older offices at Green Bay and Milwaukee, in districts where the land had mostly passed into private ownership, were abandoned. After 1848 the original office at Mineral Point remained in operation, selling mineral lands that formerly had been reserved, and to it were added others at Willow River (Hudson), Stevens Point, Menasha, La Crosse, and Superior.

When land in a given district was to be offered for the first time, a presidential proclamation was made three to six months in advance. On the appointed day a public auction began at the appropriate office. After two weeks the unsold land was put up for private sale. The minimum price was $1.25 an acre, the smallest parcel was eighty acres, and the terms were cash. So a buyer had to have on hand at least $100, the equivalent of about a half-year's wages for an unskilled laborer. He had to go in person or send an agent to the land office. On arrival he would be given small township plats showing the vacant or unentered lands. When he looked these over, he like as not would find that the choicest pieces had already been taken— by large purchasers who had bid at the auction. The least desirable lands, those remaining unsold for ten years, would

[15] D. S. Durrie, "The Public Domain," in Western Historical Company, *The History of Sauk County, Wisconsin* . . . (Chicago, 1880), 217–218; Joseph Schafer, *A History of Agriculture in Wisconsin* (Madison, 1922), 134–135; James W. Whitaker, "Wisconsin Land Speculation, 1830–1860: Case Studies of Small Scale Speculators" (master's thesis, University of Wisconsin, 1962), 48–49, and land-survey map following p. 49.

be (during the period 1854–1862) gradually reduced in price.[16]

Veterans of the War of 1812 or the Mexican War received bounties in the form of warrants entitling them each to a quarter-section (160 acres) of the public domain. In 1850 the warrants were made assignable, so that veterans or their heirs could sell them if preferring ready money to a future farm. In 1855 and 1856 the 160-acre grant was extended to all men who had participated in any battle of the Revolutionary War or had given as much as two weeks of United States service in that war or at any time thereafter. Eager for cash, recipients of the bounty warrants commonly sold them to brokers for much less than $1.25 an acre. Dealers used them to accumulate tracts for speculation or resold them to land seekers at a considerable advance in price. The business was especially brisk in Wisconsin.[17]

A settler did not have to wait until land was surveyed and put up at auction before he began to occupy, cultivate, and improve it. Under the pre-emption law, he had the right to enter his 160 acres at the minimum price before the bidding was scheduled to open. If an alien, he must have declared his intention of becoming a citizen. Native or foreign-born, he must have built a house on the land and must be living in it as his exclusive home. He must not have made any agreement to transfer the title to another person. Such was the law; but in fact pre-emption rights were bought and sold, legally or illegally. They could be sold legally when two squatters had settled on the same quarter-section. The two could divide the quarter-section and obtain rights to locate and pre-empt another eighty acres apiece within the same land district. These "floating" rights were assignable.[18]

While squatters were moving in ahead of the surveyors, plen-

[16] Ritchie, *Wisconsin and Its Resources,* 164–166; Whitaker, "Wisconsin Land Speculation," 21.

[17] Benjamin H. Hibbard, *A History of the Public Land Policies* (Madison, 1965), 124–129; Paul W. Gates, "Frontier Land Business in Wisconsin," in *WMH,* 52 (Summer, 1969), 320–321; Whitaker, "Wisconsin Land Speculation," 22–24.

[18] Ritchie, *Wisconsin and Its Resources,* 164–166; Whitaker, "Wisconsin Land Speculation," 26.

ty of land already surveyed was still available in Wisconsin.
Only a fraction of the public domain had passed into private
hands by 1857. The boundaries of Wisconsin enclosed more
than thirty-five million acres all together. During the territorial period the federal land offices had offered approximately
eleven million acres and had disposed of less than half of that
amount. Between 1849 and 1857 an additional fourteen million acres were put up for sale and only about one-third was
actually sold.[19]

Meanwhile Congress gave the state more than four million
acres for it to sell. These included grants for education, for
internal improvements, and for the reclamation of swamps.
The school lands consisted mainly of the sections numbered
sixteen in all the townships of the federal survey. Every sixteenth section was divided into forty-acre tracts, and county
appraisers set a minimum price for each tract. The minimums
ranged from $1.25 an acre in the unsettled north to $20 and
higher in the well-populated counties of the south. The internal improvement lands had to be located and appraised by
state commissioners, and since these tracts were scattered among
unsold federal lands and had to compete with them, they were
seldom priced at more than $1.25. The so-called "swamp lands,"
also located by state officials, were in fact adequately drained
or were overflowed only in seasons of unusual flooding, except
for perhaps a fourth of the total. In 1856, when the swamp
lands first became available, the legislature set the minimum
price at $5, but so little was sold that the next year it reduced
the minimum to $1.25. Like the federal government, the state
first auctioned off its lands and then put the remainder up
for private sale, and it made provision for pre-emption. Unlike the federal government, the state sold on credit. The
buyer could make a down payment of as little as 10 per cent,
or in some cases no down payment at all, and he had ten years
in which to pay the balance. He could even borrow from the

[19] These are rough calculations based on a table of "acres sold" and "acres
offered" year by year in Whitaker, "Wisconsin Land Speculation," 55.

state, on a five-year mortgage, as much as half the appraised value of the land he was buying.[20]

The land that Congress granted to the state for the construction of the Fox–Wisconsin canal, and that the state transferred to the canal company in 1853, was the subject of legal disputes and political machinations for the rest of the decade. None of the parties could agree on the amount of land involved, but it may have been as much as two-thirds of a million acres. Whatever the total, little was made available to settlers, in part because of the continuing legal tangles but also because the company preferred to hold on to the land as a speculation while borrowing against it to meet construction costs. The railroad grant of 1856 was expected to exceed two million acres once the lines had been built. It was to include odd-numbered sections in a six-mile-wide strip on each side of the right of way. After qualifying for land by laying track through it, the railroads could dispose of it on their own terms. The government would sell the land it reserved, the even-numbered sections in the checkerboard pattern, in the same way as it did the rest of the public domain, but at double the regular minimum price—at $2.50 instead of $1.25 an acre.[21]

During the late 1840's and the early 1850's, speculators were buying tremendous quantities of public land in Wisconsin and holding it for resale. Thirty-four individuals and partnerships entered more than 10,000 acres apiece, and 108 others entered

[20] Irene D. Neu, "Land Credit in Frontier Wisconsin" (master's thesis, Cornell University, 1945), 79–81; Thomas H. Patterson, "The Disposal of Wisconsin's Common School Lands, 1849–1863" (master's thesis, University of Wisconsin, 1961), 1–23, 31–32, 37–42; Malcolm J. Rohrbough, "The Acquisition and Administration of the Wisconsin Swamp Land Grant, 1850–1865" (master's thesis, University of Wisconsin, 1958), 59, 68–69, 89–94.

[21] Robert W. McCluggage, "The Fox-Wisconsin Waterway, 1836–1872: Land Speculation and Regional Rivalries, Politics and Private Enterprise" (doctoral dissertation, University of Wisconsin, 1954), 235–237, 254–258, 260–268. See also Samuel Mermin, *The Fox-Wisconsin Rivers Improvement: An Historical Study in Legal Institutions and Political Economy* (Madison, 1968). On railroads see Gordon O. Greiner, "Wisconsin National Railroad Land Grants" (master's thesis, University of Wisconsin, 1935), 11–12; and Herbert W. Rice, "Early History of the Chicago, Milwaukee and St. Paul Railway Company" (doctoral dissertation, State University of Iowa, 1938), 154–155.

1,000 to 10,000 for a total in excess of 1,250,000 acres. Many thousands of additional acres remained unsold in the hands of speculators who had made accumulations during the previous land boom of the 1830's. "We know of parties in this city," the Green Bay *Advocate* reported in 1856, "who have over 20,000 acres of good farming land which they are anxious to dispose of to actual settlers." Similar parties elsewhere were also eager to sell, year after year. The "good farming land" they offered consisted almost entirely of unbroken, unimproved, "wild" land.[22]

Thousands of owners who had started farms were also looking for buyers. In Walworth County, for example, a settler wanted to sell for $10 an acre, in 1849, an excellent farm with "great fields of corn and almost innumerable stacks of wheat & shocks of oats." In Rock County, that same year, another farm was offered for the sum of $1,000. "It contained 160 acres of prairie with a good spring on it, 65 acres prepared for a crop next year, 100 apple trees grafted fruit set out, and 40 acres of opening two miles distant." In Bad Ax (Vernon) County, seven years later, forty acres of cultivated land was worth from $500 to $1,000. By comparison, a horse cost from $100 to $200, and a yoke of oxen from $100 to $150.[23]

Thus a settler arriving in the new state could choose land at a price to fit his purse. He could get government land for as little as $1.25 an acre, but it would probably be a comparatively undesirable, leftover part of the public domain, more or less remote from existing settlements and transportation routes, and in need of clearing and breaking. He could find "any amount of second hand land" at $3 to $30 an acre, depending on the nature of the soil, the improvements, and the distance from markets. Land agents in Milwaukee and other cities stood ready to help him make a choice. They provided maps, property descriptions, bounty warrants, purchase loans, and even

[22] Gates, "Frontier Land Business," in *WMH*, 52: 324; Hibbard, *Public Land Policies,* 127n, quoting the Green Bay *Advocate,* June 12, 1856.

[23] The descriptions of the Walworth and Rock County farms are in Kenneth Duckett, ed., "A 'Down-Easter' in Wisconsin: Sears Letters, 1849, 1854," in *WMH*, 41 (Spring, 1958), 205–206; and John A. Houkam, ed., "Pioneer Kjaerkebön Writes from Coon Prairie," in *WMH*, 27 (June, 1944), 441.

horses and wagons "to take Emigrants to see farms before pay-ing their money."[24]

[4]

Americans and Europeans in search of land were swarming west-ward during the early years of Wisconsin's statehood. In the decade after 1850 one American in every four moved from one state to another, and from some of the older states of the North-east the departure rate was as high as one in three. In the same decade a larger number of Europeans migrated to America— more than two and a half million of them—than had done so in all the preceding decades together since Independence. This first great immigration wave of the nineteenth century crested during the years 1847–1854.[25]

Many a westering American was impelled by nothing more than a dimly felt urge. He was caught up by the pioneering spirit, a kind of poetic impulse, a desire for adventure, for escape from the humdrum, for an opportunity to start afresh and at the same time to assert his manhood. "The bold young American of the North Eastern States chooses a helpmate, col-lects some clothing, takes up his rifle and hatchet, and trust-ing entirely to his own prowess, marches off in the direction of the setting sun," as a contemporary put it. "There is some-thing highly exciting and grateful to youthful daring and in-dependence in travelling onward in search of a future home, and having found some sweet encouraging spot in the bosom of the wilderness, in rearing everything by his own handi-work."[26]

But there were also less romantic reasons for leaving the

[24] Gregory, *Industrial Resources of Wisconsin*, 310. Freeman, *Emigrant's Hand Book*, 103, reproduces the agent's advertisement offering transportation.

[25] *Eighth Census of the United States, 1860: Population*, xxxiii–xxxv; Marcus Lee Hansen, *The Atlantic Migration, 1607–1860: A History of the Continuing Settlement of the United States* (Cambridge, 1941), 242–306.

[26] Freeman, *Emigrant's Hand Book*, 19–20; the quotations are from p. 20. For other discussions of the romance of pioneering, with special reference to Wis-consin, see Joseph Schafer, *Four Wisconsin Counties: Prairie and Forest* (Madi-son, 1927), 117–120; Hamlin Garland, *A Son of the Middle Border* (New York, 1917), 43, 46; and Ritchie, *Wisconsin and Its Resources*, 262–266.

Northeast. Small farmers, particularly in Vermont and in western New York, found it hard to make money on their customary cash crop, wheat, as canals and then railroads brought competing grain from the farms that were being started in the Northwest. Many Yankees and New Yorkers were tempted to move west and grow wheat on more productive soil. They could sell out to richer landowners who were enlarging fields for livestock-raising and dairying. North of the border, in upper Canada, were other wheat farmers who had cause to abandon their homes and look for new ones. These English-speaking Canadians, many of them originally from the United States, had lost their protected market in Great Britain when, in 1846, the British government repealed the "corn laws" and began to accept wheat freely from the entire world. The British government's adoption of free trade also hurt the lumber industry of British America, and French-speaking lumberjacks from lower Canada and the Maritime Provinces moved south and west in growing numbers.[27]

Beyond the Atlantic, too, the urge for emigration made itself felt, among people who were becoming more and more restless. Economic and social changes increased the discontent and the numbers of the discontented. In some of the German states, for example, rising factories took business away from craftsmen and drew them along with peasants into the swelling proletariat of the industrial centers. Elsewhere in Germany large landowners consolidated small holdings and transformed the occupants into rent-paying tenants or hired laborers. As many as half the children born in certain areas were illegitimate, for young people were not allowed to marry unless they could get a place to live—or would agree to emigrate to America. In Norway, there was no industrial expansion to match a rapid population growth, and the majority of the people labored as small freeholders, renters, or farm hands on the mere 3 or 4 per cent of the land that could be tilled. In England the farm-

[27] Schafer, *Agriculture in Wisconsin*, 61–62; Marcus Lee Hansen (completed by John Bartlet Brebner), *The Mingling of the Canadian and American Peoples* (New York, 1970), 131–132.

ers feared the consequences of free trade, as they did in Canada, and the millworkers endured conditions of Dickensian horror.

A series of natural disasters gave an added stimulus to emigration. During the 1840's the potato, which had made possible the great population increase in northern Europe, repeatedly rotted in the ground. Famine resulted in parts of Norway and in Ireland, where the potato was for many families practically the only food. Though the blight was widespread on the Continent also, the hunger there was alleviated by yields of grain. During the early 1850's, however, there was a succession of bad harvests in Germany and the Low Countries.

Not all the emigrants were starving or destitute, though the great majority were far from being rich. Some were peasant proprietors or cotters whose plots were too small to support them and their families, or younger sons who had no chance to inherit the paternal estate, or more-or-less-prosperous landowners or business or professional men who had grievances other than strictly economic ones. Some, rich or poor, objected to the authority of the established church, as did the evangelical Haugeans in Norway and the Roman Catholics in certain officially Lutheran states of Germany. Some, in Norway, Belgium, and other countries, hated conscription and hoped to get away, or get their sons away, from military service. And some, having failed to make their homeland democratic, looked for democracy abroad. As Carl Schurz declared from his exile in England after the defeat of the German Revolution of 1848, "If I cannot be the citizen of a free Germany, then I would at least be a citizen of free America."[28]

Emigration was encouraged by those in Europe who stood to profit from it. Railroads and shipping companies advertised for passengers and sent agents into the hinterland to look for them. After the repeal of the British navigation acts in 1849, the shipping of all countries was open to international com-

[28] Hansen, *Atlantic Migration*, 242–279; Mack Walker, *Germany and the Emigration, 1816–1885* (Cambridge, 1964), 153–174; Theodore C. Blegen, *Norwegian Migration to America, 1825–1860* (Northfield, Minnesota, 1931), 1–23, 154–176; Schurz to Adolf Meyer, April 19, 1852, in Joseph Schafer, ed. and trans., *Intimate Letters of Carl Schurz, 1841–1869* (Madison, 1928), 109.

petition, and fares came down. Ships carrying lumber from Canada to England and Europe returned to Canada with emigrants and ballast. The Norwegian merchant marine began its rise to greatness by transporting people to America from British as well as Norwegian ports. A German company, boasting of its new screw-driven steamships, claimed that, exactly one month after leaving Bremen, a man could be settling on a Wisconsin farm. All but a few of the ships in the emigrant business, however, were much slower sailing vessels, which took as long as two or three months for the ocean crossing.

People who could do so financed the voyage by saving up for it or by selling what property they had. Many left home with more than enough money for the trip. In the early 1850's German authorities estimated that departing Germans were taking with them an average of nearly $100 apiece. But the average declined as more and more of the very poor emigrated. Their way was often paid out of charitable contributions or public funds. *Auswanderung* societies agitated to raise money for getting rid of dangerous proletarians, and the governments of Baden and a few other states subsidized the deportation of unemployables. Irish landlords sometimes bought passage for their tenants so as to avoid the responsibility of supporting them as paupers. English potters in Staffordshire contributed to a fund that enabled the unemployed among them to emigrate. Once settled in America, people of every national origin sent remittances to the old country for bringing relatives to the new.[29]

[5]

Settlers heading for Wisconsin from other states or from foreign countries usually planned to arrive in the spring, so as to have time for locating land, putting in a crop, and making

---

[29] Hansen, *Atlantic Migration*, 242–306; Blegen, *Norwegian Migration, 1825–1860*, pp. 349–352; Kligora, "German Element in Wisconsin," 22–24; Walker, *Germany and the Emigration*, 134–174; Grant Foreman, "Settlement of English Potters in Wisconsin," in *WMH*, 21 (June, 1938), 375–396.

preparations for the winter. They moved along as individuals, families, and larger groups. Unmarried men went to seek their separate fortunes, and fathers went by themselves to prepare the way for their families or, making a second trip, took their wives and children with them. Sometimes several families from the same neighborhood traveled together, and so did religious or secular colonies.[30]

Most of these people journeyed directly to Wisconsin from their home state or their port of debarkation. Practically all the Norwegians did so, and nearly all the Germans, Hollanders, and Belgians, though some Germans settled temporarily along the way, and a few Dutch stayed in the East long enough to earn money for the rest of the trip. The Irish were exceptional: as a rule they took several years to work their way to Wisconsin from the Northeastern states or Canada. Many native New Englanders, New Yorkers, and Pennsylvanians still pioneered by stages, as they had done for generations. By the time a family reached Wisconsin it might include children born in two or more states from the Northeast through Ohio, Indiana, and Illinois. But the proportion of these gradual pioneers declined as the means of transportation improved.[31]

Migrants converged upon Wisconsin by a variety of routes and modes of travel, old and new. From New York and Boston and Quebec they made their way to Buffalo by riverboat, canal boat, stagecoach, or railroad train, or some combination of them. From Buffalo they proceeded by the lakes; or partly by water and partly by rail, as segments of track were opened up; or entirely by rail after the lines had been extended to Wiscon-

[30] Theodore C. Blegen, *Norwegian Migration to America: The American Transition* (Northfield, Minnesota, 1940), 3; Mary J. Read, "A Population Study of the Driftless Hill Land During the Pioneer Period, 1832–1860" (doctoral dissertation, University of Wisconsin, 1941), 160–161. For examples of group migration, see Levi, "German Immigration," in *Wis. Hist. Colls.*, 14: 363–367, 373–374, 385–387; Henry S. Lucas, ed., *Dutch Immigrant Memoirs and Related Writings* (2 vols., Assen, Netherlands, 1955), 2: 138–139, 175–177; Foreman, "English Potters," in *WMH*, 21: 375–396.

[31] Michael P. Conzen, "Demographic Change and Urbanization in a Nineteenth Century Frontier Township" (seminar paper, University of Wisconsin, 1969), 17–19; Read, "Driftless Hill Land," 53–56, 277–280; McDonald, *Irish in Wisconsin*, 10–13; Lucas, ed., *Dutch Immigrant Memoirs*, 2: 175–177.

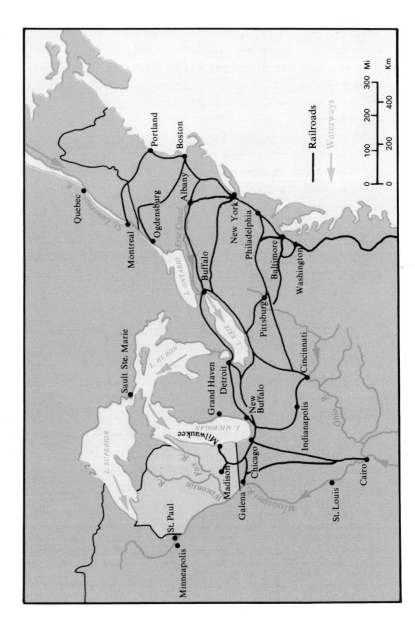

ROUTES TO WISCONSIN, 1854

sin. From New Orleans, and from Philadelphia by way of Pittsburgh and the Ohio River, they came up the Mississippi. And from states as distant as Vermont they continued to come by team and wagon, which in many cases they shipped a part of the distance by train or boat.[32]

Arriving in Wisconsin, some had no specific destination in mind and happened by chance upon a place to settle. This was the case with a Scotsman who in 1849 landed at Milwaukee with three of his children—one of them John Muir, the future world-famous naturalist, then eleven years old—and with a huge pile of heavy boxes. "In leaving Scotland," Muir was afterwards to write, "father, like many other home-seekers, burdened himself with far too much luggage, as if all America were still a wilderness in which little or nothing could be bought." At Milwaukee a farmer heading back home after bringing in a load of wheat offered to take the Muirs with their freight the hundred miles to Kingston, in Marquette (later Green Lake) County, for $30. At Kingston a land agent directed the elder Muir to a farmer on the edge of settlement, who helped Muir find a good place for a farm, while the children stayed behind in a rented room.[33]

Some settlers arrived as members of migrating communities whose leaders had determined upon a location in advance. Thus English newcomers sponsored by the Potters' Joint Stock Emigration Society or the British Temperance Emigration Society headed for the potters' settlements in Columbia and Marquette counties or the temperance people's Mazomanie Colony in Dane County. The ninety-one poor Friesians whom the wealthy Oepke Bonnema had brought over from the Netherlands joined him in founding New Amsterdam in 1853 on the Black River, at a spot he had selected as ideal for a sawmill. About a hundred German followers of the Reverend Ambrose Oschwald, founder and presiding priest of the Colony of St. Nazianz, set up their

[32] Blegen, *Norwegian Migration, 1825–1860,* pp. 349–352; Read, "Driftless Hill Land," 231–236; Gregory, *Industrial Resources of Wisconsin,* 306–307; Bayrd Still and William Herrmann, eds., "Abner Morse's Diary of Emigrant Travel, 1855–56," in *WMH,* 22 (December, 1938–March, 1939), 195–212, 329–343.

[33] John Muir, *The Story of My Boyhood and Youth* (Madison, 1965), 49–50.

religious commune (unsanctioned by the Catholic Church) near Manitowoc on 3,840 acres that he had purchased from land dealers in Milwaukee. In various parts of the state, regular priests and missionaries guided Roman Catholic Germans into compact rural settlements.[34]

Most arrivals, whatever their origin, headed for some place where people of their own kind or kindred were residing already. Thus the father of Roujet D. Marshall, a boy who was to grow up to be a distinguished lawyer and judge, made two trips from New Hampshire to Wisconsin before finding his brother-in-law's residence in a Sauk County community of New Englanders, and that community was his destination when, in 1854, he made a third trip with his family to settle on three "forties" of partially cleared woodland he had bought from a discouraged pioneer. Arriving from Norway in 1854, the father of Nils P. Haugen, a five-year-old who was to become a prominent politician, made his way to Beloit and stayed with Norwegians near there while working in the wheat fields and deciding where to make his permanent home. Meanwhile several families of Belgians, who knew of no countrymen in Wisconsin, had landed at Sheboygan and were prospecting for land thereabout but were having trouble in making themselves understood in French. When they learned that many French-speaking Canadians lived in and around Green Bay, they located in that area instead.[35]

In choosing land of their own, the newcomers generally preferred a place where they could remain among neighbors with the same language and ways of life. They also took into account the productivity of the soil, the ease of cultivating

[34] Foreman, "English Potters," in *WMH*, 21: 375–396; Lucas, ed., *Dutch Immigrant Memoirs*, 2: 138–139; Henry S. Lucas, "The Founding of New Amsterdam in La Crosse County," in *WMH*, 31 (September, 1947), 42–60; Levi, "German Immigration," in *Wis. Hist. Colls.*, 14: 385–387; Overmoehle, "Forty-Eighters in Wisconsin," 265–266.

[35] Gilson G. Glasier, ed., *Autobiography of Roujet D. Marshall, Justice of the Supreme Court of the State of Wisconsin, 1895–1918* (2 vols., Madison, 1923, 1931), 1: 95–101; Nils P. Haugen, "Pioneer and Political Reminiscences," in *WMH,* 11–13 (December, 1927–June, 1929, December, 1929), 11: 121–130; Xavier Martin, "The Belgians of Northeast Wisconsin," in *Wis. Hist. Colls.*, 13: 376–377.

it, the availability of wood and water, and the accessibility of markets. They had no way of knowing for sure how fertile a particular piece of ground would prove to be—until someone had farmed it for a while—but they believed that, on the whole, open prairie would make better farming land than would oak openings or heavy timber. They knew they could quickly break the prairie sod for putting in a crop but would have to toil long and hard to clear the timberland. Still, they needed timber for fuel, fencing, and housing. Also, they liked the shade and shelter that a grove afforded and, more important, the streams and springs and shallow wells that they were much more likely to find in wooded, hilly country than on the flat and comparatively dry prairie. Those land-seekers who had read the guidebooks or had talked with experienced settlers knew perfectly well, then, that an ideal farm would combine prairie, openings, and forest. It would also contain some marsh or meadow for natural hay, a good dam site for mill power, and perhaps a quarry for construction stone. It would lie near a lake port, a navigable river, a well-traveled road, or a rail line already built or projected. And it would be at least partially improved, with fields already plowed or planted and a house of some sort fit for immediate occupancy.[36]

Comparatively few of the land-seekers could find an ideal farm for sale, or could afford one if they found it. Roujet D. Marshall's parents did fairly well with their 120 acres near the Yankee village of Delton. They had brought with them, in two cloth belts they wore, $3,500 in banknotes and gold pieces, which was much more than enough. A well-to-do Norwegian bought, in a neighborhood of fellow Norwegians, a farm of 200 acres that included oak groves, pasture, cultivated fields,

---

[36] For an example of contemporary advice in regard to choosing land, see Wilhelm Dames, *Wie Sieht es in Wiskonsin aus? Ein Treuer Führer und Rathgeber für Auswanderer* [*What is the Outlook in Wisconsin? A True Guide and Adviser for Emigrants*] (Meurs, Prussia, 1849), as quoted and paraphrased in Schafer, *Agriculture in Wisconsin*, 38–39; a typed translation by Joseph Schafer is in the SHSW. More examples are in *America in the Forties: The Letters of Ole Munch Raeder*, travel letters of 1847–1848 originally printed in a Christiania newspaper and later edited and translated by Gunnar J. Malmin (Minneapolis, 1929), 73–74; and Gregory, *Industrial Resources of Wisconsin*, 33–34.

a quarry, and a harvested crop of wheat, corn, potatoes, and fruit, not to mention tools, a plow, and four oxen. He was able to pay the $1,250 that all this cost. But most of the new-comers, especially the foreign-born and more especially the Nor-wegians, had little or no money left by the time they reached Wisconsin. In buying land they had to be satisfied with some-thing less than the best, and they were lucky to get a good fea-ture with the bad—choice prairie and openings with a remote location, access to markets with hard-to-clear timber, an estab-lished farm with inferior soil.[37]

A great many were unable to buy land at all during their first season in Wisconsin. Or, if they bought land, they could not afford the expense of converting it into a farm. To get money they worked as hired hands on others' farms, as lumber-jacks in the northern pineries, skilled or casual laborers in vil-lages and cities, members of construction gangs on canals or railroads. The Irish in particular busied themselves with picks and shovels and wheelbarrows on the improvement projects; these projects determined the original location of Irish settle-ments within the state. After a year or two or more, some wage earners of the various nationalities had saved enough to be-come landowning farmers. Others never succeeded in doing so, or never intended to do so, but remained agricultural, in-

[37] Glasier, ed., *Autobiography of Roujet D. Marshall,* 1: 98–101; Folkedahl, ed., "Norwegians Become Americans," *Norwegian-American Studies,* 21: 108; Benja-min H. Hibbard, *The History of Agriculture in Dane County, Wisconsin* (Madi-son, 1904), 105–113; Joseph Schafer, *The Wisconsin Lead Region* (Madison, 1932), 226–231; Schafer, *Four Wisconsin Counties,* 107–121. In *Agriculture in Dane County,* 108, Hibbard suggests that New Englanders, New Yorkers, and the English preferred a combination of prairies and woods and that Germans, Nor-wegians, and the Irish preferred the forests. "The Germans and Norwegians were not at all averse to hilly land, perhaps because they were accustomed to hills at home." Schafer, *Four Wisconsin Counties,* 120–121, says: "Men from the well-wooded regions of New York, New England, Pennsylvania, and Ohio hesitated to build homes on the big, open, exposed prairies. They finally came to it. . . ." In *Wisconsin Lead Region,* 226, he also says Germans were more hesitant than Norwegians to move into the interior and were more willing to undergo the labor of clearing forests in areas (like those north of Milwaukee) that were close to markets. But in *Agriculture in Wisconsin,* 38, he says: "We have already seen that the ideal farm, to the American settler, was a combina-tion of timber, prairie or opening, and marsh. . . . Now, the above is precisely the 'ideal farm' for the ambitious immigrant as well as for the native."

dustrial, or domestic employees. Land was not for everyone. Only a little more than half the men in Wisconsin owned any real estate in 1850, and the proportion does not seem to have changed significantly by 1860.[38]

Not only prospective farmers but also business and professional men, artisans, and common laborers sought opportunities in Wisconsin. Most of these people made their way to a city or a village; they belonged to the urban rather than the rural frontier. Cautious capitalists went in person or sent agents to investigate the possibilities before committing themselves; more daring entrepreneurs simply joined the westward movement and took their chances. Some, transferring their established enterprises from an eastern state to Wisconsin, brought with them their skilled labor force as well as their capital. Christian Ficker, a recent immigrant, advised his fellow Germans that certain kinds of craftsmen, migrating on their own, would find a ready market for their services while others would not. Tailors, coopers, and lace makers, for example, could "count upon prompt support," at least in the cities. Bakers, glaziers, and barbers "might find it difficult to secure situations"—the bakers because farmers generally baked their own bread, the glaziers because home owners could buy and set factory-made windowpanes for themselves, the barbers because "colored persons" monopolized the urban hair-cutting as well as hairdressing business.[39]

[6]

"Oh, that glorious Wisconsin wilderness!" Such it seemed to young John Muir when he came upon the home his father had prepared in Marquette County, with its "charming hut,

---

[38] Blegen, *Norwegian Migration: American Transition*, 37; Schafer, *Agriculture in Wisconsin*, 130–131; McDonald, *Irish in Wisconsin*, 71–75, 91; Lee Soltow, *Patterns of Wealthholding in Wisconsin Since 1850* (Madison, 1971), 78.

[39] Alice E. Smith, *Millstone and Saw: The Origins of Neenah-Menasha* (Madison, 1966), 59–60; Joseph Schafer, ed. and trans., "Christian Traugott Ficker's Advice to Emigrants," in *WMH*, 25 (December, 1941–June, 1942), 473–474. For examples of industrialists bringing their own workers, see Chapter 3 below.

in the sunny woods, overlooking a flowery glacier meadow and a lake rimmed with white waterlilies." Not all the new arrivals were so instantly captivated as was Muir, the born nature lover. "I was very much disappointed at first; the country appeared too wild—woods, woods, nothing but woods, and only a small clearing here and there with a ramshackle building upon it," wrote Arnold Verstegen from Little Chute on the lower Fox to his father-in-law in Holland. "I felt as though I wanted to go back home right away."

It was night and raining hard when a Fox River boat brought seventeen-year-old Mary Aurelia Kimberly to her future home, the raw, frontier milltown of Neenah. Daughter of a pioneering industrialist, graduate of a New York female seminary, Mary was used to better things. Reaching the dock and "slipping in the red mud, stumbling over stumps," she and her relatives made their way to the hotel. The rooms were already full, even the kitchen, which was crowded with "squaws and bucks." Finally bedded down in the parlor, Mary and her sister cried themselves to sleep "for very homesickness." Neenah struck them as "a horrid town."[40]

At first sight, in the eyes of many arrivals, Wisconsin failed to measure up to its glowing advertisements. In "instances without number," according to one of the state's promoters, the "Old Country people" began to complain before they had even discovered what the new country was really like. Often "disappointment comes upon them from a false representation made to them before they started across the Atlantic; they commence raving against 'Yankees' and wish themselves back again." A government official from Norway, touring Wisconsin, learned that practically all the Norwegians there had been ill at one time or another. "When I told a group of Norwegians at Muskego that Mr. Fribert had written a book in which he says that Wisconsin is one of the most healthful places on earth, they

---

[40] Muir, *Boyhood and Youth*, 51–53; Lucas, ed., *Dutch Immigrant Memoirs*, 2: 151–154; Smith, *Millstone and Saw*, 165–166. The description of early Neenah is on p. 166 and is from an unpublished reminiscence, "Story of Pioneer Days" (1913), by Mary Aurelia Kimberly Hamilton, in the SHSW.

all laughed," the visitor reported. Still, he found very few who said they were dissatisfied and wanted to return to Norway, "and with some of these it was more a matter of talk than of a real desire to go."[41]

Even if they had the desire, few immigrants had the means to go back, but the discontented ones among them could usually manage, sooner or later, to go on. So, too, could the discontented ones among the American-born. If an unfavorable first impression persisted, or if original enthusiasm turned into disillusionment, settlers could look for a new location and a second chance. Uncounted numbers were doing so.

Indeed, depopulation threatened Wisconsin before the state was a year old. In December 1848 its newspapers reported President James K. Polk's announcement that gold had been discovered in territory recently acquired as a result of the war with Mexico. Some of the papers cast doubt on the President's truthfulness, the *Wisconsin Herald* of Lancaster asserting that "all the stuff about the mines of California" was "a mere attempt to throw gold dust in the people's eyes and blind them to the enormities of the war." Even when admitting that real gold was probably to be found, the editors questioned its abundance and advised their readers to stay home and stick to their business rather than risk their lives, or at least their morals, in a fruitless journey to the gold fields. Occasionally a journalist confessed his fear that the California news would draw people away from Wisconsin, depress business and property there, and hold back the development of the state.[42]

Undeterred, thousands of Wisconsinites made preparations during the winter of 1848–1849 for joining other thousands from all over the country and the world in the rush to California. The more impatient of the Wisconsin Forty-Niners, the ones who could not wait for spring, left at once for New York or New Orleans to take a roundabout passage by ship. The

[41] Freeman, *Emigrant's Hand Book*, 98–99; Malmin, ed., *Letters of Ole Raeder*, 65–66.

[42] William H. Herrmann, "Wisconsin and the California Gold Rush" (master's thesis, University of Wisconsin, 1940), 1–16; on p. 9 he quotes the Lancaster *Wisconsin Herald*, December 23, 1848.

rest, much the larger number, among them Count Agostin Haraszthy, the founder of Sauk City, began to start overland as early in March as the weather permitted. Amid feverish excitement, train after train of covered wagons and armed and mounted men set out from Wisconsin during the spring and summer of 1849. The next year the exodus was even greater. It decreased somewhat in 1851, more than recovered in 1852, fell off sharply in 1853, and gradually declined thereafter.[43]

"The California mania took a great many away," a Wisconsin promoter conceded while the rush was still going on. He claimed that by June 1850, when Wisconsin's population stood at a little over 300,000, nearly 50,000 had bypassed or left the state for the gold fields. The drain was proportionately the greatest from the lead region—the counties of Grant, Iowa, and Lafayette—in the southwestern corner of the state. Unprospering lead miners there naturally expected a relatively easy transition to becoming successful gold miners in the Far West. During the one season of 1850 more than sixty wagons and 200 persons left a single mining center, Mineral Point. Estimates of total departures from the region ran as high as one-third of the inhabitants as a whole and almost one-half of the Cornishmen. Certain localities were practically deserted, and land values dropped as much as 50 per cent. How many people all together Wisconsin lost to California (including potential settlers who bypassed Wisconsin in pursuit of gold) it is impossible to say.[44]

Some came back. They had planned to be away only long enough to strike it rich, and they had thought that that would not be very long. "I am anxious to go to California and make my fortune, and I am inclined to believe that any industrious man may make one if he goes with the intentions of making one—and saves his money, which I am resolved to do if I can get there," wrote a fairly typical Wisconsin victim of the gold

[43] Harry E. Cole, ed., *A Standard History of Sauk County, Wisconsin . . .* (2 vols., Chicago, 1918), 1: 207; Herrmann, "California Gold Rush," 24–29, 68.

[44] Freeman, *Emigrant's Hand Book,* 32; Herrmann, "California Gold Rush," 40–44; Larry Gara, "Gold Fever in Wisconsin," in *WMH,* 38 (Winter, 1954–1955), 106–108.

fever, who sought a loan from a family friend and offered to "make almost any sacrifice" by way of interest. "I do not intend to be gone more than fifteen months. . . ." Of those who returned, few had succeeded in making more than the equivalent of modest wages. One youthful Forty-Niner, the future Wisconsin governor Lucius Fairchild, reappeared in Madison after a six-year absence and let admiring friends know that he, at least, had made his "pile." Indeed, he had accumulated $10,000, though he had done so by keeping a store and grubstaking miners, not by digging gold.[45]

Wisconsin was losing people not only to California but also to other parts of the country. Though the out-migrants went in all directions, some even heading back East, much the largest number pushed on westward across the Mississippi. They were looking for better land on the farther frontier. Typical were the Norwegian settlers who in 1850 started from Muskego, paused at Koshkonong to pick up others, and then proceeded as a group of more than 100 in a caravan that included wagons with wheels "made of solid sections of oak logs." At Prairie du Chien a part of the caravan turned north, and the rest crossed the river into Iowa. Year after year other wagon trains followed, as more and more Wisconsin Norwegians resettled in Iowa and Minnesota. "I believe the entire population of Wisconsin is on the way to the west now," a woman wrote one day in 1854 while 300 wagons went creaking past. In the spring of 1857 a Wisconsin family approaching McGregor's ferry at Prairie du Chien had to stop and wait nine or ten miles back from the river—so long was the line of waiting teams ahead. By 1860 a total of 31,185 Wisconsin natives were residing out-

---

[45] L. B. Kellogg to J. C. Fairchild, January 6, 1849, in the Lucius Fairchild Papers; Sam Ross, *The Empty Sleeve: A Biography of Lucius Fairchild* (Madison, 1964), 13–17. Fairchild reports some of his experiences in Joseph Schafer, ed., *California Letters of Lucius Fairchild* (Madison, 1931). For a sampling of accounts of other gold hunters who returned to Wisconsin, see Peter J. Coleman, "The Woodhouse Family: Grant County Pioneers," in *WMH*, 42 (Summer, 1959), 267–274; John O. Holzhueter, ed., "From Waupun to Sacramento in 1849: The Gold Rush Journal of Edwin Hillyer," in *WMH*, 49 (Spring, 1966), 210–244; and J. H. A. Lacher, ed., "Visions of a Wisconsin Gold Seeker," in *WMH*, 5 (March, 1922), 290–292.

side Wisconsin, a figure which did not include former Wisconsin inhabitants who had been born in other states or in foreign countries. The states with the largest numbers of these Wisconsin-born migrants were Minnesota, Iowa, and Illinois, in that order. California was fourth.[46]

Not all the Wisconsinites on the move were leaving the state; many were resettling within its borders. In some cases their moves were frequent, like those of the Watrous family from upstate New York, one of whose five children, a boy named Jerome, was eventually to have a distinguished military career. The elder Watrous, failing repeatedly as a hotelkeeper, took his wife and their hungry brood from Sheboygan Falls west to Forest township in Fond du Lac County, then north to Brothertown in Calumet County, and then east to Hayton in Calumet, thus making three moves in a five-year period and tracing a semicircle as he did so.[47]

In most cases, however, the intrastate migrations were less meandering. People were transferring from south to north, east to west, southeast to northwest—from areas already well settled to those in the process of settlement or, in the case of the lead region, to an area in the process of resettlement as farm-makers moved in, taking advantage of depressed land prices, and replaced departing miners. Joining these migrations were old Wisconsin settlers and recent arrivals, native Americans and the foreign-born. Yankees were leaving their farms in Rock and Walworth counties, for example, and starting fresh ones in the Baraboo Valley. Norwegians were abandoning their early settlements at Muskego, Koshkonong, Rock Prairie (Rock County), and elsewhere, and were establishing

[46] The quotations are from Blegen, *Norwegian Migration: American Transition*, 487–490; the woman quoted by Blegen (p. 490) on Wisconsin's migrating population was Elizabeth Koren in her book *Fra Pioneertiden*, 168. The wait for the ferry is described in Joseph Schafer, "Ferries and Ferryboats," in *WMH*, 21 (June, 1938), 432–456. Statistics are from the *Eighth Census of the United States, 1860: Population*, xxxiii–xxxv. The census gives the number of natives of one state residing in another, but not the number of former inhabitants of one state residing in another.

[47] Jerome A. Watrous, "Fragment of an Autobiography," in *WMH*, 7 (September, 1923), 41–56.

colonies in the lead region, the Coon Valley area (including parts of Crawford, Vernon, Monroe, La Crosse, and Trempealeau counties), and St. Croix County. The Irish were spreading out from their original locations along the Fox–Wisconsin improvement in Winnebago and Columbia counties and along the railroads in various places. They were taking up farms in the surrounding townships or were moving on in search of new construction jobs. In the spring of 1855 one group of Irishmen, who had come together near Madison during the previous three years, journeyed in wagons all the way to Pleasant Valley, near Hudson. German settlers around Freistadt, Cedarburg, and Kirchhayn (all near Milwaukee) sold out and bought land in Sheboygan and Manitowoc counties, while other Germans were moving toward the interior from their settlements in the timber belt along Lake Michigan.[48]

The mobility of the Wisconsin population was dramatic. In each locality there was a continual reshuffling as some people left and others arrived. Especially was this true in places that were being newly pioneered, such as Trempealeau County, north of La Crosse. In Trempealeau County fewer than half the settlers stayed on for as long as a decade. The majority of every group, native American and foreign-born, departed within ten years for another county or another state. The turnover was higher among the non-English-speaking foreigners than among the English-speaking ones or the native Americans, higher among farm laborers than among farm operators, higher among nonagricultural than among agricultural groups, higher among the propertyless than among the propertied.[49]

[48] Read, "Driftless Hill Land," 61–67, 228–229; Cole, ed., *Sauk County*, 1: 277; Western Historical Company, *History of Sauk County*, 448–457; Blegen, *Norwegian Migration: American Transition*, 36–37; McDonald, *Irish in Wisconsin*, 91, 106–107; Levi, "German Immigration," in *Wis. Hist. Colls.*, 14: 341–352.

[49] Merle Curti, *The Making of an American Community: A Case Study of Democracy in a Frontier County* (Stanford, 1959), 65–77. Joseph Schafer suggests, without statistical evidence, that "once in possession of a tract of land, the German tended to hold on," and that "the Yankee," by contrast, tended "to regard land lightly, and to abandon one tract for another," in "The Yankee and the Teuton in Wisconsin," in *WMH*, 6–7 (December, 1922–December, 1923), 6: 125–145; see especially p. 144.

POPULATION OF WISCONSIN

Year	Population	Increase	% Increase
1842	44,478	—	—
1847	210,546	166,068	373.4%
1850	305,390	94,844	45.0%
1855	522,109	216,719	71.0%
1860	775,881	253,772	48.6%
1865	868,325	92,444	11.9%
1870	1,054,670	186,345	21.5%
1875	1,236,729	182,059	17.3%

SOURCES: Horace A. Tenney, "Census of Wisconsin From the Year 1836 to August 1860 . . ." (1842, 1847); U.S. Census of Population (1850, 1860, 1870); *Wisconsin Blue Book, 1882* (1855, 1865, 1875).

[7]

In 1850 the federal census takers found a total of 305,390 people residing in Wisconsin. With that figure in hand, one of the state's boosters predicted a population of perhaps a million by the end of the decade. He was to be disappointed, for the 1860 figure proved to be only 775,881. Not till the next decennial census was the million mark to be reached. Still, the decade's increase of 470,491 was tremendous, larger indeed than any ten-year gain the state was to make for a century. By 1860, Wisconsin had overtaken Michigan in population, was ahead of every New England state except Massachusetts, and stood fifteenth among all the thirty-four states.[50]

Within the state, the frontier of settlement had moved well to the north and west of the Fox–Wisconsin diagonal, so that the 1860 frontier line corresponded roughly to an arc drawn from Green Bay to Hudson by way of Stevens Point. The half of the state above that line remained a forested wilderness, except for identations of settlement that were being made as lumbermen advanced up the logging streams. Even in the

[50] *Seventh Census of the United States, 1850: Compendium*, 326, 333; Freeman, *Emigrant's Hand Book*, 32; William F. Raney, *Wisconsin: A Story of Progress* (New York, 1940), 138. The 1860 population figures are taken from the *Eighth Census of the United States, 1860: Population*, iv, 544–545.

southern half of the state, less than half of the area had been taken up as farms, and less than half of the state's farm acreage consisted of what the 1860 census categorized as "improved" land. Farmers and farm laborers constituted about 54 per cent of the gainfully employed, the rest of whom were engaged in nonagricultural occupations. The majority of the people lived in an essentially rural environment, either on farms or in small towns and villages. Less than 20 per cent of the population as a whole was clustered in towns of 2,500 or more. There were twenty-four such places by 1860. The largest were Milwaukee (45,246), Racine (7,882), Janesville (7,703), Madison (6,611), Oshkosh (6,086), Fond du Lac (5,450), Watertown (5,302), Sheboygan (4,262), and Beloit (4,098). Only one of the twenty-four—La Crosse (3,860)—lay to the north of the Fox–Wisconsin route. Only two—Platteville (2,865) and Hazel Green (2,543)—were located in the early-settled southwestern corner of the state. The southeast, especially Milwaukee County and adjoining counties, had become, by an increasing margin, the state's most densely populated area.[51]

On the basis of nativity, the 1860 population of Wisconsin might be divided into three parts of comparable size: one consisting of persons born in the state (247,177); the second, born elsewhere in the United States (251,777); and the third, born in foreign countries (276,927). Wisconsin, next to California, had the highest proportion of foreign-born inhabitants of all the states, yet despite the arrival of so many immigrants during the decade (166,450), the foreign-born percentage of the state's population actually had fallen a bit (from 36.2 to 35.7).[52]

Statistics regarding the foreign-born, however, fail to show the real ethnic composition of the people. The various ethnic groups included not only the immigrants themselves but also their children born in the United States. To estimate the en-

[51] In 1850 the acreage in farms was: "improved," 1,045,499; "unimproved," 1,931,159. In 1860: "improved," 3,746,167; "unimproved," 4,147,420. See the *Seventh Census of the United States, 1850*, p. 931; and the *Eighth Census of the United States, 1860: Agriculture,* 166. For population statistics, see *ibid.: Population,* 532–543, 545.

[52] *Ibid.,* xxx, 544; *Seventh Census of the United States, 1850,* p. 925; Raney, *Wisconsin,* 141.

tire number in these groups, some fraction should therefore be subtracted from the native total and added to the foreign-born. The state's population would then divide into two rather than three approximately equal parts, the one consisting of "American" families and the other of "foreign" families (the foreign-born together with their American-born children).[53]

Of the Wisconsin residents born in other states, almost half (120,637 in 1860) were natives of New York. The next largest numbers had come from Ohio (24,301), Pennsylvania (21,043), and Vermont (19,184). Many more had originated in the Northeast than in the Northwest, and very few in the Southeast and Southwest (6,265 in 1850 and 7,089 in 1860—a gain of only 824 during the decade).

Of the foreign-born, much the largest number (123,879 in 1860) had come from German countries, and the greatest share of the Germans (52,983) from Prussia. Germans made up a larger part of Wisconsin's population (nearly 16 per cent) than of any other state's. Next in order among Wisconsin's immigrants were those from Ireland (49,961), England, Scotland, and Wales (43,923); Norway (21,442—or about as many as in all the rest of the United States), British America (18,146), the Netherlands (4,906), Switzerland (4,722), and Belgium (4,647).

Milwaukee in 1860 contained a larger proportion of foreign-born inhabitants than did any other city in the nation except St. Louis. A little more than half of Milwaukee's approximately 45,000 people were immigrants, and more than two-thirds of these were Germans. Still, the foreigners in Wisconsin were

[53] Winnebago County may be taken as an example. According to the published report of the eighth census, the 1860 population of the county was approximately 29 per cent foreign-born (6,853 out of a total of 23,770). According to Robert C. Robertson, "The foreign population, computed on the basis of 'family heads' from the manuscript census, was at this time slightly less than 50 per cent." Robertson, "The Social History of Winnebago County, Wisconsin, 1850–1870" (master's thesis, University of Chicago, 1939), 6. This means that one-fourth or more of the American-born in the county were children of immigrants. If the same or nearly the same proportion should hold for the state as a whole, the entire "foreign population" could be estimated as at least 50 per cent. (The 1860 census enumerated the American-born children of foreign-born parents as an inseparable part of the native-born population.) See the *Eighth Census of the United States, 1860: Population,* 543–544.

more evenly distributed between the metropolis and the rest of the state than were those in New York, Pennsylvania, Ohio, or Illinois, where much the heaviest immigrant concentrations were to be found in New York City, Philadelphia, Cincinnati, and Chicago.[54]

Throughout Wisconsin—in the metropolis, in smaller cities and villages, and in rural townships—the people of each nationality tended to cluster in a neighborhood or larger grouping of their own. This was especially true of those whose mother tongue was not English. The Germans predominated in whole counties near Lake Michigan and in entire townships elsewhere, as in Sauk County. In New Glarus township in Green County practically every adult was Swiss by birth. A number of older settlements in Dane County and the southeast and the newer ones in Trempealeau County and Coon Valley were solidly Norwegian. Hollanders kept to themselves in scattered communities in the lower Fox Valley and other areas; the Belgians on the Door Peninsula and in Ozaukee County. Except for their colonies in Racine, Columbia, and Dane counties, the English as a whole were widely dispersed among settlers of native American stock, as were the Scots; but the Welsh and the Cornish settled in clumps, both in the lead region of the southwest. The Welsh had several communities elsewhere, particularly in Waukesha, Columbia, Winnebago, and Racine counties. The Irish were fairly well diffused throughout the state and were most numerous in places where canals or railroads had been built or planned—as in St. Croix County, where in Erin township nearly all the family heads in 1860 were natives of Ireland. In many parts of Wisconsin the ethnic localization of the people had increased with the growth of population during the 1850's.[55]

[54] *Seventh Census of the United States, 1850*, p. xxxvi; *Eighth Census of the United States, 1860: Population*, xx, xxi–xxxiii, 526–531, 543–544; Ella Lonn, *Foreigners in the Union Army and Navy* (Baton Rouge, 1951), 4–5.

[55] Levi, "German Immigration," in *Wis. Hist. Colls.*, 14: 351–352, 387–391; Read, "Driftless Hill Land," 240, 285; John D. Beck, "Acculturation and Religious Institutions: A Case Study of Acculturation in Sauk County, Wisconsin, by Special Reference to Religious Institutions" (master's thesis, University of Wisconsin, 1940), 5–9; Ruth G. Sanding, "The Norwegian Element in the Early History of Wisconsin" (master's thesis, University of Wisconsin, 1936), 86; Mc-

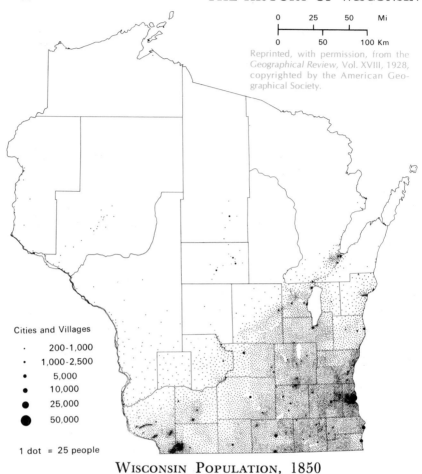

Cities and Villages

·   200-1,000
·   1,000-2,500
•   5,000
●   10,000
●   25,000
⬤   50,000

1 dot = 25 people

WISCONSIN POPULATION, 1850

Wisconsinites of African descent numbered only 1,171 according to the 1860 census. That is to say, they constituted
less than two-tenths of 1 per cent of the state's population. All
but twenty-six of the total were American-born. Most Negroes
lived in cities and towns, notably Milwaukee, Racine, and
Janesville, while somewhat smaller groups were in La Crosse,
Madison, Prairie du Chien, Kenosha, and Whitewater. Groups

Donald, *Irish in Wisconsin*, 75, 106–107; Edward G. Hartmann, *Americans from
Wales* (Boston, 1967), 71–72; Schafer, *Agriculture in Wisconsin*, 54–56.

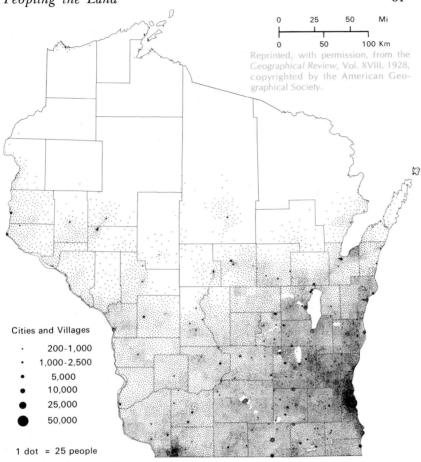

Cities and Villages

· 200-1,000
· 1,000-2,500
· 5,000
● 10,000
● 25,000
● 50,000

1 dot = 25 people

WISCONSIN POPULATION, 1860

of blacks also lived in such places as Forest in Bad Ax (Vernon) County, Caledonia (Racine County), and Trimbelle (Pierce County). Very few Negroes were found on the northern frontier except for the seventy-four who were listed as residing in Shawano and Oconto counties, who probably were of mixed black and Indian ancestry.

The 1860 census enumerated a total of 1,017 "civilized Indians," 404 of them "half breeds." Many of the latter also represented mixtures of Indian and African blood. The enumerated Indians were technically "Indians taxed," that is, property-owners and taxpayers; but the count included "broken bands and scattered remnants of tribes" who actually lived in pauperism and paid no taxes. Of the enumerated Indians the largest numbers were concentrated in Calumet (716) and Chippewa (129) counties, and the rest were scattered over the northern part of the state. Outside of Calumet, none was listed in any county lying entirely to the south of the Fox–Wisconsin line except twenty-four in Dodge and a single Indian in Rock.[56]

In addition to the thousand "civilized" and "taxed" Indians, who resided more or less among the white settlers, there were several thousand "tribal" Indians, who lived apart, untaxed, on reservations in the northeastern and northernmost reaches of the state. These tribes—the Chippewa, Menominee, Oneida, and Stockbridge—were not counted in the census, but (according to estimates by federal Indian agents) they totaled 8,000 or more as of about 1860. Another thousand or so, mostly Winnebago and Potawatomi, were classified neither as civilized nor as reservation Indians. Assigned to no reservation and attached to no agency in Wisconsin, they roamed through several western and northern counties of the state. Thus a grand total of some 10,000 of the aboriginal inhabitants remained after the white population had reached three-quarters of a million.[57]

---

[56] Eighth Census of the United States, 1860: Population, 531–544. The census of 1850 (but not that of 1860) classified many of these half breeds—particularly in Calumet County—simply as "colored," that is, Negro. See John O. Holzhueter, "Negro Admixture Among the Brotherton, Stockbridge, and Oneida Indians of Wisconsin" (1966), in the SHSW. On "enumerated" Indians, see the Ninth Census of the United States, 1870: Volume I, pp. xxi–xiii. It may be assumed that the 1860 census included the same sorts of "civilized Indians" as the 1870 census.

[57] The federal census takers themselves did not count the reservation Indians, and nobody officially counted the nomadic Winnebago and Potawatomi. Reservation and agency officials, however, provided figures in regard to reservation Indians for the census. These figures were based on both estimates and actual enumerations. The 1860 census reported only 2,833 of these Indians—a ridiculously inadequate number. The 1870 census reported 10,315. An estimate of about 8,000 for 1862, based on a study of agents' reports in the Annual Reports of the U.S. Commissioner of Indian Affairs, is given in Milo M. Quaife, "The Panic of 1862 in Wisconsin," in WMH, 4 (December, 1920), 169–170. As for the "roving Indians," a guess of "from seven hundred to nine hundred, . . . a large majority of them Winnebagoes," was presented in the U.S. Commissioner of Indian Affairs, Annual Report, 1863, p. 350.

3

Exploiting Nature's Bounty

[1]

THOSE WERE BOOM YEARS for the nation as a whole, those first years of Wisconsin's statehood. The country recovered from a recession following the Mexican War and then experienced one wave of prosperity after another, prosperity that California gold helped to stimulate. The times themselves favored the development of the state's resources, and so did the transportation improvements and the population growth. The resources to be developed—the good earth, the timber upon it, the minerals beneath it—seemed to promise for Wisconsin an early rise to industrial as well as agricultural greatness. True, coal and petroleum were lacking, but wood could be used to fuel steam engines, and streams could be harnessed for water power.

Wisconsin law encouraged the construction of milldams. On a stream designated "not navigable" a dam could be built without an official permit and without the consent of property owners whose land might be flooded by the resulting pond; they would have no legal recourse except to sue for damages. On a navigable stream no dam could be erected without the permission of the state legislature, but special acts were routinely passed for dam construction, and the rights they conveyed were generous as a rule. By 1848, there were already more than 100 water-powered mills on Wisconsin rivers and creeks, and in the first decades of statehood the number rapidly increased. By 1879, there were more than 700.[1]

Promoters of industry often talked as if Wisconsin, with its apparent potential for producing its own manufactured goods, were a separate country, one that lost money by paying for imports and stood to gain by achieving economic self-sufficiency. Patronize home industry, give "our own mechanics" the preference—such were the pleas of budding industrialists and their friends. In boosting local business, they sometimes implied that their particular city or town, as well as the state, ought to have an independent economy.[2]

If comparable to a separate country, however, the Wisconsin of the time was like an underdeveloped one. With no sizable cities except Milwaukee, the state was lacking in the readily accessible markets and sources of skilled labor necessary for the growth of complex and large-scale manufactures. Above all, the state suffered from a shortage of capital. The funds that were drawn in from the outside went largely into land speculation, which promised quicker and more dazzling profits than did most kinds of manufacturing. The state also suffered from inadequate bank credit and currency.

In any case, economic self-sufficiency would mean a comparatively low level of living. To the extent that it persisted in Wisconsin after 1848, it meant the subsistence farm, the household industry, the village craft shop, the primitive mill. Where these survived, they did so mainly because of geographical isolation. The improvement of transportation, especially railroads, stimulated commercial farming by increasing opportunities for the marketing of cash crops. At the same time, these improvements threatened local industries by exposing them to the competition of distant producers that were larger and more efficient. In short, the improvements made Wisconsin

[1] A. Allan Schmid, "Water and the Law in Wisconsin," in *WMH,* 45 (Spring, 1962, 203–204; Daniel J. Dykstra, "Law and the Lumber Industry, 1861–1881" (doctoral dissertation, University of Wisconsin, 1950), 124–129, 134, 137.

[2] Margaret Walsh, *The Manufacturing Frontier: Pioneer Industry in Antebellum Wisconsin, 1830–1860* (Madison, 1972), 1; Bayrd Still, *Milwaukee: The History of a City* (Madison, 1965), 190.

less and less self-sufficing, more and more an integral part of the national economy.[3]

The effect was to accelerate certain kinds of economic activity while slowing others down. Wisconsin began to specialize increasingly in those lines in which it had a natural advantage. Of all the state's output the farm produce as a whole was the most valuable, and wheat the single leading crop. Flour accounted for about 40 per cent of the state's industrial product in both 1850 and 1860, while the lumber industry contributed about one-fourth of the total output. Of lesser but growing importance were enterprises producing beef and pork, hides and leather, and beer. Accounting for a much smaller percentage of the industrial output than the immediate processing of goods from farm and forest were primary metal products—pig lead and shot, pig iron and castings—and the manufacture of agricultural implements and wagons. Much of the farm equipment was made in small craft shops, which served local markets, but some of it was produced in growing factories, for wider sale. These factories, along with machine shops and flouring and woodworking mills, foretold the decline of the smaller establishments and the rise of large-scale industry— though as yet most plants remained rather small, averaging all together fewer than five employees apiece. In two of the most important consumer-goods industries, those making shoes and clothes, some of the work continued to be done, by hand, in the workers' homes.[4]

[3] Walsh, *Manufacturing Frontier*, viii–x, 8, 10–11. For further information on Wisconsin's relation to the national economy and on factors which affected the condition of local industries, see Margaret Walsh, "Industrial Opportunity on the Urban Frontier: 'Rags to Riches' and Milwaukee Clothing Manufacturers, 1840–1880," in *WMH*, 57 (Spring, 1974), 175–194, especially p. 194.

[4] For statistics on Wisconsin's agricultural and industrial output as of 1860, see *Eighth Census of the United States, 1860: Agriculture*, 166–169, and *ibid.: Manufactures*, 657–658. The 1850 statistics on manufacturing are contained in *Senate Executive Documents*, 35 Cong., 2 sess., no. 39 (serial 984). For 1850 and 1860 figures on output calculated on the basis of value added by manufacture, see Walsh, *Manufacturing Frontier*, 18, 22. See also *ibid.*, 266–268, and Kathleen N. Conzen, " 'The German Athens': Milwaukee and the Accommodation of Its Immigrants, 1836–1860" (doctoral dissertation, University of Wisconsin, 1972), 202.

In the young state of Wisconsin, farm families still produced a large part of what they consumed, especially in foodstuffs. Local craftsmen met many of the needs of farmers, villagers, and city dwellers. More distant producers—lumbermen, miners, millers, manufacturers—provided other necessities through trade within the state. To a considerable extent, then, Wisconsin actually had a self-sufficing economy. But its people depended on other states for a number of essentials and paid for them by disposing of their own surpluses. A balance sheet for this rapidly increasing trade would show the following commodities coming in as the chief imports: coal, railroad iron, and salt. It would show the following going out as the main exports: wheat, flour, and lumber. Small quantities of beef and pork provisions and of butter and cheese were beginning to be exported, and a number of threshing and milling machines. The balance sheet might also contain a few "invisible items": imports of capital in the form of payments and loans, and exports of property in the form of titles to land and evidences of debt.[5]

[2]

New farms were being made at an average rate of nearly 5,000 a year in Wisconsin, though the process of farm making was laborious and slow, especially in places that were heavily timbered. A pioneer might well have been disheartened at the outset as he stood in the dank forest gloom and confronted growths of tangled brush and thick stands of maple, beech, oak, elm, and basswood, many of the trees five or six feet in diameter and some of them over a hundred feet tall. He had to chop

[5] For data on Milwaukee receipts and shipments, see William E. Derby, "A History of the Port of Milwaukee, 1835–1910" (doctoral dissertation, University of Wisconsin, 1963), 145, 150–151, 175, 196, 201. Wisconsin's exports went out by way of the Mississippi and its tributaries as well as through Milwaukee and other lake ports. "Wisconsin: Population, Resources and Statistics," in *De Bow's Review,* 14 (January, 1853), 24–28, reported that in 1851 goods worth $2,156,182.10 had left the state through the lake ports, and goods worth an estimated $1,170,000 (mostly lumber but also "furs and peltries") by way of the Mississippi.

down the smaller trees and remove the brush, while he either cut down the larger trees or killed them by girdling. Then he had to trim the fallen timber, cut it into logs of manageable size, haul them to a sawmill if there was one near enough, and pile and burn the leftover limbs and brush. Finally he had to grub out the stumps or wait for them to rot away while he planted around them. During the first spring he could make a clearing big enough for a cabin and a cultivated patch. In a whole year he would do well, even with his family's aid, to clear six or seven acres, and he would still have the task of breaking the land to the plow, all the while clearing more acres for future plantings.[6]

The work went much faster on the prairie. Here the settler could break one or two acres a day, or as much in a few days as would require a year in the forest. He would need four or five yoke of oxen to draw a heavy plow through the tough, root-matted sod and the underground "grubs," the old, still living roots of oaks, hickories, and other hardwoods whose sprouts had been repeatedly burned off by prairie fires. After harrowing, he left the overturned turf to decompose for several months or a year. When he plowed again, he might run into remaining snags, but by the third season he could expect to operate easily enough with a single ox-team.[7]

Oxen were well-nigh indispensable for clearing and breaking land. These strong and patient animals pulled steadily on yoke and chain and responded obediently to spoken commands of *gee* (for *right*) and *haw* (for *left*). Horses with their quick and jerky movements would soon have destroyed both

[6] Hjalmar R. Holand, *History of Door County, Wisconsin: The County Beautiful* (2 vols., Chicago, 1917), 1: 411–414; Joseph Schafer, ed. and trans., "Christian Traugott Ficker's Advice to Emigrants," in *WMH,* 25 (December, 1941–June, 1942), 334–336; "Journal of William Rudolph Smith," in *WMH,* 12 (December, 1928–March, 1929), 314; *Ninth Census of the United States, 1870: Volume III,* p. 340. Clarence H. Danhof, *Change in Agriculture: The Northern United States, 1820–1870* (Cambridge, 1969), 117, estimates that from ten to fifteen acres could be cleared during the first year.

[7] John Muir, *The Story of My Boyhood and Youth* (Madison, 1965), 181–184; Schafer, ed., "Ficker's Advice," in *WMH,* 25: 334–336; Daniel E. Schob, "Sod-busting on the Upper Midwestern Frontier, 1820–1860," in *Agricultural History,* 47 (January, 1973), 47–56.

harness and plow. Besides, horses cost more than twice as much. Not that oxen were cheap: the settler would have to spend a hundred dollars or more to buy a good driving team, two or three dollars a day to rent one, and between two and three dollars an acre, and even more in remote areas, to have the sod-breaking done for him. If he hired out to get the money, he could make from seventy-five cents to a dollar and a half a day on a neighboring farm. He might choose, instead, to clear and break his land without oxen, as did some of the Dutch immigrants in Brown County who—father, mother, and small boys working together—dragged logs and brush away by might and main and, their wrists aching, turned over the hard and rooty ground with grub hoes.[8]

The pioneer had to fence in his fields so as to keep out the cows and pigs that both he and his neighbors allowed to roam. Most commonly he made a rail fence by quartering logs and laying the pieces one on top of another along a zigzag line. If he could afford sawed lumber he might set posts in the ground and nail boards to them. On extensive prairies, where timber was scarce, he might resort to stringing heavy wires from post to post. Or he might trench around a field, throwing up the earth on the inner side, so as to form a ditch and embankment, or "sod fence."[9]

On rolling woodland the settler often found a ready source of drinking water in a spring, a brook, or a lake, or he could uncover a supply by digging a shallow well. On flat prairies, however, he usually had to dig or drill to a depth of twenty-

[8] Schafer, ed., "Ficker's Advice," in *WMH*, 25: 337–338; Beulah Folkedahl, ed. and trans., "Norwegians Become Americans," in *Norwegian-American Studies*, 21 (1962), 111; Josie G. Croft, ed., "A Mazomanie Pioneer of 1847," in *WMH*, 26 (December, 1942), 208–218; Ruth S. Burmester, ed., "Silas J. Seymour Letters," in *WMH*, 32 (December, 1948–June, 1949), 195; Henry S. Lucas, ed., *Dutch Immigrant Memoirs and Related Writings* (2 vols., Assen, Netherlands, 1955), 1: 184; Schob, "Sodbusting," in *Agricultural History*, 47: 48, 54.

[9] Schafer, ed., "Ficker's Advice," in *WMH*, 25: 334–336; Lucas, ed., *Dutch Immigrant Memoirs*, 2: 154–156. A "fencing & ditching machine"—by means of which, "with an ordinary breaking team of 5 yoke of oxen and 5 men a splendid *Sod-Fence, half a mile* in length, can be laid in *one day*"—was advertised in Samuel Freeman, *The Emigrant's Hand Book and Guide to Wisconsin . . .* (Milwaukee, 1851), 144.

five to 100 feet or even more. On high and dry land in Marquette County the Muirs encountered sandstone and tried without success to blast it away. Young John Muir then set to chipping the rock with hammer and chisel. Day after day, month after month, his father and brother lowered him in a wooden bucket down the slowly deepening shaft and went off to their own work. At eighty feet he nearly succumbed to "deadly choke-damp" (carbonic acid gas) before being pulled out. At ninety feet he finally struck a "fine, hearty gush of water." He then "built a fine covered top" over the well and "swung two iron-bound buckets in it."[10]

While starting a farm the pioneer might find temporary shelter in a lean-to. Before the first winter he would usually be living in a log cabin which his neighbors had helped him erect in a day or two at a "log raising." After a few years he would build himself a hewn-log or a frame, brick, or stone house. A more well-to-do pioneer could begin with an elegant dwelling of that kind. The owner of one of the better houses might have a fireplace in it, but that was a mark of the log cabin and the early hardships of pioneering, and so he might prefer the much more fashionable and efficient stove.[11]

Most early Wisconsin farms were rather small, the great majority of them ranging from twenty to 100 acres. The newer the farm, of course, the smaller the proportion of its land that was under cultivation. The fraction of improved acreage increased from slightly more than one-third of all land in farms in 1850 to nearly one-half in 1860. The number of farmers, as listed in the censuses, was considerably larger than the number of farms, although many of those enumerated as "farmers" might have been sons still working on their family's farm, retired or semi-retired older farmers, or men who spent only part of their time farming. Presumably most of the "farm-

[10] Gunnar J. Malmin, ed. and trans., *America in the Forties: The Letters of Ole Munch Raeder* (Minneapolis, 1929), 73–74; John Gregory, *Industrial Resources of Wisconsin* (Milwaukee, 1855), 33–34; Muir, *Boyhood and Youth*, 184–186.

[11] Schafer, ed., "Ficker's Advice," in *WMH*, 25: 231–233; Joseph Schafer, *A History of Agriculture in Wisconsin* (Madison, 1922), 66–69.

ers" without farms were acquiring land of their own, but even in
this era of abundant land some farm workers were propertyless
and destined to remain so.[12]

On a new farm the pioneer as a rule planted corn for his
first crop to feed his family and his oxen, and soon supplemented it with wheat and other grains, vegetables, and livestock to
provide variety for his table. From the beginning, however,
he intended to engage in commercial as well as subsistence
farming, and so he looked for surpluses and for markets in
which to dispose of them. Until the railroad opened more distant markets for him, he could find nearby ones—depending on
his location—in the lake ports, the inland villages and cities
of the well-populated southeast, the mining communities of
the southwest, and even the sawmills and lumber camps of
the thinly settled north. Indeed, at least a few observers predicted that farmers would not only follow lumbermen into
the pinery but would remain after the forest was gone and
would convert the entire northland into an agricultural paradise.

In one place or another the farmer could sell or barter a number of items, among them wheat, corn, oats, hay, potatoes, garden vegetables, pork, beef, poultry, butter, eggs, maple sugar,
and wild honey, wild cranberries, and wild rice. But most of
these, for one reason or another, paid the farmer rather poorly.
They required more of an investment than he could afford, or
more of a rigorous routine than he had the skill or the patience
or the manpower to follow. For a time he was discouraged
from raising corn because of the risk of early frost, and from
raising potatoes because of a blight like the one that had attacked them in Europe. Usually he relied on the coarse wild

[12] *Ninth Census of the United States, 1870: Volume III*, p. 340; *Eighth Census
of the United States, 1860: Population*, 545. On the "'farmer' without a farm"
in Trempealeau County, see Merle Curti, *The Making of an American Community: A Case Study of Democracy in a Frontier County* (Stanford, 1959), 59–
60. See also Paul W. Gates, *The Farmer's Age: Agriculture, 1815–1860* (New
York, 1960), 196–197, 272–275. Problems of definition make it impossible to
determine the number of farm laborers in the census. The 1850 census had
no separate category for farm laborers, although it recorded 40,865 farmers and
20,177 farms for Wisconsin. The 1860 census enumerated 31,472 farm laborers,
93,859 farmers, and 69,270 farms.

grass of meadow and marsh for his hay. Even in the winter he let his cows forage for themselves and provided them little or no shelter, though they made a pitiful scene as they stood humped and shivering through the coldest days and nights. What dairying the family did was merely incidental to providing milk and butter for home use. To make it a really profitable business, the farmer would have to take better care of his cattle and give more attention to the packing and marketing of his butter. Instead of taking it to the nearest general store—which in summer often accepted it only as axle grease —he would have to pack it in clean firkins or stone jars, store it in a cool, fresh cellar or spring house, and market it in the fall, either peddling it to local consumers or shipping it to a city commission merchant.[13]

From the first years of statehood the typical Wisconsin farmer concentrated mainly on wheat, a crop he could be sure of selling. Wheat was comparatively easy for him to produce, even with the rather primitive methods available to him. After sowing the seed, which he scattered by hand, he could leave the field unattended till harvest time. Then he would cut the standing grain with scythe and cradle, rake it and bind it into sheaves, and thresh it by having oxen tread it out. He might winnow it with the aid of a "fanning mill," which was mounted on a wagon and powered by the wheels as the wagon was moved along. A field had to be harvested within a week or so, else the last of the wheat would grow too ripe for handling without waste. Since a man could cradle no more than two or three acres a day, the crop that he could take care of, even with harvest help, was definitely limited. He could increase it if he had the means to buy or hire one of the new horse-drawn mechanical reapers, which the McCormick company had begun to manufacture in Chicago in 1846. And he could thresh the crop more expeditiously with a horse-powered

[13] Schafer, *Agriculture in Wisconsin*, 98, 105–107, 130–131, 133–134, 149–153; Vernon Carstensen, *Farms or Forests: Evolution of a State Land Policy for Northern Wisconsin, 1850–1932* (Madison, 1958), 5–6; Gregory, *Industrial Resources of Wisconsin*, 138–144.

threshing machine of the kind that Jerome I. Case was making, from the 1840's on, in Racine.[14]

Though the farmer's favorite sale crop, wheat had its disadvantages and risks. It rapidly used up the nitrogen in the soil. On one farm in central Wisconsin, fields that had yielded from twenty to twenty-five bushels an acre when first plowed, produced only five or six a few years later. The yield, even on fresh soil, varied with vagaries of the weather, and the price fluctuated according to national and international supply and demand. A succession of winters with scanty snow and then an autumn with heavy rain destroyed a large part of the Wisconsin crop in 1849, 1850, and 1851. Yet the price remained low because of a glut on the world market.[15]

The wheat disaster was a "benefit" in disguise, according to one Wisconsinite, for it was "causing farmers to turn their attention to a variety of crops." Certainly it stimulated a movement for agricultural reform. In March 1851 a group of legislators and others met in the capitol in Madison and organized Wisconsin's first successful state agricultural society. Soliciting money from interested citizens, the society sponsored a state fair and cattle show, which took place in Janesville in October 1851, in Milwaukee the next year, and in one city or another thereafter. The society also encouraged the formation of county societies in addition to the few that were already in existence. Reformers undertook to improve farming through exhibits and demonstrations at state and county fairs; through articles in the annual *Transactions* published by the state society, in the *Wisconsin Farmer and Northwestern Culti-*

[14] Schafer, *Agriculture in Wisconsin*, 87–89; Schafer, ed., "Ficker's Advice," in *WMH*, 25: 337–338; Croft, ed., "Mazomanie Pioneer," in *WMH*, 26: 208–218; Benjamin H. Hibbard, *The History of Agriculture in Dane County, Wisconsin* (Madison, 1904), 121–133; Eric E. Lampard, *The Rise of the Dairy Industry in Wisconsin: A Study in Agricultural Change, 1820–1920* (Madison, 1963), 45–46.

[15] Muir, *Boyhood and Youth*, 159; "Wisconsin: Population, Resources and Statistics," in *De Bow's Review*, 14 (January, 1853), 26–28; Gregory, *Industrial Resources of Wisconsin*, 58–63; John G. Thompson, *The Rise and Decline of the Wheat Growing Industry in Wisconsin* (Madison, 1909), 19–23; John G. Clark, *The Grain Trade in the Old Northwest* (Urbana, 1966), 96–99.

vator, a Racine weekly that had been founded in January 1849, and through other publications.[16]

The reformers advocated not only a diversification of crops but also crop rotation, careful tillage, the use of fertilizers, selective breeding of cattle and other livestock, shelters for the animals, tame grasses for hay, the making of saleable butter and cheese, wool growing, and hog raising. "It is a mistake to till more than what can be done well, as ten acres well ploughed, thoroughly drained, and carefully managed and attended to in the progress of its growth, will leave more profit than thirty scraped over and left to chance after," one reformer wrote. "I have seen the truth of this proved in many parts of this State, but in no place so fully as in the outskirts of Milwaukee, where an industrious and skillful German makes more of an acre than a country farmer does of five." Many of the Germans, both in the Milwaukee vicinity and elsewhere, did indeed provide something of a model by grubbing the stumps from their fields, cultivating a diversity of crops and doing it intensively, fertilizing with manure and gypsum, and housing their animals the year around.[17]

In response to economic pressure and the reformers' advice, some of the less careful farmers began to mend their ways. They grew clover on exhausted fields, plowed it under, and then planted corn or wheat. They looked about for early maturing varieties of corn, or cut the crop before the first autumn frost and allowed the corn to ripen in the shock. Bringing in a few pedigreed bulls and cows, they experimented with selective breeding. They improved their dairying somewhat, especially in the southeastern counties that had almost equal access to both the Milwaukee and Chicago markets.

[16] Schafer, *Agriculture in Wisconsin,* 104–108; Einar O. Hammer, "One Hundred Years of Wisconsin State Fairs," in *WMH,* 34 (Autumn, 1950), 10–11. The quotation is from "Wisconsin: Population, Resources and Statistics," in *De Bow's Review,* 14 (January, 1853), 26.

[17] Joseph Schafer, "The Yankee and the Teuton in Wisconsin," in *WMH,* 6–7 (December, 1922–December, 1923), 6: 269–279; Gregory, *Industrial Resources of Wisconsin,* 58–63. The reformer quoted is Gregory, p. 62.

They raised rapidly increasing numbers of sheep for shearing and cattle and swine for slaughtering. They produced great quantities of oats, so great that the combined output of oats and corn, both of them mainly for stock feed, exceeded the output of wheat.[18]

Yet wheat remained Wisconsin's most important crop, recovering from the four bad years. The harvest of 1853 was good and that of 1854 better. As the yield increased, so did the price, for production in the older states was declining because of soil exhaustion and an insect pest (midge larvae or "little yellow worms") that spread from Vermont to Ohio. The railroads, as construction advanced across the state, opened the eastern and world markets to farmers settled along the routes. For the time being, at least, these farmers were enjoying truly golden harvests. So long as high profits continued, the wheat growers had little incentive to develop other marketable products or to take steps to counter the depletion of their soil. The one crop took over more and more acres as Wisconsin rose, among the wheat-producing states, from ninth in 1850 to second after the bountiful harvest of 1860.[19]

While inducing farmers to depend increasingly on wheat, the abundant harvests and buoyant prices also "revived their drooping spirits," as a contemporary noted, "and placed them in comparatively affluent circumstances, which is visible by

[18] Muir, *Boyhood and Youth*, 159; Schafer, *Agriculture in Wisconsin*, 98, 115–117, 149–153. See *Ninth Census of the United States, 1870: Volume III*, pp. 86–91, for 1850 and 1860 statistics of farm production in Wisconsin and the rest of the states. Among the states, Wisconsin stood twenty-second in 1850 and eighth in 1860 in butter production. Yet, as late as 1860, Wisconsin had fewer milk cows than each of fifteen other states, including Alabama and North Carolina, and only about one-sixth as many as New York.

[19] Schafer, *Agriculture in Wisconsin*, 89–92; Thompson, *Wheat Growing Industry*, 15–36, 39–49; Clark, *Grain Trade*, 198, 206–207; *Ninth Census of the United States, 1870: Volume III*, pp. 87, 91; Frederick Merk, *Economic History of Wisconsin During the Civil War Decade* (Madison, 1916), 19. In the 1860 census, based on the 1859 harvest, Wisconsin ranked third among the wheat-producing states. After the 1860 harvest the state ranked second, ahead of Indiana but still behind Illinois.

the number of shanties which are being replaced by comfortable and sightly frame dwellings in every part of the State." All this was a sign, too, that the pioneer stage of agriculture was passing except in the most recently settled areas. Another evidence was the substitution of the horse for the ox. On the frontier of settlement the ox continued to predominate, and in the state as a whole his numbers were increasing, but not so fast as the horse total, which was beginning to exceed the ox count.[20]

[3]

While the lead industry was declining in the southwest, the lumber industry was expanding in the north, and mills, foundries, and factories were growing in the southeast, especially in the state's metropolis. Milwaukee possessed a number of advantages as a manufacturing center. It had a comparatively large local market and labor supply as well as access to distant customers and raw materials by way of its developing harbor and outreaching railroads. It got water power from a dam on the Milwaukee River and from a canal along the riverbank, where lake ships could load and unload right at the plants that used the power. During the eight years from 1849 to 1857 the annual value of products manufactured in the city increased more than sixfold from $1,714,000 to $10,500,000. Year by year the city was contributing a larger share of the state's industrial production. It was beginning to contribute between one-fifth and a quarter of the total output, though it contained only about 6 per cent of the people. In 1860 Milwaukee County, together with a half dozen other counties—Rock, Racine, Dodge,

[20] Joseph Schafer, *The Winnebago-Horicon Basin: A Type Study in Western History* (Madison, 1937), 151, 192, 197–201; Robert C. Robertson, "The Social History of Winnebago County, Wisconsin, 1850–1870" (master's thesis, University of Chicago, 1939), 8–9. The quotation is from Gregory, *Industrial Resources of Wisconsin,* 113. From 1850 to 1860 the count of oxen increased from 42,801 to 93,652; of horses (on farms), from 30,179 to 116,180. See *Ninth Census of the United States, 1870: Volume III,* pp. 86–87, 91.

Fond du Lac, Dane, and Winnebago (in order of productivity) —accounted for more than 50 per cent of the total.[21]

Capital for industrial development came largely from migrating capitalists who brought goods and money with them or borrowed from wealthy friends and relatives remaining in the Northeast. Some pioneering businessmen, arriving with stocks of merchandise, set up first as storekeepers and then invested their profits in milling and manufacturing enterprises. Small craftsmen could aspire to become large industrialists, but few succeeded in doing so, and most of these required fifteen or twenty years at least.[22]

In every new settlement a miller was needed as soon as the farmers began to harvest corn and wheat. The miller had to make a fairly large investment in order to acquire a dam site and, with the aid of a millwright, put up even a crude gristmill. Once established, he took the farmers' grain, kept part of it as pay, and returned the rest in the form of meal or flour. The wheat that he kept he made into flour for sale to villagers or townspeople in the vicinity. As transportation improved, he might concentrate more and more on buying wheat on his own account and selling the flour in distant as well as local markets. Millers like him, operating on a rather small scale, carried on their business throughout the wheat-growing areas of Wisconsin.

Some of the more successful millers, however, were beginning to operate on a larger scale, as were newly arriving enterprisers who brought capital with them. The larger-scale operators

[21] Derby, "History of the Port of Milwaukee," 214; "Wisconsin: Population, Resources and Statistics," in *De Bow's Review*, 14 (January, 1853), 25; Walsh, *Manufacturing Frontier*, 171–179; *Seventh Census of the United States, 1850: Compendium*, 179, 337; *Eighth Census of the United States, 1860: Manufactures*, 656. In 1850 Milwaukee County contributed 20.1 per cent of the state's industrial production; in 1860, 23.9 per cent. Walsh calculates Milwaukee County's contribution of the state's industrial production (as measured by value added by manufacturing) as 22.8 per cent in 1850; in 1860, 27.3 per cent.

[22] Walsh, *Manufacturing Frontier*, 10–13, 208–209; Alice E. Smith, *Millstone and Saw: The Origins of Neenah-Menasha* (Madison, 1966), 59–69. See also Margaret Walsh, "Business Success and Capital Availability in the New West: Milwaukee Ironmasters in the Middle Nineteenth Century," in the *Old Northwest*, 1 (June, 1975), 159–175.

were introducing more complex machinery, with vertical and horizontal conveyors that made the milling process nearly automatic. Milwaukee, with its advantageous location and its capital supply, benefited the most from these innovations. In 1850 the mills in both Racine and Rock counties had produced more flour than those in Milwaukee County. By 1860 Milwaukee accounted for over 16 per cent of the state's output of flour, two-thirds more than Rock, the second-ranked county, and about three to four times as much as the other leading counties—Green, Dodge, Dane, Fond du Lac, and Winnebago. Milwaukee brands such as "Sugar River," "Magnolia," and the Empire Mills's "Stone" earned premium prices in eastern markets. Milwaukee's rise to pre-eminence did not go unchallenged. Neenah, for example, already had one sizable mill in operation in 1850 when John R. and Harvey L. Kimberly, heirs of a successful building contractor, began to reassemble machinery from a mill near their former home in upstate New York in a new hewn-oak building at the rapids where Lake Winnebago empties into the lower Fox. By 1857 there were four mills on the Neenah rapids and three others on the Menasha rapids, and the twin villages with their twin power sources, both superb ones, hoped to rival Milwaukee as well as one another in flour production.[23]

Wherever Germans settled, a brewer as well as a miller was soon required. While catering to the thirst of the settlers, the brewer provided them a market for their barley and hops. Breweries sprang up in widely scattered localities, almost all of them making lager for German-speaking (or Dutch-speaking) customers, though here and there a brewery turned out English-style ale or beer for an English-speaking clientele. The biggest ones developed in Milwaukee. These were yet to make the city "famous," but during the 1850's Milwaukee County breweries were already producing more than 40 per cent of

[23] Schafer, *Agriculture in Wisconsin,* 71–72; *Eighth Census of the United States, 1860: Manufactures,* 640–657; Walsh, *Manufacturing Frontier,* 179–181; Derby, "History of the Port of Milwaukee," 214; Smith, *Millstone and Saw,* 61–65. A combined gristmill and sawmill had been established in Neenah as early as 1849.

the state's beer. They owed their development to entrepreneurs —Jacob and Philip Best, August Krug, Joseph Schlitz, John Braun, Valentin Blatz, Frederick Miller—who brought from Germany both capital and the brewmaster's art.[24]

Other important farm-related industries were meat packing and leather making. Butchers throughout the state continued to slaughter for local consumption, but a few firms in Milwaukee were beginning to cure and pack pork and beef for wider sale. The largest of these, Layton and Plankinton, a partnership formed in 1852, grew out of John Plankinton's and Frederick Layton's meat markets. Tanneries, most of them quite small, arose in a number of places where water, hides, and tanbark (preferably hemlock) were readily available. Some of those at inland locations disappeared with the disappearance of the neighboring oak or hemlock trees. Others, in lake ports and especially in Milwaukee, prospered and, if not fairly large to start with, soon grew to considerable size. For a time the Wisconsin Leather Company—the outgrowth of the leather shop which the brothers George and William Allen, tanners from Cazenovia, New York, had established in Milwaukee in 1846, and the tannery they had set up at Two Rivers two years later—carried on the largest tanning business in the entire Northwest. During the 1850's this company was rivaled by the Milwaukee firm of Guido Pfister and Fred Vogel, Württembergers who had previously been in the business in Buffalo. (In both the city and the state, Germans predominated in tanning, though not to the same extent as in brewing.) By 1872 Milwaukee was on the way to becoming the fourth-largest meat-packing center in the country and one of the largest leather-making centers in the world.[25]

[24] Walsh, *Manufacturing Frontier*, 185–188; *Eighth Census of the United States, 1860: Manufactures*, 648, 657; Still, *Milwaukee*, 188–189; Thomas C. Cochran, *The Pabst Brewing Company: The History of an American Business* (New York, 1948), 18–29.

[25] Walsh, *Manufacturing Frontier*, 188–194; Still, *Milwaukee*, 186–188; Charles E. Schefft, "The Tanning Industry in Wisconsin: A History of Its Frontier Origins and Its Development" (master's thesis, University of Wisconsin, 1938), 12–34.

Some of the leather went to Wisconsin shops making and selling harness, saddles, bridles, and luggage, such as the shop that August Ringling (Rüngeling), father of the later-to-be-famous circus brothers, opened in Baraboo in 1855. Some of the leather was converted into boots and shoes within the state. Journeymen shoemakers still traveled about or labored in small shops to make footwear to order, but in Milwaukee a few manufacturing establishments or stores already by the 1850's were offering "sale work" as well as "custom work." With little or no machinery as yet, the cutting was done in the factory and assembling in scattered shops. Pioneers in the business, among them Charles T. Bradley of the leading firm of Bradley and Metcalf, had come from eastern Massachusetts, scene of the industry's earliest and highest development. Benjamin Bosworth had brought his own craftsmen from Boston. When, in 1848, some of the men struck and others deserted, Bosworth protested he had paid their expenses to Milwaukee on the understanding that they would work for him, at a 20 per cent increase in wages, until they had repaid him out of the increase, which he was withholding.[26]

Like the shoe manufacturers and other pioneer industrialists many of the early lumbermen arrived with some previous experience at their trade. They transferred their knowledge and their capital from the depleted pineries of the Northeast (including Canada) to the fresh ones of Wisconsin. To make a start, a lumberman needed only a small investment, but he had to have finances as well as ability and luck in order to prosper and to survive the risks of fire, flood, drought, and financial panic. He might look back eastward for additional cash or credit, as did Moses M. Strong of Mineral Point, who visited Maine in 1851 "for the purpose of enlisting the attention of Capitalists." Labor as well as capital presented problems for a lumberman. Though he could find some experienced woods-

[26] J. J. Schlicher, "On the Trail of the Ringlings," in *WMH*, 26 (September, 1942), 8–22; Harold R. Quimby, *Pacemakers of Progress: The Story of Shoes and the Shoe Industry* (Chicago, 1946), 24–27, 31–32, 38. Bosworth presented his case, and his striking employees presented theirs, in the Milwaukee *Sentinel*, July 28, 29, August 1, 1848.

men who had left the older pineries, he had to depend increasingly on unskilled transients, including the many immigrants who worked as lumberjacks for only a season or two while preparing to become farmers.[27]

The early lumbermen commonly cut timber without regard to land ownership and without bothering to pay a fee. In 1849 a land-office register reported that, on the Green Bay watershed alone, the annual production was "upwards of 15,000,000 feet of pine lumber," and "every foot" of it was "plundered off the public lands." Soon the federal government sent special timber agents throughout the north woods to stop the stealing of logs. Hence some of the lumbermen gave thought to buying and logging pine lands of their own. They were convinced they had to buy, for self-protection, and so were some of the sawmill owners, when in 1853 a number of newcomers began to take up tremendous tracts of the choicest pine. Among these speculators were two who schemed to monopolize the Wisconsin pineries—Cadwallader C. Washburn and Cyrus Woodman, both of Mineral Point. With the co-operation of New England investors, the pair had accumulated 60,000 acres in Wisconsin and Minnesota Territory by 1854, though they never came close to achieving a monopoly. Washburn and Woodman promptly hired a man to keep off timber thieves and to make contracts with loggers.[28]

The lumber industry consisted of several distinct operations, and in Wisconsin separate enterprisers still carried them on. Speculators acquired pine land and sold stumpage rights—that is, the right to the standing trees. Logging contractors (the original "lumbermen") had the timber cut and the logs driven

[27] Walsh, *Manufacturing Frontier*, 216–217; Robert F. Fries, *Empire in Pine: The Story of Lumbering in Wisconsin, 1830–1900* (Madison, 1951), 13–22, 204–205. The quotation is from Fries, p. 14, who quotes Charles Durkee to Joseph Grinnell, May 25, 1851, in the Moses M. Strong Lumber Company Papers.

[28] Paul W. Gates, *The Wisconsin Pine Lands of Cornell University: A Study in Land Policy and Absentee Ownership* (Ithaca, 1943), 70–73; Paul W. Gates, "Frontier Land Business in Wisconsin," in *WMH*, 52 (Summer, 1969), 324–325; Larry Gara, *Westernized Yankee: The Story of Cyrus Woodman* (Madison, 1956), 116–118; Clare L. Marquette, "The Business Activities of C. C. Washburn" (doctoral dissertation, University of Wisconsin, 1940), 177–213.

downriver to the sawmills. Sawmill men turned the logs into rough lumber; raft and boat operators transported it to lumberyards; and wholesalers sorted, seasoned, and distributed it. Some enterprisers, however, were beginning to combine two or more of these functions and thus to make lumbering more and more an integrated industry.[29]

Among the men in the lumber business who were integrating their operations was John H. Knapp, part owner of a sawmill on the Red Cedar River (at the site of Menomonie). In 1853 he formed a partnership with Henry L. Stout, who took charge of a lumberyard at Dubuque. Knapp, Stout & Company proceeded to reinvest its profits in both timberland and additional sawmills. Another rising and diversifying lumberman was Philetus Sawyer of Oshkosh. Between 1848 and 1857 Sawyer transformed himself from a lowly mill hand and woodsman into a prosperous lumber manufacturer and dealer as well as a land speculator with 25,000 acres of Wolf River pine.[30]

As yet, Wisconsin derived from its forests mostly rough-sawed lumber—about twice as much, in worth, as the total of planed lumber, lath, shingles, and all other wood products. The state was nevertheless acquiring at least the rudiments of a sophisticated woodworking industry, which turned out such things as doors, sashes, blinds, and (from hardwoods) furniture, tubs, buckets, barrels, wagons and sleighs. Logs were sliced into rough boards by the slow, heavy, up-and-down gate saw, which required a great deal of power. (The faster and more efficient circular saw was not to come into general use in Wisconsin until after 1860.) Staves for tubs or barrels were shaped and grooved by a machine that a Milwaukeean, William Hawkins, had invented, and that had been featured in the Wisconsin exhibit at the 1851 Crystal Palace exposition in London.

---

[29] Merk, *Economic History*, 72–73.

[30] Gates, *Wisconsin Pine Lands*, 125; Richard N. Current, *Pine Logs and Politics: A Life of Philetus Sawyer, 1816–1900* (Madison, 1950), 13, 16, 22–23. Sawyer had previously rented and operated a sawmill in New York and had bought a Wisconsin farm with part of the proceeds.

With this machine, seven men could make 400 tubs in one ten-hour working day. Sawmills were already well established along some of the rivers draining the north woods, especially at Grand Rapids (Wisconsin Rapids), Stevens Point, and Big Bull Rapids (Wausau) on the Wisconsin. New mills were going up along a number of streams that offered a supply of both logs and power. But lumber manufacturing and woodworking centered more and more in such places as La Crosse, Sheboygan, Manitowoc, and above all Oshkosh, Fond du Lac, and Neenah-Menasha. In Menasha a tub and pail factory—which Elisha D. Smith, a storekeeper from Rhode Island, bought for $1,200 in 1852—employed seventy-five workers by the end of the decade and was eventually to become "the largest business of its kind in the United States."[31]

Lead mining could no longer compete with lumbering in the attraction of enterprise and capital. By 1852 some of the mining districts "appeared to be deserted, except where an occasional solitary person was employed digging up the surface, in search of mineral, his only implement being a spade." Deep shafts were needed, and pumps to empty them of water, but both would be expensive. Soon dozens of companies were formed in the hope of raising the necessary funds. One of them, Washburn and Woodman's Wisconsin Mining Company, sold stock to Easterners, bought a steam engine, leased several flooded mines near Dodgeville, and attempted to drain and deepen them. The effort failed, and the stockholders lost their money. Meanwhile Washburn and Woodman had made enough profit from their shot tower at Helena to return their original invest-

[31] Eighth Census of the United States, 1860: Manufactures, 657–658; Genivera E. Loft, "The Evolution of the Wood-Working Industries of Wisconsin" (master's thesis, University of Wisconsin, 1916), 15, 40–85; Fries, Empire in Pine, 61; Gregory, Industrial Resources of Wisconsin, 252–253; Dorothy J. Ernst, "Daniel Wells, Jr.: Wisconsin Commissioner to the Crystal Palace Exhibition of 1851," in WMH, 42 (Summer, 1959), 247; Walsh, Manufacturing Frontier, 110–111; Smith, Millstone and Saw, 65–68. The quotation is from p. 68. The stave-machine inventor was William Hawkins; the proprietor of the Menasha pail factory, Elisha D. Smith. See also Mowry Smith, Jr., and Giles Clark, One Third Crew, One Third Boat, One Third Luck: The Menasha Corporation (Menasha Wooden Ware Company) Story, 1849–1974 (Neenah, Wisconsin, 1974).

ment, but before long they found it less and less profitable.[32]

Iron mining seemed to promise more for Wisconsin's future than did lead mining. "Iron ore of unlimited extent and of great purity," an enthusiast declared in 1855, "may be found at Lake Superior, in the Baraboo district, and at the Iron Ridge in Dodge and Washington counties." In fact, the full extent of the riches of the Gogebic Range, in the far north, was not to be discovered until 1872. Only a single mine within the state, at the Iron Ridge, was as yet producing ore. In 1850 a New York ironmaster, Jonas Tower, had entered into a partnership with the mine owner for the manufacture of pig iron at Mayville. Five years later, with his employees and their families, most of them Irish, Tower moved from Crown Point, New York, to Ironton in Sauk County and started a second mine and blast furnace.[33]

From the two smelteries in Wisconsin and from others in Pennsylvania and Ohio came most of the iron for the new state's foundries and machine shops. These appeared in more than a dozen places, but they were largest and most numerous in Milwaukee, which by 1860 accounted for more than half of the state's ironwork. The shops there and elsewhere made stoves, boilers, miscellaneous castings, mill gearings, steam engines—practically everything from kettles to locomotives. In Milwaukee the Menomonee Locomotive Works was completing six locomotives, the first to be built west of Cleveland, when in 1853 the firm ran short of cash. The Reliance Works, with financing from an Ohio partner, branched out from the making of millstones to the manufacture of milling machinery and shipped its products as far as California.[34]

---

[32] Walsh, *Manufacturing Frontier,* 78; Marquette, "Business Activities of C. C. Washburn," 53–96; Gara, *Westernized Yankee,* 62–63, 110–114. The quotation is from Gregory, *Industrial Resources of Wisconsin,* 168.

[33] Merk, *Economic History,* 115–116; Gregory, *Industrial Resources of Wisconsin* (who is quoted), 169–171; Harry E. Cole, ed., *A Standard History of Sauk County, Wisconsin . . .* (2 vols., Chicago, 1918), 1: 89–90.

[34] Walsh, *Manufacturing Frontier,* 204–208; *Eighth Census of the United States, 1860: Manufactures,* 648, 657; Robert T. Hilton, "Men of Metal: A History of the Foundry Industry in Wisconsin" (master's thesis, University of Wisconsin, 1952), 1–25.

Of all the Wisconsin plants producing machinery, however, the most complex and highly developed was the Jerome I. Case factory in Racine. Case had got his start in 1842 by bringing with him from New York six threshing machines which he had bought on credit, selling five of them, and using the sixth to thresh for Wisconsin wheat growers. He purchased patent rights and made improvements of his own, developing a "sweep" model powered by horses moving in a circle and a "tread" model powered by horses on a treadmill. As early as 1850 Case was manufacturing 100 machines a year in what was said to be the "largest establishment of its kind in the West." By 1857, after adding a foundry and a machine shop, he could advertise: "Every article connected with the threshing machine is made on the premises." Meanwhile he found customers in Indiana, Illinois, and Iowa as well as Wisconsin. He traveled through these states to demonstrate machines, make repairs, and collect debts from buyers to whom he had extended credit.[35]

[4]

Wisconsin had no regular commercial banks for the first five years of its existence as a state. Its constitution forbade the chartering of banks until the voters should have approved it in a referendum. Coins being rather scarce, the notes of out-of-state banks commonly served as money, and so, to an ever greater extent, did the Wisconsin Marine and Fire Insurance Company's "certificates of deposit"—which continued to circulate even though the act incorporating the company had been repealed. This company and a few other firms performed additional banking functions, such as the making of short-term loans, the deposit of savings, the transfer of funds, and the ex-

---

[35] Reynold M. Wik, "J. I. Case: Some Experiences of an Early Wisconsin Industrialist," in *WMH*, 35 (September, 1951), 3–6, 64–67. The quotations are from pp. 5, 6. See also Stewart H. Holbrook, *Machines of Plenty: Pioneering in American Agriculture* (New York, 1955), 30–38.

change of currencies. Individuals with cash to spare engaged in money lending. Still, neither currency nor credit sufficed to meet the needs of farmers and businessmen. More and more of the people shed the anti-bank feelings they had acquired from sad experience with previous bank failures. When, in 1851, the question was put to the voters, they went for "bank" as against "no bank" by more than three to one.

The law of 1852—also subject to referendum—provided for a system of free banking on the New York model (which other northwestern states also were imitating). Any group meeting the law's requirements could go into the banking business. The firm could lend its own bank notes only after it had deposited securities with the bank comptroller, an elected state official, who alone had authority to issue the notes. As much as half of the securities might consist of Wisconsin railroad company bonds—for the law was designed in part to aid the financing of railroads. The rest of the securities were to consist of bonds of the federal government or of Wisconsin or other states. If a bank should refuse to give noteholders specie for its notes on demand, the comptroller could sell its securities and redeem the notes. Voters approved all this by a margin of nearly four to one.

The next year the first banks began to operate under the new law One of them was the Wisconsin Marine—now rechartered as the Wisconsin Marine and Fire Insurance Company Bank—which, under the Scottish-born financier Alexander Mitchell, remained the state's largest and most powerful financial institution. Between 1853 and 1859 the number of banks in the state increased from eight to 108, the loans outstanding from $640,000 to $6,480,000, and the face value of banknotes in circulation from $300,000 to $4,443,000. Some of this note issue came from wildcat banks, which kept an inadequate specie reserve. To discourage noteholders from cashing notes, such banks located their places of business or their redemption centers in out-of-the-way spots, some of which could not even be found on the map. In thinly settled northern counties the note issue per capita was ten to twenty times as large as in well-developed counties like Milwaukee or Dane.[36]

"Wisconsin has not fully recovered from the stringent times, which are incident to all new countries, but Wisconsin has got her eye teeth cut and now the times are getting good here," a Rosendale settler had written to his Vermont kin in the summer of 1853. "We never was permited by law to have any Banks, but this spring a law went into efect granting Banks, and we are having plenty of them too." Certainly the banks, by enlarging credit and the medium of exchange, helped to stimulate the prosperity that ensued. Shipments of wheat, flour, and lumber steadily and rapidly increased after having fluctuated for several years. Land sales, after falling off from 1848 to 1852, rose to new heights with an outbreak of speculative fever. By 1856, however, at least a few signs of trouble ahead had begun to appear. Milwaukee merchants were complaining of unpaid accounts and of a currency drain from the city. Farmers taking wheat to market found the price dropping.[37]

Wheat traders in Milwaukee flourished during the boom. Among them the former groceryman Daniel Newhall gained a reputation as the largest individual grain dealer in the Northwest. Operating his own fleet of twenty sailing vessels, Newhall at the height of the season sent to Buffalo as much as 15,000 bushels a day. He invested some of his profits in shipbuilding and in real estate, including the Newhall House, the city's most imposing hotel. Originally, Newhall and other dealers had met incoming farmers in person, inspected their bags of wheat, and bargained individually for it. The dealers found this less and less practicable as the volume of trade grew. Through the Board of Trade, established in 1849, the dealers

[36] Alice E. Smith, *George Smith's Money: A Scottish Investor in America* (Madison, 1966), 106, 114–117; Theodore A. Andersen, *A Century of Banking in Wisconsin* (Madison, 1954), 13–24, 34–40; Richard H. Keehn, "Market Structure and Bank Performance: Wisconsin, 1870–1900" (doctoral dissertation, University of Wisconsin, 1972), 15–21.

[37] Clinton Matteson to Isaiah Matteson, July 14, 1853, in the Clinton Matteson Letters; Derby, "History of the Port of Milwaukee," 144–149; Milwaukee *Daily American*, September 25, 1856; Smith, *Millstone and Saw*, 117–118.

organized a regular market but failed to provide a satisfactory system for grading the grain. Hence both they and the farmers were encouraged to cheat. In 1856 the Corn Exchange, an agency of the board, set vague and unsatisfactory standards, defining as "Extra" the wheat that was perfectly clean and as "No. 1" the wheat that, "in almost all cases," had been run, "with ordinary care, through a fanning mill."[38]

Grain traders and other merchants made Milwaukee even more important as a commercial than as a manufacturing center. Jobbers expanded their businesses as railroads enlarged the hinterland during the prosperous years. Henry Nazro, for one, moved in 1854 into a new wholesale and retail store that offered "three acres of iron and hardware under one roof" and aspired to be "second to none in the United States." In 1855, after several shipwrecks offshore, Milwaukee's auctioneers learned that they could dispose of practically anything labeled as damaged goods. Reportedly one auctioneer, with a stock of slow-moving merchandise on his hands, dashed water over it and then sold it at a good price.[39]

Retailers in Milwaukee specialized to the extent of selling only china and glassware, or tobacco, or confections and fancy groceries. Even in a village as small as Baraboo, with fewer than 2,000 inhabitants, a variety of stores had appeared by 1857, eight concentrating on dry goods, five on groceries, three on drugs, three on hardware and stoves, two on meat, one on jewelry, and one on stationery and books. Peddlers toured the countryside, among them the partners Henry Stern and Julius Goll, who made circuits of two and three weeks' duration out of Milwaukee. Storekeepers in rural communities offered a wide range of items for sale or barter. In a frontier settlement in Waupaca County, Thomas Knoph did business in a log building that served as a store, inn, post office, and church. On his account books he credited his customers for the cash they paid,

[38] Derby, "History of the Port of Milwaukee," 151–152, 203–207; Still, *Milwaukee,* 182–183.

[39] Derby, "History of the Port of Milwaukee," 212; Still, *Milwaukee,* 185 (source of the quotations); Milwaukee *Daily American,* December 20, 1855, reporting the story of the enterprising auctioneer.

the produce they brought in, or the labor they performed for him. He debited them for the goods they bought—spices, salt, sugar, baking soda, coffee, tea, tobacco, wine, whiskey, soap, candles, matches, nails, lead for making bullets, fine shot, powder, percussion caps, shoes, clothing, cloth, and whatnot—and for postage, lodging, meals, laundry, horseshoeing, and the rental of a horse and buggy.[40]

When the land boom of the 1850's got under way, speculators still held extensive tracts they had acquired from the public domain during the previous boom of the 1830's. An Englishman, Sir Charles Augustus Murray, for example, owned 20,000 acres of potential farming land in Grant County. Other speculators now entered even larger amounts, the firm of Washburn and Woodman the largest, more than 130,000 acres between 1846 and 1857. Dealers such as Washburn and Woodman made entries not only on their own account but also in the name of Eastern capitalists, whose holdings they then looked after. And they made "time entries" on behalf of squatters and other settlers who lacked the cash to pay the federal land office. That is, the dealer bought the land and resold it to the settler on time, boosting the price and charging interest besides. Though a state law limited the interest rate to 12 per cent (10 per cent for banks) he got a much higher effective rate through the price advance.[41]

Land speculators and "loan sharks" came to have a very bad reputation. "The money expended for lands and amassed by speculators from the toiling masses . . . ," a committee of the state legislature reported in 1851, "would, if retained by the working people, to whom it belongs, be an amount of wealth

---

[40] Freeman, *Emigrant's Hand Book,* 131–148; Western Historical Company, *History of Sauk County, Wisconsin* . . . (Chicago, 1880), 503; Henry Stern, "The Life Story of a Milwaukee Merchant," in *WMH,* 9 (September, 1925), 69; Malcolm Rosholt, "Two Men of Old Waupaca," *Norwegian-American Studies,* 22 (1965), 86–89, 98–99.

[41] Gates, *Wisconsin Pine Lands,* 65–68; Marquette, "Business Activities of C. C. Washburn," 15–19; Irene D. Neu, "Land Credit in Frontier Wisconsin" (master's thesis, Cornell University, 1945), 14–18, 41–44, 62–67.

ample for the erection of houses, barns and for other improvements, saving them from the hard necessity of resorting to
loans from usurers, at an enormous interest." Speculators, it
was often said, delayed settlement and development by accumulating land and holding it for prices that ordinary people
could not afford. To cure the evil, Wisconsin members of
the National Reform Association endorsed its demand for
laws prohibiting the sale of public land to speculators and
donating 160-acre tracts to actual settlers. One of Wisconsin's
first two United States senators, Isaac P. Walker, introduced
such a bill in the Senate, and other reformers proposed one
in the Wisconsin legislature, but neither body adopted any
effective land-limitation measure (though Congress was to
enact a homestead law in 1862).[42]

When people condemned the speculator, they usually had
in mind someone who owned land in their locality but resided
elsewhere in Wisconsin or outside the state. Such an absentee,
despite his image as a profiteer, was likely to have a hard
time making much money from his property, especially if it
consisted of prairie rather than pine. He would find few settlers willing to pay him a very high premium so long as they
could buy from the government at the minimum price. Meanwhile he had to pay taxes, and local assessors often discriminated against him as an outsider. He was at the mercy of his
agents in Wisconsin, who in locating lands were inclined to
keep the best for themselves, and who were less interested in
caring for his than for their own. The most successful dealers were those who, like Washburn and Woodman, gave close
attention to the management of their business and had the

[42] Gates, *Wisconsin Pine Lands,* 65–68; Gates, "Frontier Land Business," in
WMH, 52: 314–316 (source of the quotation); Merle Curti, "Isaac P. Walker:
Reformer in Mid-Century Politics," in *WMH,* 34 (Autumn, 1950), 5–6. Gates,
when he compares census figures of land in farms with land-office figures of
land sold, finds "a tremendous concentration of speculator-owned land" in
Wisconsin during the 1850's. See Paul W. Gates, "The Role of the Land Specu-
lator in Western Development," in the *Pennsylvania Magazine of History and
Biography,* 66 (July, 1942), 314–333.

resources and the patience to hold on through bad times as well as good.[43]

Many who denounced the speculator were themselves hoping to gain from a rise in the value of their property. Squatters were pre-empting government land with the intention of selling their claims. Farm owners were looking for buyers. Business and professional men were dabbling, or more than merely dabbling, in real estate. Carl Schurz, for one, borrowed money on a mortgage and bought a farm to make a subdivision on the edge of Watertown. Alfred Brunson, a pioneer Methodist missionary and circuit rider, caught the contagion at Prairie du Chien. "The railroads coming to the place enhanced the value of lands, and, in the spirit of others, I laid out my farm into town lots," he ruefully recalled. "I also contracted debts to build, expecting to sell lots to pay the debts."[44]

Promoters of new towns shared and inflamed the speculative frenzy. Each was confident that geography, so favorable to the state as a whole, destined his chosen spot to particular greatness—which would begin to be realized as soon as the railroad came. The fate of many a projected metropolis hung on the routing of a railroad.

The area around the mouth of Dell Creek had seemed like a promising site when, in 1849, Joseph Bailey with his wife and baby daughter occupied government land on the opposite side of the Wisconsin River. Here, on the river and the creek, was an abundance of potential water power. Here might be developed a manufacturing center and, with the completion of the Fox–Wisconsin improvement, a great inland port. Here, on both sides of the river, Bailey and a partner accumulated 400 acres. In 1852 they platted their property for a city of

[43] James W. Whitaker, "Wisconsin Land Speculation, 1830–1860: Case Studies of Small Scale Speculators" (master's thesis, University of Wisconsin, 1962), iii-iv, 34, 54–55, 102–103; Gates, *Wisconsin Pine Lands*, 81–84; Joseph Schafer, *The Wisconsin Lead Region* (Madison, 1932), 148–161; Neu, "Land Credit in Frontier Wisconsin," 73–78.

[44] Whitaker, "Wisconsin Land Speculation," iii, 100; Smith, *Millstone and Saw*, 104; Joseph Schafer, ed. and trans., *Intimate Letters of Carl Schurz, 1841–1869* (Madison, 1928), 154–155, 170–171, 413–414; Alfred Brunson, *A Western Pioneer* . . . (2 vols., Cincinnati, 1872, 1879), 2: 312.

10,000 people; Newport they called it. Before long it was booming in the expectation that a huge milldam would be built and that the railroad under construction from Milwaukee to La Crosse would bridge the river at this point. By 1856 the city had a population of more than 1,000, and lots were being resold at several times their original price. Then came the news that both the dam and the bridge were to be located a few miles upriver, where Bailey and his dam-and-railroad company associates had bought up land and laid out Kilbourn City (Wisconsin Dells) in anticipation of the rerouting. Soon long strings of oxen were dragging houses and even a hotel in that direction, and Newport was in the process of becoming a ghost town.[45]

At the western end of Lake Superior, near the mouth of the St. Louis River, a company of proprietors from St. Paul, Minnesota, had begun in 1853 to plan a city in the wilderness. Expecting a railroad to be built from this place to the Pacific— "the greatest railroad in the world," Stephen A. Douglas called it—Douglas and other nationally known politicians eagerly bought stock in the company. The city planners, on their plat, drew broad avenues and designated lots and entire blocks to be set aside for churches, schools, county buildings, a cemetery, and a park. Sales picked up in 1855, when the opening of the canal at Sault Ste. Marie made the city of Superior "the most western point accessible to ocean vessels in North America." The next year the lots on the main thoroughfare were selling for three to five hundred dollars. They "could not be had at any price" after the St. Croix and Lake Superior Railroad Company received its land grant. By 1857 the city claimed a population in excess of 2,000 and expected soon to have many thousands more. It "possesses a better site, a

[45] E. C. Dixon, "Newport: Its Rise and Fall," in *WMH*, 25 (June, 1942), 444–455; Cole, ed., *Sauk County*, 1: 534–542; C. George Extrom, "General Joseph Bailey and the Red River Dam" (unpublished paper read before the Civil War Round Table of Madison, 1965; sound recording available in the SHSW), 18–23. Extrom's account of Bailey's career as a Newport and Kilbourn City promoter is based largely on contemporary Kilbourn City, Portage, and Baraboo newspapers and quotes extensively from them.

better harbor, and greater natural advantages for a commercial city, than any other point in the Northwest," its boosters were saying; "there is no reason why Superior may not become a second Chicago." But the railroad was to be long delayed, and even longer the fulfillment of the promoters' hopes.[46]

[5]

While visiting Wisconsin in 1850, the Swedish novelist Fredrika Bremer jotted down her impression that "people in the great West" were "as yet principally occupied in the acquisition of the material portion of life, in a word by 'business!' " To her and to other cultivated Europeans, the people of Wisconsin seemed quite different from the romantic creatures, the children of nature, that Jean Jacques Rousseau had expected to grow up in the wilds of the New World. The actual Wisconsinites were materialistic and matter-of-fact.[47]

Yet there was romance in their very materialism, poetry in their seemingly prosaic life, if one Wisconsin booster was to be believed. He said a "poetical illusion," a "dream of fancy," kept the people going in their "contest" with nature to win her treasures. The dream inspired the poor frontiersman just starting out with a "small possession" and only a rough cabin to shelter his wife and babies. His heart beat high with "expectations of an extensive farm," which would become an "addition" to some future town. In his mind's eye he could already see his acres "selling at so much per lot" and himself "growing richer every day." He would then have made good the "boast of his strength and manliness" to "achieve the respectability of his family."[48]

---

[46] James S. Ritchie, *Wisconsin and Its Resources* . . . (3d revised edition, Philadelphia, 1858), 224–238. Ritchie is the source for all the quotations except Douglas' prediction, which is from Robert W. Johannsen, *Stephen A. Douglas* (New York, 1973), 435–436. See also Louise P. Kellogg, "The Rise and Fall of Old Superior," in *WMH,* 24 (September, 1940), 3–19.

[47] Fredrika Bremer, *The Homes of the New World: Impressions of America* (2 vols., New York, 1864, 1868), 1: 613–614.

[48] Ritchie, *Wisconsin and Its Resources,* 262–268.

Certainly the typical Wisconsin pioneer was no fugitive from civilization, no Daniel Boone anxious to keep ahead of its advance. On occasion he might have Boone-like moods, as even Cyrus Woodman did. When a railroad was projected to Mineral Point, Woodman told a friend he could no longer consider the place as West once "iron bands" had tied it to the East. He would then have to take his "plunder" and his family and look for a new home in "Minnesota or the Rocky Moutains or some other spot where the roar of the locomotive will not terrify the earth or vex the quiet air." But the mood would pass, as it did with Woodman, who stayed on to profit from the improvements in transportation.[49]

The Wisconsin pioneer saw himself as a bringer of civilization, a man of progress in an age of progress. What great changes he already had made in this state! Not so long ago there had been only the "dark and silent forest," the "green rolling prairie," the "roving tribes of naked Indians that claimed the wild but beautiful region as their inheritance." Now there were also the "ocean of waving crops," the "bustle of the busy reaper," and the "hum, clatter, and other sounds of industry," which were "daily and hourly banishing silence from the wilderness."[50]

Yet the "simple, coarse forms of pioneer life" remained in juxtaposition with the most modern developments, "the forms of a life of nature with those of refined living." The contrast struck a well-educated Norwegian, Pastor Johan S. Munch, as, in 1857, he voyaged up the Mississippi and, from a "most elegant" steamboat, viewed the still primitive Wisconsin countryside. "Rousseau would have been fooled here," the traveler wrote, "for if he went out into the woods crawling on all fours, he would perhaps behind his trees be vexed to see a party of Yankees camping on the river bank with their champagne bottles

---

[49] Gara, *Westernized Yankee*, 111–112.

[50] Gregory, *Industrial Resources of Wisconsin*, 6–7, 22–25, 28. The quotations are from pp. 7, 28. Contemporary comments on the rapidity of progress might be cited at length. See, for example, Lucas, ed., *Dutch Immigrant Memoirs*, 2: 160; Schafer, ed., *Intimate Letters of Carl Schurz*, 137–140, 149–150; and Freeman, *Emigrant's Hand Book*, 80–81.

and cigars and oysters, etc., etc., while the railroad whistle dinned his ear." But "every trace of the primitive," the writer believed, would have disappeared in another couple of generations.[51]

Civilization meant not only noise and litter but also water pollution. Water from streams and springs and shallow wells continued to be drunk, though it became less and less safe as the population grew denser. The incidence of typhoid fever and other communicable diseases rose. Though quite aware of the sickliness of newly settled areas, the people knew little about its real cause. They generally assumed the cause to be a miasma that arose from the decomposition of newly felled trees, freshly turned sod, and swamps and bogs. Hence they expected conditions to improve as the first stage of pioneering passed.[52]

Settlement led to the diminution of some if not most bird and animal species. It did induce bluebirds and bluejays, which had not been wintering in Wisconsin, to stay all year. It was disastrous, however, for the passenger pigeons, which were in time to be completely extinct. During the first years of statehood these birds still arrived by the millions each spring as soon as the snow was off the ground. So large was a single flock that it looked like a "mighty river in the sky," and it made a "low buzzing wing roar that could be heard a long way off." The birds feasted on wheat and oats as well as acorns. As they fed, as they roosted, as they nested each spring they were shot, or trapped in huge nets and their heads were then crushed. Many were eaten in pigeon pies, but larger numbers were killed for no purpose other than extermination.[53]

[51] J. S. Munch to his brother, November 16, 1857, in Helene Munch and Peter A. Munch, trans., *The Strange American Way: Letters of Caja Munch from Wiota, Wisconsin, 1855–1859, with An American Adventure, Excerpts from "Vita Mea" an Autobiography Written in 1903 for His Children by Johan Storm Munch, and with an essay, Social Class and Acculturation by Peter A. Munch* (Carbondale, Illinois, [1970]), 115–116.

[52] Peter T. Harstad, "Health in the Upper Mississippi River Valley, 1820 to 1861" (doctoral dissertation, University of Wisconsin, 1963), 323–326; Malmin, ed., *Letters of Ole Raeder*, 65.

[53] Muir, *Boyhood and Youth*, 111–134, whence come the quotations; Charles D. Stewart, "The Pigeon Trap," in *WMH*, 24 (September, 1940), 20–24.

A state law limited the hunting season for ducks, quail, deer, and other game, but the law was not well enforced. During the hard winter of 1856–1857, when a crust formed on the deep snow, the deer found it hard to get away from preying animals, including men on snowshoes, though deer hunting was illegal at that time of year. "And such was the general havoc among the deer from hunters and wolves that they were nearly exterminated from the country," a pioneer later recollected, "and it was several years before people could have even a taste of that delicious game."[54]

No longer did prairie fires, which the Indians used to set, fill the autumn air with a haze that dimmed the sun. "As soon as the oak openings in our neighborhood were settled, and the farmers had prevented running grass-fires," John Muir remembered of his Marquette County home, "the grubs grew up into trees and formed tall thickets so dense that it was difficult to walk through them and every trace of the sunny 'openings' vanished." In much of southern Wisconsin there were more trees in 1857 than there had been ten or twenty years earlier.[55]

But smoke still darkened the day and flames lit up the night in those areas where woods were being converted into farms. "You will be shocked when I tell you that here in Little Chute since the first settlers came, hundreds of acres of dense primeval forests have been literally destroyed," a settler wrote in 1851 to his relatives in Holland. "Except for a few timbers used to build a log house, the rest went up in smoke, because there was no sawmill and no market for the lumber, and the land was needed for grain fields and pastures." In Holland, fuel was so scarce that farmers planted hedges, from which they allowed the poor occasionally to pick dead branches. Wisconsin farmers could do the same if they ever faced a shortage of firewood. They could plant trees for their own use, or they could buy coal brought in from other states. But there was

[54] Schafer, ed., "Ficker's Advice," in *WMH*, 25: 349; Brunson, *Western Pioneer*, 2: 256.

[55] Gregory, *Industrial Resources of Wisconsin*, 275; Muir, *Boyhood and Youth*, 183–184; Carstensen, *Farms or Forests*, 6–7.

nothing urgent about the matter in the opinion of most people.[56]

One of the few who disagreed was Wisconsin's pioneer scientist, Increase A. Lapham. In the 1855 *Transactions* of the state agricultural society he made a plea for forest conservation. Trees, he explained, not only provided lumber and fuel but also maintained the balance of nature. They preserved the moisture in the ground, regulated the flow of streams, provided nourishment for the soil, and restored oxygen to the air. In an 1857 letter to the *Prairie Farmer* Lapham proposed a waste-recycling plan that went beyond the mere manuring of fields, which he along with other agricultural reformers was advocating. According to his plan, the cities would return to the countryside the animal and vegetable matter they drew from it. They would process their sewage and sell it as fertilizer.[57]

Lapham's was the voice of one crying in a vanishing wilderness. He evoked little response from his fellow citizens of Wisconsin. As farmers, businessmen, industrial workers, they were preoccupied with making a living and getting ahead. They stood to gain from the rapid development of the state's resources. This meant exploiting nature's bounty, not conserving it.

[56] Schafer, ed., "Ficker's Advice," in *WMH*, 25: 334–336. The quotation is from a letter of Arnold Verstegen to his parents-in-law, December 26, 1851, in Lucas, ed., *Dutch Immigrant Memoirs*, 2: 154–156. See also Gregory, *Industrial Resources of Wisconsin*, 79–81.

[57] Graham P. Hawks, "Increase A. Lapham: Wisconsin's First Scientist" (doctoral dissertation, University of Wisconsin, 1960), 140–142; Milo M. Quaife, "Increase Allen Lapham, Father of Forest Conservation," in *WMH*, 5 (September, 1921), 104–108; Carstensen, *Farms or Forests*, 6–7.

4

Living Together and Apart

---

[1]

"OUR ADOPTED STATE. She has gathered her sons
from many lands and given them all a home amid her bounty
and her beauty. May the elements of strength and greatness
peculiar to each be here transplanted and united to form a perfect commonwealth." Thus ran a toast that one of the Milwaukee Sons of the Pilgrims offered in December 1850 at their
annual banquet celebrating the historic landing on Plymouth
Rock. These transplanted Yankees further emphasized the
spirit of the occasion by their choice of musical entertainment.
They listened to the "martial as well as festive" music of a German band.[1]

The Irish-born promoter of immigration and real estate
John Gregory expressed a similar spirit in his 1855 book on
Wisconsin's attractions. Gregory noted, exaggerating a bit,
that the state's population was composed of "heterogeneous
masses collected together from every quarter of the globe," and
he conceded that the "admixture of different habits, customs,
passions and feelings" would generate a certain amount of
"gaseous" discord. "But though these elements may jar for
a moment, like different metals in the furnace, yet the amalgamation of the races, by intermarriage, must produce the

---

[1] Joseph Schafer, "The Yankee and the Teuton in Wisconsin," in *WMH*, 6–7
(December, 1922–December, 1923), 7: 148, 154, citing the Milwankee *Free Democrat*, December 27, 1850.

most perfect race of men that has ever appeared upon earth."

Gregory went on to say that, in America and especially in Wisconsin, the masses were "better fed, better clad, and more comfortably lodged" than anywhere else in the world. Here everyone had a vote, and "even the poorest man" could "take his seat" among those who made the laws. Every man could "engage in any useful pursuit according to his taste or inclination, without the slightest fear of loosing his position in society, or being looked down upon, or slighted by his wealthier neighbor." Here, as in all new states, the political and social conditions tended toward equality, or at least "a degree of equality." Every man "naturally" considered himself as good as any other. It was a "free country."[2]

Americans had expressed these ideals before and were often to repeat them in later years—these ideals of fusing many peoples and cultures to create a new and better society, of remaking that society according to an egalitarian model on each successive frontier of settlement. But the ideal of the melting pot never had appealed to all the people in the country, and in the 1850's it certainly did not appeal to all those in Wisconsin. Many Wisconsinites, European-born as well as American-born, prized their cultural heritage too much to be willing to dilute it. For the time being, Wisconsin remained a society made up of separate societies, each with its own churches and other organizations, its own customs, and even its own language. Yet, if there were tendencies toward conflict and repulsion, there were also tendencies toward harmony and intermingling. The image of the "metals in the furnace" had some validity as prophetic insight, despite its inadequacy as a reflection of contemporary facts. It had some validity, that is, with regard to those settlers who were white and especially those who were also English-speaking and Protestant. It had little applicability to the Indians or to the Negroes.

Every person, whatever his color or his culture, could presumably aspire to a fair share of worldly goods, yet his actual

[2] John Gregory, *Industrial Resources of Wisconsin* (Milwaukee, 1855), 12–13, 22–25.

opportunities depended in large measure on his ancestry. If he succeeded in acquiring but little, he might still consider himself as good as someone else who owned a great deal, though others would be inclined to disagree with him. In frontier Wisconsin there was no flattening out of either economic or social differences between the few and the many, the rich and the poor. During the 1850's inequality of wealth in the state was, in fact, about the same as it was to be ten or a dozen decades later.[3]

[2]

Wealth was most highly concentrated in Milwaukee County. There, as of 1860, lived eight of the eleven richest men in the state. Forty-six Milwaukeeans were worth at least $100,000 apiece; they were the equivalents of a later century's millionaires. The 218 wealthiest owned as much as all the others, the remaining 15,124. The top 10 per cent (1,534 men) held over 80 per cent of the wealth.

In Milwaukee the average property holdings of American-born men were several times as large as those of the foreign-born. In the rest of the state the difference was not so extreme, but it was nevertheless considerable. Among the native Americans, those from the eastern states owned the most. Next in order were those born in Ohio, then those from the rest of the midwestern states, followed by those from Wisconsin and the southern states. Among the immigrants, those from England, Wales, and Scotland stood the highest, with an average above that for native midwesterners. Far below were those

---

[3] On economic inequality, see Lee Soltow, *Patterns of Wealthholding in Wisconsin Since 1850* (Madison, 1971), 5, 12, 28. Merle Curti concludes that, with "several important qualifications, . . . Turner's poetical vision of free land and of relatively equal opportunity was for a great many people being realized in Trempealeau County." See Merle Curti, *The Making of an American Community: A Case Study of Democracy in a Frontier County* (Stanford, 1959), 448. But Curti uses statistics for 1880, to show an increase in the proportion of immigrants, especially those from non-English-speaking countries, who were professional men or shopkeepers as distinct from laborers. By 1880 the frontier in Trempealeau County was a thing of the past. See pp. 61–65.

from Germany and Ireland and from the Scandinavian countries.[4]

Within each nativity group there was a wide range in the ownership of wealth, and within each there was roughly the same degree of concentration. In Trempealeau County, for example, the top 10 per cent of the native Americans owned 40 per cent of all the property belonging to native Americans. The top 10 per cent of the British immigrants owned 39 per cent of all the property belonging to British immigrants. The top 10 per cent of the non-English-speaking foreigners owned 33 per cent of all the property belonging to non-English-speaking foreigners. On the whole, the distribution of wealth in this newly settled Wisconsin county was just about as uneven as in long settled townships in Vermont.[5]

Occupations in Wisconsin varied somewhat according to nationality. Though most members of every group were engaged in agriculture, a higher proportion of native Americans owned and operated their own farms, and a higher proportion of the immigrants, especially the Norwegians, worked as hired hands. Among the people in nonagricultural pursuits, a disproportionate number of the American-born made a living from a business or a profession. A disproportionate number of the Irish and the non-English-speaking foreigners depended on the wages of daily work. "Most of the Americans," it seemed to an Irish publicist, "devote themselves to trade or commerce of some kind—they seldom work at hard labor."[6]

[4] Soltow, *Wealthholding in Wisconsin,* 30–34, 36, 40–41, 100–102. The rankings are based on the average wealth of a sample of forty-year-old males born in these states and countries. Pp. 89–90, 95, also show that on the whole Norwegians in Wisconsin were better off than those in Norway.

[5] Curti, *Making of an American Community,* 77–83. The Trempealeau County figures are for 1870, but figures for 1860 would probably be quite similar. When taking all groups together the top 10 per cent owned 39 per cent of the property in both 1860 and 1870.

[6] See, for example, Curti, *Making of an American Community,* 61–65; Alice E. Smith, *Millstone and Saw: The Origins of Neenah-Menasha* (Madison, 1966), 156–158; Schafer, "Yankee and Teuton in Wisconsin," in *WMH,* 7: 148–158; Gregory, *Industrial Resources of Wisconsin,* 249–250; the quotation is on p. 250. In the 1850's in Milwaukee, the Irish in particular were at the bottom of the occupational ladder, working as unskilled or semiskilled laborers. German

The richest man in Milwaukee (according to the 1860 census) was the Scottish-born banker Alexander Mitchell. Three of the next four wealthiest listed themselves as dealers in real estate, including the last of the four, railroad promoter Byron Kilbourn, who descended from old New England stock. Of the forty-six with property worth $100,000 or more, only seven besides Mitchell were immigrants. One of these was the Roman Catholic Bishop of Milwaukee, John M. Henni, born in Switzerland, but church property probably was listed under his name. Only four of the forty-six were principally engaged in industry—two millers, a lumber manufacturer, and a distiller. Except for a man who put himself down as a hotelkeeper and another who listed himself as an insurance company president, all the rest regarded themselves primarily as bankers, merchants, lawyers, or dealers in real estate.[7]

Along with the larger share of highly remunerative and prestigious occupations, the American-born also enjoyed more of the other amenities of life. The house a successful Yankee businessman provided for his family—such as the Italian villa with an indoor privy that was built for the Janesville perfume manufacturer William Tallman in 1857—was a far cry from the slab shanty of an Irish canal digger or the dugout of a newly arrived Norwegian settler, neither of whom was likely to have even on outdoor privy. "In a number of homes at Madison, Elkhorn, and Janesville," a traveler from abroad had noted as early as 1847, "I found all the comforts and all the elegance that we generally associate with the upper classes in Europe." Some of the "gentlemen of the higher classes" in Wisconsin, he observed, no longer polished their own shoes. These gentlemen had Irish, German, or Norwegian servants to perform such chores.[8]

---

laborers tended to have more semiskilled and skilled jobs, although a high proportion of the more recent German immigrants performed day labor. See Kathleen N. Conzen, " 'The German Athens': Milwaukee and the Accommodation of Its Immigrants, 1836–1860" (doctoral dissertation, University of Wisconsin, 1972), 158–163.

[7] Soltow, *Wealthholding in Wisconsin*, 31–33.

[8] The quotations are from Gunnar J. Malmin, ed. and trans., *America in the*

No Wisconsin laboring man or woman, native American or foreign-born, was likely to get rich from the proceeds of his or her labor. In the state as a whole (as of 1860) skilled workers such as carpenters earned an average of $1.73 a day. Ordinary day laborers averaged $1.05. Farm hands received their board and $13.96 a month, female domestics their board and $1.30 a week. All these averages were slightly below those for the rest of the country.[9]

Even in Milwaukee the wage earners themselves had too little economic strength and group consciousness to maintain a continuing and effective labor movement, though some of them did form unions and engage in occasional strikes for higher pay or shorter hours. In 1848 the Ship Carpenters' and Caulkers' Association successfully struck a shipbuilding company, but few if any other unions won a strike during the next several years. Employers played upon ethnic differences among their workers. When his journeymen shoemakers quit work in 1848, Benjamin Bosworth threatened to replace them with "true blooded Yankees" who would not be "humbugged by foreigners"—apparently referring to German socialist organizers. On the other hand, when the journeymen tailors struck in 1853, they complained of "many of the Bosses taking advantage of Old Countrymen, who don't understand the language, and getting them for less than they are worth, to the detriment of the Trade." Regarding a strike of railroad construction hands in 1854, the Milwaukee *Sentinel* reported, "The German laborers refused to work at the prices paid for labor, and drove off the Irish laborers who were willing to work at the present prices paid by the contractors."[10]

Forties: The Letters of Ole Munch Raeder (Minneapolis, 1929), 149–151. For a brief account and a picture of the Tallman house, see Richard W. E. Perrin, *The Architecture of Wisconsin* (Madison, 1967), 90–91. See also Rachel Salisbury, "1860–The Last Year of Peace: Augusta Tallman's Diary," in *WMH,* 44 (Winter, 1960–1961), 85–94. There is no evidence for the story, here repeated, that the Tallman house served as a station on the "underground railroad" for slaves escaping from the South.

[9] *Eighth Census of the United States, 1860: Mortality and Miscellaneous Statistics,* 512.

[10] Thomas W. Gavett, *Development of the Labor Movement in Milwaukee* (Madison, 1965), 5–9. The quotations are from the Milwaukee *Sentinel,* August 1, 1848, September 12, 1853, and March 9, 1854.

Workingmen, whatever their nationality, disliked the competition of working women, who could be hired to do the same jobs for less pay. One of the objectives of the tailors', shoemakers', cigar makers', and printers' unions was to keep down the number of female employees. The men at a Milwaukee print shop, themselves Germans, refused to set type for Mathilde Franziska Anneke, who had published the first women's newspaper in Germany, the *Frauen Zeitung,* and was trying to re-establish it in Wisconsin. She not only advocated that women be given the suffrage but also insisted that they be employed as compositors for her paper. She managed to have six issues printed at another German shop.

Despite the efforts of Mathilde Anneke and other feminists, the women of Wisconsin failed to get the vote. They gained some rights through a law of 1850 entitling them to property separate from their husbands' and a law of 1855 allowing them to dispose of their own wages or profits without their husbands' interference (in cases of the husbands' nonsupport). Yet they remained economically and legally far inferior to their menfolk, no matter what their ethnic group or social class.[11]

[3]

The Germans of Milwaukee, who made up more than 40 per cent of the city's population, occupied several areas of their own, including "German Town," located in the center of the city on both sides of the Milwaukee River. "Here one sees German houses, German inscriptions over the doors or signs, German physiognomies. Here are published German newspapers; and many Germans live here who never learn English, and seldom go beyond the German town." So reported Fredri-

---

[11] Gavett, *Labor Movement in Milwaukee,* 7; Donald J. Berthrong, "Social Legislation in Wisconsin, 1836–1900" (doctoral dissertation, University of Wisconsin, 1951), 103–104, 119–120; Lawrence L. Graves, "The Wisconsin Woman Suffrage Movement, 1846–1920" (doctoral dissertation, University of Wisconsin, 1954), 1–19. In 1850 and 1860 wages for women averaged about 40 per cent of male wages. See Margaret Walsh, "The Manufacturing Frontier: Pioneer Industry in Antebellum Wisconsin, 1830–1860" (doctoral dissertation, University of Wisconsin, 1969), 491n.

ka Bremer after her 1850 visit. "Their music and dances, and other popular pleasures, distinguish them from the Anglo-American people, who, particularly in the West, have no other pleasure than 'business.' "[12]

Milwaukee's German Town was the largest and most highly developed of the immigrant communities in Wisconsin, but others scattered throughout the state also lived more or less to themselves and maintained in some degree their Old Country languages and customs. These traits distinguished the various minorities from the majority, the "Anglo-American people," which included most of the British-born as well as the native-born of American stock, but did not include the Irish (as distinct from the Scotch-Irish).

Germans, Swiss, Norwegians, and others clung as best they could to their traditional dress as well as diet, the Dutch and the Belgians and some of the Germans keeping their wooden shoes. But they often found it hard to replace the materials for the clothes or to obtain the ingredients for the dishes. And, as a Norwegian in Madison explained to relatives in Norway, employers would not hire women unless they wore American dress. Some of the immigrants, especially the more youthful ones, were not reluctant but eager to cast off the old ways and adopt the new. Norwegian boys were quick to pick up English; "as soon as they learned 'to guess' and 'to calculate,' " their elders complained, "they at once become strangers to their less fortunate countrymen and are very loath to admit their Norwegian origin."[13]

[12] Fredrika Bremer, *The Homes of the New World: Impressions of America* (2 vols., New York, 1864, 1868), 1: 615–616. See also Conzen, " 'German Athens'," 291–294. For a discussion of the proportionate size of Milwaukee's German population, see fn. 5 on p. 5 above.

[13] Letter from a Washington County resident to the Boston *Pilot*, August 20, 1859, quoted in M. Justille McDonald, *History of the Irish in Wisconsin in the Nineteenth Century* (Washington, D.C., 1954), 205–206; Malmin, ed., *Letters of Ole Raeder*, 15–20, 40–41; the quotation is from p. 40. See also Theodore C. Blegen, *Norwegian Migration to America: The American Transition* (Northfield, Minnesota, 1940), 195; John D. Beck, "Acculturation and Religious Institutions: A Case Study of Acculturation in Sauk County, Wisconsin, by Special Reference to Religious Institutions" (master's thesis, University of Wisconsin, 1940), 69; Kate Everest Levi, "Geographical Origin of German Immigration to

One striking and persisting difference between the European-born and the American-born could be seen in their respective farm homes, as observers of various nationalities agreed. "If a place looks really filthy and disreputable, you must expect to meet either Norwegians or Swiss or Irish ('Eirisa,' as the Norwegians call them)," remarked a Norwegian scholar traveling through the state. After visiting some "Norwegian peasant houses" in the Koshkonong settlement, the Swedish Fredrika Bremer found a "want of neatness and order" that "contrasted strongly with the condition of the poor American cottages." Her fellow countryman, the Episcopal minister Gustav Unonius, said that upon entering an American cabin he usually saw "a broom at one side of the door and a wash basin at the other—things that do not litter up the German house, for the simple reason that they are so rarely used." Of all the immigrants, he believed, "the Germans longer than others retain the European lack of cleanliness, unless the patriotism of the Norwegian mountaineers expresses itself in that fashion to an even greater degree." The German author of an immigrant guidebook, who resided in Fond du Lac County, wrote that the German dwellings there, which reminded him of "peasant houses in Germany," were "dark and cheerless," while the "log houses of the Yankees" were "light and clean." Carl Schurz was even more emphatic. "You cannot believe how greatly the house and the whole domestic management of the American farmer surpass in cleanliness and clever arrangements those of the Germans," he told his wife after a trip from Watertown to Columbus and back. "If you enter the most insignificant hut of the Americans you will at least find the

Wisconsin," in *Wis. Hist. Colls.*, 14: 362-363; Henry S. Lucas, ed., *Dutch Immigrant Memoirs and Related Writings* (2 vols., Assen, Netherlands, 1955), 2: 175–177; Letter from Madison, December 18, 1849, in Beulah Folkedahl, ed. and trans., "Norwegians Become Americans," *Norwegian-American Studies,* 21 (1962), 103; Caja Munch to sisters-in-law, [February 23,] 1857, in Helene Munch and Peter A. Munch, trans., *The Strange American Way: Letters of Caja Munch from Wiota, Wisconsin, 1855–1859, with An American Adventure, Excerpts from "Vita Mea" an Autobiography Written in 1903 for His Children by Johan Storm Munch, and with an essay, Social Class and Acculturation by Peter A. Munch* (Carbondale, Illinois, [1970]), 74–75.

walls speckessly white, all utensils brightly scoured, the windows shining, furniture in order, no farm tools inside the house, and all the female occupants arrayed with a certain degree of taste."[14]

The women and girls of native American farm families generally, though not invariably, confined themselves to housework and to such other chores as tending gardens and chickens. "It is the men in this country who milk the cows," Bremer noted with some surprise, "as well as attend to all kinds of out-of-door business." Accepting this custom of the new country, a Swedish wife at Pine Lake, in the presence of the visitor from abroad, reminded her husband to be sure to "milk the white cow well again to-night." But many of the European and especially the German women continued to do not only the milking but also much of the heavy labor in the fields.[15]

Cornish miners quit work at noon on Saturday and spent the afternoon smoking, drinking, and talking with friends in a "kiddlywink," a beer and soft-drink tavern. Dutch (Catholic) and Belgian farmers allowed themselves little or no time for recreation except on Sundays and holidays. On Sunday afternoons, gathering at one of the houses in a Dutch neighborhood,

[14] Malmin, ed., *Letters of Ole Raeder,* 37–38; Bremer, *Homes of the New World,* 1: 634–635; Nils W. Olsson, ed., *A Pioneer in Northwest America, 1841–1858: The Memoirs of Gustaf Unonius,* trans. Jonas O. Backlund (2 vols., Minneapolis, [1950, 1960]), 2: 82; Carl de Haas, *Nordamerika, Wisconsin, Calumet: Winke für Auswanderer* (Elberfeld, 1848), quoted in Joseph Schafer, *The Winnebago-Horicon Basin: A Type Study in Western History* (Madison, 1937), 193–194; Schurz to his wife, September 3, 1855, in Joseph Schafer, ed. and trans., *Intimate Letters of Carl Schurz, 1841–1869* (Madison, 1928), 150. Schafer takes the Carl de Haas quotation as indicating the "difference between the homes of the most advanced American settlers and those of the poorer immigrants," and he comments on the Schurz letter: "Of course Schurz had seen only the better types of American settlers and he had apparently not seen the superior types of German settlers." But Haas appears to have ordinary "log houses of the Yankees" in mind, and Schurz refers in so many words to even "the most insignificant hut of the Americans." Raeder does not say he is comparing poor immigrant homes with well-to-do native ones. Bremer makes her contrast with the "poor American cottages," and Unonius, too, includes the humblest American dwellings in his comparison.

[15] Bremer, *Homes of the New World,* 1: 624. See also Alice E. Smith, *The History of Wisconsin. Volume I: From Exploration to Statehood* (Madison, 1973), 493–494.

the men "played cards and took an occasional drink from a jug of liquor," the women "sipped their tea or coffee and chatted," and the boys "found amusement in innocent games." The Belgians celebrated Sunday first with mass and then with many rounds of weak beer, a feast, patriotic French and Belgian songs, contests and other pastimes such as the "swinging of the flags," and finally dancing until late at night. During the Kermiss, or harvest festival, the fun was prolonged through the week. Germans, too, enjoyed a convivial Sunday, with beer drinking, target shooting, bowling, and dancing.[16]

Sunday was quieter among most of the old-stock Americans. While staying with a prominent Madison family, Bremer wished to take advantage of fine October weather and enjoy an excursion on one of the lakes after church. " 'But—it is Sunday,' was the answer which I received with a smile, and on Sundays people must not amuse themselves, not even in God's beautiful scenery." Some Madisonians of American ancestry did amuse themselves in God's scenery on God's day—a local newspaper, with implied disapproval, reported the governor and other state officials one Sunday putting off in a boat with "guns, fishing tackle, &c.," and with "a plentiful supply of excitants."[17]

Certainly, on other days and nights, the families of native background had ways of enjoying their leisure, despite Bremer's impression that the "Anglo-American people" knew "no other pleasure than 'business.' " At the capital the fashionable young folk had the most "gayety in a social way" during the sessions of the legislature. On New Year's Day, friends dropped in on one another in Madison as they did in New York. On this

---

[16] Louis A. Copeland, "The Cornish in Southwest Wisconsin," in *Wis. Hist. Colls.*, 14: 333–334; Lucas, ed., *Dutch Immigrant Memoirs*, 2: 177–179 (the quotation is from p. 179); Hjalmar R. Holand, *History of Door County, Wisconsin: The County Beautiful* (2 vols., Chicago, 1917), 1: 416–419; Xavier Martin, "The Belgians of Northeast Wisconsin," in *Wis. Hist. Colls.*, 13: 386–387; Lee W. Metzner, "The First Kirmess," in *WMH*, 14 (June, 1931), 339–353, Schurz describes a German Sunday near Watertown in a letter to his wife, August 12, 1855, in Schafer, ed., *Intimate Letters of Carl Schurz*, 147.

[17] Bremer, *Homes of the New World*, 1: 630–631; Madison *Wisconsin Express*, October 30, 1849, quoted in Aaron M. Boom, "The Development of Sectional Attitudes in Wisconsin, 1848–1861" (doctoral dissertation, University of Chicago, 1948), 17–18.

and other holidays the leaders of high society in Madison, Milwaukee, and lesser cities arranged elaborate balls, often at hotels, where couples ate, drank, and danced the cotillion, paying as much as a dollar apiece for tickets. The less well-to-do, including those on the farms, also got together from time to time for private parties and picnics, for sleigh rides, oyster suppers, and square dances, and for log raisings, husking bees, and other occasions combining pleasure with work.[18]

People organized for sociability and recreation according to their ethnic background. Those of remote or recent British origin met together as members of the same lodges, as Masons, Odd Fellows, Good Templars. Germans had their own fraternal as well as musical, theatrical, gymnastic, and other clubs. The Irish had some, though fewer, organizations, among them the Hibernian Benevolent Society, which paid sickness and death benefits, and militia companies which gave added verve and color to St. Patrick's Day. Whether native or foreign-born, people of the various religious affiliations centered much of their social life upon their respective churches.[19]

Public recreation and entertainment also were available in Milwaukee and to a lesser extent in other places. Even a small town as a rule had its saloon, bowling alley, and billiard hall. By 1857 horse racing and betting on the horses were well established, at least in some parts of the state. Meanwhile circus troupes had begun to tour the state, and so had entertainers of other kinds, offering Shakespearean readings and other theatrical as well as musical performances, which supplemented the more frequent appearances of local bands, glee clubs, and dra-

[18] George Paine to Lucius Fairchild, February 4, 1848, and Sarah Fairchild Dean to Elizabeth Gordon, April 16, 1848, in the Lucius Fairchild Papers; Elizabeth Gordon to Charlotte Gordon, January 25, 1850, in the Elizabeth Gordon Correspondence; Robert C. Robertson, "The Social History of Winnebago County, Wisconsin, 1850–1870" (master's thesis, University of Chicago, 1939), 101–104; Eugene Wiggins, "Pioneer Days in Fall City," in Menomonie *Dunn County News*, June 14, 1923; "Frank Bowe, Pioneer, Can Recall Day When Fond du Lac Had 500 Inhabitants and Rosendale 15," in Fond du Lac *Commonwealth-Reporter*, July 17, 1929.

[19] Robertson, "Social History of Winnebago County," 105; Bayrd Still, *Milwaukee: The History of a City* (Madison, 1965), 127, 130; McDonald, *Irish in Wisconsin*, 235, 248.

Above: State capitol, ca. 1868. Below: Racine schoolhouse, 1860's.

De Pere, 1870.

Steamboat moored at an Eau Claire landing, 1868.

Yellow Thunder, a Winnebago chief.

Emmeline S. Whitney.

William A. Barstow.

Oshkosh waterfront, ca. 1855.

Milwaukee, ca. 1868.

De Pere fire department, ca. 1872.

Hide-laden steamer docking at Appleton tannery; Lawrence University in the background.

Carl Schurz.

Edward P. Allis.

Unidentified.

Chippewa River landing, Eau Claire, ca. 1870.

Julia Chamberlain Drake.

Sherman Booth.

Unidentified.

St. John's Cathedral, Milwaukee, 1860.

matic groups. In Milwaukee the *Musikverein,* under the leadership of the Forty-Eighter Hans Balatka from 1849 to 1855, sponsored an orchestra, a male chorus, and string quartets and presented concerts, oratorios, and operas of very high quality. "I do not believe they can perform any better in most of the small capitals of Germany," Carl Schurz declared. In 1855 the *Musikverein* sent out a small traveling company to give an "operatic concert," consisting of selections from the opera *Norma,* in Watertown and other Wisconsin cities. Some of the most famous performers of Europe, such as the "Swedish nightingale" Jenny Lind and the Norwegian violinist Ole Bull, included Milwaukee in the American tours of the 1850's, and Bull appeared also in Madison. To hear Jenny Lind, wealthy Wisconsinites from as far as Madison and Menasha made their way to Milwaukee, and thereafter they were known as "Jenny Linders," which implied not only that they were members of a privileged class but also that they had pretensions to aristocracy.[20]

The Fourth of July was one occasion that, in the larger towns at least, the various groups could and did often celebrate together. At the approach of July 4, 1856, however, many Milwaukee Germans still wondered whether they should not observe the day in their own manner and apart from the "Yankees." The performances of German musicians provided other occasions for the sharing of leisure. Native Americans supported the Milwaukee *Musikverein* with both subscriptions and attendance; they made up well over one-third of the audience at the performance of *Czaar und Zimmermann* on April 8, 1853. The beer and music and festivities of the German Sunday sometimes drew young "Anglo-American" men, and, it seemed to Bremer, "those strong, blooming German

[20] Robertson, "Social History of Winnebago County," 29, 104; Schafer, *Winnebago-Horicon Basin,* 200; circus and other advertisements in Menasha *Conservator,* August 7, 1856, November 4, 1858, and March 19 and April 2, 1859; Still, *Milwaukee,* 206–216; J. J. Schlicher, "Hans Balatka and the Milwaukee Musical Society," in *WMH,* 27 (September, 1943), 40–55. The Schurz quotation is from a letter to his wife, September 4, 1855, in Schafer, ed., *Intimate Letters of Carl Schurz,* 151.

girls" also sometimes attracted them, and quite "irresistibly."[21]

Whatever truth there may have been in that, the fact is that very few native boys married German girls. Intermarriage between native American men or women and immigrants from any country of continental Europe or from Ireland, or between individuals of different European nationalities, was as yet extremely rare.[22]

[4]

"The religious institutions of Wisconsin bear, in good degree, the impress of New England." So declared a Congregational minister when the state was only a few years old. The Puritan faith, which had made New England "lovely and renowned," might yet do the same for the rising West. But the friends of Zion faced no easy task. On the frontier, they realized, even the settlers from good Christian backgrounds in the older states were likely to backslide. Other settlers had "no saving knowledge of Christ and his Gospel" to begin with. "A large portion of these have come to our soil from foreign lands, where superstition and formalism and infidelity have wound themselves around the tree of christianity and pressed out its life." Missionaries of New England birth or descent felt a duty toward these less fortunate people, a duty to "give them the Gospel in its simplicity and purity and living power."[23]

Puritans were not the only ones campaigning to win the souls of Wisconsinites. Other native American Protestant evangelizers were also active in the same mission field. So were the agents of the European Protestant churches whose communi-

---

[21] Still, *Milwaukee*, 115–120, 224–226; Milwaukee *Banner und Volksfreund*, July 6, 1855; Bremer, *Homes of the New World*, 1: 615–616.

[22] Conzen, " 'German Athens'," 509; Joseph Schafer, *Four Wisconsin Counties: Prairie and Forest* (Madison, 1927), 174.

[23] The first quotation is from Stephen Peet, *History of the Presbyterian and Congregational Churches and Ministers in Wisconsin: Including an Account of the Organization of the Convention and the Plan of Union* (Milwaukee, 1851), 187. The others are from a report, "Wisconsin: Wants of the State," in the *Home Missionary*, 22 (December, 1849), 191.

cants were settling in the state. And so were the Roman Catholics, whose American leaders were beginning to take a frankly aggressive stand. Anti-Catholic extremists had long feared what they considered a popish plot to capture the Mississippi Valley. Their fears appeared to be confirmed when, in 1850, Archbishop John Hughes of New York spoke out to announce the impending collapse of Protestantism and the impending triumph of Rome. There was no secret about "the intention of the Pope with regard to the Valley of the Mississippi," the archbishop declared. "Everybody should know that we have for our mission to convert the world—including the inhabitants of the United States. . . ."[24]

Even without the conversion of many Protestants, the mere process of settlement seemed likely to make Wisconsin a predominantly Roman Catholic state in time. Among its immigrants, practically all the Belgians and the French Canadians, the great majority of the Irish, about half of the Dutch, and a third or more of the Germans were at least nominally members of the church of Rome. During the 1850's the number of Catholics grew steadily, to a point where they constituted nearly one-fourth of the state's total population.[25]

The spiritual leader of Wisconsin Catholics, the Swiss-born, German-speaking Bishop of Milwaukee, John Martin Henni, was a determined foe of what he viewed as the errors of American Protestantism. Bishop Henni ably kept up the great work he had set for himself, which was both to attract Catholic settlers and to maintain them in their faith. He had the continued

[24] Ray A. Billington, *The Protestant Crusade, 1800–1860: A Study of the Origins of American Nativism* (New York, 1938), 129, 289–291; the quotation from p. 291 is from the New York *Freeman's Journal*, November 23, 1850.

[25] "By 1861 the Catholic population of Wisconsin had risen to 190,000. . . ." Peter Leo Johnson, *Crosier on the Frontier: A Life of John Martin Henni, Archbishop of Milwaukee* (Madison, 1959), 134–135. Johnson's figure of 190,000 is slightly less than 25 per cent of the total population of 775,881 as given in the 1860 census. *The Metropolitan Catholic Almanac and Laity's Directory for the United States, Canada, and the British Provinces, 1861* (Baltimore, 1860), 174, also gives the Catholic population of Wisconsin as "about" 190,000. See also Martin, "Belgians of Northeast Wisconsin," in *Wis. Hist. Colls.*, 13: 384.

support of devoted missionaries, such as Samuel Charles Mazzuchelli, Adelbert Inama, and Martin Kundig, who received
financial aid from Bavarian and Austrian missionary societies.
Yet he was hard put to find money and priests enough to provide regular care for all his rapidly expanding flock. Much
of his financing he obtained from abroad, especially from the
Ludwigmissionsverein in Munich. In 1848–1849 he traveled
to Europe to raise funds, recruit members of religious orders,
and secure hard-to-get church supplies. Later he visited Mexico
and Cuba to gather alms. Under his episcopacy a hospital
serving Catholics and non-Catholics alike was opened, a handsome cathedral was erected in Milwaukee, and a priest-training
seminary was founded near the city. New church buildings
continued to rise throughout the diocese, the bishop blessing
twenty-three of them in 1856 and twice as many the following
year.[26]

Bishop Henni found his task complicated by the nationality
differences among Wisconsin Catholics. Not that he wished
to see any of them lose their ethnic identity, for he was sure
that keeping their language helped them to keep their faith.
Mit der Sprache geht der Glaube. The bishop conceived of himself as the special champion of Catholic Germans, and he had
planned the seminary as, in large part, a means of assuring
an ample supply of German-speaking priests. In each parish he
hoped to have a priest of the same nationality as the majority
of the parishioners, but he could not always manage to do so,
and when he did, the minority was almost bound to be dissatisfied. Generally he pleased the Germans, though he had
trouble with some who demanded lay control of church property, provoked schisms, and in one Bavarian parish even threatened armed revolt. He was often criticized by Irish Catholics,
and sooner or later they withdrew from mixed parishes to form
separate congregations of their own. Catholics of other nationalities did the same. When, in 1857, the bishop visited

[26] Johnson, *Crosier on the Frontier*, 32–33, 82–85, 88–94, 98–99, 101–102, 158–164.

the French and German churches in Green Bay—and spoke on "the necessity of union in faith"—the Irish were about to leave the French and form an Irish church, and the Hollanders were already separating from the Germans and beginning to worship in a brand-new Dutch church.[27]

During the 1850's the Lutherans in Wisconsin were increasing about as fast as the Catholics, but they were suffering much more from differences among themselves. They had no single organization such as the Catholics had. Most of them had belonged to a state church in one or another of the German or Scandinavian countries, each church having its distinctive forms of governance, worship, and doctrine. The new arrivals in a given locality might join to form a congregation that, at least temporarily, had no connection with any larger Lutheran group. Sooner or later the congregation might be linked with others under the authority of one of several American synods.

In 1848 the Reverend J. Muehlhaueser, a Lutheran missionary from Rochester, New York, had entered Wisconsin as an agent for the American Tract Society. Muehlhaueser found the new state a challenge because of its growing number of churchless German Lutherans. In 1849 he with three other ministers founded the Synod of Wisconsin. They received reinforcements of pastors from the Rhenish Missionary Seminary at Barmen, where he himself had been educated, and financial assistance from the Ministerium of Pennsylvania. Many of the German Lutherans in Wisconsin, however, affiliated with older synods, Buffalo or Missouri, and some with the Iowa Synod, which was formed in 1854 by seceders from the Missouri group.[28]

[27] McDonald, *Irish in Wisconsin*, 203–206; Johnson, *Crosier on the Frontier*, 123–125, 133–135; the Rev. F. J. Bonduel, Green Bay, to the editor of the Boston *Pilot*, October 20, 1857, typed transcription in File No. 21, Milwaukee Archdiocese Chancery Archives.

[28] Henry E. Jacobs, *A History of the Evangelical Lutheran Church in the United States* (New York, 1899), 21, 406–410; John P. Koehler, *The History of the Wisconsin Synod*, ed. Leigh D. Jordahl (St. Cloud, Minnesota, 1970), 33, 39–43.

Pastors and parishioners of different synodical affiliations devoted a great deal of time and effort to quarreling with one another. The Buffalo and Missouri synods, which engaged in continual polemics over fine doctrinal points, centered much of their attention on issues arising in the Milwaukee area. The Wisconsin and Missouri synods, also disagreeing about doctrine, clashed most bitterly over the control of a Racine church. Some German Lutherans divided in consequence of differences having nothing to do with either the polity or the policy of a synod. Pomeranians and Mecklenburgers, "both of the same shade of the Lutheran faith" but living on opposite sides of the Wolf (Ahnapee) River in Door County, could not agree on where their church should stand. They ended by building two churches, only a mile apart.[29]

Many of the early Norwegian settlers in Wisconsin were Haugeans, that is, pietistic Lutherans who wished to reform the state church of Norway. In Wisconsin they found a leader in Elling Eielsen, a lay preacher and revivalist who, in 1846, had set up a synod of his own. Already, however, a few orthodox and university-trained pastors had arrived, among them the Reverend J. W. Dietrichson, who by 1848 was taking care of two congregations totaling 1,400 people in the Koshkonong area. In 1851, delegates from eighteen or nineteen congregations met in the hope of bringing them together, but Haugeans and orthodox Lutherans could come to no agreement. In 1853 Herman A. Preus and other orthodox pastors of Wisconsin succeeded in forming the Norwegian Evangelical Lutheran Church in America. They transferred to this country the ritual and dogma of the official church of Norway. Norwegian congregations remained divided as between the new Norwegian Synod and the older Eielsen one, between the high church and the low. Within their own congregations, pastors of the regular synod had constantly to contend with both pious Haugeans and irreligious rowdies who flouted ecclesiastical authority.

[29] Roy A. Suelflow, *A Plan for Survival* (New York, 1965), 88, 95; Holand, *History of Door County*, 1: 434–438; the quotation is from p. 437.

Many of the Haugeans were ripe for conversion to one or another of the American evangelistic sects.[30]

The pietism of the Moravians, for example, attracted a few Norwegians in Wisconsin, and in 1850 the wealthy Nils Otto Tank, who had become a Moravian convert before arriving in Wisconsin, bought land near Green Bay and set up a colony, which lasted only a few years, for his impoverished fellow believers. Much more numerous than the Moravians were the Calvinists from the Reformed churches of Germany, Switzerland, and the Netherlands. Some of the German Calvinists and Lutherans had already been combined in their home countries, and some formed "unionist" congregations after their arrival in Wisconsin. Some, when pastors of their own faith were unavailable, accepted men provided by the Evangelical Association of America—a German-speaking denomination similar to the Methodist—which had originated in Pennsylvania. The Dutch Protestants were divided between the Netherlands-oriented Christian Reformed Church and the long Americanized Reformed Church in America.[31]

Among the German immigrants, especially the Forty-Eighters, were a number of humanists and freethinkers. The most notable of them, the former Catholic priest Eduard Schröter, had founded a Free Congregation *(Freie Gemeinde)* in Hesse-Darmstadt and another in New York City before he came to Milwaukee in 1851 at the invitation of a Lutheran-Reformed group and established a third. For this Milwaukee Free Congregation he drew up a set of Fundamental Principles committing the members to "reason and the great teachings of nature

---

[30] Munch, trans., *Letters of Caja Munch*, 203–210; Blegen, *Norwegian Migration: American Transition*, 141, 160, 163–170; Folkedahl, ed., "Norwegians Become Americans," *Norwegian-American Studies*, 21: 98. A travel account and Koshkonong parish journal by Dietrichson are published in E. Clifford Nelson, ed., *A Pioneer Churchman: J. W. C. Dietrichson in Wisconsin, 1844–1850*, trans. Malcolm Rosholt and Harris E. Kaasa (New York, 1973).

[31] Joseph Schafer, "Scandinavian Moravians in Wisconsin," in *WMH*, 24 (September, 1940), 25–38; Beck, "Acculturation and Religious Institutions," 18–21; John Hoffman, "The Dutch Settlements of Sheboygan County," in *WMH*, 2 (June, 1919), 464–466.

and history." He also published the *Humanist*, which soon reached a circulation of more than a thousand. By the end of 1852 there were twenty-nine Free Congregations in the state. The next year Schröter abandoned the paper and moved to Sauk City to serve as a regular salaried lecturer for a group of about ninety members there. For thirty-five years he was to hold this position while he also farmed and visited neighboring communities with missionary zeal. Meantime the Milwaukee Free Congregation federated with the more extreme and atheistic Society of Free Men *(Verein Freier Männer)*, and most of the other freethinking organizations in the state declined and disappeared.[32]

The Jews in Wisconsin, who came mostly from the German countries, were concentrated in Milwaukee, where by 1856 they comprised about two hundred families. At first they had held services in one another's homes, without any formal organization. In 1848 they founded a Jewish cemetery association, which as the first Jewish congregation observed the Holy Days of 1849 in a room above a grocery store. Later members from different countries disagreed over liturgical customs, and the congregation broke into three groups. The pioneer of Reform Judaism in America, the Bohemian-born Rabbi Isaac Mayer Wise of Cincinnati, visited Milwaukee in 1856 and undertook to "rouse our people" and reunite them. Two of the groups consolidated (and were soon joined by a third), brought in their first regular rabbi, and began to build a "neat and substantial" synagogue.[33]

The native American Protestants—the Methodists, Congregationalists and Presbyterians, Baptists, Episcopalians, and members of smaller denominations—recognized a certain spir-

---

[32] Beck, "Acculturation and Religious Institutions," 55–61; J. J. Schlicher, "Eduard Schroeter the Humanist," in *WMH*, 28 (December, 1944–March, 1945), 169–183, 307–324; the quotation is from p. 177. By 1862 Schröter lamented the declining membership and growing apathy within the groups. See Berenice Cooper, "Die Freien Gemeinden in Wisconsin," in the *Transactions of the Wisconsin Academy of Sciences, Arts and Letters,* 53 (1964), 53–65.

[33] Louis J. Swichkow and Lloyd P. Gartner, *The History of the Jews of Milwaukee* (Philadelphia, 1963), 11–12, 33–41.

itual kinship among themselves. All of them, in the words of Wisconsin's Presbyterian-Congregationalist leader Dexter Clary, contributed to the "full evangelical religious strength in Wisconsin." All of them drew a sharp distinction between "evangelical" Protestantism, on the one hand, and both Catholicism and Lutheranism on the other. They did not recognize the Lutherans as evangelical in the same sense that they themselves were. But they accepted, as true Protestants, the Dutch Reformed and many of the German and other foreign Calvinistic or pietistic sects.

The "spirit of union and co-operation" among true Protestants had steadily grown, Clary reported at the end of the 1850's. Not only had his own Presbyterian-Congregational Convention maintained itself as an interdenominational enterprise (the two churches' Plan of Union persisting in Wisconsin after having been abandoned in other states), but the Convention had entered into "fraternal correspondence with other evangelical denominations" and had sent delegates to and received them from those churches' annual conferences. Yet there were trends toward fragmentation as well as unification, even among the Presbyterians. Instead of going along with the Plan of Union, some of the presbyteries aligned themselves with either of two independent state synods, the one Old School (strictly Calvinistic) and the other New School (which placed less emphasis on such traditional doctrines as predestination). Cornish congregations in the mining region seceded from the Wisconsin Methodist Episcopal Conference and joined the Primitive Methodist Church. Seventh-Day Baptists remained apart from the regular Baptists of the Wisconsin Baptist State Association.[34]

Missionaries and ministers of the various denominations competed as much as they co-operated in their conversion efforts. Denominational rivalries and jealousies often became bitter.

[34] Dexter Clary, *History of the Churches and Ministers Connected with the Presbyterian and Congregational Convention of Wisconsin, and of the Operations of the American Home Missionary Society in the State for the Past Ten Years* (Beloit, 1861), 11–12, 37–38, 65–66, 121–128; P. S. Bennett and James Lawson, *History of Methodism in Wisconsin* (Cincinnati, 1890), 110.

The pioneer Methodist missionary Alfred Brunson, laboring in La Crosse, suspected Baptist and Congregationalist preachers of enticing Methodist families into their churches and taking advantage of his revival meetings to gain additional converts. "Union among Christians, upon terms of equality, I am favorable to," Brunson said, "but a union to be all on one side and be made to play into the hands of others, but nothing into ours, is not agreeable to my views of propriety, and I would not submit to it." Another Methodist missionary, who received Presbyterian financial support on his mission to Superior and its environs, complained to his diary: "I feel very much trameled and embarressed in my ministerial labor, for every time I turn around I hit my elbows against some other denominational prejudices, and feel that I am infringing upon the customs & usages of others, and especially so as the Presbyterians tried to keep me from being a Methodist. . . ."[35]

The evangelistic churches had difficulty, as the Catholic and Lutheran did, in keeping up with the needs of their own members who migrated to the Wisconsin frontier. Settlers were seldom willing or able to pay the full costs of maintaining religious services. Of 126 Presbyterian and Congregational churches in 1850, only ten supported their preachers without missionary aid. Of more than 200 such churches in 1861, only forty were self-supporting. During the 1850's the American Home Missionary Society contributed more than 90 per cent of the combined denominations' operating expenses in Wisconsin, in addition to the money that the society spent on agents and missionaries in the state. For the most part, the congregations paid for the erection of their own houses of worship, but the Home Missionary Society and the General Convention of the Congregational Church financed nearly 10 per cent of the total building cost.[36]

Despite their limited resources, the evangelistic churches

[35] Alfred Brunson, *A Western Pioneer* . . . (2 vols., Cincinnati, 1872, 1879), 2: 235–237; James Peet Diaries, August 20, 1857.

[36] Clary, *Presbyterian and Congregational Convention of Wisconsin,* 101, 113–120.

managed to support missionary work among the immigrants, and they gained some converts among those foreign-born Protestants whose religious views most resembled their own. Norwegians readily became Baptists, Episcopalians, Congregationalists, Presbyterians, and Methodists. A Danish convert laboring for the Methodist Home Missionary Society, Christian B. Willerup, had a stone church built in Cambridge in 1851—"the first Norwegian Methodist house of worship in the world." Willerup organized several other Methodist congregations among Norwegians in the state and then left, in 1856, to carry Methodism to Norway. Missionaries of the German Methodist Episcopal Church, which had originated in western Pennsylvania and Ohio in the 1830's, canvassed German communities and found some "more fruitful" than others, depending on the "different degrees in which the people were intrenched in superstition and infidelity." Germans also formed a few Congregational churches, and Hollanders a few Presbyterian churches, these being scarcely distinguishable from the Dutch Reformed. Welsh settlers constituted twenty Congregational churches, which were "becoming Americanized very fast." But the great mass of immigrants, especially the Catholics, remained untouched by American proselyting efforts.[37]

The activities of churchmen of many persuasions helped to change the face if not the soul of Wisconsin. When the state was new, arrivals from Europe were struck by the relative absence of church edifices and chiming bells, which had been all around them at home. Already there were a few "splendid temples" in some of the cities, but even in "such a prosperous little town as Janesville" there were no churches before 1848. Throughout the state the great majority of worshipers met at first in a school building, courthouse, store, or log or frame structure with only a wooden cross to mark it as a house of God. Then, during the 1850's, the number of church build-

[37] Blegen, *Norwegian Migration: American Transition*, 119–121; Bennett and Lawson, *Methodism in Wisconsin*, 127, 149, 455–458; Clary, *Presbyterian and Congregational Convention of Wisconsin*, 92–93, 101, 110. The quotation about the Welsh is from Clary, p. 92; the others are from Bennett and Lawson, pp. 127, 457.

ings more than tripled. Most of these had steeples but no bells, and many more were built of wood rather than brick or stone. (As of 1860, of the Presbyterian-Congregational Convention's 165 houses of worship, 139 were of frame, twenty-one of brick, and five of stone construction, and only thirty-four were equipped with bells.) By the end of the decade the Methodists led in church accommodations, the Catholics were second, the Congregationalists were third, though they ranked fifth in number of churches, and the Baptists, Lutherans, Presbyterians, and Episcopalians followed in that order. The religious institutions of Wisconsin now bore less of the New England stamp than they formerly had done. As a whole, the native evangelistic churches could still claim much the largest membership, but relatively they had lost ground, and they felt more and more on the defensive.[38]

[5]

To Americans of old stock the ways of the foreigners, especially the Roman Catholics, often seemed outlandish. A Methodist missionary in Superior, referring to an Irishman who had drowned in the lake, remarked contemptuously that "his friends had an Irish drunken revel over his corpse." To foreign-born Catholics or Lutherans the behavior of some of the American sects was equally absurd. A German settler, after attending a Methodist revival near Mequon, said he had "never been in an insane asylum, but truly it could not be worse there." Evangelistic preachers regularly denounced the Church of Rome

[38] Malmin, ed., *Letters of Ole Raeder*, 139–140; the Janesville quotation is from p. 140. See also Joseph Schafer, ed. and trans., "Christian Traugott Ficker's Advice to Emigrants," in *WMH*, 25 (December, 1941–June, 1942), 461; Clary, *Presbyterian and Congregational Convention of Wisconsin*, 113–120, 128; William Blake, *Cross and Flame in Wisconsin: The Story of United Methodism in the Badger State* (Sun Prairie, Wisconsin, 1973), 57–82; Robertson, "Social History of Winnebago County," 35. For figures on church accommodations in 1850 and 1860 as well as 1870, see *Ninth Census of the United States, 1870: Volume I*, pp. 506–525. Though not completely reliable, these census figures may give a general indication of comparative accommodations; for the evangelistic denominations, the figures on accommodations correspond roughly to those on memberships as provided by Clary, p. 128.

and offered their pulpits to self-proclaimed former monks or priests who promised "awful disclosures" about the wickedness within it. Good Catholics were not always in a mood to permit that kind of free speech. When, in 1851, "Father" E. M. Leahy appeared in a Milwaukee Methodist church, an Irish mob stormed into the building, drove out the lecturer and his listeners, and demolished the pews.[39]

Tension between Catholics and Protestants was not due merely to bigotry on either side. Between the two were fundamental differences in outlook regarding this world as well as the next. The Catholics, though viewing the earth as a sinful place, were inclined to believe that it had to be accepted as such. The Protestants, especially the more evangelistic ones, felt that they had a duty to save mankind from what they considered sin and to create, according to their own lights, a heaven on earth. On this issue many of the Lutherans occupied a middle position. They were anti-Catholic—the Missouri Synod still endorsed the old doctrine that the pope was Antichrist— and yet they shared some of the Catholic distaste for the aims and methods of the Protestant social reformers.[40]

The Wisconsin Presbyterian and Congregational Convention of 1853 resolved that "the ministry and churches" were "bound to rebuke all sin, to labor earnestly for the removal of oppression, and to withhold Christian fellowship from all those who persist in holding in slavery their fellow men." At the 1854 meeting of the Methodist Conference of the state the "most absorbing subject, aside from the direct work of leading souls to Christ, was that of slavery." Slavery, a sin, had come to be the worst social wrong of the time, in the view of most evangelical leaders, and the sinners in this case were of course

[39] For the comment on the Irish wake, see James Peet Diaries, August 2, 1856. The comparison to an asylum is in Schafer, ed., "Ficker's Advice," in *WMH,* 25: 463–466. For the reaction to Leahy's appearance, see Leonard G. Koerber, "Anti-Catholic Agitation in Milwaukee, 1843–1860" (master's thesis, Marquette University, 1960), 77–78.

[40] For a discussion of "ritualistic" and "pietistic" religious groups and their respective social values, see Paul Kleppner, *The Cross of Culture: A Social Analysis of Midwestern Politics, 1850–1900* (New York, 1970), 71–73, 91. On the pope as "Antichrist," see Jacobs, *Evangelical Lutheran Church,* 408.

the slaveholders of the distant South. But there remained, close at hand, a number of serious though lesser evils—dancing, gambling, smoking, drinking, and Sabbath-breaking—against which the leading Methodists, Congregationalists, Presbyterians, and Baptists continually inveighed. The guilty in such matters, the leaders realized, included people of these very denominations; a Baptist preacher in Arena sadly noted one day that his own children had stayed at a party "until 2 & 3 o'clock this morning & engaged in dancing also." The worst offenders, however, seemed to be the foreign-born of other faiths.[41]

In Wisconsin a "Sunday law" remained on the books from territorial times (and was to continue almost unchanged into the twentieth century). The 1839 law read: "No person shall keep open his shop, warehouse or workhouse, or shall do any manner of business, or work, except only works of necessity or charity, or be present at any dancing, or any public diversion, show or entertainment, or take part in any sport, game or play on the Lord's day, commonly called Sunday; and every person so offending shall be punished by a fine not exceeding two dollars for each offense." But the law seldom was enforced in those communities that opposed it. The Germans disregarded it in enjoying their Sunday *Gemütlichkeit*.[42]

Puritanical Americans desired legislation not only against revelry on the Sabbath but against inebriety at any time. The Sons of Temperance, with more than three thousand Wisconsin members in 1849, gave added momentum to the cause. A state law of that year provided for a most unusual method of liquor control. It required saloonkeepers to post a bond and made

---

[41] Clary, *Presbyterian and Congregational Convention of Wisconsin*, 51–52, 58–62 (p. 52 for the quotation on withholding Christian fellowship from slaveholders); Bennett and Lawson, *Methodism in Wisconsin*, 119, 131–133, 146–148 (p. 146 for the 1854 Methodist Conference); Frank L. Byrne, "Cold Water Crusade: The Ante-Bellum Wisconsin Temperance Movement" (master's thesis, University of Wisconsin, 1951), 146; Charles J. Kennedy, "The Congregationalists and the Presbyterians on the Wisconsin Frontier" (doctoral dissertation, University of Wisconsin, 1940), 48, 367–370, 374–376. On the Baptist preacher's children, see the William H. Brisbane diary, January 19, 1856, in the William H. Brisbane Papers.

[42] Schafer, *Four Wisconsin Counties*, 188–189.

them personally responsible for the harm their drunken customers might do. Germans called for repeal, but in 1850 the act was strengthened by anti-drink legislators, prominent among them John B. Smith, recently the head of the state Sons of Temperance. A crowd of three or four hundred infuriated Germans then marched upon Smith's house in Milwaukee and smashed the windows. The next year, the legislature gave in and replaced the liability law with an ordinary licensing act.

The advocates of strict control now turned to outright prohibition. Maine had just prohibited the manufacture or sale of alcoholic beverages, and in Wisconsin the Methodist, Congregational, Presbyterian, and Baptist churches, the Sons of Temperance, the Good Templars, and other reformist organizations began to demand that their state do the same. Norwegian Lutheran churchmen, deploring the widespread drunkenness among their people, saw to the formation of abstinence societies and joined in the campaign for a "Maine law." A few Roman Catholic priests, who viewed drinking as no sin but excessive drinking as unwise, organized temperance groups among their Irish parishioners but advocated individual self-control and opposed the passage of a prohibitory act. Frustrated at the failure of the Wisconsin prohibition crusade, some Methodist women of Baraboo resorted to direct action in 1854 after their pastor had wished to God that "the thunderbolts of heaven would shiver the brick tavern." Early one morning, before the arrival of the proprietor, the women invaded the tavern and emptied or broke all the bottles in the place.[43]

Like German Catholics and Lutherans, the German freethinkers had no sympathy with the Yankee sabbatarians and prohibitionists. The Forty-Eighters and other liberals or radicals were also fond of their beer and their Sunday conviviality, and they looked upon blue laws as infringements of personal liberty that were out of place in a free republic. At the same

[43] Byrne, "Cold Water Crusade," 84, 99–116; Blegen, *Norwegian Migration: American Transition,* 205–206; Johnson, *Crosier on the Frontier,* 170; Peter Leo Johnson, *Stuffed Saddlebags: The Life of Martin Kundig, Priest, 1805–1879* (Milwaukee, 1942), 230–232; Western Historical Company, *The History of Sauk County, Wisconsin* . . . (Chicago, 1880), 517–519 (the quotation is from p. 517).

time, they viewed the Catholic Church, the bulwark of the old order in Europe, as a threat to the republic itself. The radicals were both anticlerical and anticapitalist, the constitution of the Milwaukee *Turnverein* declaring in favor of the "Red Flag of Socialism" and against the Jesuits and the "political Reaction" of Rome. Liberal German-language newspapers such as the *Banner* and the *Volksfreund* (the two were combined in 1855) kept up a constant firing on the church. To reply to them, Father Joseph Salzmann in 1852 founded the Milwaukee *Seebote*, which served as the semi-official organ of the state's hierarchy. For several years the German anti-Catholics caused the church leaders much more concern than did the Yankee zealots. "Here we have four daily English papers," Father Michael Heiss wrote from Milwaukee to a friend in Germany in 1853, "in which you can hardly ever find anything that could be called an attack on the Catholic faith. . . . The English press does not hamper the progress of Catholicity."[44]

Two years later, in 1855, an English-language newspaper appeared that persistently attacked not only the Catholic faith but also its freethinking critics and indeed all foreigners. This was the Milwaukee *Daily American*, the voice of Wisconsin's so-called Know Nothings, members of a national organization so secret they pretended in the presence of outsiders to know nothing about it. Councils of the order were being formed in various parts of the state. "You cannot have failed to observe the significant transition of the foreigner and Romanist from a character quiet, retiring, and even abject, to one bold, threatening, turbulent, and *despotic* in its appearance and assumptions," initiates were told. Besides taking an oath of secrecy, they had to swear that they were American-born of Protestant parents or were American-born and "reared under Protestant influence," and that since they were "in favor of

[44] Koerber, "Anti-Catholic Agitation in Milwaukee," 65–68, 84; M. Hedwigis Overmoehle, "The Anti-Clerical Activities of the Forty-Eighters in Wisconsin, 1848–1860: A Study in German-American Liberalism" (doctoral dissertation, St. Louis University, 1941), 139, 171–172, 215–216; Heiss to Kilian Kleiner, July 6, 1853, trans. J. Rainer, in the *Salesianum*, 10 (January, 1915), 14–27. See also Conzen, " 'German Athens'," 379–388.

Americans ruling America," they would oppose anyone of foreign birth or of the Catholic faith running for public office. The *Daily American* openly denounced those "heathen" from abroad who violated the Sabbath and made it a "day of noise, bustle, and confusion," who ran "riot and rampant over the civil and religious institutions, in founding which our fathers sacrificed their property and their lives." Those "peculiar traits of *foreignism,* coming under heads of Socialism and Red Republicanism," the editor declared, were "ten thousand times more to be feared" than even the "worst features of Catholicism." He appealed to his readers: "Let us keep *down* the newly arrived flood of emigration until they understand our language and our laws . . . while their *children* are educated and become Americanized—then we are safe."[45]

[6]

Once, when the territorial council of Wisconsin was discussing statehood, a delegate from Mineral Point had spoken up to say that "niggers" should not be allowed to vote. A delegate from Racine objected to the use of "the contemptuous epithet, 'niggers,'" and argued that Negroes deserved the "privileges of freemen" as much as many of the whites and more than some of them, that the Negroes were "more intelligent, more civilized, better acquainted with our institutions than the Norwegians." A second delegate from Mineral Point joined the first in opposing suffrage for Negroes, since "to encourage them was to encourage amalgamation," and this would be "most deleterious to the offspring."[46]

[45] Milwaukee *Daily American,* October 19, 1855. The summary and quotation of the ritual are from a tiny, 24-page pamphlet bearing no date or place of publication and no title except *Ritual of the First Degree* on the cover and *Ritual of the Second Degree* on p. 20. The pamphlet identifies the organization only as "the Order." The copy in the SHSW library (call number F902/8 AM) has been labeled in handwriting "American Party—Wisconsin." See especially pp. 6, 9, and 16 for the passages here quoted or paraphrased.

[46] Milo M. Quaife, ed., *The Movement for Statehood, 1845–1846* (Madison, 1918), 95–96, 99, 104–105. The delegates from Mineral Point were Moses M. Strong and John Catlin, both Vermonters by birth. The delegate from Racine was Marshall M. Strong, born in Massachusetts.

Reflecting the division of opinion, the state constitution of 1848 did not extend the vote to Negroes but authorized the legislature and the voting public to do so. The wording of the constitutional provision was critical, for upon the interpretation of the words was to depend the ultimate disposition of the matter. These were the words: "the legislature may at any time extend by law the right of suffrage to persons not herein enumerated; but no such law shall be in force until the same shall have been submitted to a vote of the people at a general election, and approved by a majority of all the votes cast at such election."[47]

In 1849 the legislature passed a bill for "equal suffrage to colored persons" and submitted it to the voters in separate balloting at the general election. Of the ballots cast on the suffrage referendum, there were 5,265 Yes and 4,075 No. But in the general election more than 31,000 votes were polled. Fewer than a third of the voters had bothered to express themselves on the suffrage bill. Though it had received more affirmative than negative votes, it had not received in its favor a majority of all the votes cast at the election, and even its proponents therefore considered it as lost.[48]

So the few blacks of Wisconsin, a tiny minority, continued to be deprived of the franchise, and they were also excluded from other phases of community life. A territorial law, still in effect, made them ineligible for the militia, and the highway act of 1849 exempted them from service with neighborhood road crews; it required a poll tax payable in labor from all male inhabitants "excepting persons of color, paupers, idiots and lunatics." In 1850 the national office of the Sons of Temperance forbade the enrollment of Negroes in the order (the Kenosha division gave up its charter in protest).[49]

---

[47] Leslie H. Fishel, Jr., "Wisconsin and Negro Suffrage," in *WMH*, 46 (Spring, 1963), 184; State Constitution, Art. 3, sec. 1, *Wisconsin Statutes*, 1849, p. 22.

[48] Milwaukee *Sentinel*, March 29, November 8, 21, December 24, 1849.

[49] William J. Vollmar, "The Negro in a Midwest Frontier City: Milwaukee, 1835–1870" (master's thesis, Marquette University, 1968), 27–28; Milwaukee *Sentinel*, July 20, 1850. The 1849 act is given in Wisconsin State Highway Com-

Yet the Negroes in Wisconsin enjoyed greater legal rights than did those in some of the other northern states. In Wisconsin there was no law against interracial marriage, and in Milwaukee as of 1850 five of the twenty-five married black men had white wives. Negroes were legally entitled to travel about, engage in any occupation, own property, send their children to the public schools, appeal to the courts, testify against white men, serve on juries, and hold private or public meetings.

In Milwaukee, Racine, and other cities, where most of the blacks were concentrated, they practically monopolized the barbering and hairdressing trade. They also worked as cooks, waiters, domestics, sailors, artisans, and common laborers. A few operated grocery stores, millinery and dress shops, or other businesses. Jesse Epps, who advertised as a "wholesale and retail dealer in pies, cakes, maple sugar, fruit, cider vinegar mulled, etc.," carried on his business in an abandoned shack in Milwaukee for several years, until the owner forced him out by having the shack torn down. Some of the Negroes managed to accumulate property of their own. As early as 1850 at least five of those in Milwaukee (whose entire black population then numbered only 101) were worth $300 or more, and three were worth $1,000 or more.[50]

The blacks of Wisconsin began to exercise one of their few political rights—their right to assemble and protest—when Congress passed, as part of the Compromise of 1850, a fugitive-slave law that left them along with other Negroes in the North, freemen as well as runaway slaves, at the mercy of Southerners who claimed them as their chattels. At a Milwaukee mass meeting a black leader warned his people that they must either accept the risk of re-enslavement or stand together and, with the aid

mission and United States Public Roads Administration, *A History of Wisconsin Highway Development, 1835–1945* (Madison, 1947), 16.

[50] Vollmar, "Negro in Milwaukee," 22–27, 35–38. The description of Jesse Epps is from an unidentified 1855 Milwaukee newspaper quoted in James S. Buck, *Pioneer History of Milwaukee* (4 vols., Milwaukee, 1876–1886), 4: 99. A German advised prospective immigrants from Germany that they would find few opportunities as barbers in Wisconsin cities, because "colored persons" usually served as barbers and hairdressers. See Schafer, ed., "Ficker's Advice," in *WMH,* 25: 473.

of friendly whites, prevent the enforcement of the law. His
hearers adopted resolutions in which they promised to resist
—"we pledge ourselves to come forward at any alarm given and
rescue our fugitive brethren even unto death." The very next
year, kidnapers made off with a Milwaukee Negro boy, George
Wells, but during the 1850's the blacks of Wisconsin, with the
co-operation of sympathetic whites, assisted a number of southern runaways along the "underground railroad" to freedom.
Blacks had a part in Wisconsin's most spectacular rescue, that
of the fugitive Joshua Glover in 1854. Three years later the
legislature finally passed a "personal liberty" law to grant
fugitives the right of trial by jury and to prevent the kidnaping
of Negroes in the state.[51]

Meanwhile, exercising both their right to assemble and their
right to petition, the Negroes of Wisconsin continued to seek
the most important political right, the suffrage. At another
mass meeting, held in Milwaukee in 1855, it was resolved that,
whereas the vote had been extended "to all persons, irrespec-
tive of birth, creed, or clime, except to the colored man," the
legislature should again be called upon to grant him "this
God given right." Negroes circulated petitions for the signa-
tures of both blacks and whites throughout the state. The
legislature responded with another equal-suffrage bill in 1857,
but this referendum failed 41,345 to 28,235, to gain a majority even among those who voted on it at the general election.[52]

Like other ethnic groups in Wisconsin, the Negroes had a
special holiday of their own. This was August 1, the anniversary of the emancipation in 1838 of the slaves in the British
West Indies. Undoubtedly such celebrations by the Negroes,
along with their co-operative efforts to improve their status,
helped to give them a sense of group consciousness and self-

[51] Vollmar, "Negro in Milwaukee," 28–33, 49. For scattered references to fugitive slaves in the state, see the Janesville (weekly) *Gazette,* March 26, 1853;
the Milwaukee *Sentinel,* July 13, 1854, and October 26, 1858; and the Milwaukee
Daily American, December 13, 1855. The Milwaukee *Sentinel,* October 11, 1850,
contains the proceedings and resolutions of the mass meeting.
[52] Vollmar, "Negro in Milwaukee," 46–48, quoting the Milwaukee *Sentinel,*
November 10, 1855.

esteem. Yet, in the face of prejudice and discrimination more extreme than were applied to other minorities, the maintenance of dignity was a never-ending challenge for individual blacks. They met it in a variety of ways. Lyman Benjamin, a Milwaukee hotel cook, wishing to show the world what "the colored people of Wisconsin" could do, collected examples of their handiwork and took them to England to exhibit them at the Crystal Palace Exposition of 1851. W. H. Noland, the best-known black of Madison and the barber of its leading citizens, proudly but politely declined to serve one of his regular customers after the man had assisted in the capture of the fugitive slave Joshua Glover. "Nigger Dick," a lone "character" of Baraboo, when he was refused a drink in a local hotel, rode his horse into the lobby and threatened to wreck the place. He got the drink and, indeed, got drunk.[53]

[7]

The Indian tribes of Wisconsin, like those of other states and territories, were subject to laws enacted by Congress and administered by the Bureau of Indian Affairs, which in 1849 was shifted from the War Department to the Interior Department. Federal policies with regard to the Indians were contradictory. On the one hand, the aim, as laid down in an act of 1819, was to foster education "for the purpose of providing against the further decline and final extinction of the Indian tribes" and "introducing among them the habits and arts of civilization." Money from congressional appropriations and, by treaty arrangement, from Indian annuities was used to assist white missionaries in operating Indian schools. On the other hand, the policy sanctioned in a law of 1830 was to remove the tribes to the far frontier, in effect to places generally inferior to their original habitats, where they might have great

---

[53] Vollmar, "Negro in Milwaukee," 33; Milwaukee *Sentinel,* July 13, 1854 (quoting the *Wisconsin State Journal,* July 10, 1854), and August 5, 1857; Harry E. Cole, *Stagecoach and Tavern Days in the Baraboo Region* (Baraboo, Wisconsin, 1923), 50.

difficulty surviving—and always would be forced to adapt—
and where they would be the least exposed to civilizing in-
fluences. Because such wholesale removal was involuntary, it
was in itself disrupting and demoralizing. And, if missionaries
were authorized to go among them, so were traders who had a
very different conception of the Indians' welfare.[54]

Both the Episcopalians and the Methodists were active among
the Oneida Indians, trying to help them—as well as they could
—against the "hostile designs formed by avaricious and in-
triguing white men." The Presbyterians and Congregationalists
gave support to the Stockbridge, not only in providing "minis-
trations of the Gospel" but also in petitioning the federal government to respect the Indians' rights. The Roman Catholics
maintained missions and schools among both the Chippewa
and the Menominee. One treaty with the Chippewa had called
for the employment of full or mixed-blood Chippewa teachers
whenever competent ones could be found.[55]

Missionaries had to vie with traders for influence among the
Indians, and the agents of the Indian Bureau generally sided
with the traders. One missionary, the Belgian-born priest
Florimond J. Bonduel, opposed the removal of the Menominee
to Minnesota and also opposed the immediate payment, as part
of their annuities, of interest on a fund for the promotion of
agriculture and education. Father Bonduel felt that traders
rather than the Indians would benefit from the extra cash. As
a result of his stand, he incurred the enmity of the traders, who
intrigued against him with both Chief Oshkosh and the Green
Bay agent of the Indian Bureau. When the Menominee were

[54] Martha E. Layman, "A History of Indian Education in the United States"
(doctoral dissertation, University of Minnesota, 1942), 117–118, 156–157; Clyde A.
Morley, "A General Survey of the Schooling Provided for the American Indian
Throughout Our Country's History, with a Special Study of Conditions in Wis-
consin" (master's thesis, University of Wisconsin, 1927), 29–30; *United States
Statutes at Large*, 3: 516.

[55] "A Mission to the Menominee: Alfred Cope's Green Bay Diary," in *WMH*,
49–50 (Summer, 1966–Spring, 1967), 50: 135–144; Samuel Freeman, *The Emigrant's Hand Book and Guide to Wisconsin* . . . (Milwaukee, 1851), 41 (on
"hostile designs"); Clary, *Presbyterian and Congregational Convention of Wisconsin*, 46–47; Layman, "History of Indian Education," 134, 188, 221–222.

resettled on their Wolf River reservation, the priest accompanied them and, at Keshena, began to teach in a new school. Soon his teaching stipend from the government was mysteriously cut off and he left Keshena. The school continued under other teachers.[56]

Whenever government agents distributed money or goods among the Indians, a "flock of harpies" was always ready to "pounce upon the spoil." Payments to the Menominee, before the tribe was put on its reservation, were made at the traditional site of its council fire on the southern shore of Lake Poygan. Here each Indian passed through a cabin and received his pile of coins in a corner of his blanket. On the way out he was met by a trader or a trader's representative collecting debts. If he tried to run or refused to pay, he was seized and the amount claimed was taken from him. A company or two of United States troops were at hand to preserve order and prevent resistance. What money the Indians had left, the traders were eager to obtain through new sales, and one of the fastest-selling items was whiskey.[57]

The white man's liquor, his reservation policy, his annuities, even his missions and schools—all had a destructive effect on the tribal organizations and cultures, which were already becoming strained and distorted as white settlement encroached on Indian territories. At the same time, the tribes were slow to take on the "habits and arts of civilization." Most of the Indians found themselves in a kind of cultural limbo between the old and the new.

The native Wisconsin tribes—the Winnebago, Potawatomi, Chippewa, and Menominee—were perforce abandoning their old economy of agriculture, gathering, and hunting as they lost their territories, but only a few actually had made a transition to single-family farming in the style of the white settlers. Fugitives from their Minnesota reservation, the Winnebago wan-

[56] Johnson, *Crosier on the Frontier,* 146–148.

[57] "Alfred Cope's Green Bay Diary," in *WMH,* 49: 312; the quotation is from 50: 22. See also A. T. Glaze, "The Indians of Early Days," in the Fond du Lac *Commonwealth,* May 20, 1905. The state liquor-control law of 1849 prohibited liquor sales to Indians but was not well enforced and was repealed in 1851.

dering in Wisconsin could not even depend on annuities, which the government would pay only to those who stayed on the reservation. They tried to make a living as they always had, by hunting, sometimes planting, and gathering wild berries, nuts, and roots, but more and more they had to turn to doing odd jobs for white settlers or begging and stealing from them. All these tribes continued to speak their own languages and wear their traditional dress, which long since had come to include trade goods such as cloth, jewelry, and hats. A minority of the people were converts to Christianity. In the case of the Menominee, at least, the conversions put a strain upon the polity of the tribe, for the chiefs were divided between a Catholic faction and a faction which held to the tribe's traditional beliefs. The Indians accepted the white man's drink more readily than his religion. Among whites, the Menominee had a special reputation for drunkenness, and Chief Oshkosh (one of the non-Christians) was considered the worst of the lot.[58]

The "New York Tribes"—the Stockbridge-Munsee, Oneida, and Brothertown—had already become somewhat successful farmers, by white standards, by the time they migrated to Wisconsin. During the Stockbridge's stay in Calumet County, they were said to "live comfortably and farm their lands well." It was reported that the Oneida were "quite superior as farmers" to the settlers of French descent in the Green Bay area (who generally were only a slight remove from voyageur status), and that the Brothertown were even more successful than the Oneida. These people and most of the Stockbridge held land on tribal allotments, but the Brothertown held theirs by private ownership. Stockbridge and Oneida men but not women and Brothertown women as well as men wore clothing essentially like that of their white neighbors. Most of the Stockbridge and Oneida could speak English, and the Brothertown

---

[58] George W. Thatcher, "The Winnebago Indians, 1827–1932" (master's thesis, University of Wisconsin, 1935), 148–149; Johnson, *Crosier on the Frontier,* 146–148; "Alfred Cope's Green Bay Diary," in *WMH,* 49: 310, 312; 50: 19, 22–26, 31, 218–219.

(descendants of various tribes) had long since given up their native languages entirely. Among the three groups taken as a whole, a majority of the people worshiped as Christians—Episcopalians, Methodists, Presbyterians, Congregationalists. The Oneida supported the temperance cause and prohibited the selling of liquor on their reservation. They retained their tribal organization, and so did the Stockbridge, but some of the latter were landowners and citizens. The Stockbridge patriarch, John W. Quinney, struggled against the citizen party in an effort to hold the tribe together, maintain its cultural identity, and keep intact his family's vested financial interests in tribal affairs. To whites, Quinney said: "Our God hath made us distinct from you—we must remain so or perish." At the other extreme, the Brothertown took part in politics as citizens and members of the white community. One of them, Alonzo Dick, ran for the state assembly in 1849 and was elected.[59]

People of mixed white and Indian blood generally lived in poverty and closer to the Indians than to the whites. But there were exceptions, such as the prominent Juneau and Grignon families, whose ancestry was French-Menominee. These and others like them were well educated and well-to-do, even rich. "They were very little like Indians," as a Green Bay visitor from Pennsylvania was surprised to learn, and "some of the women were esteemed the most attractive and accomplished of their sex in Green Bay and moved in what was considered the first society there."[60]

Except for such mixed-bloods and some of the citizen purebloods, however, the Indians had no place in white society. A few of the white settlers admired them for their skill as hunters

---

[59] Schafer, *Winnebago-Horicon Basin*, 61–64, 67–73; "Alfred Cope's Green Bay Diary," in *WMH*, 49: 313–318; 50: 135–144; see pp. 314 and 137 for quotations on the Stockbridge and the Oneida. The Quinney quotation is from U.S. Commissioner of Indian Affairs, *Annual Report*, 1847, p. 69. Schafer, 64n, states that John W. Quinney was probably the author of the document from which the quotation is drawn. Cope was favorably impressed by the Stockbridge as well as the Oneida and Brothertown when he visited them in 1849. Schafer, however, refers to the "progress of the Stockbridges," while in Calumet County, as "negative."

[60] "Alfred Cope's Green Bay Diary," in *WMH*, 50: 36–37.

of game or trainers of ponies or practitioners of herb medicine. Many were curious about their ceremonials, and crowds flocked to Lake Poygan, when the Menominee gathered there for annuity payments, to watch the dancing and hear the tom-tom and flute playing. But most of the whites, with no awareness of the cultural stress to which the Indians were subjected, viewed them as lazy, drunken, thieving members of a degenerate race. Settlers seldom had any contact with an Indian except as a beggar and a nuisance. On outlying farms the housewives in particular dreaded his approach.[61]

Tension between the races was fairly constant, and from time to time violence broke out. On July 4, 1849, several lumberjacks left their holiday celebration in a Chippewa Falls saloon for some fun at a nearby wigwam. When one of them, Martial Caznobia, attempted to take liberties with a Chippewa woman, her husband drove him off with a knife, inflicting a supposedly fatal wound (Caznobia recovered from it). A mob of whites hanged the Indian to the limb of a pine tree. More than a thousand of his fellow tribesmen then descended upon the town and threatened to burn it unless the killers were turned over to them. Finally the chiefs agreed to let the mob leaders be punished according to the white man's law. Three men were arrested and put on a boat to be sent to Prairie du Chien for trial. They escaped on the way.[62]

When the Menominee objected to relocation in Minnesota, and impatient whites moved into the tribe's Wisconsin lands, a white friend of the Indians reported: "Irritation has followed and blood has flowed." A son and a female relative of Chief Oshkosh were murdered. In anticipation of serious trouble, the long-empty Fort Howard was regarrisoned in the fall of

[61] For examples of white attitudes toward Indians, see Mary J. Atwood, "John Wilson, a Sauk County Pioneer," in *WMH*, 8 (September, 1924), 67–70; John Muir, *The Story of My Boyhood and Youth* (Madison, 1965), 78, 84–85, 136–137; Glaze, "Indians of Early Days," in the Fond du Lac *Commonwealth*, May 20, 1905; Western Historical Company, *History of Northern Wisconsin* . . . (Chicago, 1881), 164; diary of Jabez Brown, August 30, 1855, in the Jabez Brown Papers; reminiscences of C. A. Verwyst, in Lucas, ed., *Dutch Immigrant Memoirs*, 2: 180–181; Milwaukee *Sentinel*, July 22, 1853.

[62] Western Historical Company, *History of Northern Wisconsin*, 195.

1849 with two companies of troops. Again, when some of the Stockbridge (not landowners and citizens) refused to leave Calumet County for their new reservation, the incoming settlers complained that the Indians were destroying property, threatening lives, and actually causing bloodshed.[63]

Settlers had a ready answer for anyone who questioned their right to dispossess the Indians. When a Scottish farmer in Marquette County questioned it, expressing his pity for the "children of Nature" who were "being robbed of their lands and pushed ruthlessly back," John Muir's father expostulated that "surely it could never have been the intention of God to allow Indians to rove and hunt over so fertile a country and hold it forever in unproductive wilderness, while Scotch and Irish and English farmers could put it to so much better use." Muir's neighbor replied that these farmers themselves were rather inexperienced and inefficient, and he asked "how should we like to have specially trained and educated farmers drive us out of our homes and farms . . . making use of the same argument . . . ?"[64]

[63] The quotation is from "Alfred Cope's Green Bay Diary," in *WMH*, 50: 239. See also U.S. Commissioner of Indian Affairs, *Annual Report*, 1858, p. 29; Schafer, *Winnebago-Horicon Basin*, 65–66.

[64] Muir, *Boyhood and Youth*, 174–175. Even a missionary could use the same rationalization for the whites dispossessing the Indians. Father Anthony M. Gachet, who succeeded Father Bonduel among the Menominee, once wrote: "In looking at this question from an elevated point of view, and analyzing the injustices of which these Indians have been the victims, are we not obliged to consider the views of Providence which would not so long permit great stretches of the earth to remain uncultivated and preserved from the works of man?" See Anthony M. Gachet, "Five Years in America: Journal of a Missionary among the Redskins—Journal, 1859," in *WMH*, 18 (September, 1934–March, 1935), 346.

5

Enlarging
Community Affairs

---

[1]

THE PEOPLE of Wisconsin had looked to the federal government for the gift of statehood. They kept on looking to it for other benefits: the survey and sale of public land, the encouragement of waterways and railways by means of land grants, the removal of Indians and the protection of the frontier, the awarding of federal patronage, the delivery of mail. Yet the people viewed the federal government as rather distant and as touching their lives indirectly and infrequently in comparison with the state and local governments.

The state government gave or withheld the boon of suffrage. It, too, had lands for sale or for donation. It chartered banks, railroads, and other companies. It laid out counties (which divided themselves into towns), incorporated villages and cities, and conferred upon them certain powers of government. In their separate capacities the state and local authorities arranged for the levying of taxes, the construction and repair of roads and streets (almost exclusively a local function), the operation of schools and other educational agencies, the promotion of the public welfare, and the maintenance of law and order. Much the closest to the individual, much the most concerned with his daily needs, was the government of the town, the village, or the city.

WISCONSIN CITIES AND VILLAGES, 1848–1873

The activity of local in comparison with state government was roughly indicated by tax collections. These amounted to almost exactly the same per capita in Wisconsin as in the United States as a whole—about three dollars a year. In Wisconsin, however, the local units (counties, towns, villages, cities, and school and road districts) took in more than 86 per cent of the total. This was a much larger proportion than the average for all the states, which was less than 64 per cent. Most of the state and local revenue in Wisconsin arose from the taxation of real property, though the counties also levied taxes on personal property such as livestock, wagons, watches, and pianos.[1]

The formation of counties and towns proceeded along with or even ahead of the advance of settlement. By 1848, thirty counties already were in existence, and during the early years of statehood new ones were formed at the rate of two a year. Real-estate promoters lobbied with the legislature to induce it to carve new counties out of existing ones and locate county seats where these would enhance the value of the promoters' landholdings. Rivals sometimes undertook to have the seat relocated, as when, in 1855, the boosters of Dodgeville began a four-year struggle, eventually successful, to take the Iowa County courthouse away from Mineral Point.[2]

The four counties of the southwestern mining region—Iowa, Grant, Lafayette, and Green—together with Sauk County, retained the southern type of county government (without town government) that early settlers had brought from Missouri. The rest of the counties followed the New York pattern of county-and-town government. According to this pattern, the county was divided into towns (or civil townships, which did not necessarily coincide with the six-mile-square townships of the federal land survey). At an annual town meeting the voters discussed town affairs and elected officials, the most important of which were the chairman and two fellow members of the town board of supervisors. The chairmen of the various

[1] These are the tax figures as of 1860. For comparison, the annual per capita tax in Iowa was $3.52; in Illinois, $3.58; in Minnesota, $3.87; in New York, $3.96; in Massachusetts, $6.04. On the other hand, the average in North Carolina was only $1.05; in Alabama, about $0.88; and in Georgia, $0.76. See *Eighth Census of the United States, 1860: Mortality and Miscellaneous Statistics,* 511. On personal property taxes in Trempealeau County, see Merle Curti, *The Making of an American Community: A Case Study of Democracy in a Frontier County* (Stanford, 1959), 270–272.

[2] A. O. Barton, "Wisconsin's Oldest Courthouse," in *WMH,* 2 (March, 1919), 332–334. On the conversion of a La Crosse County township into Trempealeau County, see Curti, *Making of an American Community,* 260–261. Twenty-nine Wisconsin counties were created between 1848 and 1862. See Wisconsin Historical Records Survey of the Work Projects Administration, *Origin and Legislative History of County Boundaries in Wisconsin* (mimeographed, Madison, 1942), *passim,* and *Wisconsin Blue Book, 1975,* p. 664.

town boards made up the county board of supervisors. The
county board created new towns by splitting existent ones in
response to population growth and popular demand.[3]

When part of a town became rather thickly settled, and the
residents of that part began to desire increased autonomy and
more public services than the town or county government was
willing to provide, they might petition the state legislature
for an act incorporating a village. The charters the state granted spelled out the structure, powers, and functions of the village government in great detail, which varied from one case
to another. The Menasha charter of 1853, for example, contained fifty-one sections and covered sixteen pages of text.
It authorized the village board, after receiving approval by
referendum, to levy a tax or borrow up to $5,000 to build a
bridge across Little Lake Butte des Morts. It set no limit on
the tax rate—unlike the Appleton charter of the same year,
which limited the rate to two mills except under extraordinary
conditions when high rates might be approved by referendum.
The Sauk City charter of 1854 empowered the newly created
village to borrow as much as $2,500 for the construction of a
causeway that would connect with a ferry across the Wisconsin
River. Improvement projects like those of Menasha and Sauk
City often provided a motive for village incorporation. Settlements as large or larger but lacking such a motive remained
unincorporated.[4]

A village growing in population and desiring still greater
self-rule might get a city charter from the state legislature;
size in itself did not make a city. There was one city in Wisconsin when the state was formed—Milwaukee. An observer
in the 1850's said, however, that Milwaukee was not really

[3] George S. Wehrwein, "County Government in Wisconsin," *Wisconsin Blue Book, 1933*, pp. 87–89; George S. Wehrwein, "Town Government in Wisconsin," *Wisconsin Blue Book, 1935*, pp. 95–99. Sauk County retained the southern type of county government until 1849, with no town governments and with three commissioners elected from the county. See Harry E. Cole, ed., *A Standard History of Sauk County, Wisconsin . . .* (2 vols., Chicago, 1918), 1: 226–227.

[4] Alice E. Smith, *Millstone and Saw: The Origins of Neenah-Menasha* (Madison, 1966), 176–177; Western Historical Company, *The History of Sauk County, Wisconsin . . .* (Chicago, 1880), 601–602.

a city but only "five villages slightly connected together." It was in truth "more a municipal confederation than a real municipality," for each of the five wards was a separate corporation that could contract debts and carry out projects on its own initiative. The mayor presided over five sets of more of less independent aldermen, three for each ward. Smaller cities that were chartered in the 1850's, such as Green Bay in 1854, were provided with more centralized forms of government.[5]

From top to bottom the layers of government in Wisconsin were open to talent and ambition. Practically all men residing in the state—except for Negroes and noncitizen Indians—could meet the legal requirements for voting and officeholding. Terms of office were short, ranging from one to two years, so that the offices could be passed around among a comparatively large number of the citizens if the voters wished it. Thus, constitutionally, state and local government was quite representative.

In another sense, however, it was much less so. The officeholders actually chosen did not represent the people in the sense of constituting a cross section in regard to wealth, occupation, or nationality. Lawyers and businessmen held office in much more than proportional numbers, farmers in less than proportional numbers, and laborers hardly at all. Men of foreign birth were elected much less frequently than the size of the foreign-born population would seem to justify.[6]

As immigrants concentrated more and more in particular localities, and as some advanced in wealth and in familiarity with American ways, the number of foreign-born officeholders

[5] The quotations are from Bayrd Still, *Milwaukee: The History of a City* (Madison, 1965), 106–107. See also Donald A. DeBats, "The Political Sieve: A Study of Green Bay, Wisconsin, 1854–1880" (master's thesis, University of Wisconsin, 1967), 10–11.

[6] These generalizations are admittedly based on the findings of only a few sample studies. See William F. Dickinson, "The Personnel of the Wisconsin Legislature for the Years 1850, 1860, and 1870" (bachelor's thesis, University of Wisconsin, 1901), 2–7; Curti, *Making of an American Community*, 309, 338, 341–343; DeBats, "Political Sieve," 43–44, 58, 76–77, and *passim;* Still, *Milwaukee*, 144–146.

began to increase. For example, in the newer townships of Trempealeau County, populated largely by Norwegians, and in the town of Holland in Sheboygan County, settled mainly by the Dutch, the immigrant voters elected a larger and larger number of men of their own nationality. In predominantly German-speaking Sauk City, the second village election (1855) brought into office as president and trustees men with the names of Hantzsch, Halasz, Scharff, Deininger, Conradi, and Heller. In Green Bay the British, the Canadians, and the Prussians were beginning to be represented on the council in rough proportion to their numbers in the city, while the Austrians lagged somewhat and only the Dutch and the Belgians remained far behind.[7]

Though local officeholders belonged to a kind of political elite, they seldom formed a continuous governing clique. Almost everywhere, during the early years of statehood, there was a constant turnover of jobs, the same man rarely serving more than one term, or, at the most, more than two or three terms. Yet machine rule was already making its appearance in the city of Milwaukee. The Milwaukee boss, Jackson Hadley, derived his support from contractors and laborers who, in turn, benefited from the rage for municipal improvements.[8]

[2]

"No one measure of governmental policy can contribute more to the stability of our institutions and the permanent welfare of the whole community, than a well regulated system of public instruction, of common schools, open and free to all." So declared Governor Nelson Dewey in his first message to the state legislature, which assembled in Madison in June 1848. During the next few years other friends of public education

[7] Curti, *Making of an American Community*, 296; Henry S. Lucas, ed., *Dutch Immigrant Memoirs and Related Writings* (2 vols., Assen, Netherlands, 1955), 2: 117–121; Western Historical Company, *History of Sauk County*, 602; DeBats, "Political Sieve," 43–44.

[8] *Ibid.*, 87–88; Curti, *Making of an American Community*, 341–343; Still, *Milwaukee*, 144–146.

elaborated upon its aims and its anticipated benefits. It ought to inculcate virtue and morality, since children growing up in "ignorance and consequent vice" would become a danger and a burden to society, filling the poorhouses and jails. Besides producing "moral and intelligent citizens," it could be expected to counteract the "aristocratic tendencies of hereditary wealth," for knowledge was the "great leveler," the "true democracy," the element without which the "boasted political equality of which we dream" would prove a mere illusion. Public education presumably would also bring together the children of native stock and those of immigrant backgrounds, teach the latter the rudiments of Americanism, and fuse them into a "homogeneous whole."[9]

The state constitution and the school law of 1848, revised in 1849, reflected and reinforced a free-school movement that had been under way in the territory for several years. The law, modeled on that of New York, provided for a highly localized system of common schools. In each town there was to be an annually elected school superintendent, with authority to divide the town into districts. Within each district the voters were to meet yearly to elect a school board and decide on such matters as the construction of a building and the purchase of equipment. A state superintendent of public instruction, elected for two years, was to supervise all the schools, see to the enforcement of the school law, and make supplementary rules, but he was given little power except that of persuasion. Money for school construction and equipment was to come from a district tax, and money for teachers' salaries was to come from both town taxes and the state school fund, which consisted of the receipts from the sale of certain categories of public lands that had been set aside for the purpose.

[9] Alan W. Brownsword, "Educational Ideas in Early Wisconsin, 1848–1870" (master's thesis, University of Wisconsin, 1958), 28, 31; *Wisconsin Journal of Education*, 1 (April, 1856), 60; Merle Curti and Vernon Carstensen, *The University of Wisconsin: A History, 1848–1925* (2 vols., Madison, 1949), 1: 51 (quoting Governor Dewey), 64; Fredrika Bremer, *The Homes of the New World: Impressions of America* (2 vols., New York, 1864, 1868), 1: 636–642; Milwaukee *Daily American*, February 27, 1856; Still, *Milwaukee*, 218.

Once the new system was in operation, the state school fund proved a disappointment, seldom yielding an average of more than fifty cents a year for each child of school age. Some districts had an adequate tax base, but others did not, and local jealousies led to the subdivision of districts that already were too small to raise sufficient revenue. Every district acted almost like a "separate, independent republic," as one of the state superintendents complained. These superintendents urged consolidation but made little headway outside a few cities and villages.[10]

Teaching in early Wisconsin was sometimes described as an almost sacred calling—and teachers were referred to as "educational missionaries"—but in fact it was not yet a true profession nor even a regular occupation. It was usually a part-time job, and an average teaching career lasted only eighteen months. The pay ranged from a little more than thirty-five dollars to less than ten dollars a month and averaged half as much for women as for men. Accordingly, school officials tended to hire women teachers, who thus outnumbered men (except in German communities, where women teachers were rare). Few teachers had any special training; many were fresh graduates of the common schools. Some efforts at professionalization, however, were being made. In 1853 the Wisconsin State Teachers' Association was founded, and two years later it decided to sponsor the *Wisconsin Journal of Education*.[11]

Originally most of the schoolhouses were rather primitive log cabins. As late as 1854 there were 176 log, 174 frame, and only eight stone or brick school buildings in the four counties of Dodge, Fond du Lac, Winnebago, and Calumet. There, as elsewhere in the state, log cabins continued to prevail in rural

[10] Lloyd P. Jorgenson, "The Origins of Public Education in Wisconsin," in *WMH*, 33 (September, 1949), 27; Lloyd P. Jorgenson, *The Founding of Public Education in Wisconsin* (Madison, 1956), 94–110 (the quotation from p. 98). See also Conrad E. Patzer, *Public Education in Wisconsin* (Madison, 1924), 54–56, 103–113; Still, *Milwaukee,* 216–218; Helen F. Patton, "Public School Architecture in Racine, Wisconsin, and Vicinity from the Time of Settlement to 1900" (doctoral dissertation, University of Wisconsin, 1965), 125–127.

[11] Jorgenson, *Founding of Public Education,* 155–164, 167–177, 200–201.

districts that were heavily forested, frame buildings were more common in the openings and prairie areas, and nearly all the stone or brick structures were located in the villages and cities. Few of the country schools were equipped with more than a single outhouse, and typically this was a flimsy, rough-boarded affair that provided a "very poor and inadequate screen." Many schools had no privy of any description; the "scholars, male and female," were turned "promiscuously and simultaneously into the public highway, without the shelter of so much as a stump as a covert to the calls of nature."[12]

In a village or city school the pupils were usually grouped, according to age and attainment, in two or three or more classes or departments. In a country school as many as a hundred or more (the 1860 average was about forty) children of all ages recited in a single room. The state superintendents attempted to bring about a statewide uniformity in textbooks, but even the better schools were slow to achieve it, and some of the poorer districts continued to make do with whatever miscellaneous books the teacher happened to have or the children could bring from home.[13]

Subjects to be taught in every district school, according to the law of 1849, were orthography, reading, writing, English grammar, geography, arithmetic, and "such other branches of education" as the local school board might choose. The law implied but did not make clear that instruction should be in English except for the "other branches," which might include

[12] Joseph Schafer, *The Winnebago-Horicon Basin: A Type Study in Western History* (Madison, 1937), 194–196; Jorgenson, *Founding of Public Education,* 136; State Superintendent of Public Instruction, *Annual Report,* 1860, pp. 58–59, quoting the superintendents of New York and Connecticut on conditions in their states and applying the same strictures to Wisconsin. Newer city schools, such as two built in Racine in 1855, had carefully separated privies and playgrounds for girls and boys. See Patton, "Public School Architecture in Racine," 285.

[13] Jorgenson, *Founding of Public Education,* 134–143; Menasha *Conservator,* May 14 and October 30, 1856, on schools in Neenah and Menasha; Milwaukee *Daily American,* September 27, 1855, on schools in Racine; "Memoirs of Mary D. Bradford," in *WMH,* 14–16 (September, 1930–September, 1932), 14: 3–47, on schools in Kenosha County; Eleazer Root to G. Nichols, June 14, 1850, and Azel P. Ladd to E. B. Ransome, July 15, 1852, in Decisions in Appeals, vol. 1, pp. 60, 333, Series 650, Records of the State Superintendent of Schools, WSA.

foreign languages. In most German communities, however, every subject was taught in German. An act of 1854 definitely required that English be the medium of instruction for all but the optional courses. "A district School taught in the German or any other than the English language," the state superintendent then declared, "is not such a School as will entitle the district to receive any portion of the public funds." Nevertheless, German continued to be used exclusively in many of the district schools.[14]

The Wisconsin constitution not only prohibited state aid to any religious organization but also, going beyond other state constitutions of the time, contained the following stipulation with regard to the public schools: "No sectarian instruction shall be allowed therein." Did this exclude all religious education and such exercises as Bible-reading and prayer?

When the question arose in 1850, State Superintendent Eleazer Root said the district boards must answer it for themselves. Root thought that, religion being the basis of morality, the schools should not neglect religious education. But he hastened to explain, "By 'religious education' I must not be understood to mean anything having any whatever bearing upon sectarian differences—either between Christian sects, or even between the Christian and Jewish religions." He ruled that the Bible was "not regarded as a sectarian book" and that prayer was not necessarily a sectarian exercise, but he recommended that each district board "pursue such a course on this subject" as would be "calculated to produce harmony in the district."

By 1854 the question was "assuming some prominence in various parts of the State," as Root's successor Hiram A. Wright observed. Wright now modified Root's ruling and discouraged Bible-reading in class and prayer during school hours. "There are different versions of the Bible in use by different denomi-

---

[14] Jorgenson, *Founding of Public Education*, 143–148; H. A. Wright (the superintendent quoted) to Daniel Mahoney, February 17, 1854, in Decisions in Appeals, vol. 1, p. 414, Series 650, Records of the State Superintendent of Schools, WSA.

nations, and the common English version is wholly repudiated by a very large class of our population," Wright pointed out. He concluded that there was "no medium between sectarian instruction and the broadest toleration," and that all religious teaching should therefore be "consigned to the family circle, the Sabbath-school and the church, leaving the school-house neutral ground." But later superintendents were to disagree with Wright, and the schoolhouse was to remain a field of sectarian battle.[15]

Lutheran or Roman Catholic leaders could exert some influence upon the public schools in districts where Lutherans or Catholics predominated, but many such leaders preferred to set up church schools which they could completely control and through which they could maintain the traditional faith. Among the Lutherans in Germany and in Norway it had been the duty of each pastor of the state church to provide schooling for the young of his congregation, and some of the pastors of the more conservative synods wanted to resume the tradition in Wisconsin, together with instruction in the old-country language. From the beginning Bishop John Martin Henni had been eager to carry out in the state the Catholic Church's national aim of establishing parochial schools, and in the 1850's he made considerable progress, though the Catholics were disappointed in their hope of tapping the state school fund. Con-

[15] Eleazer Root to C. K. Eachron, December 3, 1850, to E. Bixby, July 29, 1851, and to William Butler, August 28, 1851; Hiram A. Wright to L. C. Jacobs, January 4, 1854, to C. A. Hastings, February 4, 1854, to W. W. Treadway, June 10, 1854, and to G. A. Gardiner, September 13, 1854, in Decisions in Appeals, vol. 1, pp. 94, 226–227, 240, 403, 410, 451–452, 465–466, Series 650, Records of the State Superintendent of Schools, WSA; see also letter of Wright, dated September 13, 1854, published in the New York *Tribune*, October 14, 1854. During the 1850's the use of the Bible in the public schools was a hot issue also in New York, Ohio, and other northern states. See Ray A. Billington, *The Protestant Crusade, 1800–1860: A Study of the Origins of American Nativism* (New York, 1938), 315–316. As late as 1875 there was only one other state (Nevada) with a constitutional prohibition of sectarian instruction. See Brownsword, "Educational Ideas in Early Wisconsin," 53. Not till 1889, however, did the Wisconsin supreme court rule that Bible reading in the public schools was unconstitutional. See Jorgenson, *Founding of Public Education*, 122. See also William W. Updegrove, "Bibles and Brickbats: Religious Conflict in Wisconsin's Public School System during the Nineteenth Century" (master's thesis, University of Wisconsin, 1970).

servative Norwegian Synod pastors often found their congregations preferred public schools to parochial schools. Both Lutherans and Catholics were handicapped by the cost of providing their own schools while being taxed for public education.[16]

Not only Catholic and some Lutheran immigrants but also some Protestants of old American stock hesitated to send their children to the public schools. Often the well-to-do preferred to send them to private or "select" schools and thus keep them from mingling with the children of the poor, while supposedly enabling them to learn from better teachers. Many of the select schools were temporary enterprises that occupied rented quarters and remained in business only so long as the proprietors continued to make a profit. The usual tuition charge was three dollars for an eleven-week term. Most of the private institutions were located in villages or cities, where prosperous families of the business and professional class provided a clientele. In Fond du Lac, for example, there were in 1857 a half dozen private schools as compared with only two public ones. In Watertown at that time Mrs. Carl Schurz was operating a special kind of private school—the first kindergarten in the United States—but this lasted for less than two years.[17]

In the state as a whole the district schools attracted much larger numbers than did the private and church schools together. Of every hundred enrolled, more than ninety-five were

[16] Theodore C. Blegen, *Norwegian Migration to America: The American Transition* (Northfield, Minnesota, 1940), 241–253; Roy A. Suelflow, *A Plan for Survival* (New York, 1965), 177–178; Peter Leo Johnson, *Crosier on the Frontier: A Life of John Martin Henni, Archbishop of Milwaukee* (Madison, 1959), 112–113; James S. Buck, *Pioneer History of Milwaukee* (4 vols., Milwaukee, 1876–1886), 3: 459; 4: 29; M. Hedwigis Overmoehle, "The Anti-Clerical Activities of the Forty-Eighters in Wisconsin, 1848–1860: A Study in German-American Liberalism" (doctoral dissertation, St. Louis University, 1941), 140–141. See also E. Clifford Nelson and Eugene L. Fevold, *The Lutheran Church Among Norwegian-Americans: A History of the Evangelical Lutheran Church* (2 vols., Minneapolis, 1960), 1: 184.

[17] Jorgenson, *Founding of Public Education*, 188–190; Menasha *Conservator*, September 18, 1856, and April 30, 1857, announcing the opening of select schools in Menasha and Neenah; Elizabeth Jenkins, "How the Kindergarten Found Its Way to America," in *WMH*, 14 (September, 1930), 48–62. In Fond du Lac there was, in 1857, a public high school in addition to the two district schools.

in public schools. But in 1854 the state superintendent estimated that a fifth or more of all the children aged four to sixteen were not signed up for a school of any kind, and a third
or more of those on the lists were likely to be absent on a typical day. Attendance was not compulsory. Educators worried
about the large numbers out of school who were making
themselves "fit candidates for the penitentiary," but many
parents opposed compulsory attendance as an infringement
upon their family rights. Even the most faithful schoolgoers
might get comparatively little schooling. By law the term was
to run at least three months, and in some districts it actually
totaled eight or more, but in others as little as a single month
had to suffice.[18]

It would be hard to say to what extent the system of common
schools in early Wisconsin succeeded in the professed aims of
fostering morality, democracy, and Americanization while also
instilling the essentials of learning. So far as Americanization
was concerned, the result depended in part on the degree to
which children of native and immigrant parents were brought
together in the same classroom. "We had in our district school
a good mixture of nationalities: mostly Norwegians, but some
Americans, Irish, French, and at least one German family,"
Nils Haugen recalled about his Pierce County boyhood. "The
melting pot was doing its work. . . . In an adjoining district
every family was Norwegian, and English was not acquired so
easily."[19]

Schools comparable to this latter one—with all or nearly
all the pupils coming from the same ethnic background—must
have been fairly numerous in the state. Since so many of the
various groups, native and foreign, had settled in their separate

[18] Jorgenson, *Founding of Public Education,* 134–143; Brownsword, "Educational Ideas in Early Wisconsin," 41, quoting state superintendent Lyman Draper.
For 1850, the total number of pupils in "all classes" of schools (including high
schools and academies) is given as 61,615; in public schools, 58,817; and in non-
public colleges, academies, and other schools, 2,798. For 1860, the respective
figures are 209,998; 198,676; and 11,322. See *Ninth Census of the United States,
1870: Volume I,* pp. 451–457.

[19] Nils P. Haugen, *Pioneer and Political Reminiscences* (Madison, n.d.), 17–18.

localities, a large number of the school districts, highly localized as these were, would presumably have contained fairly homogeneous populations. To the extent that they did so, the common school could hardly have been a very effective agent of Americanization.

[3]

On a fall afternoon in 1850 the sun was setting as Chancellor John H. Lathrop and his wife showed their distinguished foreign guest the new university's first building, soon to be finished, on College Hill. A plain but well-proportioned stone structure, it commanded a breathtaking view of lakes and woods and the village of Madison. The visitor, the Swedish novelist Fredrika Bremer, was struck by the beauty of the scene and especially by the sun's brilliant reflection on the windows of the university hall. This momentary temple of the sun, she mused, was to be a lasting temple of light. Her host had hopes equally glorious, if less poetically expressed, for the future of the University of Wisconsin. Chancellor Lathrop envisioned his institution as the apex of a grand system of free, public education, a system that would include secondary as well as primary schools.[20]

The chancellor's dream was not to be realized during his tenure at the university (1849–1859) nor for many years after that. For the time being, both secondary and higher education, quite unlike elementary education, were left mainly to private enterprise or church support.

In 1850 there were but nine secondary schools in the entire state, and only one of these was a public high school. The rest were proprietary or church-related academies or seminaries or else college or university preparatory departments. During the prosperous years of the 1850's the number of academies rapidly increased, until practically every village with a thousand or more residents and with "any pretensions to enterprise

<hr />

[20] Bremer, *Homes of the New World,* 1: 636–642; Curti and Carstensen, *University of Wisconsin,* 1: 161–162.

and enlightenment" could boast of at least one. Some were
for boys, others for girls, and still others co-educational. In
general the academies and seminaries, like the "select" schools
at the elementary level, attracted the children of the well-to-do.
Community leaders who paid tuition to academies were often
opposed to paying taxes for the support of high schools.

The early advocates of public secondary education gained
success only in a few places. Of these the first was Southport,
where the newspaperman and reformer Michael Frank led a
movement that culminated in the opening of a free high
school in 1849. The second was Racine, where one boy and
four girls formed a high-school class in 1853. Milwaukee had
no public secondary schools until 1858, when two of them were
started. No school boards in the state took advantage of an
1856 law that authorized them to combine adjoining common-
school districts so as to form union high-school districts.[21]

While private academies were springing up, so were private
colleges—in smaller numbers, to be sure, and yet in large enough
numbers that the state, while still young, could claim to be
better supplied than any except nine or ten of the older states.
Not all the "colleges" and "universities," however, deserved
the name. Brockway College (later Ripon College) was not
to develop into anything more than an academy until the
1860's, and Galesville University (Trempealeau County) and
Wayland University (Beaver Dam) were never to do so. Some
other colleges began with only a preparatory department and
continued to enroll the majority of their students in that department after adding a collegiate curriculum.[22]

When Wisconsin became a state, Beloit College was already
operating as an institution of higher learning, having admitted

[21] Patzer, *Public Education in Wisconsin,* 80–83; Joseph Schafer, "Genesis of
Wisconsin's Free High School System," in *WMH,* 10 (December, 1926), 123–141;
Patton, "Public School Architecture in Racine," 196, 200; Still, *Milwaukee,*
216–218; Western Historical Company, *History of Sauk County,* 531–532.

[22] On Brockway, Galesville, and Wayland, see William F. Allen and David
E. Spencer, *Higher Education in Wisconsin* (Washington, D.C., 1889), 55–57,
66–67. The federal census of 1860 credited Wisconsin with a total of twelve
"colleges" of one kind or another. See *Eighth Census of the United States, 1860:
Mortality and Miscellaneous Statistics,* 510.

five young men to its first freshman class the previous year.
"Beloit College," as one of its graduates of the 1850's was later
to describe it, "is as truly the child of New England Puritanism
as though its walls were standing on Plymouth Rock." It had
been founded and was supported by the Presbyterian-Congregational Convention of Wisconsin, and its main object was the
training of Presbyterian and Congregational ministers. In
the beginning its two professors, its president, and the head of
its board of trustees were Yale alumni, and for many years its
friends referred to it as the "Yale of the West." It got assistance
from prominent Beloit villagers, interested in the community's
development, who donated land for the campus and money for
buildings.[23]

The same year, 1847, that Beloit College began with five
students, St. Thomas College opened with eighteen. Founded
by Father Samuel Mazzuchelli at Sinsinawa Mound, in the
extreme southwestern corner of the state, St. Thomas flourished
during the early 1850's. It was one of two Roman Catholic institutions of higher learning in Wisconsin after the establishment of St. Francis Seminary south of Milwaukee, for the
training of priests, in 1856. But only the exertions of Mazzuchelli kept St. Thomas College alive. He was unable to get
the financial aid he needed from outside the diocese, and the
college was to survive its founder, who died in 1864, by only
one year.[24]

Before 1848 the Boston capitalist Amos Lawrence had offered
money for a college in Wisconsin, the Methodists of the state
had agreed to sponsor it, and two landowners had donated
sixty-two acres in Grand Chute (Appleton) on the condition
that it be located there. Another Boston capitalist, Nathan
Appleton, gave an endowment for a library. The Lawrence
University of Wisconsin began to offer preparatory studies in

[23] Allen and Spencer, *Higher Education in Wisconsin*, 45, 47–48. The quotation is from Frank N. Dexter, ed., *A Hundred Years of Congregational History
in Wisconsin* ([Fond du Lac, Wisconsin], 1933), 146. See also Robert K. Richardson, "'Yale of the West'—A Study of Academic Sectionalism," in *WMH*, 36
(Summer, 1953), 258–260.

[24] Johnson, *Crosier on the Frontier*, 119–120.

1849 and college courses in 1854. The only co-educational college in the state at the time, Lawrence graduated its first class,
consisting of "four gentlemen and three ladies," in 1857.[25]

Carroll College, an outgrowth of Prairieville Academy in
Waukesha, existed little more than in name before 1850, when
the trustees started a preparatory department. College classes
began in 1853, after the recently organized Wisconsin Presbyterian synod (Old School) had taken over the institution. With
financial difficulties far more serious than Lawrence's, Carroll
during the 1860's would be forced to close and reopen several
times before it finally reverted to the status of an academy
in 1872.[26]

Racine College opened in 1852 under the auspices of the
Wisconsin diocese of the Episcopal Church. Its founder was
the pioneer Episcopal missionary, Bishop Jackson Kemper, who
was also one of the founders of the church's theological seminary in 1841, Nashotah House, the oldest institution of higher
learning in Wisconsin. The new college received its ninety-
acre lake-front site and contributions for its first buildings from
citizens of Racine. It emulated the great "public schools" of
England. By 1857 it had eighty students, who were taught in
an extreme high-church atmosphere and with a strict Christian
discipline.[27]

The first women's college in Wisconsin originated as the
Milwaukee Female Seminary, run by the wife of the pastor of
the independent Free Congregational Church. The school came
to the attention of Catharine Beecher, elder sister of the soon-
to-be-famous Harriet Beecher Stowe and well-known in her own
right as an educational reformer. In 1850 Catharine Beecher
visited Milwaukee and offered financial aid for converting the
seminary into a nondenominational college that would embody

[25] Allen and Spencer, *Higher Education in Wisconsin,* 51–54; P. S. Bennett
and James Lawson, *History of Methodism in Wisconsin* (Cincinnati, 1890), 153,
162–163, 169; Samuel Plantz, "Lawrence College," in *WMH,* 6 (December, 1922),
146–164.

[26] Allen and Spencer, *Higher Education in Wisconsin,* 67; Dorothy G. Fowler,
"Wisconsin's Carroll College," in *WMH,* 29 (December, 1945), 137–156.

[27] Allen and Spencer, *Higher Education in Wisconsin,* 58–61.

her ideas of intellectual, physical, and vocational education adapted to the special needs of women. Her offer was accepted. Increase A. Lapham donated fifteen acres of land and became a trustee. With other trustees and patrons he launched a campaign to raise additional funds for the reorganized institution, which in 1852 was renamed the Milwaukee Female College, and in 1895 was to become Milwaukee-Downer College. It had an enrollment of more than two hundred, but for several years it remained in a precarious financial condition, even Beecher's grant being jeopardized by bickering between her and the trustees.[28]

Each of the private colleges had its own special purposes in addition to its general aim of furthering higher education. Quite different in conception was the University of Wisconsin, which the first state legislature established in 1848 in accordance with the state constitution and with a congressional act of 1838 that set aside land for the support of a "Seminary of Learning" in the territory. The university was to embody the idea, already taking form in other western states, of an inclusive, secular, democratic, and utilitarian as well as intellectual institution. Tuition was to be free as soon as income from the university fund, to be realized from land sales, would permit.

The board of regents promptly got to work under the leadership of Eleazer Root, one of the founders of Carroll College and soon to be the first state superintendent of public instruction. They hired as chancellor the president of the University of Missouri, John H. Lathrop, purchased a site for the campus, and arranged for the construction of the first building, getting a loan from the legislature to pay expenses while awaiting the growth of the university fund. Meanwhile, in 1849, twenty boys enrolled in the preparatory department and began to

---

[28] Dexter, ed., *Congregational History in Wisconsin,* 173–177; Grace N. Kieckhefer, "Milwaukee-Downer College Rediscovers Its Past," in *WMH,* 34 (Summer, 1951), 210–214; Grace N. Kieckhefer, *The History of Milwaukee-Downer College, 1851–1951* (Milwaukee, [1950]), 1–18; Louise P. Kellogg, "The Origins of Milwaukee College," in *WMH,* 9 (July, 1926), 386–408; Graham P. Hawks, "Increase A. Lapham: Wisconsin's First Scientist" (doctoral dissertation, University of Wisconsin, 1960), 114–121.

attend classes in a room made available in the Madison Female Academy. The next year the first college students met in the university's new hall, and in 1854 the first college class of two young men was graduated.

By 1857 the university appeared to be thriving financially, its lands selling well, though it was to receive no regular tax support for nearly twenty years. Two buildings, North Hall and South Hall, were in use, and a third, much later to be known as Bascom Hall, was being built. Except for its prosperity and its aspirations, however, this state institution as yet differed little from its private competitors. With its $1,000 salaries it could lure their best professors, such as the natural scientist S. P. Lathrop, who would have gotten $700 at Beloit. But for the most part the state university's professors taught the same classical courses and taught them in the same way, with textbook recitations. Both its professors and its students were required to attend daily chapel services. Even its enrollment failed to distinguish it from its rivals. The state university had never numbered many more than 300 students, the majority of them in the preparatory department, at a time when Lawrence University totaled well over 400.[29]

In certain respects the private colleges as well as the state university were public institutions. The state chartered them, authorized them to grant degrees, and favored them with tax exemption. Potentially they had even more of a public character, for the constitution provided that the state could associate other colleges with the university as branches of it. Struggling to make ends meet, some of the colleges demanded that they be recognized as branches of the university and be given a share of the proceeds from the university lands. In 1855 and 1856, bills were introduced in the legislature for distributing the university fund among all the colleges of the state, but the proposals received practically no support.[30]

[29] Curti and Carstensen, *University of Wisconsin,* 1: 21, 41, 51–55, 57–68, 79, 82, 84, 135, 176–177, 185, 296; Hawks, "Increase A. Lapham," 123; Fowler, "Carroll College," in *WMH,* 29: 138.

[30] Curti and Carstensen, *University of Wisconsin,* 1: 90–92; Allen and Spencer, *Higher Education in Wisconsin,* 24–25; Patzer, *Public Education in Wisconsin,* 238–239.

The next year, the hungry colleges diverted their attention to another public source of income, the "swamp lands" that the federal government had donated to the state. Some advocates of teacher training hoped to use the proceeds from the sale of swamp lands to finance tuition-free state normal schools. The University of Wisconsin, with its normal department, already aspired to be the "school of the schoolmaster," and most of the private academies and colleges also considered themselves teacher-training institutions. When proponents of state normal schools saw to the introduction of their bill in the legislature, a "college lobby"—consisting of the Lawrence, Beloit, and Carroll presidents and the Milton Academy principal—proposed a substitute bill. The upshot was the normal-school law of 1857. This set up a normal (swamp land) fund and divided the income among all the universities (except the state university), colleges, and academies that would adopt a teacher-training curriculum. The law also allowed any locality providing a site and a building to apply for aid to a normal school.[31]

[4]

Wisconsin's schools and colleges were by no means its only agencies of education or of intellectual life. Others were newspapers, lyceums, libraries, and a variety of literary or scientific organizations. Some of these received public support, but most of them had to depend entirely on private contributions of money and effort.

"At present, in this country, as well as in all other new countries," one of the state's boosters apologized, "the great and paramount object of every individual is to procure the actual necessaries of life—food and raiment." Hence, for a time, Wisconsin was bound to lag behind her "older sisters" in the march of "intellectual and social improvement." The great obstacle, as another Wisconsin friend of enlightenment complained, was the "perverted taste and general apathy of the

[31] William H. Herrmann, "The Rise of the Public Normal School System in Wisconsin" (doctoral dissertation, University of Wisconsin, 1953), 27, 31–33, 36–47, 50–56, 60–61.

masses in reference to any movement calculated to really benefit and elevate the standard of morals and intelligence." On
the whole the masses had at least the advantage of literacy,
though a considerable number of the adult immigrants could
not read or write their own language, to say nothing of English.[32]

Literate Wisconsinites, for the most part, had no lack of
newspapers to read. These appeared and disappeared, combined with one another, changed their managements and their
titles, or transformed themselves from weeklies to dailies or
from dailies back to weeklies at a bewildering rate. Most were
party organs, and some existed only for the duration of a political campaign. Editors needed little experience or capital, no
more than a secondhand press and font, to get a start. "They
are of a kind of mushroom origin," as the first newspaperman
in Oshkosh said, "—spring up full blown without any body's
knowing whence they come." Only a comparative few of the
journals had a long life or a wide influence.

In 1848 three daily newspapers were already being published
in the State— the *Sentinel*, the *Wisconsin*, and the *News*—all of
them in Milwaukee. The *Sentinel* had begun its weekly edition in 1837 and its daily edition in 1844. As editor from
1845 to 1861, Rufus King, a native of New York City and a
graduate of the United States Military Academy at West Point,
made it a power in state politics, at first as a Whig and then
as a Republican paper. During the 1850's several other Milwaukee dailies, four of them in the German language, made an
appearance, but none of them was to last nearly so long as
the *Sentinel*. In the single year 1852 no fewer than six local
dailies were available in Madison. Only one of these, the
Wisconsin State Journal, was to exist more than a few years.
At one time or another during the decade one or more dailies

[32] The quotations are from John Gregory, *Industrial Resources of Wisconsin*
(Milwaukee, 1855), 24–26, and the Menasha *Conservator*, April 2, 1850. For
1850, the census takers reported 1,551 American-born persons aged twenty and
over who could not read and write, and 4,902 foreign-born. For 1860, the figures
were 2,663 and 13,883. See *Ninth Census of the United States, 1870: Volume I*,
pp. 394–397.

also appeared in each of the following places: Racine, Janesville, Oshkosh, Fond du Lac, Kenosha, and La Crosse.

As of 1857, more than 100 weeklies were being issued in the state. Of these, some fourteen were in German and three in Norwegian; one was in Dutch. Over sixty communities had at least one weekly apiece, but several entire counties, including thinly settled Marquette and Trempealeau, had none at all.[33]

Some of the foreign-language papers aimed to preserve and strengthen the old-country culture, as did the German Milwaukee *Seebote*, the semi-official organ of the Roman Catholic hierarchy in the state. Others attempted to hasten the assimilation of their readers, as did the *Banner* and the *Volksfreund*, two Milwaukee German dailies, which were combined in 1855, whose freethinking and anticlerical tendencies the *Seebote* undertook to combat. The Norwegian *Emigranten* announced its purpose in a special message in English: "Through our paper we hope to hurry the process of Americanization of our immigrated countrymen." *Emigranten* and other Norwegian papers gave prominence to translations of writings illustrative of American history and political traditions, including the Declaration of Independence and the Wisconsin constitution.[34]

Newspapers, magazines, and books from eastern states and foreign countries found buyers and readers among at least

[33] Richard N. Current, "The First Newspaperman in Oshkosh [James Densmore]," in *WMH*, 30 (June, 1947), 408–422. The quotation is from the Oshkosh *True Democrat*, February 9, 1849. The Milwaukee *News* was titled the *Commercial Advertiser* from 1848 to early 1852. On Rufus King, see the *DWB*. The number of daily and weekly publications is derived from a count of those listed in Donald E. Oehlerts, comp., *Guide to Wisconsin Newspapers, 1833–1957* (Madison, 1958). The figures are tentative, since Oehlerts' listing is not quite complete.

[34] Overmoehle, "Forty-Eighters in Wisconsin," 139, 150–154, 229–232; Leonard G. Koerber, "Anti-Catholic Agitation in Milwaukee, 1843–1860" (master's thesis, Marquette University, 1960), 68, 84; Blegen, *Norwegian Migration: American Transition*, 303–312, quoting the *Emigranten* on p. 307. See also Arlow W. Andersen, "Venturing into Politics: The Norwegian-American Press of the 1850's," in *WMH*, 32 (September, 1948), 58–79; Olaf H. Spetland, "The Americanizing Aspects of the Norwegian Language Press in Wisconsin, 1847–1865, with Particular Reference to Its Role in Local, State, and National Politics" (master's thesis, University of Wisconsin, 1960), 12, 30. The census of 1860 gave a total of fifty-six Wisconsin establishments engaged in printing and eight in bookbinding. See *Eighth Census of the United States, 1860: Manufactures*, 657–658.

a minority of Wisconsinites. A family coming from the East might continue for years to take the old, familiar "home paper." The well-off and well-educated subscribed to such periodicals as *Ballou's Pictorial, Leslie's Illustrated Weekly, Godey's Ladies' Book*, the *Saturday Evening Post, Harper's Monthly, Harper's Weekly*, and after its appearance in 1857 the *Atlantic Monthly*, which a Menasha editor hailed as containing material "far above the sickly trash" to be found in *Godey's* and other women's publications. Not more than one family in six subscribed to any periodical besides a newspaper, at least in Oshkosh, where by the end of the decade the post office received slightly more than 250 copies of monthly magazines. In Milwaukee there were dealers advertising German, French, and English as well as American periodicals and books. Other cities and some of the larger villages also had book and stationery stores, though most of these kept only a limited stock. House-to-house canvassers sold encyclopedias and other books by subscription. Sent to Milwaukee by a Chicago bookseller in 1856, the young Henry Villard expected to peddle a history of American literature among his fellow Germans but was soon disheartened on finding they "knew nothing of American literature and did not care much for it."[35]

Lyceums and other organizations—especially churches—undertook to make periodicals and books more widely available and also to promote public lectures and discussions. The Young Men's Association of Milwaukee began in 1850 to enlist local ministers, lawyers, and teachers for its lecture series and then, in the prosperity of the middle fifties, attracted such national figures as Horace Greeley, Ralph Waldo Emerson, and Henry Ward Beecher. Meanwhile the association accumulated

[35] Mary D. Bradford, *Memoirs of Mary D. Bradford: Autobiographical and Historical Reminiscences of Education in Wisconsin, Through Progressive Service From Rural School Teaching to City Superintendent* (Evansville, Wisconsin, 1932), 90–91; Menasha *Conservator*, November 5, 1857; Robert C. Robertson, "The Social History of Winnebago County, Wisconsin, 1850–1870" (master's thesis, University of Chicago, 1939), 89–95; Samuel Freeman, *The Emigrant's Hand Book and Guide to Wisconsin* . . . (Milwaukee, 1851), 131, 136; *Memoirs of Henry Villard: Journalist and Financier, 1835–1900* (2 vols., Boston, 1904), 1: 47–50.

a library of nearly four thousand volumes. Outside Milwaukee and Madison, audiences generally had to be content with rather obscure talent. In Oshkosh a debating club of "young mechanics" put on weekly debates before large crowds. In Neenah the local lyceum invited "any Gentleman or Lady" to read an original essay at one of the Monday evening meetings. In Menasha the Aletheon Institute opened a reading room where —for three cents a day, fifty cents a month, or three dollars a year—the public had access to a wide selection of newspapers and magazines. In various places library associations solicited subscriptions and book donations to found libraries open to subscribers.[36]

Besides the libraries that voluntary groups formed, and that in most cases were "public" in the sense of being open to all who paid the required fees, the young state contained hundreds of school, Sunday school, college, church, and private libraries. After gathering such statistics as he could, Lyman C. Draper calculated in 1857 that Wisconsin then had a grand total of 201,278 volumes. "It is questionable," Draper declared, "if any [other] Western State can make any such exhibit of books—the great source of intelligence, knowledge and power." Possibly, in his enthusiasm, he exaggerated a bit.[37]

Lyman C. Draper, absorbed by frontier history since his boyhood in western New York, was the forming and guiding spirit of the State Historical Society of Wisconsin. This society, a feeble infant from its birth in 1846 and its rebirth in 1849, was chartered by the state in 1853 and, under Draper's leadership, was reorganized and invigorated in 1854. That year the legislature appropriated $500 for the purchase of books and other materials—the first time, a Madison newspaper

[36] Still, *Milwaukee*, 206–216; Menasha *Conservator*, January 28, 1858, and June 18, 1859; Robertson, "Social History of Winnebago County," 95–97; Hawks, "Increase A. Lapham," 106.

[37] William B. Hesseltine, *Pioneer's Mission: The Story of Lyman Copeland Draper* (Madison, 1954), 150. The 1860 census credited Wisconsin with 150,559 library volumes (not including books in private collections). This figure placed Wisconsin twenty-third among all the states—ahead of Minnesota, Iowa, Kansas, and California but behind Michigan, Indiana, Illinois, and Missouri. See *Eighth Census of the United States, 1860: Mortality and Miscellaneous Statistics*, 505.

claimed, that a state had ever given direct aid to a historical society. The next year the legislature added another $500 for Draper's salary as corresponding secretary. Under his editorship appeared in 1855, from the press of the Madison *Argus*, the first of ten volumes of the society's *Collections* that he was to edit. The 1857 volume contained the recollections of Augustin Grignon, grandson of the Sieur Charles de Langlade, recollections that Draper had obtained by skillful interviewing. He devoted himself to making the society a broadly based and energetic agency for collecting and disseminating historical knowledge about Wisconsin and the West—rather than a club with restricted membership and ceremonial functions of the kind some of his associates had envisioned.[38]

While Draper was busy recording Wisconsin's history, the versatile Increase A. Lapham kept diligently at investigating both its prehistory and its natural history. Lapham surveyed its mysterious "antiquities," its widely scattered man-made mounds, which were already being plowed up and obliterated. The Smithsonian Institution published in 1855 his descriptions, his fifty-three scale drawings, and his unconventional opinion that the mound builders had been not Aztecs, except perhaps in the case of the Aztalan mounds, but ancestors of Indians still living in the state. The Wisconsin Natural History Association, which he led, accomplished little except to operate a museum in Madison for a time. Lapham himself, however, published in the *Transactions* of the state agricultural society a series of studies of Wisconsin's forests, grasses, fauna and flora, geological formations, and meteorological phenomena. He discovered and described the lunar tide on Lake Michigan. While he financed his researches as best he could, the state government sponsored its own geological survey, the first report of which was published in 1854.[39]

[38] Hesseltine, *Pioneer's Mission*, 104–136, 153–154; Clifford L. Lord and Carl Ubbelohde, *Clio's Servant: The State Historical Society of Wisconsin, 1846–1954* (Madison, 1967), 3–27.
[39] Hawks, "Increase A. Lapham," 87–91, 93–94, 150–155; A. W. Schorger, "The Wisconsin Natural History Association," in *WMH,* 31 (December, 1947), 168–177; Lawrence Martin, *The Physical Geography of Wisconsin* (Madison, 1965),

Lapham and other observers accurately delineated the state's topography, but they could not agree on what had produced those remarkable features—the strange ridges and depressions in some places, the boulders and pebbles scattered over most of the state, and the absence of all these things in a large area of the southwest. Though the Swiss-born Harvard professor Louis Agassiz had already put forth the glacial theory, some geologists still clung to the notion of a flood. Lapham did not fully accept either the ice or the water explanation. Regarding the "back bones" (drumlins and eskers) near Watertown, which were "supposed to be the projecting vertebral ridge of some subterranean monster," he said, "this monstrous theory is certainly preferable to that which attributes them to diluvial action, icebergs, glaciers, etc." He preferred to believe the formations had resulted from erosion.[40]

When a traveling lecturer spoke to a Mineral Point audience on geology, the pioneer Methodist missionary Alfred Brunson was shocked to hear an account of the earth's development that contradicted the Bible story. Brunson replied with arguments that, according to his memoirs, "astounded, confounded, and confused" the speaker. You talk of "drift" covering most of the state, he challenged, but Lakes Superior, Huron, and Michigan are hundreds of feet deep, and obviously it is impossible for "this vast amount of granite soil, gravel, and bowlders to have been drifted across those lakes" by either water or ice. And even if it were somehow possible, why did the drift stop before reaching the Mississippi and filling the entire valley? "Why not admit at once the creative act of God in all this?" Two Presbyterian ministers, also present, were "so fascinated with the word *science*" they failed to see the

---

531. A Wisconsin ornithologist already well known in the 1850's was Thure Kumlien. Born in Sweden and educated at Uppsala University, he later taught at Albion Academy. See Angie Kumlien Main, "Thure Kumlien, Koshkonong Naturalist," in *WMH*, 27 (September, 1943–March, 1944), 17–39, 194–220, 321–343.

40 Hawks, "Increase A. Lapham," 132–140, 156–162; the quotation, from Lapham's letter to the Milwaukee *Sentinel*, May 28, 1852, is on p. 157. On early observations regarding the "driftless area," see Martin, *Physical Geography of Wisconsin*, 102–110.

"infidel influence against the Bible," but believers in such "humbuggery" were "greatly in the minority in the community at large."[41]

Clearly, science and learning in early Wisconsin had more to contend against than either the preoccupation of individual settlers with the actual necessaries of life or the perverted taste and general apathy of the masses.

[5]

In Wisconsin, as in the rest of the country, state and local government during the 1850's was becoming slowly and unevenly a provider of public services and a promoter of social welfare. The larger a community grew, the greater the government's role was likely to be. Yet even in the largest, Milwaukee, many important cares and concerns eventually to become governmental responsibilities were still left to the self-help of the individual or the family, to the good will of a voluntary association, or to the profit-seeking of a private enterprise.

Streets and sidewalks were prime concerns for most municipal authorities. Wooden sidewalks fronted the stores in many communities, but paved streets were rare even in Milwaukee. Alternate mud and dust, well manured by horses and other animals, was an inescapable fact of urban as well as rural life. Ordinances forbade letting hogs run loose, yet they continued to run, in Milwaukee as in smaller towns. One day in 1855 a Milwaukeean on a downtown stroll chased a hog to rescue a tiny child the beast had carried off. Horses constituted a more frequent danger, and the regulation of them—or of their owners—was a recurring problem. Despite laws against leaving teams unhitched, runaways caused many accidents. So did fast drivers and galloping riders, especially when drunk.[42]

Municipalities assumed responsibility for fire protection to

[41] Alfred Brunson, *A Western Pioneer* . . . (2 vols., Cincinnati, 1872, 1879), 2: 215–216, 220–221, 227.

[42] Still, *Milwaukee,* 237–239; Eugene Wiggins, "Pioneer Days in Fall City," in Menomonie *Dunn County News,* June 14, 1923; Milwaukee *Sentinel,* July 27, 1848, November 30, December 5, 1854, November 30, 1855, August 16, 1858.

the extent of adopting safety codes and giving financial assistance to fire companies, but the task of fire fighting continued to be left to volunteers. In Milwaukee the code required every householder to have two buckets ready in case
of emergency and prohibited the construction of wooden buildings in the central business district, the dumping of ashes
where they might cause fires, the carrying of fire in the streets,
and the use of unenclosed candles in livery stables. Prominent
businessmen took an active part in fire fighting. They also
held benefit concerts and other performances and sought contributions to augment the public funds that went to the
support of the volunteer companies. These, like competing
athletic clubs, carried on a spirited rivalry with one another.
"We have now got the best Company in town, we have now
52 members of stout men, and not a dead head in the Company," wrote a proud Milwaukee fireman in 1853. He went on
to describe the rather gaudy uniform, including a red pleated
shirt with black braid and brass buttons, a sky-blue tarpaulin
hat with the company's name ("Ocean 5") on the front, and
a black patent-leather belt. Even the newest fire engines were,
as yet, equipped only with hand-operated pumps.[43]

Villagers were likely to form their first fire company in
response to some particularly destructive conflagration. After
the oldest house in Sauk City burned in 1854, a series of public
meetings led to the organization of a company and to subscriptions for a small piece of apparatus. Later the village authorities were to provide an engine house and to purchase a larger
engine and additional equipment as cast-offs from the Madison fire department.[44]

No city in Wisconsin, and none in the whole region except
Chicago, had a central water system in the 1850's. Milwaukee
was not to have one until 1873. Some cities maintained public
pumps, but most city as well as village dwellers had to depend
on private wells. Both private and public wells were likely to
be contaminated by sewage. Even Milwaukee possessed no cen-

---

[43] Still, *Milwaukee*, 233–234. The quotations are from Joseph D. Sprague to
Joseph A. Denny, April 17, 1853, in the Joseph D. Sprague Correspondence.
[44] Western Historical Company, *History of Sauk County*, 606–607.

tral sewerage system, though the separate wards had laid some primitive wooden sewers. Privies were commonly located without regard to the protection of the water supply. There were no privies at all in some of the newly settled rural areas. Regarding these areas a doctor recalled, "The discharges of both the sick and the well were deposited in the open, where they were accessible to hogs and chickens, as well as to the myriads of flies which always infested the homes, for no window screens were used."[45]

Cholera epidemics swept Wisconsin, as they did much of the nation, in every year from 1849 through 1854, with Milwaukee enduring severe attacks in 1849, 1850, and 1854. Other epidemics threatened from time to time as when, in 1850, the propeller *Alleghany* brought to Milwaukee about three hundred Norwegians and Swedes, most of whom were dead or dying of typhus. Municipal leaders were concerned about the city's healthfulness, for economic as well as humanitarian reasons, since the fear of contagion might turn away prospective settlers and discourage business. The city council therefore, by ordinances of 1846 and 1855, ordered fines for ship captains and stage drivers bringing in sick passengers and set up a board of health with authority to investigate the causes of disease, remove nuisances, and provide a pesthouse. The council, by a law of 1847, also required all residents to be vaccinated against smallpox. Some smaller communities provided vaccination for school children. Many towns, villages, and cities undertook campaigns to clean up streets and vacant lots, on the assumption that cholera was due to effluvia arising from heaps of filth and rotting matter. As a result, the cholera bacteria had fewer chances to spread.[46]

---

[45] Still, *Milwaukee*, 247–248; Peter T. Harstad, "Health in the Upper Mississippi River Valley, 1820 to 1861" (doctoral dissertation, University of Wisconsin, 1963), 71 (quotation), 101. From 1852 on, some Milwaukee streets and buildings were lighted with gas supplied by a private corporation, the Milwaukee Gas Light Company. See Still, *Milwaukee*, 246–247.

[46] Peter T. Harstad, "Disease and Sickness on the Wisconsin Frontier: Cholera," in *WMH*, 43 (Spring, 1960), 203–220; Johnson, *Crosier on the Frontier*, 102; Still, *Milwaukee*, 240. In 1855 a doctor from Reedsburg vaccinated children at a school in Marston township. See diary of Jabez Brown, December 3, 1855, in the Jabez Brown Papers.

Early Wisconsin appeared to have more than its share of physicians—one for every 526 persons as compared with one for every 572 in the nation as a whole, according to the census of 1850. But the state also had comparatively lax requirements for admission to medical practice. The law required only that a candidate be approved by one of the county medical societies. Their standards varied but were rather low at best, and the law itself was not well enforced. Hence a great variety of practitioners, trained and untrained, were competing for patients and fees. In addition to the regular doctors—the old-fashioned allopaths who prescribed mineral medicines like calomel and still resorted to bleeding—there was a host of newcomers including homeopaths, hydropaths, botanics, and eclectics. To lessen the competition, the regulars wanted the state to set and enforce strict standards. When a regulatory bill finally came before the legislature in 1861, it was rejected on the ground that the state ought to do nothing either for the "protection of the practice of those physicians who have diplomas, or for the protection of the people who will employ irregular practitioners, charlatans, and quacks."[47]

Institutions for the care of the sick were few. When the *Alleghany* put in at Milwaukee, the typhus-stricken passengers were transferred to some empty federal buildings on the waterfront or to an improvised hospital on Jones Island. The mayor asked the Sisters of Charity, who operated St. John's Hospital, to look after the patients. Remembering the heroic services of the Sisters of Charity, Protestant as well as Catholic Milwaukeeans contributed to the fund the nuns raised in 1856–1857 for the construction of a new building, which was renamed St. Mary's Hospital. This Catholic institution served the entire community.[48]

The "poor laws," which were carried over from the territorial period and codified in 1848 and revised in 1849, gave county commissioners or township authorities "superintendence

---

[47] Harstad, "Health in the Upper Mississippi Valley," 251–252, 283–285, 314; the quotation is from pp. 284–285. For figures on the number of physicians in the United States in 1850, see *Seventh Census of the United States, 1850,* p. lxxiv.

[48] Johnson, *Crosier on the Frontier,* 102–103; Peter Leo Johnson, *Daughters of Charity in Milwaukee, 1846–1946* (Milwaukee, 1946), 46–48, 71–73, 79–80.

of the poor," who were defined as persons incapable of obtaining a livelihood because of "bodily infirmity, idiocy, lunacy, or other unavoidable cause." Parents, children, grandparents, and brothers and sisters were to provide for their indigent relatives when able to do so and, if unwilling, were to compensate the local government for the relief it furnished. No one could apply for aid before residing twelve months in the locality, and town or county authorities could remove nonresident paupers. The authorities were to arrange for the maintenance of the eligible poor, inside or outside of poorhouses, but could bind out to some "respectable householder" any minor likely to become a public charge.[49]

Counties tried to shift responsibility for the poor to the townships, and these tried to avoid as much of it as they could. The towns were careful to screen out transients, many of whom had no legal residence anywhere. Thus the relief load and the tax burden were kept down. On June 1, 1850, for example, only 238 persons in the entire state were being publicly supported in whole or in part, and this number plus all those who had received aid at any time during the preceding fiscal year came to no more than 666, of whom 169 were American-born and 497 foreign-born. The tax money spent on the poor that year totaled $14,743, an average of about $22 per recipient.[50]

Private charities helped take care of some of the needy. Fraternal societies such as the Independent Order of Odd Fellows provided sickness and death benefits for their own dues-paying members. Church groups and other benevolent societies held benefit concerts and donation parties and solicited gifts for the poor. The Milwaukee Relief Society undertook, from 1855 on, to systematize collections; it raised a little over $1,000 the first year. In Milwaukee and elsewhere in the Wisconsin diocese, Roman Catholic orders founded a number of orphanages,

[49] Donald J. Berthrong, "Social Legislation in Wisconsin, 1836–1900" (doctoral dissertation, University of Wisconsin, 1951), 7–10.

[50] Curti, *Making of an American Community,* 313; *Ninth Census of the United States, 1870: Volume I,* p. 970; *Seventh Census of the United States, 1850: Compendium,* 162–163.

which received some financial aid from county and state government.[51]

In assisting the blind and the deaf and dumb, philanthropic individuals took the initiative and then persuaded the state to add its support. A resident of Janesville began to teach a private class for the blind in 1849. The next year he and others in the Janesville area induced the legislature to incorporate the Wisconsin Institute for the Education of the Blind and to pay the board, lodging, and other expenses of Wisconsin residents attending the institute. In 1850 a young woman graduate of the New York Institution for the Deaf and Dumb started a school for deaf-mutes near Delavan. It soon had to close for lack of funds. In response to petitions circulated throughout the county, the state in 1852 chartered the Wisconsin Institute for the Deaf and Dumb and gave it financial aid. The trustees and instructors urged that the deaf-mutes be taught shoemaking, cabinetmaking, and other occupations which would render them self-supporting and keep them from becoming "pests to society."

The mentally ill, unless their relatives took care of them at home, were kept in poorhouses or, if violent, in jails. In both places they were exposed to cruel treatment, some of them living in chains and wallowing in their own filth, and they often made themselves a nuisance to other inmates and to the surrounding community. The state took a step toward assuming responsibility and providing better care when, in 1854, the legislature passed an act to establish an asylum. Opposition soon arose, however, some critics charging that the project was tainted by political corruption, others insisting that the insane in Wisconsin were too few to justify the expense. "We are in favor of the Lunatic Asylum being completed without delay," the Jefferson *Jeffersonian* replied, citing the case of a deranged prisoner in the Jefferson County jail who for two or three years had been yelling night and day and making

[51] Still, *Milwaukee*, 235–236; Johnson, *Crosier on the Frontier*, 103–108. *Seventh Census of the United States, 1850: Compendium*, 162–163, gives figures for the Wisconsin Odd Fellows' relief expenditures, 1843–1853.

himself heard all over the village. The legislature repealed the asylum act but soon, in 1857, passed a new one, which was to result three years later in the opening of the Wisconsin State Hospital for the Insane near Madison.[52]

[6]

Wisconsin seemed like a completely "free country" and yet a remarkably law-abiding one to some of the immigrants who were familiar with the burdensome regulations and the ubiquitous police of Europe. In this new state "only a few necessary and useful laws" were made. "And with few laws and few officers to enforce them, the people have respect for the law and like to see it enforced; as a whole the people cooperate with the officers, so that transgressions are few." That was what a well-to-do Dutch settler, in 1852, after two years in Little Chute, told his relatives in Holland. "There are policemen in the cities, but we never see one; still we don't have to lock the house or the stable or keep a vicious watchdog to frighten burglars away." In 1853 a German residing in Mequon, north of Milwaukee, wrote, "The members of the police organization are elected by the people and therefore are closely bound to them and become friends with them, and it does not occur to anyone to agitate against them." He added, "On account of the variety of nationalities which make up the American people and the minimum police control which is directed against evildoers, it is a marvel that there is not more crime."[53]

Certainly the law-enforcement system was rudimentary, but not all Wisconsinites believed that it was adequate or that crime was negligible. Each county had its sheriff, district at-

---

[52] Berthrong, "Social Legislation in Wisconsin," 16–17, 32–44 ("pests" quotation on p. 44), 53–56; Milwaukee *Daily American,* February 2, 1856, quoting the Jefferson *Jeffersonian,* date unspecified. See also Bernett O. Odegard and George M. Keith, *A History of the State Board of Control of Wisconsin and the State Institutions, 1849–1939* (Madison, [1939]), 77, 107–108, 159–160.

[53] Arnoldus Verstegen to his wife's parents, June 16, 1852, in Lucas, ed., *Dutch Immigrant Memoirs,* 2: 157–159; Joseph Schafer, ed. and trans., "Christian Traugott Ficker's Advice to Emigrants," in *WMH,* 25 (December, 1941– June, 1942), 460.

torney, and coroner, and each town or village its constables, all of them elected for short terms and few of them noted for either professionalism or proficiency. Even Milwaukee, at first, was equipped with no more than a city marshal and ward constables, who inspired so little confidence that many citizens carried guns for self-protection or hired private guards. In 1852 the city temporarily provided night watchmen, fifteen of them, to maintain order and report fires. After a series of thefts, murders, and incendiary burnings, the city in 1855 set up its first police department, with a chief and twelve patrolmen, who were given badges but no uniforms. In Neenah and Menasha—only a few miles from Little Chute, where there was said to be no fear of burglars in 1852—a rash of burglaries broke out only a few years later. The Menasha *Conservator* advised "every family to be prepared with one or more good revolvers" and blamed the "depredations" on the "laxity of our courts."[54]

Local officers had difficulty in putting down riots, which were fairly frequent in Milwaukee. When in 1853 three or four hundred construction workers, mostly Germans, marched upon a railroad company office to demand back pay, the mayor along with several aldermen and constables met them and tried to dissuade them from violence but failed. The mayor then called on the firemen, who used their hoses to help disperse the crowd. When Germans and Irishmen got into a fight at a polling place, the sheriff was powerless to stop them, and he and several other persons were badly hurt by flying bricks and stones.[55]

Militia companies were expected to assist, when necessary, in maintaining law and order. According to a state law of 1851, all able-bodied white males between the ages of eighteen

[54] Still, *Milwaukee*, 230–232; Menasha *Conservator*, July 1, 1858. Reports of suspects escaping from the custody of constables were fairly frequent. Within the space of a little over a month, in 1851, the Watertown *Register* reported two suspected horse thieves getting away from one constable and a third from another in the Watertown area. See Milwaukee *Sentinel*, July 17 and August 20, 1851.

[55] Milwaukee *Sentinel*, July 12, 1853, March 8, 1854; Madison *Capital Times*, March 23, 1967.

and forty-five were to be enrolled in the militia, but in fact only volunteer companies were formed, and only about twenty of these by 1855. The state provided arms, which it received from the federal government, but the volunteers had to supply their own uniforms and other equipment. Uniforms were colorful, the Kenosha City Rifles choosing scarlet jackets faced with blue velvet; the Black Yaegers, a Milwaukee German company, black coats with green collars and cuffs and black hats with green plumes. More showy than efficient, the companies drilled and paraded but got little or no real military training. They were essentially mere social clubs.[56]

Until Wisconsin established a state prison, all convicted criminals served their sentences in county jails. The number of such persons was not large: only 267 were convicted during the year ending June 1, 1850, and on that day but sixty-one (twenty-six of them American-born, thirty-five foreign-born) were still in jail. Governor Nelson Dewey and other reformers criticized the jail system as expensive, insecure, and unfair, some of the convicts being confined in unhealthful cells, others being allowed to roam at will. Above all, the critics denounced the system as offering no opportunity for the reformation of the criminal. In response, the legislature provided in 1851 for a penitentiary to be located at Waupun, and construction of a permanent structure began in 1852 with prisoners doing the work. By 1855 the number in the prison had not yet reached 100; many criminals with short sentences continued to be assigned to jails. Taxpayers complained of the cost of maintaining able-bodied criminals at Waupun and demanded that the prison pay for itself. So the warden began to lease convict labor to private contractors, though this interfered with the aim of reforming criminals through penitentiary discipline and enforced meditation.

In the early years offenders old and young were herded together in county jails and even in the state prison. At least

[56] Jerry M. Cooper, "The Wisconsin Militia, 1832–1900" (master's thesis, University of Wisconsin, 1968), 84, 89–91, 95–97, 134n.

sixty-one youths under sixteen were sent to the Milwaukee County jail in a single year, and boys as young as nine were imprisoned at Waupun. In 1857 the legislature directed that a "house of refuge," or reform school, be set up at Waukesha. Counties had to pay a dollar a week for the maintenance of each of their children committed to the school. Often the county authorities resorted to the cheaper expedient of a brief term in the local jail.[57]

The establishment of the state prison gave added impetus to a movement for eliminating the death penalty, since there was now the alternative of secure and presumably redemptive life imprisonment. Executions in Wisconsin had been few— only four from 1836 to 1851, two of them with Indians as the victims—but the fourth, which proved to be the last, was particularly shocking to humanitarians. This was the public hanging, near Kenosha, of John McCaffary, who had been convicted of drowning his wife Bridget in a hogshead in the backyard of their Kenosha home. Two or three thousand spectators crowded around the gallows, most of them in a holiday mood. It was "murder before the people, with its horrors removed by the respectability of those engaged in its execution," the Madison *Democrat* editorialized. Assemblyman Christopher Latham Sholes quoted this approvingly in his newspaper, the Kenosha *Telegraph*. Sholes in the assembly and Marvin Bovee, a Waukesha County farmer, in the senate led the struggle to make Wisconsin the third of the states to put an end to capital punishment. Bovee's bill finally passed in 1853.[58]

The next year saw a lynching in Wisconsin, and the follow-

[57] Berthrong, "Social Legislation in Wisconsin," 66–76; Miriam Z. Langsam, "The Nineteenth Century Wisconsin Criminal: Ideologies and Institutions" (doctoral dissertation, University of Wisconsin, 1967), 34–38, 165–172; *Ninth Census of the United States, 1870: Volume I,* p. 570.

[58] Kenosha *Telegraph*, August 22, 1851; Langsam, "Nineteenth Century Wisconsin Criminal," 86–89; Carrie Cropley, "The Case of John McCaffary," in *WMH,* 35 (Summer, 1952), 281–288; Elwood R. McIntyre, "A Farmer Halts the Hangman: The Story of Marvin Bovee," in *WMH,* 42 (Autumn, 1958), 3–12. The quotation from the Madison *Democrat* is from the August 29, 1851 issue of the Kenosha *Telegraph*.

ing year two more, these two within a month of one another.
First of the victims in 1855 was David F. Mayberry of Rockford, Illinois, a Tennessee-born Mormon convert and a horse
thief recently released from an Illinois prison, whom the Rock
County circuit court had sentenced to life at Waupun, with
frequent periods of solitary confinement, for the extraordinar-
ily brutal and cold-blooded robbery-murder of a highly respected Johnson's Creek lumber raftsman and dealer. After the
sentencing, a throng of two or three thousand was waiting outside the Janesville court house for Mayberry to appear on his
way to the nearby jail. "Many were from abroad, though several men of Janesville were but too active, and there was an
apathy among those who did not join the mob, that made it
difficult to procure a force to maintain the law, though quite
a number volunteered and were sworn in as special constables."
Judge James Doolittle came out and appealed to the crowd, with
little effect. Finally the judge, the city marshal, the sheriff and
his deputies, and the special constables emerged with the prisoner. The mob quickly overpowered them, clubbed the desperately resisting Mayberry into unconsciousness, then strung
him up to a tree limb.[59]

That was on July 12. On August 7 occurred the second
lynching of the year, this one in Washington County, where
most of the people were German-born but most of the local
officials were native Americans. George DeBar, the victim, a

[59] The 1854 lynching occurred in Waushara County after Frederick Cartwright,
freed on bail while awaiting trial for the murder of a quarreling neighbor, shot
and killed two friends of the dead man when they attempted to break into his
house in order—as it was alleged—to "get him out of the way *dead or alive*."
After a nearly two-day siege, a mob of about 100 men managed to seize Cartwright and hang him. See Ripon *Herald*, February 29, 1854, quoted in the
Milwaukee *Sentinel*, March 6, 1854. See also the *Sentinel* for March 8, 1854.
Eyewitness reports of the Mayberry lynching are in an extra edition of the Janesville *Democratic Standard*, July 12, 1855, and in the Milwaukee *Sentinel*, July 14,
1855. For a full contemporary account, see Ira C. Jenks, *Trial of David F.
Mayberry, for the Murder of Andrew Alger, Before the Rock Co. Circuit Court,
Judge Doolittle Presiding, July 10th and 11th, 1855, Containing the Arguments
of the Attorneys, and a Full and Correct Account of His Death by a Mob* (Janesville, 1855, a rare 48-page pamphlet in the SHSW. The quotation is from p. 47.

physically and mentally weak nineteen-year-old native of New York, had worked as a farmhand for John Muehr, an immigrant from Germany. Apparently DeBar held a grudge against Muehr, who he said had struck him during a town election dispute (DeBar wore the white hat that some Know Nothings used as a badge) and had mistreated him at work. Going to Muehr's house one night to collect wages owed him, DeBar in a frenzy attacked and wounded Muehr and Mrs. Muehr and killed their hired boy, Paul Winderling, with a knife. DeBar was arrested in Milwaukee and jailed in West Bend. Hundreds of angry Germans poured into the village. Judge Charles H. Larrabee hoped to avert a lynching by giving DeBar a speedy trial and then hurrying him off to Waupun. Meanwhile the judge and the sheriff called for militia, and the Union Guards, also known, as the Ozaukee Rifles, of Port Washington, and the Washington Artillery of Milwaukee promptly arrived. Both companies were German. Some of their members were seen hobnobbing with the crowds in the local beer halls. After DeBar's indictment, the militiamen, about fifty of them, surrounded the prisoner as the sheriff started to lead him from the courthouse to the jail, but when the roaring mob made a sudden rush, the militiamen fell back with practically no resistance. The mob knocked DeBar down, trampled him, pounded him with stones, tied a rope to his legs, dragged him half a mile, dangled him head downwards from a tree, dragged and clubbed him again, kicked him off a bridge into the Milwaukee River, and finally hanged him by the neck.[60]

No action was being taken against the Janesville lynchers—a fact which, it was said, had emboldened the West Bend mob leaders—but several men were eventually brought to trial for the killing of DeBar. The predominantly German jury acquitted the defendants on a technicality: the indictment charged

[60] The events were thoroughly covered by the Milwaukee *Sentinel* in its daily issues of August 3–13, 1855. Included in the *Sentinel* were accounts by witnesses and participants, among them Captain J. A. Liebhaber of the Washington Artillery (issue of August 10), West Bend resident Ansel Tupper (August 20), and Undersheriff G. Weiss (August 24).

them with strangling DeBar by means of a rope around his neck, but the jury was of the opinion that he was already dead when he was at last strung up![61]

The DeBar lynching both reflected and reinforced ethnic tensions in Washington County and elsewhere in the state. Native Americans residing in the county blamed the lynching on "hideous monsters" with an anti-American blood lust and accused the militia companies and their officers—with one notable exception—of complicity in the affair. The undersheriff, G. Weiss, denounced the lynchers but defended the actions of some, if not all, of the militia. He said the mob had comprised the "rudest part of the population of Washington County" and had been "inspired with *religious* fanaticism," the implication being that it had consisted mainly of Roman Catholics. Another German also referred to a "mob enraged by religious fanaticism." Convinced that the Union Guards and the Washington Artillery were "guilty of fraternizing with the MOB," 186 residents of West Bend and its vicinity signed a petition urging the governor to disband the two companies; he declined to do so. A hundred Milwaukeeans volunteered for a newly formed outfit, the Milwaukee Light Guards. "In a city where all the arms are held by foreign born citizens," commented the local Know Nothing paper, "it is gratifying to know that this company is composed of Americans, which is another way to say they are brave and patriotic fellows, who will do their duty when called upon to protect the laws of the land or guard the rights of its citizens."[62]

[61] Milwaukee *Sentinel,* February 16, May 8, 1856. Brought to trial a second time, the defendants were again acquitted, this time on a plea of double jeopardy—despite a statute that read: "If any person . . . be acquitted upon the ground of a variance between the indictment and the proof . . . he may be arraigned again on a new indictment, and may be tried and convicted for the same offence, notwithstanding such formal acquittal." See Milwaukee *Sentinel,* March 31, April 18, 1857.

[62] Milwaukee *Sentinel,* August 20, 22, 24, 1855; Milwaukee *Daily American,* September 10, 1855. Lieutenant Charles Beger of the Union Guards—"about the only soldier" who "did his duty"—received an appropriately inscribed silver goblet from the appreciative "Ladies of Ozaukee." See Fond du Lac *Union,* date unspecified, quoted in the Milwaukee *Daily American,* November 5, 1855.

Meanwhile the lynchings provoked a demand for the revival of capital punishment. "In three cases of murder, in the State, 'lynch law' has done, what under the death penalty would have been done by the executioner," one Milwaukeean declared. "There must be an end of this sickly sympathy for the murderer," another maintained. "The first and chief aim of all punishment is to *protect society,* not the *criminal.* Let capital punishment be restored, and we shall have no more Lynch Law." The agitation rose to new heights when, two months after the DeBar lynching, an angry bank patron, a German, shot and killed one Milwaukee banker and wounded another. Alexander Mitchell and some sixty other business leaders of the city called a mass meeting to express sympathy for the dead banker's family and to petition the legislature for repeal of the 1853 law and re-enactment of the death penalty. A large majority of the newspapers throughout the state favored repeal. Bills for that purpose were introduced during the session of 1856, and during each of the next four annual sessions, but none of the bills quite managed to win the approval of both houses.[63]

"Wisconsin is rapidly gaining a reputation for disregard of law and contempt for legal tribunals," the New York *Times* had observed in 1855. Civic leaders in Wisconsin were concerned about the good name of their state and their particular communities. A Janesville editor, after watching the Mayberry lynching from his office window, feared that it would be "heralded throughout the country as an evidence of mob-spirit" and would leave "an ineffaceable blot upon the escutcheon of our fair young city." The truth, he implied, was that the majority of the inhabitants were essentially peaceable and

[63] Milwaukee *Sentinel,* August 10, 1855 (second quote), February 16, 1856 (first quote); Milwaukee *Daily American,* October 17, 19, 30, 1855; Berthrong, "Social Legislation in Wisconsin," 134–137. An attempted lynching near Portage was averted by an alert and determined sheriff in 1857. See Western Historical Company, *The History of Columbia County, Wisconsin . . .* (Chicago, 1880), 493–494; Franklin F. Lewis, "The Career of Edward F. Lewis," in *WMH,* 3 (June, 1920), 434–442.

law-abiding. Probably they were, and likewise those of the rest of the state. Nevertheless, as the events demonstrated, a vast potential for violence lay beneath the surface of Wisconsin society, ready to erupt, and the forces of law and order were hardly adequate for coping with the occasional eruptions.[64]

[64] New York *Times*, date unspecified, quoted in the Milwaukee *Sentinel*, August 13, 1855; Janesville *Democratic Standard*, July 12, 1855.

6

Reshaping Party Politics

[1]

PARTY POLITICS kept politicians fairly busy in the early years of Wisconsin's statehood. Every year there were state assemblymen as well as local officers to be elected by popular vote. Every second year there were state senators and administrative officials, including a governor, in addition to congressmen. And every fourth year, of course, there were electors for a President of the United States.

When Wisconsin entered the Union on May 29, 1848, the Democratic party controlled the state as well as the federal government. At the recent elections, held in anticipation of statehood, the Democrats had won the governorship, all the other state offices, the two congressional seats, and a majority of the places in both houses of the legislature. At its first session, convening on June 5, 1848, the legislature chose two Democrats as United States senators. Though on top for the moment, the Democratic organization still had to face the determined opposition of the other major party, the Whig. Neither Democrats nor Whigs appeared to have much to fear from the third party, the Liberty party, which in the recent gubernatorial election had polled only 1,134 votes for its candidate as compared with 14,621 for the Whig and 19,875 for the Democrat.[1]

Nevertheless, in Wisconsin as in the rest of the country, both Democratic and Whig organizations were beginning to suffer from new disruptive strains, tensions of a kind to which the Liberty party was immune. The war with Mexico was over—it officially ended the day after Wisconsin became a state, the peace treaty being proclaimed on May 30, 1848—but the domestic quarrel the war had provoked was growing more and more bitter and divisive. The point in dispute was the future of slavery in the newly acquired territories. In Wisconsin and elsewhere in the North, both Whigs and Democrats disagreed among themselves about the Wilmot Proviso, a resolution proposed in Congress to exclude slavery from the entire Mexican cession. At the war's end both parties in the state were therefore trying to ignore the issue. But not the Liberty men, all of whom gave wholehearted support to the principle of "free soil."

For the time being the Democratic party in Wisconsin managed to patch over its old factionalism resulting from personal and local attachments. Earlier the party's center of gravity had lain in the lead region of the southwest, and its outstanding leader had been Colonel Henry Dodge, who had twice served as territorial governor. With the growth of population and party strength in the southeastern counties, politicians in that area began to contest the dominance of the Dodge faction. By 1848, Josiah A. Noonan of Milwaukee was on the way to becoming the Democratic boss of the state. Born in 1813 in Amsterdam, New York, of Irish ancestry, Noonan was described as a man of "heavy frame, red hair, florid complexion, big head, gray eyes, aggressive manners, self-assertive, voluble speech and quick wit, indicative of his Celtic origin." He based his power not only on his job as Milwaukee postmaster but

[1] C. W. Butterfield, "History of Wisconsin," in Western Historical Company, *The History of Sauk County, Wisconsin* . . . (Chicago, 1880), 53–54; Frederick J. Blue, "The Free Soil Party and the Election of 1848 in Wisconsin" (master's thesis, University of Wisconsin, 1962), 9. Unless otherwise noted, all gubernatorial election totals are from the *Wisconsin Blue Book, 1975,* p. 657.

also on his paper and type-foundry business, which gave him influence with editors throughout the state who "had unsettled accounts with him" and "felt under obligations to him." In nominating the first state governor the Dodge and Noonan factions were able to compromise on Nelson Dewey, of Cassville, because of Dewey's retiring disposition and inoffensive, rather colorless personality. In choosing the first United States senators, they balanced west and east by agreeing on Dodge himself for the one seat and Isaac Walker, a thirty-four-year-old Milwaukee lawyer, for the other.[2]

With James K. Polk in the White House, the Wisconsin Democrats had the benefit of federal patronage. They also had the advantage of their reputation, dating from Andrew Jackson's time, as the party of the common man. They could claim to be defending the people against the "money power" by opposing the legalization of banks. They could appeal to the foreign-born by virtue of having sponsored the state constitution's liberal suffrage clause, which permitted aliens to vote after a year's residence in the state. Democratic in image as well as in name, the party at first attracted nearly all the Irish, German, and Norwegian immigrants who took advantage of their voting opportunities. The Irish were quickly drawn into politics, but many of the Germans and Norwegians, though Democratic in sympathy, were slow to take an active part.[3]

---

[2] Alexander M. Thomson, *A Political History of Wisconsin* (Milwaukee, 1900), 63–72.

[3] Joseph Schafer, *Four Wisconsin Counties: Prairie and Forest* (Madison, 1927), 150–155; M. Justille McDonald, *History of the Irish in Wisconsin in the Nineteenth Century* (Washington, D.C., 1954), 127–128; Roy A. Suelflow, *A Plan for Survival* (New York, 1965), 176–177; Olaf H. Spetland, "The Americanizing Aspects of the Norwegian Language Press in Wisconsin, 1847–1865, with Particular Reference to Its Role in Local, State, and National Politics" (master's thesis, University of Wisconsin, 1960), 9–16.

The federal patronage consisted of appointive jobs on the federal payroll and contracts let to provide such services as the delivery of the mail. Neither was particularly large in the early days of Wisconsin. In 1849 there were approximately 325 federal appointments in the state, nearly 90 per cent of which were to jobs with the post office, and the total amount of all the mail contracts was only slightly more than $20,000. But the postmasters, together with the federal judges and the surveyors, receivers, and registers of the Department of the Interior—if not the five lighthouse keepers—were persons of prestige in

The Democrats of Wisconsin were handicapped as well as benefited by their affiliation with the national party. Under the leadership of the Tennesseean Polk, the party seemed more willing to advance Southern than Northern interests. By his veto of an 1847 rivers-and-harbors appropriation bill, President Polk had shown his opposition to federal spending for transportation improvements, which most Wisconsinites enthusiastically approved. The Wisconsin party boldly declared itself in favor of federally financed "internal improvements" but could not avoid embarrassment as a result of the national party's stand on the question.[4]

Wisconsin Whigs did not suffer the same embarrassment. They could point to their party's record of advocating the improvements expenditures that Polk resisted. But the Whig party had other handicaps. In the nation as a whole it bore a stigma as the party of the rich and also as the party of the nativists. In Wisconsin it did include some (though by no means all) of the wealthiest men. The Whigs could nevertheless hope to attract the American-born poor by posing as the defenders of American institutions, but in doing so they repelled the immigrants, at least those whose religion was Roman Catholic or whose native tongue was other than English. "The party professing to be democratic, has taken foreign pauperism into its alliance and has beaten us with the votes of aliens," the Whig *Grant County Herald* complained after the spring elections of 1848. "Our Sovereigns are the ragged rabble of

most communities and exercised a political influence in local affairs far beyond their number. See U.S. Department of State, *Register of all Officers and Agents, Civil, Military, and Naval, in the Service of the United States*, 1849, pp. 107, 123, 133, 136, 138, 140, 148, 151, 247, 515–526, 534, 689–691, 708.

The first Norwegian newspaper in Wisconsin and in the United States, *Nordlyset*, which began publication at Norway in 1847, was Democratic. Its editor, James D. Reymert, was elected to the Wisconsin legislature as a Democrat in 1848. Apparently he was the first person of Norwegian birth to serve in any state legislature. See Spetland, as cited above. See also Theodore C. Blegen, *Norwegian Migration to America: The American Transition* (Northfield, Minnesota, 1940), 286–299.

[4] Richard L. Hanneman, "The First Republican Campaign in Wisconsin, 1854" (master's thesis, University of Wisconsin, 1966), 8–9.

Europe." Whatever its weaknesses, the Whig party had over-turned the Democrats in the southwestern counties of Iowa and Grant. And it continued to have a powerful voice in the Milwaukee *Sentinel* under the editorship of Rufus King.[5]

The Liberty party was an outgrowth of the antislavery movement, which had its main centers in New England and New York. Migrants from that region had organized antislavery societies in Wisconsin as early as 1840. While the Liberty party included abolitionists, it did not itself propose the abolition of slavery in the southern states (only in the District of Columbia), though insisting on the exclusion of slavery from the western territories. The party had an organ in Milwaukee, the *American Freeman*. Just ten days before Wisconsin was admitted to the Union, a new editor arrived to take charge of the paper and infuse vigor into the cause. He was Sherman M. Booth, a thirty-five-year-old native of upstate New York, who had helped to organize the Liberty party in Connecticut. A fanatic on the temperance as well as the slavery question, Booth was to antagonize those Germans who otherwise might have joined the antislavery movement. A forceful speaker and writer but often erratic and tactless, he was also to repel many native Americans who were otherwise inclined to share his aims. Nevertheless, much was to be heard of him, and from him, in the years ahead.[6]

Between 1848 and 1857 the party system was to undergo a revolution in both the nation and the state. The Democratic party was to be badly shaken and the Whig party completely shattered. Some of the Democrats and most of the Whigs were to join with Liberty men—Rufus King with Sherman Booth—

[5] Joseph Schafer, *The Wisconsin Lead Region* (Madison, 1932), 74–91; David B. Leonard, "A Biography of Alexander Mitchell, 1817–1887" (master's thesis, University of Wisconsin, 1951), 113; Aaron M. Boom, "The Development of Sectional Attitudes in Wisconsin, 1848–1861" (doctoral dissertation, University of Chicago, 1948), 35. The quotation is from the Lancaster *Grant County Herald,* May 20, 1848.

[6] Blue, "Free Soil Party," 9–19; Theodore C. Smith, "The Free Soil Party in Wisconsin," in *SHSW Proceedings*, 1894, pp. 99–108; Thomson, *Political History*, 57–58.

to form a new party, for which some would claim Wisconsin as the place of birth. By 1857 the new Republican party, though not yet in control of the federal government, would dominate the politics and government of Wisconsin.

[2]

In its immediate consequences the slavery dispute threatened the unity of the Democrats more than that of the Whigs. As the parties prepared for the fall elections of 1848, the Democratic ranks began to divide. The national Democratic platform made no mention of slavery in the territories, and the presidential candidate, Lewis Cass of Michigan, was known to oppose the Wilmot Proviso and to advocate "squatter sovereignty," which would have allowed the settlers in a territory to adopt slavery if a majority of them approved it. Cass was anathema to antislavery Democrats throughout the North. They found no acceptable alternative if they looked to the Whig candidate, Zachary Taylor, for Taylor owned slaves in Louisiana, and he was running with no platform whatsoever. The disaffected Democrats of New York state, the "Barnburners," took steps to organize a new party and nominate a third candidate, former President Martin Van Buren. They arranged for a national Free Soil convention to meet in Buffalo, New York.

The disaffected Democrats of Wisconsin, who began to refer to themselves as Barnburners also, announced a mass meeting to be held in Janesville for choosing delegates to the Buffalo convention. The leaders of the Liberty party in Wisconsin, after a heated debate among themselves, decided to join the new movement, though Booth insisted, "If it shall nominate a man, who like Mr. Van Buren, is opposed to abolishing Slavery in the District of Columbia, we can't go for him." Of those who gathered for the Janesville meeting on July 26, 1848, it was reported that they were "about three parts Democracy, one part Abolition, one or two *scruples* of Whiggery and a grain of

National Reform." The delegation that was sent to Buffalo also consisted mainly of Democrats, though it included Booth.[7]

After the adjournment of the Buffalo convention, which had done the expected by nominating Van Buren, the Wisconsin Barnburners reassembled in Janesville to organize the state Free Soil party, endorse the Buffalo candidate and platform, add planks for internal improvements and land reform, and plan the fall campaign. The Liberty men swallowed their objections to Van Buren, and Booth himself took on the editorship of a Free Soil campaign newspaper in Milwaukee, the *Wisconsin Barnburner*. The Free Soilers also had the support of Booth's *Wisconsin Freeman* (successor to the *American Freeman*), the state's only Free Soil daily, and several other weeklies, prominent among them the Southport *Telegraph* and the Racine *Advocate*. The new party appealed to Germans through A. H. Bielfeld's *Volksfreund* ("People's Friend") in Milwaukee, and to Norwegians through James D. Reymert's *Nordlyset* ("The Northern Light") in Norway, Racine County.[8]

Alarmed by the defection of the Free Soilers, the regular Democrats in Wisconsin claimed to be the true "free soil" party. The Milwaukee *Wisconsin* and other Democratic papers carried the banner "Cass and free soil." They claimed that their candidate had changed his mind on the territorial question, and they pointed out that Wisconsin's two congressmen, both Democrats, had voted for the Wilmot Proviso. When a Democratic district convention in Mineral Point referred to the proviso as an "impractical abstraction," the convention's

[7] Albert J. Cole, "The Barnburner Element in the Republican Party" (master's thesis, University of Wisconsin, 1951), 33–34; Smith, "Free Soil Party in Wisconsin," in *SHSW Proceedings,* 1894, pp. 109–118, quoting on p. 113 Booth in the Milwaukee *American Freeman,* August 2, 1848, and the Milwaukee *Sentinel,* August 1, 1848. Delegates are listed in the "Official Proceedings of the National Free Soil Convention, Assembled at Buffalo, N. Y., August 9th and 10th, 1848," an extra edition of the Buffalo *Republic,* n.d., a copy of which is in the SHSW.

[8] Cole, "Barnburner Element," 34–35; Smith, "Free Soil Party in Wisconsin," in *SHSW Proceedings,* 1894, pp. 150–154; Blue, "Free Soil Party," 57; Spetland, "Norwegian Language Press in Wisconsin," 13.

nominee for Congress repudiated the statement, insisting that he was "opposed to the extension of slavery under any pretext." At first the Wisconsin Whigs assumed complacently that the Barnburner revolt would hurt only the Democrats, but soon the Whigs also took alarm and began to pass resolutions against slavery in the territories. "Resolved," a Walworth County convention proclaimed, "that the Free Soil party has stolen the Whig thunder and hopes to ride into office on Whig principles."[9]

In Wisconsin's fall elections of 1848 the Democrats lost many voters—far more than the Whigs did—to the Free Soil party. The Democrats carried the state for their presidential candidate, but with a plurality of only 38 per cent of the votes (Cass receiving 15,001, Taylor 13,747, and Van Buren 10,418). The Wisconsin Whigs could take comfort, however, in their candidate's success in the nation at large. With Taylor elected, they could look forward to four years' benefit of the federal patronage. Had it not been for the Free Soil competition, the Democrats would have captured all the Wisconsin congressional seats, which had been increased to three. As it was, each of the three parties secured one congressman. Without the party split, the Democrats would have won a majority in both houses of the state legislature. In fact, they gained a majority in the senate (twelve Democrats, five Free Soilers, four Whigs) but only a plurality in the assembly (thirty-two Democrats, eighteen Free Soilers, sixteen Whigs). With more than a fourth of the total vote, the Free Soilers in Wisconsin did proportionally better than those in any other state, except Vermont and Massachusetts.

In Wisconsin the Free Soilers made their best showing in the southeastern counties—especially Racine (then including Kenosha) and Walworth—that had been settled mainly by people from New England and New York. The Democrats were strongest in the lakeshore counties farther north, among them

[9] Smith, "Free Soil Party in Wisconsin," in *SHSW Proceedings*, 1894, pp. 109–117, quoting the Walworth County resolutions; Blue, "Free Soil Party," 31–36; Robert R. Flatley, "The Wisconsin Congressional Delegation from Statehood to Secession, 1848–1861" (bachelor's thesis, University of Wisconsin, 1951), 12, quoting the nominee for Congress.

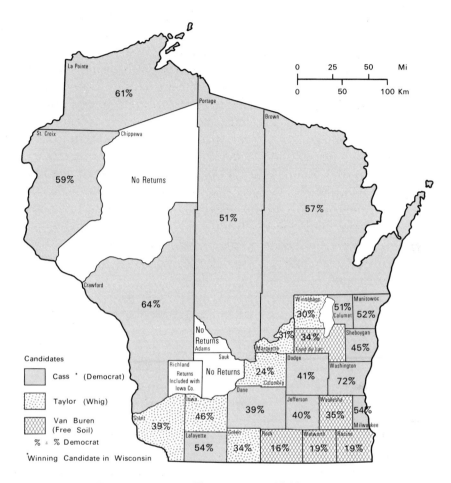

PRESIDENTIAL ELECTION, 1848

Milwaukee and above all Washington (then including Ozaukee), which contained the heaviest concentrations of German
immigrants. The Whigs had a plurality in six counties, among
them Grant and Iowa (but not Lafayette) in the southwest,
where people of Southern and of British stock were comparatively numerous.[10]

<hr />

[10] Smith, "Free Soil Party in Wisconsin," in *SHSW Proceedings,* 1894, pp.
115–118; Blue, "Free Soil Party," 75–87; Frederick J. Blue, *The Free Soilers:
Third Party Politics, 1848–54* (Urbana, 1973), 142–146. Unless otherwise noted,
all presidential election totals are from the *Wisconsin Blue Book, 1954,* p. 535.

When the legislature met in January 1849, one of the Free Soil assemblymen undertook to commit the state officially to his party's principles. He moved that the legislature instruct the United States senators from Wisconsin, and request the representatives, to oppose the formation of any territorial government without a slavery prohibition, to oppose the admission of any more slave states, and to seek the abolition of both slavery and the slave trade in the District of Columbia and in all other places under federal jurisdiction. In this set of resolutions the Democratic *Wisconsin* discovered an abolitionist plot. The paper charged that the extreme position taken was intended to provoke the negative votes of Democrats and thus allow the abolitionists to pose as the only true friends of free soil. Nevertheless, so popular did free soil appear to be that only three members of the entire legislature voted against the resolutions.[11]

A few weeks later, Senator Isaac P. Walker, whom the legislature had just re-elected for a regular six-year term, proposed to amend a Senate bill so as to extend federal laws over the Mexican cession without excluding slavery. "If the constitution will extend slavery to the land, then let it go," Walker declared. "If by the constitution slavery is extended, I am willing to stand by that constitution. If we cannot put a check upon slavery without doing violence to the constitution, I say let it be unchecked. For slavery, and the opposition to it, are creating a feeling disastrous—a state of things from which our country can reap nothing but disaster, in my opinion, and the agitation of which must enhance that disaster." When the news reached Wisconsin, even his Democratic friends thought he had "erred—sadly erred." Democrats joined with Whigs and Free Soilers in the legislature to censure him and demand that he either conform to the wishes of his constituents or resign. He did neither.[12]

By disavowing Walker, the Wisconsin Democrats hoped to

[11] Smith, "Free Soil Party in Wisconsin," in *SHSW Proceedings,* 1894, p. 123; Mary B. Mueller, "Crystallization of Antislavery Sentiment in Wisconsin and the Compromise of 1850" (master's thesis, Marquette University, 1954), 31–32.

[12] Flatley, "Wisconsin Congressional Delegation," 18–20, quoting the Madison (weekly) *Wisconsin Argus,* March 27, 1849, on Walker having "sadly erred."

maintain their credentials as true devotees of free soil. They reaffirmed their stand by again endorsing the principle in anticipation of the state elections of 1849. The regular party leaders now took the position that there was no need for a separate Free Soil organization. They welcomed the return of straying Democrats as individuals but rebuffed the Free Soilers when they proposed a combination of the two parties.

Once more in 1849, the two ran separate tickets with similar platforms, except for the Free Soil planks urging such populistic reforms as the direct election of the President and United States senators. The Whigs also tried again to lure voters away from the Free Soil party by means of an antislavery platform, but the Free Soilers ignored the Whig slate and concentrated their attacks on the Democratic ticket. "The ticket is composed of the most rabid proslavery Hunkers [the name given to the New York faction opposed to the Barnburners]," the Southport *Telegraph* contended, "to take whom as the representatives of the Free Soil resolutions which were adopted is simply humbug, so transparent that none should be deceived by it."

Deceived or not, the voters of Wisconsin elected the entire Democratic state ticket, headed again by Nelson Dewey, running for re-election as governor. The Democrats polled even more votes in 1849 than in 1848, a presidential election year. The Whigs suffered only a slight decline, but the Free Soilers lost more than 60 per cent of their previous support. Most of the Barnburners had gone back to the Democratic party, and that party had, for the time being, triumphantly survived the disruptive thrust of the slavery issue in Wisconsin.[13]

[3]

While the Democrats remained strong, the Whig party was seriously weakened, both in Wisconsin and in the country at

On Walker's career as a whole, see Merle Curti, "Isaac P. Walker: Reformer in Mid-Century Politics," in *WMH,* 34 (Autumn, 1950), 3-6, 58-62, quoting from Walker's speech in the U.S. Senate.

[13] Smith, "Free Soil Party in Wisconsin," in *SHSW Proceedings,* 1894, pp. 119-131, quoting on p. 128 from the Southport *Telegraph,* September 14, 1849; Boom, "Development of Sectional Attitudes in Wisconsin," 41-42.

large, as a consequence of the sectional crisis of 1850. The crisis was precipitated when President Taylor, to the consternation of Southern Whigs and Democrats alike, demanded the prompt admission of California as a free state. Southern politicians threatened that, if California thus came in, the slave states would go out. Congress began to consider proposals for compromising all the most urgent sectional disagreements and thereby heading off secession. These proposals would concede to the North the admission of California, the abolition of the slave trade (but not slavery itself) in the District of Columbia, and a decision for New Mexico in its boundary dispute with Texas. They would concede to the South the organization of New Mexico and Utah as territories without a prohibition of slavery, the federal government's assumption of the Texan public debt, and the passage of a new and stringent law for the return of fugitive slaves.

As each of the compromise bills was put to a vote, the Wisconsin delegation "presented an unbroken front on the right side," in the words of the *Wisconsin Express* of Madison. The state's two senators, both Democratic, and three representatives —a Democrat, a Whig, and a Free Soiler—voted for none of the measures except the admission of California and the abolition of the slave trade in the District of Columbia. All voted against the organization of Utah and New Mexico and against the fugitive-slave bill. They "stood up manfully," the Milwaukee *Sentinel* said, "in the defense of Northern Interests and Human Rights, and in resistance of Southern aggression and Slavery propagandism." Nevertheless, the pro-Southern as well as the pro-Northern measures passed both houses of Congress and received the signature of President Millard Fillmore to form the Compromise of 1850.[14]

To antislavery people in Wisconsin, as elsewhere in the North, the fugitive-slave law was the worst feature of the hated compromise. In the Milwaukee *Free Democrat* (successor to

[14] *Ibid.,* 50, quoting the Madison *Wisconsin Express,* August 1, 1850, and the Milwaukee *Sentinel,* September 2, 1850. See also Flatley, "Wisconsin Congressional Delegation," 22.

the *Wisconsin Freeman*) abolitionist editor Sherman M. Booth called upon all Wisconsinites "with a human heart in their bosoms" to defy the law. "It ain't a question of *niggers*," Booth wrote. "It's a question of humanity—whether we will be *men*, or barbarians and *brutes.*" Rufus King of the Whig *Sentinel* joined Booth and other antislavery editors in a demand for repeal. All over the state, opponents of the law, both whites and blacks, held protest meetings. A gathering in Winnebago County resolved: "The Fugitive Law has no binding force upon us, and therefore we will continue, as heretofore, to help the slave escape."[15]

In the Wisconsin elections of 1850 the compromise was not a party issue, however, since all three parties took the same stand on it. Again, each of the three elected a congressman. One incumbent, James Duane Doty, the former territorial governor appointed by the Whigs, had switched sides in 1848 and had accepted the nomination of the Democrats. Since then they had turned against him because his pro-tariff views conflicted with those of the party, and he now ran as an independent. The Whigs, making no nomination in his district, accepted Doty as their own candidate, and he won. Similarly, the Whigs refrained from opposing the Free Soil incumbent, the former Liberty man Charles Durkee, and helped to re-elect him also. The Democrats retained control of the assembly as well as the state senate.[16]

By 1851 the slavery question seemed to have lost most of its importance in Wisconsin politics. The Democrats in the legislature rescinded the 1849 censure of Senator Walker, since he voted for none of the compromise bills except the admission of California. Soon after the removal of the censure, Walker

---

[15] Boom, "Development of Sectional Attitudes in Wisconsin," 51–52, quoting the Milwaukee *Free Democrat*, October 2, 1850; Curtis W. Miller, "Rufus King and the Problems of His Era" (master's thesis, Marquette University, 1963), 47; Robert C. Robertson, "The Social History of Winnebago County, Wisconsin, 1850–1870" (master's thesis, University of Chicago, 1939), 48, quoting the Winnebago County resolution.

[16] Smith, "Free Soil Party in Wisconsin," in *SHSW Proceedings*, 1894, pp. 131–132; Flatley, "Wisconsin Congressional Delegation," 24–29.

in a Milwaukee speech made bold to endorse the compromise, fugitive-slave law and all. "Upon our soul," the Free Soil Kenosha *Telegraph* commented, "we cannot divine the object of his tergiversations, whifflings, somersets, and double-shuffles on the slavery question."[17]

That fall the Wisconsin Democrats resolved to stand on old Democratic principles and shun "all extraneous issues and sectional tests of party strength." The Free Soilers, now consisting mainly of Liberty party veterans, had little choice but to look again, as they had done the previous year, for Whig support. They decided to head their state ticket with Leonard J. Farwell, a wealthy Madison real-estate promoter ("owning nearly one half of the town site") and a prominent Whig. "I spent two or three days with Farwell at his bachelor home at Madison," Booth afterward recalled, "and rode half a day with him on the ice over the lake, trying to convince him that he had a call to be Governor of Wisconsin." Reluctantly accepting both the Free Soil and the Whig nomination, Farwell won the governorship by the narrow margin of about five hundred votes, 22,319 to 21,812. All the other Whig and Free Soil candidates for state offices, running on separate tickets, went down in defeat, though a Whig majority was sent to the assembly.[18]

The Farwell victory gave Wisconsin Free Soilers hopes of wielding the balance of power in state politics in 1852. "Whenever the Democratic party will dissolve its alliance with Slavery . . . we shall act with it," Booth announced. "Or, should the Whig party take the ground of Human Rights . . . we shall co-operate with *it*." Neither Democrats nor Whigs responded to the Free Soil offer.[19]

[17] Curti, "Isaac P. Walker," in *WMH,* 34: 60, quoting the Kenosha *Telegraph,* May 5, 1851.

[18] Smith, "Free Soil Party in Wisconsin," in *SHSW Proceedings,* 1894, pp. 132–135, for the quotation on "all extraneous issues"; Thomson, *Political History,* 76–80, for the quotations on Farwell.

[19] Smith, "Free Soil Party in Wisconsin," in *SHSW Proceedings,* 1894, pp. 135–136. The Booth quotation is from the Milwaukee (weekly) *Wisconsin Free Democrat,* January 14, 1852.

In 1852 the national Democratic convention enthusiastically and unanimously approved the Compromise of 1850 as a final settlement of the sectional controversy. For the Presidency, the Democrats chose the "dark horse" Franklin Pierce of New Hampshire, whom antislavery Northerners considered a "dough-face"—a Northern man with Southern principles. The Whig convention, with much less unanimity, only "acquiesced in" the compromise as a temporary adjustment. The Whigs again nominated a military hero of the Mexican War, this time General Winfield Scott of Virginia, whose attitude toward the compromise was unknown. The Free Soilers, with a platform re-affirming the Wilmot Proviso and denouncing the fugitive-slave law, picked as their candidate a former Liberty party leader, Senator John P. Hale of New Hampshire.

In Wisconsin the Whigs played down the slavery question and tried to make an issue of Franklin Pierce's opposition to internal improvements at federal expense. The Democrats could reply, however, that the Democratic senators and representatives from Wisconsin had always supported measures of that kind. Even Senator Walker, unwilling to disobey the state legislature a second time, had followed instructions and voted for a land grant to the Rock River Valley Union Railroad, though that road would lead to Chicago and not to Milwaukee, Walker's home. He said, "It will have the effect to drain the state of its very marrow and vitality, as it were, but the Legislature of Wisconsin have acted in favor of the measure, and it is not for me to oppose my wishes to theirs."

Internal improvements constituted the main issue in the congressional campaigns of 1852. None of the candidates opposed federal aid in itself, but they gave priority to different projects —the Fox–Wisconsin waterway, one Lake Michigan harbor or another, or this or that railroad line. This time the Whigs refused to co-operate with the Free Soilers in backing Congressman Durkee. The national Whig platform called for tariff raises, but Durkee was a free trader as well as a Free Soiler. Besides, he had failed to get an appropriation, which his constituents were demanding, for the dredging of the harbor at

Racine. Promoters of particular improvements poured thousands of dollars into the congressional campaigns, especially in what had been Doty's northeastern district, where large numbers of voters were aroused and brought to the polls.[20]

The presidential contest of 1852, in Wisconsin as in most of the nation, was exceedingly dull. One of the candidates, the Free Soiler John P. Hale, visited the state and stirred up a flurry of enthusiasm among his followers. The Wisconsin Democrats made strenuous efforts to bring out the foreign-born voters. Senator Walker, identifying himself with the "Young America" group in the national party, spectacularly offered "the blood and treasure of our land" to save liberty-loving people from despotism throughout the world. Democrats in the legislature carried a resolution expressing sympathy for the Irish in their struggle against British rule—which resolution the Whig governor, Farwell, vetoed on the ground that it cast gratuitous aspersions on the British. Whig papers tried to offset the Democratic appeal by describing Franklin Pierce as anti-Irish: he opposed a protective tariff, which Irish revolutionaries favored as a means of weakening Great Britain by reducing her foreign trade. To attract Norwegians, the Democratic Norwegian-language paper *Emigranten*, of Rock County, ran a Pierce campaign biography in installments. The Whigs countered with a Norwegian version of a Scott biography and one of Horace Greeley's book *Why I Am a Whig*. Despite all the efforts to excite Wisconsin voters, there was little or no proportional increase in the number of voters who went to the polls in 1852 as compared to the turnout for the presidential election four years earlier.

The Democrats carried the state for Pierce, though only by a narrow majority (33,658 for Pierce to 22,210 for Scott and 8,814 for Hale), while he won by a landslide in the electoral college. The Democrats also swept all three congressional elections and sent a large majority to both houses of the legislature. In the nation the Pierce victory meant an endorsement of the

[20] Flatley, "Wisconsin Congressional Delegation," 46–52, quoting Walker.

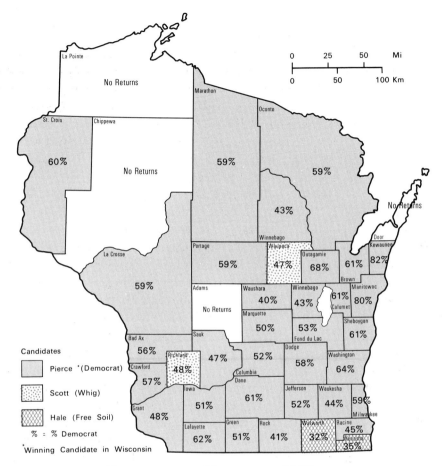

PRESIDENTIAL ELECTION, 1852

Compromise of 1850 and a temporary quieting of the sectional controversy. But the election left the Whig party irreparably torn as between its Northern and Southern members. Southern Whigs began to move into the Democratic party, but Northern Whigs—including those in Wisconsin—could seldom bring themselves to make that choice. They needed a new party.[21]

[21] Smith, "Free Soil Party in Wisconsin," in *SHSW Proceedings,* 1894, pp. 135–138; Curti, "Isaac P. Walker," in *WMH,* 34: 61–62, quoting Walker; McDonald, *Irish in Wisconsin,* 134–136; Blegen, *Norwegian Migration: American Transition,* 302–312.

[4]

By 1853 the Wisconsin Whigs were growing desperate. Again the Democrats controlled the government in both Washington and Madison—except for the governorship, still occupied by the Whig Farwell. His election had been the fruit of Whig co-operation with the Free Soilers. For Whigs, the lesson seemed clear. If they were to recover power in the state, they must agree to a complete Whig and Free Soil coalition. The Free Soilers were willing, as they had been for some time.

The two parties did co-operate in support of a single "People's" ticket. In the state elections in September 1852 for the newly established supreme court the candidate for chief justice on the People's ticket won, though the two candidates for associate justice lost. In the Milwaukee city election in March 1853 the combination, which had the backing of both Rufus King's Milwaukee *Sentinel* and Sherman Booth's *Free Democrat,* carried four of the five wards and elected a mayor.

These victories encouraged Whig and Free Soil leaders to make a combined slate for the fall election of state administrative officials. The coalitionists begged Governor Farwell to head the ticket but, more interested in business than in politics, he repeatedly declined to run again. This set back the coalition movement. At first the Whigs and the Free Soilers made separate nominations. When they finally agreed on a People's ticket, the Whig nominee for governor, Henry S. Baird, refused to withdraw in favor of the Free Soil nominee, who was now the People's candidate—Edward D. Holton, a well-to-do Milwaukee businessman and one of the founders of the Liberty party in Wisconsin.

The more or less united Whigs and Free Soilers continued to make an issue of the Compromise of 1850 and especially the fugitive-slave law. In 1853 a Free Soil member of the legislature, Christopher Latham Sholes, editor of the Kenosha *Telegraph,* introduced a "personal liberty" bill, which would have guaranteed a jury trial to persons claimed as fugitives, but the Democratic majority defeated the measure.

In the campaign for the People's ticket, the Free Soilers emphasized another and, they hoped, more effective vote-getting cause. This was temperance, which could be expected to appeal to the native Protestant majority, though it would certainly antagonize most of the immigrant minority, including the free-soil sympathizers among the German-born. At the election there was to be a referendum on the question of a "Maine law" for Wisconsin, that is, a law like the one in Maine prohibiting the manufacture or sale of alcoholic beverages. The People's candidates were known as thorough Maine-law men, and Holton promised that, as governor, he would gladly sign a prohibition act.[22]

While the Whigs and Free Soilers were drawing together, the Democrats in Wisconsin were showing a tendency to fall apart. Josiah Noonan, the Democratic boss, faced a factional revolt at the time he was reinstated as Milwaukee postmaster upon Pierce's inauguration in 1853. One of Noonan's most determined foes was the fiery Irish-born lawyer Edward G. Ryan, and one of Noonan's closest allies was circuit judge Levi Hubbell, a suave and handsome widower, from upstate New York. At Ryan's instigation, Hubbell had been impeached and was on trial for taking bribes, embezzling funds, usurping tyrannical authority, and "inducing females interested in suits before his court to submit themselves to be debauched by him." It was a case of Democrats against Democrats. Though Hubbell was finally acquitted, his reputation was badly damaged, and so was the cohesion of the party.[23]

[22] The supreme court was newly established in the sense that legislation enacted in 1852 provided for the organization of a separate court with three elected justices. From 1848 to 1852 as many as five elected district justices, when sitting *en banc*, comprised the supreme court. See *Laws of Wisconsin*, 1852, Chapter 395. See also Smith, "Free Soil Party in Wisconsin," in *SHSW Proceedings*, 1894, pp. 138–147; Hanneman, "First Republican Campaign in Wisconsin," 11–15. The German Free Soil leader, A. H. Bielfeld, made a desperate effort to exclude the temperance issue from the campaign. On temperance in Wisconsin, see Frank L. Byrne, "Cold Water Crusade: The Ante-Bellum Wisconsin Temperance Movement" (master's thesis, University of Wisconsin, 1951).

[23] Alfons J. Beitzinger, *Edward G. Ryan, Lion of the Law* (Madison, 1960), 31–39; Parker M. Reed, *The Bench and Bar of Wisconsin: History and Biography* (Milwaukee, 1882), 491–496; the quotation is from p. 494.

Ryan was not the only prominent Democrat to challenge
Noonan's party leadership. There was also William A. Barstow,
who had come from Connecticut, where he was born in 1813,
and had prospered as a merchant in Waukesha. Barstow was
one of the Barnburners who had returned to the party after
bolting it in 1848, and his faction included others who had done
the same. He was known as a magnetic person but an unscrupulous politician. Opponents spoke of him and his friends as
"Barstow and the balance" or "Barstow and the Forty Thieves."
The first phrase, originating while he was secretary of state,
came from the letter of a Madison newspaperman who was seeking a state printing contract and who assured his associates that
they would get it even if they had to "buy up Barstow and the
balance," that is, the balance of state officials responsible for
the letting. The second phrase came from Barstow's presumed
role as one of the lobbyists for the Rock River Valley Union
Railroad, who were dubbed "The Forty Thieves" because of
their insatiable demands.[24]

To Noonan's disgust, Barstow won the nomination for governor at the party convention in 1853. Barstow and his fellow
Democrats opposed a prohibition act, but during the campaign
he yielded to pressure from the temperance groups so far as to
make the equivocal statement that he would "feel it his duty,
if the representatives of the people pass a *constitutional* law, to
approve the same." Even without Noonan's help Barstow won
the governorship by a decisive majority (30,405 votes to 21,886
for Holton and only 3,304 for Baird). The Democrats also
carried the rest of their slate of administrative officials and
retained control of the legislature. In the referendum the prohibition forces nevertheless managed to gain an endorsement
of the Maine law by a vote of 27,519 to 24,109.[25]

After the election, Booth's *Free Democrat* and King's *Sentinel* urged the next legislature to carry out the popular will by

[24] Reuben Gold Thwaites, *The Story of Wisconsin* (Boston, 1890), 237–239.
[25] Hanneman, "First Republican Campaign in Wisconsin," 16–17; Smith,
"Free Soil Party in Wisconsin," in *SHSW Proceedings*, 1894, pp. 145–148, quoting Barstow (italics added). Unless otherwise noted, all referenda results are
from the *Wisconsin Blue Book, 1940*, p. 225.

quickly passing a prohibition act. When the legislature met, however, Governor Barstow merely noted the referendum result without taking a position on the question. The assembly chose as its speaker a Prussian-born opponent of temperance legislation, Frederick W. Horn. King began to advocate a compromise, suggesting a law that would exempt lager beer. Turning on his late ally, King now denounced Booth as a fanatic. "He would like nothing better than to get you all to quarreling about negro slavery, the Maine Law, woman's rights, or some such ridiculous trash." During the 1854 session the senate and the assembly finally passed separate liquor bills but failed to concur. So the state remained without a prohibition law.[26]

The Whig and Free Soil coalition, a loose patchwork to begin with, was torn by disagreements over the temperance issue. But the Democratic party was holding together no better as its factional disputes intensified. After the party's 1853 victory, won with little or no co-operation from Boss Noonan, the Ryan and Barstow Democrats determined to overthrow him. They deluged President Pierce and his postmaster general with letters demanding Noonan's removal from the Milwaukee post office. A delegation headed by Ryan and Barstow went to Washington to present their case in person. Some members of the group also urged the President to use his influence for the passage of a Rock River Valley Union Railroad land grant, which Noonan opposed (as did many prominent Milwaukeeans, including King and other Whigs). Pierce did nothing to save the railroad bill, nor did he remove Noonan from office. One thing he did do: he vetoed a rivers-and-harbors bill that was of great interest to many Wisconsinites. The "real effective" Democrats in Wisconsin, as Ryan said, were cooling toward the Pierce administration because of its ingratitude to them.[27]

By early 1854, parties and factions were fluxing in Wisconsin

[26] Hanneman, "First Republican Campaign in Wisconsin," 18, quoting the Milwaukee *Sentinel*, January 17, 1854; Joseph Schafer, "Prohibition in Early Wisconsin," in *WMH*, 8 (March, 1925), 294–295.

[27] Hanneman, "First Republican Campaign in Wisconsin," 52; Beitzinger, *Ryan*, 40–42.

as in many other states. A rearrangement of the floating pieces was about to be made, with a fusion of some of them to form a new and potent political organization. This was to result from dramatic events already unfolding on both the national and the Wisconsin scene.

[5]

In January 1854 the Democratic senator from Illinois, Stephen A. Douglas, presented Congress with his bill to organize the territories of Kansas and Nebraska. That area had been closed to slavery by the Missouri Compromise of 1820. But, as amended, the Douglas bill would repeal the antislavery provision of the Missouri Compromise and would allow the settlers in each of the two new territories to decide for themselves, under the principle of "popular sovereignty," whether or not to make slaveowning legal. As further amended, the measure would deny aliens the right to vote or hold office in either of the territories.

In Wisconsin, as in other northern states, the Kansas-Nebraska bill provoked immediate and unrelenting cries of outrage. Though it had the support of the Democratic Pierce administration, the bill met disapproval not only in Wisconsin's Whig and Free Soil newspapers but also in the great majority of the state's Democratic journals, including most of the foreign-language press, which deplored the amendment disfranchising aliens if not also the provision opening the territories to slavery. Here and there throughout the state, Free Soil leaders organized protest meetings. A Ripon gathering adopted the following resolution: "Resolved, that the passage of this bill (if pass it should) will be the call to arms of a great Northern party, such an one as the country has not hitherto seen, composed of Whigs, Democrats, and Free Soilers, every man with a heart in him united under the single banner cry of Repeal! Repeal!" The organizer of the Ripon meeting, Alvan E. Bovay, a lawyer born in New York state and college-educated in Vermont, proposed the name "Republican" for the new party. That name, he afterwards explained, was "suggestive of equality," had been "used by the party of Jefferson in its best and purest days," and was "the cherished name with our foreign population of every nationality."[28]

Both the Free Soiler Sherman Booth, in the *Free Democrat*, and the Whig Rufus King, in the Milwaukee *Sentinel*, called upon the state legislature to express itself in opposition to the Kansas-Nebraska bill. The senate failed to do so, but the assembly, with a majority of the Democratic members going along, urged the state's congressmen to oppose the measure. Taking heed, both of the Wisconsin senators and all three of the congressmen voted against it. When it nevertheless became a law, as it did in May, though without the amendment disfranchising aliens, the proponents of a new party were ready to act.[29]

Their determination had been reinforced, and the excitement over slavery had been intensified, as a result of recent events in their own state. These events began on a March night in 1854 when a deputy federal marshal and three associates entered a shack, about four miles north of Racine, where Joshua Glover, a runaway slave from Missouri, was playing cards with two other black men. The intruders bludgeoned Glover and, after a desperate struggle, manacled him and took him away in a wagon.

The next morning, Booth in Milwaukee received a telegram from the Racine mayor asking him to find out if a warrant had

[28] Hanneman, "First Republican Campaign in Wisconsin," 21, 25–26, 28, and quoting the Ripon resolution on p. 43 from the Milwaukee *Free Democrat,* May 11, 1854; Thomson, *Political History,* 110–111, quoting Bovay's statement to Henry Wilson regarding the name "Republican." Bovay claimed Ripon as the birthplace and February 28, 1854, as the birthdate and himself as the father of the Republican party. In fact, the Ripon meeting only proposed and did not organize a new party. Other "anti-Nebraska" meetings, throughout the North, also recommended a new organization. The term "Republican" seems to have occurred to a number of the protesters at about the same time. In Jackson, Michigan, a convention to form a state Republican organization met on July 6, 1854, one week before a similar convention met in Madison, Wisconsin. See Andrew W. Crandall, *The Early History of the Republican Party* (Boston, 1930), 20–21, and George H. Mayer, *The Republican Party, 1854–1964* (New York, 1964), 26–27.

[29] Hanneman, "First Republican Campaign in Wisconsin," 22–23, 29–30; Flatley, "Wisconsin Congressional Delegation," 57.

been issued for Glover's arrest. Making inquiries, Booth learned from the federal district judge that the slave's owner, Bennami Garland, had secured a warrant in accordance with the fugitive-slave act of 1850 and that the slave himself was lodged in the Milwaukee jail. Booth asked for a fair and open trial, but the act of 1850 made no provision for such. Rebuffed, he "mounted a dark, blazed-face horse, and full-bearded, bald-headed, and in trumpet tones, riding through the principal streets," called interested citizens to a meeting in the courthouse square. At the meeting, early in the afternoon, a crowd of several thousand adopted resolutions demanding Glover's release on a writ of habeas corpus.[30]

Late in the afternoon a hundred men from Racine landed at the Milwaukee wharf. They were led by the Racine County sheriff, who had a warrant for the arrest of the slaveowner and the deputy federal marshal for assault and battery on Glover. The hundred marched to the jail and joined a gathering mob. Booth advised against violence. Glover's volunteer counsel, G. K. Watkins, insisted that the prisoner, bloody and bruised as he was, must not be left without medical aid. Watkins told the people to ponder whether they should take matters into their own hands. Eventually, the mob made a rush for the jail door, rammed it open with a large timber, and set Glover free. A buggy took him to Waukesha, outdistancing pursuers. Later, sympathizers spirited him by night to Racine and put him on a boat, which carried him to Canada and safety.[31]

For the Glover rescue, Booth received more credit—or blame—than he deserved. He was arrested on a federal charge of violating the fugitive-slave act by aiding and abetting the escape. Jailed briefly, he was released on bond for later trial. He could

[30] The quotation is from Reed, *Bench and Bar*, 496–504. Some witnesses later testified that Booth on his horseback ride shouted "Freemen, to the rescue!" Reed's account and many others describe him as doing so, but Booth always denied making any such appeal. See William J. Maher, "The Antislavery Movement in Milwaukee and Vicinity, 1842–1860" (master's thesis, Marquette University, 1954), 53n.

[31] This account is based mainly on Maher, "Antislavery Movement in Milwaukee," 50–72, and partly on Reed, *Bench and Bar*, 496–504.

now appear as a martyr in the cause of human liberty. At his call, a mass meeting was held in Milwaukee, including delegates sent from meetings elsewhere in the state, to demand repeal of the fugitive-slave law and to lay plans for preventing slave recaptures. Thus Booth and others added freedom in Wisconsin itself to freedom in the western territories as an issue justifying the prompt formation of a new "Freedom Party."[32]

For tactical reasons, Booth wanted the Whigs to take the initiative in calling a convention to organize the new party, but Whig leaders hesitated, many of them hoping for a revival rather than a replacement of the old Whig organization. Finally, on June 9, Booth through his paper proposed a convention to meet in Madison on July 13. King in the *Sentinel* and Horace Rublee in the *Wisconsin State Journal* promptly followed suit, and before long almost all the Whig editors in the state did the same. Meanwhile local meetings either invited mass attendance at the Madison convention or elected delegates, including Democrats as well as Free Soilers and Whigs.

By the afternoon of July 13, so many delegates had poured into Madison—more than a thousand all together, hundreds by way of the recently opened railroad from Milwaukee—that the convention had to move from the confinement of the capitol to the warm and pleasant summer air outside. Most of those present were idealistic amateurs unused to the machinations of politics, and their enthusiasm ran high. But experienced Whig and Free Soil politicians controlled the proceedings, which they had carefully planned in advance. The members resolved "That we accept this issue [freedom or slavery], forced upon us by the slave power, and in the defense of freedom will cooperate and be known as Republicans." They elected a state central committee, applauded a string of speeches, and adjourned with resounding cheers for the new Republican party.

[32] Hanneman, "First Republican Campaign in Wisconsin," 46–49. Booth later said: "I aimed simply to secure for Glover a fair trial and competent counsel." See the Chicago *Chronicle*, May 2, 1897, clipping on file in the SHSW.

The Wisconsin Republican party, as it emerged in 1854, was an extension of the People's coalition of the previous year, with the addition of a number of Democrats. Former Whigs dominated the new party. As they got ready for the fall campaign, many local Whig organizations simply began to call themselves Republican and invited Free Soilers and Democrats to join. Yet the Republican politicians, whatever their party background, played down the continuities with the past and did their best to present themselves as newcomers to politics, as political innocents crusading for a high moral cause. Shrewdly they concentrated on the single issue of slavery—the one issue on which all Republicans could agree—and avoided any mention of temperance or any hint of nativism.[33]

With a fresh image for their party, the Republicans could hope to attract the votes of foreigners who in previous years had spurned the Whig and Free Soil candidates and the combined People's ticket. To reach the immigrant voters, the Republicans would have to break the Democrats' near monopoly of the foreign-language press. The new party won over several of the papers, including the Norwegian *Emigranten* of Inmansville, the Dutch *Nieuwsbode* of Sheboygan, and the German *Demokrat* of Manitowoc, *Zeitung* of Oshkosh, and *Pionier am Wisconsin* of Sauk City. In Milwaukee, however, the three German newspapers remained steadfastly Democratic, and so the Republicans set up a new one, *Korsar*, under the editorship of Bernhard Domschcke, a youthful Forty-Eighter who had just arrived in the city and had immediately distinguished himself by the virulence of his attacks on both the Roman Catholic Church and what he called the "Democratic Church."[34]

The Democratic "church" in Wisconsin was beset by schisms and heresies as it went into the campaign of 1854. The Kansas-Nebraska issue had widened the split between Governor Bar-

[33] Hanneman, "First Republican Campaign in Wisconsin," 49–50, 58–60, 71–77, 83–85. The resolution quoted is reported in the Madison *Argus and Democrat,* July 17, 1854, and the Milwaukee *Sentinel,* July 15, 1854.

[34] Blegen, *Norwegian Migration: American Transition,* 313–316; Hanneman, "First Republican Campaign in Wisconsin," 94–95; J. J. Schlicher, "Bernhard Domschcke," in *WMH,* 29 (March–June, 1946), 325–328.

stow and Postmaster Noonan. Barstow and his followers opposed the Kansas-Nebraska act and defied the Pierce administration, which attempted to make the act a test of party loyalty. Some of the "anti-Nebraska" Democrats wavered between the Barstow faction and the Republican party. Several Democratic candidates ran as Independents, with Republican support. The Noonan or Pierce Democrats used the federal patronage against their dissident fellow partisans and denounced them along with the Republicans.

To counteract the new party's appeal to immigrants, Democratic papers reminded them of that party's Whig antecedents and of the nativist streak in Whiggery. Noonan's Milwaukee *News,* for one, countered nativism with racism. Any "Adopted Citizen" who casts his ballot for a Republican, the *News* warned Milwaukee Germans, "votes to *rob himself of his religion and political rights,* and to put in power a party that seeks to elevate the native negro *at the expense of the foreignborn white man.*"

On election day the slavery issue brought out swarms of excited voters in most of the counties, especially in those that were heavily populated by native Protestants. In Milwaukee and the other lakeshore counties to the north of it, however, many of the Germans apparently found it hard to choose between the nativist stigma of the Republicans and the proslavery taint of the Democrats. These Germans could resolve their dilemma by staying home. The number of people who went to the polls, in the largely German counties, was smaller in 1854 than it had been in 1853. Thus, in its first campaign, the Republican party seemingly profited from the non-voting of certain German Democrats. It also gained from the voting of some Germans and other foreigners—though probably few if any Catholics—who now switched from Democratic to Republican ballots.[35]

When the 1854 election returns were in, the Republicans

---

[35] Suelflow, *A Plan for Survival,* 176–177, refers to the political dilemma of Lutherans. Hanneman, "First Republican Campaign in Wisconsin," 143–152, interprets the behavior of foreign-born voters in 1854, though without giving statistics. The Milwaukee *News* quotation is from the Milwaukee *Free Democrat,* November 6, 1854.

had good reason for self-congratulation. They had won two of the three congressional races, losing only in the first (south-eastern) district, where the incumbent Daniel Wells, Jr., an anti-Nebraska Democrat, polled a large enough majority in Milwaukee County to overcome the Republican majorities in Racine, Kenosha, and Walworth counties. In the next state legislature the Republicans, together with Independents and hold-over Whigs, would not quite have a senate majority but would nevertheless be in a position to control a joint ballot of the two houses and choose a Republican as United States senator.[36]

When the legislature met, in January 1855, the senate Democrats at first refused to agree to a joint session, hoping to delay the choice of a senator until the rival ambitions of former Whigs and Free Soilers had divided the Republicans and opened the way for the election of a Democrat. But the Republicans managed to agree on Charles Durkee, the former Free Soil congressman, and Durkee was finally elected to take the place of the controversial Democrat Isaac Walker, who in his six-year term had left a most equivocal record on the matter of slavery extension.[37]

One of two United States senators, two of three national representatives, and a majority of the state assemblymen, besides a large number of local officials had been elected! The new party, in less than a year, had done remarkably well. And it could expect, within the next twelve months, to add a governor and other state officers to its list.[38]

[6]

The Republicans were indeed to make one of their men the next governor, but only after an electoral dispute that for a time aroused fears of a civil war within the state.

The new party's prospects for the election of 1855 looked

[36] Flatley, "Wisconsin Congressional Delegation," 61–66; Hanneman, "First Republican Campaign in Wisconsin," 129–132, 139.

[37] Flatley, "Wisconsin Congressional Delegation," 68–70.

[38] *Wisconsin State Journal*, January 9, 1855; Madison *Argus and Democrat*, January 8, 1855.

better than ever when, early in the year, Republicans in the legislature uncovered evidence that pointed to mismanagement if not misfeasance on the part of the Barstow administration. One investigating committee reported that the contracts for the building of the state insane asylum had been let without fair bidding and had far exceeded the authorized sum. Another committee revealed that school lands had been sold to insiders for less than the value at auction, that the school fund had been depleted by improper loans and withdrawals, and that the books of the state treasurer and land commissioners were in "almost hopeless confusion." The state treasurer was the German-born Edward H. Janssen, whom the Democrats had twice put on their ticket in order to attract German voters.[39]

The Republicans in the 1855 legislature hurt their party's chances, however, when they made the mistake of reviving the temperance issue, which the party had wisely left alone during the recent electoral campaign. They did this at the insistence of Yankee "Maine law" members of the party and over the objections of German Republicans, who warned desperately against the danger to partisan unity. Temperance advocates introduced and passed two prohibition bills, the first exempting beer and light wine, the second prohibiting the sale—though not, as in Maine, the manufacture as well—of all alcoholic beverages. Governor Barstow vetoed both measures. Germans praised the Democratic governor for his good sense and condemned the Republican legislators for their "pious pretensions" and "Puritan bigotry."[40]

By espousing prohibition, the Republicans had thus laid themselves open to charges of nativism. The issue of nativism was intensified when, in June 1855, a national American

---

[39] Thomson, *Political History*, 121–122 (quotation); Malcolm J. Rohrbough, "The Acquisition and Administration of the Wisconsin Swamp Land Grant, 1850–1865" (master's thesis, University of Wisconsin, 1958), 79–80; Thomas H. Patterson, "The Disposal of Wisconsin's Common School Lands, 1849–1863" (master's thesis, University of Wisconsin, 1961), 64–77.

[40] Schafer, "Prohibition in Early Wisconsin," in *WMH*, 8: 296–297; Frank L. Byrne, "Maine Law Versus Lager Beer: A Dilemma of Wisconsin's Young Republican Party," in *WMH*, 42 (Winter, 1958–1959), 118–119; Milwaukee *Banner und Volksfreund*, October 16, 1855.

(Know Nothing) party was formed in Philadelphia, with a platform for excluding the foreign-born and all Catholics from public office. A party press, the *Daily American*, was set up in Milwaukee, and secret lodges multiplied throughout the state. Feeling against the nativist movement found expression, that summer, in the West Bend lynching of the Know Nothing youth George DeBar at the hands of a German mob.

The Democrats were ready to exploit the resentment on the part of German and other immigrants. Democratic newspapers treated the West Bend occurrence with circumspection. Some blamed Republicans for setting an example of lawlessness by flouting the law themselves—the federal fugitive-slave act. The DeBar lynching, Democratic editors said, was a natural consequence of the Glover rescue! At their state convention in Madison on August 31 the Democrats adopted a resolution thoroughly denouncing the nativist movement. They renominated Barstow for governor, though one delegate asserted that Barstow was himself a member of a Know Nothing lodge. They again named a German for state treasurer, Charles Kuehn, who took the place of the discredited incumbent, Janssen, on the ticket.[41]

The Republicans, at their state convention in Madison a few days later, also did their best to dissociate themselves from the Know Nothings. The convention declared itself in favor of the "equal rights of all men" and in opposition to "all secret political organizations" that advocated proscription on account of "birthplace, religion, or color." It nominated Coles Bashford for governor and Charles Roeser for state treasurer. Bashford, an Oshkosh lawyer, born in New York state, had led one of the senate committees in exposing the misdeeds of the Barstow regime, but he had also played a large role in the fight for a prohibition law. Roeser, born in Germany, editor of the Republican German-language paper in Manitowoc, assured his readers that Bashford was now putting prohibition aside and devoting himself to the "great issue of freedom." Again the Republicans were subordinating the temperance question to

[41] Joseph Schafer, "The Yankee and the Teuton in Wisconsin," in *WMH*, 6–7 (December, 1922–December, 1923), 7: 166–170.

the slavery question, but this time they had the additional issue of governmental corruption. They also had a German candidate to match the one on the Democratic slate.[42]

The Wisconsin leaders of the American party, according to the *Daily American*, had intended to present a ticket of their own, but they changed their minds after the Republican convention had met. The Republican candidates proved to be "mostly Americans, in *sentiment* and in *principle*, as well as in *name*." So the state council of the American party secretly directed the local councils to "poll the entire vote of the organization for Bashford, and the remainder of the Republican ticket." To the embarrassment of Republicans, the *Daily American* announced the Know Nothing endorsement shortly before the election. On the day after the election, the paper proclaimed: "The American organization of Wisconsin, has achieved, for the Republican party, its victory—if victory it has obtained."[43]

But *had* the Republicans won a victory? They had lost control of the legislature, gaining a majority of one in the senate but yielding a large majority to the Democrats in the assembly. The Republicans had not elected their German candidate for state treasurer, who had run far behind the rest of the ticket, many Know Nothing voters apparently having scratched his name. Indeed, the Republicans had carried none of their candidates for state offices—with the possible exception of their candidate for governor. For several weeks the outcome of the gubernatorial contest remained in doubt. Not till mid-December did the state board of canvassers, consisting of the secretary of state, the state treasurer, and the attorney general, and having the legal duty to certify the returns, give its final report. The canvassers certified their fellow Democrat, Barstow, as the winner by a mere 157 votes.[44]

[42] The first quotations are from Joseph Schafer, "Know-Nothingism in Wisconsin," in *WMH*, 8 (September, 1924), 12–18; the last is from Byrne, "Maine Law Versus Lager Beer," in *WMH*, 42: 119.

[43] Milwaukee *Daily American*, October 27, November 6, 7, 10, 1855.

[44] Schafer, "Know-Nothingism in Wisconsin," in *WMH*, 8: 20n; Reed, *Bench and Bar*, 481–482; Milwaukee *Daily American*, December 17, 1855.

Republicans charged the canvassers with fraud, and Bashford decided to contest the election. Excitement on both sides grew with the approach of inauguration day, January 7, 1856. Rumor had it that Bashford and his Republican friends were conspiring to occupy the capitol and use force to prevent the induction of Barstow. The Barstow men prepared a cache of arms and brought from Milwaukee and Watertown more than 250 Irish and German militiamen, all loyal Democrats. Inauguration day was bitterly cold, and the soldiers "presented a sorry sight as they paraded the streets with their benumbed fingers and frozen ears." The Republicans attempted no coup d'état. Without disturbance, Barstow was sworn in by a lower court judge for a second term. On the same day, however, Bashford appeared before Chief Justice Edward V. Whiton, a Republican, and took the oath as governor.[45]

When the legislature met, the assembly, with its large Democratic majority, promptly passed a joint resolution to communicate with "His Excellency William A. Barstow, Governor of the State." The senate, with its Republican majority of one, rejected the assembly resolution, but after defeating efforts to substitute Bashford's name for Barstow's and to insert the phrase "de facto Governor," adopted a resolution addressed merely to "His Excellency, the Governor of the State." The assembly concurred. For redress, Bashford looked not to the legislature but to the supreme court, two of whose three members were Republicans.

In the case of *Bashford v. Barstow*, the most conspicuous of the attorneys for the defense was Matthew H. Carpenter, a rising young Democratic lawyer of Beloit. Recently Carpenter had won a disputed election as district attorney for Rock County by persuading a circuit court and jury to look into returns that the local board of canvassers had disallowed. The supreme court had upheld the decision. Now, as Barstow's counsel, Carpenter reversed himself and contended that the supreme court had no constitutional power to go behind the

[45] The quotation is from Reed, *Bench and Bar*, 482–483. See also Beitzinger, *Ryan*, 43.

certificate of the canvassing board that had declared Barstow elected. But the court rejected a defense motion to dismiss the case for want of jurisdiction.[46]

Thereupon the defense surprisingly withdrew from the case. And, even more surprising, after having served only six weeks of his second term, Barstow resigned as governor. The lieutenant-governor, Arthur McArthur, immediately took over the executive office. By this maneuver, the Democrats could hope to hold on to the governorship, no matter what the court's ultimate decision might be, since the validity of McArthur's election as lieutenant-governor was not in question.[47]

The court proceeded to consider the evidence and argument of the prosecution, which was led by Edward G. Ryan, the head of one of the state's Democratic factions. And amazing evidence it proved to be. On the previous December 13 and 14, "after all the official returns had been in some days," as Ryan summed it up, a "shower of supplements" came in and "changed the entire result." Most if not all of the supplementary returns were forgeries. For example, those from Spring Creek, a nonexistent precinct purported to be somewhere in Polk County, and the returns from Gilberts Mills, a tiny settlement near Menomonie, in Dunn County, were written on the same unusual kind of watermarked paper, with the same peculiar phrasing, and in the same handwriting. Since the information for each place was written on half sheets of paper that had originally been a single full sheet, it became all the more apparent that the state canvassers in Madison had—at the very least—blundered by accepting bogus supplementary returns. The canvassers also certified returns from a second nonexistent precinct, Bridge Creek in Chippewa County, and they had tallied far more votes than there were legal voters for Waupaca, while raising Barstow's count there from 288 to 547 and lowering

---

[46] *Wisconsin Assembly Journal*, 1856, pp. 10–15, 22; *Wisconsin Senate Journal*, 1856, pp. 7–9; E. Bruce Thompson, *Matthew Hale Carpenter: Webster of the West* (Madison, 1954), 35–36, 40–45.

[47] Arthur McArthur was the father of General Arthur MacArthur (who changed the spelling of the surname) and the grandfather of General Douglas MacArthur. See *DWB*.

Bashford's from 219 to 59. Ryan expostulated, "It is a grievous reproach upon the whole State—a bitter and terrible reproach —that any man can be found to claim the meanest and lowest office—even that of fence-viewer or dog-catcher—on such frauds as these."[48]

On March 24, 1856, three days after Barstow's resignation, the supreme court gave its unanimous judgment that Coles Bashford had been elected governor on November 6, 1855. On the morning after the decision, Bashford along with Ryan and about twenty other men called on McArthur at the executive office and demanded possession of it. Yielding to an implied threat of force, McArthur rose from the governor's chair and left the room. When Governor Bashford sent his first message to the legislature, the Democrats in the assembly refused for a day to receive the message and then accepted it after drawing up a protest.[49]

The final victory of Bashford over Barstow turned out to be no triumph of virtue over vice. At the 1856 session, when the legislature disposed of Wisconsin's first federal land grants for railroad construction, overeager railroad enterprisers distributed favors among a number of legislators and state officials, Governor Bashford above all. Rumors of wrongdoing circulated at the time, but the full story was not to come out for two years. There was then to be revealed a political scandal fully as shocking as the attempt to steal the gubernatorial election of 1855.

[7]

For the time being, during the presidential election year of 1856, the Republicans in Wisconsin and other Northern states gained in popularity as public attention focused on events in "Bleeding Kansas," events that seemed to give added urgency

[48] *The Trial in the Supreme Court, of the Information in the Nature of a Quo Warranto Filed by the Attorney General, on the Relation of Coles Bashford vs. Wm. A. Barstow, Contesting the Right to the Office of Governor of Wisconsin* (Madison, 1856), 297, 300, 328, 340, 342.

[49] Beitzinger, *Ryan*, 45-46; Reed, *Bench and Bar*, 485-487.

to the cause of free soil. With the support of the Pierce administration, migrants from the South and "border ruffians" from Missouri were trying to make Kansas Territory a slave state. Without official authorization, arrivals from the North set up their own territorial government and formed a constitution for a free state. Guerrilla warfare broke out when a federal posse arrested free-state leaders and sacked the town of Lawrence, and John Brown and his followers in retaliation killed five proslavery settlers. To multiply the free-state voters and fighters, voluntary associations in the North stepped up the work of encouraging migration to Kansas, a work that the New England Emigrant Aid Company had begun.

In March 1856 a group of prominent Republicans and Know Nothings held a mass meeting in Milwaukee and organized the Kansas Emigrant Aid Society of Wisconsin. Promptly an agent of the society left for Kansas to spy out the land, and the leaders started to raise funds and recruit emigrants. Women assisted through a Ladies' Kansas Aid Society, which sponsored a concert and a dinner to raise money, solicited cloth as well as cash, and met in sewing circles to make clothing for needy pilgrims. In the spring a well-equipped train of fifty-five large wagons and several hundred men and women, who had gathered from all over the state, left Milwaukee for Kansas, and in the fall another expedition set out. The Wisconsinites in Kansas founded at least three towns, among them Holton, which they named in honor of Edward D. Holton, a generous sponsor of the Emigrant Aid Society. With letters sent back home telling of brushes with "border ruffians" and of a determination to make Kansas free, the emigrants helped to keep the issue alive in Wisconsin politics.[50]

Wisconsin voters were to have a choice among three presidential candidates: the Americans' and Whigs' Millard Fillmore, who as President had insisted on strict enforcement of the fugitive-slave law; the Democrats' James Buchanan, who, like

[50] The activities of the Emigrant Aid Society may be followed in the Milwaukee *Daily American,* March 7, 8, August 27, 30, September 8, 12, 20, 22, 26, October 8, 10, 11, 1856; Milwaukee *Sentinel,* March 6, 7, 1856.

Pierce, had a reputation as a "doughface"; and the Republicans' John C. Frémont, who was famous as an explorer but unknown as a politician. Most of the Americans in the North repudiated Fillmore and endorsed Frémont. Only a handful of those in Wisconsin—die-hard Whigs who were not yet sure that the Republican party had a future—were willing to back a state ticket of Fillmore electors. And several prominent Wisconsin Democrats, one after another, publicly defected to the Republican side.[51]

Campaigning with the slogan "Free Speech, Free Soil, Free Press, Free Kansas, and Frémont," the Wisconsin Republicans got considerable help from recent political enemies who appeared at Frémont rallies to tell why they were deserting the "Border Ruffian Democracy." But the open support by avowed Know Nothings and their organ, the Milwaukee *Daily American,* exposed the Republicans once more to the risk of alienating foreign-born voters, even those who were outraged by what the Democrats were doing in Kansas. The Democratic Norwegian-language paper *Norske Amerikaner* of Madison warned its readers against the "Republican Know Nothing[s]," the party of "all sorts of tinker-politicians, abolitionists, spiritualists, Whigs, desperate turncoats, and dissatisfied, sulking Democrats." On behalf of the Republicans, *Emigranten* of Inmansville countered by describing the election as a battle between "liberty, equality, and enlightenment on the one side, and slavery, despotism, and ignorance on the other."[52]

The Republicans redoubled their efforts to attract German voters. Party leaders purchased the Democratic paper *Volks-*

[51] Heading the list of Fillmore electors in Wisconsin was Harrison Ludington, a rising Milwaukee lumberman. Most of the leading Know Nothings in the state—the Frémont as well as the Fillmore adherents—appear to have been young business or professional men on the make. On their role in 1856, see the Milwaukee *Daily American* (which supported Frémont), August 18, September 11, 19, 24, 1856.

[52] *Ibid.,* September 5, 6, 13, 1856; Blegen, *Norwegian Migration: American Transition,* 316–317, quoting from *Den Norske Amerikaner,* November 1, 1856, and *Emigranten,* November 21, 1856. The Republican slogan, as quoted in the *Daily American,* September 13, 1856, is a variant of the more familiar "Free Soil, Free Labor, Free Men, Frémont."

blatt in Racine and brought the youthful Bavarian Henry Villard from Chicago to edit it and to give campaign speeches in both German and English. They acquired another and a very effective stump speaker in the Watertown Forty-Eighter Carl Schurz, who carried the Republican message in German to communities that previously had not heard it—and to some that did not want to hear it. Other German-speaking orators joined with English-speaking campaigners at huge rallies of both immigrants and natives in Milwaukee and elsewhere.[53]

While hoping to win over Protestants among the foreign-born, the Republicans could hardly expect to make converts of Catholics, either Irish or German. Know Nothing supporters of the Republican party, who generally identified it with the American party, were more than content to leave foreign-born Catholics with the Democratic party. The Milwaukee *Daily American* had seen evidence of "foreign influence and papal powers" in the 1855 Democratic nominations for the city—the candidate for state senator and four of the five candidates for assemblymen being either Irish or German Catholics. "In a year or two more," the *Daily American* had predicted, "the democratic party will consist almost entirely of priest-led foreigners, and opposed to it will stand the American party, *upheld in a great measure, by the protestant foreign population.*"[54]

In the presidential election of 1856 almost twice as many Wisconsinites voted as had done so in 1852. They cast 66,090 ballots for Frémont, 52,843 for Buchanan, and only 579 for Fillmore. These returns were quite different from those in the nation as a whole, where the combined Frémont and Fillmore tallies made a majority but Buchanan won with a plurality of the popular vote. In Wisconsin, as was to be expected, the Republicans did best in townships and counties having the highest proportion of English-speaking (except Irish) and Scandinavian inhabitants. The Democrats ran strongest in

[53] *Memoirs of Henry Villard: Journalist and Financier, 1835–1900* (2 vols., Boston, 1904), 1: 59–67; Chester V. Easum, *The Americanization of Carl Schurz* (Chicago, 1929), 121–122, 147; Milwaukee *Daily American*, August 28, September 13, 1856.

[54] *Ibid.*, November 6, 1855.

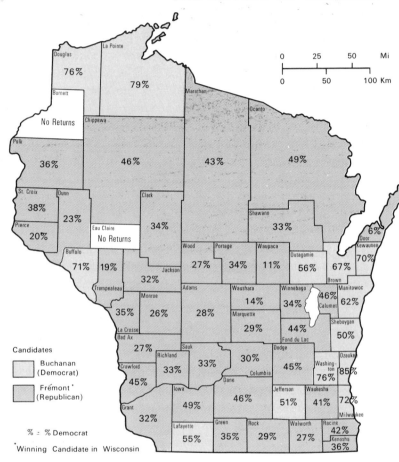

PRESIDENTIAL ELECTION, 1856

places containing the largest numbers of Irish, German, or
other non-English-speaking (except Scandinavian) immigrants.
Thus Buchanan got nearly 72 per cent of the vote in Milwaukee County while receiving less than 42 per cent in the rest of
the state.[55]

[55] Schafer, *Four Wisconsin Counties*, 140–158; Joseph Schafer, *The Winnebago-
Horicon Basin: A Type Study in Western History* (Madison, 1937), 307–324;
Bayrd Still, *Milwaukee: The History of a City* (Madison, 1965), 591, giving
returns supplied by the Division of Records and Elections of the State of
Wisconsin.

In the western and northern districts the Republicans easily re-elected their congressmen, Cadwallader C. Washburn and Charles Billinghurst. In the southeastern district, where their candidate was John Fox Potter, they had a scare when his Democratic opponent ran up a tremendous majority in Milwaukee County, but Potter accumulated enough votes in Kenosha, Racine, Walworth, and Waukesha counties to take the election, though by a margin of only 306 in a total of 28,000.[56]

The Republicans won a large majority of both the senate and the assembly seats. Once again, they were in a position to choose a United States senator. But, when the legislature met in January 1857, the Republican members were so badly divided that they had to hold four caucuses and go through nineteen ballots before finally making a choice.

Republicans differed among themselves over the clash between the federal and state courts in proceedings arising from Sherman Booth's rescue of Joshua Glover. On three occasions in 1854 and 1855, the Wisconsin supreme court had issued writs of habeas corpus freeing Booth from federal court jurisdiction on the grounds that the fugitive-slave act, under which he had been indicted and convicted, was unconstitutional. The state supreme court had also refused to send the records of the Booth proceedings to the United States supreme court in response to a writ of error. In effect, the state was nullifying a federal law.[57]

When it came to choosing a United States senator, Booth and other antislavery radicals made state rights a test of Republican orthodoxy. They refused to vote for anyone who would not endorse the principles of the Virginia and Kentucky Resolutions of 1798–1799 (to the effect that each state had the

[56] Flatley, "Wisconsin Congressional Delegation," 75–77.
[57] Maher, "Antislavery Movement in Milwaukee," 64–68; Joseph Schafer, "Stormy Days in Court—The Booth Case," in *WMH*, 20 (September, 1936), 89–110. The cases and issues involved have frequently been confused with a separate civil court proceeding known as *Garland v. Booth,* arising from a suit by Garland, Glover's former owner, to recover damages. See Gilbert S. Roe, ed., *Selected Opinions of Luther S. Dixon and Edward G. Ryan* (Chicago, 1907), 96–101, for a summary of the various criminal and civil proceedings. See also pp. 270–271, 276, below.

right to decide whether federal laws were constitutional) and who would not uphold the Wisconsin supreme court in "shielding the inhabitants of the state from the operation of unconstitutional enactments." The leading contender, Timothy O. Howe of Green Bay, himself a former state supreme court judge, balked at the idea that a state court could exercise appellate jurisdiction over a federal court. So the nomination went to James R. Doolittle of Racine, a resigned state circuit court judge who had only recently left the Democratic party, bolting in mid-campaign after failing to get the Democratic nomination for congressman, but who had managed to satisfy the anti-slavery Republicans of his devotion to state rights. Doolittle defeated the Democrats' senatorial nominee by a vote of seventy-nine to thirty-seven.[58]

Thus, by 1857, the Republicans had come to dominate the politics of Wisconsin, having elected the governor, an overwhelming majority of the state legislators, all three of the congressmen, and both of the United States senators—not to mention the five presidential electors.

[58] James L. Sellers, "Republicanism and State Rights in Wisconsin," in the *Mississippi Valley Historical Review,* 17 (September, 1930), 217–220; Flatley, "Wisconsin Congressional Delegation," 77–82. The resolutions from which the quotation is taken appeared in the *Wisconsin State Journal,* January 20, 1857.

7

Panic and Depression

[1]

" Business is very quiet; money matters in the whole United States are depressed," Carl Schurz wrote in Watertown on September 20, 1857. "How far the financial crisis which has recently broken upon us may go is still hard to determine." In fact, the depression following the Panic of 1857 was to go deeper and last longer in Wisconsin than in most other states. In the North as a whole the business collapse (as measured by total liabilities of bankrupts) was less than a fourth as bad for 1858 as for the year of the crash. In Wisconsin it was nearly twice as bad. Not until late 1860 was the state on the way to recovery, and then was to come the secession of the South, bringing on a new financial crisis in Wisconsin and throughout the North.[1]

The Panic of 1857 provoked runs on the banks as holders of banknotes tried desperately to turn them in for cash. Though no Wisconsin banks failed, many of them temporarily suspended specie payments. Wildcat banks continued to evade noteholders by maintaining offices in remote and inaccessible locations. At the onset of the panic, forty-five bankers met in Milwaukee to consider setting up a bankers' association and a central note-redemption system. In 1858, at the bottom of the depression, they succeeded in forming the Association of Banks of Wisconsin, but the forty-five members represented only

[1] Joseph Schafer, ed. and trans., *Intimate Letters of Carl Schurz, 1841–1869* (Madison, 1928), 179; Frederick Merk, *Economic History of Wisconsin During the Civil War Decade* (Madison, 1916), 222–223.

about half of the banks in the state, and nothing came of the redemption proposal. That same year, the legislature amended the banking act of 1852 so as to require every bank to keep a redemption center in a town having at least 200 voters, but the law had little effect.[2]

While the association banks tightly restricted their own lending and note issuing, others went on printing promises to pay that had little or no backing. For two or three years, Wisconsin suffered from an extreme scarcity of coin and reliable bank money, and from a great overabundance of banknotes with uncertain and fluctuating value. Businessmen had difficulty in finding means of payment that would be acceptable to creditors in the East. Wheat dealers could usually get loans from sound Wisconsin banks, since wheat sales would bring in Eastern money. Merchants and manufacturers selling in the Wisconsin market, however, often were unable to obtain bank credit.[3]

Because of the "money famine," merchants and manufacturers had to barter with their customers in order to stay in business. A Menasha sash-and-door manufacturer, for example, carried on many of his transactions by "swapping accounts." In return for his wood products he received "hay, hams, town lots, horses, cows, and Village orders," using these to pay his suppliers and his employees. Even in good times, J. I. Case had run into trouble as he toured the countryside and tried to collect from buyers of his Racine-made threshers. During the hard times he returned from his tours with horses, wagons, hogs, cattle, lumber, land titles, and gold watches, which he accepted from farmers who simply had no money.[4]

Some impoverished Wisconsinites looked for economic salvation in a then fairly common plant that grew wild, close to

[2] Theodore A. Andersen, *A Century of Banking in Wisconsin* (Madison, 1954), 34–40.

[3] William E. Derby, "A History of the Port of Milwaukee, 1835–1910" (doctoral dissertation, University of Wisconsin, 1963), 209–212.

[4] Schafer, ed., *Intimate Letters of Carl Schurz*, 182–183; Alice E. Smith, *Millstone and Saw: The Origins of Neenah-Menasha* (Madison, 1966), 119–120; Stewart H. Holbrook, *Machines of Plenty: Pioneering in American Agriculture* (New York, 1955), 43–44.

the ground, in shady places. This was ginseng. Its man-shaped, aromatic root found a ready market in China, where it was prized as a medicine of almost magical properties. During the summer of 1858, when the depression was at its worst, a ginseng craze developed in parts of Wisconsin, especially in Bad Ax (Vernon), Richland, and Sauk counties. "Men go out with wagons and teams and provisions and bedding, and camp in the woods to dig Gin Sang," recorded one of the enthusiasts, who was gathering roots in the vicinity of Ironton (Sauk County). "All classes of men are digging, some make as high as three dollars per day," he said. "In the extreme money pressure it is all the article that will fetch cash. . . ."[5]

[2]

The land boom of the mid-fifties gave way to a land bust in the last years of the decade. Sales of federal land in the state fell off dramatically—from 1,730,508 acres in 1855 and 1,538,652 in 1856 to 195,960 in 1857, 78,139 in 1858, 45,280 in 1859, and 36,882 in 1860.[6]

Even the largest and most successful land speculators were hard-pressed. Cadwallader C. Washburn retrenched by closing his Mineral Point office, moving to La Crosse, and discontinuing a part of his lumber business. He searched the country for loans with which to pay taxes on his holdings and interest on his debts, which his borrowing increased. Many small speculators lost heavily. Carl Schurz, for one, was left with an embarrassing burden of debt when Watertown stopped growing and the lots in his subdivision remained unsold. Townsite promoters were ruined. Within a year after the panic, the population of Superior City, lately such a booming place, had dropped from 2,500 to 500.[7]

[5] Diary of Jabez Brown, September 18, 1858, in the Jabez Brown Papers.
[6] James W. Whitaker, "Wisconsin Land Speculation, 1830–1860: Case Studies of Small Scale Speculators" (master's thesis, University of Wisconsin, 1962), 55.
[7] Clare L. Marquette, "The Business Activities of C. C. Washburn" (doctoral dissertation, University of Wisconsin, 1940), 218; Chester V. Easum, *The Americanization of Carl Schurz* (Chicago, 1929), 157–158; Louise P. Kellogg, "The Rise and Fall of Old Superior," in *WMH*, 24 (September, 1940), 3–19.

Some disappointed Wisconsinites joined the Colorado gold rush, which began in 1858. Yet, despite the depression, the booster spirit in Wisconsin was not entirely crushed. People in Prescott, a village of 1,000 at the juncture of the St. Croix and the Mississippi, still expected the village to become eventually the metropolis of the upper Midwest. "Pike's Peak is nowhere in comparison," the local editor assured his readers at the beginning of 1860; "a bright future is before us."[8]

The depression set back the industrial development of the state. Large-scale manufacturers with reserve funds or available credit generally managed to survive, though not to expand. Small, individual enterprisers or two-man or three-man partnerships, with only a few hundred dollars invested and with little or no machinery, were in many cases forced out of business; but they were usually able to make a new start, since they needed only minimal financing to do so. On the whole the medium-sized firms, with an investment of several thousand dollars, were the hardest hit. Once they had collapsed, they seldom succeeded in obtaining sufficient funds to resume operations at the same level.[9]

Lumbering, along with flour milling the state's dominant industry, went through three discouraging years after the panic. During the first year, receipts of lumber at the port of Milwaukee (the figures provide a rough measure of production on the Green Bay watershed) decreased by more than half—from 71,135,000 feet in 1857 to 32,127,700 in 1858. In the Chippewa Valley, the crash ended a speculative boom that had produced approximately 75,000,000 feet of lumber in 1855. Lead mining, already deteriorating before the crash, hastened in decline thereafter, as operators abandoned marginal mines in despair. But flour milling continued to grow and prosper in counter to the general downward trend. Milwaukee millers by 1860 produced about 300,000 barrels for commercial use, while flour shipments from the port of Milwaukee rose from 188,000 bar-

[8] Lawrence H. Larsen, "Pierce County in 1860," in *WMH*, 42 (Spring, 1959), 177.

[9] Margaret Walsh, *The Manufacturing Frontier: Pioneer Industry in Antebellum Wisconsin, 1830–1860* (Madison, 1972), 10–11n.

rels in 1856 to 298,000 in 1858 and 458,000 in 1860.[10]

Wheat growing predominated more and more in Wisconsin agriculture. The acreage planted in wheat—which had been increasing with the stimulus of high prices and railroad construction during the boom years—continued to increase during the hard times after 1857. For the farmer, wheat had the advantage of being a readily marketable cash crop. By 1860, wheat cultivation had spread north of the Wisconsin River and to the thinly wooded valleys of the Driftless Area. Indeed, it had assumed greater and greater importance in all the settled parts of the state except in the extreme southeast, where it already had been most highly developed.[11]

The state's wheat harvest in 1857 was fairly large—about 14 million bushels—but the price was low. In 1858 and again in 1859 the crop fell short because of persisting drought. Then came a mild and open winter, an early spring, and abundant rainfall during the growing season. The size of the crop harvested in 1860 was amazing: nearly 29 million bushels, almost twice as large as any before. And the price was higher than it had been at any time since the panic. Farmers would remember 1860 as the "golden year." After the 1860 harvest, Wisconsin stood second only to Illinois among all the wheat-producing states.[12]

Wisconsin farmers, as well as those on the Iowa and Minnesota wheat frontier, depended mainly on the railroads for carrying wheat—and the railroads depended largely on the farmers for traffic—especially after the lines from Milwaukee reached the Mississippi River at Prairie du Chien (1857) and La Crosse (1858). True, the growers could still dispose of some of their grain in local markets, and at first the railroads seemed likely to enlarge these markets by providing an out-

[10] Merk, *Economic History*, 61, 111; Robert F. Fries, *Empire in Pine: The Story of Lumbering in Wisconsin, 1830–1900* (Madison, 1951), 20–21; Walsh, *Manufacturing Frontier*, 181; Derby, "History of the Port of Milwaukee," 196, 243.

[11] John G. Thompson, *The Rise and Decline of the Wheat Growing Industry in Wisconsin* (Madison, 1909), 39–56, 139–141.

[12] Merk, *Economic History*, 16–19; Joseph Schafer, *A History of Agriculture in Wisconsin* (Madison, 1922), 91–92.

let for local flour mills. Thus, after the La Crosse and Milwaukee had reached Kilbourn City (Wisconsin Dells), a new mill was built in Baraboo, sixteen miles away. The neighboring farmers, as one of them later recalled, "began to think they were in the swim, by having a flouring mill at hand to buy their wheat and a railroad so near"; they expected to make extra money by hauling barrels of flour from the mill to the depot. With the improvement of the lower Fox River, farmers and millers along the route could send their products to market by boat, and the quantities of wheat and flour passing through the Appleton locks increased a great deal from 1857 to 1860. But Milwaukee became more and more the entrepôt for Wisconsin wheat, plus much of the Iowa and Minnesota wheat. By 1858, only about one-sixth of the Milwaukee grain receipts was still arriving by team and wagon; the rest came by rail.[13]

The railroads' rate policies added to the difficulties of many Wisconsin wheat growers during the lean years of the depression and subtracted from the gains of the growers during the "golden year" of 1860. All farmers, of course, had welcomed the railroads in the expectation that they would lower the cost of marketing crops. For a time, the railroads actually did so, and with the coming of the depression they reduced their charges over those stretches where they faced competition. Where no competing line existed, however, the railroads made up for the reductions by keeping rates high. Thus the Milwaukee and Mississippi charged more for carrying the wheat of Wisconsin farmers from Madison to Milwaukee than for carrying the wheat of Iowa and Minnesota farmers all the way from Prairie du Chien to Milwaukee. In 1857 the *Wisconsin State Journal* complained that it cost as much for Dane County growers to ship their grain to Milwaukee by rail as by wagon (and that it cost as much to haul freight from Milwaukee to Madison as to bring it from "eastern ports" to Milwaukee). In the autumn of that year, in response to protests, the Mil-

[13] Harry E. Cole, ed., *A Standard History of Sauk County, Wisconsin* . . . (2 vols., Chicago, 1918), 1: 93; Smith, *Millstone and Saw*, 126; Derby, "History of the Port of Milwaukee," 174.

waukee and Mississippi reduced its rates on wheat from Madison to Milwaukee, but restored them to the previous level after less than three weeks.[14]

After a slight decline in 1857, the wheat trade of Milwaukee recovered and shipments increased dramatically in the ensuing years from 2.6 million bushels in 1857 to 4 million in 1858 and 4.6 million in 1859, while those of Chicago were falling from 9.5 to 8.7 and 7.3 million. Concerned Milwaukeeans had to improve their facilities for taking care of the rapidly swelling volume of grain. In 1858 grain dealers, railroad companies, and bankers converted the Corn Exchange into the Chamber of Commerce and devised a new grading system for wheat, a system well adapted to bulk handling and the use of elevators. The Milwaukee and Mississippi guaranteed a monopoly of its grain-storage business to anyone who would erect an adequate structure, and then the La Crosse and Milwaukee did the same. As a consequence, two large, modern steam elevators were built.[15]

Though wheat cargoes leaving Wisconsin ports increased during the depression, lake shipping as a whole diminished. The amount of lumber reaching the port of Milwaukee fell by nearly a third between 1858 and 1860, while clearances at the port for vessels engaged in foreign trade declined through the end of the decade. Full recovery for the merchant marine was not to come until the big harvests of 1860 and 1861 and the outbreak of the Civil War.[16]

[3]

No Wisconsin enterprises suffered more from the depression than did the railroads. One after another they went bank-

[14] Thompson, *Wheat Growing Industry*, 143–147; Benjamin H. Hibbard, *The History of Agriculture in Dane County, Wisconsin* (Madison, 1904), 140–142; Herbert W. Rice, "Early History of the Chicago, Milwaukee and St. Paul Railway Company" (doctoral dissertation, State University of Iowa, 1938), 237–238.
[15] Derby, "History of the Port of Milwaukee," 177–178, 203–209.
[16] Merk, *Economic History*, 372–373; Derby, "History of the Port of Milwaukee," 245, 250.

rupt, and the bondholders took control of them under receiver-
ships. This threatened ruin to the several thousand farmers
who had helped to build the railroads by mortgaging their
farms and exchanging the mortgages for railroad stock. The
stock, which the farmers had expected to yield a profit in
addition to covering the interest on the mortgages, now ceased
to pay dividends and became practically worthless. The mortgages were in the hands of the bondholders, most of them Easterners, who had been induced to lend to Wisconsin railroads
by the pledge of Wisconsin farm land as security. If the bondholders should foreclose, the mortgagers would have to pay
up or lose their farms—unless they could find a way out of
their dilemma.

Farmers, who recently had greeted the railroad as their best
friend, now began to look upon it as their worst enemy. Their
feelings were intensified by the discriminatory and, as they
saw it, extortionate freights they were charged and also by
revelations of mismanagement, corruption, and fraud on the
part of the railroad companies. Company officers were shown
to have watered their stock, misused corporate funds for private ventures, contracted with construction firms in which they
were secretly interested, and defrauded stockholders in various
other ways. Three corporations—the Milwaukee and Superior,
the Milwaukee and Beloit, and the Wisconsin Central—had
received a total of more than $800,000 in farm mortgages and
loans from local governments and had dissipated the entire
proceeds without putting into operation a single mile of track.
The mortgagers were convinced that the railroads' financial
collapse and their own resulting plight were due not so much
to the general business depression as to the specific wrongdoing
of the railroad managers.[17]

The worst scandal, one that by itself seemed to confirm the
farmers' view, involved president Byron Kilbourn and other
officials of the La Crosse and Milwaukee. These officials had

[17] Rice, "Chicago, Milwaukee and St. Paul Railway," 125–126; Merk, *Economic
History*, 243–245. The Wisconsin Central should not be confused with the Wisconsin Central Railroad Company incorporated in 1870.

overloaded the company with obligations in their campaign to obtain a large portion of the federal land grant in 1856. Kilbourn's report for 1857, published when the railroad was on the verge of bankruptcy, confessed that the land grant, "so eagerly sought," had, "by the expenses of the contest for its possession," contributed largely to the "present embarrassments of the Company." The report listed bonds totaling $2,210,000 and stock in the amount of $90,000 which the company had issued for the purchase of other railroads with claims to the grant (the St. Croix and Lake Superior and the Milwaukee and Watertown) and also for unspecified and mysterious "services" and "charter expenses." Rumors arose to the effect that Kilbourn and his associates had used a large part of these funds as bribes to induce the legislature to favor the La Crosse and Milwaukee in assigning the grant.

The rumors were verified when the legislature got around to making an investigation in 1858. As the investigating committee discovered, the company officials had distributed more than $800,000 in bonds and money, mostly in bonds, as "pecuniary compliments." Of this total, the sum of $530,000, in parcels ranging from $5,000 to $25,000, went to the fifty-nine assemblymen and thirteen senators who had voted for the land-grant bill. Nothing was given to the twelve assemblymen and thirteen senators who had voted against it. Governor Coles Bashford received $50,000 for signing the measure. Another $16,000 provided tokens of appreciation for compliant clerks of the two houses and various state officials, and $246,000 was divided among such helpful men of influence as Alexander Mitchell, Daniel Wells, Jr., James Ludington, and Milwaukee *Sentinel* editor Rufus King. The rest of the bonds were divided among Kilbourn and the company directors as a reward for their services in the transaction.[18]

Kilbourn and his friends justified this wholesale bribery on

[18] Rice, "Chicago, Milwaukee and St. Paul Railway," 158–160, quoting from the *Annual Report* of the La Crosse and Milwaukee Railroad Company, 1858, p. 16, and from the *Wisconsin Assembly Journal Appendix*, 1858, pp. 4–10, 47, which contains a listing of those who co-operated with the La Crosse and Milwaukee officials.

the ground that his company had been compelled to counteract the similar methods of a rival Chicago-based company. The act of 1856 to dispose of the federal grant, while conferring the western portion upon the La Crosse and Milwaukee, had awarded the eastern portion to the Wisconsin and Superior. The Chicago, St. Paul and Fond du Lac had then got its own people on the board of the Wisconsin and Superior by paying its previous directors to resign, and had thereby acquired the eastern grant. Though exposing this much, the investigating committee of 1858 refrained from pursuing the charges that the Chicago firm also had bribed or plotted to bribe some of the legislators. But Kilbourn insisted that it had done so, that it had schemed to monopolize the entire grant, the western as well as the eastern part, and that his own company had acted in the best interest of Wisconsin as well as itself by heading off the danger from outside. "Suppose we had failed, and offered as an excuse that it would have cost a million dollars to have secured the grant, while at the same time by the expenditure of a million and a half, payable in its stock, the Chicago Company should have secured the prize?" So Kilbourn asked in a pamphlet he wrote in reply to the legislative committee's report. "Would not every citizen and every stockholder have blamed us for our stupidity? Would they not have taunted us with the loss of land worth ten or twelve millions?"[19]

The La Crosse and Milwaukee grant was worth even more than that, according to the commissioner of the road's land department, Moses Strong, who somehow had arrived at the precise figure of $17,345,600. Whatever the value of the land, the company's officials were never to obtain title to it. After going to such ruinous expense to influence the legislature, they failed to lay track over the route the law required them to follow in order to secure confirmation of the grant. Thus

[19] Frank N. Elliott, "The Causes and the Growth of Railroad Regulation in Wisconsin, 1848–1876" (doctoral dissertation, University of Wisconsin, 1956), 162–167, quoting from Byron Kilbourn, *Review of the Report Made by the Committee of Investigation to the Legislature of Wisconsin Relating to the Land Grant* (Milwaukee, 1858), 22.

the company lost the one great asset that might have served to liquidate the stockholders' mortgages and save their farms. Organizing what they called a "home league," the mortgagers demanded that the state set aside the forfeited land and use the proceeds from its sale to relieve them from their debts.[20]

While the farmer stockholders of the bankrupt La Crosse and Milwaukee grew more and more desperate, those of the tottering Milwaukee and Mississippi were trying to salvage their company and safeguard their farms by getting rid of what they considered the dishonest and incapable management. Earlier, when they pledged their farms for stock, they had been told that, as stockholders, they themselves rather than out-of-state capitalists would own and control the company. Now, in 1858, they were putting the idea of the farmer's railroad to the test. They appealed to the eastern investors for support, sending them a circular letter that asked them to visit Wisconsin and look into the misconduct of the corporation directors. A representative of the Easterners came to the state and talked with some of the farmers, but at the stockholders' meeting he sided with the directors, and the farmers' candidates to replace them were defeated. Soon afterward the company defaulted on its interest payments, and the bondholders instituted foreclosure proceedings in a United States district court in New York.[21]

As the threat to their homes came closer, the farm mortgagers of all the railroads turned to the legislature for relief. They now made much of a legal point they had ignored when they were eagerly swapping mortgage notes for railroad stocks in the expectation of a sure profit. The transactions, the farmers in their adversity asserted, had been void from the beginning, for all the railroad charters had specifically required money payment for the stock. So, in collecting mortgages, the railroad

[20] Rice, "Chicago, Milwaukee and St. Paul Railway," 160–161; Merk, *Economic History*, 250. Strong's figure was probably inflated as an inducement to investors.

[21] Philip A. Schilling, "Farmers and Railroads: A Case Study of Farmer Attitudes in the Promotion of the Milwaukee and Mississippi Railroad Company" (master's thesis, University of Wisconsin, 1964), 59–61, 64–65.

companies had been guilty of fraud! Responding to this argument, the legislature passed a series of stay laws. An act of
1858 stopped foreclosure proceedings in cases where the mortgagers could prove they had signed their notes under the persuasion of "fraudulent representations by the railroad agent,"
and denied to mortgage holders the right to plead that they
were "innocent purchasers without notice." An act of 1859
lengthened and complicated the procedure of foreclosing, and
an act of 1860 made it possible to advance the charge of fraud
as a defense even against unknown holders of the notes.[22]

Understandably, these laws provoked an outcry on the part
of the eastern bondholders, who insisted with some justice that
they had purchased the mortgages along with the bonds in good
faith. Throughout the East, Wisconsin acquired a reputation
as a repudiating state, one that was attempting to spare its people from the responsibility of their just debts. Within the state
many businessmen, especially those from Milwaukee, deplored
the legislation, fearing that it would worsen their already
serious difficulties in obtaining out-of-state capital and credit.
To the relief of both eastern bondholders and Wisconsin businessmen, and to the distress of Wisconsin farmers, the state
supreme court declared the stay laws unconstitutional in 1860,
as soon as it had a chance to review cases involving them. The
court ruled, in *Clark v. Farrington* and *Blunt v. Walker,* that
the farm mortgages were valid contracts and that the holders
were entitled to foreclose.[23]

In reaction to the court's decisions, the mortgagers promptly
set up a Grand State League to co-ordinate the existing local
leagues and to represent the farmer stockholders of all the
railroads involved (a total of eight companies). Among the
leaders of the movement were large and well-to-do landowners,
including former railroad officials. The organization sponsored

[22]Elliott, "Railroad Regulation in Wisconsin," 57–59, quoting from the
Laws of Wisconsin, 1858, p. 47.
[23]Schilling, "Farmers and Railroads," 56–57, 67; Merk, *Economic History,*
250–251.

a weekly paper, the *Home League,* which Alexander M. Thomson edited and published (1860–1864) at Hartford (Washington County). Thomson described the controversy as a struggle between vice and virtue: on the one hand, the "Railroad thieves and their apologists," who were "in the pay of Wall Street"; on the other hand, "five or six thousand men who have been cheated and defrauded in the most shameful and disgraceful manner." Under pressure from the Grand State League, the legislature passed a succession of new acts to protect the mortgagers, but again the state supreme court eventually disallowed the more efficacious ones. Between 1858 and 1863 a total of fourteen such measures were adopted, ten of which the court declared unconstitutional.[24]

While they were in effect, the debtor-protection laws intimidated eastern creditors into considering compromise settlements. The disallowance of the laws left a mortgager with little choice but to accept a compromise if one was offered. The farmer's only alternatives were dismal: to pay his debt if he could, a debt that was steadily increasing because of the accumulating interest; to submit to foreclosure and the loss of his farm; or forcibly to resist any attempt at collection.

"Will you *force* us from our homes?" the Grand State League demanded. *"We will meet that force in kind."* When a Milwaukee lawyer arrived in Prairie du Chien to foreclose some thirty mortgages, "a large body of men took peaceable possession of him," as the Milwaukee *Sentinel* reported, "shut him up, burned his papers, and kept him close till the next train started, when he was put on board and 'ticketed through' to Milwaukee." In a few instances farmers resorted to violence, putting obstructions on tracks, removing rails, destroying bridges, cutting telegraph poles, even setting fire to a depot. But resistance was futile. Sooner or later many farmers who could not or would not pay were evicted along with their families. Probably few of the mortgagers ever paid their notes in

[24] Schilling, "Farmers and Railroads," 69–72; Merk, *Economic History,* 247–248, 254–255.

full. Some escaped foreclosure by accepting compromises; several hundred of the Milwaukee and Mississippi stockholders settled by surrendering their stock and paying a fraction (one-fourth or less) of the principal due on their mortgages. To compensate La Crosse and Milwaukee stockholders who had lost money on their mortgages, a part of the corporation's forfeited land grant was eventually (1868) turned over to the Wisconsin Railroad Farm Mortgage Land Company to be sold for their benefit. This company grossly mismanaged its land sales, and netted less than $250,000, which had to be divided among more than a thousand mortgagers whose verified claims exceeded $1,300,000.[25]

The question of the railroad farm mortgages was to drag on for many years (the Wisconsin Railroad Farm Mortgage Land Company was not to wind up its affairs until 1883). To the end of their lives the distressed farmers and their sympathizers were never to forget the agonies of uncertainty, of monetary sacrifice, of complete impoverishment. With these feelings went an undying hatred of "Wall Street" and the railroads.

[4]

During the depression a great many property owners besides the railroad farm mortgagers found themselves burdened with debts that became increasingly difficult to carry. In Trempealeau County alone, as of 1860, though there were only 2,560 people and 291 farms, there were 367 mortgages, including those on village property. Throughout the state, warned a correspondent in the *Wisconsin Farmer* of April 1, 1860, foreclosures threatened to bring about "thousands of unjust sacrifices of farms and homesteads, for a little or nothing, to rapacious and heartless creditors," though another writer in the same issue insisted that fewer than one in four of the people

[25] Rice, "Chicago, Milwaukee and St. Paul Railway," 136–137, 161; Schilling, "Farmers and Railroads," 84, 92–96; Merk, *Economic History*, 261–270, quoting from the Milwaukee *Sentinel*, January 16, 1861.

were in debt and that most of the debtors could "get out even in the present hard times" with one or two good crops. In fact, many did so with the golden wheat harvest of that year.[26]

Worse off than property owners, even those with heavy debts, were propertyless workers who lost their jobs with the retrenchment or the bankruptcy of their employers. Often workmen lost back pay along with their jobs. When a Milwaukee lumber firm went out of business, several employees who said they had "worked for the establishment a long time without receiving anything but due bills," and who were "greatly incensed at not getting what was due them when they were discharged," broke into the company office, smashed the furniture, and threatened one of the company executives with violence if he did not settle with them immediately. They were arrested, but, "no one appearing to complain against them," were released, still without their wages. Amid the widespread unemployment, workers who kept their jobs hesitated to strike, whatever their grievances.[27]

Thousands of the jobless and their families sank into pauperism. They could look to neither the state nor the federal governments for assistance, but had to depend on local authorities and private groups. At a time when revenue was falling off, town and county boards faced the necessity of spending more and more to take care of the poor. During 1859–1860 they provided relief, in or out of poorhouses, for 5,256 indigents (as compared with 666 in 1849–1850) at a total cost of

[26] *Eighth Census of the United States, 1860: Population,* 544; *ibid.: Agriculture,* 219; Merle Curti, *The Making of an American Community: A Case Study of Democracy in a Frontier County* (Stanford, 1959), 156–159; Paul W. Gates, "Frontier Land Business in Wisconsin," in *WMH,* 52 (Summer, 1969), 318–319, quoting from the *Wisconsin Farmer,* April 1, 1860. Gates on 319n observes: "No study has been made for Wisconsin or any other state of the proportions of entries and of land acquired directly by potential farm makers from the government, nor are there available data concerning the number and acreage of entries that were promptly mortgaged."

[27] Milwaukee *Sentinel,* September 17, 1858. The *Sentinel* of July 27, 1860, when a business recovery was under way, reported a successful strike of 250 journeyman tailors.

$126,500 (more than eight times the $14,743 of a decade earlier).[28]

Private charity supplemented public aid, especially in the cities. The Milwaukee Relief Society, founded in 1855, set up soup kitchens which fed more than 700 persons during the winter of 1857–1858 and more than 900 during that of 1859–1860. The society financed its operations partly by selling meal tickets to those who could afford them and wished to donate them to the poor. It trusted to "the benevolence of our citizens for the food to be supplied." The Roman Catholic Society of St. Vincent de Paul, organized about 1850 to help the needy immigrants of Milwaukee, was nearly bankrupted by the demands made upon it after the panic. Reorganized in 1858, this society distributed flour, wood, candles, cloth, soap, and clothing to more than seventy families during the winter of 1859–1860. A German relief association, formed in 1857, assisted the German poor in Milwaukee, and the benevolent societies of various native and foreign groups, in Milwaukee and elsewhere, cushioned the shock of the depression for their respective members.[29]

Public and private relief together fell short of meeting the wants if not the needs of all the unemployed. Some turned to begging, stealing, or robbing. In the spring of 1858 one desperate character waylaid a Neenah businessman returning from Appleton after selling window shades there, knocked him down, cut his throat, and made off with the proceeds of the sales—nine dollars. Horse thieves became increasingly numerous and active throughout the state. One of them, captured and held in the Richland County jail, was said to have given the names of twenty-six gang members who formed a chain extending from Lone Rock to Sparta. Horse owners, taking matters into their own hands, organized anti-horse-thief societies (the first one apparently in Sheboygan in 1857)

[28] Curti, *Making of an American Community*, 284; Donald J. Berthrong, "Social Legislation in Wisconsin, 1836–1900" (doctoral dissertation, University of Wisconsin, 1951), 19; *Eighth Census of the United States, 1860: Mortality and Miscellaneous Statistics*, 512.

[29] Bayrd Still, *Milwaukee: The History of a City* (Madison, 1965), 236–237; Peter Leo Johnson, *Crosier on the Frontier: A Life of John Martin Henni, Archbishop of Milwaukee* (Madison, 1959), 109; Smith, *Millstone and Saw*, 91.

to offer rewards, recover stolen property, and ferret out the culprits. While crime appeared to increase, police protection was diminishing. To economize, the city of Milwaukee not only halted street and bridge construction, thus incidentally lessening job opportunities, but also cut down the size of the police force. After that, Milwaukeeans complained continually about the inadequacy of police protection. Among offenders who were caught, tried, and convicted in the state, immigrants outnumbered native Americans by more than two to one (542 to 212 for the year ending June 1, 1860).[30]

No community service suffered more than education. "We hear all about us the cry of *hard times,*" one educator wrote during the first depression winter, "and it is weighing heavily upon our Common Schools." Already most of them were shortening the winter term so as to save money; fewer than ever were going to remain in session for the legal minimum of three months. The writer argued that the amount spent on tobacco in any district would enable a school to maintain and even lengthen its regular term. "When will men be wise and curb appetite, instead of robbing the minds of their children?" Another educator remonstrated, after the worsening depression had brought even more serious consequences for the schools: "Whiskey, Beer, Race Horses, Chess, Billiards, Land Sharking, Gambling, &c. will pay but educating people will not."[31]

In 1859 the state superintendent of public instruction reported that in Columbia County alone 1,000 children were being kept out of school because their parents were so impoverished they could not provide adequate clothing. He rec-

---

[30] Menasha *Conservator*, April 1, 1858; Milwaukee *Sentinel*, October 7, 1857, and July 12, December 10, 1860, for accounts of horse thievery. The legislature eventually passed a bill for the more effectual punishment of horse thieves, providing a two-to-fifteen-year sentence. See the Milwaukee *Sentinel*, February 6, 1861, and *Laws of Wisconsin*, 1861, p. 57. See also Still, *Milwaukee*, 233, 238; *Eighth Census of the United States, 1860: Mortality and Miscellaneous Statistics*, 512.

[31] *Wisconsin Journal of Education*, 2 (February, 1858), 246; William H. Herrmann, "The Rise of the Public Normal School System in Wisconsin" (doctoral dissertation, University of Wisconsin, 1953), 87, quoting William S. Baker to Henry Barnard, June 8, 1859[?], in the Henry Barnard Manuscripts, New York University.

ommended that the length of the legal school year be left at three months instead of being extended to four as he had earlier proposed. At the state teachers' convention in 1860, attendance was extremely low, and the reason given was the "long-continued pressure of hard times and the consequent non-payment of teachers."

By 1860, even the larger city school systems were in serious trouble. In Milwaukee, after falling far behind in paying teachers, the school board suspended all classes for two months, until the city council could provide funds. When the council did so, the board found it had to cut the annual budget by more than half, from $70,000 to $32,000. Sixteen teachers were dropped, though there was already an average of sixty-one pupils per instructor. The two high schools, opened in 1858, were closed. In Madison, where a schoolhouse had been planned for each of the four wards, the two buildings under construction were completed in 1857, but plans for the other two were abandoned. The Madison school year was reduced to two twelve-week terms from the previous three. Before long the high school was to be discontinued so that the two ward schools could be maintained. In Racine the school board expected only a third of its usual income, so much had tax collections fallen off. Anticipating a $3,000 deficit for the next school year, the Racine board considered closing the schools but finally decided to keep them open as long as teachers could be "obtained with the means at our disposal, trusting to the interest and good sense of the people—asking them to come forward and pay their School Tax and educate their children."[32]

The depression set back the development of higher educa-

[32] Lloyd P. Jorgenson, *The Founding of Public Education in Wisconsin* (Madison, 1956), 190–192; Still, *Milwaukee*, 218–220; Helen F. Patton, "Public School Architecture in Racine, Wisconsin and Vicinity from the Time of Settlement to 1900" (doctoral dissertation, University of Wisconsin, 1965), 343–344, quoting from the Proceedings of the Racine Board of Education, April 12, 1860. In May 1860 the Milwaukee city council approved a $25,000 appropriation to add to the $7,000 the schools received from state funds. See Augustus J. Rogers, "History of Education and the Public School System," in Henry E. Conrad, ed., *History of Milwaukee from Its First Settlement to the Year 1895* (3 vols., Chicago, [1896]), 1: 131.

tion as well as primary and secondary schooling. Private colleges, already scrimping to make ends meet before the panic struck, had to resort to even stricter economies afterward. Having managed to obtain enough subscriptions to a building fund, Racine College authorities in 1857 celebrated the Fourth of July by laying the cornerstone for Kemper Hall, then suddenly found it impossible to collect on the pledges that had been made. The Episcopal Church, sponsor of both Racine College and Nashotah Seminary, economized in 1859 by transferring the seminary's preparatory department to Racine and combining it with the college.

Friends of the academy in Ripon had to postpone their plans for converting it into an institution of collegiate rank. The chancellor and trustees of the University of Milwaukee abandoned the charter they had obtained at the height of the boom, in 1855. Forgotten now were the expansive words with which the chancellor had then announced the founding. He had declared that a city destined for greatness ought to have a university and that enterprising citizens, by supporting it with their donations, would be contributing not only to "the welfare of their children, and the interests of solid learning" but also to "the material prosperity of our favored city" and to "the value and augmentation of their own private fortunes."[33]

With that potential rival stillborn, and with other private institutions struggling to stay alive, the state university at Madison might have been expected to establish its pre-eminence. But the University of Wisconsin also was suffering from the shrinkage of its financial resources. By an 1860 ordinance the regents limited the faculty to five professors and one tutor and cut their salaries. To complete a building program already under way, the regents vainly sought a loan from the legislature and had to reduce operating expenses and draw from current income. They persuaded Henry Barnard, the

[33] William F. Allen and David E. Spencer, *Higher Education in Wisconsin* (Washington, D.C., 1889), 55–59. The quotation is from Still, *Milwaukee*, 223. Racine College was to survive the panics of 1857 and 1873, but was to go under during the depression of the 1930's.

school superintendent of Connecticut, nationally famous as
an advocate of public education, to come to Madison and
serve as both chancellor of the university and general agent
of the board of normal-school regents. Barnard proved to be
much more interested in teacher training than in university
administration. Afflicted with illness and frustrated by the
lack of finances, he left Wisconsin in 1860, a year after his
arrival.[34]

While the normal-school fund dwindled, more and more
academies and colleges sought a share of the fund under the
law of 1857 that provided for state aid to private institutions
maintaining normal departments. As a result, the number of
students preparing to be teachers grew—at a time when employment opportunities for them were declining—and the subsidy per student and per institution decreased. The payment
to Lawrence University, for example, fell from $2,400 for
1857–1858 to $1,620 for the following academic year, while
enrollment in the college's normal department rose by ten.[35]

Education for the handicapped underwent a temporary re-
verse after 1858, when, in a mood of retrenchment, the legislature decided that only the children of indigents, with certification from local authorities that the parents were financially
unable to provide support, should be educated at state expense.
Enrollment at the Wisconsin Institute for the Education of the
Blind, in Janesville, immediately fell from twenty-five to five.
The next year the school's annual report protested that such
institutions were "necessary features of a liberal system of popular education," and the school's head visited the capitol with
his students to demonstrate the teaching methods. Thus persuaded, the legislature repealed the act of 1858, and thirty-two
pupils were enrolled in 1859–1860.[36]

Cultural activities in general faltered as voluntary groups

[34] Merle Curti and Vernon Carstensen, *The University of Wisconsin: A History,
1848–1925* (2 vols., Madison, 1949), 1: 114, 120–152; Herrmann, "Normal School
System," 83–86; Allen and Spencer, *Higher Education in Wisconsin*, 27–28.

[35] Herrmann, "Normal School System," 105–108.

[36] Berthrong, "Social Legislation in Wisconsin," 36–38, quoting from Wisconsin
Institute for the Education of the Blind, *Annual Report*, 1858, p. 30.

promoting them ran into financial difficulties. For instance, the Young Men's Association of Milwaukee had to curtail its lecture program for a time. Even the *Musikverein,* whose subscribers had kept its treasury full during the prosperous years, found its resources badly depleted after the panic.[37]

[5]

It would be impossible to measure the traumatic effect that the hard times had on the people of Wisconsin, but certainly a great many of them experienced a psychological as well as an economic and social shock. During the prosperous years they had assumed that, with a bit of luck and a good deal of labor, they could hardly fail to get ahead. The panic and depression must surely have caused them to lose some of their faith in themselves.

It must also have caused them to question their belief in the almost automatic progress, moral as well as material, of the society of which they were a part. While preoccupied with making their individual fortunes, people could ignore or forget the public evils that were reported around them: the mob lawlessness and the lynching, the skulduggery in politics that extended to the stealing of a gubernatorial election. It was harder to dismiss the evils that came to light after the panic: the spectacular frauds on the part of corporation insiders, the unblushing bribery of legislators and other officeholders. Other states too had their scandals, of course; but the cumulative news from Wisconsin gave this state a special reputation for wrongdoing, a reputation that grew still worse in many quarters when the legislature abetted thousands of residents in their attempt to repudiate their debts to nonresidents.

At least a few of the state's more thoughtful men began to question the soundness of the Wisconsin character, to ponder the reasons for its apparent deterioration, and to consider rem-

[37] Still, *Milwaukee,* 119, 215.

edies that might yet make possible the realization of the earlier promise. One of these philosophers was the German-born Carl Schurz, a lawyer-politician who was a liberal and a Republican. Another was the Irish-born Edward G. Ryan, also a lawyer-politician but a conservative and a Democrat.

Schurz developed the theme of degeneration and regeneration when, in July 1859, as a regent of the University of Wisconsin, he gave the address of welcome to the new university chancellor, Henry Barnard. Most of the people of Wisconsin, he began, had come here to improve their condition. That was right and proper, and the people had done amazingly well by dint of their boldness, energy, hard work, and skill at mechanical arts and sciences. But, he went on, there was a "dark side of the picture." The "spirit of materialism" and the "pursuit of gain" had gone too far: they had "almost exclusively presided over our councils" and had taken almost "exclusive possession" of the people's souls. "It is but natural that a tendency like this should have left its mark on the character of a social organization which like ours was founded on the basis of material interest," Schurz concluded. "This is the point where a higher order of popular education has to interpose its ennobling influence." Education, then, was the remedy.[38]

Addressing the annual meeting of the State Historical Society of Wisconsin in February 1860, Ryan described the same symptoms as Schurz had done but differed with him in regard to the cause and the cure. In territorial days, Ryan said, the pioneers had been industrious and honest, the laws fair, the government well-administered. Now, after only a dozen years of statehood, corruption had permeated government, business, and society itself. Wisconsin, which Ryan once had called the "paradise of western civilization," seemed at present about to become a "paradise of folly and knavery." Success was valued above honor; money above intellect or integrity. The fundamental reason: in migrating to Wisconsin from far-off, scattered places, from eastern states and European countries,

[38] Schurz had recently given essentially the same speech at Beloit College. Easum, *Schurz*, 207–210.

too many of the people had left behind the moral standards and controls of their various home communities. The only solution: a new society must be fused from the diverse elements in the state. Until this was done, Wisconsin "would probably remain less a community than a mob."[39]

The society had not yet jelled, the political system had not yet attained responsibility and trustworthiness, and the economy had not yet fully recovered when Wisconsin was confronted with a new and terrible trial. Immature though the state was, it had to face the disruption of the Union of which it was a part, and then had to meet the challenge of the Civil War.

[39] Alfons J. Beitzinger, *Edward G. Ryan, Lion of the Law* (Madison, 1960), 52–54.

8

State Rights or the Union?

IN 1860–1861 eleven states of the South, asserting the doctrine of state rights in an extreme form, were to defy the authority of the federal government by seceding from the Union. For several years before that, however, the most thoroughgoing champion of state rights in defiance of federal authority was none of the Southern states. It was Wisconsin.

Unlike the Southern states, Wisconsin invoked the doctrine in opposition to, rather than in support of, the institution of Negro slavery. The Wisconsin stand dated from the rescue of the fugitive slave Joshua Glover in 1854 and the state supreme court's refusal to yield his rescuer Sherman M. Booth to federal jurisdiction in 1854 and again in 1855.

As of 1857, still the antislavery hero, Booth stood at the peak of his influence in Wisconsin politics. He and other antislavery radicals dominated the Republican party, the party that prevailed at the state capital. Early in the year, the legislature finally passed a "personal liberty law," following the example of other legislatures in the North. This law, designed to frustrate the federal fugitive-slave act of 1850, assured the right of habeas corpus to persons detained as fugitive slaves, and it prohibited the use of any state agency to assist in their detention. At the same session, the legislature also provided for a new referendum which, if the voters should approve at the fall election, would at last give the ballot to Wisconsin's blacks.[1]

But the Democrats continued to hold power in Washington, and the national Democratic party remained under the domination of its Southern and proslavery elements. President James Buchanan, inaugurated in March, was quite acceptable to them. Shortly after he took office the Supreme Court, under Chief Justice Roger B. Taney, a former slaveholder, rejected the suit of Dred Scott, a Missouri slave who was seeking his freedom on the basis of long residence in Wisconsin Territory (in a part that later became the state of Minnesota) at a time when slavery was prohibited there by federal law. Taney held that, so far as the federal Constitution was concerned, Scott was not a citizen and therefore had no right to sue, and that indeed blacks had no constitutional rights at all that whites were "bound to respect." Taney and a majority of his colleagues went on to rule that, in any event, Congress had no constitutional power to exclude slavery from any of the territories.

Booth and his friends held a mass meeting in Milwaukee, on June 17, to consider the Dred Scott case "and other matters." Among the speakers, in addition to Booth, were two abolitionists of much greater notoriety—Gerrit Smith, a financier of reform from New York state; and John Brown, a grim, fierce-eyed man from Kansas, who the year before had seen to the revenge killing of five proslavery settlers there, and who two years later was to attempt a much more far-reaching antislavery enterprise at Harpers Ferry, Virginia, with Smith's financial as well as moral support. The Milwaukee meeting adopted resolutions denouncing both the Dred Scott decision and the fugitive-slave law. Democrats ridiculed the gathering, the Milwaukee *News* reporting it under the headline "The Negro Worshippers in Council." Some Republicans were embarrassed

[1] Robert N. Kroncke, "Race and Politics in Wisconsin, 1854–1865" (master's thesis, University of Wisconsin, 1968), 23; Leslie H. Fishel, Jr., "Wisconsin and Negro Suffrage," in *WMH*, 46 (Spring, 1963), 185–187.

by it and took pains to dissociate themselves from it as an unauthorized scheme to "abolitionize" their party.

When, in September, the Republican state convention met in Madison, it nevertheless adopted a platform reaffirming the resolutions of the June mass meeting and declaring that the Taney opinion, in denying citizenship to Negroes, ignored the "great political truth" that, "in the absence of positive enactments to the contrary, birth upon the American soil constitutes the best of our titles to American citizenship." But the Republicans cautiously avoided a direct endorsement of the proposition to make Negroes full citizens in Wisconsin by giving them the right to vote. Instead, the Republicans merely resolved that they were "utterly hostile to the proscription of any man on account of birthplace, religion, or color"—thus seeking to absolve themselves of Know Nothing prejudice against the foreign-born as well as racist prejudice against native blacks. Democrats insisted that the Republicans had indeed come out for Negro suffrage and that, "by that action republicanism and *niggerism* became one in Wisconsin." The Democratic convention, assembled in Madison in August, had put forth a platform that explicitly denounced suffrage for blacks and roundly condemned the "odious doctrine of negro equality."[2]

Turning to nominations for state offices, the Republican convention had run into a deadlock over the governorship. One of the two leading contenders was Walter D. McIndoe, a Scotsman by birth and "neither a church member nor a moralist." The other was Edward D. Holton, a New Englander and a Congregationalist, whose zeal in the temperance cause was sure to make him unpopular among German voters, even the freethinkers and Protestants. Finally a majority of the delegates settled upon Alexander W. Randall, a Waukesha lawyer from New York state, as a compromise candidate. The jaunty, tou-

[2] Kroncke, "Race and Politics in Wisconsin," 24–27, refers to the Republican resolutions printed in the Milwaukee *Sentinel*, September 7, 1857; he quotes the Democratic platform as it was published in the Madison *Argus and Democrat* on September 5, 1857. A Democratic reaction to the convention was published in the *Argus and Democrat*, September 4, 1857.

pee-wearing Randall, already bald though not yet thirty-eight, was a prominent Methodist layman but was reputed to have no aversion to playing cards or taking a drink in private. His political record was various. Originally a Whig, he had become successively a regular Democrat, a Free Soiler, and an independent Democrat before running for attorney general, and losing, on the Republican ticket in 1855. In 1857 he was acceptable to antislavery radicals because of his Free Soil principles and his early, as early as 1846, advocacy of Negro suffrage. He was approved by many delegates because of his Democratic background, which was expected to draw Democratic votes, and because of his effectiveness as a stump speaker, one who knew how to "fit the vein" of any audience.[3]

When it came to choosing a Republican candidate for lieutenant governor, Booth took the floor to make an impassioned speech on behalf of a recently arrived revolutionist from Germany, Carl Schurz. Though as yet unknown to many of the delegates, Schurz was quickly nominated. Some had their doubts about him when they got their first glimpse of him as he went forward to make an acceptance speech. "His tall, lank form and long legs were heightened by his dress, which was seedy, threadbare and ill-fitting," one of the delegates later recalled. "His coat sleeves and his trouser legs were much too short, and his Emersonian nose, adorned with the ever-present gold-bowed spectacles, gave him a novel and picturesque appearance." But, as he spoke, the assembled Republicans grew "amazed at his eloquence and the charm and power of his masterly oratory." With this remarkable German on their ticket, they could hope to do better than ever before in drawing German voters away from the Democratic party.[4]

The Republicans' prospects of gaining German votes seemed

[3] Alexander M. Thomson, *A Political History of Wisconsin* (Milwaukee, 1900), 138–141, recalling his impression of Schurz. See also Robert H. Jacobi, "Wisconsin Civil War Governors" (master's thesis, University of Wisconsin, 1948), 16–17; and William B. Hesseltine, "Lincoln's Problems in Wisconsin," in *WMH*, 48 (Spring, 1965), 190–191.

[4] Thomson, *Political History*, 141–142; Chester V. Easum, *The Americanization of Carl Schurz* (Chicago, 1929), 161–164.

to improve still more as a result of the Democrats' choice for governor. Aspiring for the Democratic nomination was the German-born Dr. Franz Huebschmann, since 1842 a physician and a leader of the German community in Milwaukee. Instead of Huebschmann, however, the convention named another Milwaukee pioneer, one of New York birth, the lawyer, businessman, and, from 1855 to 1857, mayor James B. Cross. When Huebschmann and his followers muttered about a rigged convention and threatened to bolt, other Democrats tried to explain that the good doctor had no following outside the city. "Politically he cannot complain if the voice of the State was against his nomination," one Democratic paper said; "then why divide the Democracy now?" Undeterred by such appeals, a number of Milwaukee Germans, "lifelong" Democrats, switched their support to the Republican ticket before election day.[5]

In the campaign of 1857 the corruption issue had a place. Cross was vulnerable because of fiscal irregularities during his mayoralty and because of his friendship with William A. Barstow, the former governor whom election frauds had brought into disrepute. Randall was handicapped by his political association with the incumbent governor, Coles Bashford, whose acceptance of a bribe had not yet been exposed but was already being rumored. The question the campaigners emphasized the most, however, was that of Negro rights as opposed to immigrant rights.

Democrats charged that the Republicans were problack and antiforeigner. Republicans were essentially Know Nothings, the German-language *Banner und Volksfreund* of Milwaukee contended, and they were conspiring to take the vote away from the immigrant and give it to the black. The Milwaukee *News* editorialized, "Negroes, in the opinion of the Republicans, 'are

[5] Milwaukee (weekly) *American*, September 30, October 28, 1857. The *American*, formerly a Know Nothing paper, supported the Democratic ticket in 1857. This paper admitted that Milwaukee Know Nothings, formerly Whigs, who had declared for the Fillmore ticket in 1856, had since turned Democratic. "To-day those same whigs prefer Democracy untainted, to voting for a candidate [Randall] whose political history 'is all round my hat.'" *Ibid.*, September 23, 1857.

born to command' equally with native white men—are inherently the superiors of the representatives of the German, Celtic, French, English, and Norse races among us." Taking it for granted that political equality would mean social equality and would lead to amalgamation, the Madison *Argus and Democrat* asked in horror, "Shall negroes marry our sisters and daughters and smutty wenches be married by our brothers and sons?" Thus did Democrats play upon the widespread Negrophobia among the foreign-born.

In the face of the Democratic resort to raw racism, some of the Republicans hesitated to avow the Negro suffrage proposal as their own. Booth himself declared it was not a *"party measure,"* though he thought Republicans ought to vote for it. But most of the Republican newspapers gave it their full support. " 'All men are created equal' is the first proposition in our political catechism," the Hudson *Chronicle* declared, "and there is no reason why the few hundred persons of African descent who reside in Wisconsin should be denied its benefits, except a stupid prejudice against 'niggers,' which every sensible man ought to be heartily ashamed of." The Republican Milwaukee *Sentinel* replied to the charge of nativism by repeating the "Republican creed" of equal rights for all, pointing out that former Know Nothings were backing Cross for governor, and reminding the voters of the German candidate for lieutenant governor on the Republican ticket.[6]

The Republican candidates themselves campaigned very hard, Schurz appearing on the stump almost daily during October, sometimes with Randall, when Schurz spoke in German, and at other times by himself, when he usually spoke first in English and then in German. The "financial crisis was claiming the attention of everyone," Schurz explained afterward, "so that we could easily lose our majority and the election." He felt that the panic would disadvantage the Republicans. "Since our party is composed chiefly of the most reliable ele-

[6] Kroncke, "Race and Politics in Wisconsin," 27–32; Milwaukee *Sentinel,* August 7, 18, 22 (quoting the Hudson *Chronicle*), 28, September 9, 10, 1857. On Cross, see the *DWB.*

ment of the population—namely, the native American farmers, who follow politics with a great deal of conscientiousness but with little zeal, unless particularly exciting questions happen to be up for decision—we feared lest many, more than usually concerned about their business, should fail to go to the polls and leave us in the lurch." It was different with the Democrats. "The strength of our opponents lies mainly in the populous cities, and consists largely of the Irish and the uneducated mass of German immigrants, and in the nature of things is easier to assemble and to handle."

"The result justified our concern," Schurz pointed out. On November 3, 1857, only about 90,000 men bothered to go to the polls. More Republicans than Democrats stayed at home, the Republican vote totaling 21,000 less than in 1856 (a presidential year, of course) and the Democratic vote only 8,500 less. Schurz himself went down in defeat, losing by the narrow margin of 107 votes. Randall and two others on the state ticket managed to win, though barely, with majorities of less than 600 each. Undoubtedly some Democrats—German evangelicals but few if any Lutherans or Catholics—had scratched their ballots in favor of Schurz. But obviously a larger number of Republicans had scratched theirs against him.[7]

For the Republican candidates, the Negro suffrage proposal was a heavy burden. About four out of five voters who cast ballots in the gubernatorial election cast them also in the suffrage referendum. They turned down the proposition by the overwhelming vote of 41,345 to 28,235. In most localities the division on this issue corresponded at least roughly to the division on the governorship. That is, the proposition got the largest favorable vote, though a smaller one than Randall himself, in those places that Randall carried by the largest majority, such as the southeastern counties having a relatively high proportion of settlers from New England and New York. It re-

[7] Schurz to Henry Meyer, November 25, 1857, January 15, 1858, in Joseph Schafer, ed. and trans., *Intimate Letters of Carl Schurz, 1841–1869* (Madison, 1928), 179–181; Easum, *Schurz*, 172–173, 184–188. *Wisconsin Blue Book, 1954*, p. 535; *ibid., 1975*, p. 657.

ceived the least support in the areas where Cross ran the strongest, such as the city of Milwaukee and the counties north of it, where the German population was greatest.[8]

After the election black leaders proposed to hold a hundred public meetings for "indoctrinating the people of this State into the true principles" of democracy and then to appeal to the people once more for equal rights. Few Republican politicians, however, were any longer in a mood to take up the suffrage cause and thereby risk defeat. When the legislature, still under Republican control, met early in 1858, Governor Randall in his inaugural did speak out boldly as an antislavery radical, insisting it was the duty of Congress to prohibit the extension of slavery in the territories. But, turning to Wisconsin affairs, he adopted the role of a political rather than a social reformer. For some time Josiah Noonan, the Democratic boss of Milwaukee, had been demanding an investigation of the alleged corruption in the passage of the legislature's 1856 act granting land to the La Crosse and Milwaukee Railroad. Noonan hoped thereby to discredit his Democratic rivals of the Barstow clique. Apparently agreeing that exposure would hurt Democrats worse than Republicans, Randall now called for an investigation; he said the people had a right to know whether their representatives could be "bought and sold like slaves in the market, or like cattle in the shambles."[9]

The ensuing investigation reached a dramatic climax when

[8] Fishel, "Wisconsin and Negro Suffrage," in *WMH*, 46: 185–189; *Wisconsin Blue Book, 1940*, p. 225. A partial geographic analysis may be made from scattered returns given in the Milwaukee *Sentinel*, November 5–7, 9, 11–14, 16–19, 21, 1857. In the city of Milwaukee the vote was 1,301 for Negro suffrage and 4,592 against, 1,705 for Randall and 4,258 for Cross. In Washington County, 300 for and 1,467 against, 341 Randall and 1,433 Cross. In Ozaukee County, 168 for and 1,357 against, 266 Randall and 1,167 Cross. In Kenosha County, 784 for and 743 against, 932 Randall and 693 Cross. In Racine County, a majority of 192 for Negro suffrage and 300 for Randall. In Rock County, a majority of 1,432 for suffrage and 1,792 for Randall. All gubernatorial figures except Milwaukee's are from James R. Donoghue, *How Wisconsin Voted, 1848–1972* (Madison, 1974), 93.

[9] Milwaukee *Sentinel*, November 18, 1857; Jacobi, "Wisconsin Civil War Governors," 17; Frank N. Elliott, "The Causes and the Growth of Railroad Regulation in Wisconsin, 1848–1876" (doctoral dissertation, University of Wisconsin, 1956), 156–159, quotes Governor Randall's 1858 message.

the investigating committee subpoenaed Moses Strong, a La Crosse and Milwaukee official and a prominent Democrat, and he refused to testify. In March 1858 the legislature met in an all-night session to hear the contempt charge that the committee had brought against Strong. Spectators jammed the capitol, in which, with doors and windows shut against the chill outside, the atmosphere was "like that of a furnace." The proceedings dragged on because of the delaying tactics of the Democrats. Impatient members passed the time with frequent visits to the post office adjoining the chamber for refreshments, solid and liquid. At one point the speaker ordered Strong to sit down, and when Strong stood his ground the sergeant-at-arms pulled him off the floor. Finally, at four in the morning, a resolution citing him for contempt was passed. After six days in jail he agreed to answer questions, and from then on the facts about the massive bribery rapidly came out.[10]

Having emerged from the investigation comparatively clean, despite the revealing of Republican ex-governor Bashford's guilt, the Republicans played up the corruption issue in the campaign of 1858, in which legislators and congressmen were to be elected. "Look Out for the Corruptionists!" was a slogan of the Republicans. They reminded voters that none of their candidates had been tainted by the scandal, while the Democrats were running five men who had received a total of $305,000 in railroad bonds. At the same time, the Republicans played down the question of Negro rights. The party platform, with a cynical appeal to racists, no longer referred to the extension of slavery but opposed "all further extension of the African race upon this continent." The revised position of the Republicans did not deter the German-language Milwaukee *Seebote* from continuing to denounce them as "nigger worshippers." Added the *Seebote*: "Temperance men, abolitionists, haters of foreigners, sacrilegious despoilers of churches . . . , killers of

[10] Kenneth W. Duckett, "Politics, Brown Bread, and Bologna," in *WMH*, 36 (Spring, 1953), 178–181, 202, 215–217.

Catholics—these are the infernal ingredients of which this loathesome Republican monstrosity is composed."[11]

In the congressional elections the Kansas question again aroused excitement. This problem had strained the national Democratic party as President Buchanan tried to impose a pro-slavery constitution on the incipient state and Senator Stephen A. Douglas insisted on an honest application of his principle of popular sovereignty. Douglas' contest for re-election, against his Illinois rival Abraham Lincoln, was attracting the attention of the whole country. On the floor of Congress the Kansas dispute had provoked a fist fight in which Wisconsin representatives Cadwallader C. Washburn and John F. Potter engaged a group of Southerners. Potter scored a coup when he "scalped" a Mississippi congressman by making off with his wig. In Madison Governor Randall suggested that the wig be deposited with the state historical society, and he made both Potter and Washburn honorary colonels of the state militia.

A hero among Republicans, Potter had no difficulty in winning re-election from the first (southeastern) district. Running against the former Madison editor Beriah Brown, whom Republicans accused of having accepted $52,000 in La Crosse and Milwaukee securities, Potter gained a majority of more than 3,000 votes, as compared with only about 300 two years earlier. From the second (western) district the land speculator Washburn also was sent back to Congress, though his margin had shrunk to less than 4,000 from more than 10,000. From the third (northern) dsitrict, however, the Republican incumbent, Charles Billinghurst, was not to return. Too conservative on the slavery question, Billinghurst had little or no support from radical state-righters, having "forfeited the good

[11] Elliott, "Railroad Regulation in Wisconsin," 167–169; Kroncke, "Race and Politics in Wisconsin," 39, quoting the Republican platform from the Milwaukee *Sentinel*, October 8, 1858; Ernest Bruncken, "The Political Activity of Wisconsin Germans, 1854–1860," in *SHSW Proceedings*, 1901, p. 197, translating and quoting the *Seebote* of November 6, 1858.

will of a great many," as Schurz said. Billinghurst lost a close race, 21,514 to 22,667, to Judge Charles Larrabee, who was a friend of Senator Douglas and had resigned from a state circuit court at the senator's request in order to show the Douglas strength in the Northwest.[12]

Though the Republicans retained majorities in both houses of the legislature, the future of the party in Wisconsin looked uncertain at best after the elections of 1858. And more scandal was soon to come, this time to embarrass the Republicans, especially the antislavery radicals.

[2]

Troubles were descending on Sherman M. Booth, the great symbol of idealism and morality in Wisconsin politics. Early in 1859 the cases of *Ableman v. Booth* and *U.S. v. Booth* appeared on the docket of the United States Supreme Court, despite the refusal of the Wisconsin supreme court to respond to writs of error and send in the records of its proceedings. S. V. R. Ableman, the federal marshal in Milwaukee, a herculean figure of more than three hundred pounds, was suing for the custody of Booth, whom the federal district court had convicted of violating the fugitive-slave law but whom the state court had several times freed on writs of habeas corpus. Booth now refused to appear in Washington or to be represented by counsel. He merely submitted a pamphlet containing the argument of his former attorney Byron Paine before the Wisconsin courts—urging the unconstitutionality of the fugitive-slave act—and also copies of the opinions of the state judges, claiming final jurisdiction in the matter. On March 7, 1859, Chief Justice Taney announced the Supreme Court's decision reversing the Wisconsin court's. The federal district judge in

[12] Robert R. Flatley, "The Wisconsin Congressional Delegation from Statehood to Secession, 1848–1861" (bachelor's thesis, University of Wisconsin, 1951), 87–91; on p. 91 he quotes Schurz to Moses Davis, August 24, 1858, in the Moses M. Davis Papers.

Milwaukee then ordered the marshal to rearrest and imprison Booth.[13]

In its immediate consequences, all this was, for Booth, no unmitigated disaster. Though denied a writ of habeas corpus by the state supreme court, he remained at liberty for the time being. Meanwhile the action against him confirmed his martyr role and enhanced his political importance. Promptly the legislature passed resolutions, with a solid Republican vote and Governor Randall's endorsement, condemning the Supreme Court's "arbitrary act of power" and declaring it "void and of no force." To justify Wisconsin's nullification of federal law, Schurz delivered a fiery public address on "State Rights and Byron Paine." "It is a splendid thing," Timothy Howe wrote in regard to Schurz's speech, "but he has struck the cause of Republicanism the hardest blow it ever received. Hitherto, it has only been denounced as fanatical. Hereafter, it will be stigmatized as traitorous and disloyal." But Howe, a conservative Republican and a former state supreme court judge, confined his misgivings to a private letter. In April 1859 Paine was elected to the court on the strength of his defense of Booth. For the moment, Booth and the state-rights radicals were riding high.[14]

At that very time, however, Booth was already confronting another and quite different legal action, one that bore the threat of completely undermining his private reputation and, along with it, his public influence. This was a morals case.

[13] William J. Maher, "The Antislavery Movement in Milwaukee and Vicinity, 1842–1860" (master's thesis, Marquette University, 1954), 67–69. On Ableman, see Harry E. Cole, ed., *A Standard History of Sauk County, Wisconsin . . .* (2 vols., Chicago, 1918), 1: 513–514. On legal and constitutional aspects of the controversy, see Alfons J. Beitzinger, "Federal Law Enforcement and the Booth Cases," in the *Marquette Law Review*, 41 (Summer, 1957), 7–32; Arthur Bestor, "State Sovereignty and Slavery: A Reinterpretation of Proslavery Constitutional Doctrine, 1846–1860," in the *Journal of the Illinois State Historical Society*, 54 (Summer, 1961), 117–180; and Joseph Schafer, "Stormy Days in Court—the Booth Case," in *WMH*, 20 (September, 1936), 89–110.

[14] Parker M. Reed, *The Bench and Bar of Wisconsin: History and Biography* (Milwaukee, 1882), 496–504; Sherman Miller Booth in *DWB*; Easum, *Schurz*, 237–240, quotes Howe's letter to Horace Rublee, March 27, 1859, published in the Milwaukee *Sentinel*, December 15, 1889.

On February 28, 1859, a week and a day before the Supreme
Court was to hand down its decision against him, Booth, then
forty-six, had remained at home in Milwaukee while his wife
was away attending a wedding in Waukesha. Also spending
the night at the Booth house, to look after the children, was
Caroline N. Cook, a well-developed girl of fourteen, the
daughter of a workingman who lived across the street. Afterwards she talked to her father, and he complained to the authorities. On April 3, 1859, Booth was indicted on a charge
of seducing Caroline and having "illicit connection" with her.

At the trial, which began in July before a packed courtroom,
Caroline took the stand to tell her story of that February night.
"Mr. Booth," she related, "was undressed . . . got in bed with
me . . . put his hand in my bosom . . . got on to me . . . took his
hand and put *it* in me." Booth himself, who declined to testify,
was quoted as having told the father that, yes, he had got into
bed with Caroline but, no, he had not done anything to her.
"For the purposes of the present argument," Booth's lawyer
Matthew H. Carpenter frankly said, "I concede that Booth was
in bed with the girl."

Nevertheless, Carpenter pointed out, Booth was not guilty
under the Wisconsin statute, which reflected the extreme anti-
feminine bias of the contemporary social and legal order, unless it could be proved that there had been both seduction and
penetration and, moreover, that the girl had been of a previous "chaste character." The defense brought in neighbors
as witnesses against Caroline. Among them, one woman told
how the girl, when playing in her yard or skipping across the
street to the Booths', often "exposed her person"; that is, she
allowed her hoopskirt to fly up and reveal her legs above the
knee. A man added that Caroline was not always careful
about concealing her breasts; even from his second-floor shop
he had been able to see her nipples. Disregarding the prurience
of the witnesses, Carpenter presented their testimony as evidence that Caroline was a "lewd woman," and he implied
that "this little gipsy" might well have seduced Booth—if indeed
there had been a seduction. But there had been no such thing,

he maintained. The whole prosecution was simply a "Democratic conspiracy" (he was speaking as a Democrat himself) to bring down the "great champion of Republicanism."

The jurors disagreed among themselves, seven voting for conviction, five against. Booth was acquitted, but the defamation of Caroline's character had not safeguarded his. The trial had been extensively reported in the newspapers, and a book detailing the proceedings was rushed into print. Never again was Booth to speak with quite the same moral authority he once had wielded.[15]

Not only was Booth himself politically weakened, but so was the radical faction of the Republicans. Some of his fellow radicals now shied away from him. The fastidious Schurz, for one, while holding fast to the same state-rights principles, felt a strong aversion to Booth personally. Schurz's ambition further divided the party when the state Republican convention met in September 1859. His German friends demanded that the party nominate him for governor, so as clearly to "condemn the proscription of foreign-born citizens." Schurz himself was determined to replace Randall, who he felt had undercut him when they were running mates in 1857. But Schurz faced the

[15] This account is based upon the proceedings as contained in the book that Wm. E. Tunis & Co. immediately brought out: *The Trial of Sherman M. Booth for Seduction: Evidence and Summing up of Counsel in the Case of the State* versus *S. M. Booth, for Seducing Caroline N. Cook* (Milwaukee, 1859), 3, 7, 116, 121, 140, 146–147, 159, 209, 294, and *passim*. For a brief, accurate summary of the case, see Alfons J. Beitzinger, *Edward G. Ryan, Lion of the Law* (Madison, 1960), 63–64. As a voluntary assistant to the district attorney, Ryan took the main responsibility for the prosecution. Though a Democrat, Ryan was a factional foe of Josiah Noonan, who is said to have persuaded Carpenter to oppose Ryan and serve for the defense. See E. Bruce Thompson, *Matthew Hale Carpenter, Webster of the West* (Madison, 1954), 61–62. Thompson assumes that Booth was innocent. He states: "The Democratic strategists now sought to ruin him by means of a trumped-up charge of seduction." For his nearly two-page account of the case, however, Thompson provides only one footnote, and that one refers to pp. 103–110 of Frank A. Flower's biography of Carpenter. In his own "Essay on Authorities" (pp. 312–313) Thompson has this to say about Flower's book: It bears the grandiose title *Life of Matthew Hale Carpenter: A View of the Honors and Achievements That, in the American Republic, Are the Fruits of Well-Directed Ambition and Persistent Industry* (Madison, 1883). As the title suggests, the book is mostly an apology and a panegyric; it canonizes Carpenter and anathematizes his enemies."

opposition of Howe and other conservatives, who looked upon Randall as the lesser of radical evils. Schurz refused to consider any place on the ticket except the first, and when the infuriated Randall finally won renomination, the party went before the people without a German among its candidates for state offices.[16]

As an earnest of their repudiation of nativism, however, the Republicans did put a Norwegian on their ticket in 1859. He was Hans Christian Heg, who in 1840, at the age of ten, had come from Norway to Wisconsin with his parents, and whose father had helped to found the first Norwegian-language newspaper in the United States, the Free Soil *Nordlyset*. Heg was running for the post of prison commissioner against another Norwegian, Henry C. Fleck, whom the Democrats had nominated. "Mr. Heg is completely Americanized, speaks English as clearly and fluently as a native citizen," the Milwaukee *Free Democrat* (a Republican paper) declared. Indeed, he was so completely Americanized that he had become indifferent to the Norwegians, the Democratic Norwegian-language paper *Emigranten* replied. In any event he was to be the first Norwegian immigrant ever elected, it appears, to a state office in the United States.[17]

For governor, the Democrats nominated Harrison C. Hobart, a Massachusetts-born, Dartmouth-educated lawyer of Calumet County. Though an experienced politician and an able campaigner, Hobart failed to hold the united support of his party. In a joint debate at Horicon, Randall so focused the issue on the corruption of the Democratic Barstow administration that Hobart was driven to disavow Barstow, who then denounced Hobart. The candidate could no longer hope for many, if any, votes from Barstow's followers.[18]

[16] Thomson, *Political History*, 142–145; Easum, *Schurz*, 249–251, writes about Schurz's friends at the convention.

[17] Theodore C. Blegen, "Colonel Hans Christian Heg," in *WMH*, 4 (December, 1920), 140–165, quotes the *Free Democrat*, September 14, 1859, on p. 148. See also Theodore C. Blegen, ed., *The Civil War Letters of Colonel Hans Christian Heg* (Northfield, Minnesota, 1936), 17–18; and Theodore C. Blegen, *Norwegian Migration to America: The American Transition* (Northfield, Minnesota, 1940), 317–322.

[18] Thomson, *Political History*, 145–146; Harrison Carroll Hobart in *DWB*.

At the height of the campaign, in mid-October 1859, came news that again embarrassed the Republicans, especially the antislavery extremists. This was the news of John Brown's raid on the federal arsenal at Harpers Ferry. According to report, his aim was to get weapons with which to arm blacks and start a slave insurrection. Democrats, in Wisconsin as in other states, accused Republicans of complicity for having spread treasonable doctrines. In Wisconsin a few radicals defended Brown, but most Republicans condemned his raid, while giving their approval, at least in private, to his idealism and bravery. Even Howe, stout opponent of Booth and the radicals though he was, sympathized with Brown. In a personal letter Howe denied that Brown represented Republican principles, but confided that he himself thought the deed a courageous one, aimed "not at the slave but at the fetters which bound him, not to destroy the oppressor even but to end the oppression."[19]

Apparently the Democratic factionalism on the part of the Barstow men more than offset the Republican embarrassment over Harpers Ferry. At any rate, the Republicans won a sweeping victory on election day. The turnout at the polls was unusually large for a gubernatorial election—considerably larger than it had been in 1857 or was to be in 1861. Of the total of 122,991 ballots cast, 63,466 or about 52 per cent went to Randall. Along with the governor the Republicans, for the first time, carried their entire slate of executive officials. They also held on to their majority in the legislature.[20]

During the next several months, while a fear of Republican-inspired slave revolts swept through the Southern states and these states began to build up their military defenses, the state-rights issue in a different form remained alive in Wisconsin,

[19] Kroncke, "Race and Politics in Wisconsin," 41–43, quoting Howe to Horace Rublee, October 26, 1859, in the Timothy O. Howe Papers.

[20] Donoghue, *How Wisconsin Voted*, 94, gives 63,466 for Randall and 59,525 for Hobart, a total of 122,991. The *Wisconsin Blue Book* for 1975, p. 657, gives 59,999 for Randall, 52,539 for Hobart, and 134 scattered, a total of 112,755. The discrepancy arises from the fact that the *Blue Book* omits returns from Buffalo, Door, Eau Claire, and Milwaukee counties that the state board of canvassers rejected because of irregularities.

continuing to divide the Republican party. The state-righters were angered when, in February 1860, a Republican convention nominated Luther S. Dixon for a continuing position as the state's chief justice, for Dixon was willing to yield to the federal Supreme Court's decision in the cases of *Ableman v. Booth* and *U.S. v. Booth.* Schurz and his fellow radicals disavowed the convention's work and nominated their own state-rights candidate. The Democrats threw their support to Dixon. In April he was elected. Soon the three-man court took up, for final disposition, the question of habeas corpus for Booth. Justice Paine, as Booth's former attorney, disqualified himself. Justice Orsamus Cole favored the writ, but Chief Justice Dixon opposed it, and on the tie vote it was denied.[21]

Already the federal marshal had levied on Booth's property because of his nonpayment of the $1,000 as restitution to the slaveowner Garland. Booth was forced into bankruptcy and his printing press was sold, yet the judgment remained unsatisfied. He was imprisoned in the Milwaukee customs house. Two friends compelled a guard to free him, but after a couple of months in hiding he was recaptured. Finally, on March 3, 1861, the day before leaving office, President Buchanan pardoned him. Sherman Booth had forty-three years of life remaining, but his glory was behind him.[22]

[3]

While the Wisconsin supreme court was weakening in its resistance to federal authority, the Wisconsin governor took occasion to reassert in his own way the sovereignty of the state. As commander in chief of the state militia, he dared to challenge, at least hypothetically, the President's power as commander in chief of the army and navy of the United States. The governor's actions set going a chain of events that, as fate would

[21] Beitzinger, *Ryan,* 65; Easum, *Schurz,* 255–258; Jacobi, "Wisconsin Civil War Governors," 19–20.
[22] Maher, "Antislavery Movement in Milwaukee," 70–72; Reed, *Bench and Bar,* 496–504; Thomson, *Political History,* 101; Sherman M. Booth in *DWB.*

have it, were to culminate in one of the most horrendous disasters in all the nautical history of the Great Lakes—the wreck of the *Lady Elgin*.

The fateful events began in March 1860, at the time when the federal marshal had just retaken custody of Sherman Booth. One of Booth's persisting admirers, Assemblyman Ben Hunkins of Waukesha, introduced in the legislature a startling resolution: "*Whereas* . . . the United States of America (whose relations with this State were formerly friendly) have recently restrained of his liberty, for the third or fourth time, one of our citizens, who has long been regarded as a martyr of freedom," and "*Whereas,* the State is honorably bound to protect the liberty of its citizens against foreign powers," therefore "*Resolved* . . . that the Governor be . . . directed to declare war against the United States." Once the clerk had read the resolution, the speaker of the assembly ruled it unconstitutional, and that was the end of it.

If a war declaration was only Assemblyman Hunkins' whim, and not to be taken seriously, the possibility of some kind of clash of arms nevertheless seemed very real. At any rate, Governor Randall and his associates expressed concern about the dependability of some of the state's militia officers in case a showdown with the federal government should come. Particularly suspect was Captain Garrett Barry of the Union Guards.

Captain Barry, of Irish extraction, was a Democratic politician, the treasurer of Milwaukee County. He was also a well-trained soldier, having received a military education at West Point. For the Union Guards, he had recruited seventy young Irishmen and drilled them to perfection. Their weapons, like those of other militia companies, had been furnished by the state, to which they had been lent by the federal government. Uniforms and other equipment the men had provided for themselves, raising the money through dues, picnics, banquets, and other benefits. The Union Guards and their dashing captain were the pride of Milwaukee's Irish south side.

"It is reported . . . ," Captain Barry read in a communication from James A. Swain, adjutant general of Wisconsin, on March

5, 1860, "that you have stated that, in the possible contingency of a conflict between the U.S. authorities and those of this State, you, as an officer of a military organization under the laws of this State[,] would obey a call for your company to turn out, made by the U.S. authorities, but would *not* obey a call by your superior officers, under the State laws." Replying immediately, Barry admitted that, on being questioned, he had said he would not obey an illegal order from the governor. "With all due respect to State authority," he added, "I don't believe the Governor would dream for a moment of giving an order so *clearly illegal,* as to amount to an order to the military of this State to commit the crime of treason, in obeying which, I and my men would deserve to be hung, or at least forfeit all rights of citizenship."

Two days later Governor Randall proclaimed an order disbanding the Union Guards and revoking Barry's commission as their captain. At the same time, Adjutant General Swain ordered that "all arms and stores of all kinds, belonging to the State, in possession of the volunteer company," be handed over forthwith, to be forwarded to Madison. Barry finally complied, after a contumacious correspondence with Randall and Swain.

Democrats continued to insist, however, that constitutionality and legality were all on Barry's side. The *Wisconsin Patriot* of Madison asserted, "The President of the United States is, by the Constitution of the United States, the laws of Congress, and the statutes of this State, the commander-in-chief of the militia of the State, when called into the actual service of the United States." A congressional act of 1795, the *Wisconsin Patriot* pointed out, provided that whenever federal laws should be opposed by "combinations too powerful to be suppressed by the ordinary course of judicial proceedings" within any state, it would be lawful for the President to call upon the militia of that and other states, and officers and privates of the militia who failed to obey the President's orders would be liable to penalties. There could be no doubt, then, the paper concluded, that if the "laws of the United States, under which

Booth is convicted," should be obstructed in Wisconsin, any orders of the governor in opposition to those of the President would be illegal and should not be obeyed.

Governor Randall himself seemed to have some doubt about the legality of his stand. To the legislature he sent a special message on the "inadequacy of the militia laws of the State." After reciting the article of the Wisconsin constitution that made the governor the commander in chief of the militia, he quoted the clause of the Wisconsin statute: "except when called into the service of the United States." He then remarked that either the constitution or the statute was wrong. "They materially disagree."

German Catholics sympathized with Barry and his Irishmen, the Milwaukee *Seebote* calling the disbandment of the Union Guards an act of Know Nothing prejudice. Some non-Catholic Germans disagreed. Opined the Milwaukee *Atlas,* a Republican German-language paper edited by the freethinker Bernhard Domschcke, "if ever Governor Randall has done anything that commands the absolute approbation, it is the disbandment of that *Democratic Patrick,* who thinks, in his world-known position as commander of twenty-five shillelah bearers, he can be guilty of insubordination with impunity."[23]

But Barry and his "shillelah bearers" had no intention of disbanding. They determined to keep the Union Guards together as an independent unit. Hoping to get guns directly from the federal government, they appealed to Charles Larrabee, Wisconsin's lone Democratic representative in Washington. Congressman Larrabee found that, since the company was no longer a part of the state militia, he could not obtain the weapons free, but he managed to buy eighty muskets at the bargain price of two dollars each. To pay for the purchase, the

---

[23] The Madison *Wisconsin Patriot,* March 10, 12, 1860, reprinted Hunkins' resolution and the correspondence between Barry and the state authorities, quoted other newspapers, and published a long statement defending Barry. These items from the *Patriot* are reproduced in Charles M. Scanlan, "Captain Garret Barry and the 'Lady Elgyn' Disaster," in the *Journal of the American Irish Historical Society,* 16 (July, 1917), 190–200. This account is based upon the documents as reproduced therein.

Union Guards and their friends got up a grand benefit, an excursion to Chicago on a lake steamer. They chose the *Lady Elgin*, a fast and magnificent triple-decked sidewheeler, about 300 feet from stem to stern, one of the favorites on the lakes in those days.

On Thursday evening, September 6, 1860, the *Lady Elgin* left Milwaukee with about 400 excursionists on board, among them members of two German militia companies, the Black Yaegers and the Green Yaegers, as well as Captain Barry and his Union Guards. The next morning, on landing at Chicago, the Union Guards received an ovation from an admiring Irish crowd. After a day of sightseeing, Barry's fellow tourists honored him and his men with a gala dinner and an evening of drinking toasts.

At about eleven o'clock that night the *Lady Elgin* steamed out of Chicago harbor, with the excursionists and a hundred or more additional passengers, for the return trip. A German band was playing, and still unwearied young people were singing and dancing. Around midnight a thick fog and a cold breeze drove most of them off the decks, but the merrymaking continued in the saloon below. The wind turned into a squall, with heavy rain. Suddenly, about two in the morning, when some nine miles off Winnetka, the *Lady Elgin* shook with a loud crash and listed to one side. She had been rammed amidships by the *Augusta,* a schooner heavily loaded with lumber. As the storm-driven schooner drew off into the darkness, the *Lady Elgin* with her hull gaping rolled over, righted herself, began to break apart, and finally sank.

At daylight, Saturday, September 8, the yet rough water was covered with bobbing pieces of wreckage to which men, women, and children clung. Dozens went under within sight of the shore, but others managed to make their way through the breakers to the safety of the narrow beach beneath the Winnetka bluffs. As bodies were recovered—227 eventually—there was a continual dirge in Milwaukee, one mass funeral following another at St. John's cathedral, while much of the city was draped in black. The number of victims, perhaps 300 or more, was never exactly known, for the passenger list went down with the ship, and many of the lost were never found. For weeks and months, bodies kept appearing at widely scattered points. The body of Captain Barry's schoolboy son Willie was washed ashore only two days after the sinking, but the body of the captain himself not until two months afterward, on November 8, 1860, in Lake County, Indiana.[24]

[4]

November 6, 1860, was election day in a presidential year. The grieving over the victims of the *Lady Elgin* disaster coincided with the political campaign, and the poor prospects for Wisconsin Democrats did nothing to assuage the grief. "I suppose we Democrats have got to make up our minds to remain in the minority in the state for a long while to come," one of them had written a year earlier. "Well perhaps it is just as well since our worst political enemies are in our own ranks." If the party in the state was weakened by dissension, the party in the nation was, by now, completely split. The Northern Democrats were supporting Stephen A. Douglas for President. The Southern Democrats were running a candidate of their own, John C. Breckinridge of Kentucky. With the opposition thus divided, the Republicans were almost certain to carry the day for Abraham Lincoln.[25]

Lincoln had not been the first choice of Wisconsin Republicans. Of course, he was well known, in the words of one of them, for the "able manner he conducted the campaign with

[24] The sinking of the *Lady Elgin* was reported, in varying degrees of detail, by newspapers throughout the country, but almost none of them so much as mentioned the political background of the ill-fated excursion. Several accounts by survivors are quoted by Clark S. Matteson, *The History of Wisconsin from Prehistoric to Present Periods* (Milwaukee, 1893), 461–477. A good brief treatment of the background as well as the accident is in Scanlan, "'Lady Elgyn' Disaster," in the *Journal of the American Irish Historical Society,* 16: 200–203. For a warmly partisan retelling of the entire story, see Charles M. Scanlan, *The Lady Elgin Disaster, September 8, 1860* (Milwaukee, 1928).

[25] The quotation is from a letter of Jackson Hadley to Moses Strong, November 14, 1859, in the Moses M. Strong Papers, as quoted in Flatley, "Wisconsin Congressional Delegation," 98.

Douglas in Illinois" in 1858, a contest that had "given him a world wide fame as a debator and sound reasoner." But he possessed no wide or deep personal acquaintanceship among Wisconsin leaders. He had made no great impression when he visited the state in late September and early October 1859. At the state fair near Milwaukee he then delivered a nonpolitical address in praise of agriculture, labor, invention, education, and opportunity. At the Newhall House, where he was staying, he talked politics with prominent men of both parties who called to pay their respects. On his way home he made brief and unspectacular appearances in Janesville and Beloit.[26]

When, in May 1860, the Republicans met in Chicago, the chairman, Schurz, and the rest of the Wisconsin delegation were prepared to give their support to the preconvention favorite, the senator from New York, William H. Seward, who was noted for his statement that there was an "irrepressible conflict" between the North and the South. Schurz seconded the nomination of Seward. But when, after the third ballot, a vote switch gave Lincoln a narrow majority, Schurz seconded a motion to make Lincoln's nomination unanimous, and the Wisconsin delegates joined the stampede. "Next to Mr. Seward . . . ," the Milwaukee *Sentinel* commented, "Mr. Lincoln was probably the most acceptable candidate that could be presented to Wisconsin." Lincoln was familiar with the problems of the West, and he was dead set against any extension of slavery. He deserved the vote of everyone who believed that "the interests of FREE rather than Slave labor should be the chief care of the Federal Government."[27]

[26] Thomson, *Political History*, 149–153; "Lincoln's 1859 Address at Milwaukee," in *WMH*, 10 (March, 1927), 243–258; Stanley E. Lathrop, "Lincoln at Beloit in 1859," in the *Wisconsin Magazine*, 2 (January–February, 1924), 3–4. The quotation is from a letter by Wilson Colwell, La Crosse, to John A. Colwell, May 27, 1860, published in "Lincoln's Sponsor in La Crosse, 1860," in *WMH*, 10 (June, 1927), 453. A far-fetched thesis that Lincoln visited Wisconsin three times— not only in 1859 and in 1832 during the Black Hawk War, but also in 1835, while grieving over the death of Ann Rutledge—is presented by Julius E. Olson, "Lincoln in Wisconsin," in *WMH*, 4 (September, 1920), 44–54.

[27] Easum, *Schurz*, 272–275; "The Chicago Convention of 1860," in *WMH*, 5 (June, 1921), 99–104; Curtis W. Miller, "Rufus King and the Problems of His Era" (master's thesis, Marquette University, 1963), 90–93, quoting the Milwaukee *Sentinel*, May 22, August 1, 1860.

Having retreated a long way from their 1857 stand supporting Negro rights, the Wisconsin Republicans in the 1860 campaign were stressing the "interests of free rather than slave labor," the rights of white men rather than black. Many shared the views of Senator James R. Doolittle, who had espoused the state-rights doctrines of the antislavery radicals at the time of his election in 1857, but who since then had made himself the foremost congressional spokesman for the "colonization" of free blacks outside the United States. Doolittle, a solemn and unctuous but highly effective orator, was proud of his speaking ability. He once wrote his wife: The publisher of the congressional debates "says of my voice and pronunciation that it is the finest and clearest he ever heard on the floor of the Senate." At a tremendous 1860 campaign rally in Madison, Doolittle applied his eloquence to the "solution of the whole negro question," which he said was the "mission" of the Republican party. "The Caucassian was planted in the temperate zone," but "the ultimate, permanent, natural and normal home of the African is in the tropics," Doolittle intoned. There was only one way to right the wrong of slavery, solve the race problem, and end the "irrepressible conflict," he concluded. That was to restore the African "to his tropical zone, and to his rights as a man," and leave "our temperate territories" for the Caucasian to cultivate.[28]

With this new emphasis on removing the Negro while removing slavery, the Wisconsin Republicans could hope to lessen the antagonism of Negrophobes, especially among the foreign-born. But the party also took more positive steps to gain the foreign vote, both in Wisconsin and in other states. The Chicago platform contained a plank, of Schurz's authorship, that promised no abridgment of the immigrant's political rights.

[28] Flatley, "Wisconsin Congressional Delegation," 82–85, including a quotation of Doolittle to Mary Doolittle, January 30, 1858, in the James R. Doolittle Papers. For a personality sketch of Doolittle, see Thomson, *Political History,* 181–183. On Doolittle's early years in the Senate, see also James L. Sellers, "James R. Doolittle," in *WMH,* 17–18 (December, 1933–December, 1934), 17: 277–306. Doolittle's 1860 Madison speech was printed in full, almost a year later, in the Milwaukee *Sentinel,* June 24, 1861, which is the source for this summary of it.

Schurz, a member of the Republican national executive committee, took charge of its "foreign department." As he reported to Lincoln, he planned to organize squads of speakers and set up a system of correspondence among Germans, Scandinavians, and Hollanders throughout the North. Schurz himself stumped the states of Pennsylvania, Illinois, Missouri, Indiana, and New York before returning to Wisconsin for a climactic effort.

On arriving in Milwaukee, Schurz was greeted by a demonstration that typified the enthusiastic Republican campaign everywhere. That evening a torchlight procession moved past him at the Newhall House, which was "illuminated from top to bottom." In the parade were some 3,000 Wide Awakes, members of a Republican youth organization wearing distinctive capes and caps and carrying a banner with Schurz's picture on it. "Then came the citizens of all classes—Mitchell, Crocker, Tweedy, and all the first people of the city, carrying torches and marching in the procession." What a show of unity among Republicans, old and young, rich and poor, conservative and radical! "In marching by the Newhall House the whole tremendous column, which was more than a mile and half long, fired off rockets and shouted hurrahs."

In Watertown the Wide Awakes had enlisted more than forty Germans among the nearly 200 members. When the Watertown group first paraded, the marchers encountered a shower of bricks as they strode past Bieber's saloon. They completed their route, then returned and battered open the locked saloon, where their assailants, German Democrats of the "Rothe band," had taken refuge. The Wide Awakes got the better of Rothe and his followers in a wild melee. This made Watertown temporarily safe for Republicans, but fights at the polling places were common, and when going to vote many of the Republicans banded together for protection against German and Irish Democratic toughs.[29]

---

[29] Easum, *Schurz*, 275–300. Schurz describes the demonstrations in letters to Mrs. Schurz, October 25, 29, 1860, in Schafer, ed., *Intimate Letters of Carl Schurz*, 227–229. Also see William F. Whyte, "Chronicles of Early Watertown," in *WMH*,

The enthusiasm of Wisconsin Republicans contrasted with the discouragement of Wisconsin Democrats. True, the Democrats had the continuing support of almost all the German press, including the anti-Catholic *Banner und Volksfreund* as well as the Catholic *Seebote* in Milwaukee. Playing upon familiar Democratic themes, the *Banner und Volksfreund* condemned Lincoln and Breckinridge alike as sectional candidates, the election of either of whom might have revolutionary consequences. It kept lauding Douglas as a national statesman whose victory would assure Union and peace. "We Democrats don't want Congress to discuss the slavery question any more," the paper added. "It only causes disturbance; and other, more important business is neglected." True also, the Democrats had strengthened their ticket among foreigners by nominating a larger number of them than the Republicans had done for local offices. Thus for eight Dane County positions the Democratic slate included an Irishman, a Pole, a German, a Scot, a Dane, and only three native Americans as compared with the Republican list of one Norwegian and seven Yankees.[30]

Still, the Democrats had little chance of carrying Wisconsin for Douglas or of winning any of the three congressional contests. In the western congressional district they had picked James D. Reymert, of Madison, a native of Norway and former editor of *Nordlyset,* only after the American-born George D. Smith had declined consideration because he felt the race would be hopeless for any Democrat. In the northeastern district Congressman Larrabee, running for re-election, could count upon the affection of Irish voters after his assistance to the Union Guards, but he had lost popularity wtih other

---

4 (March, 1921), 288–290. Alexander Mitchell was the well-known banker; Hans Crocker, an associate of Mitchell and a traditional Democrat; and John H. Tweedy, an important Republican, a wealthy businessman, and Crocker's one-time law partner; see the *DWB*.

[30] Mary D. Meyer, "The Germans in Wisconsin and the Civil War: Their Attitude Toward the Union, the Republicans, Slavery, and Lincoln" (master's thesis, Catholic University of America, 1937), 20–27, citing the *Banner und Volksfreund,* July 6, August 5, November 4, 1860; Jacob O. Stampen, "The Norwegian Element of Madison, Wisconsin, 1850–1900" (master's thesis, University of Wisconsin, 1965), 59.

groups as a result of his blatantly proslavery remarks in the House.

Certainly no realistic Democrat could expect to beat John F. Potter in the southeastern district. Already famous for having dewigged a Southern congressman in a scuffle, Potter had enhanced his heroic stature in the eyes of Republicans with another and even greater anti-Southern exploit. In April 1860, with fisticuffs again threatening on the House floor, he sprang to the defense of Illinois Representative Owen Lovejoy against Virginia's Roger A. Pryor. Others restored order before Potter and Pryor came to blows, but Pryor later tried to provoke Potter into a duel. Potter hesitated, explaining that the Wisconsin constitution debarred duelists from public office. So Pryor issued a direct challenge. He had a reputation as an expert marksman with a pistol. The choice of weapons, however, was up to Potter as the challenged party. After consulting with friends he specified bowie knives. Pryor backed out, and Potter became a national figure. While contemned in the South, he received bowie knives as gifts from admirers all over the North and West—including one from Missouri Republicans that was seven feet long and inscribed "Will always meet a 'Pryor' engagement." The affair and the reaction to it gave some measure of the extent to which, in spirit, Northerners and Southerners were drifting apart.[31]

On election night the great expectations of Republicans were confirmed. A crowd of prominent Milwaukeeans, who had gathered in the Chamber of Commerce to get telegraphic reports, cheered from time to time as the tallies for Lincoln mounted in the Northern states. By two o'clock in the morning his majority in the electoral college was assured. "The cannon was now dragged out," as Schurz informed his wife, "and we woke up the Democrats, they having withdrawn from the streets pretty early in the evening."[32]

---

[31] Flatley, "Wisconsin Congressional Delegation," 91–99; William B. Hesseltine, "The Pryor-Potter Duel," in *WMH*, 27 (June, 1944), 400–409.

[32] Schurz to Mrs. Schurz, November 7, 1860, in Schafer, ed., *Intimate Letters of Carl Schurz*, 230–231.

When the final returns were in (86,113 to 65,021), it was clear that Lincoln had carried Wisconsin by a majority of more than 20,000 over Douglas and the other two candidates (Breckinridge and the Constitutional Union party's John Bell, who together got only about 1,000 votes in the state). Lincoln's margin was more than 7,000 larger than Frémont's had been in 1856. Schurz claimed credit for a large part of the increase, and certainly German voters contributed to it. Later the notion was to gain currency that, in Wisconsin and in other states of the Northwest, the Germans had elected Lincoln. A close look at the returns, however, would have shown that, in Wisconsin at least, this was by no means the case.

In Wisconsin it appears that the German Catholics, along with the Irish Catholics, voted almost unanimously for Douglas. The German Lutherans also favored him, though with somewhat less than unanimity. The German Reformed communities were more divided, but in at least one town they preferred Douglas by nearly two to one. On the other hand, the evangelicals, such as the Methodists, went largely for Lincoln, and the freethinkers mainly for him—especially the Forty-Eighters, the revolutionary émigrés. For them, Schurz had a strong appeal; to Catholics and Lutherans he was anathema, a godless fanatic. The Catholics constituted about half of the state's German population, and the Lutherans made up much the largest part of the remainder. All together, fewer than one-sixth of Wisconsin's German voters cast their ballots for Lincoln, and he would have carried the state handily even if none of them had done so.[33]

---

[33] *Wisconsin Blue Book, 1954*, p. 535; Easum, *Schurz*, 300–309. The generalizations regarding the German vote are derived (with some extrapolation) from Joseph Schafer, "Who Elected Lincoln?" in the *American Historical Review*, 47 (October, 1941), 51–63. Schafer produces some striking correlations from an analysis of the voting in sample townships, some of which were also election precincts. For instance, in the town of Marshfield, Fond du Lac County, where there were 229 German and ten non-German family heads, there were 193 votes for Douglas and six for Lincoln. In Rosendale, in the same county, where there were 140 native American and forty-three British family heads to only twelve Irish and sixteen German, there were 215 votes for Lincoln and twenty-two for Douglas.

On the whole, the Norwegians supported Lincoln, though there were exceptions. In Dane County some were attracted to the Democratic ticket by the name of Reymert, the Democrats' Norwegian candidate for Congress. In Pierce County, Norwegians gave Douglas a number of the votes he received in Wisconsin. From the town of Martell one of the Stortroen brothers explained to relatives in Norway that "the northern states are free, and the Southern states are slave states. We are not well-informed enough to judge which of these are right. We and most of the Norwegians around here voted for the Southern Democrat [Douglas] for president, however."[34]

The bulk of Lincoln's Wisconsin backing, however, came from native Americans of New York and New England stock and from English, Welsh, and Scottish immigrants. They, not the Germans and certainly not the Irish, were mainly responsible for the state's five electoral votes going to Lincoln.

Their party, the Republican party, was now more firmly entrenched than ever in Wisconsin politics. All three of the state's congressmen-elect were Republicans, as were both of the incumbent senators. So were sizable majorities in the two houses of the state legislature. Republicans remained in the governorship and all the administrative offices. Henceforth the Wisconsin party would have the benefit of the federal patronage. As yet, however, the effective head of that party was Governor Randall, not the President-elect.

[5]

With the election of a Republican to the Presidency, the state-rights doctrine lost its charm for its quondam advocates in Wisconsin. The doctrine now was put to the test by South Carolina, which took Lincoln's election as sufficient cause to adopt an ordinance of secession on December 20, 1860. Seces-

[34] Schafer, "Who Elected Lincoln?" in *American Historical Review*, 47: 56–57; Blegen, *Norwegian Migration: American Transition*, 322–324; Stampen, "Norwegian Element of Madison," 58; Anders Jensen Stortroen to his parents, January 1862, in "Norwegian Immigrant Letters," in *WMH*, 15 (March, 1932), 367–368.

sionists in other slave states demanded that these follow the South Carolina example. By the time Congress met, at the beginning of December, both the Congress and the country faced an impending crisis of disunion. What to do about it? Three general proposals were in the air: to use force against the seceders, to "let the erring sisters go in peace," or to find some Union-saving compromise.

Wisconsin Republicans held firm convictions on the subject. "Let it be settled there shall be no more slave territory," Senator Doolittle the colonizationist was writing to his wife. "If our folks back down now," Representative Potter of bowie-knife fame confided to a friend, "the Republican party will be buried in 6 months and the Union irreparably dissolved." At a special convention in Ripon, on December 12, delegates from around the state reaffirmed the old principles of free men and free soil by adopting two stern resolutions. The first of these denounced the fugitive-slave act of 1850. The second read: *"Resolved,* That we can make no compromise which will appease the South without yielding the whole ground which brought the Republican party into existence."

In the House of Representatives the lame-duck Democrat from Wisconsin, Larrabee, gave expression to a very different, conciliatory spirit. He introduced a resolution for calling a national convention—an idea that was highly popular in the border states—to propose constitutional amendments that would settle the sectional dispute. His resolution never came to a vote. The House, with his approval, did set up a committee of thirty-three, one member from each state, to consider compromise plans. Cadwallader C. Washburn took Wisconsin's place on the committee, though he along with Potter had voted against creating it. In the Senate a committee of thirteen, one of them Doolittle, was appointed for the same purpose.[35]

[35] Robert L. Schwab, "Wisconsin and Compromise Efforts on the Eve of the Civil War" (master's thesis, Marquette University, 1957), 15–16, 19, 29–36; p. 36 quotes Doolittle to his wife, December 2, 1860, in the James R. Doolittle Papers. Potter's remarks were written to Jerome Brigham on December 8, 1860, and are in the Jerome R. Brigham Papers. The convention's resolutions are published in the *Wisconsin State Journal,* December 18, 1860.

Expressing the urgent concern of border-state people, who would be caught in the middle in case of a civil war, Senator John J. Crittenden of Kentucky offered a compromise consisting of several constitutional amendments. The most controversial of these—requiring the Republicans to recede from their position on the extension of slavery—would have drawn an east-west line across the territories and allowed the introduction of slaves to the south of it. Doolittle rejected the plan, saying the "people of the United States" would never consent to change the fundamental law so as to make it a "slavery-extending Constitution by force of its own terms." He proposed, instead, an amendment explicitly declaring that no state had or ever would have the right to secede. Opposed by extremists from both North and South, the Crittenden Compromise bogged down in the Senate committee of thirteen.[36]

It fared little better in the House committee of thirty-three. Here Wisconsin's Washburn made himself the spokesman for no-compromise Republicans from all the Northern states. The personal-liberty laws, which most of these states had enacted, constituted one of the Southern grievances to which he addressed himself. Wisconsin Democrats sympathized with the Southerners on this score among others. "Wisconsin has upon her statute books a law nullifying the Constitution, and denying to citizens of the Southern States rights secured to them under that Constitution," the *Wisconsin Patriot* of Madison urged, "—let that law be repealed promptly, and on the motion of the majority Republican party." But Washburn, as author of one of his committee's minority reports, upheld the constitutionality as well as the justice of the personal-liberty laws. "The clamor now against them is a mere excuse for long meditated treason." As for changing the Constitution, "it needs to be obeyed rather than amended"; the way out of present difficulties is to "preserve and protect the public property and enforce the

---

[36] Biagino M. Marone, "Senator James Rood Doolittle and the Struggle Against Radicalism, 1857–1866" (master's thesis, Marquette University, 1955), 8–9, quoting the *Congressional Globe*, 36 Cong., 2 sess., 197.

laws." Republicans must not retreat. Washburn urged on the floor of the House: "Let us have disunion and, if need be, civil war rather than dishonor."[37]

Washburn's solicitude to "preserve and protect the public property" had reference in particular to Fort Sumter in Charleston harbor. On December 26, 1860, six days after South Carolina's secession, Major Robert Anderson had moved his garrison from the hostile mainland to the more defensible though still unfinished fort. This fort became the focus of attention throughout the country as the South Carolina hotheads proceeded to encircle it with menacing shore batteries. On January 8, 1861, the seceders' guns fired upon and turned away the *Star of the West*, a merchant ship that President Buchanan had chartered to carry supplies and, below deck, troop reinforcements to the beleaguered Sumter garrison. This news reached Wisconsin at a time when, throughout the state, the dread possibility of bloodshed was already an engrossing topic of conversation. In the cities the newspapers predicted war— "civil strife seems inevitable"—and in some rural areas they assumed it had already begun.

Such was the atmosphere when, on January 10, Governor Randall delivered his annual message to the legislature, now convening for its regular session. On this occasion the governor repeated none of his old state-rights challenges to federal authority. Far from it. He defended the state's personal-liberty law but advised the legislators to change any of its provisions which, on close scrutiny, they might feel were in conflict with the Constitution of the United States. He concluded with a resoundingly nationalistic peroration. "The Government must be sustained, the laws shall be enforced!" he exclaimed. "Secession is revolution, revolution is war; war against the government of the United States is treason."

---

[37] Schwab, "Wisconsin and Compromise Efforts," 9, 38, 46–48, quoting the *Wisconsin Patriot*, December 3, 1860; pp. 4 and 11 of the minority report by Washburn and Mason W. Tappan in *House Reports*, 36 Cong., 2 sess., no. 31 (serial 1104); and Washburn from the *Congressional Globe*, 36 Cong., 2 sess., 513.

The legislature responded with a joint resolution tendering to the President of the United States, "through the Chief Magistrate of our own State, whatever aid in men and money," might be required to "enable him to enforce the laws and uphold the authority of the Federal Government, and in defense of the more perfect Union. . . ." Over the strong objections of the Democratic members, the legislature endorsed Washburn's uncompromising minority report to Congress. The Democrats failed to repeal the personal-liberty law, despite persisting efforts, and the Republicans declined to modify it.[38]

While hurrying to get out his no-compromise report, Congressman Washburn had one eye on Charles Durkee's seat in the upcoming Wisconsin senatorial election, as did Governor Randall when delivering his bellicose speech to the legislature. Washburn, who had refrained from running again for the House in anticipation of being elevated to the Senate, polled the largest vote when the Republican legislators first balloted in caucus, on January 18. But Washburn lacked a majority, for there was a third man in the race—the slender, handsome, sprightly former judge, Timothy O. Howe of Green Bay. Always a foe of those who would "involve Wisconsin in the guilt of nullification," Howe had lost the senatorship four years earlier because of his unwillingness to cater to the then prevailing sentiment for state rights. That was now a dead issue in Wisconsin politics. "When the National Government was in the hands of the Slavocracy, it was important to have, in our national council, representatives who watched with zealous care every encroachment upon the reserved rights of the States," the Racine *Advocate* was saying, but since a Republican administration was now about to take charge in Washington, such care was no longer necessary. After several days of futile balloting, Randall threw his support and the nomination to Howe,

<hr>

[38] Walter S. Glazer, "Wisconsin Goes to War: April, 1861" (master's thesis, University of Wisconsin, 1963), 1–8; Schwab, "Wisconsin and Compromise Efforts," 57–58, 61–72; p. 58 quotes Randall in the *Wisconsin Senate Journal,* 1861, p. 33. For the joint resolution, see *ibid.,* 40–41.

and Howe easily defeated the pro forma Democratic candidate, ninety-two to thirty-four.[39]

Many people in Wisconsin had second thoughts about the sectional crisis as, during January, the states of the lower South withdrew from the Union and prepared to form a new confederacy, calling a convention to meet in Montgomery, Alabama, on February 4. Republican editors began to agree with Democratic editors in bespeaking moderation for Wisconsinites. The Beloit *Journal and Courier*—which a couple of weeks before had announced: "The day for conciliation is past and the time for action has arrived"—on January 21 discovered: "A decided reaction of sentiment is taking place." Public opinion in Wisconsin seemed to be receptive when the legislature of Virginia invited all the states to send delegates to a peace conference, to meet in Washington on the same day the Southern convention was to assemble in Montgomery. Businessmen were especially favorable to the idea. More than 800 members of the Milwaukee Chamber of Commerce signed a statement endorsing it as a means to "appease Southern fears." Prominent citizens, Republicans joining with Democrats, got up "Union meetings" in various parts of the state. The banker Alexander Mitchell presided over a huge Union meeting in Milwaukee on February 4, the day the Washington peace conference began.[40]

No Wisconsin delegates were at the conference. The Wisconsin legislature was still debating the question whether to accept the Virginia legislature's invitation. One group of anti-

[39] Flatley, "Wisconsin Congressional Delegation," 99–100, quotes Howe to John Tweedy, April 11, 1859, in the John H. Tweedy Papers. James L. Sellers, "Republicanism and State Rights in Wisconsin," in the *Mississippi Valley Historical Review*, 17 (September, 1930), 228–229, quotes the *Advocate's* statement as printed in the *Wisconsin State Journal*, January 11, 1861. See William H. Russell, "Timothy O. Howe, Stalwart Republican," in *WMH*, 35 (Winter, 1951), 90–99.

[40] Glazer, "Wisconsin Goes to War," 10–12, quoting the Beloit paper and the Milwaukee Chamber of Commerce; Schwab, "Wisconsin and Compromise Efforts," 84–86; David B. Leonard, "A Biography of Alexander Mitchell, 1817–1887" (master's thesis, University of Wisconsin, 1951), 114.

slavery radicals in the assembly denounced the overture as a scheme to compromise "the honor and dignity of Wisconsin," though other radicals in and out of the legislature thought it politic to send a delegation, one composed of unyielding anti-slavery men. Schurz, on a lecture tour in Ohio, dispatched a rather cryptic telegram to Randall: "Appoint commissioners —me one—to help our side." On February 26, after the legislature had failed to agree and the governor had refused to act, an unofficial gathering of Republicans and Democrats in the assembly hall chose five conservative personages as Wisconsin's peace commissioners. The very next day the Washington conference adjourned, having accomplished nothing except a vast amount of speechifying.[41]

After the inauguration of Lincoln, on March 4, Wisconsin Republicans were more patient with him than they had been with his predecessor, Buchanan. They had criticized Buchanan for irresolution and inaction, but they bore with Lincoln for three weeks or longer while he appeared to do nothing to assert his authority in the South. Most of the Republican papers even gave their approval when the rumor spread that he intended to withdraw the federal garrison and let Fort Sumter go. The Milwaukee *Sentinel*, for one, said it was wise and proper for the North to "win the South back by kindness." At the same time, however, in his maiden speech in Congress late in March, Senator Howe talked about the blood that freedom had shed "upon all her battlefields, from Marathon to Yorktown." Such was the blood of the Northern people: "They have not forgotten how to die, they never knew how to surrender."

By the beginning of April some party leaders had such misgivings about a policy of kindness that Governor Randall traveled to Washington to consult personally with the President. He assured Lincoln that Wisconsin would support him wholeheartedly in a resolute stand. The New York *Times*

<hr/>

[41] Jacobi, "Wisconsin Civil War Governors," 22–23. The quotation is from Wyman Spooner in the *Wisconsin Assembly Journal*, 1861, pp. 183–184. Robert G. Gunderson, *Old Gentlemen's Convention: The Washington Peace Conference of 1861* (Madison, 1961), 75–79, recounts the incident of Schurz's telegram.

reported Randall's telling a friend that Sumter's evacuation would disrupt the Republican party in Wisconsin, but the *Wisconsin State Journal* repudiated the story and insisted that the state's Republicans were "prepared to sustain a policy of evacuation."

According to news reports reaching Wisconsin on April 11, Lincoln apparently was not going to give up the fort but, instead, was sending an expedition to provision and strengthen it. Some editors doubted the reports, and others predicted that the Confederates would allow a peaceful provisioning. On April 12, however, the telegraph brought news that the Confederate artillery around Charleston harbor had opened fire, and two days later that the Sumter garrison had surrendered. Disbelief gave way to numbing realization, but as yet there was no certainty as to where the events might lead. "What shall be done?" a reporter found everyone vaguely asking as he toured the southern part of the state. "The rebels must be put down," the Janesville *Gazette* answered, and practically all Wisconsin papers, Democratic as well as Republican, agreed.[42]

On April 15 newspaper readers learned of President Lincoln's proclamation calling upon the state governors for troops. The proclamation was based upon and embodied the language of the act of 1795 that authorized the President, as commander in chief of the army and navy, to call the state militia into federal service in order to put down "combinations too powerful to be suppressed by the ordinary course of judicial proceedings." It was the same law that Governor Randall had been willing to disregard at the time of his clash with Garrett Barry and the Union Guards only a year before. The governor's response was far different now.

[42] Glazer, "Wisconsin Goes to War," 16–51, quoting the Milwaukee *Sentinel*, March 23, 1861 (p. 20), the *Wisconsin State Journal*, April 6, 1861 (p. 28n), the Waukesha *Freeman*, April 17, 1861 (p. 50), and the Janesville *Gazette*, April 15, 1861 (p. 48); William D. Love, *Wisconsin in the War of the Rebellion; A History of All Regiments and Batteries the State Has Sent to the Field, And deeds of her Citizens, Governors and other Military Officers, and State and National Legislators to suppress the Rebellion* (Chicago, 1866), 114–117; William B. Hesseltine, *Lincoln and the War Governors* (New York, 1948), 141. Howe's speech is in the *Congressional Globe*, 37 Cong., special sess., 1501.

9

The Call to Arms

[1]

A TELEGRAM from Washington, April 15, 1861, called upon Wisconsin for one regiment of militia, totaling 780 men, to serve for three months. Without delay, Governor Alexander W. Randall replied by wiring his assurance that the call would be "promptly met, and further calls when made." The next day the governor issued a proclamation to the people of the state. "All good citizens, everywhere, must join in making common cause against a common enemy." Opportunities for enlistment would be "immediately offered to all existing military companies."[1]

There were, at the time, more than fifty companies of militia in Wisconsin, but some were no more than lists of names on muster rolls, and few if any were filled, trained, equipped, and ready to march. During the recent weeks of sectional crisis, anticipating a presidential call for troops, Randall had urged upon the legislature various measures for preparedness. The legislature had responded by authorizing the acceptance of seventy-five-man companies, appropriating $100,000 for uniforms and equipment, and sanctioning a $200,000 war loan. True, the constitution prohibited a state debt in excess of

---

[1] *The War of the Rebellion: A Compilation of the Official Records of the Union and Confederate Armies* (128 vols., Washington, D.C., 1880–1901), series 3, vol. 1: 72, hereinafter cited as *Official Records*; William D. Love, *Wisconsin in the War of the Rebellion . . .* (Chicago, 1866), 124–125.

$100,000, and that limit had already been reached by the issuance of bonds for the enlargement of the capitol and for the construction of the insane asylum. But the constitution also permitted borrowing for defense, and in the emergency, acting on the very day of the Sumter attack, the majority of the legislators took this constitutional provision as a warrant for going over the debt limit.[2]

Responding to the President's and the governor's proclamation, people throughout the state attended patriotic meetings and flag raisings to encourage volunteering and pledge moral and financial support to the Union cause. Men with money gladly offered some of it to persuade other men to leave their families and go off to war. The mass meetings turned to procuring funds for the maintenance of volunteers' dependents. In Waupun, the subscriptions quickly totaled $3,000; in Kenosha, $3,543; in Fond du Lac, $4,000; in Madison, $7,490; and in Milwaukee, more than $30,000, of which wealthy banker Alexander Mitchell contributed $1,000.

"Wisconsin speaks but one voice today," Senator James R. Doolittle declared at a Union prayer meeting in Racine. "From town and hamlet, from native and foreign born, from old and young, from Republican and Democrat, there comes but one response, 'The Constitution and Union must be maintained. . . .'" For the moment, Democrats were indeed standing together with Republicans, immigrants with old Americans, Catholics with Protestants. The Catholic priest F. J. Bonduel, for one, at Bay Settlement near Green Bay, had been "advocating compromise and counselling peace," but now he was for "asserting the power of the Government with the Bible in one hand and the sword in the other." It was a tribute to Lincoln's Sumter policy that so many diverse Wisconsinites found themselves temporarily united in patriotism. The Southern rebels had fired the first shot—not the Lincoln

[2] Robert H. Jacobi, "Wisconsin Civil War Governors" (master's thesis, University of Wisconsin, 1948), 23–26; Jerry M. Cooper, "The Wisconsin Militia, 1832–1900" (master's thesis, University of Wisconsin, 1968), 143–144; Spencer C. Scott, "The Financial Effects of the Civil War on the State of Wisconsin" (master's thesis, University of Wisconsin, 1939), 101–103.

government. "It has carefully refrained from even the appearance of a purpose to strike a blow at the South," as the Milwaukee *Sentinel* explained. "Its late mission to Sumter was only one of common humanity—of mercy."[3]

Yet it was an exaggeration to say, even during the first days of the war, that Wisconsin spoke with a single voice. There was considerable dissent, and there would have been more if there had been complete freedom of speech and of the press. In Green Bay Senator Timothy O. Howe thought it urgent to stage a war meeting because, as he informed Randall, even some of the native-born citizens "gloried in our defeat" at Sumter and the "whole Irish host was rejoicing." In Madison the former Democratic mayor George E. Smith confessed at a patriotic gathering: "I would forgive the South in many things —even for firing on the American flag when we sent a steamer into Charleston." In Manitowoc the Democratic editor Jere Crowley was still more daring: he told a crowd that Jefferson Davis was no traitor but "the bravest man that ever lived." The crowd overwhelmed the speaker with boos and hisses and a week later they assembled again to "assist" him in "raising the Stars and Stripes over his newspaper office." In Milwaukee the Democratic *News* and the German Catholic *Seebote* questioned the administration's "excuse" for war. "Last Monday [April 15] the excitement here was so great that a movement to destroy the printing establishments of the *News* and the *Seebote* was only barely averted," Carl Schurz wrote to his wife from Milwaukee two days later. "The *News* has already become distinctly tame and the *Seebote* will hardly escape its doom unless it changes its course betimes."[4]

[3] Love, *Wisconsin in the War*, 126–139, 150–151. The Doolittle quotation is from p. 151. The Milwaukee *Sentinel* quotation is from April 17, 1861. The reference to Father Bonduel is from a stray note dated April 13, 1861, a typed copy of which is in File No. 21, Milwaukee Archdiocese Chancery Archives.

[4] Walter S. Glazer, "Wisconsin Goes to War: April, 1861" (master's thesis, University of Wisconsin, 1963), 48–49, 68, 85, 87, 105. The Howe quotation is from Howe to Randall, April 20, 1861, in the Timothy O. Howe Papers; the Smith quotation from the Milwaukee *Wisconsin*, April 16, 1861. The Schurz quotation is from Joseph Schafer, ed. and trans., *Intimate Letters of Carl Schurz, 1841–1869* (Madison, 1928), 253–254.

Meanwhile the militiamen of Wisconsin were giving a mixed response to the governor's appeal for volunteers. Many of the men suddenly discovered familial, financial, or other obligations that would make it impossible for them to serve. Some had political objections as well. Especially reluctant were the Democrats of Irish or German birth. The Hibernian Guards of Fond du Lac, an Irish outfit, decided to disband. So did the Watertown Rifles and the Governor's Artillery (also of Watertown), both German units. None of the four companies in predominantly German Ozaukee and Washington counties volunteered. The captain of the recalcitrant Cedarburg Rifles, of Ozaukee County, was Frederick W. Horn, who had come from Prussia and, as the former state immigration commissioner, had encouraged others to come. On resigning his commission, Horn denounced the war as a scheme to strengthen the Republican party and the business interests of the Northeast. He also feared that it might turn into an anti-Catholic crusade. In Republican areas some captains, more willing than Horn and more willing than their own men, made promises they had difficulty in carrying out. The captain of the Park City Grays (Kenosha) was one of the first to offer his company's service, but he and other Kenoshans had to work hard to fill the company's ranks in time.

Within one week the required ten companies were available, and the governor had accepted them, for three-months' duty— one each from Kenosha, Beloit, Horicon, and Fond du Lac; two from Madison; and four from Milwaukee. On Monday, April 22, Randall telegraphed to Secretary of War Simon Cameron: "I have the honor to inform you that the First Regiment of Wisconsin active militia is enrolled and officered, and will be at the command of the Government at Milwaukee on Saturday of the present week."[5]

By now a surge of enthusiasm for war service was rising in

[5] Glazer, "Wisconsin Goes to War," 62–64, 75–85, 101–104; Cooper, "Wisconsin Militia," 148–156; Frank Klement, "Copperheads and Copperheadism in Wisconsin: Democratic Opposition to the Lincoln Administration," in *WMH*, 42 (Spring, 1959), 183, 186. The quotation is from *Official Records*, series 3, vol. 1: 102.

the state. This was in part a delayed reaction to the Sumter attack and in part a response to what seemed like new aggression when, on April 19, a pro-Confederate mob fell upon Massachusetts troops as they passed through Baltimore on the way to the defense of Washington. Men eager to put down the rebels began to take over inactive militia companies or to recruit and organize new ones. Offers of service flooded the governor's office. "We have no parties now," Randall exulted. "The people will not be content to furnish one regiment alone." He proceeded to authorize several more regiments, but the War Department refused to accept any of these.[6]

Randall became more and more concerned as a result of what seemed to him like indifference and inefficiency on the part of the Lincoln administration. There appeared to be a growing threat to the Northern states and particularly to those of the Mississippi Valley. The people themselves were rising magnificently—"there is a spirit evoked by this rebellion among the liberty-loving people of the country that is driving them to action"—but the federal government was slow to harness this spirit and use it for victory. Other Northern governors shared Randall's anxiety. He gladly accepted when the Ohio governor invited all those west of New England to a conference in Cleveland. The conference met on May 3, with representatives from seven states in attendance. They delegated to Randall the task of presenting their views to Lincoln.

After returning to Madison, Randall on behalf of himself and his fellow governors composed a long letter in which he lectured Lincoln on the President's duties. Now that Washington was safe, the President must see to the protection of the border farther west. He must keep the Ohio and Mississippi rivers open for the trade of Wisconsin and the other northwestern states. To meet the needs of the hour, he should "call into the field at once 300,000 men" in addition to the 75,000 he had already called for. If the federal government should

---

[6] Glazer, "Wisconsin Goes to War," 104; Jacobi, "Wisconsin Civil War Governors," 33–34, quoting Randall to Cameron, April 19, 1861, in the *Official Records*, series 3, vol. 1: 91.

fail to act immediately and decisively, the states and their people would have to take matters into their own hands and "act for themselves." If, on the other hand, the Lincoln administration should promptly live up to its responsibilities, then "it would have the right as well as power of ultimate direction and control, without the confusion that otherwise might arise between the States and the Government."

Lincoln had anticipated the demands of Randall and the rest of the impatient governors. Already, on May 3, the President had issued a new call for forty regiments of volunteers. These were not to consist of state militia serving for three months. Instead, they were to be soldiers "subject to the laws and regulations governing the army of the United States," and they were to enlist for three years or for the duration of the war (if it should end in less than three years). Lincoln had taken charge.[7]

[2]

"This war began where Charleston *is;* it should end where Charleston *was,*" Governor Randall declaimed on May 15, 1861, one month after the original call to arms. "These gathering armies are the instruments of His vengeance, to execute His just judgments; they are His flails wherewith on God's great Southern threshing floor, He will pound rebellion for its sins!" Thus, mixing his Methodism with his Republicanism, the governor addressed the legislators whom he had convened in a special session to provide for the gathering troops.[8]

He had assured the War Department that Wisconsin was "anxious to furnish at least five regiments" for three years or the duration of the war. He expected no difficulty in raising enough men, since thousands of three-month volunteers were

[7] William B. Hesseltine, *Lincoln and the War Governors* (New York, 1948), 161–165; Randall to Lincoln, May 6, 1861; the other quotations are from *Official Records,* series 3, vol. 1: 151–157, 167–170.

[8] P. Marcus Schmidt, "The Dependence of the Lincoln Administration on the Northwestern Governors" (master's thesis, University of Wisconsin, 1936), 85, quoting from the *Assembly Journal, Extra Session,* 1861, p. 12.

willing to extend their terms, and thousands of others apparently were eager to enlist for the duration. But he needed money
to feed, house, clothe, and pay the recruits. The federal government was promising to supply arms, to take care of the men
once they were mustered into the federal service, and to reim-
burse the state for its expenses in maintaining them until then.
For the time being, some captains-to-be were recruiting companies and paying the men out of their own pockets while rely-
ing on the local communities to provide board and lodging.
This could not go on indefinitely, as the governor knew from
the letters that filled his mail, clamoring for the state to assume
the entire burden.

At its May session the legislature gave the governor the
authority he asked for to organize and subsist three-year regiments. The legislature also voted a war loan of $1,000,000 in
addition to the previous one of $200,000. This first issue of
bonds had not been selling, partly because of a stipulation that
they must be sold only at par. The new bonds were free from
this restriction, yet they also proved hard to sell. There was
doubt about their constitutionality in view of the state constitution's debt ceiling. Randall removed this obstacle by taking an unprecedented step and getting an advisory opinion from
the Wisconsin supreme court, which approved of borrowing
without limit for defense. There remained the handicap of
Wisconsin's low credit rating among Eastern financiers, who
were all too keenly aware of the state's recent efforts to prevent
Eastern creditors from collecting from Wisconsin's railroad
farm mortgagers. The problems of public finance, already serious, were made desperate by the impending collapse of the state's
banking system.[9]

Before the war, many Wisconsin banks had invested heavily
in the bonds of Southern states—especially Missouri, Virginia,
Tennessee, North Carolina, and Louisiana—since these bonds
could be bought below par and yielded high interest rates.

[9] Randall to Cameron, May 11, 1861, in *Official Records*, series 3, vol. 1: 189
(quotation); Scott, "Financial Effects of the Civil War," 7, 102–105; Jacobi, "Wisconsin Civil War Governors," 36, 45–51.

Deposited with the bank comptroller, the Southern bonds served as backing for more than half of the banknotes that were issued in Wisconsin to circulate as currency. At the start of secession the bonds began to fall in value, and after the firing on Fort Sumter they dropped still faster. Repeatedly the comptroller demanded additional security to make up for the depreciation of the bonds. When some of the banks were unable to comply, others refused to accept their notes. By late April, $2,000,000 of the notes had been discredited, and unlucky holders of this dubious money were trying desperately to get rid of it. Only seventy of the 111 banks remained in good standing.

To maintain confidence in the seventy unscathed banks and their currency ($2,500,000 of it), the members of the Wisconsin Bankers' Association, under the leadership of Alexander Mitchell, guaranteed the notes by agreeing to receive them at par. The price of Southern bonds continued to decline, however, and in early June, when the comptroller again required further security, eighteen of the seventy banks failed to respond, and ten of the eighteen closed down. On June 21 Mitchell and the other Milwaukee bankers met and decided they would no longer accept the notes of the ten insolvent banks. The Milwaukee bankers kept their decision secret until after banking hours the next morning, a Saturday. When the announcement was made, it started a rumor, probably true, that the bankers had been unloading the notes they were about to repudiate. Businessmen charged the bankers with a breach of faith, and workingmen were even angrier, especially those who had just received their wages in the now nearly worthless bills.

On Monday morning a crowd consisting mostly of Germans marched behind a brass band to the office of Mitchell's bank, the Wisconsin Marine and Fire Insurance Company. Confronting the protesters at the bank's entrance, Mitchell along with the mayor and the police chief attempted to calm them. Soon stones were flying. Mitchell got away with slight injuries, but one of his clerks was caught and badly mauled. The mob surged into the bank and into several neighboring ones, threw furniture and records into the street, and turned the piles of wreckage into bonfires. After police with the aid of militia had put down the riot, threats of renewed violence persisted for the rest of the week. Four companies of troops, with cannon, patrolled the banking district, and a detachment from the Montgomery Guard (an Irish company) protected Mitchell's residence.

Already Mitchell had proposed and the state authorities had accepted a plan to rescue the banks and at the same time to dispose of the war loan. The idea was simple: the banks would buy Wisconsin bonds and use them to replace the Southern bonds as security for the banknotes. A committee of bankers concluded negotiations with the state bank comptroller and the state loan commissioners on the day after the bank riot. According to the agreement, the bankers were to take $800,000 of the $1,000,000 bond issue. They were to pay down 70 per cent of the $800,000, partly in coin or New York exchange and partly in Wisconsin par currency. The remaining 30 per cent they were to pay in installments over a period of fifteen years. During this time they were to receive interest at 6 per cent on the entire sum, including the unpaid portion of it. These terms were highly favorable to the bankers, and yet the deal was also advantageous to the state. Not only did the banking system return to stability, but the government could now realize some immediate proceeds from the war loan.[10]

Nevertheless, Governor Randall soon found himself in financial difficulties again as he continued busily to organize troops. He pleaded with the Lincoln administration to accept six regiments instead of the three it had asked for. He finally won his point on the condition that the six be ready early in July. After these regiments had departed, the Wisconsin secretary of the treasury billed the federal government for $512,000

[10] Frederick Merk, *Economic History of Wisconsin During the Civil War Decade* (Madison, 1916), 187–209; David B. Leonard, "A Biography of Alexander Mitchell, 1817–1887" (master's thesis, University of Wisconsin, 1951), 64–70; Scott, "Financial Effects of the Civil War," 106–112; Theodore A. Andersen, *A Century of Banking in Wisconsin* (Madison, 1954), 48–49.

Above: John H. and John W. Fonda of Prairie du Chien, father-and-son enlistees at the outbreak of the Civil War. Below: First Wisconsin Artillery encampment near Chattanooga, Tennessee, 1864.

Officers of the Iron Brigade: Rufus King, John C. Starkweather, and George B. Bingham.

Above: Henry A. Cooper. Right: Arthur McArthur, Jr., colonel of the Twenty-Fourth Wisconsin Volunteer Infantry.

Soldiers' Orphans' Home, Madison, in the former home of Governor Leonard J. Farwell on Spaight Street.

Above: James R. Doolittle.
Above right: Young sports.

Bishop Jackson Kemper.

Cream City baseball team, Milwaukee.

The Herman Band, Sheboygan, 1871.

Above: Summertime croquet, ca. 1870. Below: Well-equipped German huntsmen.

Devils Lake beach, with Cliff House in background.

*The Wisconsin Dells, photographed by Henry H. Bennett, ca. 1870.
(Photo courtesy H. H. Bennett Studio.)*

*Wedding party, Dane County, photographed by Andreas L. Dahl
in the 1870's.*

but got no reimbursement until September, and then only $205,000.

While delaying to pay its bills and to provide the necessary arms, the federal government was making new demands for troops. By August the relationship between the governor and the War Department had been reversed. Previously he had been begging a reluctant administration to accept more and more Wisconsin men. Now he was making excuses for holding back. He was confident that the war spirit among his people remained high, though the federal rout at Bull Run, on July 21, had dispelled the early expectations of a quick victory and a short war. He explained that the farmers needed to harvest their crops, and he therefore wished to postpone recruiting the seventh and eighth regiments until September.

Having nearly exhausted the available state funds, Randall kept pressing the federal government for the means with which to pay for additional troops. At the same time he renewed his efforts to raise them. "If we get any money from Government," he wired the war secretary on October 26, "can furnish in all seventeen regiments infantry, a full regiment artillery, and a full regiment of cavalry." In November he went to Washington and succeeded in making arrangements to collect another $205,000 on the state's long outstanding claim for reimbursement. (Neither he nor his wartime successors in the governorship were ever to collect all they claimed as due the state.) [11]

An order from the War Department, dated December, 3, 1861, instructed Randall along with the rest of the loyal governors to raise no more regiments except for those already in the process of formation. The order added that, in the future, federal superintendents would take charge of the recruiting service in the various states. By the time the order took effect, there had been organized in Wisconsin thirteen regiments of infantry (including the three-month First Regiment, reorganized as a three-year unit), an additional company of infantry and one company each of cavalry and sharpshooters, and four batteries

[11] *Official Records,* series 3, vol. 1: 289, 600 (quotation); Jacobi, "Wisconsin Civil War Governors," 53–61; Scott, "Financial Effects of the Civil War," 127–135.

of artillery. All were in active service. By the end of the year, there were also, either organized or in the process of being organized, six regiments of infantry, three regiments of cavalry, and five companies of artillery. These were still encamped within the state, "only waiting for the visit of the U.S. paymaster and marching orders."[12]

[3]

According to the state adjutant general's count, the first thirteen regiments of infantry, together with the company of sharpshooters and the first company of cavalry, came to a total of 14,002 men. Of these, 10,334 were American natives and 3,668 were foreign-born. That is to say, the foreigners constituted a little over a fourth (26.2 per cent) of the total. According to census data, immigrants made up about a third of Wisconsin's population as a whole and more than half of its men of military age, eighteen to forty-five. Thus, in response to the first calls for troops, the young men of foreign birth volunteered in much less than proportionate numbers, and those of American birth in considerably more than proportionate numbers. Indeed, the natives enlisted at nearly three times the rate of the foreign-born.[13]

[12] *Official Records,* series 3, vol. 1: 880–881, 941; the quotation is from p. 880. See also E. B. Quiner, *The Military History of Wisconsin: A Record of the Civil and Military Patriotism of the State in the War for the Union, With a History of the Campaigns in which Wisconsin Soldiers have been Conspicuous—Regimental Histories—Sketches of Distinguished Officers—The Roll of the Illustrious Dead—Movements of the Legislature and State Officers, etc.* (Chicago, 1866), 98–99.

[13] Wisconsin Adjutant General, *Annual Report,* 1861, p. 54. Foreign-born included those from the "German States, including Switzerland and Holland; Irish; Norwegians and Swedes; English, Canadians, Welsh, and Scotch; and Scattering." The 1860 census gives 159,335 as the number of white males of military age in Wiconsin, but does not provide separate figures for the native and foreign-born of this group, though it does for the population as a whole. See *Eighth Census of the United States, 1860: Population,* xvii, xxx-xxxii, 543–544. The 1870 census gives 192,331 as the number of males of military age and divides this into 86,593 American-born and 105,738 foreign-born, which means approximately 45 per cent American and 55 per cent foreign in 1870. See *Ninth Census of the United States, 1870: Volume I,* p. 619. Since there is less than a 5 per cent change between 1860 and 1870 in the native and foreign-born proportions of the total population, in the proportion of military-age citizens in the

The recruits of 1861 were true volunteers, who came forward without compulsion except for that of their own principles, ambitions, or necessities. They responded to appeals that were based on self-interest as well as patriotism, like the August appeal of a Menasha editor. "Let a few of our patriotic young men walk up and enlist," this editor urged. They might win fame and at least they could make a good livelihood, what with the enlistment bounty, the soldier's pay, and the allowance for his family. "In view of the hard times and almost universal stagnation of business of every kind . . . there is nothing which offers so great an inducement as the army."[14]

Among the Germans of Wisconsin, the Protestant liberals and the freethinking radicals, both strong adherents of the Republican party, were the earliest to volunteer. Such Germans formed practically an entire company of the Second Regiment. A Schuetzen Corps of Milwaukee Turners comprised one company of the Fifth, and other Germans predominated in most if not all its companies. When Governor Randall invited immigrants from Germany to provide a whole regiment, one member of a Milwaukee Forty-Eighter family took the lead in raising and his brother commanded what came to be known as the Ninth or "German" Regiment. Germans also helped to fill the ranks of other regiments that were organized in 1861, especially the Eighteenth.[15]

Scattered Irishmen were to be found in each of the original thirteen regiments except perhaps for the German Ninth. In

total population, and in the proportion of males 18–45 in the American-born and foreign-born population, it is clear that the proportions of American-born and foreign-born of military age must have been almost the same for 1860 as for 1870.

[14] Menasha *Weekly Manufacturer*, August 8, 29, 1861, quoted in Alice E. Smith, *Millstone and Saw: The Origins of Neenah-Menasha* (Madison, 1966), 186.

[15] Ella Lonn, *Foreigners in the Union Army and Navy* (Baton Rouge, 1951), 110–111. The manuscript Muster and Descriptive Roll of the Wisconsin regiments, Series 1144 in the WSA, indicates that all but a few of the first nineteen regiments included some Germans among the original recruits. On the prompt volunteering of the Turners, as distinct from the German Catholics, see also M. Hedwigis Overmoehle, "The Anti-Clerical Activities of the Forty-Eighters in Wisconsin, 1848–1860: A Study in German-American Liberalism" (doctoral dissertation, St. Louis University, 1941), 260.

the early volunteering the immigrants from Ireland apparently lagged behind the other English-speaking immigrants—those from England, Scotland, Wales, and British North America. Later the Hibernian proportion of the Wisconsin troops increased with the recruiting of the Seventeenth Regiment, which was called the "Irish Brigade" and consisted mainly though not entirely of men from Ireland.[16]

To many Norwegians the army was attractive both because of their Republican convictions and because of their desperate poverty. Leaders of the Norwegian community added an appeal to ethnic pride: the Norwegians must not let the Germans or the Irish get ahead of them in springing to the defense of their adopted land. Answering the governor's very first call, a group of Dane County Norwegians became the nucleus of Company K of the Third Regiment. Others, a few here and a few there, enlisted in most of the companies being formed. Much the largest number signed up for a Scandinavian regiment after Hans Christian Heg and other prominent Norwegians began to organize it in September. Heg and his fellow recruiters sought Danes and Swedes as well as Norwegians and looked to Illinois, Iowa, and Minnesota as well as Wisconsin. Nevertheless, the great majority of the men of the Fifteenth, when it finally took form, proved to be Wisconsinites from Norway.[17]

[16] M. Justille McDonald, *History of the Irish in Wisconsin in the Nineteenth Century* (Washington, D.C., 1954), 140–141. The manuscript Muster and Descriptive Roll unfortunately lists no birthplaces for the First Regiment and only about three-fourths of those of the next eleven regiments (excluding the Ninth). Of the birthplaces given, 965 are in England, Scotland, Wales, or British North America (omitting those of British North Americans with French names), 336 in Ireland. Lonn, *Foreigners in the Union Army*, 125, describes the Eleventh as "chiefly Irish" and the Seventeenth as "completely Irish." She is incorrect in regard to both. Among the 920 original recruits of the Eleventh whose nativities are given in the Muster and Descriptive Roll, only fifty-four or fewer than 6 per cent were of Irish birth. In Company D of the Seventeenth—the one company of that regiment for which nativities are completely given—only twenty-seven of 112 were born in Ireland (a plurality of thirty-eight were born in Germany).

[17] Lonn, *Foreigners in the Union Army*, 132, 136–138; Theodore C. Blegen, ed., *The Civil War Letters of Colonel Hans Christian Heg* (Northfield, Minnesota, 1936), 20–26.

After the first thirteen regiments had been completed, and while the next five were being raised, the Wisconsin adjutant general predicted that these five would contain more men of foreign than of American birth. He estimated that, of 5,230 additional men, only 2,430 would be Americans. Among the foreign-born, the Irish, "supposing the 17th to fill," would number 1,200; and the Norwegians, "supposing the 15th to fill," would number 1,050. In fact, by the end of 1861 the Seventeenth had reached scarcely half of its projected strength, with only 500 men, and the Fifteenth also had fallen short, with 600. Yet the delayed surge of Irish and Norwegian volunteering had helped to raise the over-all percentage of immigrants among the Wisconsin troops. Once the first nineteen regiments had been filled, the American-born no longer constituted nearly three-fourths of the total and no longer led in volunteering by nearly three to one. Nevertheless, of these approximately 20,000 volunteers, the Americans still constituted at least two-thirds. They still led, in proportion to numbers of military age, by more than two to one.[18]

[4]

Despite his success at raising troops, Governor Randall ran into a great deal of criticism for his handling of the war effort. Carpers complained that he wasted state funds, provided shoddy uniforms, and misused the patronage in his appointments of purchasing agents and special governor's representatives who traveled with the regiments to see that the men were properly cared for. Weary of the attacks on his administration, he decided not to seek a third term as governor but, instead, to

[18] Even accepting the adjutant general's estimate for the Fourteenth to Eighteenth regiments, as well as his calculation for the first thirteen, the figure for the American-born would be 12,764 in a total of 19,232—that is, 66.4 per cent. Wisconsin Adjutant General, *Annual Report*, 1861, pp. 44, 47, 56. Citing p. 56 of this report, Alan T. Nolan erroneously says the adjutant general "found that approximately 50 per cent of the Wisconsin volunteers were American born"; *The Iron Brigade: A Military History* (New York, 1961), 32.

accept President Lincoln's offer of the diplomatic post of minister to Rome.

Randall's succesor in the governorship was his former secretary of state, the Connecticut-born Louis Powell Harvey, a man who had made few enemies and who, as the *Wisconsin State Journal* once said, had "never been associated with any dishonorable transactions." Taking office in January 1862, Governor Harvey was fated to serve for just over 100 days. In that time he succeeded in making arrangements for the collection of most of Wisconsin's claims against the federal government. Congress had levied a direct tax on each of the states, a tax that the state authorities were required to collect and turn over to the federal treasury. Following the example of other governors, Harvey secured permission for Wisconsin to keep its share of the direct tax and use the money to offset the state's claims. He also made a reputation as the special friend of Wisconsin soldiers. Though he withdrew Randall's traveling representatives, he assigned agents to fixed locations for looking after the soldiers' needs. And he went personally on Samaritan missions to the troops.

In April, after returning from a visit with Wisconsin soldiers in St. Louis, Harvey learned that four Wisconsin regiments had suffered losses in the Battle of Shiloh. Promptly he set out for the battlefield with medical supplies and a group of surgeons. On the way he visited hospitals and hospital boats at Cairo and Mound City, Illinois, and Paducah, Kentucky, to greet and reassure the sick and wounded from Wisconsin. At Pittsburgh Landing, Tennessee, he offered cheer and praise to Wisconsin survivors of the recent battle. On the dark and rainy night of April 19 he was about to step from one riverboat to another for the return trip. He slipped, fell between the two vessels, and disappeared. Days later some children found his body sixty-five miles downstream.

Harvey's death brought Edward Salomon to the governorship. Only thirty-three years old, Salomon was a Prussian by birth and a Lutheran in faith. While a student at the University of Berlin he had supported the revolutionary movement of

1848, and after its suppression he had left for the United States, to make his home for a time in Manitowoc. In ten years' residence in Milwaukee he had established himself at the local bar but had taken little part in politics until the Republicans nominated him for lieutenant governor. They chose him simply because he was a German and a Democrat who supported the war (one of his brothers organized and another commanded the Ninth Regiment) and who could be expected to draw German Democratic voters to the Republican cause. In the election he may have attracted some of those voters, but he certainly repelled a number of regular Republicans, for he ran behind the rest of the Republican ticket. Now that an accident had made this man governor, many Wisconsinites anxiously wondered whether he would be up to the exacting wartime demands of the office. He would be, indeed, as he soon proceeded to demonstrate.[19]

On May 19, one month after Harvey's drowning, Governor Salomon received a telegram from the new secretary of war, Edwin M. Stanton. Recently Stanton in an optimistic mood had closed the federal recruiting offices, but since then the need for men had suddenly increased, and again the War Department was looking to the governors for troops. Salomon promised to raise the three more regiments requested from Wisconsin, but only if the War Department should meet certain conditions. The department would have to pay all expenses promptly, and it would have to name a man of Salomon's choice as federal disbursing and mustering officer for the state. He delayed the organization of the first of the new regiments, the Twentieth, until Secretary Stanton agreed to pay the officers while they were recruiting. Though the War Department revived its own recruiting service on June 6, enlistments in Wisconsin continued to lag. Then, on July 2, President Lincoln issued a call for 300,000 additional three-year men, 11,904 of

[19] Jacobi, "Wisconsin Civil War Governors," 65–67, 75–79, 81–82; Hesseltine, *Lincoln and the War Governors,* 225–226, quoting from the *Wisconsin State Journal,* September 27, 1861; Love, *Wisconsin in the War,* 434–437; Alexander M. Thomson, *A Political History of Wisconsin* (Milwaukee, 1900), 158.

them from Wisconsin. The War Department now was offering each recruit, in advance, one month's pay, or $13, and $25 of the $100 federal bounty. Salomon prevailed on some of the Wisconsin counties to give a $50 local bounty besides. The money stimulated volunteering, and so did the federal militia act of July 17. By September enough men had come forward in Wisconsin to fill a total of fourteen new regiments (the Twentieth through the Thirty-Third) of three-year volunteers. The number was considerably above what the state had been asked for.[20]

This militia act of 1862 was essentially a revision of the militia act of 1795. Like the old law, the new one authorized the President to call out the militia for as much as nine months of federal service, but the new one also gave the President the power to "make all necessary rules and regulations"—by implication the power to use the draft—for raising troops in states that did not themselves make adequate provision for doing so. Under the act the War Department on August 4 sent the governors yet another call, this one for nine-month militiamen. Once more, the total for all the states was 300,000 and for Wisconsin 11,904. The governors were ordered to produce their quotas in less than two weeks, by August 15. If any of the governors should fail to do so, the draft would go into effect in his state.[21]

Governor Salomon now had to assign a quota for each Wisconsin county. He instructed every sheriff to compile a list of men eighteen to forty-five who were eligible for military service. Soon he ran into difficulty. "What course shall I take," he inquired of Secretary Stanton, "where in a township no man will serve as enrolling officer and the people refuse

[20] Jacobi, "Wisconsin Civil War Governors," 83–90, 134–135; Schmidt, "Northwestern Governors," 50–52; Quiner, Military History of Wisconsin, 132. The Nineteenth began organizing in December 1861, but did not leave Madison until June 1862. See Wisconsin Adjutant General, Annual Report, 1862, pp. 28–29.

[21] Fred A. Shannon, The Organization and Administration of the Union Army, 1861–1865 (2 vols., Cleveland, 1928), 1: 275–289; Quiner, Military History of Wisconsin, 139–140.

to give their names and abandon their houses when an officer comes to enroll them?" Stanton responded, "Let them slide." Salomon also wondered what to do with members of fire companies, which were now "being filled by shirks at a fearful rate," by men taking advantage of a state law that exempted firemen from militia duty. Stanton thought those who had joined fire companies since April 1861 should be considered liable to the draft. Salomon was especially troubled on account of the large numbers of his fellow immigrants who claimed exemption on the grounds of alienage. "About one-half of the able-bodied men between eighteen and forty-five years in this State are foreign born. They have declared their intention to become citizens of the United States," he reported to Stanton. "Cannot those who are not willing to subject themselves to draft be ordered to leave the country?" Those who had exercised the right to vote, Stanton replied, were properly subject to the draft.

Once Salomon had set the county quotas as best he could, he persuaded Stanton to postpone the draft in Wisconsin, in the hope that all the quotas could be filled by volunteering. Things would go better after the harvest, Salomon believed. They did go well enough in most parts of the state. Before the end of October, volunteering had sufficed in all the counties except for several of those, near Lake Michigan, where Roman Catholic immigrants were especially numerous.[22]

That summer an Austrian-born priest of Port Washington, the Reverend Francis Fulleder, had written, "Two recruiting officers approached me last fall with the question why so few Catholics enlisted." Fulleder said he had answered that every Catholic desired the "consolations of his religion in the hour of danger and death," but these consolations were inadequately provided. So far, only a single Wisconsin regiment, the Irish Seventeenth, had a Catholic chaplain (for every regiment the

[22] The quotations are from *Official Records*, series 3, vol. 2: 369, 395–396, 471, 477. See also Schmidt, "Northwestern Governors," 57–61; Linn I. Schoonover, "A History of the Civil War Draft in Wisconsin" (master's thesis, University of Wisconsin, 1915), 6–12.

officers chose a chaplain, and only the Seventeenth contained a majority of Catholics). According to Fulleder, German Catholics would volunteer more readily if, in the army, they could be assured of access to a German-speaking priest. He himself had acted as an unofficial "visiting chaplain" to various Wisconsin units until Governor Salomon told him there was no law for such an appointment. When the predominantly German Twenty-Fourth Regiment was formed, Fulleder received a commission, on September 3, 1862, as its chaplain, but by then many of his coreligionists were convinced that the army discriminated against them. "According to my judgment," he said, "this accounts for the German Catholic reluctance to enlist."[23]

A more general reason for the reluctance of German Catholics was their lack of enthusiasm for the Lincoln administration, the administration of a party that to them was tainted by abolitionism, nativism, and the godlessness of German anti-church liberals. Many German Catholics would lose what little enthusiasm they had if the administration should openly avow abolitionism and make it a war aim. This was what the native Protestant churches had been advocating all along, the state Baptist, Methodist, and Presbyterian and Congregational conventions having early declared themselves in favor of a crusade to free the slaves. Then, on September 22, 1862, Lincoln issued his preliminary Emancipation Proclamation. The Milwaukee *Seebote*, the pre-eminent voice of Wisconsin's German Catholics, expressed its horror that European immigrants should be "used as fodder for cannons" in an abolitionist war. Under Lincoln's edict the editor exclaimed, the "Germans and Irish must be annihilated, to make room for the Negro. . . ."[24]

In such a cause as that, the draft was especially hateful to

[23] Peter Leo Johnson, "Port Washington Draft Riot of 1862," in *Mid-America*, new series, 1 (January, 1930), 219–222.

[24] Antislavery statements of native Protestant preachers and organizations are quoted and summarized in Love, *Wisconsin in the War*, 180–207; the *Seebote*, October 25, 1862, is quoted in Mary D. Meyer, "The Germans in Wisconsin and the Civil War: Their Attitude Toward the Union, the Republicans, Slavery, and Lincoln" (master's thesis, Catholic University of America, 1937), 45–46.

people who viewed conscription as intolerable in itself. Many of the immigrants had left the Old Country with the hope of escaping compulsory military service. Particularly opposed to conscription were the German-speaking Catholics from Luxemburg, who or whose fathers in the homeland had been compelled to leave their fields and go off to serve foreign rulers, either Belgian or Dutch. To people such as the Luxemburgers it seemed that surely, in a democratic country like the United States, forced service in an army could have no rightful place. Some leaders of the Democratic party, above all the Irish-born Edward G. Ryan, gave them to believe that the draft was indeed unconstitutional and therefore could be disregarded with impunity, though President Lincoln proclaimed on September 24, 1862, that all persons discouraging enlistment or resisting the draft would be subject to court-martial.[25]

According to Governor Salomon's order, drafting was finally scheduled to begin, town by town in the laggard counties, on November 10, 1862. In each locality, after granting exemptions, the governor's appointed draft commissioner was to have a blindfolded person draw names from a drum or box, enough of them to make up the difference between the town's quota and the number of its volunteers.

On November 10 and 11 antidraft rioting broke out in several places. In Brown County hundreds of Belgian farmers armed themselves with guns and scythes and marched upon the Green Bay home of Senator Howe, whom they blamed for the conscription law. Howe, "pale as death, stood upon the upper piazza of his residence and addressed the malcontents, but the majority understood not a word of English. . . ." Unable to quiet the menacing crowd, the senator sneaked out by a side entrance and sped off in a carriage. In Washington County fifteen or twenty Germans descended on West Bend, attacked the draft commissioner, and drove him out of town.

---

[25] Kate Everest Levi, "Geographical Origin of German Immigration to Wisconsin," in *Wis. Hist. Colls.*, 14: 374–379; Alfons J. Beitzinger, *Edward G. Ryan, Lion of the Law* (Madison, 1960), 72; Quiner, *Military History of Wisconsin*, 139–140.

Salomon ordered four companies of the newly formed Thirtieth Regiment to the scene, and with their support the commissioner was finally able to carry out the draft.[26]

In Ozaukee County, Catholic farmers from Luxemburg practically declared a civil war of their own against the Protestant German and native American businessmen of the county seat and trading center, Port Washington. Here the draft commissioner, William Pors, was a German and a Democrat, but he was also a Protestant and a Mason, and he was accused of exempting his Masonic friends from military service. When Pors got ready to start the drawing of names in the courthouse, a drunken mob of Luxemburgers dragged him to the door, threw him down the steps, and pelted him with stones as he fled for his life. The rioters destroyed the boxes containing the names and then roamed through the town looking for Masons to vent their anger on. In several hours of "pillage and plunder" the mob severely damaged the Masonic hall, looted a warehouse, and smashed windows and furniture in several fine residences, one of these belonging to Pors himself and others to businessmen with such names as Hunt, Stillman, Blair, and Loomis. To Port Washington the governor sent eight companies of the Twenty-Eighth Regiment, which surrounded and then occupied the town. On the governor's orders, the provost marshal proceeded to make dozens of arrests.[27]

In Milwaukee County the governor had put off the drafting for another nine days, until November 19, after hearing from a committee of Milwaukeeans that trouble was to be expected there. The sheriff had exaggerated the number of volunteers from the county so as to minimize the number of con-

[26] Peter T. Harstad, ed., "A Civil War Medical Examiner: The Report of Dr. Horace O. Crane," in *WMH*, 48 (Spring, 1965), 223. The quotation is from Deborah B. Martin, *History of Brown County, Wisconsin, Past and Present* (2 vols., Chicago, 1913), 1: 205. See also Quiner, *Military History of Wisconsin*, 147.

[27] Lawrence H. Larsen, "Draft Riot in Wisconsin, 1862," in *Civil War History*, 7 (December, 1961), 421–423, quoting from the Milwaukee *Sentinel*, November 13, 1862; Western Historical Company, *History of Washington and Ozaukee Counties, Wisconsin* . . . (Chicago, 1881), 493–495; Quiner, *Military History of Wisconsin*, 145–147.

scripts needed, and the draft commissioner had had to correct the figures. "Evil disposed persons, operating upon the minds of the foreign-born citizens, had incited threats of resistance, so much so as to induce the Draft Commissioner to resign his position." Salomon used the extra time to make thorough preparations. By November 19 Colonel John C. Starkweather and the First Regiment were ready to back up the governor's proclamation to the disaffected Milwaukeeans: "The disgraceful scenes that recently occurred in a neighboring county shall not be re-enacted in your community." Soldiers picketed all roads leading into the city, a squad was on the alert in every ward, and companies marched and countermarched through the streets. The drawing went off without a hitch.[28]

It was one thing to carry out the drawing of names, but it was quite another to bring the drafted men into the army. Of the 4,537 selected, more than a third (1,662) failed to report for duty. Of those who did report, a large number were discharged or deferred for one reason or another, and only 1,739 were actually mustered in. Many of these took the option of joining old regiments for three years with advance pay and bounty or for nine months without. The rest, most of them Germans, formed a special regiment of nine-month conscripts, the Thirty-Fourth. Such was the yield, besides the direct and indirect stimulus to volunteering, of the 1862 draft in Wisconsin, the only one of the western states except for Indiana that had been compelled to resort to it.

And Wisconsin should not have been compelled to do so, as Governor Salomon learned too late. The War Department had informed other governors, but not him, that if a state exceeded its quota of three-year volunteers it could apply the excess against its quota of nine-month militiamen, counting every surplus three-year recruit as the equivalent of four nine-month recruits. Under the earlier calls of 1862 the state had raised so many extra men for the full term that their number, multiplied by four, would have more than made up for the shortage

---

[28] Schoonover, "Civil War Draft," 12–13. The quotations are from Quiner, *Military History of Wisconsin,* 145, 147–148.

under the later, more limited call. In the light of all this the 1862 draft in Wisconsin, so disruptive and so unproductive, was also quite unjustified.[29]

After the suppression of the Ozaukee County draft riot, Salomon was left with about 150 of the rioters on his hands. He was holding these men under Lincoln's September 24 proclamation, which subjected draft resisters to martial law and denied them the writ of habeas corpus. The proclamation meant that the prisoners from Ozaukee County could either be court-martialed or be held indefinitely without a hearing of any kind. "I am very anxious to be rid of them," Salomon assured Stanton, who finally directed him to release them to the custody of Major General John Pope, commander of the Department of the Northwest. On turning them over to Pope, Salomon urged Stanton to see that they were promptly tried.

While the Lincoln administration was trying to decide what to do with the prisoners, some of them applied to the Wisconsin judiciary for relief. In January 1863 the state supreme court held, in the case of Nicholas Kemp, a leader of the riotous Luxemburgers, that only Congress and not the President had the power to suspend the writ of habeas corpus. Again, as in the case of Sherman Booth a few years earlier, the state of Wisconsin stood in confrontation with the federal government. To avoid a showdown, the state court delayed serving its writ for Kemp's release, and the governor recommended to Stanton that he discharge all the prisoners at once. Instead of complying, Stanton sent Senator Howe to Madison as a special War Department counsel with instructions to arrange for an appeal to the Supreme Court of the United States. On Howe's advice, Stanton agreed to parole the prisoners while awaiting the Supreme Court's review of the case. The review soon proved unnecessary. In a second case involving Ozaukee rioters the Wisconsin supreme court, without abandoning its stand against presidential suspension of habeas corpus, con-

[29] Shannon, *Union Army,* 1: 289–290; Quiner, *Military History of Wisconsin,* 148–149; Love, *Wisconsin in the War,* 849–850; Jacobi, "Wisconsin Civil War Governors," 134–135.

ceded that the President had the power to order and execute the draft. Before long, the issue of the Kemp case became moot when Congress granted the President the power to suspend the writ. Both the state and the federal authorities were satisfied. As for the paroled rioters, they remained at liberty.[30]

[5]

In the midst of his struggle to carry out the draft, Governor Salomon had to turn aside to deal with what seemed, for the moment, a much more urgent task. If he needed arms and men to help preserve the Union, he needed them even more desperately to protect the people of Wisconsin. So he believed as a great wave of fear swept over the state in the summer of 1862.

The terror began with an Indian outbreak in the neighboring state of Minnesota. On August 17 a group of Sioux youth murdered five settlers in the Minnesota Valley. The next day Sioux raiders fell upon white settlements with a continuing onslaught that, by the time federal troops got control nearly six weeks later, was to leave several hundred civilians dead. Some 40,000 Minnesotans took to flight, many of them crossing the Mississippi River into Wisconsin.[31]

Into Wisconsin the panic also spread. It struck hardest and lasted longest at Superior City, where the few hundred isolated inhabitants expected the Chippewa to follow the example of the Sioux. Thirty persons departed by the first lake steamer. From Menomonie, which soon filled with fugitives from the surrounding countryside, the epidemic moved swiftly toward the east and southeast. At the cry "The Indians are coming!" farmers left their harvesting, loaded their families into wagons, and took to the roads in search of security. Those streaming into Fond du Lac from Calumet brought word that the "red

[30] *Official Records*, series 2, vol. 5: 174, 190; series 3, vol. 2: 761, 765, 786, 843, 861 (quotation), 867–868, 935; series 3, vol. 3: 15, 17; Shannon, *Union Army*, 2: 200–204; Beitzinger, *Ryan*, 72–73.

[31] Charles M. Oehler, *The Great Sioux Uprising* (New York, 1959), vii-viii, xiii-xvi, 74.

devils" had plundered and burned Manitowoc and Sheboygan and were advancing toward Fond du Lac. People heading for Sheboygan, about 4,000 of them, made it over the single draw-bridge into the town, but later arrivals found the bridge up, it having been raised to keep the Indians out. By September 4 the terror had reached the outskirts of Milwaukee, and all that day and night an unbroken string of teams and wagons passed through Wauwatosa, seeking refuge in the city.[32]

From various parts of the state the governor received appeals for protection. Many newspapers ridiculed the popular excitement, and from Hudson an army captain with the assignment of pacifying the Indians reported: "So far as I can judge, the fear is mutual, and tne Indians and Whites are striving to outdo each other in conceding Territory—i.e. while the Whites are running in one direction the Indians are running in the other." But Salomon took the matter seriously. He was convinced that some of the Indians had been "tampered with by rebel agents." So was the federal Indian agent at Appleton, M. M. Davis. While trusting the reservation tribes, Davis was sure that individuals among the roving Winnebago and Potawatomi, in particular a Winnebago chief, Dandy, were disloyal and were plotting mischief. From friendly Menominee Davis had heard that Dandy's scheme was to organize the malcontents and, at the strategic moment, to stage an uprising in support of the Confederacy. "I do not propose to wait until butchery commences, as in Minnesota," Salomon avowed to Stanton, "but to arm people for defense, and thus enable them to take care of themselves, so that our troops can leave for the South and the East."

Salomon encouraged the prompt formation of home guards in the seemingly endangered localities, especially in the Lake Superior region, and he distributed among the guards all the arms available to him, about two thousand of them. He kept pressing Stanton for more arms and ammunition and for author-

[32] Milo M. Quaife, "The Panic of 1862 in Wisconsin," in *WMH*, 4 (December, 1920), 166–195; Louise Phelps Kellogg, "Sioux War of 1862 at Superior," in *WMH*, 3 (June, 1920), 473–477.

ity to use some of the newly recruited soldiers for local defense. Stanton demanded evidence of a "reasonable necessity" for the requests. Salomon insisted that, as chief executive of the state, he must be the judge of its needs. Stanton replied, "The President must be the judge." Another confrontation between the state and the federal government was averted when it became obvious to all that Wisconsin Indians were not on the warpath, and the great fear of 1862 subsided.[33]

Still, some uneasiness on the part of Wisconsinites persisted, and the next summer the governor had to contend with another Indian scare, one that was less extensive but more serious and one that again brought state and federal authorities into disagreement. The trouble centered in Juneau County. Concentrating here, the Winnebago not only gathered wild berries and peddled them to white farmers but also begged, entered houses to demand provisions, threatened housewives, grazed ponies in grainfields, and otherwise annoyed and intimidated the whites. General Pope planned to send troops for removing the Winnebago from the state, but the acting commissioner of Indian affairs, after consulting the secretaries of interior and war, refused to co-operate, protesting that the Indians in question were "old residents of Wisconsin" and that the Indian bureau had "neither agent nor money to take care of these Indians."

Apparently, as Pope told Salomon, the bureau intended to "leave the whole matter to the State of Wisconsin." Salomon was of two minds about removing the Winnebago. It was a necessity, he thought, yet it would antagonize Chief Dandy, who swore he would never leave the land where God had first shown him the light. During the winter Dandy had sent Salomon a peace pipe to smoke, and Salomon wished to keep the peace. He thoroughly agreed with Pope, however, that the federal government ought to assume responsibility for the Wisconsin Winnebago. "The frenzy of a drunken Indian, or

---

[33] U.S. Commissioner of Indian Affairs, *Annual Report,* 1862, pp. 333–334. The quotations are from *Official Records,* series 3, vol. 2: 508–509, 511, 515, 518, 522–523. See also Jacobi, "Wisconsin Civil War Governors," 103–107.

the machinations of bad men," he wrote to Lincoln's secretary of the interior on July 10, 1863, "may at any moment plunge our defenceless border settlers into the horrors of Indian outrages like those of Minnesota, and the prompt action of the [federal] government is invoked by the unanimous voice of the people of this State."[34]

Just four days after the governor's warning, a party of Winnebago visited the farmhouse of George Salter, six miles north of New Lisbon, while he was away. He returned with his children to find the house ransacked and his wife dead. She had been badly beaten, her throat had been cut, and she had apparently been raped. When a drunken Indian appeared near the house, Salter killed him, and a German neighbor took a grubhoe, cut off the dead Indian's head, and stuck it on a pole. When another Indian came by, Salter beat him to death with an axe handle. About two weeks after Mrs. Salter's death, another Juneau County farm wife nearly suffered the same fate. Mrs. J. Austin was at home with her two small children, five miles from New Lisbon, while her husband was at work in the fields. She locked the door when Indians approached, but they broke in through a window, attacked her with knives, and attempted to seize the children. She barely managed to fight off the intruders with a rifle and with the aid of a large dog, which was seriously wounded.

While farm families flocked to the villages for safety, the citizens of Juneau County got up a petition asserting that there were in the county from one to two thousand Indians who could "utterly destroy" them "at any hour," asking the government to "remove these barbarians," and threatening, "in self-defence, to exterminate them" if they were not removed. In nearby Monroe County, the people of Tomah and its vicinity circulated a similar petition: "We cannot consent to allow the horrible scenes of the Minnesota massacre to be re-enacted in

<hr>

[34] Pope to W. P. Dole, July 1; Charles E. Mix to Pope, July 2; Salomon to Pope, July 2; Pope to Salomon, July 3; Salomon to J. P. Usher, July 10; Davis to William P. Dole, August 4; W. D. McIndoe to Dole, September 25, 1863, in U.S. Commissioner of Indian Affairs, *Annual Report*, 1863, pp. 356–361, 367, 371.

our midst." In New Lisbon men were saying they would not organize a company for the Union army until the Indians were got rid of.

Governor Salomon forwarded petitions and letters to Washington and reiterated his pleas for action by the federal authorities. General Pope dispatched to New Lisbon a company of the Thirtieth Regiment, for the protection of the Indians as well as the whites. The military also arrested several Winnebago leaders, including Chief Dandy, and held them "more for their own protection against the excited white settlers than for any crimes or depredations." While under arrest, Dandy told Indian Agent Davis he would be willing to turn over Mrs. Salter's murderers to the white authorities but could not do so until he had been freed. After his release he talked with Salomon and gave assurances for the good behavior of his tribespeople.

By summer's end in 1863 a relative calm had returned to the New Lisbon area. As the hunting season began, the Winnebago—perhaps 1,000 men, women, and children altogether—broke up as usual into several small bands under chiefs Dandy, Caramonee, Little Snake, Dekorah, Yellow Thunder, and Indian Jim. These bands were scattered over a distance of seventy-five to 100 miles, from Wood County through Juneau, Sauk, and Columbia. "From the fact of the Indians having separated into small parties," reported Congressman W. D. McIndoe, whom the Commissioner of Indian Affairs had appointed as a special investigator, "I apprehend no further difficulty from them at present, and trust they may remain so until Congress can make an appropriation for their removal, which, in my judgment, must be as early as possible next spring." In fact, the next attempt at removal was not to come for another decade.[35]

[35] J. T. Kingston to Salomon, July 19; Pope to J. C. Kalton, July 21; Salomon to Usher, July 21, 24, 28; Stanton to Usher, July 27; Davis to Dole, August 4; McIndoe to Dole, August 29, September 25, 1863, in U.S. Commissioner of Indian Affairs, *Annual Report*, 1863, pp. 35, 361–367, 370–374. According to the *Annual Report*, 367, George Salter's "business, to a large extent, appears to have been to furnish the Indians with whiskey."

[6]

While concerning himself with the exaggerated Indian menace in Wisconsin, Governor Salomon had no rest from his labors in helping to preserve the Union. In the Civil War the year 1863 was climactic, bringing the prospect of ultimate victory for the North with the triumphs at Gettysburg and Vicksburg. Still the war went on, and the demand for men to fight and die in it seemed endless. The governors continued to share in the responsibility for procuring them, even though the federal government now took direct charge of the draft.

According to the conscription act of March 1863, every state was divided into draft districts coinciding with congressional districts, Wisconsin therefore having six of them, and each of these was divided into subdistricts consisting of townships or city wards. Each district acquired a set of federal draft officials—a provost marshal, a commissioner, an examining physician, and a board of enrollment. The board was to make a list of men liable for military duty, omitting those it considered exempt on physical or other grounds. On the basis of the lists the War Department would set quotas for subsequent troop calls. The draft, where necessary, would take place in individual subdistricts. Once a man's name was drawn, he would have ten days in which to report for duty, furnish a substitute, or buy exemption by paying a $300 commutation fee.[36]

When the Wisconsin enrollment began in May, it proceeded without serious incident except in Milwaukee and in Dodge County. In Milwaukee, on the first day, "one of the enrolling officers was attacked by an Irishman with a spade and received a severe cut in the face," as the state's acting assistant provost marshal general related. "The Irishman was assisted by several women, who pelted the enrolling officer with stones, &c." On hearing about it the provost marshal for the first district, Captain J. M. Tillapaugh, grew almost hysterical. He frantically demanded a sizable military force, insisting that Milwaukee

[36] Quiner, *Military History of Wisconsin,* 156; Schoonover, "Civil War Draft," 30–33.

was a "disloyal place," the scene of "seven mobs and riots" in the past twelve years, its population mostly "German and Irish of the most desperate character." General Pope, commander of the Department of the Northwest, with headquarters in Milwaukee, pooh-poohed Tillapaugh's alarm and preferred to rely on the civilian authorities. About a month later he reported with satisfaction that the Milwaukee enrollment had been completed "by the aid of the municipal police force alone." To Salomon, however, he gave this reassurance: "By the time the draft is ordered a sufficient force will be here to make resistance absurd and impossible."

In Dodge County one of the enrolling officers was murdered by an unknown assailant. General Pope deployed seven companies of the Thirtieth Regiment in the county to see that the enrollment was carried out. In the town of Lebanon a crowd of two or three hundred Germans, most of them armed, gathered at a schoolhouse to demonstrate their determination to resist. They scattered when a company of soldiers appeared, and resistance throughout the county soon collapsed.[37]

After Lincoln, in July, issued his first call for troops under the new conscription act, Salomon determined to see that Wisconsin was compelled to make no greater sacrifices than other states. Hence he got into a series of disputes with Stanton and with the federal provost marshal general, James B. Fry. Salomon complained that Wisconsin's quota was too large, that the state had been given insufficient credit for the surplus it had provided on previous calls. He made a trip to Washington to argue the point but finally lost that argument. He won another, however, when he insisted that the draft be postponed in Wisconsin, as it had been in New Jersey, to allow time for trying to fill the quota by volunteering. And to encourage volunteering he persuaded the War Department to pay the same bounty in his state as in Ohio and Indiana, that is, $302 instead of the usual $100 for each new recruit. In the four predominantly Republican districts there proved to be more than enough

[37] *Official Records*, series 1, vol. 27, part 3: 222–223; series 3, vol. 3: 238–239, 247–249, 368, 395–396, 544–545 (quotations); Schoonover, "Civil War Draft," 37–38.

volunteers, but there was a deficiency in both of the Democratic districts, which included the heavily German counties of Milwaukee, Dodge, Ozaukee, Washington, and Sheboygan.

That autumn the draft in the deficient localities went off quietly. It was not very productive. Of the nearly 15,000 whose names were drawn, about 2,700 failed to report, and more than 5,000 hired substitutes or paid the $300 commutation fee. Many got the money from draft insurance associations, which they had joined at a cost of $25 to $50. Of the remaining draftees, some were exempted for alienage and most of the others were discharged for various reasons. Fewer than 900 were actually mustered in.[38]

Already, in October, Lincoln had made another call, the Wisconsin quota being 10,281, to be filled by January 5, 1864. By that time, Salomon would be out of office, yet he continued to work hard to stimulate volunteering and avoid another draft. He was more and more distressed because of the growing numbers of his fellow immigrants who had declared their intention of becoming citizens and had exercised the right to vote but now were claiming foreign nationality as an excuse for staying out of the army. Lincoln had announced on May 8, 1863, that no such aliens were exempt, and the War Department had laid down the rule that anyone asserting the right of alienage must present to his enrollment board an affidavit swearing he had neither declared for citizenship nor cast a ballot. The board was to refer doubtful cases to the Department of State. In December Salomon requested Secretary of State William H. Seward to consider no Wisconsin cases until Salomon himself had passed upon them. He explained that some persons were making a business of preparing fraudulent affidavits. Seward agreed to Salomon's request.[39]

For nearly two years Salomon as governor had done his best to serve the Union cause and at the same time to protect Wisconsin's interests. If he seemed excitable and irascible on occa-

[38] *Official Records,* series 3, vol. 3: 592–593, 611, 782–783, 799, 850, 874–875, 908, 941–942; Schmidt, "Northwestern Governors," 112–113; Quiner, *Military History of Wisconsin,* 161; Schoonover, "Civil War Draft," 39, 45–50.

[39] Lonn, *Foreigners in the Union Army,* 441–444; *Official Records,* series 3, vol. 3: 545; Schmidt, "Northwestern Governors," 113.

sion, he was consistently honest and impartial. Such a man in such a time could hardly have been popular, even if he had been a better politician than Salomon was. Democrats blamed him for the draft, and Republicans concluded he had lost his usefulness as a vote getter among Germans. He was not renominated. At the end of his term he resumed his law practice in Milwaukee and, after five years, transferred it to New York City. In 1894 he went back to Germany, where he lived in obscure retirement until his death in 1909.[40]

[7]

James T. Lewis, secretary of state in the administration of Salomon, succeeded him as governor, taking office on January 4, 1864. Once a schoolteacher in New York state, Lewis had arrived in Wisconsin in 1845, to practice law in Columbus and to rise in politics as first a Democrat and then a Republican. As governor, he took up where Salomon had left off. He strove consistently to see that Wisconsin contributed its fair share—but no more than its fair share—to the Union war effort.

Another draft was impending, the one that had been set for January 5, the day after Lewis assumed the governorship. Immediately he undertook to get the draft postponed, as other governors were already trying to do. It was twice delayed, until April 1, and by that time Wisconsin had filled its quota by volunteering. Sensitive to the growing war weariness among Wisconsinites as among other Northerners, Lewis was anxious to save the state from further conscription. He therefore joined with the governors of Ohio, Indiana, Illinois, and Iowa in going to Washington and, on April 21, offering to raise a total of 85,000 militia for 100 days' service. Lincoln accepted the proposal, and Lewis issued a call for 5,000 men from Wisconsin. Volunteering was slow, even though the term of service was so short. By June, only 2,134 had come forward, many of them university and college students.

Casualties on the Southern battlefields mounted during the spring and summer of 1864 as the Union launched its campaigns

[41] Jacobi, "Wisconsin Civil War Governors," 160–164; Edward Salomon in *DWB*.

for Richmond and Atlanta. Twice again, on July 18 and December 19, the President made calls for troops under the conscription act. As before, Governor Lewis managed to secure postponements of the draft. He now also protested the size of Wisconsin's quota, maintaining that previous excess enlistments had not been properly credited to the state. After the July call he succeeded in reducing the quota by nearly half, from 19,032 to 10,683. After the December call he failed to get the reduction he claimed was due. In exasperation he finally sent the President a memorial from the legislature asking him to remove Provost Marshal General Fry on account of Fry's "manifest injustice" to Wisconsin.[41]

In a strenuous effort to fill the quotas, Lewis along with his fellow governors persuaded the War Department to continue the high bounty of $302 for new three-year recruits, or $100 a year for those who signed up for less than three years. Before the end of 1863 some Wisconsin counties and municipalities had begun to offer additional bounties. These varied from place to place, ranging from $100 in Eau Claire, for example, to $200 in Madison, Baraboo, and Beloit, and $300 in Clinton Junction (Rock County). A volunteer received the bounty of the locality in which he enlisted, and he was counted toward the quota of that locality. The more generous localities drew men from others, and these found it hard to raise enough recruits.

Hence, in February 1864 the legislature took up a bill to provide a uniform bounty from state funds. The *Wisconsin State Journal* objected, arguing that a state law should not be passed "to help Milwaukee, Washington, Ozaukee and similar localities fill up their deficiencies" when "so many other localities" had "provided bounties and almost filled their quotas." The *Grant County Witness,* of Platteville, opposed both state and local bounties on the grounds that they were unfair to veterans who had not received them. Instead of providing for a state bounty, the legislature passed a law limiting local bounties to $200.

[41] Jacobi, "Wisconsin Civil War Governors," 169–170, 179–184; *Official Records,* series 3, vol. 4: 137–138, 1179, 1192–1194; series 3, vol. 5: 736–737.

Despite the law, competition among localities continued and intensified. By 1865, much the largest local bounties were being paid in the fourth district (including Washington and Ozaukee counties), where recruits were collecting an average of $625 apiece in addition to the federal bounty. By this time, as the result of a business boom, wages were higher and job opportunities more abundant than they had been earlier in the war. Without bounty increases, army service would have become less and less financially attractive in comparison with civilian life. Still, the increases meant that, so far as bounties were concerned, some of the men who joined the latest and served the least were paid the most.[42]

The desperate need for soldiers caused both the state and the federal authorities to look, in the last year and a half of the war, to two groups they previously had spurned—the Negroes and the Indians. Negroes had been excluded from the Wisconsin militia since territorial days. When Governor Randall issued his very first call for volunteers, in April 1861, a leading black citizen of Madison, W. H. Noland, wrote to inquire whether the governor would accept a company of blacks on equal terms with whites. Many of his race in Wisconsin, Noland said, were eager to "hurl back" the charge that they were "neither brave or loyal, and not reliable in an emergency like the present." Randall turned down the proposal. Later in 1861 a fur trader offered the service of 500 Chippewa braves under his command, and another white man tendered 200 Menominee warriors, "all well armed with rifles, sure at forty rods," but the state's attorney general doubted the propriety of using Indians "in the present contest with our brothers." The next year Governor Salomon telegraphed to Secretary of War Stanton: "I am applied to by parties who offer to raise a battalion or more of friendly Indians in this

---

[42] Schoonover, "Civil War Draft," 67; Western Historical Company, *The History of Sauk County, Wisconsin* . . . (Chicago, 1880), 395; Quiner, *Military History of Wisconsin,* 175–176; Scott, "Financial Effects of the Civil War," 53; Donald E. Rasmussen, "Wisconsin Editors and the Civil War: A Study of the Reaction of Wisconsin Editors to the Major Controversial Issues of the Civil War" (master's thesis, University of Wisconsin, 1952), 44–46; *Official Records,* series 3, vol. 5: 748–749. The quotation is from the *Wisconsin State Journal,* February 4, 1864.

State; also one or more companies of colored citizens." He got a prompt answer: "The President declines to receive Indians or negroes as troops."[43]

Finally, in the summer of 1863, Salomon obtained authorization from the War Department to raise a regiment or any number of companies of "colored men," who were to be paid no bounty and only $10 per month, instead of the usual $15. Blacks were now subject to the draft. A black conscript protested to Salomon: "Other men . . . who were drafted the same day I was have been allowed to inlist and received the Bounty, and I think it is a hard case, for me to be Compell'd to fight for a country whose laws does not recognize me as a man." The governor made little headway in raising black troops during the summer and fall of 1863, but a recruiter from Chicago, himself a Negro, did much better in the spring of 1864. From the summer of 1864 on blacks were given the federal bounty, were granted equal pay, and were allowed to substitute for whites.

Altogether, 363 "colored troops" were credited to Wisconsin. The total of "free colored males between the ages of 18 and 45" in the state, according to the 1860 manuscript census, was only 292. Thus Wisconsin appears to have provided a considerably larger number of black soldiers than its entire black male population of military age. The reason for the discrepancy is that many of the Negroes credited to the state were actually recruited elsewhere. They were attracted by agents of white men, especially in Milwaukee, who were trying to escape the draft. Of the Negroes who enlisted in the summer of 1864 or after, one-half or more were substitutes. These and practically all the other blacks credited to Wisconsin were put in segregated units, most of them in the Twenty-Ninth Regiment of United States Colored Troops.[44]

[43] Edward Noyes, "The Negro in Wisconsin's Civil War Effort," in the *Lincoln Herald*, 69 (Summer, 1967), 72–74; Quaife, "Panic of 1862," in *WMH*, 4: 170–172; *Official Records*, series 3, vol. 2: 297, 314.

[44] Noyes, "Negro in Wisconsin's Civil War Effort," in the *Lincoln Herald*, 69: 74–78 (quoting the black conscript); William J. Vollmar, "The Negro in a Midwest Frontier City: Milwaukee, 1835–1870" (master's thesis, Marquette

By the spring of 1864, recruiters were also busy on the Indian reservations of Wisconsin. During the recent Indian scares the Menominee had taken pains to demonstrate their loyalty to the United States, the chiefs on one occasion telling an interpreter, "We wish our great Father, the President, at Washington, to know, through our agent, that we do not like the Winnebagoes and Pottawatomies, because they are some of his bad red children. . . ." The reservation Indians had nothing to fear from the draft (all those "not taxed" were exempt), but they were barely able to scratch together an existence on the poor lands that had been assigned them, and many responded to the lure of the military bounties and the soldier pay—if not to dreams of battle glory or the call of patriotic duty. Out of a total population of about 3,300, the Menominee, Oneida and Stockbridge reservations contributed 279 men to the army, a larger number than came from many a white community of the same size. Menominee filled much of Company K of the Thirty-Seventh Wisconsin Regiment.[45]

Despite the best efforts of Governor Lewis and others to save Wisconsin from another draft—by getting deadlines postponed and quotas reduced, by paying generous bounties, and by recruiting black and red troops—the threat of conscription continued to hang over the state. Eventually some of the previously laggard towns and counties again fell behind, and a new drawing began in the deficient districts on September 19, 1864. This time there was no violent resistance, but there was, as before, a good deal of evasion. No longer could a man escape by paying the $300 commutation fee, unless he could prove

---

University, 1968), 73–76; *Roster of Wisconsin Volunteers, War of the Rebellion, 1861–1865* (2 vols., Madison, 1886), 1: 955–960, 977–979; *Official Records,* series 3, vol. 3: 43–44, 598; series 3, vol. 4: 1270.

[45] Quaife, "Panic of 1862," in *WMH,* 4: 170–172; U.S. Commissioner of Indian Affairs, *Annual Report,* 1863, pp. 368–369 (quotation); *ibid.,* 1865, pp. 51–53; Quiner, *Military History of Wisconsin,* 835–844; R. C. Eden, *The Sword and the Gun, A History of the 37th Wis. Volunteer Infantry, From its First Organization to its Final Muster Out* (Madison, 1865), 106–109; Muster and Descriptive Roll, Company K, Thirty-Seventh Regiment, Series 1144 in the WSA. Altogether some 500 or 600 reservation Indians enlisted in Wisconsin regiments.

himself a conscientious objector, as very few could. He could, however, still hire a substitute if he could afford the price, which began to soar, going as high as $1,000. In some cases he could get exemption on the grounds of alienage or of physical incapacity. As a last resort he could always run or hide.

The examining surgeon for the fifth district, Horace O. Crane, stationed in Green Bay, reported it difficult to obtain enlistments in those areas of the district where the people were, in his words, "mostly Roman Catholics, and as such generally *hostile to the conscription act.*" Among the poor, hard-working Belgians who cleared the heavy timber by hand "for the want of a team," Dr. Crane found a "large proportion of cases of hernia, varicocele, and varicose veins of the inferior extremities, together with necrosis of tibia, fractures, and dislocations"—which, with bad surgery or none at all, had "produced many cripples." He also discovered some ingenious deceptions, especially among the Bohemians he examined. Men pretended to be blind in one eye, or used belladonna "to get up an inordinate action of the heart," or claimed to have hernia "of a peculiar character" that had "baffled the surgeons in Europe." The scrotum was "evidently inflamed, tender, and much thickened, feeling much like a large, solid, corrugated orange." Dr. Crane solved this mystery. He ascertained that an incision had been made in the scrotum, "a blowpipe inserted, and the surrounding parts completely filled with air." The exposure of frauds, however, failed to make the draft effective in those areas where it was most unpopular. "Usually the strong and able-bodied ran away, while the cripples, those of overage, and aliens [nonvoting foreigners who were exempt] alone reported."[46]

To one Milwaukee priest, an Austrian-born professor in St. Francis Seminary, the "inhuman draft" seemed like the destroying angel of the Bible, striking every parish and every household. Certainly the draft had a destructive effect upon the seminary. "On one day no less than a whole dozen of

[46] Harstad, "Report of Dr. Horace O. Crane," in *WMH,* 48: 227–230.

our Seminarians escaped to Canada for fear of being drafted," the seminary's rector, Michael Heiss, had written home to Germany before the drawing in 1863. The rector himself was exempt as a subject of Bavaria. "But all who can take to flight, for no one cares to risk his life for such a wretched cause as is this war." Before the next draft, in 1864, the rector wrote that "within two days about sixty of our one hundred students had disappeared. The professors too, priests and laymen, took to flight."[47]

As the dreaded day in September approached, alarmists turned to Governor Lewis with warnings that Wisconsin was "being depopulated of men liable to the draft" and with demands that he do something to stop the "stampede from our State." The postmaster of Platteville wrote him, "I have information, which I consider reliable, that an organization exists in Galena, connected with Benton, New Diggings, and Elk Grove, in this State, which organization is prepared with arms and ammunition, and they are ready and declare they will resist the draft, if there is any." Lewis turned the letters over to the state's acting assistant provost marshal general, who forwarded them to Provost Marshal General Fry.

After the draft of September 1864, more than a third of those whose names were drawn—7,901 of 20,804—failed to report. After the final draft, early in 1865, when the number drawn was 2,656, the number refusing to respond was 1,144. These figures brought to 11,742 the total of Wisconsin draft dodgers for the entire war. Provost marshals searched the state, especially the lumber camps of the north woods, but rounded up comparatively few of the evaders.[48]

[47] Michael Heiss to Kilian Kleiner, July 4, 1863, and July 4, 1864, "Letters of the Late Archbishop Michael Heiss," in the *Salesianium,* 11 (April, 1916), 19–22; Joseph Salzmann to the *Ludwigmissionsverein,* Munich, October 3, 1864, in the *Salesianium,* 42 (January, 1947), 19–25.

[48] C. S. Lovell to Fry, September 1, 1864, enclosing letters to Lewis, *Official Records,* series 3, vol. 4: 682–684. The experiences of one provost marshal in pursuit of draft dodgers are related in William W. Winterbotham, "Memoirs of a Civil War Sleuth," in *WMH,* 19 (December, 1935–March, 1936), 131–160, 276–293. The figure here given for the total of Wisconsin draft dodgers—11,742—is the sum of the figures for those who "failed to report" after drafts under

On April 13, 1865, four days after General Robert E. Lee's surrender to General U. S. Grant at Appomattox, an order came from the War Department to discontinue recruiting in Wisconsin and to discharge all drafted men who had not yet been mustered in. Governor Lewis, glad to be relieved of the struggle for enlistments, could take justifiable pride in his record. During his administration the state had furnished more than 38,000 troops, including 6,000 veterans who had re-enlisted. Many of these went to fill depleted regiments, but eighteen new ones were formed, bringing the total of Wisconsin infantry regiments to fifty-three. The Thirty-Sixth was the last to consist entirely of three-year enlistments. The Thirty-Seventh and Thirty-Eighth included men who signed up for one, two, or three years. The Thirty-Ninth, Fortieth, and Forty-First contained the one-hundred-day men. All the rest were made up of enlistees for only one year.[49]

In its contribution to the Union army, Wisconsin had done less well than other states of the Midwest. It lagged behind Indiana, Illinois, Ohio, Minnesota, Iowa, and Michigan in the number of troops furnished in proportion to the number of white males of military age and also in proportion to total population. The grand total of white men recruited in Wisconsin, counting re-enlistments, came to approximately 91,000. The net number of individual soldiers was about 80,000. Of these, roughly 40 per cent were foreign-born. This is higher than the roughly 33 per cent that the foreign-born constituted among the original 20,000 recruits, those who volunteered during the first year of the war. Obviously the proportion of immigrants enlisting had risen considerably during the last three

the 1863 conscription act, as given in *Official Records*, series 3, vol. 5: 730–737. After the war the state published a *List of Persons, Residents of the State of Wisconsin, Reported as Deserters from the Military and Naval Service of the United States* (Madison, 1868), bound in *Wisconsin Miscellaneous Pamphlets*, vol. 17. This named approximately 8,600 persons as "Non-Reporting Drafted Men and Deserters after Reporting under Various Drafts" in addition to more than 3,000 "Deserters from Regiments."

[49] C. W. Butterfield, "History of Wisconsin," in Western Historical Company, *History of Sauk County*, 88, 90–91; Frank L. Klement, *Wisconsin and the Civil War* (Madison, 1963), 83–84, 86.

years, when the threat of conscription and the lure of generous bounties were in effect. Since, however, the foreign-born made up more than 50 per cent of the state's men of military age, their 40 per cent share of Wisconsin troops as a whole was still comparatively low.[50]

It cost the people of Wisconsin about $12,000,000 to raise troops for the four years of war. Some $4,000,000 of this sum was paid by the state and the remainder by counties and towns. Most of the money went to provide bounties for soldiers and aid for their dependent families. The total expense amounted to $150 for every man, woman, and child in the state.[51]

[50] Wisconsin and the six other states furnished troops in the following proportions:

State	Troops Furnished as a Percentage of White Males, 18–45	Troops Furnished per 1,000 of Total Population
Indiana	74.0	145
Illinois	69.1	151
Ohio	68.2	134
Minnesota	58.3	140
Iowa	54.7	113
Michigan	53.3	116
Wisconsin	49.7	102

See also *Official Records*, series 3, vol. 4: 1264–1270. When reduced to the equivalent of men serving a full three years, the total for Wisconsin was 79,500 (including 133 in the navy). Of these, 47,972 were American-born. See Benjamin A. Gould, *Investigations in the Military and Anthropological Statistics of American Soldiers* (New York, 1869), 27. Albert B. Faust, *The German Element in the United States, with Special Reference to its Political, Moral, Social, and Educational Influence* (2 vols., Boston, 1909), 1: 524–525, contends, on the basis of Gould's statistics, that, in the soldier statistics for the North as a whole, the "foreigners in every case show an increase over the number which would naturally be expected of them," but "the native American stock fell short of its due proportion." Faust's reasoning, if applied to Wisconsin, would lead to the conclusion that the Germans in that state contributed more than double their due share since they made up 33 per cent of the Wisconsin soldiery but only 16 per cent of the state's population. (See the table he gives for the country as a whole on p. 524.) He fails to note that the foreign-born constituted a higher percentage of men of military age than of the population as a whole. He also fails to note that a comparatively large proportion of the foreign-born soldiers, at least in Wisconsin, were late recruits who served for relatively short periods and saw little action.

[51] Quiner, *Military History of Wisconsin*, 973; Scott, "Financial Effects of the Civil War," 68–69; Schmidt, "Northwestern Governors," 109.

10

Badger Boys in Blue

THE EARLY VOLUNTEERS from Wisconsin, like those from other states in the Civil War, enlisted by companies, joining as a rule with friends and neighbors or other like-minded men from the same general locality. First there were the militia units, already in existence as social clubs, like the Governor's Guards, consisting of young businessmen and professional men from Madison, or the Montgomery Guards, led by Captain John O'Rourke and filled by fellow Irishmen from Milwaukee. Then there were the new companies, recruited here and there throughout the state.

Men who aspired to be captains or lieutenants took the lead in gathering volunteers. One such was Rufus R. Dawes, a twenty-two-year-old Ohioan who had spent two years at the University of Wisconsin and who happened to be in Juneau County on business with his father when Fort Sumter was fired on. Like his great grandfather William Dawes, who in 1775 had made the famous ride with Paul Revere, young Rufus Dawes now helped to rouse the countryside, riding day and night to get pledges of service. When he had signed up the necessary hundred men, including a number of raftsmen from the pineries, he called them all to a rally in Mauston. There, on the Lemonweir River, they elected officers (Dawes winning the captaincy without opposition) and chose a name for their outfit—the Lemonweir Minute Men.

While impatiently awaiting orders to report for duty, Captain Dawes had little chance to provide any training for his company, since his men were too widely scattered to be brought together easily. He kept busy trying to hold them to their pledges and finding replacements for men who changed their minds. Some other companies spent part of the time in what they took to be military exercises. The Wisconsin River Volunteers, with a veteran of the First (three-month) Regiment as drillmaster, performed evolutions to fife and drum in Delton, to the delight of village girls who gathered to watch. Off the drill ground, however, there was little discipline. The captain of the company, Abraham Vanderpoel, a wealthy landowner of Newport, was fifty-five years old. But most of the recruits, like those of other early companies, were young, unmarried men, between seventeen and twenty-one. To them, the soldier's life as yet was a lark.[1]

The recruits would get a further initiation at one of the state's training camps, which were operated by the state government until January 1862 and by the federal government thereafter. The first ten companies of three-month volunteers had rendezvoused at Camp Scott, Milwaukee, in April 1861, while the camp was still in the process of hasty construction, to form the one regiment that President Lincoln had originally requested from Wisconsin. There were twenty companies left over, and instead of disbanding these, as Secretary of War Stanton suggested, Governor Randall assembled them at the State Agricultural Society's fairgrounds outside of Madison. The colonel of the first regiment to be formed here, the Second Wisconsin, named the grounds Camp Randall. The Third Regiment rendezvoused at a camp near Fond du Lac, and the Fourth at Camp Utley in Racine. A number of later regiments were to gather at camps in Milwaukee, Racine, and a few other places, but in the course of the war the great major-

[1] Rufus R. Dawes, *Service with the Sixth Wisconsin Volunteers*, ed. Alan T. Nolan (Madison, 1962), v–xv, 6–11; [Hosea W. Rood], *Story of the Service of Company E, and of the Twelfth Wisconsin Regiment, Veteran Volunteer Infantry, in the War of the Rebellion* (Milwaukee, 1893), 33–35, 40, 42.

ity of Wisconsin troops—some 70,000 of them—were mustered at Camp Randall.[2]

For many a boy from village or farm, the trip to camp was the first adventure into the outside world. Thrilled and self-conscious were the Eau Claire Eagles as, in September 1861, they marched down to the Chippewa River—"with bands playing, banners flying, and people shouting"—to go by boat to La Crosse and then by train to Madison. Apparently enjoying the excitement as much as anybody was the company's mascot, a live and nearly full-grown eagle, the object of attention at every stop as he sat proudly on his perch. He was later to be famous as "Old Abe." Not only for the eagle but for most of the men, this was the first train ride. "It was a new experience to me, I was wide awake the whole way," confessed a member of another company later making the same trip from La Crosse. "I was afraid we were off the track every time we crossed a switch or came to a river. At the towns, girls swarmed on the platforms to ask the boys for their pictures and to kiss the best looking ones." Fifteen-year-old Elisha Stockwell, who had signed up at a war meeting in the log schoolhouse at Alma, feared he would miss the fun when his company left without him. His father would not let him go. The boy later drove his father's ox team into Black River Falls, left the team and wagon on the street, walked to Sparta, took the train to Fond du Lac, and caught up with his company in camp. He was to be wounded twice in the battle of Shiloh.[3]

[2] Frank L. Klement, *Wisconsin and the Civil War* (Madison, 1963), 18–23; Carolyn J. Mattern, "Soldiers When They Go: The Story of Camp Randall, 1861–1865" (master's thesis, University of Wisconsin, 1968), 59.

[3] [John M. Williams], *"The Eagle Regiment," 8th Wis. Inf'ty Vols., A Sketch of Its Marches, Battles and Campaigns, From 1861 to 1865, With a Complete Regimental and Company Roster, And a Few Portraits and Sketches of Its Officers and Commanders, By a "Non-Vet" of Co. "H."* (Belleville, Wisconsin, 1890), 40–44; "Letters of a Badger Boy in Blue," in *WMH*, 4–5 (September, 1920–September, 1921), 4: 209. The quoted soldier traveling from La Crosse to Madison was Chauncey H. Cooke, whose series of letters also described army life on the Minnesota frontier, at Camp Randall, in Kentucky, and at Vicksburg and Atlanta during the campaigns there. See also Edgar P. Houghton, "History of Company I, Fourteenth Wisconsin Infantry, from October 19, 1861, to October 9, 1865," in *WMH*, 11 (September, 1927), 47–48.

On the last day of October 1861 a string of thirteen farm wagons, each carrying eight men seated on planks laid across the wagon boxes, moved out from the village of Delton as soon as a local preacher had ended his benediction. Friends and relatives, some with tearful adieus, others laughing and bantering, walked alongside the wagons as far as the low, narrow bridge over Dell Creek. When the procession had wound up the high bank on the other side, and the last fluttering handkerchief at the bridge was lost to sight, the men of the Wisconsin River Volunteers turned to the enjoyment of what their historian was to recall as a "jolly ride," though a rough one. They sang, shouted, laughed, teased dogs, foraged in turnip patches, "helped" farmers drive their oxen in the fields by geeing and hawing. As the wagons creaked through Baraboo, the townspeople waved flags, fired off a Fourth-of-July cannon, and "hurrahed till they were hoarse." After crossing the river at Matt's Ferry the men were met by a brass band, which led them into Lodi, where they spent the night. The next morning they passed a young man digging potatoes in a field. He asked to join the company. Would he have done so, the historian of the company much later wondered, if he had known the journey would take him ultimately, on July 28, 1864, to his death in the fighting near Atlanta?[4]

Once at camp, the companies were brought together and organized, ten to a regiment. They now lost the homelike and distinctive names with which they had started out. The Chippewa Valley Guards, for example, became simply Company G of the Sixteenth Regiment. As the recruits put on uniforms, they also lost the individuality of their previous motley dress, which ranged from the red shirts of raftsmen to the homespun and the drooping straw hats of farmers and the broadcloth and the silk hats of businessmen. The uniforms provided by the state for the first eight regiments were gray. When the federal government ordered that these be replaced by regular army blue, the Wisconsin wearers of the gray complained because

[4] Rood, *Service of Company E,* 64–70.

they had to pay a second time for uniforms and because they considered the new ones sleazy by comparison.

In camp the recruits found that there was more to military life than just a pleasant outing. Now they began their day at 5 A.M., when they were awakened by a cannon shot. With or without muskets, they drilled for most of the morning and the afternoon. Often they had to line up for a dress parade in the evening. Since the regular army provided neither instructors nor instructions, the state camps had to depend on such drillmasters as happened to appear. Here and there a company was fortunate to have a captain or a lieutenant who had served in the Mexican War or in European wars, such a man as Lieutenant Werner von Bachelle or Captain J. F. Hauser, the latter a graduate of a Swiss military school. Inexperienced young officers like Captain Dawes stayed up late to pore over the manual of arms and textbooks on tactics. All in all, the trainees spent a great deal of time on drill and parade, very little on the use of weapons or on battle practice.

At Camp Randall many of the men slept in barracks that formerly had been used as stables and cowsheds for the state fair. The men itched from the flea-ridden straw in their bunks, while shivering in cold weather and sweltering in hot. More fortunate were those who stayed in large conical tents that were pitched on the grounds, even though a tent often filled with smoke from the heating arrangement—a square hole dug in the earth, covered with sheet iron, and equipped with an underground flue on one side to let in the air and on the other, supposedly, to let out the smoke. As many as 3,000 at a time could eat in the huge mess hall, the fair's machinery exhibition building, measuring 150 by 240 feet. The men blamed bad food, especially the sour bread and spoiled beef, for their ill health. Certainly there was much sickness, though the soldier must have been exaggerating who wrote home that the men of his regiment were dying at the rate of one a day. The hospital, in Floral Hall (which also contained officers' quarters and storerooms), had no lack of patients.

The ten acres of Camp Randall were surrounded by a board

fence eight feet high, with two guarded gates on the Madison side. Townspeople visited the camp to watch parades or call on friends, and soldiers on passes went to town to do the things that soldiers on leave have always done, even to attend church. Vexed by the carryings-on of the rowdier elements from the camp, some Madisonians complained that passes were too freely given, but most of the soldiers thought them too hard to get. When confined to the monotony of barrack life, many of the men amused themselves with gambling and drinking. During the first year, sutlers were allowed to sell beer and liquor in the camp; after that, the soldiers had to smuggle in their drinks, or else do their drinking outside.

Drunkenness was one of the offenses for which men might be confined to the guardhouse. For serious infractions of the rules they were sometimes bucked and gagged. Yet discipline at times was tenuous. Once a group of Norwegians from the Fifteenth Regiment attempted to free a couple of their friends who had been confined. Irishmen from the Seventeenth sprang to the support of the guards, who were Irish. The Sixteenth had to be stationed between the Fifteenth and the Seventeenth to keep the two whole regiments from coming to blows. On another occasion, members of a regiment burned down a guardhouse in an effort to release some of their comrades. When the Seventeenth was scheduled to leave camp, and the pay due the men was delayed, most of them refused to board the waiting train. Some got drunk and roamed the streets of Madison, to the alarm of the citizens. For a time, the officers completely lost control of the regiment, and six days passed before the last of its members had been persuaded to depart.[5]

Conditions were worst at Camp Randall during an interlude

[5] Mattern, "Soldiers When They Go," 59–62; Dawes, *Sixth Wisconsin Volunteers,* 11–15; Rood, *Service of Company E,* 71–92; "Badger Boy in Blue," in *WMH,* 4: 209–210; Daniel R. Porter, "The Colonel and the Private Go to War," in *WMH,* 42 (Winter, 1958–1959), 124–127; Spencer C. Scott, "The Financial Effects of the Civil War on the State of Wisconsin" (master's thesis, University of Wisconsin, 1939), 9–12; E. B. Quiner, *The Military History of Wisconsin . . .* (Chicago, 1866), 90; William D. Love, *Wisconsin in the War of the Rebellion . . .* (Chicago, 1866), 493–495.

of a few months, from April to June 1862, when it was used
as a prison camp for Confederates taken at the capture of
Island No. 10 in the Mississippi River. The federal authorities
soon realized that, except for its accessibility from the battlefield by riverboat to Prairie du Chien and by train from there,
Camp Randall was wholly unsuitable for the purpose. Escape
was so easy that a whole regiment was required to "guard less
than double their own numbers," about 1,260 prisoners. To
guard the camp, the Nineteenth Wisconsin was brought to
Madison from training at Racine. The Nineteenth was "perfectly raw," had insufficient arms, and showed an "utter want of
discipline." Officers and soldiers diverted to their own use
much of the supplies that were intended for the prisoners,
disposing of all the liquor in the medical stores—168 pint
bottles of it—in just five days. Adequate bedding had been
sent, yet some of the 200 or more ill prisoners lay helpless
on the bare floor of the hospital. After only one month in
the camp, the toll of prisoners dying from disease had reached
ninety-four. Well prisoners were "very insolent and abusive"
to sentinels, "throwing missiles and water at them and . . .
threatening their lives." One prisoner insisted on squatting
to defecate near the guard post of seventeen-year-old Private
Clarence Wicks, and defied Wicks's order that he go to a
sink. When several other prisoners rushed toward Wicks, he
fired at the foremost of them, killing him.[6]

The Wisconsin troops who trained at Camp Randall stayed
there, as a rule, from a few weeks to two months or more.
When the time came for a regiment to be mustered into the
United States service, there was, in the case of the earlier regiments, a grand "jollification." For the Sixth, there were about
6,000 visitors, and there was a "fine supper, the gift of the
ladies of Dane County." Again, when the early regiments en-
trained for the departure from Madison, there were elaborate
farewells, with the governor and other notables giving speeches,

<hr />

[6] *The War of the Rebellion: A Compilation of the Official Records of the
Union and Confederate Armies* (128 vols., Washington, D.C., 1880–1901), series
2, vol. 3: 435, 509, 539–541, 578–586 (hereinafter cited as *Official Records*).

brass bands playing, church bells ringing, and tremendous crowds applauding. When the Sixth Wisconsin left, in July 1861, the enthusiasm was still high, and its signs were seen all along the way. "At Milwaukee an abundant table was spread for us. At Racine, Kenosha, and Chicago, the haversacks of our men were crammed with every delicacy."

With the passage of time, however, the departure of troops became routine. When the Twenty-Fifth left Madison, early in 1863, the city itself was no longer providing much of a show. But "the sweethearts and wives of the boys from all parts of the state swarmed about the station to say good bye." When the Thirty-Sixth departed, in May 1864, the soldiers themselves were no longer the eager young bachelors who had filled the ranks in the beginning. The men of the Thirty-Sixth had received still less training than most of their predecessors. They had had their muskets for only a few days. Some of them feared, regarding their colonel, that it was "his intention to rush us right into the thickest of it without having had a chance to try our arms." But, then, few if any of the soldiers were ready, when they left their home state, for what they were to find on distant fields of battle.[7]

[2]

Among Wisconsin infantry, only the first three regiments saw any action during the opening year of the war. All three were sent east, to the Washington area. From there the First Regiment of three-month volunteers went to Harpers Ferry, then moved up the Shenandoah Valley. In a skirmish at Falling Waters, Virginia, on July 2, 1861, two of the regiment's members fell—the first Wisconsinites to die fighting for the Union. Later that same month the Second Wisconsin marched with

---

[7] Klement, *Wisconsin and the Civil War*, 19–21. The quotations describing the send-off given the Sixth are from Dawes, *Sixth Wisconsin Volunteers*, 15–16, while the quotation about the Twenty-Fifth's departure is from "Badger Boy in Blue," in *WMH*, 4: 322. See Frank L. Byrne and Andrew T. Weaver, eds., *Haskell of Gettysburg: His Life and Civil War Papers* (Madison, 1970), 243–244, for the remark of the colonel.

General Irvin McDowell's army to Manassas, Virginia, aided
in driving back the Confederates, and then was caught in the
disorderly retreat which followed this first battle of Bull Run.
Only four of McDowell's regiments suffered heavier losses,
which for the Second Wisconsin amounted to twenty-three
dead, sixty-five wounded, and sixty-three missing (mostly prisoners). In September the Third Wisconsin carried out a blood-
less mission, arresting secessionist delegates to a "bogus" legislature in Maryland and thus helping to hold that state in the
Union.

In 1862 a total of six Wisconsin regiments served with the
Army of the Potomac under General George B. McClellan.
The Fifth Wisconsin distinguished itself when, during the
Peninsular campaign, it broke the Confederate line at Wil-
liamsburg and opened the way to Richmond. *"Through you,
we won the day . . . ,"* McClellan told the men of the Fifth. "I
cannot thank you enough." The Third won special praise
from its commander, General Nathaniel P. Banks, for its part
in the battle of Cedar Mountain, in which the Federals fought
the Confederates to a draw. Then the Third and the Fifth,
along with the Second, Sixth, and Seventh Wisconsin, joined
in McClellan's effort to head off Robert E. Lee as the latter,
in September, entered Maryland on his first invasion of the
North.[8]

In the ensuing battles of South Mountain and Antietam,
Wisconsin troops were in the thickest of the fighting. At
Antietam the Sixth led a charge through a strip of woods and
into a cornfield, to meet the opening and devastating salvos
of the enemy. "Men are falling in their places or running
back into the corn," Colonel Rufus Dawes related. "The
soldier who is shooting is furious in his energy. The soldier
who is shot looks around for help with an imploring agony
of death on his face." To stop a "headlong flight," Dawes
"took the blue color of the state of Wisconsin, and waving it,
called a rally of Wisconsin men." Of 280 of his men who had

[8] Klement, *Wisconsin and the Civil War,* 19–23, 65–68; Love, *Wisconsin in the War,* 253–257, 260–287, 319–339 (the quotation of McClellan is on p. 253).

been in the cornfield, 150 were now dead or wounded. After the battle, rows and heaps of corpses, with blue and gray uniforms indiscriminately mingled, lay bloating in the hot September sun. Heavy contributions to these rows and heaps had come from all the five regiments from the Badger state.[9]

Three of the Wisconsin regiments—the Second, Sixth, and Seventh—had been combined with the Nineteenth Indiana to form the only all-western brigade in the Army of the Potomac. From the distinctive plumed black hats the men wore, it had come to be known as the Black Hat Brigade, and Confederates had learned to respect "those damned Black Hats." Watching the men move without flinching into enemy fire at South Mountain, McClellan remarked: "They must be made of iron." After Antietam the name was changed to the Iron Brigade, and the Twenty-Fourth Michigan was added to make up for the recent losses. For a time, the brigade was one of the most colorful and heroic in the entire Union army. After suffering heavy losses again at Gettysburg, the brigade incorporated Easterners and lost its distinctive character and name.[10]

At Gettysburg, in 1863, were present not only the Wisconsin units of the Iron Brigade but also three others of the state's regiments—the Third, the Fifth, and the principally German Twenty-Sixth—besides a company of its sharpshooters. When the accidental engagement began, on the morning of July 1, the Second Wisconsin was one of the first Union infantry units to arrive on the scene. The regiment ran into a Confederate fusillade that knocked out of combat nearly a third of the men, among them Colonel Lucius Fairchild, his left arm shattered. The First Corps (of which the Iron Brigade was the First Brigade of the First Division) of the Army of the Potomac

[9] Dawes, *Sixth Wisconsin Volunteers*, 87–95. The quotations are from pp. 90–91. See also General Edward Bragg to Cornelia Bragg, September 21, 1862, in Elizabeth A. Bascom, "Why They Fought: A Comparative Study of the Impact of the Civil War on Five Wisconsin Soldiers, with Selections from Their War Letters" (master's thesis, University of Wisconsin, 1941), 55.

[10] Alan T. Nolan, *The Iron Brigade: A Military History* (New York, 1961), 28, 53–54, 98, 149–167, 263, 335–336, and *passim*. The quotation about the men of iron is on p. 335, while the statement about the Black Hats is from Klement, *Wisconsin and the Civil War*, 59.

was compelled to give ground. "Making its last stand upon what is called 'Seminary Ridge,' not far from the town," wrote Frank A. Haskell, adjutant of the Sixth Wisconsin, in what was to become the classic eyewitness account of the battle, "it fell back in considerable confusion, through the South-West part of the town, making brave resistance, however, but with considerable loss." Indeed, the First Corps with a total of 9,403 men counted more than 6,000 casualties in that one day's fighting. "Them Wisconsin fellers . . . fit terribly," as a Gettysburg veteran of the War of 1812 who fought alongside them remarked in admiration. Together with their First Corps comrades, they made it possible for General George Gordon Meade to seize the high ground south of the Pennsylvania borough and, after two more days of bloody combat, to turn back Lee's second and last invasion of the North.[11]

While some Wisconsin troops were helping to contain and to wear down the enemy on the eastern front, a still larger number were campaigning west of the Appalachian range, to open the Mississippi River and, having done that, to drive yet another wedge into the sundered Confederacy. With Ulysses S. Grant, as he advanced up the Tennessee River in 1862, were five regiments of infantry and five batteries of artillery from the Badger state. Grant praised the Fourteenth Wisconsin for its performance at Shiloh, and brigade commanders cited the Eighth, Fourteenth, and Seventeenth regiments for heroism at Corinth, in northeastern Mississippi. The Eighth, its brigadier general said, consisted of "big burly fellows, who could march a mule off its feet," and who proved at Corinth "that they could *fight* as well as march." Their mascot, the eagle Old Abe, celebrated the victory by "whirling and dancing on his perch." The Fourteenth was "the regiment to rely upon in every emergency; always cool, steady, and vigorous." The Seventeenth, its Irishmen leading a bayonet attack with the Gaelic

[11] Love, *Wisconsin in the War*, 403–422; Sam Ross, *The Empty Sleeve: A Biography of Lucius Fairchild* (Madison, 1964), 48–49. The quotations are from Byrne and Weaver, eds., *Haskell of Gettysburg*, 96–97. See also Nolan, *Iron Brigade*, 255, 258–259.

battle cry "Faugh a ballagh!" ("Clear the way!"), were credited by their commander with "the most glorious charge in the campaign."

When Grant undertook his long, hard struggle to capture Vicksburg, in 1863, he had with him a Wisconsin contingent that had grown to some ten thousand or more—twelve regiments of infantry, one regiment of cavalry, and three batteries of artillery. In the taking of Jackson, Mississippi, at the rear of Vicksburg, the Eleventh Wisconsin left 348 of its men wounded, killed, or dead of disease. On a thrust to the east of Jackson, members of the Twelfth passed a roadside gate that was bespattered with the brains of a rebel soldier. By now battle-hardened, one of the men "picked up a piece of the poor fellow who had lost the brains" and kept it as a souvenir. After a long siege, Vicksburg surrendered on July 4, the same day that Lee withdrew from Gettysburg. More than a year earlier, a Union naval and military expedition had come up the Mississippi from its mouth and, with the Fourth Wisconsin striking the Confederate river forts from the rear, had occupied New Orleans. Now the Fourth took part in the seizure of Port Hudson, Louisiana, the last of the Mississippi River posts remaining in rebel hands. The Father of Waters, in President Lincoln's words, went "again unvexed to the sea."[12]

In the autumn of 1862, while Lee's army was moving northward from Virginia into Maryland, another Confederate army had been making a parallel incursion from Tennessee into Kentucky. Five infantry regiments and three artillery batteries from Wisconsin were among the bluecoats who met the rebels' surprise assault near Perryville, Kentucky, on October 8. The First and the Twenty-Fourth Wisconsin led in fierce counterattacks that threw the Confederates back. When the Union army caught up with the Confederates near Murfreesboro,

[12] Klement, *Wisconsin and the Civil War,* 66–72, 79–80. The quotations about the Eighth and Fourteenth regiments are on pp. 70, 79. Love, *Wisconsin in the War,* 493–525, 641–668, on p. 516 includes the quotation about the Seventeenth, while Williams, "*Eagle Regiment,*" 47–48, depicts Old Abe's antics. See Rood, *Service of Company E,* 244, for the quotation about the bespattered brains.

Tennessee, at the end of the year, the same regiments again distinguished themselves, along with others from Wisconsin, including the (Scandinavian) Fifteenth. The Twenty-Fourth counted nearly 40 per cent of its men and almost all its officers as casualties in this three-day battle of Stone's River.

By September 1863 the Federals had pushed the Confederates southward across Tennessee and into northern Georgia. Here, along Chickamauga Creek, the Federals were hit by an over-whelming attack—in resisting which the Fifteenth Wisconsin again displayed "true courage" and its Colonel Hans C. Heg was among the many who were killed—and were compelled to retreat to Chattanooga, which was soon beleaguered. Arriving from the Mississippi to take charge and break the siege, General Grant finally ordered a series of strikes against the encircling Confederates. The Twenty-Fourth Wisconsin was with a force that, on November 25, received orders to take the first line of rifle pits at the foot of Missionary Ridge. Instead of stopping there, the Federals spontaneously charged on up the hill, the Confederates fleeing before them. Among the foremost of the pursuers were the Twenty-Fourth and its adjutant, Arthur McArthur, who picked up the regimental flag from the wounded color bearer and planted it on the crest. For his performance in this battle, McArthur was awarded a Medal of Honor and, though only eighteen years old, was promoted from first lieutenant to major and was given command of the regiment. (Brevetted a colonel in March 1865, he was to be remembered as the "gallant boy colonel" of the Civil War before he gained fame as a lieutenant general in the Philippines, 1898–1901.) [13]

With Tennessee in Federal control, Grant went east early in 1864 to oversee, as general in chief, the final campaigns of all the Union armies while accompanying and directing the Army of the Potomac. While Grant in northern Virginia prepared to move toward Richmond, and William T. Sherman in

[13] Klement, *Wisconsin and the Civil War*, 64–66, 70–71, 80; Love, *Wisconsin in the War*, 607–641, 674–697; D. Clayton James, *The Years of MacArthur* (2 vols., Boston, 1970, 1975), 1: 13–16; Bell I. Wiley, *The Life of Billy Yank: The Common Soldier of the Union* (Indianapolis, 1952), 301–302.

northern Georgia got ready to advance on Atlanta, Nathaniel P. Banks in Louisiana began an ill-conceived expedition up the Red River toward Texas. Wisconsin soldiers played a conspicuous part in each of the three undertakings, as indeed they did in all the important campaigns of the war.

When Banks was forced to retreat down the Red River, a Wisconsin man saved the expedition from threatened disaster. Accompanying the army, in addition to seven regiments of Wisconsin infantry, were the Fourth Cavalry and Lieutenant Colonel Joseph Bailey of Kilbourn City, who had been responsible for a number of engineering exploits with the Fourth both as an infantry and as a cavalry regiment. Now, at the end of April 1864, as Banks's retreating flotilla of ten gunboats approached the rapids at Alexandria, the water was too low for the boats to pass over and make their escape. Bailey got 3,000 men from Banks, including experienced loggers and log drivers from the Twenty-Third and Twenty-Ninth Wisconsin, and set them to building a hasty, improvised dam. The vessels floated into the resulting pool and then were borne downstream when the dam gate was opened. Afterward Congress gave Bailey a vote of thanks (he was one of only fifteen officers whom Congress thus honored during the war) and the navy presented him a gold sword and a silver punch bowl.[14]

With Grant on his bloody Wilderness campaign in northern Virginia were eight Wisconsin regiments of infantry and one battery of artillery. These included many raw recruits. The newly raised Thirty-Sixth went into battle on May 31, just three weeks after leaving Madison. During the next week this regiment lost its colonel, Frank A. Haskell, at Cold Harbor, and a total of 400 others, counting the wounded. When the survivors of the Army of the Potomac had got below Richmond, the army set off a tremendous mine, July 30, to break the Confederate lines outside Petersburg. Into the crater went, among others, recently arrived red men and black from Wis-

[14] Love, *Wisconsin in the War*, 743–760; Ludwell H. Johnson, *Red River Campaign: Politics and Cotton in the Civil War* (Baltimore, 1958), 248–250, 260–264; C. George Extrom, "General Joseph Bailey and the Red River Dam" (unpublished paper read before the Civil War Round Table of Madison, 1965; sound recording available in the SHSW), 1–17, 23–32.

consin. Charging ahead were Company K, consisting mostly of Menominee Indians, and other companies of the Thirty-Seventh Wisconsin, in addition to the Wisconsin unit, Company F of the Twenty-Ninth United States Colored Troops. Trapped by the enfilading fire of the quickly recovered Confederates, the Union soldiers remained in the crater, helpless, for several hours. Of 250 men from the Thirty-Seventh, only ninety-five emerged in shape to answer roll call that evening. Fifty-seven were dead or dying, among them Corporal Hahpah-tonwahiquette and Privates Kenosha, Jeco, Nahwahquah, Nash-ahkahappah, and Wahtahnotte. Of the eighty-five blacks in Company F, eleven lost their lives in the day's action.[15]

The largest Wisconsin contingent to participate in any phase of the war—fourteen regiments of infantry, one regiment of cavalry, and two batteries of artillery—accompanied Sherman on his campaign, May–September 1864, from Dalton, Georgia, to Atlanta. Referring to Sherman's entire host, a private in the Third Wisconsin wrote in mid-campaign: "Our line extends some 10 or twelve miles in length and besides the cavalrys on each flank." This soldier went for more than two months without taking his shoes off as the army marched and entrenched and marched again, generally avoiding pitched battles until approaching Atlanta. When the army besieged, set fire to, and finally entered the still-burning city, he was impressed by the desolation all around—"it looks like a waste place."[16]

While some of the Wisconsin regiments, after the fall of Atlanta, headed north to take care of the enemy in the rear, and to fight in the battles of Franklin and Nashville, eleven of the regiments and several batteries went with Sherman, November–December 1864, on his famous march to the sea. It was a

[15] Love, *Wisconsin in the War*, 933–956; Byrne and Weaver, eds., *Haskell of Gettysburg*, 245–246; Quiner, *Military History of Wisconsin*, 835–844; Robert C. Eden, *The Sword and the Gun: A History of the 37th Wis. Volunteer Infantry, From Its First Organization to Its Final Muster Out* (Madison, 1865), 30–32, 106–109; Edward Noyes, "The Negro in Wisconsin's Civil War Effort," in the *Lincoln Herald*, 69 (Summer, 1967), 75–76.

[16] Love, *Wisconsin in the War*, 698–742; John O. Holzhueter, ed., "William Wallace's Civil War Letters: The Atlanta Campaign," in *WMH*, 57 (Autumn, 1973–Winter, 1973–1974), 100–101, 104–106, 109–110. The quotations are from pp. 100, 110.

"long and tedious march," as one of the Wisconsin boys summed it up after reaching Savannah, but "we made a clean sweep of everything that came in our way." Another regretted the "indiscriminate destruction of property" and the ransacking of houses by stragglers. Heading up through South Carolina and finding Columbia in flames, "some of our men who were partly under the influence of liquor," recalled a member of the Twelfth Wisconsin, "would whoop and yell, and say, 'This is the nest where the first secession egg was hatched! *Let 'er burn!*'" North of Columbia the troops continued to tear up railroad tracks, make bonfires of the ties, heat the rails, and bend them out of shape. A Wisconsin soldier improved the technique by devising "a sort of cant-hook, which, in the hands of a man at each end of the rail, pushing in opposite directions, easily twisted the hot part of it into the shape of a huge auger." After entering North Carolina the army became much less destructive. "We all felt that the state was about half loyal. . . ." Sherman's men ended their trek in March 1865, after fifty days of tramping and only ten of resting since their departure from Savannah.

In April 1865, as Lee withdrew from Richmond, to be overtaken by Grant at Appomattox, Jefferson Davis fled with members of his cabinet into Georgia. There the following month the First Wisconsin Cavalry had a share in apprehending the fugitive president of the collapsed Confederacy.[17]

[3]

Soldiers from Wisconsin rivaled those from other Northern states in giving the "last full measure of devotion" to the

[17] Klement, *Wisconsin and the Civil War*, 82–83; Love, *Wisconsin in the War*, 957–964. The quotations are from Holzhueter, "Wallace's Civil War Letters," in *WMH*, 57: 113; Frank L. Byrne, ed., *The View from Headquarters: Civil War Letters of Harvey Reid* (Madison, 1965), 203; and Rood, *Service of Company E*, 407, 410, 418, 421–422. Jefferson Davis was taken by the Fourth Michigan Cavalry, and when the First Wisconsin arrived on the scene, there was an exchange of gunfire between the two Union regiments, each mistaking the other for the enemy. Nevertheless, the commanding officer of the entire corps reported: "The credit due the First Wisconsin . . . is scarcely less than that to the actual captors." *Official Records*, series 1, vol. 49, part 2: 721–722, 782.

Union cause. Yet, as among themselves, the Badger boys in blue bore quite unequally the burden of war service and sacrifice. Some, including many of the early volunteers, served as long as three and even four years, saw a great deal of battle action, and were frequently exposed to the risk of disablement or death. Others, especially the latest to be recruited, experienced little or no hardship or danger.

Of approximately 2,000 regiments in all the Union armies, 200 were afterward listed as "fighting regiments" that had lost 10 per cent or more of their numbers in killed or mortally wounded. Among the 200 were ten from Wisconsin. Of forty-five that had lost more than 200 men in battle, three were Wisconsin infantry regiments: the Seventh (third on the list, with 281 killed), the Sixth, and the Second. Among the twenty-two with the highest percentage of total battle deaths, the Second Wisconsin stood at the top, with nearly 20 per cent. Also on the list were the Twenty-Sixth (consisting mostly of German Turners), the Seventh, and the Thirty-Sixth.[18]

The Twenty-Sixth was fourth among Wisconsin regiments in numbers killed or mortally wounded, with a total of 188, and it was followed by nine others with more than 100 each: the Fifth, Third, Thirty-Seventh, First, Sixteenth, Thirty-Sixth, Twenty-First, Fourth, and Fourteenth. If deaths from disease are added to battle deaths, the total losses for thirteen Wisconsin regiments amount to 300 or more, or from nearly a third to nearly a half of the original strength of the regiment. These were the First and Second Cavalry, the Fourth Infantry (which became the Fourth Cavalry), and the Fifth, Sixth, Seventh, Eleventh, Twelfth, Fifteenth, Sixteenth, Twenty-Fifth, and Twenty-Ninth Infantry regiments.

The first dozen infantry regiments to leave the state lost altogether 1,729 men in battle action. Twelve of the last regiments to be formed did not lose a single man to enemy fire, though they suffered wastage from disease. A few of the earlier regiments, through no fault of their own, also failed

[18] William F. Fox, *Regimental Losses in the American Civil War, 1861–1865: A Treatise on the Extent and Nature of the Mortuary Losses in the Union Regiments, With Full and Exhaustive Statistics Compiled from the Official Records on File in the State Military Bureaus and at Washington* (Albany, New York, 1889), 1–3, 8, 10–14.

to see much fighting. The Thirteenth spent its time beyond the Mississippi in the Southwest, far from the main theaters of war, and only five of its men died from enemy action. Though, like the Thirteenth, eager enough for active campaigning, the Thirtieth merely patrolled in Minnesota after the 1862 Indian uprising and then did guard duty in the South; this regiment had but two men killed.

One regiment understandably had no stomach for the war— the Thirty-Fourth, which consisted entirely of nine-month conscripts, practically all of them immigrants, mostly Germans. These men stayed well behind the lines, doing garrison duty in Kentucky, Illinois, and Tennessee. In the short space of nine months, 283 of the original 961 deserted. One drowned himself, another was killed in an accident, and eighteen others died of disease. None felt or even heard any enemy gunfire. The Thirty-Ninth, Fortieth, and Forty-First served a still shorter time, they being hundred-day troops whose mission was mainly to guard communications and thus relieve other forces for the battlefield. Three of the hundred-day men were killed. The war was over before the rest of the regiments, the Forty-Second through the Fifty-Third, could see much if any action. One of these, the Fiftieth, was kept in the army for about a year after the war was over, to garrison the forts against the Sioux in Dakota Territory; it lost one man in hostilities.[19]

Instead of seeing so many new regiments formed, the men of the earlier outfits would have preferred to keep these filled. "The prime fault of our military system," Colonel Rufus Dawes of the Sixth Wisconsin complained in 1863, "has been to continue to send new organizations into the field, raw and green, while the old regiments, trained and tried, and their officers made fit by experience to lead, are allowed to dwindle down to nothing." Some of the officers sent recruiters back to Wisconsin, but these had to compete with the organizers of fresh regiments.

Veteran units therefore looked to the draft act of 1863 for

[19] Love, *Wisconsin in the War*, 781–787, 834–839, 849–850, 856–860, 875, 1056–1136; Klement, *Wisconsin and the Civil War*, 81–82. Comparative losses of Wisconsin regiments have been derived from a table of "Wisconsin Losses in the Civil War," which is conveniently reproduced on the inside of the back cover of Klement.

help. "They like the conscription law or any other law that promises to fill the shattered ranks of their battalions," Dawes said at the time. When conscripts began to arrive, however, he was disappointed to see such a "sorry looking set." Many, he suspected, were substitutes who had signed up for money and who would repeat what they had done before—desert and sign up again. "What a contrast between such hounds and the enthusiastic and eager volunteers of 1861." A soldier in another veteran regiment feared that "the 3d Wisconsin *volunteers*" would become "the 3d Regt. of *conscripts*." Regarding a "lot of new recruits" that appeared in 1864, a member of the Twelfth Wisconsin observed with some contempt: "The most of these were foreigners, and were either drafted men or substitutes for drafted men."[20]

As a result of losses and replacements, the composition of the early regiments was, indeed, drastically changed. The First Wisconsin, for example, had an original strength of 945. In the course of the war, it lost 527 in dead, missing, and discharged for disabling illness or wounds, and it gained 548 in new recruits, 407 of them draftees. When the three-year enlistments of early volunteers approached an end, these men were encouragd to re-enlist by the offer of a $402 bounty. If three-fourths of a regiment's veterans agreed to stay on, they also received a thirty-day furlough. These inducements apparently had some effect (a total of 5,784 Wisconsin veterans re-enlisted) but in some of the early regiments the veterans remaining at the end of three years were decidedly few. In the Sixth Wisconsin, for example, only 290 were left when, in 1864, three-fourths of them chose to extend their service.[21]

Naturally the conscripts—and the substitutes as well—were less willing to fight, more ready to desert, than were the volunteers, especially the volunteers who enlisted before there was

---

[20] Dawes, *Sixth Wisconsin Volunteers*, 123, 127, 202, 231, is the critic of the new recruits, while the quotation about the Third is from Wiley, *Life of Billy Yank*, 325–326. The quotation about new recruits in the Twelfth is from Rood, *Service with Company E*, 352.

[21] Quiner, *Military History of Wisconsin*, 175–176, 437, 973; Dawes, *Sixth Wisconsin Volunteers*, 235.

any draft. The desertion rate for the all-conscript regiment, the Thirty-Fourth, came to 294 per thousand in only nine months of service. The rate for the Wisconsin company of the Twenty-Ninth United States Colored Troops, Company F, many of whom were substitutes, was considerably less than half as high, 114 per thousand, and that for about sixteen months in the army. But the over-all desertion ratio for the whole body of Wisconsin troops throughout the war was much, much lower—not quite forty-three per thousand. This was about the same as the ratio of battle deaths per thousand.

In comparison with other states, Wisconsin had a creditable record with respect both to desertions and to battle deaths. While the desertion rate for Wisconsin was less than forty-three, the rate for the western states as a group was more than forty-five, and for the entire North it was about sixty-two (for New York it was eighty-nine; for New Jersey, 107; and for Connecticut, 117). The proportion of killed and mortally wounded per thousand in uniform was slightly more than forty-two for Wisconsin, less than thirty-seven for the western states taken together, and about thirty-five for the North as a whole (but nearly forty-five for New England).

Of the estimated 80,595 individual enlistments from Wisconsin, more than 11,000 men died from wounds or disease or were reported missing in action. There were, besides, approximately 15,000 men discharged for disabilities incurred in the service. This is to say that, roughly, one soldier in every three became a casualty of some kind, and one in every seven failed to survive the war.[22]

[4]

For the Wisconsin men who took part in it, the Civil War was

[22] *Official Records,* series 3, vol. 5: 667–669; Quiner, *Military History of Wisconsin,* 973; Noyes, "Negro in Wisconsin's Civil War Effort," in the *Lincoln Herald,* 69: 78. In *Desertion During the Civil War* (New York, 1928), 152, Ella Lonn says that "Indiana, Wisconsin, and Iowa, where there was considerable disaffection, rank relatively high [in desertions] in proportion to their population," but the figures in the *Official Records* and in Quiner, as well as those Lonn herself gives on p. 234, do not bear this out with regard to Wisconsin.

both a unifying and a divisive experience. It brought them together in the comradeship of arms, yet by no means did it fuse them into a single, like-minded mass. They differed in the reasons why they fought and in their responses to the South and its people. They disagreed on questions of army politics, of rivalries for military leadership, as well as questions of party politics. In the life of the camp they were cliquish, sorting themselves into groups of their own choosing.

Money—the soldier's pay together with the bounties—was a common incentive for going to war, as some of the enlisted men frankly avowed. One of them, a Norwegian, said that he felt "compelled to go in order to get out of debt" and to buy a farm that was his wife's "dearest wish." If a man waited too long and was caught in the draft, he would fail to get the bounties, and so he might decide to enlist in order to avoid conscription, as another Norwegian did late in the war. "I am not going to trye to make mi self a meletary man eney moer than to doue mi duty thil mi year is up," this man explained in his quite adequate English.

Adventure and travel were additional motives. Still another Norwegian, newly arrived in Wisconsin in 1861, worked in a sawmill for a few weeks and then decided he could do better by joining the Scandinavian Fifteenth Regiment and receiving the bounty, the pay, and the free food. "This seemed good enough to me, and furthermore, I would have an opportunity to travel and to see a great deal." A Wisconsinite of Yankee stock wrote from Cincinnati in 1862: "We are almost in Dixie at last. I have accomplished a great part of one thing I volunteered for—seen some of our United States."[23]

Patriotism inspired many of the foreign-born as well as many of the native Americans. One immigrant from Norway identi-

---

[23] William O. Wettleson to his parents, October 12, 1861, translated from the Norwegian, in Wiley, *Life of Billy Yank*, 38; Peter Larsen to his wife, November 25, 1864, and January 14, 1865, and Harvey Reid to his parents, September 18, 1862, in Bascom, "Why They Fought," 253, 267, 387; Bersven Nelson, in Waldemar Ager, ed., *Oberst Heg og hans Gutter ved Waldemar Ager* (Eau Claire, Wisconsin, 1916), as quoted in Ella Lonn, *Foreigners in the Union Army and Navy* (Baton Rouge, 1951), 75.

fied himself as completely with the Union cause as if he had
been the grandson of some Revolutionary hero of New England:
"Let our countrymen remember that this war is waged for
our children and grand-children, just as our forefathers fought
in the Revolution against England to assure us freedom, we now
justly are proud of, so it is our holy duty now to take up
arms to preserve this splendid gift for our descendants." Another Norwegian, lying seriously wounded on the battlefield
of Stone's River, took pride in the confirmation of his American identity when the rebels came upon him and one of them
said: "Here is a damn Yankee." A Hollander, waking in a
Georgia camp to find that two shallow graves had been made
beside him during the night, sermonized about the importance
of being ready to sacrifice one's life for one's country. At the
end of the war an Irishman rejoiced: "How glad that the sons
of Erin's Isle have helped to save this our dear land."[24]

Cynicism also had a place in the thinking of Wisconsin troops.
"Dearest, take my word for it, the whole war from beginning
to end is nothing but a humbug and a swindle," a German
Catholic assured his wife. "This war doesn't concern the
Union but the almighty purses of the officers and contractors,
speculators and dealers." He believed that the privates and
the company officers of his regiment, the German Twenty-Sixth,
had little enthusiasm for the war. "They simply do not want
to fight for the niggers."

Emancipation was, indeed, the concern of only a comparative
few. One of the few was Chauncey H. Cooke, a Buffalo County
farm boy who went south with the Twenty-Fifth Regiment at
the age of sixteen. "There is nothing farther from my mind
at this writing than a wish to die for anybody or anything,"

[24] Letter to the *Emigranten*, December 23, 1861, quoted in Lonn, *Foreigners in the Union Army*, 78; Lars O. Dokken to his relatives, March, 1862, quoted in Theodore C. Blegen, *Norwegian Migration to America: The American Transition* (Northfield, Minnesota, 1940), 396, quoting from Ager, ed., *Oberst Heg*, 101–120; Peter J. Williamson to his wife, July 20, 1864, in Henry L. Swint, ed., "With the First Wisconsin Cavalry, 1862–1865: The Letters of Peter J. Williamson," in *WMH*, 26 (March, 1943–June, 1943), 439; James Lockney to to his parents, August 14, 1865, in Bascom, "Why They Fought," 227.

Cooke reported to his mother after reaching Kentucky early in 1863. As the regiment advanced through the land of slavery, he became more and more concerned about the institution as a moral wrong, but he found his comrades unsympathetic. "I tell the boys right to their face I am in the war for the freedom of the slave," he wrote from Mississippi after the fall of Vicksburg. "Most of the boys have their laugh at me for helping the 'Niggers.' "[25]

Opposition to slavery did not necessarily mean sympathy for the enslaved. Some Wisconsinites, like the Irish-born liberal and apostate from Catholicism James Lockney, wished to get rid of both slavery and the Negro. Lockney thought slavery was the cause of the rebellion and must therefore be abolished, but he also believed that "having the Blacks among us in a state of unrestrained freedom" would "still be very objectionable" and that they should be colonized in Africa as soon as they were freed. He feared that, if they remained in America, they would forever suffer from the prejudice of whites. "I have seen," he reported, "some of the soldiers of the so-called *gallant 28* Wis as well as others insult, by disrespectful & indecent language many, very many blacks, *men & women*, as well as many whites, *some ladies*."

Runaway slaves, or "contrabands," who swarmed around the Union armies in the South, looking to them for deliverance, got a mixed reception from the Wisconsin regiments. "Pathetic, indeed, was the sight of these poor, tired, hungry people," one Wisconsin veteran wrote in retrospect. At first, some of the blacks were well received, were given employment as cooks, personal servants, or common laborers, or were treated as pets, though most had to go on shifting for themselves. As the novelty wore off, however, the welcome diminished. With the Twenty-Second Wisconsin, the "romance of coaxing negroes into the camp" had "about 'played out' in soldier's parlance"

[25] Adam Muenzenberger to his wife, December 21, 1862, [March 7], 1863, in Bascom, "Why They Fought," 327, 341; Cooke to his mother, April 10, July 28, 1863, in "Badger Boy in Blue," in *WMH*, 4: 333, 455.

as early as November 1862, according to one of the regiment's men. "They find them lazy, saucy, and lousy, and, but for the name of it, nearly all in the camp would be sent out of it."[26]

Poverty and backwardness were the features of the Southern landscape that most impressed Wisconsin soldiers, who generally put the blame on slavery and the presumably consequent shiftlessness of Southern whites, without taking adequately into account the destructive and demoralizing effects of the war itself. From northern Alabama a Wisconsin boy informed a friend back home: "The folks [here] is poo[r]er than skim piss." From Dalton, Georgia, another wrote to his Norwegian relatives: "I would not give one farm in Koshkonong for the whole South." From Arkansas a third reported that, in a march of fifty-five miles, "we saw one pretty nice church, but schoolhouses were not to be seen, as if the darkness & gloom of Death had always covered the land," which was "very thinly settled" even though "this was a State long before Wis."

In the minds of some Badger boys, however, the balmy South had real advantages over Wisconsin, "where the Winter King rules so long each year." Once slavery and the slaves had been removed, the South with its undeveloped resources might become an even more promising frontier of settlement than the Northwest. Already, here and there, men from Wisconsin were taking advantage of the opportunities they saw. By early 1864, for example, two men of the Twenty-Second, in Tennessee, had rented plantations and were starting to "hire negroes and buy mules and go into cotton raising, expecting to make an immense fortune out of it." Other Wisconsin soldiers in various parts of the South were looking forward to future residence there. "I doubt very much if I get back safe & well whether I Pass one half my future years in Wis. or as far North in any

[26] James Lockney to his niece, February 26, 1863, and to his brother, June 20, July 13, 1863, in Bascom, "Why They Fought," 135, 146–148, 152; Rood, *Service of Company E,* 249–250 (the quoted veteran); Dawes, *Sixth Wisconsin Volunteers,* 48. The quoted soldier from the Twenty-Second is Harvey Reid to his sisters, November 11, 1862, in Byrne, ed., *Civil War Letters of Harvey Reid,* 15–16.

other state," said one, ". . . I think I may seek a home in some milder clime."[27]

For many of the men from Wisconsin, the war signified something besides a livelihood, an unavoidable duty, a patriotic sacrifice, an idealistic crusade, or a chance to travel and see the country. The war also meant an opportunity for personal achievement, for the play of ambition both military and political. "I desire promotion—am ambitious—as much as any man . . . ," the heroic Frank A. Haskell confessed. From his enlistment as a lieutenant in 1861 to his death as a colonel in 1864, Haskell was continually campaigning for higher rank and envying those who got ahead of him. "My being a Col. is a wonderful remote point . . . ," Captain Edward Bragg of the Sixth Wisconsin told his wife in 1861. "The most I expect to be is Lieut. Col., which I soon shall be if our Col. is promoted, which as you know we are working hard for. . . ." By 1863 Bragg had a full colonelship. "And as I have to stay in the service, I fight for 'a Star' or a coffin." Before the end of the war he had his star, as a brigadier general of volunteers. After the war he won election to Congress. He was only one of a number of officer veterans who, in peacetime, converted their war records into political assets.

While captains aspired to be colonels, and colonels to be generals, privates had hopes of becoming corporals, and corporals of becoming sergeants or even captains. The earnings of a captain were almost ten times those of a private, and a captain had some patronage at his disposal: he could name the noncommissioned officers of his company. Harvey Reid of the Twenty-Second Wisconsin finally received a promotion in 1864, when the "dropping out of two lieutenants" occasioned

[27] Thomas Wall to Andrew Weld, March 21, 1864, and William O. Wettleson to his family, November 27, 1864, in Wiley, *Life of Billy Yank,* 96, 187; James Lockney to his sister, August 21, 1863, and to his brother, September 28, 1863, in Bascom, "Why They Fought," 156–157, 162–164; Harvey Reid to his sister, February 21, 1864, in Byrne, ed., *Civil War Letters of Harvey Reid,* 119; David H. Overy, Jr., "The Wisconsin Carpetbagger: A Group Portrait," in *WMH,* 44 (Autumn, 1960), 18–21.

"an advance of the whole line of company officers," two corporals moving up to be sergeants, and Reid and another private rising to be corporals. There was a good reason, as Reid recognized, why he had not been promoted earlier. He was from Union Grove, the "Grove boys" had got more than their fair share of the offices when the company was formed, and the captain had "endeavored to 'equalize the spoils.' "[28]

Veterans in old regiments advanced less rapidly, as a rule, than did recent recruits in newly formed ones, since the creation of new outfits multiplied the number of offices to be filled. "The chances for promotion," as Colonel Dawes contended, "were therefore in inverse ratio to the service performed." This was undoubtedly true in many cases. It was both a reason for the organization of so many new regiments and a reason for the opposition to the practice.

From the beginning the governor appointed the officers of the Wisconsin regiments, and after the first year of war he also named the commissioned officers of the companies. One private expressed a widely shared disgust when Edward Salomon, that "miserable Dutch governor," took from the men the traditional privilege of electing their own company leaders. Throughout the war, ambitious officers sought to improve their rank by bringing pressure to bear upon the governor either directly or through fellow officers or friendly politicians.

Disappointment led to bitterness. Frank A. Haskell, with some justification, accused Salomon of favoring the politically influential over the militarily experienced. Salomon refused to promote him despite the intercession of Brigadier General Lysander Cutler, like Haskell a Wisconsinite of old New England stock. Haskell took what satisfaction he could from repeating Cutler's statement—tinged with a bit of anti-Semitism

---

[28] Byrne and Weaver, eds., *Haskell of Gettysburg*, 15–22; the quotation (p. 238) is from Haskell to his brother, January 17, 1864. Bragg told of his expectations in letters to his wife, December 7, 1861, and March 22, 1863, in Bascom, "Why They Fought," 37, 72. See also Dawes, *Sixth Wisconsin Volunteers*, 14, and Harvey Reid to his sister, April 12, 1864, in Byrne, ed., *Civil War Letters of Harvey Reid*, 125.

arising from the rumor of Salomon's having Jewish ancestry
—that "the Ex-Dutchman, from Judea," had lost his chances
for renomination because of his refusal to promote Haskell.

Regimental politics went to extremes in the Twenty-Second
Wisconsin. Its colonel, William L. Utley, was a former assemblyman from Racine and (in 1861) state adjutant general,
who in 1862 received his regimental appointment from Governor Salomon by virtue of his standing in the Republican party.
The regiment's lieutenant colonel, Edward Bloodgood, the
son of a West Point graduate, had been active in the peacetime
militia, had volunteered early, and had risen through the ranks.
Between Utley and Bloodgood there arose a feud that, for
months, so demoralized the regiment as to make it unfit for
combat. Siding with Bloodgood, twenty-three of twenty-seven
line officers charged Utley with incompetence and petitioned
him to resign. Utley countered by threatening to court-martial
the officers who opposed him and by cultivating the sympathy
of the enlisted men. He gained the support of Governor Lewis,
who (as one of the soldiers heard) promised to "respect his
recommendations for the commissioning of officers," and he
"adopted the plan of letting the companies vote upon promo-
tions." Finally, in July 1864, Utley resigned "on the plea of
ill health"; but before he left he had a last confrontation with
his adversary, when Bloodgood called him a liar and he struck
Bloodgood and nearly knocked him down.[29]

Ethnic differences between officers and men sometimes occasioned ill feeling. Except in companies or regiments consisting exclusively or overwhelmingly of men of a particular
immigrant nationality, a disproportionate number of the officers were Americans of native background. War Secretary
Simon Cameron early recommended to the governors the em-

[29] Dawes, *Sixth Wisconsin Volunteers*, 244–245; Quiner, *Military History of Wisconsin*, 132. The quotation about Salomon's background is from Haskell to his brother, January 17, 1864, in Byrne and Weaver, eds., *Haskell of Gettysburg*, 239. The quotations concerning the Utley-Bloodgood feud and the "Dutch governor" are from Byrne, ed., *Civil War Letters of Harvey Reid*, xii–xiii, 76–78, 114, 117, 167–168.

ployment of "foreign officers of military education and experience," who had "tendered their services" to the federal government in large numbers. Governor Randall replied that Wisconsin citizens were "very sensitive as to being placed under the command of foreigners." He said he had appointed one such foreigner, who had been highly recommended and had been "for some time a resident of this State," but the man could not get along with his fellow officers. Though not naming him, the governor was referring to Joseph Vandor, a Hungarian, who at the outset was colonel of the Seventh Wisconsin. Apparently the common soldiers liked Vandor well enough, despite his strict discipline, but the officers resented his habit of pointing out their deficiencies in front of the men. The officers eventually forced his resignation.

If most American-born citizens favored American-born officers, most of the immigrants preferred leaders of their own kind. Certainly the Irishmen of the Sixth Wisconsin's Company D, the old Montgomery Guards of the prewar militia, were proud to serve under Captain John O'Rourke and his associates. In 1861, while still colonel of the Sixth, the Yankee from Massachusetts Lysander Cutler weeded out the line officers who "for various reasons were not acceptable to him" under the "thin disguise" of failure to pass an examination that he required. In the process, the colonel stripped the Irish company of its Irish officers. "This appointment of strangers to command of the company, and disregard of their natural and reasonable preference as to nationality, made bad feeling among the men of that company," recalled Rufus Dawes, then a captain and later the colonel of the regiment.

Still, there were ethnically mixed companies that got along quite happily with foreign-born as well as native officers. A good example was Company C of the Eighth Wisconsin. Its roster included English or "American" names like Dodge and Morse, German like Selb and Stahlmann, Irish like McGinnes and McCauley, and Scandinavian like Oleson and Swenson. When they first organized, the men chose John E. Perkins as captain, Victor Wolf as first lieutenant, and Frank McGuire as second lieutenant. Wolf, born in Germany, had gained military experience there. On Perkins' death, early in the war, Wolf succeeded to the captaincy, and the men willingly followed him through nearly three years of hard campaigning.[30]

Party politics heightened tensions among the Wisconsin troops, especially at election times, when the men were allowed, by state law, to vote in the field. On election day, 1862, a German Catholic in the Twenty-Sixth Regiment complained that his company did not have a chance to vote. "Our officers are all Republicans and our soldiers are all Democrats," he said, "and so they've cheated us—or rather the candidates." In regiments containing a great majority of Republicans, it was sometimes unsafe for anyone to cast a Democratic ballot. When a member of the Twenty-Second was caught doing so in 1863, a mob of other men from the regiment rode him on a rail and threatened to duck him in a river. That year only one Wisconsin regiment went Democratic—the Seventeenth, the so-called Irish Brigade. "I suppose that regiment would vote for Jeff. Davis," an American-born veteran of the Sixth remarked, "if they were told that he was a Democrat." As the presidential election of 1864 approached, even some of the Republicans were at first inclined to vote for the Democratic candidate, since he was George B. McClellan, the former general-in-chief who had been extremely popular among the rank and file. But Republicanism reasserted itself before election day.[31]

Like soldiers from other states, those from Wisconsin usually developed a sense of identification first with their company,

[30] The Cameron-Randall exchange is contained in *Official Records*, series 3, vol. 1: 756, 763–764, 880. See also Dawes, *Sixth Wisconsin Volunteers*, 26; Williams, *"Eagle Regiment,"* 111–113, 154; Mattern, "Soldiers When They Go," 31–32.

[31] The quoted German Catholic is Adam Muenzenberger to his wife, November 29, 1862, in Bascom, "Why They Fought," 320. The quotation about the Irish Brigade is from D. K. Noyes to Dawes, December 8, 1863, in Dawes, *Sixth Wisconsin Volunteers*, 231. See also Harvey Reid to his sister, November 10, 1863, in Bascom, "Why They Fought," 425–426, and Reid to his father, November 8, 1864, in Byrne, ed., *Civil War Letters of Harvey Reid*, 198.

next with their regiment, and then to a lesser degree with their brigade, corps, and army. Within the company, however, the men divided into informal groupings of congenial spirits, for sociability and for mess, and such groupings attracted much the strongest feelings of kinship and loyalty. Hence, though practically every Wisconsin company sooner or later included at least a few foreign-born, these men did not necessarily mingle as intimates with the American-born. Close friendships were even less likely to arise between the native Americans and those immigrants who belonged to companies and whole regiments of their own nationality.

At every level there were instances of exclusiveness if not antagonism. As Westerners, the Wisconsin members of Sherman's army looked down upon the Army of the Potomac as an outfit of Easterners, even though it too contained Wisconsinites. A Wisconsin private in the Department of the Gulf noted after the arrival of some troops from the East: "They and the Western boys fight every time we meet. I think either side would rather shoot at each other than the Johnnies." Men of the Twenty-Second Wisconsin—mostly from the New York and New England settlements in Racine, Walworth, Rock, and Green counties—objected to being assigned to the Eleventh Corps as part of the only western brigade in it, not only because of the "incurable jealousy between the Potomac and western Armies" but also because of a "natural repugnance to being joined to a corps composed almost entirely of Germans." James D. McVicar, born in British America, of Scottish ancestry, had a similar repugnance to being assigned to Company G of the Sixteenth Wisconsin—"there was so manny Irishman in our Company that I could not live with them"—and he escaped by contriving to get a job in the quartermaster's department.

Even when native Americans were well disposed, they were likely to be condescending toward immigrants, particularly the Irish, whom they looked upon good-naturedly as humorous objects. There was, for example, the "typical Irishman, from another regiment," who amused the men of the Twelfth with his exclamations "in a rich brogue" as shell after shell whistled past during the battle of Kenesaw Mountain: "the murtherin' thing will be afther killin' every wan av us if ye don't get *close down!*" In the case of the Germans, communication could be difficult because of the language barrier. One day some men of the Twelfth, while stationed in Missouri, were pleased to observe the arrival of another Wisconsin regiment, the Ninth. "The most of us went over to visit with them," the historian of Company E of the Twelfth remembered, "but, as they were all Germans, we could not talk much." When the Seventh received fourteen Chippewa recruits, "apparently wild from the woods," some of them unable to speak English, the veterans viewed them as curiosities and gathered to watch as the Indians performed a war dance for them.[32]

Prejudice led many of the American-born whites to belittle the fighting qualities of their fellow soldiers from other ethnic groups. Quite unfairly, Haskell accused the Eleventh Corps "Dutchmen" of running at the battle at Chancellorsville "before they had delivered a shot" and of fleeing on the first day of Gettysburg in a "disgraceful rout and panic." Of Irishmen it was said they usually had "more vehemence than discretion" and, though they were courageous, their courage was the result of "impulse rather than the result of deliberate valor." Officers commanding Indians reported that these men were "good soldiers, being unsurpassed for scouting or picket duty, but quite unable to stand a charge or artillery fire." Blacks were given less credit for bravery than the Indians. Unsurprisingly, a Wisconsin army surgeon of Yankee background came to the following conclusion: "the descendants of the early settlers of New England, New York, Pennsylvania, and Ohio, where physical development and courage are combined with intelligence and patriotism, make the best soldiers the world has

[32] Wiley, *Life of Billy Yank*, 322–323, 325–326, 340 (quotation of the Wisconsin private is on p. 323). The comments about assignment to the Eleventh Corps are from Harvey Reid to his sister, January 9, 1864, in Byrne, ed., *Civil War Letters of Harvey Reid*, 112–113. Porter, "The Colonel and the Private Go to War," in *WMH*, 42: 126, quotes McVicar, and the quotations about immigrants in the Twelfth are from Rood, *Service of Company E*, 99, 299. See also Dawes, *Sixth Wisconsin Volunteers*, 46–47, 202, 248–249.

ever seen, and as a class by far excel the representatives of any European state."[33]

Thus, to a considerable extent, the shared experience of the Civil War reinforced rather than modified the mental stereotypes that already prevailed among the native white Wisconsinites when thinking about immigrants or Indians or blacks. Many though by no means all of the foreign-born soldiers got from their service a heightened sense of identification with the ideals and fortunes of the United States. Yet, on balance, it may be questioned whether the war's assimilative influence outweighed its divisive effects.

[5]

"I've tho't of home and you so many times," a youthful Wisconsin soldier wrote after several months in the army. "Don't think I am homesick, mother. . . ." A year later, addressing his father, he summed up the feeling of thousands of his fellows: "If the folks at home could know what happy fools it made of us to get letters, they would write more of them and longer ones." Husbands appealed to their wives for more frequent communications, and unmarried men to their sweethearts or even to total strangers, as in an advertisement that appeared in a Milwaukee paper: "CORRESPONDENCE WANTED.— Three young gentlemen wish the correspondence of a limited number of young ladies."[34]

Soldiers filled their letters with details of their day-to-day

---

[33] See Byrne and Weaver, eds., *Haskell of Gettysburg*, 80–81, 96, for Haskell's criticisms. Peter T. Harstad, ed., "A Civil War Medical Examiner: The Report of Dr. Horace O. Crane," in *WMH*, 48 (Spring, 1965), contains the quotations about the Irish, Indian, and Yankee soldiers. On the fighting ability of blacks, see Noyes, "Negro in Wisconsin's Civil War Effort," in the *Lincoln Herald*, 69: 78. In 1866 Love stated in *Wisconsin in the War*, 1032: "The Indian names found in the roll of the dead of some regiments testify to the valor of Wisconsin red men. They who witnessed them on the field, can give many of them a good name."

[34] "Badger Boy in Blue," in *WMH*, 4: 84, 442 (quotations from the youthful soldier); Milwaukee *Sentinel*, September 24, 1864. For other examples of soldier letters with similar themes, see Bascom, "Why They Fought," 247–248, 249–250; Leo M. Kaiser, ed., "Civil War Letters of Charles W. Carr of the 21st Wisconsin Volunteers," in *WMH*, 43 (Summer, 1960), 264–272; and R. G. Plumb, ed., "Letters of a Fifth Wisconsin Volunteer," in *WMH*, 3 (September, 1919), 52–83.

living—the rain and mud, the sleeping on the ground, the army
rations and the foraging to supplement them, the frequent
diarrhea and other illnesses, the sights along the way, the battle
action and the wounds, the deaths of comrades. The writers
also related their impressions of war aims, of slavery, of the
Southern foe. Thus, by sharing their experiences with the
folks at home, the soldiers influenced the thinking of civilians.
Indeed, some of the men in uniform believed that, because
of their service, they had a special right to be heard. As one
put it, "soldiers have sacrificed enough and suffered enough
to be allowed to have an opinion as to how this war should
be settled and how conducted." Many, including some from
Democratic families, expressed their contempt for war evaders and war opponents, especially the antiwar Democrats, or
Copperheads as they were called. "It is manifest that the
cowardly sneaks who stay at home intend to sell out the country," said Rufus Dawes. Another Wisconsinite, a Norwegian,
after telling how he and his comrades had torn down a Virginia
farmer's outbuilding to get brick and lumber, went on to say
he would like for some of the Wisconsin Copperheads to have
their farms "in the same fix."[35]

Some men with families worried continually about the wives
and children they had left behind. Such men were glad enough
to contribute to their families' support. Others forgetfully
spent or gambled off most of their soldier's pay. In any case,
it was risky for soldiers to send money home by mail. Beginning in 1862, commissioners from each state made the rounds
of the camps to collect allotments of pay and remit these to
dependents. Before the end of 1863, a total of 12,637 Wisconsin troops had made such allotments.[36]

The state undertook officially to reassure the soldiers in the

[35] Harvey Reid to his father, August 26, 1864, in Byrne, ed., *Civil War Letters
of Harvey Reid*, 180–182; Dawes, *Sixth Wisconsin Volunteers*, 105–106; Peter
Larsen to his wife and children, December 24, 1864, in Bascom, "Why They
Fought," 262.
[36] Scott, "Financial Effects of the Civil War," 56–57; James W. Shannon, "State
Aid to Wisconsin Soldiers and Their Families: Financial and Humanitarian"
(master's thesis, University of Wisconsin, 1915), 2–3.

field that the people of Wisconsin were concerned about them. "The history of all wars tells us that both during their continuance and after their close thousands of soldiers, sick and diseased and maimed, go wandering homeward, suffering with privation and want, begging their weary way, and meeting that curious public gaze which has no sympathy or kindness in it." So wrote Governor Randall on July 4, 1861, in an eloquent letter to each of the governors of the other Northern states. On behalf of Wisconsin he said he was determined that every disabled man should be "safely and comfortably returned to this State and to his family or friends." He asked the other governors to adopt his plan of sending state agents to look out for the welfare of the troops. Some of the others did so, and his successors in Wisconsin renewed the practice, with the aid of modest appropriations by the legislature. Wisconsin and other states insisted on caring for their own men even after the United States Sanitary Commission began to provide for the "sanitary" needs of all Union soldiers.[37]

Serving as the governor's personal representatives, the Wisconsin agents visited and inspected hospitals and camps, reported the numbers of sick and wounded, arranged for transporting them home, distributed gifts and medical supplies, and made available extra surgeons and nurses. Certainly the most famous and probably the most effective of the agents was Cordelia Harvey, the governor's widow, who took up his Samaritan work after his untimely death. On board a river steamer, during the fighting around Vicksburg, Mrs. Harvey found the deck covered with dead and wounded, many of the latter suffering for want of attention. "I hastened away," she reported, "and soon returned with everything needed, shirts, drawers, socks, lemons, sugar, wines, canned peaches, jellies, nice fresh crackers, peaches, tumblers, wash basins, sponges, soap, towels, handkerchiefs, cloth, and lint." There were many

[37] *Official Records*, series 3, vol. 1: 330–331 (quotations); P. Marcus Schmidt, "The Dependence of the Lincoln Administration on the Northwestern Governors" (master's thesis, University of Wisconsin, 1936), 126–128. The legislature granted appropriations in 1863–1865, but not in 1862. See Shannon, "State Aid to Wisconsin Soldiers," 54–56.

Wisconsin men on board, but she did not confine her ministra-
tions to them. "If you ask for men from any state it makes
hearts so sad. . . ." Besides sending representatives, Governors
Salomon and Lewis also made personal visits to Wisconsin soldiers in hospitals and in the field.

In 1863 the army ceased to allow the sick and wounded to go
home on furlough and began to keep them (except for those
it discharged as unfit for further service) in military hospitals.
This made more urgent the demand, which Salomon and other
Northern governors had already voiced, that army hospitals
be located in their own states, where the boys would be near
their relatives and friends. Mrs. Harvey took up the cause.
After visiting hospitals as far south as New Orleans, she had
concluded that only the bracing northern air would restore
many of the Wisconsin invalids to health. She carried to Washington a petition signed by 8,000 people of the state, and after
repeated conferences with War Secretary Edwin M. Stanton
and President Lincoln she finally got action. In October 1863,
the Harvey United States Army General Hospital, named for
her husband, began to function in the Farwell house, a three-
storied octagonal building on the edge of Lake Monona in Madison. The following year, similar hospitals were opened in
Milwaukee and Prairie du Chien.[38]

Throughout the war, soldiers who were discharged for disability or for other reasons made their way homeward. By
1864 the numbers of returning men had begun to grow as
veterans completed their terms and went home either to stay
or to spend the furlough that was part of the reward for those
who re-enlisted. Then, in 1865, occurred the grand demobilization. Meanwhile public-spirited citizens made preparations
to receive the ex-soldiers.

Passing through Milwaukee were thousands of them, sick,
disabled, or destitute, who often were compelled to beg in

[38] *Ibid.*, 44–75. The quotations are on pp. 65–66. See also Robert H. Jacobi,
"Wisconsin Civil War Governors" (master's thesis, University of Wisconsin, 1948),
169–176; Ethel A. Hurn, *Wisconsin Women in the War Between the States*
(Madison, 1911), 118–144.

order to get food, lodging, and transportation to their homes. In the spring of 1864 a group of Milwaukee women decided to do something about this. They formed the Wisconsin Soldiers' Home Association, solicited contributions, and rented rooms on West Water Street. "Here the soldier could come and be provided with temporary rest and entertainment, and when too sick to proceed on his journey, he could receive such medical aid as was required, and kind and careful nursing." In the spring of 1865 the women held a fair to raise money, with the eagle Old Abe as one of the main attractions, and bought property of their own. From April 1864 to July 1866 the Wisconsin Soldiers' Home sheltered a total of 31,650 veterans. Later its property went to the federal government for a National Asylum for Disabled Soldiers.

When, early in 1864, the re-enlisting veterans of the Sixth Wisconsin arrived in Milwaukee on furlough, they dined as guests of the Board of Trade and then listened to flattering speeches by politicians. That year the legislature authorized the governor to use state funds, not exceeding 50 cents per man, to provide a reception and entertainment for any returning regiment, company, or battery. In 1865 the legislature asked the federal government to favor, first, disabled soldiers and, next, other veterans in awarding postal and other jobs. Private philanthropists, with the endorsement of the Wisconsin Soldiers' Aid Society, set up a Bureau of Employment for Discharged Soldiers at the headquarters of the Young Men's Christian Association in Milwaukee. The bureau urged that the "light occupations of all towns and communities" be given to the men who had incapacitated themselves for heavier work by "giving their limbs, their health, and their blood to the nation."[39]

As the war drew to an end, in May 1865, the War Department designated Milwaukee and Madison as the places where the Wisconsin troops still in the army would get their final pay-

[39] Shannon, "State Aid to Wisconsin Soldiers," 77–80; Hurn, *Wisconsin Women in the War*, 161–176; Dawes, *Sixth Wisconsin Volunteers*, 236–237. The quotations are from Quiner, *Military History of Wisconsin*, 241–242, 245–246.

ment and discharge—to the delight of local businessmen, who expected to profit from the estimated $3 million the soldiers would receive. Most of these men were then encamped in the vicinity of Washington, where many of them paraded in the last "grand review" of Union forces. Transferred to Louisville, Kentucky, the Wisconsin troops were shipped northward from there, many of them in boxcars or on flatcars. There were irksome delays, because of red tape, especially for the members of the older regiments. These men complained that those who had enlisted for large bonuses late in the war were let go first, while those who had served longer "for less money" were held back.

The earliest returnees also received the most enthusiastic public welcomes when, in June, they arrived at Madison or Milwaukee. They were greeted with free banquets, patriotic speechmaking, rousing music, and gratifying banners, such as the one that proclaimed: "The only national debt we can never pay—the debt we owe our soldiers." As time passed, the Madison and Milwaukee homecoming receptions became routine, and both attendance and enthusiasm declined. Individual heroes continued to be honored at celebrations in their home localities, as General Joseph Bailey, hero of the Red River campaign, was in Kilbourn City and again in Baraboo.[40]

But the ex-soldiers could not subsist on honor, and many veterans of long service now found it difficult to pick up their lives and jobs where they had left them three or even four years earlier. Bailey, for one, could not resume his previous position, since the hydraulic company he formerly worked for had gone out of business. Failing to get the federal appointment he sought, he moved to a farm in Missouri, where he was elected sheriff and, in 1867, was shot and killed while bringing in a couple of desperadoes. A great many other restless veterans —perhaps as many as one-third of the Wisconsin total—left the

[40] Jackson R. Horton, "The Demobilization of Wisconsin Troops after the Civil War" (master's thesis, University of Wisconsin, 1952), 15–19, 29–33 (quotations); Baraboo *Republic*, July 5, 12, 1865.

state soon after their return (while large numbers of foot-
loose veterans from other states were taking up residence in
Wisconsin). Most of the migrating Wisconsinites went to
Iowa and Minnesota, many others to the Far West, and some
back to the recently conquered South. Wisconsin newspapers
deplored the exodus and urged the former soldiers to stay home
and help develop the still bounteous resources of the state.[41]

[41] Horton, "Demobilization of Wisconsin Troops," 50–59; Extrom, "General
Joseph Bailey," 30–32; Overy, "Wisconsin Carpetbagger," in *WMH,* 44: 31, 49.

11

Civilian Life in Wartime

[1]

AFTER Wisconsin's financial shock in early 1861, resulting from the secession of the Southern states, the Civil War brought prosperity to Wisconsin as it did to the rest of the North. Wisconsin barely felt the financial crisis of late 1861, which struck elsewhere almost as hard as the Panic of 1857, through with a less lasting effect. By 1862, throughout the Union, recovery was beginning, and by 1863 the boom was on.

In Wisconsin the boom developed in spite of banking policies that make for tight money and credit. According to a state law of 1861, the banks could use only the bonds of Wisconsin or the United States as backing for their notes, and these were limited to three times the amount of capital actually paid in. Besides, each bank was to keep at least $15,000 in cash on hand and was to maintain in Milwaukee or in Madison an agent ready at all times to redeem its currency. The object was to prevent a resurgence of wildcat banking. Under the presidency of Alexander Mitchell, the Wisconsin Bankers' Association took upon itself the responsibility of policing the banks and holding them to even stricter rules. The association determined to prevent new banks from going into business and to prevent existing ones from putting out additional notes without the approval of its board of directors. Members enforced the association's rules by rejecting the notes of unapproved banks and by collecting large batches and then demanding immediate redemption of the notes of banks that made unauthorized issues, thus draining the offenders of specie and forcing them out of business. Between October 1861 and October 1862 the number of Wisconsin banks fell from 107 to sixty-five. The banknote circulation, which had shrunk from $4,580,832 to $1,590,691 during 1861, increased but slowly thereafter—by less than $150,000 during 1863. Mitchell's own institution, the Wisconsin Marine and Fire Insurance Company Bank, remained dominant, controlling more than an eighth of all the bank resources and handling almost a fifth of all the bank loans in the state.

The money scarcity was alleviated when, early in 1862, the federal government began to issue its legal tender notes, or greenbacks. There was still a shortage of small change, however, since people were withholding coins. To make up for this lack, banks had pasteboard coupons printed, merchants made change with their own private notes ("shinplasters"), and Congress defined postage stamps as legal tender. The glue made the stamps a nuisance, and counterfeiting as well as fragility gave bank coupons and shinplasters a bad name. These expedients lasted only about a year. They were replaced by stamps without glue, which the post office sold in denominations of 5, 10, 25, and 50 cents.

Congressional acts of 1863 and 1864 set up a national banking system. Banks joining it could issue federally guaranteed notes after buying United States bonds and depositing them with the Treasury Department as security. At first, few Wisconsin banks joined—only fifteen by the end of 1864—since most of them were already loaded down with Wisconsin bonds, which they could not easily dispose of. Most of them had little choice, however, after March 3, 1865, when Congress imposed a 10 per cent tax on state banknotes so as to drive them out of circulation. In order to become national banks, purchase United States bonds, and issue national banknotes, the state banks now had to unload their state bonds; but there was no market for these. Once again Wisconsin's financial wizard, Alexander Mitchell, devised a scheme to meet a banking emergency. He dispatched his lawyer from Milwaukee to Madison with the draft of a bill, which the legislature quickly passed. The new law required every Wisconsin insurance company to deposit with the state treasurer, as surety for policy holders, state bonds in the amount of the business the company had done the previous year. Thus, against strenuous resistance on their part, the insurance companies were brought to the rescue, and the transition from state banks to national banks was eased.[1]

In 1863 the farmers of Wisconsin entered upon a period of greater prosperity than they had ever enjoyed, a period that was to last for several years. Farm owners on the whole realized good profits, improved their properties, invested in new lands and equipment, and paid off accumulated debts. All this they did in spite of rising costs. Credit was scarce and interest rates were high, around 10 per cent. Labor, with the departure of men in uniform, also became scarce, and wages for hired hands during harvest time went up from $1 or $1.50 a day in 1861 to $4 or $4.50 in 1864. Transportation charges more than tripled in the course of the war. Fortunately for the farmers, the prices of their crops also multiplied, the Milwaukee price of wheat increasing from under 70 cents a bushel in 1861 to $2.26 three years later.

"Wheat is king, and Wisconsin is the center of the Empire," the Milwaukee *Sentinel* crowed in November 1861, when serious trouble threatened between Great Britain and the United States, and Southerners were counting on "King Cotton" to bring about British and French intervention on the side of the Confederacy. Wisconsinites were convinced that Europe's need for wheat would prevail over her need for cotton and thus would keep European nations out of the American war. Among the wheat-producing states, Wisconsin remained second only to Illinois. Wheat continued to be Wisconsin's largest single crop year after year, with a harvest of 20,842,359 bushels in

[1] Frederick Merk, *Economic History of Wisconsin During the Civil War Decade* (Madison, 1916), 208–219, 229–234; David B. Leonard, "A Biography of Alexander Mitchell, 1817–1887" (master's thesis, University of Wisconsin, 1951), 72–75.

1863, though in 1864 the yield fell off somewhat because of chinch bugs and a drought. After the 1864 harvest of 14,168,317 bushels, the 1865 harvest rose to 20,307,920. Even larger was the combined output of other grains—oats, corn, rye, and barley—but these were grown mainly for local consumption, not for large-scale export. Wheat production was still expanding toward the north and west within the state. Only in the southeastern counties, where the cost of production was high and years of cropping had taxed the soil, did King Wheat fail to extend his sway or even to hold his own.

The war gave some stimulus to the mechanization of Wisconsin farms. In the absence of so many men, the harvesting of the vast wheat fields posed a serious challenge. A mechanical reaper would do the work of four to six men. At the start of the war, such reapers were already in fairly common use, Wisconsin farmers having bought at least 3,000 of them in 1860 alone. They purchased still more in the succeeding years. Once they had gathered their grain, however, they still faced the task of threshing it, a very laborious task with hand-swung flails. As late as 1860 the threshing machine was something of a novelty in Wisconsin. On buying one that year, a well-to-do Dutch farmer near Little Chute felt compelled to describe the new invention in some detail—a "power plant" resembling a huge "coffee grinder" in the yard, a pole attached to it and propelled by horses going around in a wide circle, a long overhead shaft transmitting the power to the barn, and inside the barn the device that did the work, with a "big open mouth full of teeth," some of them stationary, others moving with a revolving drum. The proud owner had paid "close to a $100" for the machine, but with it and the "help of a few assistants" he could thresh 100 bushels a day. During the war other farmers in increasing numbers bought threshers of similar design.[2]

[2] Merk, *Economic History*, 16–19, 36–37, 52–54, 57–58; the Milwaukee *Sentinel*, November 8, 1861, is quoted on p. 16. See also John G. Thompson, *The Rise and Decline of the Wheat Growing Industry in Wisconsin* (Madison, 1909), 57–69, 133, 162–163, 196; Benjamin H. Hibbard, *The History of Agriculture in Dane County* (Madison, 1904), 121–133; Willard F. Miller, "A History of Eau Claire County During the Civil War" (master's thesis, University of Wisconsin,

Especially in southeastern Wisconsin, where wheat culture was faltering, the war also stimulated the production of a variety of crops, especially wool. Since Southern cotton was in short supply, while the manufacture of army uniforms created a large demand, both cotton and its substitutes went up in price, wool from 25 cents a pound in 1861 to $1.05 in 1864. In response, so many Wisconsin farmers turned to sheep raising that between 1860 and 1865 the number of sheep in the state increased from 332,954 to 1,260,900 and the wool output from 1 million to 4 million pounds. Some farmers tried growing flax, and a few linen factories and linseed oil plants appeared in the state. In the absence of Southern sugar and molasses, a small number of Wisconsinites experimented with sugar beets and a much larger number planted sorghum, producing syrup in quantities that approached a million gallons a year by the end of the war (compared with 19,854 gallons in 1860). The state's tobacco crop, more and more of which was grown by Norwegians in Dane and Rock counties, practically doubled during the war years. Cattle raising and dairying, however, had made little advance as yet.[3]

The wartime steps toward agricultural diversification resulted from temporary and abnormal market conditions rather than deliberate, long-range planning. For the time being, the application of farm science was retarded. As secretary of the Wisconsin Agricultural Society and editor of the *Wisconsin Farmer*, John Wesley Hoyt kept trying to spread ideas of scientific farming, both through his publications and through lectures that he traveled widely to deliver. The society held no state fair, however, in 1861, 1862, or 1863. Agricultural education received federal encouragement in the Morrill Act

1954), 34–36, 45–50, 57–60; and Arnold Verstegen, Little Chute, to relatives, August 20, 1860, in Henry S. Lucas, ed., *Dutch Immigrant Memoirs and Related Writings* (2 vols., Assen, Netherlands, 1955), 2: 164–165. The authorities agree that the use of farm machinery in Wisconsin increased during the war, but unfortunately they do not provide statistics that would make possible a reliable quantitative statement.

[3] Merk, *Economic History*, 20–21, 30–37; Eric E. Lampard, *The Rise of the Dairy Industry in Wisconsin: A Study in Agricultural Change, 1820–1920* (Madison, 1963), 49–56, 68–89.

of 1862, which provided land grants to the states for the support of agricultural colleges. Though favoring such education, most Wisconsinites disliked that particular law, for it would enable speculators, especially those in the East, to acquire large tracts of federal land in Wisconsin.[4]

Lumbering, continuing to be a most important economic activity, also benefited from wartime prices and demand. From $6.75 in 1861, the Chicago price for 1,000 board feet of mixed lumber reached the unprecedented height of $23 in 1864. Federal contracts helped to keep Wisconsin lumber firms busy. Daniel Shaw and Company, of Eau Claire, ·cut an annual average of 1.5 million board feet for the army during the first three years and received an order of 3 million more for the last year of the war. When sales were at their liveliest, however, the lumbermen of the northwestern part of the state were unable to take full advantage of the market. During the dry summers of 1863 and 1864, low water in the Mississippi's tributaries delayed the delivery of lumber and logs, and destructive fires swept through the pineries. With the competition thus reduced, lumbermen in northeastern Wisconsin prospered all the more. Sawmills in Oshkosh and Fond du Lac ran day and night, and the firm of P. Sawyer & Son alone attained an annual output of more than 5 million feet of lumber. Spring floods in 1865 floated the accumulations of lumber down the Chippewa and other northwestern rivers, but the price dropped with the advent of peace.[5]

As the price of lead rose, from $4.90 per hundredweight in

[4] Merk, *Economic History*, 50–51; Joseph Schafer, *A History of Agriculture in Wisconsin* (Madison, 1922), 108–109; Paul W. Gates, *The Wisconsin Pine Lands of Cornell University: A Study in Land Policy and Absentee Ownership* (Ithaca, 1943), 1–26, 75–77. Speculators opposed the principle of a homestead law—the cry of "Land to the landless," a Connecticut partner cautioned the Wisconsin speculator Moses M. Strong, "bodes no good to present holders" (Gates, 76)—but they were relieved by the terms of the Homestead Act of 1862, which interposed no bar to their continuing their acquisitions.

[5] Merk, *Economic History*, 59–64, 101–102; Miller, "Eau Claire County During tht Civil War," 26–27, 30–31; Bill Hooker, "Anecdotes of Civil War Days in 'Lower Town' Are Related by Pioneer Newspaper Man" in Fond lu Lac *Commonwealth-Reporter*, September 27, 1935; Richard N. Current, *Pine Logs and Politics: A Life of Philetus Sawyer, 1816–1900* (Madison, 1950), 27–30.

1861 to $15 in 1865, corporations with Eastern capital took over mines that former owners had abandoned after the Panic of 1857 in the southwestern counties of Grant, Iowa, and La-fayette. The new enterprisers invested large sums in deepening shafts and providing drains, but could not maintain the initial boost in production, which reached 17 million pounds in 1862 but declined to only about 14 million in 1865. They compensated for the declining yield from the galena, however, by exploiting the zinc ores they found in conjunction with it, ores that most previous miners had refused to bother with. Zinc output increased from a mere 320,000 pounds in 1860 to more than 4 million in 1865.

Flour milling, one of the state's foremost industries, ex-panded less during the boom years than it might have done had it not been handicapped by discriminatory policies of railroads and grain elevators, which charged excessive rates for transferring and storing wheat for Wisconsin mills. Oth-er farm-related industries thrived, among them meat packing and leather making, both of which had unwonted govern-ment orders to fill. Brewers benefited from a high federal excise tax on liquors; this made beer cheaper than ever by comparison, and lager was started on the way to becoming the favorite drink of old-stock Americans as well as German im-migrants.

Manufacturers of farm machinery strained against the limi-tations of capital and credit in an effort to keep up with sales. "The several agricultural shops in this city," the La Crosse Democrat reported in 1863, "are driven with work and hardly able to meet the demands on them for threshing machines, reapers, fanning mills, &c. A million more dollars could be profitably invested here in the manufacture of farm tools and labor saving implements of all kinds." In 1863 J. I. Case, taking in three partners, reorganized and enlarged his firm in Racine. By the end of the war it was turning out 500 threshing ma-chines a year (as compared with 300 in 1860) and ranked as one of the largest manufacturers of such machines in the entire country.[6]

Railroad construction during the war lagged even more in Wisconsin than in the North as a whole, only a few miles of track being added to the 900 already existing in the state in 1861. In 1862 a line was extended from Appleton to Green Bay and, later, to the upper peninsula of Michigan. "A big crew of men is working with shovels and pickaxes and scrapers drawn by horses, making a perfectly level roadbed," wrote a Little Chute resident in June 1862. "It is surprising that in these times of uncertainty, funds can be found to finance so big an undertaking, and that with so many young men joining the army enough labor is available." The writer expected the project to be a "great boon" for the Fox Valley, perhaps eventually making Little Chute a "big city." Certainly a new line running from Doty Island proved a tremendous benefit to the industrializing community of Neenah-Menasha, which now had direct access north to Green Bay or south, via Fond du Lac and Janesville, to Chicago. While investing little in new trackage within the state, Wisconsin railroad companies were contributing to the extension of lines across Iowa and Minnesota, lines that would generate traffic for the railroads running from the Mississippi to Milwaukee.[7]

Consolidation rather than construction was the keynote in Wisconsin, as two large railroad systems began to emerge—the Chicago and North Western and the Milwaukee and St. Paul. Originating in 1859 as an association of bondholders

[6] Merk, *Economic History*, 111–115, 129–130, 144–146, 151–155, 370–371; the La Crosse *Democrat*, July 28, 1863, is quoted on pp. 145–146. See also William E. Derby, "A History of the Port of Milwaukee, 1835–1910" (doctoral dissertation, University of Wisconsin, 1963), 242, 270; Charles E. Schefft, "The Tanning Industry in Wisconsin: A History of Its Frontier Origins and Its Development" (master's thesis, University of Wisconsin, 1938), 34–43; and Stewart H. Holbrook, *Machines of Plenty: Pioneering in American Agriculture* (New York, 1955), 48–50.

[7] Merk, *Economic History*, 271–277; Arnold Verstegen to relatives, June 19, 1862, in Lucas, ed., *Dutch Immigrant Memoirs*, 2: 169–170; Alice E. Smith, *Millstone and Saw: The Origins of Neenah-Menasha* (Madison, 1966), 53–55.

and other creditors of the longest north–south line in the state (the Chicago, St. Paul and Fond du Lac), the C. & N. W. turned to acquiring other companies after completing its extension to Green Bay. It got a controlling interest in the Kenosha, Rockford and Rock Island; absorbed the Galena and Chicago Union and, along with it, the Beloit and Madison (completed during the war); and quietly bought a majority of the stock of the Chicago and Milwaukee. The Milwaukee and St. Paul grew out of the bankrupt La Crosse and Milwaukee, which the bondholders foreclosed and reorganized in 1863. After taking over three short lines in receivership, the M. & St. P. made repeated offers to purchase the Milwaukee and Prairie du Chien (the former Milwaukee and Mississippi) so as to monopolize the through east–west routes across the state. But the Milwaukee and Prairie du Chien, prospering under new management, refused to sell. Alexander Mitchell was president of both the Milwaukee and St. Paul and the Chicago and Milwaukee, so the North Western's acquisition of C. & M. stock amounted to an encroachment on the interests of the M. & St. P.

With the closing of the lower Mississippi as a result of the war, the Wisconsin railroads no longer had to fear the competition of that river-and-ocean route to eastern markets. Steamboats on the upper Mississippi continued to serve as feeders for the railroads that ran from the river to Lake Michigan. Early in the war the boats began to add to their capacity by towing barges, as many as three to a boat, each of them carrying as much grain as the boat itself. Already the ownership of the boat lines was highly concentrated, and by 1863 a pair of related companies dominated the river traffic between St. Paul and Galena. The railroads controlled these companies through an interlocking directorate.

Taking advantage of their monopolistic position, the railroads proceeded to push up their rates. For hauling a bushel of wheat from Hudson to Milwaukee, by river and rail, the charge was 35 cents in the spring of 1865 (it had been only 12 cents in the spring of 1861). From Madison to Milwaukee the charge for wheat ran 5 or 6 cents higher than from La Crosse or Prairie du Chien. To ship cattle from Mauston to Milwaukee, 131 miles, it cost $46 per car load, a buyer found in 1864. "By driving his cattle to La Crosse, 69 miles from here, and 200 from Milwaukee," the Mauston *Star* remonstrated, "he gets them sent to Milwaukee by the same railroad company for $24 a car load." As in the prewar period, the railroads could get away with charging more for the short than the long haul because they had even less competition over the short haul.

These monopolistic practices renewed old anti-railroad feelings on the part of the railroads' former owners, the farm mortgagers and other Wisconsin stockholders who had been "cleaned out" in the course of the bankruptcies and reorganizations. The fear of monopoly peaked in 1863, when the rumor ran that the two big companies, the North Western and the Milwaukee and St. Paul, were about to merge. Soon, according to a widely circulated broadside, Wisconsin would become a second New Jersey, the plaything of outside interests, its people helpless to resist the "mercenary demands of a gigantic corporation" whose "principal proprietors" were "Wall Street sharpers and European Hebrews." Reformers clamored for laws to prohibit consolidations and to limit rates, but no such laws were passed and the agitation soon died down. It was to be revived and greatly intensified after the war.[8]

Before the war, Chicago, Milwaukee, and to a lesser extent St. Louis had been competing for the grain trade of the Northwest. Then St. Louis was temporarily eliminated from the competition as a result of the disruption of commerce on the lower Mississippi. Wheat exports from Milwaukee were almost twice as large in 1860 as in 1859, and they nearly doubled again the following year. By 1862, Milwaukee had surpassed Chicago as the greatest primary wheat market in the world. Milwaukee did not hold its lead for long. It had the advantage

[8] Merk, *Economic History*, 296–308, 322–324, 348–355; Herbert W. Rice, "Early History of the Chicago, Milwaukee and St. Paul Railway Company" (doctoral dissertation, State University of Iowa, 1938), 187–189, 244–246; the Mauston *Star* article, reprinted in the Hartford *Home League*, January 9, 1864, is quoted by Rice on p. 238. The broadside, quoted by Rice on p. 192, was published by the Milwaukee *Daily Life*, June 27, 1863; a copy is in the SHSW.

of proximity to the wheat fields of the upper Mississippi Valley, but this advantage was soon offset when the Wisconsin and Illinois railroads equalized their grain rates from the upper Mississippi to Milwaukee and Chicago. In forwarding wheat to eastern markets, the grain dealers of Milwaukee maintained a parity with those of Chicago on freight charges by way of the all-rail route through Chicago to the East. The Milwaukee merchants did so by virtue of the shipping alternatives they enjoyed—through the Great Lakes in the summer and across Lake Michigan to the railhead at Grand Haven in the winter.

As a distributing center for commodities from the East, Milwaukee also did extremely well during the war. Milwaukee wholesalers sent their agents not only through Wisconsin but across its borders into the neighboring states, even into northern Illinois, where they came "directly in the path of Chicago" and "succeeded in competing with the trade of that city," as the Milwaukee Chamber of Commerce boasted. By 1863, the chamber asserted, Milwaukee jobbers were handling three-quarters of the goods sold in the western and northwestern hinterlands. More and more, the railroads were bringing manufactures to Milwaukee from the East, but lake boats continued to carry, in increasing quantities, the bulky items such as salt, sugar, coal, lumber, and nails.[9]

[2]

The wartime prosperity was quite unevenly shared in Wisconsin. Despite the scarcity of labor, wages on the whole rose belatedly and by comparatively small increments, though there were some notable exceptions. In the remote lumber camps of the northwest, for example, where work was both seasonal and rough, the pay for ordinary laborers soared from $12 to $25 a month plus board in 1861 to $3 to $4 a day plus board in 1864. Increases were even greater for rivermen, and espe-

---

[9] Merk, *Economic History*, 363–372; Derby, "History of the Port of Milwaukee," 228–229, 232–233, 253–255; Bayrd Still, *Milwaukee: The History of a City* (Madison, 1965), 185–186; on p. 185, Still quotes the Milwaukee Chamber of Commerce, *Annual Statement*, 1860, p. 12.

cially for raft pilots. But the daily wage for most unskilled workers advanced from $1 in 1861 to only $1.25 in 1863, though it went as high as $1.75, and even $2 on some railroad projects, in 1864.

The benefits of the boom fell more largely to farm owners, and, still more, to businessmen. War profits swelled the incomes of wealthy Milwaukeeans so much that the number of them receiving more than $10,000 a year almost doubled in one year, going from forty-four in 1863 to eighty-three in 1864. Four of the eighty-three were getting more than $50,000 apiece, and one of these was getting more than $100,000—John Plankinton, a meat packer who was profiting from shrewd investments in wool. Including those living in Milwaukee County, in 1864 there were 101 men declaring incomes between $5,000 and $10,000; 846 between $1,000 and $5,000; and 842 between $600 and $1,000. There were 16,326 other adult males in the county; each of them made less than $600 a year and therefore did not have to report his earnings for the wartime federal income tax. Apparently, income inequality was greater at that time than a century later.

The cost of living went up faster than most wages did; the consumer price index, if fixed at 100 for 1860, was 139 for 1863 and 176 for 1864. Some wages had caught up by 1864; in that year, according to one estimate, the average yearly earnings of workers in Milwaukee County, as measured in 1860 dollars, were higher ($287) than they had been in 1860 ($264). Consumers in 1864 were complaining of the exorbitant price of practically everything they had to buy. "Groceries are high and so is clothing," a father wrote to his son in the army; "boots and shoes are extravagantly high with no prospect of a change for some time to come. . . . It is difficult to keep up with the times."[10]

Skilled workers often felt the erosion of their status even more keenly than the unskilled. Labor in Milwaukee and other

[10] Merk, *Economic History,* 108–109, 158–169, 225–227; Lee Soltow, *Patterns of Wealthholding in Wisconsin Since 1850* (Madison, 1971), 129–130, 132, 151; Soltow's income data are for 1864, 1929, and 1959. John Gibbons to son Robert Gibbons, April 23, November 29, 1864, in the John Gibbons Papers, describes inflation of prices.

cities now developed a new self-consciousness and a new militancy. For the first time, the various crafts began to unionize on a large scale, among them the bricklayers and masons, carpenters and joiners, machinists, blacksmiths, iron molders, custom tailors, sailors, and shipwrights. By 1864, strikes had become more frequent than ever, on the part of common laborers as well as artisans. Workmen grading a roadbed near Watertown, for example, struck for 12 shillings (about $1.50) and a ten-hour day; the railroad contractors were willing to settle for 12 shillings and eleven hours. Deck hands on Mississippi steamboats, who had been receiving $60 a month, quit work and demanded $75. Some strikes were at least partly successful, but a larger number were lost, since the strikers usually had to contend against the combined power of the organized employers and the local government.[11]

When, in 1861, the Society of Shipwrights and Caulkers struck, the shipbuilders and repairers of Milwaukee, five firms acting in accord, "adopted the novel plan of hiring mechanics and laborers from other branches and pursuits to the exclusion of the regular shipwrights." The shipbuilders also appealed to the city's vessel owners and masters, and these, approximately forty of them, "most heartily" approved of "the action of the builders in endeavoring to put down the monopoly existing among the shipwrights and caulkers." After their defeat, some of the shipwrights withdrew from the union and formed a co-operative shipbuilding association, which, beginning with small repair jobs, grew and prospered and was converted into a private, profit-making business which eventually became the Milwaukee Dry Dock Company, on Jones Island. The withdrawal of leading members, however, left the union seriously weakened.

When, in 1862, sailors in Milwaukee "struck for higher wages, and proceeded in a body on board of several vessels in the harbor, and endeavored to prevent others from working," the police arrested three of the leaders for "endeavoring to make a riot." The sailors struck again in the spring of 1864. They now "had a regular organization, with a President, &c.," and they had the support of "a Chicago association of a like nature," whose president met with them at the Blue Anchor saloon. They "resolved to go on board all vessels about to leave port and take off by force any sailors who had engaged themselves for less than $3.00 per day." Sixty or more ships then in port were hiring crews for $2.25 and even as little as $2. When the first of the ships sailed, "several policemen were detailed to protect the officers and crew," but "no disturbance occurred."[12]

In June 1864 the sawmill workers of Oshkosh walked out, demanding a pay raise. "They marched in crowds to some of the mills and compelled their fellows to join them." There was, however, "a general determination on the part of the mill owners not to accede to the demands of the strikers." The lumbermen—the most important of whom was Philetus Sawyer, then mayor of Oshkosh—got together in the common council room of the city hall and "formed themselves into an association for the purpose of promoting their interests." Rebuffed, the strikers determined to stop all the mills, most of which were still operating, though short-handed. But when the strikers attempted to "put their threat into execution," they were "met by the sheriff, who told them the consequences of such folly, upon which they disappeared."[13]

Confronted by the manpower shortage and the wage demands, and willing to try any source of abundant, cheap, and docile labor, some employers turned to what were for them unaccustomed categories—white women or black men. This might have meant new and lasting opportunities for both groups, but these opportunities were severely limited because of the prejudices of the time.

[12] Gavett, *Labor Movement in Milwaukee*, 19–20. Quotations are from the Milwaukee *Sentinel*, December 20, 1861, April 3, 1862, and April 26, 1864.

[13] Current, *Pine Logs and Politics*, 29–30, quotes the Oshkosh *Northwestern*, June 30, 1864, describing the strike and the lumbermen's meeting. Also see the Oshkosh *Courier*, quoted in the Milwaukee *Sentinel*, July 8, 1864.

Employers accepted women in a number of trades previously occupied by men only, but a large printing firm (the printer of the Milwaukee *Sentinel*) ran into trouble when, in 1863, it began to hire "female compositors." The army had "taken a large number of printers" as well as other breadwinners, leaving publishers short of help and families without support, the *Sentinel* explained. "We have received hundreds of letters from various portions of the State, written by young ladies thus situated, who were anxious to learn type-setting, in order to earn a decent support for themselves and those dependent on them." After accepting and training about a dozen applicants, the company put them to work in a separate building, away from the men. Members of the Milwaukee Typographical Union promptly left their jobs. The firm let them go and managed to keep on putting out the paper with women and nonunion men. Eventually, so many union members enlisted in the army that the union temporarily disbanded in 1864.

Women who continued to work at one of the occupations already open to them, such as tailoring, gained little or nothing from the rising wage trend. Indeed, the "unfortunate tailoress" in Milwaukee was paid no more in 1864 than she had been four years earlier. She got considerably less than a man doing the same work, even if she were a widow with young children to support. To make as much as $3 a week, she had to cut, stitch, and press from early in the morning to late at night, working at home, where out of her earnings she had to pay for her own sewing machine and for extra fuel to keep her irons hot. All her costs were going up, as were the profits of the clothing store that employed her. She felt that she was not even as well off as a washerwoman, who went out to work, had few expenses, quit at six o'clock, and received about 75 cents a day plus her board. Yet the desperate seamstresses dared not strike. The most they did was to write letters to a local newspaper, calling attention to their plight and pleading for higher piece rates.[14]

[14] Ethel A. Hurn, *Wisconsin Women in the War Between the States* (Madison, 1911), 83–84; Gavett, *Labor Movement in Milwaukee*, 10–12. For quotations see the Milwaukee *Sentinel*, January 12, 1863, January 16, 19, 1864.

Much the largest number of women and girls worked on farms. Except among some of the immigrants, especially the Germans, the women had rarely labored in the fields before the war. Those of Yankee stock had confined themselves almost entirely to household duties and to such outdoor chores as gathering berries or fruit, garden vegetables, and eggs. The war brought a startling change, as a woman from the East observed upon traveling through Wisconsin and Iowa in a private carriage during the summer of 1863. "Women were in the field everywhere," she afterward wrote, "driving the reapers, binding and shocking, and loading grain, until then an unusual sight." Stopping by a field where six women and two men were at work, the inquiring traveler spoke to a woman of forty-five or fifty who sat on a reaper while resting her horses. "Yes, ma'am," the woman on the reaper said, "the men have all gone to the war, so that my man can't hire help at any price, and I told my girls we must turn to and give him a lift with the harvestin'." "You are not German? You are surely one of my own countrywomen—American?" "Yes, ma'am," was the reply; "we moved here from Cattaraugus County, New York State." While native women such as these toiled on their own farms, some German women even worked away from home.[15]

Prejudice was a much greater bar to the employment of blacks, male or female, and it was especially strong among Irish and German immigrants. At the time of the 1860 census the black community of Milwaukee numbered 122, including twenty-four married couples, of which eight were biracial (seven black men with white wives, one white man with a black wife). On Saturday evening, September 6, 1861, two young black men, Marshall Clark and James B. Shelton, were escorting two white girls on Milwaukee Street when a couple

[15] Hurn, *Wisconsin Women in the War*, 78–83; George W. Carter, "Pioneer Women," in the Fond du Lac *Commonwealth*, August 27, 1906. Mary E. Livermore recounts her talk with the woman working on the harvest in *My Story of the War: A Woman's Narrative of Four Years Personal Experience as Nurse in the Union Army, and in Relief Work at Home, in Hospitals, Camps, and at the Front, During the War of the Rebellion. With Anecdotes, Pathetic Incidents, and Thrilling Reminiscences Portraying the Lights and Shadows of Hospital Life and the Sanitary Service of the War* (Hartford, 1889), 146–147.

of Irishmen approached them and provoked a fight. Drawing a knife, Shelton slashed one of the assailants and stabbed the other, who died several hours later after identifying Shelton as the knife wielder. A largely Irish crowd formed immediately and broke into the jail where Clark and Shelton had been lodged. Shelton managed to escape, but Clark was dragged out, beaten, "tried" in the firehouse of an Irish fire company, and finally hanged from a piledriver. The next day, in search of Shelton, "some two or three hundred Irishmen" went down to a wharf from which a Chicago-bound steamer was about to depart with a dozen or more panic-stricken Negroes fleeing the city. "Be Jasus, let us kill all the damned nagers," a Milwaukee *News* reporter heard a member of the mob cry out, "and then we'll be sure to get the right one." But the crowd apparently was satisfied to find that Shelton was not aboard. Later recaptured and tried for murder, Shelton was acquitted on a plea of self-defense. He was then spirited out of town and to safety in Chicago. Still later six Irishmen were tried for the lynching, but they got off when the jury failed to agree.[16]

For a time the lynching of Marshall Clark resulted in a decrease in Wisconsin's black population, as other black Milwaukeeans, continuing to feel a threat from the Irish, followed the first fugitives in moving out of the state. Before long, however, this outward movement was more than offset by an in-migration of blacks who were attracted by the state's war-created job opportunities.

Many white Wisconsinites welcomed the newcomers. In the fall of 1862 a newspaper in Racine noted the arrival there of "a number of 'contrabands' from West Tennessee," opined that they had "come in good time on account of the scarcity of laborers," and added that there was "room for five thousand more in that county." To Fond du Lac were brought seventy-five Negroes from Alabama, to be employed as servants and laborers. In Berlin, the local paper reported, a "pair

<hr>

[16] William J. Vollmar, "The Negro in a Midwest Frontier City: Milwaukee, 1835–1870" (master's thesis, Marquette University, 1968), 54, 60–61, 65–73. The quotations are from the Milwaukee *News*, September 10, 1861. For a description of the trial, see the Milwaukee *Sentinel*, October 8, November 14, 16–22, 1861.

of contrabands, late from Alabama," who had been sent north by a Badger artillery captain, were "working for wages"; the men were "thorough bred" and "robust as a logging team." The next year, 1863, farmers in Trempealeau County expressed an interest in obtaining Negro hands, and a group in Dodge County succeeded in doing so, bringing in about forty emancipated slaves from Cairo, Illinois.

Some whites in the state began to fear an inundation by blacks, who they thought were coming north "by car and steamboat loads" and "flocking into Wisconsin." By supposedly turning loose millions of slaves, Lincoln's emancipation proclamations of September 22, 1862, and January 1, 1863, intensified the fears. Emancipation, the German Catholic *Seebote* of Milwaukee asserted, was really a scheme of employers who desired a pool of cheap labor. In the legislature the editor of the *Seebote,* serving as an assemblyman, insisted that something must be done to prevent the impoverishment of white workers and to protect the homes of soldiers away at the front. Apprehensive Wisconsinites showered the legislature with more than sixty petitions, demanding a law to prohibit persons of African descent from settling in the state. Such a bill was introduced in 1862 and again in 1863, but it got little support on either occasion. Also failing to pass was a resolution of 1863, declaring that Wisconsin was underpopulated and would welcome settlers of any race.

The anti-black excitement was hardly justified by the number of Negroes—several hundred—who actually entered Wisconsin during the war. The black population remained very small for the state as a whole, mainly clustered in certain places, and nonexistent in most areas. In Sheboygan, for example, as a local paper reported in January 1865, there was not a single "fellow citizen of African descent," and there had not been one for five years.[17]

[17] Edward Noyes, "The Negro in Wisconsin's Civil War Effort," in the *Lincoln Herald,* 69 (Summer, 1967), 70–71; Robert N. Kroncke, "Race and Politics in Wisconsin, 1854–1865" (master's thesis, University of Wisconsin, 1968), 51–52, 55–56; Merk, *Economic History,* 56n; Milwaukee *Sentinel,* October 13, December 22, 1862, March 28, 1863, January 30, 1865; quotations are from the two 1862 and the 1865 issues.

[3]

At home, it was a sad time for many with friends or relatives in the army, and especially for families with fathers absent. "I did not know what war meant," one Wisconsinite remembered of his boyhood, "except that it was something that made me afraid and then Ma cried every day and Pa was going to war." During the war years the boy noticed that grownups "went about with tense faces" and were "frantic for news" from or about the men at the front. All too often the dreaded word came, and children ceased to be strangers to grief. For the families of surviving soldiers, the homecoming was an unforgettable event. Afterward Hamlin Garland, not quite five years old when the war ended, had no memory of his mother's "agony of waiting" on the farm in Green's Coulee, near La Crosse. But he clearly recalled his father's return with mementos of his service, including one of those canteens that, in peacetime, "made excellent water-bottles for the men in the harvest fields."[18]

While sons, fathers, and husbands were away in uniform, their womenfolk in many if not most cases were too much preoccupied with home cares to provide more than letters and perhaps an occasional gift for the absent ones. Women with enough leisure, especially those in villages and cities, gave their time to the provision of soldier comforts on a larger scale. Wisconsin women of New England background were used to gathering in church-sponsored missionary and sewing societies, and at the start of the war they naturally formed ladies' aid societies, usually in connection with a church, to scrape lint (for dressing wounds), roll bandages, knit socks and mittens, make "housewives" or "hussies" (small bags containing needles, thread, buttons, and other mending necessities), and prepare foods and delicacies for the soldiers from the church or community. Immigrant women did much the same for their friends and relatives, each ethnic group for its own. More

[18] "Frank: Memories of Childhood, Youth and Old Age," typewritten reminiscences of Frank Coffeen, pp. 3, 6, in the Frank Coffeen Papers; Hamlin Garland, *A Son of the Middle Border* (New York, 1917), 1, 6–7, 11–12.

broadly based soldiers' aid societies, including men as well as women, early appeared in the larger towns of the state. These eventually affiliated with the Milwaukee group, the oldest one, to form the Wisconsin Aid Society. After 1862, at the governor's request, the aid societies directed their packages to Wisconsin troops in general, no longer to friends and neighbors in specific companies. Increasingly the Wisconsin societies cooperated with the United States Sanitary Commission, sending most of their supplies through its Chicago branch, to be distributed among Union soldiers without regard to their home states.

To raise money for soldier aid, the societies depended on voluntary contributions. Churches sometimes announced that the collection for a particular Sunday would go to the cause. When, in 1864, the Milwaukee Chamber of Commerce protested that it could no longer afford to contribute, a famed army nurse and fund raiser from Kansas, Mary Anne ("Mother") Bickerdyke, delivered this public rebuke on a Milwaukee visit: "And you, merchants and rich men of Milwaukee, living at your ease, dressed in your broadcloth, knowing little of and caring less for the sufferings of these soldiers from hunger and thirst, from cold and nakedness, from sickness and wounds, from pain and death, all incurred that you may roll in wealth, and your houses and little ones be safe. . . . Shame on you." Chastened, the Milwaukee Chamber of Commerce promised $1,000 a month. Though the Wisconsin aid societies held no fair of their own, they donated goods to the sanitary commission for its "Sanitary Fair" in Chicago in the fall of 1863. Even the Germans participated—although many were unhappy with the war—thanks to the efforts of Elisa Salomon, the governor's wife. She solicited her countrymen's support and gifts, promising that their contributions would be separately identified and displayed at the fair.[19]

While some women busied themselves with aid to distant

[19] Hurn, *Wisconsin Women in the War*, 18–60, quoting Mary Anne Bickerdyke on p. 56; Spencer C. Scott, "The Financial Effects of the Civil War on the State of Wisconsin" (master's thesis, University of Wisconsin, 1939), 69–83; Ella Lonn, *Foreigners in the Union Army and Navy* (Baton Rouge, 1951), 553.

soldiers, others struggled at home to keep alive their temporarily or permanently fatherless children. Few men of the laboring class had enough savings to tide their families over an absence of even a few months. In the flush of war enthusiasm immediately after the firing on Fort Sumter, well-to-do patriots at rallies throughout the state subscribed thousands of dollars for the support of volunteers' dependents. But, after the passing of this first frenzy, some subscribers failed to redeem their pledges. In any event, private charity could hardly have been expected to meet the tremendous need that arose as the war lengthened and the army took larger and larger numbers of married men. The Wisconsin Aid Society gave some assistance to soldiers' families. It set up an industrial aid department to help wives and mothers and widows and orphans find jobs. Its corresponding secretary, Henrietta Colt, the widow of a Milwaukee lawyer, went to Washington and, from the quartermaster-general, obtained a contract for the making of army clothing by soldiers' dependents. She put 475 Milwaukee women to work on the project.[20]

In the main, however, the relief of soldiers' families became a public responsibility. As early as May 1861 the legislature voted a supplement of $5 a month to the pay of each Wisconsin soldier with a family to support. This money was to be credited to the soldier's account with the state treasurer, and the wife or person in charge of the dependent family was to apply for payment from the state. At the same time, the legislature authorized local governments to levy taxes for additional relief. In accordance with a federal law of 1862, the state appointed and paid the salaries of commissioners who visited soldiers in the field and arranged for allotments from regular pay to be transmitted to relatives at home. A state law of 1863 extended the $5-a-month payment for a period of six months after a soldier's death or discharge for disability—except in a case where the family was already receiving the $8-a-month

[20] Hurn, *Wisconsin Women in the War*, 57–60; Scott, "Financial Effects of the Civil War," 47, 51, 72; Donald J. Berthrong, "Social Legislation in Wisconsin, 1836–1900" (doctoral dissertation, University of Wisconsin, 1951), 21.

federal pension. An act of 1864 provided for the six-months'
continuation of state pay whether or not the federal pension
was being received.

The local governments—county, town, village, and city—
bore much the largest part of the burden of relief. The state
provided a comparatively small share, and the soldiers themselves a still smaller one. For the wartime and immediate postwar years (1861–1867) the totals were as follows: local expenditures, $7,752,506; direct state aid, $2,698,999; soldier
allotments, $1,051,520. These sums would have been inade-
quate even if they had been promptly and fairly distributed.
In fact, there were serious inequities and delays. The generosity of local governments varied from place to place and was
embarrassingly restricted in some areas, as in Richland County, where a woman had to swear she was a pauper before she
could get her pittance. Since Negro soldiers served in national
rather than state units, until 1866 they were considered ineligible for state aid. For want of funds, the state stopped its payments to all families for several months in 1862 and 1863. At
other times these payments were held up by bureaucratic bun-
gling, as were soldier allotments on many occasions. Some
destitute families received little public assistance or none at
all. As a result, there was considerable suffering throughout
the state, an extreme instance being that of a war widow who,
with her brood of nine children, the oldest only thirteen, almost starved to death.[21]

If impoverished families of soldiers had difficulties, the poor
who lacked a special claim to public bounty were likely to be
still worse off. The war emergency did little to enlarge ideas
about government responsibility for social welfare, except in
cases that were directly related to the war. Even the principle
of state aid to soldier families ran into strong opposition from
legislators who argued that it would foster pauperism and that

[21] James W. Shannon, "State Aid to Wisconsin Soldiers and Their Families:
Financial and Humanitarian" (master's thesis, University of Wisconsin, 1915),
14–37; Scott, "Financial Effects of the Civil War," 47–65; Noyes, "Negro in
Wisconsin's Civil War Effort," in the *Lincoln Herald*, 69: 77–78; Hurn, *Wisconsin Women in the War*, 63–78.

soldiers had an obligation to support their families from their own pay.

With needs increasing during the war, churches and benevolent societies expanded their regular charitable work, the Milwaukee Relief Society feeding as many as 750 families a winter in an effort to do away with begging on the city streets. The charity of Wisconsinites reached far beyond the borders of the state. In 1863, when the cotton shortage shut down the textile mills of Manchester, England, the St. George's Society of Wisconsin called for contributions to relieve the English unemployed, and the Madison chapter of the society sent them fifty-three barrels of flour. In 1864 a group in Whitewater organized a freedmen's aid society, to secure clothing and other necessities for homeless former slaves in the South. The Wisconsin Conference of the Methodist Church, whose "benevolent collections" increased from $2,131.41 in 1860 to $10,409.54 in 1866, used a part of these collections to assist the work of freedmen's aid societies. Yet some unfortunates within the state had to look abroad for help. When, in 1863, two women of the Trempealeau German community came to Wilhelmina Melchior with their problems—beastly, drunken husbands, too many children and pregnant again, no money, not enough to eat—she wrote to a cousin for one woman and to Germany for the other to ask for financial aid.[22]

The lot of the poor, especially in towns and cities, was made worse by wartime scarcities and the high price of food, clothing, fuel, and shelter. In the circumstances, the cruel Wisconsin winter was more than ever to be dreaded, and the winter of 1863–1864 was one of the cruelest. On January 1, 1864, the temperature dropped to thirty-three degrees below zero in Racine County—making that day the "Coaldest & Most Tedious I ever Saw in Wisconsin," as one resident noted—and the frigid spell lasted more than a week, while snow blocked the rail-

[22] Berthrong, "Social Legislation in Wisconsin," 24; Scott, "Financial Effects of the Civil War," 75, 83; Still, Milwaukee, 236–237; P. S. Bennett and James Lawson, History of Methodism in Wisconsin (Cincinnati, 1890), 219; "Sample Letters of Immigrants," in WMH, 20 (June, 1937), 436–446.

roads. New Year's Day was even colder in the Baraboo area, thirty-seven below, and several stage drivers pulled in at Kilbourn City with frozen hands and feet. "There is a sad need of tenement houses in Neenah and Menasha," a local paper reported as the following autumn approached, "and it is next to impossibility for a newcomer to secure a dwelling, on any terms of rent."[23]

Insufficient though public welfare was, its cost put a severe strain on local government. This happened at a time when county government was adapting to a structural change that the state legislature had seen fit to impose. An act of 1861 abolished the old county board of supervisors, consisting of a representative from each of the town boards, and replaced it with a board of three commissioners who were elected from the three districts into which every county (regardless of size or population) now was arbitrarily divided. The new system was generally unpopular, critics charging that it fostered irresponsibility and graft. During the war the county commissioners were preoccupied with the financial problems of providing bounties for soldiers and relief for their dependents. Since so many taxpayers were absent in the army, much of the tax collection had to be postponed. The counties were compelled to economize on their ordinary functions, as were other units of local government. Construction and repair of roads, bridges, streets, and sidewalks were usually neglected.[24]

In the interest of economy, the mayor and common council of Milwaukee decided, on April 11, 1861, to cut the city police force from twenty-four to twenty (later eighteen) men and to reduce their pay by 20 per cent. Very soon occurred the bank riot, a few months later the Clark lynching, and then

---

[23] Hiram David Morse Diary, January 1, 1864 (typewritten copy); Harry E. Cole, ed., *A Standard History of Sauk County, Wisconsin* . . . (2 vols., Chicago, 1918), 1: 323. For the quotation see the Neenah-Menasha *Island City Times*, September 15, 1864.

[24] Merle Curti, *The Making of an American Community: A Case Study of Democracy in a Frontier County* (Stanford, 1959), 287–291; Hjalmar R. Holand, *History of Door County, Wisconsin: The County Beautiful* (2 vols., Chicago, 1917), 1: 94–99; Still, *Milwaukee*, 238.

in 1862 and 1863 the violence in opposition to the draft. In every instance the mobs were mostly German or Irish, and property owners of the native American middle and upper classes took alarm. "Do eighteen men constitute a police force sufficient for fifty thousand heterogeneous people?" the *Sentinel* demanded after the Clark lynching. "Are those eighteen the right kind of men?" A reader signing himself Publicola replied in the negative. The police force, he said, no longer "evenly represented the different nations . . . Germans, Irish, Americans" of which Milwaukee was made up, and "only a few of the old and really efficient privates" remained. He proposed that the city, or if necessary the state, set up a special force of 100 men "of unquestioned good character" to act only in emergencies. Let "all good law-and-order men combine" in support of the idea, he urged. This provoked the wrath of Mayor James S. Brown, a Democrat from Maine. In a rabble-rousing speech to his German followers, the mayor denounced the plan as a scheme to set up a revolutionary "Vigilance Committee," and he concluded with the challenge of the old German verse: *"Dem Freunde die Hand, Dem Feinde die Brust."* Thus the city government exacerbated ethnic tensions while seemingly condoning lawlessness.[25]

Apparently the wartime juxtaposition of prosperity and poverty led to an increase in larceny, burglary, and robbery, at least in some parts of the state. In Oshkosh, for example, there seemed to be a rising crime wave in 1863 and 1864. The Oshkosh common council raised the city marshal's salary by $100 in 1863 but did not provide for much of a police force. In January 1864 the *Northwestern* complained that robberies by

[25] Milwaukee *Sentinel*, September 10, 11 (police force quotation), 17 (Publicola quotation and mayor's speech), 1861. The German lines in English are: "To the friend my hand, To the enemy my breast." The lynch mob of 1861 took Clark from the same jail which the abolitionist mob of 1854 had taken the fugitive Glover from. The mayor and his defenders made much of the supposed parallel between the two cases. Said the Democratic Milwaukee *News,* September 12, 1861: "The mob of last Saturday had just as much right to hang the negro [Clark], as the mob under the lead of Mr. Booth, had to free the negro Glover. No more and no less." An interesting comparison between liberation and murder, yet the point perhaps had some merit if the question was strictly one of legality, and certainly the mayor's Republican critics in 1861 were putting a heavy if not exclusive emphasis on the "law and order" theme.

then had become "almost of daily occurrence." Concluding
that the city's night watchman was ineffective, local merchants
soon began to hire youths to stay in their stores at night.[26]

While reorganizing county government, the state legislature
also undertook to reform the school system. An act of 1861
abolished the office of town superintendent of schools and
replaced it with the office of county superintendent. At the
beginning of the next year, 743 town superintendents stepped
aside and fifty-four county superintendents, newly elected, took
over. While experts also advocated appointment by school
boards rather than popular election, this was a move in the
direction of centralization of control and elevation of standards.
Also progressive was a law of 1862 that set new and comparatively strict requirements for teacher certification. This law authorized the county superintendent to issue one of three grades
of certificates after examining an applicant in specified subjects. Perhaps fortunately, in view of the teacher shortage
that was soon to develop, the superintendent could award third-
grade certificates, valid for less than a year and only in one
or another particular district, to persons of limited preparation.
Another act of 1862 was hardly in the long-run interest of
public education and could be justified only as a war measure.
This directed the commissioners of school and university lands
to invest the school fund—the proceeds from the sale of the
school lands—in state bonds. Thus the schools gave up a productive, independent source of revenue in exchange for the
fixed interest of assets that depended on state taxes.

When the war began, public education had not yet recovered
from the effects of the Panic of 1857, and with the bank crisis
and the financial stringency of 1861 it suffered another setback.
Teachers' salaries were cut, and some schools were closed. Then
education began to prosper with the economy. By 1863 the
state superintendent could boast that the schools were "better
filled, better taught, and better supported" than they had ever
been. Already, however, the schools were feeling the strain of

[26] Robert C. Robertson, "The Social History of Winnebago County, Wisconsin,
1850–1870" (master's thesis, University of Chicago, 1939), 25–27.

war, with more than 600 teachers in the army. The next year
the Wisconsin teachers' association skipped its summer meeting because so many of its members were away. Meanwhile the
proportion of women teachers increased, and so did their
salaries, somewhat. Public education in Wisconsin was on the
way to surviving the shocks of both depression and war.[27]

By 1861 the University of Wisconsin found itself so heavily
burdened with debt that the interest was eating up a large
part of the income of the university fund (derived chiefly from
the sale of university lands). In 1862 the legislature authorized
the regents to pay the debts out of capital, leaving the fund reduced but the proceeds unencumbered. By 1864 the net income was considerably higher than it had been three years
before. Already, however, the professors had been forced to
take another salary cut, their pay falling from $1,500 in 1858
to $1,000 in 1860 and $900 in 1863.

Meanwhile the university's enrollments were declining from
a peak of more than 300, including preparatory and special
students, to a low of sixty-three, of whom only twenty-nine were
taking collegiate courses. In 1863, fearing the possible loss of
all college-level students, the regents started a full normal department and admitted women to it on equal terms with men.
Thus, out of an exigency of the war, the University of Wisconsin reluctantly became co-educational at a time when several
institutions of higher learning in the country had long since
done so, among them Lawrence University in the same state.
For the 1863 fall term, a total of 197 students enrolled at Madison, 162 of them in the normal department, and of these 119
were "young ladies." During the academic year the number of
women rose to 180. Most of the remaining young males, feeling themselves a humiliated minority, refused to recognize the
presence of the university's first co-eds. All but one member

[27] Lloyd P. Jorgenson, *The Founding of Public Education in Wisconsin* (Madison, 1956), 104, 163–164, 191; on p. 192 he quotes the state superintendent from
the *Wisconsin Journal of Education*, 8 (April, 1864), 309. See also Conrad E.
Patzer, *Public Education in Wisconsin* (Madison, 1924), 56–60, 69–70, 114–115,
125–128; William H. Herrmann, "The Rise of the Public Normal School System
in Wisconsin" (doctoral dissertation, University of Wisconsin, 1953), 1–6.

of the class of 1864 having joined the army, there was no commencement that year.[28]

The private colleges were barely able to survive the war, and Carroll failed to do so, going out of existence temporarily. Brockway College was an exception; though it, too, closed briefly, it emerged as a college during the war. At first a struggling preparatory school with collegiate aspirations, it leased its grounds as a training camp for the First Wisconsin Cavalry in 1861. Then the Winnebago District Convention of the Presbyterians and Congregationalists began a money-raising campaign so as to reopen the school and pay off its debts. In 1863 it admitted its first college class, with men and women enjoying "equal advantages." The next year, with its name changed from Brockway to Ripon College, it started a new, debt-free career.[29]

[4]

So far as political parties were concerned, the war's main effect was to divide and weaken the Democrats and, by the same token, to confirm the Republicans in their dominance in the state. The Republicans, associated as they were with the Lincoln administration, had the benefit of both the federal patronage and the Union propaganda. True, they also suffered from the handicap—a serious one at least temporarily—of sharing responsibility for unpopular government policies such as conscription and emancipation. For a time, indeed, the advantage seemed to lie with the Democrats.

At the outset there was on both sides much talk of a patriotic stay of partisanship. To minimize the odium of their national party's recent affiliation with secessionist Southern Democrats,

[28] Merle Curti and Vernon Carstensen, *The University of Wisconsin: A History, 1848–1925* (2 vols., Madison, 1949), 1: 116, 138–147, 185, 196, 370; William F. Allen and David E. Spencer, *Higher Education in Wisconsin* (Washington, D.C., 1889), 27–28; Patzer, *Public Education in Wisconsin,* 261.

[29] Allen and Spencer, *Higher Education in Wisconsin,* 55–57; Samuel M. Pedrick, "Early History of Ripon College, 1850–1864," in *WMH,* 8 (September, 1924), 22–37.

Wisconsin party leaders made a show of recruiting troops and leading them to battle. State Democratic organs asked people to forget the past and unite for the present. "We need union among all parties for the sake of the union," said the Fond du Lac *Saturday Reporter*, for one. "We hold the man to be an enemy of the union who at this time promulgates party views or discusses the agency of parties in bringing on the war." On behalf of Republicans, the *Wisconsin State Journal* expressed its pleasure that people throughout the North were united in the Union cause and that "party feeling so rife and embittered" had "almost disappeared." During the spring and summer of 1861, some Democrats and Republicans considered the possibility of merging to form a "union party" for the duration, but by fall many in both parties were suspicious. Republicans, the La Crosse *Democrat* charged, were "very busy circulating their no party ideas" in order to keep themselves in power. There was a "deliberate plot among certain politicians mainly of the Democratic faith," the *State Journal* countered, to "break up the Republican organization" and restore the "sway of Democracy."

Nevertheless, some Republicans and some Democrats did cooperate in a union movement for the state campaign of 1861. The participating Republicans favored Louis P. Harvey against Alexander Randall for the governorship, and they put Harvey at the head of a slate that included a Democrat, William S. Allen, for the lieutenant-governorship. After replacing Allen with another disaffected Democrat, the German Edward Salomon, the regular Republicans endorsed the union ticket. The Republicans not only elected these state officials but also maintained a majority in the senate, though they could be sure of only a plurality in the assembly, since a number of the assemblymen had run as union candidates.[30]

[30] Fond du Lac *Saturday Reporter*, April 27, 1861, reprinted in Fond du Lac *Reporter*, January 6, 1916; *Wisconsin State Journal*, May 6 and November 14, 1861, and La Crosse *Democrat*, July 17, 1861, in Donald E. Rasmussen, "Wisconsin Editors and the Civil War: A Study of the Reaction of Wisconsin Editors to the Major Controversial Issues of the Civil War" (master's thesis, University of Wisconsin, 1952), 27–31; Robert H. Jacobi, "Wisconsin Civil War Governors" (master's thesis, University of Wisconsin, 1948), 66–68; C. W. Butterfield, "History of Wisconsin," in Western Historical Company, *The History of Sauk County, Wisconsin* . . . (Chicago, 1880), 76. The gubernatorial vote was 53,777 to 45,456.

Difficult as it was for the two parties in Wisconsin to come together while they shared a simple war aim, the restoration of the Union, it became still more difficult when in 1862 the Republican President and the Republican-controlled Congress advanced toward the espousal of a second war aim, the abolition of slavery. Wisconsin Republicans themselves were divided on aspects of this issue. When Lincoln proposed a plan for freeing the slaves gradually and resettling them outside the country, Senator James R. Doolittle heartily approved the application of his favorite theme, "colonization," and repeated his familiar argument (citing Thomas Jefferson as an authority) that whites and blacks simply could not and would not "live together upon a footing of equality." Other Wisconsin Republicans rejected Doolittle's "wild notions of colonization" and insisted that, once slavery was abolished, Negroes in the South would be glad to remain there and those in Wisconsin and elsewhere in the North would "soon leave and go there" —so that "the Northern States would be speedily cleared of their present free colored population." Dissatisfied with Lincoln's gradualism, the radical antislavery Republicans in Wisconsin joined with those in other states to demand that Lincoln take more immediate steps, both to free the blacks and to use them as troops. Governor Salomon accepted an invitation to meet with other Republican governors in Altoona, Pennsylvania, and arrange to bring concerted pressure upon the President. While the governors were on the way to Altoona, Lincoln forestalled them by announcing his preliminary proclamation of emancipation, on September 22, 1862. Wisconsin Republicans then rallied in support of the emancipationist cause.[31]

Far different was the response of most Wisconsin Democrats. Democratic newspapers continued to harp upon the fears of German and Irish laborers that, once freed, Southern blacks

[31] Biagino M. Marone, "Senator James Rood Doolittle and the Struggle Against Radicalism, 1857–1866" (master's thesis, Marquette University, 1955), 12–13, 17–21; on p. 12 he quotes Doolittle's speech published in the *Congressional Globe, Appendix*, 37 Cong., 2 sess., 83–86. David Noggle to Doolittle, May 30, 1862, in Jacque Voegeli, "The Northwest and the Race Issue, 1861–1862," in the *Mississippi Valley Historical Review*, 50 (September, 1963), 242, opines that blacks would all choose to settle in a free South, making colonization unnecessary. See also the Milwaukee *Sentinel*, June 9, 1862; and William B. Hesseltine, *Lincoln and the War Governors* (New York, 1948), 203.

would swarm northward to compete for jobs. Already the Democratic leader Edward G. Ryan had aggressively challenged the Republican policy and completely repudiated all thought of a party truce. In Milwaukee, on September 3, he had presented and the state Democratic convention had adopted a remarkable "Address to the People by the Democracy of Wisconsin," which the party then printed in both German and English and circulated throughout the state, more than 100,000 copies within a month. "We hold this country to be the possession of the white race," the address ran, "and this Government to be instituted by white men for white men." The "proper condition of the African was subjection in some form to the white." The Republicans were to blame for secession and the war: "The abolition party at the North produced the disunion party at the South." Especially culpable were the Republicans of Wisconsin, for they had asserted the doctrine of state rights and nullification "as broadly" as it had "ever been asserted by any Southern States." This Ryan address instantly became the "Bible of Copperheadism" in Wisconsin, and its author the foremost of the state's Copperheads, or antiwar Democrats.

Not all Wisconsin Democrats could swear by the new Bible. Ryan's one-time law partner Matthew Hale Carpenter stood apart to condemn the address and approve the emancipation proclamation, which he justified as a war measure, an "overloaded gun" to be sure, but a gun pointed at the enemy. Agreeing with Carpenter were his close friends, the prominent Democrats Levi Hubbell and Arthur McArthur, both of them state judges, and Charles D. Robinson, editor of the Green Bay *Advocate*. These men led an emerging faction that was to be known as the Loyal Democracy. For the time being, they remained within the regular organization. Carpenter still criticized Lincoln for "honest incapacity" and referred to the Democratic party as the "last and only hope for the country."[32]

---

[32] Frank Klement, "Copperheads and Copperheadism in Wisconsin: Democratic Opposition to the Lincoln Administration," in *WMH*, 42 (Spring, 1959), 185–187; William D. Love reprints much of Ryan's speech in *Wisconsin in the*

As Wisconsin Republicans looked ahead to the election of 1862, they had reason to be concerned. They could expect many voters to be alienated not only because of the emancipationist trend but also because of frustration over the prolonged war, disgust with the draft and the threat of military arrests, and discontent with economic conditions that were yet to make their spectacular improvement. Besides, as Governor Salomon told the legislature when he called it into special session in September, many thousands of "loyal" (that is, Republican) voters were off in the service of their country and would be unable to go to the polls. Responding readily to Salomon's request, the legislature passed a law to allow soldiers to cast their ballots in the field, as the legislatures of Missouri and Iowa had already done.

The Wisconsin soldier vote in 1862 (8,373 Republican and 2,046 Democratic) helped enable the Republicans to win three of the state's congressional seats—now raised to a total of six—even though the home vote was decidedly Democratic (62,112 to 53,466). The soldier vote also helped Republicans to hold on to narrow majorities in both houses of the legislature. Thus, when the new legislature met in January 1863, Wisconsin's Republicans were able to retain the seat in the United States Senate that was contested that year. Running against the incumbent, Senator Doolittle, was the Copperhead chief himself, Edward G. Ryan; and Ryan did not even get the ballots of all the Democrats in the legislature.

Already the Democrats had challenged the constitutionality of the law permitting soldiers to vote, and the case was before the state supreme court. Chief Justice Luther S. Dixon, who

---

War of the Rebellion . . . (Chicago, 1866), 163–165. Of course, there was more to Ryan's address of 1862 and more to Copperheadism than merely racism and anti-Republicanism. Ryan also presented a constitutional argument for opposing the Lincoln administration's conduct of the war. With some justice he charged the federal government with violations of the Bill of Rights, and he insisted that citizens owed loyalty above all to the Constitution itself, and to the men in office only insofar as they conformed to its requirements. See also Alfons J. Beitzinger, *Edward G. Ryan, Lion of the Law* (Madison, 1960), 67–71; and E. Bruce Thompson, *Matthew Hale Carpenter: Webster of the West* (Madison, 1954), 64–72; Carpenter is quoted on p. 69.

had been elected as a Republican, was up for re-election in the spring. Dixon could expect strong if not insuperable opposition, both because of the Democratic resurgence and because of the court's unpopular decisions in favor of the railroads and against the railroad farm mortgagers. The soldiers' ballots would be of great benefit to him, but under the existing law they could not be counted in judicial elections. While the court's decision on the law was pending, the legislature amended it so as to allow soldiers to vote for judges. A week later the court upheld the original act. After the April election it appeared at first that Dixon's Democratic opponent, Montgomery M. Cothren, had won, with a home vote of 56,840 to Dixon's 51,948. But when the soldier vote came in—9,440 for Dixon to 1,747 for Cothren—it saved the day for Dixon.[33]

In preparation for the fall election of 1863, Ryan meanwhile pressed the advantage that his Copperheadism seemed to have given the Democrats. He took up the cause of the imprisoned Port Washington draft resisters and persuaded the state supreme court to rule against Lincoln's suspension of habeas corpus, though he failed to get the court to declare the conscription act itself unconstitutional. At party rallies, his face glowing and his eyes bulging, he called Lincoln both a Constitution-breaker as bad as Jefferson Davis and a helpless tool—a "mere doll, worked by springs"—of conspirators who were "growing rich on the misfortunes of the nation." When the Democrats held their state convention in Madison on August 6, they reaffirmed his address of the previous year and nominated for governor a Milwaukee lawyer and executive of the Northwestern Mutual Life Insurance Company, Henry L. Palmer, who had a reputation as a friend of the railroads.

Republicans rejoiced when Carpenter, McArthur, Hubbell, Robinson, and a number of other Democratic leaders repudiated their party's platform and ticket and proposed a separate convention of War Democrats. At once the Republicans began to

[33] Love, *Wisconsin in the War*, 672; Frank Klement, "The Soldier Vote in Wisconsin During the Civil War," in *WMH*, 28 (September, 1944), 37–45; Marone, "Senator James Rood Doolittle," 23–25; Merk, *Economic History*, 255–261.

woo the dissidents. They asked Carpenter to run for attorney general on their own ticket, but he declined, suggesting instead that the Republicans join with the War Democrats in drawing up a combined "Union" slate. The Republicans went ahead with their regular convention, gathering in Madison on August 19 to choose other candidates with a Democratic aura and appeal—for governor, James T. Lewis, a recent (1861) convert from the Democracy; for secretary of state, Lucius Fairchild, a War Democrat as well as a war hero. Carpenter and his associates went ahead with their plans for a separate convention, meeting in Janesville on September 17, but they created no third party. Instead, a little later, Carpenter, Robinson, and three fellow leaders of the aborted "Union" movement accepted appointment as members of the Republican state central committee. Thus the War Democrats merged with the Republicans to form the Union Republican party for the 1863 campaign.

By their continued extremism the regular or Ryan Democrats had lost the contest long before election day. Among Wisconsin voters, economic grievances were abating with the onset of the boom, emancipation was becoming more and more acceptable in view of the prospect of black soldiers substituting for white, and hopes of winning the war were rising in consequence of the glorious victories of July 1863 at Gettysburg and Vicksburg. The voters now saw and heard well-known Democrats, like the persuasive Carpenter, stumping for Republican candidates. Veterans and their families were especially attracted to one of the candidates, Colonel Lucius Fairchild, his empty sleeve a badge of patriotism and a reminder of his sacrifice at Gettysburg. At the height of the campaign regular Democrats pointed out that, under the Wisconsin constitution, Fairchild, as the holder of an army commission, was ineligible for state office. Colonel Fairchild thereupon went to Washington, talked with Lincoln, and received from him a promotion to brigadier general. Then, as a general at the age of thirty, Fairchild resigned from the army a few days before the election. When the returns were in, the Republicans did not need the soldier vote, except to widen the margin of their triumph. And a remarkable triumph it was. James T. Lewis got a larger majority (72,717 to 49,053) than any Republican gubernatorial candidate in Wisconsin before him, and Fairchild ran ahead of Lewis and the rest of the ticket by 2,200 votes.[34]

After its debacle of 1863, the Democratic party of Wisconsin remained a comparative ruin, and Ryan himself, his influence in it gone, dropped into a political limbo. By contrast, the Republican party continued its development, already under way, toward becoming a well-led, tightly knit, highly efficient organization. Emerging as the dominant machine within the party was the so-called Madison Regency, headed by a Madison lawyer and insurance salesman with a knack for political maneuvering, Elisha W. Keyes, in partnership with former governor Alexander W. Randall. Since 1861 Keyes had held the Madison postmastership, and in 1862 Randall was appointed first assistant postmaster general in Washington. One of their main sources of strength was the postal patronage that, between them, the two controlled.

Keyes and Randall, along with other Republican leaders, were determined in 1864 not only to keep the three congressional seats their party already held but also to take the three that the Democrats had captured in 1862. In the summer of 1864 Keyes visited Randall to discuss tactics and candidates. One of the districts to be recovered was the fifth, which included Oshkosh. For this district Randall recommended the millionaire lumberman Philetus Sawyer, and Randall appointed Keyes as a special agent of the Post Office Department with free transportation on the railroads and with instructions to see all the postmasters in the district and set them to work in Sawyer's behalf. Sawyer agreed to run on the condition that Keyes per-

---

[34] Alfons J. Beitzinger, "The Father of Copperheadism in Wisconsin," in *WMH*, 39 (Autumn, 1955), 17–25, on p. 21 quotes Ryan's remarks which were published in the Milwaukee (weekly) *News*, July 18, 1863. See also Beitzinger, *Ryan*, 74–82; Thompson, *Carpenter*, 72–79; Sam Ross, *The Empty Sleeve: A Biography of Lucius Fairchild* (Madison, 1964), 54–62; and Jacobi, "Wisconsin Civil War Governors," 164–166.

suade Carpenter and Doolittle, each of them as eloquent as Sawyer was inarticulate, to campaign for him.

In this congressional contest the Democrats had patriotism on their side, since their candidate was Gabriel Bouck, like Sawyer a native of Vermont but unlike him a veteran of the army. "Col. Bouck has been three years in the war to the neglect and sacrifice of his pecuniary interest," the Democratic Oshkosh *Union* pointed out. "Where has Mr. Sawyer been all this time? Has he not been at home making fabulous profits upon the rise of lumber in consequence of the war . . . ?" In two other congressional races, however, the Republicans entered military officers who were still on active service. The candidate in the first district (the five southeastern counties) was Halbert E. Paine of Milwaukee, the erstwhile colonel of the Fourth Wisconsin, now a brigadier general. Running for re-election in the third district (in the southwestern counties) was Amasa Cobb of Mineral Point, who had resigned as colonel of the Fifth Wisconsin before going to Congress in 1863, but who during the congressional recess of 1864 was recruiting a new regiment, the Forty-Third. Cobb was to serve as colonel of this regiment while completing his congressional term.[35]

The national ticket—with Andrew Johnson, a Democrat from Tennessee, as Lincoln's running mate—gave credibility to the name that Republicans adopted for the 1864 campaign. They called themselves the Union party, so as to appeal to Democratic voters while reinforcing the charge that the opposition was the disunion party. But the Union party itself suffered from disunity. A splinter group of antislavery extremists

[35] In 1863 the Post Office employed more than 1,000 postmasters, clerks, and agents in Wisconsin, and contracted or otherwise paid for mail delivery totaling more than $165,000, a notable increase in the patronage from the days of early statehood (see above, Chapter 6, fn. 3 on p. 199); U.S. Department of the Interior, *Register of Officers and Agents, Civil, Military, and Naval, in the Service of the United States,* 1863, pp. 682–696, 715–718, 728, 734–735, 740–741, 793–796, 799. See also Richard W. Hantke, "Elisha W. Keyes and the Radical Republicans," in *WMH,* 35 (Spring, 1952), 203; and Beitzinger, *Ryan,* 81–82. Current, *Pine Logs and Politics,* 38–43, quotes the Oshkosh *Union* on p. 41. On Paine and Cobb, see the *DWB.*

was supporting a separate ticket, headed by John C. Frémont, and was calling for an abolition amendment. Though the regular Republicans, the Union men, included such an amendment in their own platform, a number of the more radical leaders questioned Lincoln's sincerity as an emancipationist and condemned his "ten percent" plan for the reconstruction of the South as much too lenient toward the rebels. During the summer some of the radicals started a move to force the withdrawal of both Lincoln and Frémont and to replace them with a single candidate who might reunite the party.

The controversy strained but did not disrupt the party in Wisconsin. Both Senator Doolittle and Senator Timothy O. Howe endorsed the proposed Thirteenth Amendment, which had passed the Senate but had yet to pass the House. Doolittle did so with reluctance, however, and with continued insistence on colonization. Howe, leaning more and more to the radicals, repudiated the notion that freed blacks could not exist in harmony with the rest of the American people and that they did not have an equal right to live and labor in this country. Doolittle campaigned much the more enthusiastically for Lincoln, another colonizationist. "Fellow citizens," he declaimed, on a side trip to Lincoln's home town, Springfield, Illinois, "I believe in God. Under Him I believe in Abraham Lincoln."[36]

Wisconsin Republicans importuned the War Democrats to come to Lincoln's support. At first, Carpenter positively refused to consider aiding anyone so "perfectly *idiotic*" and so thoroughly abolitionist as Lincoln seemed to him to have become. The movement to revoke Lincoln's nomination struck him as the "most wonderful thing" he had ever heard of. But when the national Democratic convention finally met, at the end of August, Carpenter was even more disgusted with its work. Its Copperhead platform, calling for an immediate cease-fire, he considered "even worse" than the Ryan address

[36] Kroncke, "Race and Politics in Wisconsin," 70–73; Marone, "Senator James Rood Doolittle," 29–31. Doolittle is quoted in Duane Mowry, "A Memorable Speech at Springfield and a Bystander's Account of It," in the *Journal of the Illinois State Historical Society,* 2 (April, 1909), 40–43.

of 1862. The Loyal Democracy now split. Some of its leaders got to work for the Democratic candidate, George B. McClellan. Others came out for Lincoln. Making what was to prove an irreparable break with his political past, Carpenter labored for the Union ticket with the zeal of a convert. Throughout the state he went, giving a Union speech practically every night and as many as three speeches a day.

The Wisconsin Copperheads, the remnants of a once-powerful movement, denounced Lincoln with all the bitterness and shrillness of a frustrated minority. One of the most scurrilous of the Lincoln haters in the entire country was Marcus M. ("Brick") Pomeroy, editor of the La Crosse *Democrat*. After a visit to the front in 1863, Pomeroy had concluded not only that the war was horrible but also that it benefited only abolitionists and profiteers. In 1864, on the front page of his paper, he put a cartoon of Lincoln with the caption: "The Widow-Maker of the 19th Century." Week after week the editor grew more and more strident, until he capped the crescendo with the charge that Lincoln was warring "against the constitution of our country" and was therefore a traitor. "And if he is elected to misgovern for another four years, we trust some bold hand will pierce his heart with dagger point for the public good."

Such rhetoric on the part of Democrats made it all the easier for Republican campaigners to sell the idea that the Union party was the patriot's and the soldier's friend. "Show yourselves as true to your country when citizens as you have been when soldiers," Secretary of State Fairchild told the discharged veterans of the Second Wisconsin, and they could understand perfectly that he meant for them to vote Republican. Fairchild kept up an extensive correspondence with soldiers in the field, and he performed many favors for veterans and their families at home. Some were much distressed that numbers of Badger boys were still left to rot in Confederate prisons. In mid-campaign, with a good deal of fanfare, Fairchild arranged for Doolittle to make a dramatic departure for Washington to "do something" about the prisoners of war.

As it turned out, the ballots of soldiers in the field, with

their overwhelming Lincoln vote of 11,372 against 2,428, were
not needed to carry Wisconsin for the Lincoln-Johnson ticket,
which took the state's eight electoral votes by a comfortable
margin (65,750 to 61,839) on election day. Sawyer carried the
fifth district for the Republicans by almost 5,000 votes. Only
when the soldiers' ballots were in, however, was the Republican
candidate for Congress from the first district, General Paine,
assured of victory. All together, the Republicans won five of
six congressional seats, losing only the fourth district, which
included Washington, Ozaukee, and Sheboygan counties.[37]

Taking the national returns as a mandate for the Thirteenth
Amendment, Lincoln persuaded the House of Representatives
to approve it, at the end of January 1865. Promptly in February
the Wisconsin legislature, with a safe Republican Union majority in both houses, ratified the amendment. On April 10,
Governor Lewis formally reported to the legislature the surrender of Robert E. Lee the previous day. "Let us rejoice,"
the governor exhorted, "and thank the Ruler of the Universe
for victory and the prospects of an honorable peace." The
people of Wisconsin required no urging. All at once Milwaukee became "one vast lunacy of joy," with festoons of red,
white, and blue bedecking the city by day and bonfires and
fireworks brightening it by night. Other towns across the
state celebrated in much the same way; in far-off Superior the
celebrants cracked a church bell ringing out the tidings. Within a week, black crepe had replaced the joyous colors, flags
everywhere were hanging at half-mast, and solemnity and gloom

[37] Thompson, *Carpenter*, 79–82; on pp. 80–81, Thompson quotes letters from
Carpenter to Charles Robinson, August 20 and September 4, 1864, in the Charles
D. Robinson Papers. For Pomeroy's statements, see Frank Klement, "Brick
Pomeroy: Copperhead and Curmudgeon," in *WMH*, 35 (Winter, 1951), 106;
and the La Crosse (daily) *Democrat*, August 25, 1864. Ross, *Empty Sleeve*,
63–66, quotes Fairchild and Doolittle's resolve to "do something." See Klement,
"Soldier Vote in Wisconsin," in *WMH*, 28: 46–47. James R. Donoghue, *How
Wisconsin Voted, 1848–1972* (Madison, 1974), 75, gives the separate civilian and
military votes for President, with a total of 80,122 for the Republicans and
64,267 for the Democrats; the *Wisconsin Blue Book, 1954*, p. 535, gives higher
totals of 83,458 and 65,884. For names and parties of congressmen, see the
Wisconsin Blue Book, 1865, p. 150.

prevailed. An assassin had done his work—not with a dagger stroke but with a pistol shot.

Politics went on, in Wisconsin as in the rest of the country. While speculating on the future under the Johnson administration, Republican politicians, Governor Fairchild conspicuous among them, continued to make a point of greeting and cultivating the Wisconsin troops as they returned. Almost half of the state's men of voting age had worn the uniform. The veterans were bound to constitute a tremendous force in the postwar politics of Wisconsin.[38]

[38] Governor Lewis is quoted in Butterfield, "History of Wisconsin," in Western Historical Company, *History of Sauk County,* 86. Still, *Milwaukee,* 160–161, quotes the Milwaukee *Sentinel,* April 11, 1865. See also Jackson R. Horton, "The Demobilization of Wisconsin Troops after the Civil War" (master's thesis, University of Wisconsin, 1952), 31–32; and the *Eighth Census of the United States, 1860: Population,* xvii.

12

Filling in the Contours

[1]

D URING the immediate postwar years, 1865–1873, the settlement of Wisconsin proceeded along the lines already laid down before the war. The population grew faster than during the period 1860–1865, though not so fast as during the 1850's. The ethnic mix stayed essentially the same as it had been, with some changes in proportions. As the frontier of settlement continued to advance steadily northward, the disposal of the public land remaining in the north proceeded much more rapidly than its actual occupation, and much more rapidly than in previous years. Tracts of unprecedented size passed into private ownership. Railroads began to penetrate the north, as the total trackage in the state more than doubled, marking a new phase of the transportation revolution· that had got under way earlier.

In 1865 the state census takers counted a total of 868,325 people in Wisconsin. By 1870, according to the federal census, the figure had gone up to more than a million—1,054,670. During the decade since the previous federal count, the population of the state had grown by nearly 36 per cent, while the population of the country as a whole was growing by only about 22 per cent. Wisconsin remained in fifteenth place among the states, but there was now a total of thirty-seven of them, as compared with thirty-four in 1860. During the decade the

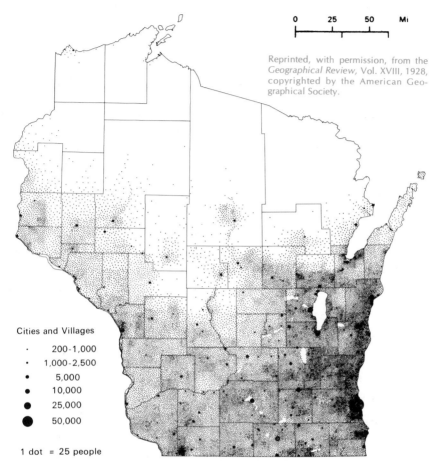

0   25   50   Mɪ

Cities and Villages

·	200-1,000
·	1,000-2,500
•	5,000
●	10,000
●	25,000
⬤	50,000

1 dot = 25 people

WISCONSIN POPULATION, 1870

number of Wisconsin-born persons in the state had increased
by more than 82 per cent, from 247,177 to 450,272; the number born elsewhere in the United States had decreased by
nearly 5 per cent, from 251,777 to 239,899; and the number
born in foreign countries had increased by approximately 32
per cent, from 276,927 to 364,499. Wisconsin in 1870, with
about the same proportion of immigrants (over 34 per cent) as
ten years earlier, still contained proportionally the largest num-

ber of the foreign-born except for California, Nevada, and Minnesota.[1]

As in previous censuses, the percentage of foreign-born in the census of 1870 did not reflect the true ethnic composition of Wisconsin. The "foreign" element was actually about twice as large as the approximately 34 per cent who were born abroad, since more than 68 per cent of the people (717,832 of them) had at least one parent of foreign birth, and nearly 64 per cent (670,759) had both a father and a mother of foreign birth. There were 29,643 persons with foreign-born fathers and American-born mothers, and 17,480 with foreign-born mothers and American-born fathers. With few exceptions, the native husbands of immigrant women and the native wives of immigrant men were themselves of foreign parentage. Generally the spouses were of the same national and religious background. German immigrants who married native Americans, for example, usually married sons or daughters of German immigrants. Intermarriage between men and women of different European nationalities, or between persons of foreign birth or parentage and those of old American stock, was as yet extremely rare.[2]

Once again the state was officially taking steps to attract immigrants. A law of 1867 had set up a board of immigration, consisting of the governor, the secretary of state, and six other members serving without pay. The board saw to the publica-

[1] *Ninth Census of the United States, 1870: Volume I,* pp. ix-xii, 73, 324, 328, 334; *ibid.: Compendium,* 376; *Eighth Census of the United States, 1860: Population,* xxiii, xxxi. Figures from both federal and state censuses for 1840–1875 are reproduced in C. W. Butterfield, "History of Wisconsin," in Western Historical Company, *The History of Sauk County, Wisconsin . . .* (Chicago, 1880), 258.

[2] *Ninth Census of the United States, 1870: Compendium,* 376. Joseph Schafer, *Four Wisconsin Counties: Prairie and Forest* (Madison, 1927), 173–188, finds that, in Milwaukee, intermarriage between Germans and Americans of old stock, "negligible" in 1850, was still very uncommon in 1870, though intermarriage between English-speaking foreigners and Americans of old stock was somewhat more frequent. Merle Curti, *The Making of an American Community: A Case Study of Democracy in a Frontier County* (Stanford, 1959), 104–106, suggests that, in Trempealeau County also, the "non-English-speaking foreign-born" were "least inclined to marry native Americans," and there was "relatively little" intermarriage between "different groups of British settlers," though more than between Germans and Norwegians.

tion of a pamphlet written by Increase A. Lapham, which in thirty-two pages undertook to describe the state's location, topographical features, waterpower, rivers, small lakes, climate, health, geology, lead mines, zinc, iron ores, clays, peat and marl, native animals, fishes, forests, pine regions, agriculture, chief crops in 1866, livestock, farm products, agricultural implements, wages of farm laborers, manufactures, railroads, occupations, markets, population, newspapers, churches, principal cities, lands, surveys, the Homestead Law, land tenure, value of property, government, personal rights, office holding, rights of married women, revenues and expenditures of the state, schools, state institutions, libraries, post offices, and routes from the seaboard. Stressed in the pamphlet was the cheapness of Wisconsin land. Besides the English edition, translations appeared in German, Welsh, French, Norwegian, Dutch, and Swedish. Under the law the governor appointed a committee of three in each county to gather names of friends and relatives in the old country. These names were to constitute a mailing list for the pamphlet.

A Milwaukee German newspaper complained that the immigration board's authority was too limited and its budget too small. The paper said the board ought to have the authority and the means to give financial assistance to immigrants willing to come to Wisconsin. "Other states are doing far more in this area. . . . Every dollar the state spends for the transportation of the immigrants is repaid a hundred times over." A law of 1869 empowered the board to appoint a general agent to direct its work and two field agents, one in Milwaukee and the other in Chicago, to aid Wisconsin-bound immigrants. The new law also authorized the board to spend money to assist immigrant travel.

An act of 1871 replaced the board with an elective commissioner of immigration, who was to be stationed in Milwaukee and was to employ a part-time agent in Chicago. The first commissioner to be elected was Ole C. Johnson, a Norwegian by birth. Johnson promptly decided that he must reach prospective immigrants before they departed for America, since

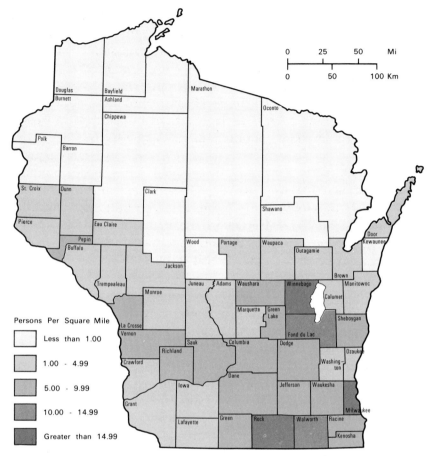

Persons Per Square Mile

☐ Less than 1.00

▨ 1.00 - 4.99

▨ 5.00 - 9.99

▨ 10.00 - 14.99

■ Greater than 14.99

NATIVE-BORN FROM EASTERN STATES, 1870

he believed they knew less about Wisconsin than about some other states. He therefore had pamphlets published and distributed in foreign countries—England, Germany, Belgium, Denmark, Norway. He also arranged with the Milwaukee and St. Paul Railway to provide free travel for arriving women, children, or elderly men who lacked the money to pay their way from Milwaukee to their Wisconsin destination.[3]

[3] Wisconsin Board of Immigration, *Statistics, Exhibiting the History, Climate and Productions of the State of Wisconsin* (Madison, 1867). Theodore C. Blegen, "The Competition of the Northwestern States for Immigrants," in *WMH*, 3

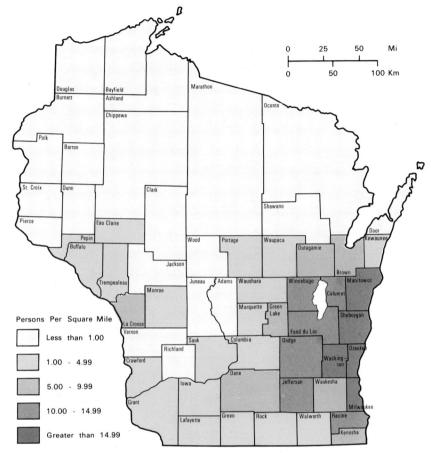

Persons Per Square Mile

Less than 1.00

1.00 - 4.99

5.00 - 9.99

10.00 - 14.99

Greater than 14.99

GERMAN-BORN IN WISCONSIN, 1870

The response to Wisconsin's appeal varied greatly among the different European nationalities. Germans continued to arrive in large numbers. After falling off in the late 1850's, emigration from Germany had started to rise again in 1864–1865, as warfare was beginning in Europe and coming to an end in the United States. The *Auswanderung* fell off again in 1870–1871 but reached a new peak in 1872–1873. Between

(September, 1919), 3–29; Ira J. Kligora, "The German Element in Wisconsin, 1940–1880" (master's thesis, University of Wisconsin, 1937), 57–64. The quotation is from the *Herold*, June 7, 1867.

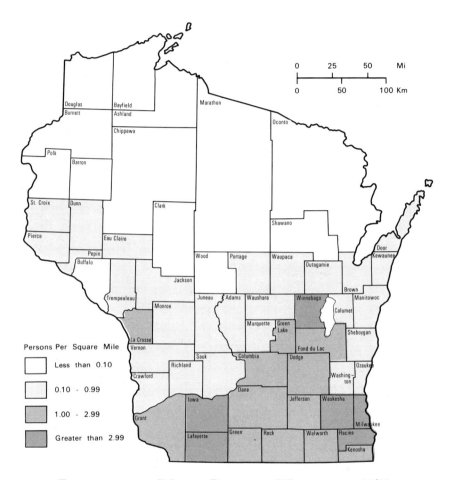

ENGLISH- AND WELSH-BORN IN WISCONSIN, 1870

1860 and 1870 the number of people born in the German countries who were in Wisconsin increased by 45,516 (from 116,798 to 162,234, of whom 103,423 were from Prussia), or by 39 per cent. This was a rate of increase only slightly greater than that of the state's population as a whole, nearly 36 per cent. Yet the relative size of the German element had become considerably larger than before. Probably a third or more of the Wisconsin-born who were counted in the 1870 census were of German parentage. When these are added to

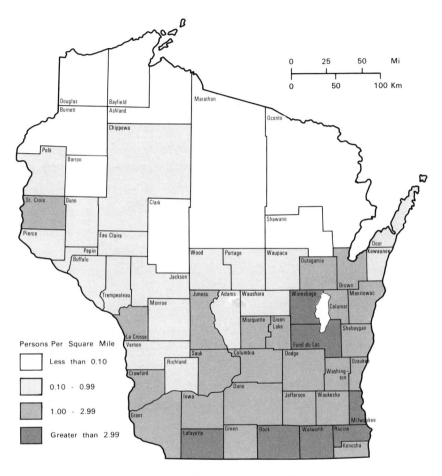

IRISH-BORN IN WISCONSIN, 1870

those of German birth, the sum amounts to over a third of the entire Wisconsin population.

The German proportion is still higher if the German-speaking people from the Austro-Hungarian Empire are included. Their numbers, though comparatively small, increased dramatically during the decade of the sixties, from 7,081 to 15,056, or more than 100 per cent. Of the 15,056, over two-thirds, or 10,570, were classified as Bohemians. They may be presumed to have been mostly Germans or Germanized Czechs.

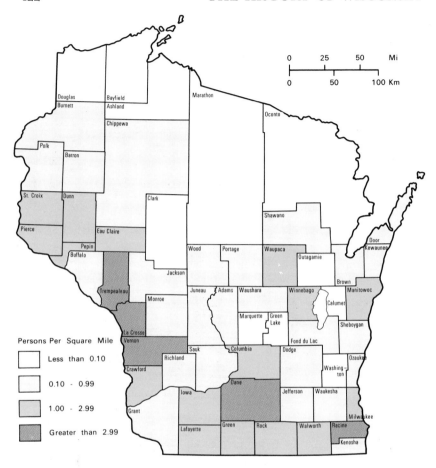

SWEDISH- AND NORWEGIAN-BORN IN WISCONSIN, 1870

The Swiss, on the other hand, experienced only a modest increase, from 4,722 to 6,069.

Among the major nationality groups in Wisconsin, the Scandinavians made the most striking gain, as their numbers more than doubled during the decade, rising from 23,265 to 48,057, of whom 40,046 were Norwegians. By contrast, the Irish total actually declined, falling from 49,961 to 48,479, a figure barely larger than the one the Scandinavians had attained. In January 1866 an Irish Emigration Aid Society had been organized in Madison for the purpose of attracting Irishmen to the state,

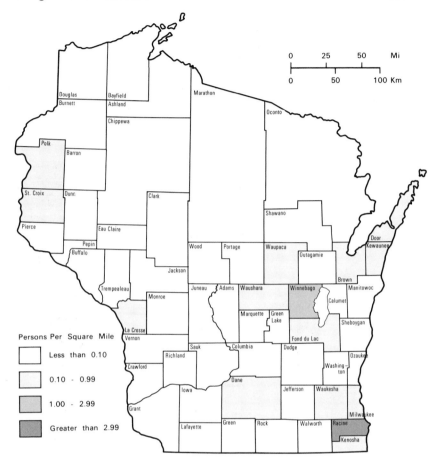

Persons Per Square Mile

Less than 0.10

0.10 - 0.99

1.00 - 2.99

Greater than 2.99

DANISH-BORN IN WISCONSIN, 1870

but the society could accomplish little. Of 14,576 immigrants who entered Wisconsin through Milwaukee in seven months of 1869, only fifty were Irish. During the decade the number of British-born (English, Scottish, Welsh) decreased even more than the number of Irish—from 43,923 to 41,522. The next largest group, the Canadian-born, grew almost in proportion to the state's growth, yielding a total of 22,741 in 1870. The Dutch increased rather little, from 4,906 to 5,990, and the Belgians still less, from 4,647 to 4,804. One other nationality, eventually to have a sizable representation in Wisconsin, had

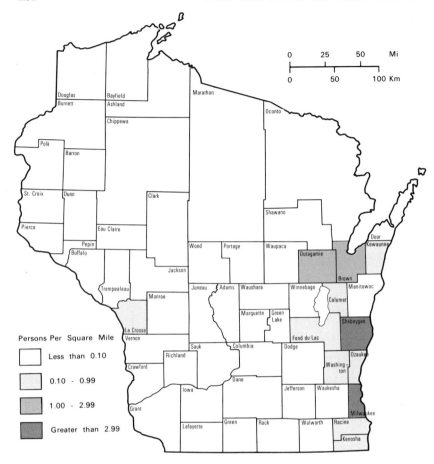

DUTCH-BORN IN WISCONSIN, 1870

very few representatives as late as 1870—the Polish, with a
count of only 1,290, though an indeterminate number of additional Poles, from German-occupied Poland, were classified
as Germans.[4]

As the comparative numbers of the various immigrant groups

---

[4] *Ninth Census of the United States, 1870: Volume I*, pp. 337–342; *Eighth Census of the United States, 1860: Population*, 544; Mack Walker, *Germany and
the Emigration, 1816–1885* (Cambridge, 1964), 175; M. Justille McDonald, *History of the Irish in Wisconsin in the Nineteenth Century* (Washington, D.C.,
1954), 27–28, 36.

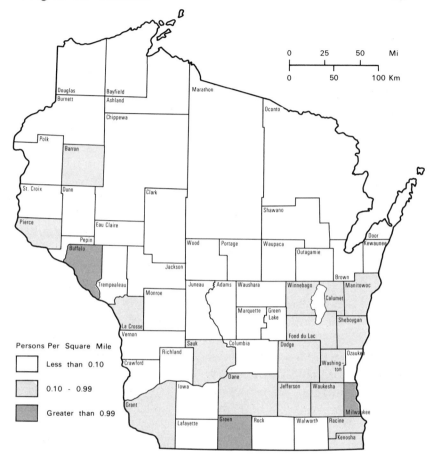

Persons Per Square Mile

☐ Less than 0.10

▨ 0.10 - 0.99

▨ Greater than 0.99

SWISS-BORN IN WISCONSIN, 1870

changed, so did their geographical distribution. The multi-plying Germans, in search of extra room for settlement, often displaced previous settlers of other nationalities. Especially in such southern counties as Dodge, Jefferson, and Waukesha, the Germans after 1865 occupied land that formerly had been held by settlers from New England, Ireland, or Norway. Mi-grating Norwegians also took the places of others. About 1870, for example, there was an exodus of Norwegians from Manito-woc County to Door County, where they bought farms that Yankees and Irishmen had started in 1855 and 1856. Meanwhile Norwegians continued to move in a northwesterly direction from Dane and other counties of the south and east.

In 1870 there were nearly 97,000 natives of Wisconsin residing in other states and territories, about half of them in Iowa and Minnesota, where settlement was now expanding more rapidly than in Wisconsin, and close to 1,000 of them in the eleven states of the former Confederacy. These statistics, however, give no adequate measure of the out-migration from Wisconsin. A larger total of former residents, other than Wisconsin natives, had left the state during the previous decade, as is indicated by the decline in the state's population of British, Irish, and eastern American nativity. A great many Norwegians also had moved on beyond the state's borders, though others had arrived in sufficient numbers to double the total of the Scandinavian-born remaining in the state.[5]

By 1870 the population of Wisconsin had spread far enough to the state's northeastern and northwestern regions, that a frontier line could be drawn, roughly, as an arc extending from Green Bay through Stevens Point and Eau Claire to Hudson on the St. Croix. Such a line would divide the state's area approximately into halves. In the southern half lived nearly a million people, with the heaviest concentrations of them in the counties of Milwaukee (89,930), Dane (53,096), Dodge (47,035), and Fond du Lac (46,273). Except for Racine, the counties of the southeastern region had grown little if any since 1860, and two of them had actually suffered a net loss—Walworth, down from 26,496 to 25,972, and Kenosha, from 13,900 to 13,147. In the northern half of the state there were in 1870 fewer than 60,000 people, all told. On the whole the north remained a wilderness, broken only by a few settlements, most of them lumbering centers such as Wausau and Marinette. In the northernmost counties of Ashland, Bay-

[5] Kate Everest Levi, "Geographical Origin of German Immigration to Wisconsin," in *Wis. Hist. Colls.*, 14: 352–354; McDonald, *Irish in Wisconsin*, 82–83; Hjalmar R. Holand, *History of Door County, Wisconsin: The County Beautiful* (2 vols., Chicago, 1917), 1: 443–444; Anton Jarstad, "The Melting Pot in Northeastern Wisconsin," in *WMH*, 26 (June, 1943), 426–432; *Ninth Census of the United States, 1870: Volume I*, pp. 334, 337–342.

field, and Douglas, including Superior City, the total population had increased by only 260 during the decade, from 1,377 to 1,637.[6]

The rate of urbanization was uneven. From 1865 to 1870 the thirty-three largest villages and cities grew only 5 per cent faster than the countryside, though from 1860 to 1865 they had been growing more than 15 per cent faster. The manufacturing center of Milwaukee, however, accelerated its growth by 28 per cent after 1865. Developing proportionately even more rapidly during the decade 1860–1870 were the lumbering and sawmilling centers of Marinette, Oconto, Peshtigo, Wausau, Stevens Point, Grand Rapids (Wisconsin Rapids), Black River Falls, Eau Claire, Chippewa Falls, La Crosse, Green Bay, Oshkosh, and Fond du Lac. Their combined population increased four times as fast as that of the state as a whole. Yet, despite the urbanizing trend, the proportion of employed Wisconsinites who were engaged in agriculture remained practically unchanged. It was 53.9 per cent in 1860 and 54.6 per cent in 1870.[7]

The occupational distribution of the people in 1870 varied somewhat according to their national origins. Those of American birth constituted less than half (46.1 per cent) of all the "persons occupied." The American-born made up a roughly proportionate share (44.1 per cent) of all those engaged in agriculture, and a somewhat larger share (55.1 per cent and 54.8 per cent) of those working as agricultural laborers and as domestic servants. But they held a very high proportion, about 70 per cent or more, of the positions as government officials and employees, physicians and surgeons, and printers, and a still higher proportion, 80 per cent or more, of the positions as bankers and stockbrokers, teachers, journalists, and lawyers.

The German-born filled 23.3 per cent of the occupations as

[6] Joseph Schafer, *A History of Agriculture in Wisconsin* (Madison, 1922), 136–138; *Ninth Census of the United States, 1870: Volume I*, p. 73.

[7] Frederick Merk, *Economic History of Wisconsin During the Civil War Decade* (Madison, 1916), 227–228; Wisconsin Secretary of State, *Annual Report*, 1865, p. 111; *Ninth Census of the United States, 1870: Volume I*, pp. 287–295, 764; *Eighth Census of the United States, 1860: Population*, 545.

a whole. They held about the same proportion of places in agriculture and a somewhat smaller proportion of the jobs as agricultural laborers. They predominated among the cigarmakers and tobacco workers and bakers, more than 50 per cent, and among the tanners and leather finishers, distillers, and brewers, more than 60 per cent. Persons of Scandinavian birth, who made up 6.8 per cent of all those occupied, were more or less proportionately represented among farmers, farm workers, and common laborers, and disproportionately represented among domestic servants (11.2 per cent), sailors and other watermen (12.3 per cent), sawmill operatives (13.5 per cent), and especially shipbuilders (23.5 per cent).

The British-born, 6 per cent of the occupation force, constituted a comparable percentage of the farmers (6.7), a higher percentage of the masons (12.6) and machinists (9.3), and nearly a majority of the miners (43.8 per cent). The Irish-born comprised 7.9 per cent of the persons occupied and 8.7 per cent of those engaged in agriculture, but only 4 per cent of the farm laborers. In the state as a whole, they were not yet getting even their fair share of political jobs—they were only 6.7 per cent of government officials and employees—but they were comparatively numerous among the draymen and teamsters (11.6 per cent), the common laborers (13.3 per cent), and of course the railroad workers (21.6 per cent). The conception of the typical Irishman as working on the railroad, however, is far off the mark. There were only 608 Irish employees of railroad companies as compared with 13,914 Irish farmers and farm laborers, though some of the 3,289 Irish common laborers were engaged in railroad construction.

During the 1860's the number of Wisconsinites of African descent grew by more than 80 per cent, but this was an increase of less than a thousand, from 1,171 to 2,113. In 1870 the Negroes again constituted only about two-tenths of one per cent of the state's population. Of the 2,113 total, 611 had been born in Wisconsin, 979 in the former slave states of the border and the South, 478 in other states and territories, and 45 in foreign countries. At the same time, 315 Wisconsin-born blacks were residing outside of Wisconsin, 111 of them in Illinois. The largest concentration in Wisconsin was to be found in Fond du Lac County (an increase from fifty-nine in 1860 to 209 in 1870), the next largest in Racine County (from 135 to 194) and in Rock County (from 93 to 194), and the next in Milwaukee County (from 107 to 185). "It is stated as a fact," the Milwaukee *Sentinel* reported in 1873, "that the little burg of Patch Grove has a greater number of colored residents, in proportion to its population, than any other town in the State." The blacks who migrated to Patch Grove after the Civil War, combined with others near Beetown, gave Grant County a black population of ninety-eight in 1870, as compared with thirty-five in 1860. More than half of the state's counties, twenty-seven of the fifty-one, contained fewer than twenty blacks apiece as late as 1870.

Included in the 1870 "constitutional population" of 1,054,670 for Wisconsin—that is, the count on which congressional representation was to be based—were 1,206 "Indians taxed," that is, "civilized" Indians not residing on reservations. Of these Indians, the largest numbers were recorded in the counties of Calumet (597), Brown (ninety-five), Shawano (eighty-three), Oconto (sixty), and Polk (fifty-nine). In addition, there were in Wisconsin 10,315 Indians "not taxed," that is, people "maintaining their tribal relations" on reservations or at agencies, according to partial counts and supplementary estimates. This figure did not necessarily include all the wandering Winnebago, not taxed and yet not confined on any reservation. Even so, the recorded total of Indians in Wisconsin—11,521—was much larger than that in any other state east of the Mississippi. When the Indians not enumerated in the census were added to the census figures, the presumed "true population" of Wisconsin in 1870 came to 1,064,985.[8]

---

[8] These analyses are based on figures given in *Ninth Census of the United States, 1870: Volume I*, pp. ix–xiii, xvi–xvii, 73–74, 334, 764. The Milwaukee *Sentinel*, September 27, 1873, is the source of the quotation. The totals for blacks and Indians are very unreliable since both often were overlooked by census takers. Indians living outside a reservation were seldom counted. See p. 82n above about the difficulty of counting Indians and blacks in Calumet County.

[2]

At the end of the Civil War there was still an abundance of unsold land in Wisconsin. The public domain, most of it in the north, embraced 10 or 11 million acres, nearly one-third of the state's entire area. Comparatively little of the remaining federal land was considered suitable for farming, but most of it was highly desirable for lumbering. As the best timberland in lower Michigan had been sold, and the pineries of the states farther east were nearing exhaustion, timber seekers focused their attention on Wisconsin's extensive and excellent stands of white pine. The federal government obliged the timber seekers by disposing generously of much of the land through grants to railroads, gifts to the various states under the Morrill Act, and sales of vast tracts at very moderate prices. Meanwhile the government transferred a much smaller quantity of land to settlers taking advantage of the homestead law.[9]

By congressional acts of 1856 and 1864, more than 3,750,000 acres of the public domain in Wisconsin had been set aside for the encouragement of railroad construction. These grants were assigned to various railroad companies, were renewed or revoked and reassigned to other companies, and were in some cases again forfeited or rejected, so as to leave a most confusing history. By 1873 only a small fraction of the 3,750,000 acres, not more than one-fifth of that amount, had actually been earned and acquired by any of the grantees, though eventually most of it was to be awarded to qualifying railroads.

After the lands offered under the 1856 law had been forfeited, Congress renewed and enlarged the offer by the act of 1864. This provded for three grants—one for a northwestern route from either the St. Croix river or lake to the west end of Lake Superior and continuing on to Bayfield, another for a line between Tomah and the St. Croix, and a third for a

[9] Paul W. Gates, "Frontier Land Business in Wisconsin," in *WMH*, 52 (Summer, 1969), 326–327, and Paul W. Gates, *The Wisconsin Pine Lands of Cornell University: A Study in Land Policy and Absentee Ownership* (Ithaca, 1943), 90.

north-central route from Portage, Berlin, Doty's Island, or Fond du Lac to Bayfield and Superior City. To qualify for the grants, the first two railroads were required to complete construction within five years, the third within ten. In 1865 Congress also extended the time required to lay tracks from Green Bay "northerly to the state line." In each case the railroad company was to receive every other section of land within a strip twenty miles wide, ten miles on each side of the right of way.

By 1869 the St. Croix and Lake Superior Railroad Company, which was to have built from Hudson to Bayfield and Superior City, had not laid a single mile of track. Having failed to meet the five-year limit, this company lost its claim on any part of the northwestern or St. Croix grant. The status of the lands involved was now uncertain. Had they reverted to the federal government, or did the state have the right to designate another grantee? The legislature proceeded to select a new corporation, the North Wisconsin Railway Company, and make it the beneficiary of any right that the state might have in regard to the lands.

Friends of the company lobbied in Washington, hoping to get from Congress a definite renewal of the grant. They ran into opposition from promoters of a Minnesota railroad terminating at Duluth, and the controversy became entangled in a quarrel between the rival lake ports of Duluth and Superior City. Citizens of Superior considered their town a more logical railroad terminus than Duluth, for, as they pointed out, Superior had a better harbor and a terrain that would more easily accommodate the growth of a large city. They were angered when Duluth tried to improve its harbor by cutting a canal and diverting the flow of the St. Louis River. The people of Duluth, for their part, were determined to keep Superior from becoming a railroad competitor. They had the help of Jay Cooke, of Philadelphia, the nation's leading investment banker. Cooke, who had an interest in the Minnesota railroad, got control of the North Wisconsin and, while pretending to lobby for both companies, secretly used his influence to the

disadvantage of the Wisconsin line. Congress did nothing to
renew the St. Croix grant, and in four years the Wisconsin
company managed to extend its rails only seventeen miles
northeast from Hudson.

The North Wisconsin was by 1872 under the control of
the Chicago and North Western, and the rival Milwaukee
and St. Paul was attempting to persuade the legislature to
award it the state's claim to the St. Croix grant. Finally the
legislature did so. To the consternation of most Wisconsinites,
President Alexander Mitchell of the Milwaukee road announced, in May 1873, that his company was rejecting the award.
Mitchell explained that the Wisconsin title to the lands was
more questionable than he and his fellow directors had earlier
supposed. Some newspapers took a different view, typical head-
lines being "Swindle, Act of Treachery, Downright Robbery."
One man said the Milwaukee road was like Aesop's dog in the
manger: "It won't eat the hay or let the oxen eat it." Wisconsin had to wait until 1883 for the completion of the St. Croix
line and for the disposal of the St. Croix grant.

Meanwhile one company succeeded in acquiring a small portion of the land that had been set aside in that area. Commenc-
ing in 1869, the West Wisconsin Railway Company (originally
the Tomah and St. Croix) pushed its work from Tomah northwestward through Eau Claire to Hudson. In 1873 Congress rewarded the West Wisconsin by allowing it to take 20,000 acres
in the St. Croix Valley.

Less frustrating and less complex was the story of the railroad grant in the northeast. The lands here were offered to the
Chicago and North Western as the successor of the original
grantee. In 1868 Congress again changed the requirements for
the grant, authorizing the C. & N. W. to lay its track to Marinette rather than "northerly to the state line" but to select its
lands along the originally plotted route farther to the west,
where more and better timberland was available. By 1871 the
C. & N. W. had completed the track and gained title to more
than half a million acres.

The disposal of the north-central grant, however, was delayed. In 1866 the legislature divided the lands between two

Women making yarn.

Left: 1870's barber shop.
Right: Racine College, ca.
1869.

Lumberjacks.

Above: Pontoon railroad bridge over the Mississippi River at Prairie du Chien. Below: Ferry across the Wisconsin River at Grand Rapids.

Right: Ice-encrusted three-masted schooner at Milwaukee, 1871. B e l o w : Brewery, Mineral Point, ca. 1860.

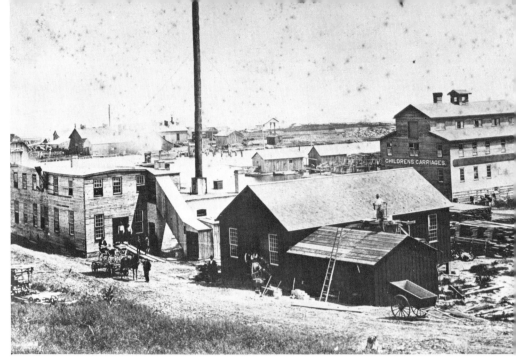

Children's carriage factory, Sheboygan, ca. 1870.

Centralia Mills, Wood County, in what is now part of Wisconsin Rapids.

Brewery (left) and residence (right) originally owned by C. T. Melms, on Virginia Street in Milwaukee, ca. 1870.

Creamery, southern Wisconsin.

Alexander Mitchell.

Railway conductor.

Railroad company stock certificate.

Chicago and North Western engine decorated for July Fourth, 1869.

Loading grain on a lake steamer, Milwaukee.

Post-Civil War farmstead, southern Wisconsin.

companies, the Winnebago and Lake Superior and the Portage and Superior, which later merged and in 1871 assumed the name of the Wisconsin Central Railroad Company. The legislature had directed the companies to build lines separately from Menasha and Portage to Stevens Point and jointly from there to Superior City. Construction proceeded rapidly on the Menasha branch but was delayed on the Portage branch. After an extension of time for completing the work, the Wisconsin Central in 1877 was to reach Ashland, though not Superior City, and qualify for more than 835,000 acres of valuable timberland.

Until after 1873 the railroad men offered for sale very little of the government land they had acquired. They used it as security for loans, cut trees to make ties and bridge timbers, and obtained cash by selling stumpage to sawmill operators. But they preferred to hold on to the land itself, since they expected it to rise in value as settlement increased.[10]

During the early postwar years a much larger part of the public domain in Wisconsin passed into private ownership through the workings of the Morrill Act of 1862 than through the railroad grants. Most Wisconsinites favored the encouragement of agricultural colleges, but few approved the terms of the Morrill Act. It bestowed land scrip on the states in quantities proportionate to their representation in Congress, the most populous eastern states receiving the largest amounts. To raise money for the support of agricultural colleges, the states could sell the scrip, and the buyers could exchange it for lands wherever they could locate them in the available portions of the public domain. Wisconsinites feared that outside speculators would accumulate the scrip and use it to monopolize the best of the unsold and ungranted land remaining in the state. So, indeed, events were to prove.

In 1866 the federal land office opened for entry the last big previously unoffered tract in Wisconsin. This comprised

[10] Merk, *Economic History*, 277–288; *United States Statutes at Large*, 13: 66–68, 520; Frank N. Elliott, "The Causes and the Growth of Railroad Regulation in Wisconsin, 1848–1876" (doctoral dissertation, University of Wisconsin, 1956), 170–171, 194–196, 204–218; Gordon O. Greiner, "Wisconsin National Railroad Land Grants" (master's thesis, University of Wisconsin, 1935), 12, 17–36.

6,423,984 acres, much of it in the Chippewa pinery. Agricultural college scrip in the amount of 7,500,000 acres had recently been sold, much of it for less than a dollar an acre. The buyers now rushed to locate their lands, and during the next two years they entered 1,334,460 acres in Wisconsin. Over two-thirds of this acreage went to capitalists from Michigan, Pennsylvania, and New York.

The largest and most valuable share went to Ezra Cornell, who had taken over New York's scrip and was investing it on behalf of Cornell University. He acquired 499,126 acres, including some of the finest stands of white pine in the Chippewa Valley. In achieving this coup he had the indispensable help of Wisconsin partners, among them the clerk of the Eau Claire land office, who used his position to turn away competing land seekers and to see that Cornell got the choicest parcels in the district. Two of his associates obtained an additional 101,000 acres for themselves. Eventually Cornell University was to gain an endowment of about $5 million from the sale of its Wisconsin lands.

The University of Wisconsin was to benefit far less from the 240,000 acres' worth of scrip that had been assigned to the state. By 1866 the state land commissioners had located the lands, more than half of them in the counties of Marathon and Polk and the rest in Chippewa, Clark, Dunn, Oconto, and Shawano. Most of the land was sold to large buyers, that is, to those purchasing 800 acres or more. The largest sale, about 33,000 acres in Polk County, was to Caleb Cushing, of Massachusetts, organizer of the Great European American Emigration Land Company, which planned to bring in settlers from Europe. By 1872 the state had disposed of about two-thirds of its agricultural college land. When it had sold the remainder, it realized a grand total of just over $300,000.[11]

Wisconsin speculators and lumbermen resented the intru-

[11] Gates, *Wisconsin Pine Lands*, 73–77, 90–110, 246; Gates, "Frontier Land Business," in *WMH*, 52: 326–327; Merle Curti and Vernon Carstensen, *The University of Wisconsin: A History, 1848–1925* (2 vols., Madison, 1949), 1: 299–302; Wilbur H. Glover, "The Agricultural College Lands in Wisconsin," in *WMH*, 30 (March, 1947), 261–272; Alice E. Smith, "Caleb Cushing's Investments in the St. Croix Valley," in *WMH*, 28 (September, 1944), 14–19.

sion of large-scale land dealers from other states. The partners Cyrus Woodman and Cadwallader Washburn, two of the
biggest speculators among the Wisconsinites, had had their own
eyes on the white pine of the Chippewa Valley. As Woodman
ruefully confessed to Washburn in 1869, the two had been out-
smarted when they "let Cornell & Michigan men come in and
gobble up such an enormous quantity of valuable pine there
with college scrip." Woodman and Washburn continued to
look for choice tracts of timberland and enter them quietly at
the land offices for the minimum price, $1.25 an acre. So did
lumbermen and sawmill owners such as Pound, Halbert &
Company of Chippewa Falls, Smith & Buffington and Carson
& Rand of Eau Claire, Knapp, Stout & Company of Menomonie,
Ludington, Stephenson & Company of Marinette, and P. Sawyer
& Son of Oshkosh. Secretly these and other firms sent "timber
cruisers" through the forests to appraise remote stands and
record their location. Or the proprietors tramped the woods
in person, since they could not always trust a cruiser, who might
save the best finds for himself or sell his knowledge to a rival
of his employer.

An opportunity for sawmill owners on the Chippewa seemed
at hand when, in 1869, the federal government ordered a public
sale of the last sizable tract it still owned in the valley. This
consisted of 247,680 acres that had been withheld for railroad
grants. On the day of the auction, at Eau Claire, the local
lumbermen were dismayed to find buyers present from other
parts of Wisconsin and from Michigan and eastern states. The
heavy bidding soon drove the price up to $6 an acre. Cornell's
agent then proposed and the other buyers agreed to divide the
land among themselves and make no more competitive bids.
The price quickly dropped. When, in 1873, a smaller lot of
pine land was auctioned off, the buyers formed a similar ring
and again kept competition within bounds.[12]

While speculators in the postwar years were mainly interested

---

[12] Gates, *Wisconsin Pine Lands,* 103–120; Gates, "Frontier Land Business," in
WMH, 52: 326–327 (quotation); Robert F. Fries, *Empire in Pine: The Story
of Lumbering in Wisconsin, 1830–1900* (Madison, 1951), 161–178; Willard F.
Miller, "A History of Eau Claire County During the Civil War" (master's thesis,
University of Wisconsin, 1954), 14.

in pine land, they also held tens of thousands of acres that were suitable for agriculture. The prospective farmer, if he bought from a speculator, would have to pay more than if he purchased directly from the land office, but he could usually get better soil from the private dealer. Settlers had the option of taking up land under the homestead law of 1862, and 3,489 of them in Wisconsin had done so by the end of 1865. It was not easy, however, for the homesteader to develop a farm, even if he could find a good location for it in what was left of the public domain. True, he could obtain 160 acres without charge, except for a $10 entry fee. Still, to gain title to the land, he had to improve it and live on it for five years. Some homesteaders were so poor they had to borrow to pay the $10 fee, and most of them needed loans in order to make the necessary improvements. Yet they could not mortgage the land until the five years were up and the title was theirs. Many converted their homestead entries into pre-emption entries, at $1.25 an acre, so that they could get the title immediately and use the land as security for borrowing. Of the 7,495 persons who took up Wisconsin homesteads from 1863 to 1868, only about a half, or 3,743, had succeeded in acquiring ownership of them by the end of 1873.[13]

Settlers as well as lumbermen and speculators could still purchase land from the state, which had hundreds of thousands of acres left over from its federal swamp land grant. This land was cheap, the minimum price being 75 cents per acre for most of it and, after 1867, only 50 cents for some in certain badly overflowed areas. As a rule, however, the expense of drainage made wet land a poor bargain for prospective farmers. They continued, as in prewar years, to have the alternative, if they could afford it, of purchasing from previous settlers. When, for example, Olaf Erickson moved to a new Norwegian settlement west of Ontario (Vernon County) in 1868, he could

[13] Irene D. Neu, "Land Credit in Frontier Wisconsin" (master's thesis, Cornell University, 1945), 26–28; Thomas Donaldson, *The Public Domain: Its History with Statistics . . . ,* in *House Miscellaneous Documents,* 47 Cong., 2 sess., no. 45, pt. 4 (serial 2158), 351–355; Gates, *Wisconsin Pine Lands,* 101.

find in the vicinity no land except what was already privately owned, and he bought eighty acres for $600 with a loan at 12 per cent.[14]

[3]

Railroad building had boomed in Wisconsin during the prosperous years of the 1850's and then had slackened in consequence of the Panic of 1857 and the coming of the war. From 1868 through 1873 the construction of railroads recovered and went ahead faster than ever. During these six years the trackage in the state lengthened from 1,030 to 2,379 miles. The prewar drive had been mainly from east to west, to connect Lake Michigan with the Mississippi River. The postwar thrust was largely to the north. By 1873, however, it had only begun to extend beyond the frontier of settlement, with the lines to Marinette and to points somewhat above Stevens Point and Hudson.

Only a part of the recent construction was the work of the land-grant railroads. These were the Chicago and North Western from Green Bay to Marinette, the Wisconsin Central from Menasha to Stevens Point and beyond, the West Wisconsin from Tomah to Hudson, and the North Wisconsin from Hudson a short distance northeast. On the stretch from Menasha to Stevens Point the Menasha contractor, Reuben Scott, set something of a construction record. With rails brought up the Fox River from Green Bay, and with the labor of 100 yoke of oxen, 600 horses, and 2,000 men, Scott laid the sixty-three miles of track in 120 days. On a stretch near Tomah the West Wisconsin gained a distinction of a different kind. After receiving its land grant for building to Hudson from Tomah, as had been required, the company relaid some of its track so as to bypass Tomah on the north and make a terminus about ten miles farther east. People in and around Tomah protested, and the

[14] Malcolm J. Rohrbough, "The Acquisition and Administration of the Wisconsin Swamp Land Grant, 1850–1865" (master's thesis, University of Wisconsin, 1958), 122–125; Oluf Erickson, "Olaf Erickson, Scandinavian Frontiersman," in *WMH,* 31 (September, 1947–March, 1948), 11.

RAILROADS IN WISCONSIN, 1865

RAILROADS IN WISCONSIN, 1873

legislature, in 1873, acted to compel the company to restore rail access to the town.

There was no mystery about the motives of the West Wisconsin in relocating its main line. The company wished to make a direct connection at Camp Douglas with a new road that the Chicago and North Western was building from Madison by way of Merrimac to Baraboo, Reedsburg, and Elroy. This key segment of the emerging C. & N. W. system in Wisconsin was one of several railroads that were being built without the encouragement of a gift of federal land. Among other important rail projects that went ahead without land grants were the Madison and Portage line (the company angled in vain for a grant), the Northwestern Union Railway from Milwaukee to Fond du Lac, the Milwaukee and Northern's road straight north (between Lake Michigan and Lake Winnebago) to Green Bay, the Milwaukee, Lake Shore and Western's route along Lake Michigan toward Sheboygan and Manitowoc, and the Green Bay and Lake Pepin's line westward through Grand Rapids to the Mississippi River.[15]

Even for the land-grant railroads, the financing of new lines presented difficulties, since rail construction had to be completed to acquire the lands, and eastern capitalists were still reluctant to risk their money on new Wisconsin ventures. The question of financing divided Wisconsinites as between those who lived in the north or had interests there and those whose homes and interests were in the south. Some people in the south opposed all public assistance to railroad enterprises, including the grants of federal land to them. "What is the public domain good for while it remains public domain?" a reader of the *Chippewa Herald* indignantly responded. "We

[15] Merk, *Economic History*, 277–278; William E. Derby, "A History of the Port of Milwaukee, 1835–1910" (doctoral dissertation, University of Wisconsin, 1963), 285–287; Alice E. Smith, *Millstone and Saw: The Origins of Neenah-Menasha* (Madison, 1966), 55–58; Elliott, "Railroad Regulation in Wisconsin," 202. Wisconsin Railroad Commissioners, *Annual Report*, 1874, contains a summary of the activity of each railroad chartered in Wisconsin to 1874, though the most accurate record of track laid for each year is James P. Kaysen, *The Railroads of Wisconsin, 1827–1937* (Boston, 1937).

want cattle—not buffalo. We want sheep—not antelopes. We want emigrants—not Indians. Railroads will not be built through a howling wilderness without aid."

Promoters of northern railroads hoped to get generous aid from the state. To do so, they would have to change the constitution, since it prohibited the state from giving financial assistance to internal improvements. Yielding to the pressure of railroad lobbyists, the legislature in 1867 approved a constitutional amendment, with a solid vote from northern and a divided vote from southern members, to empower the state to contribute $100,000 for every twenty miles of future construction. Before a proposed amendment could be submitted to the people, however, it had to be repassed by the next legislature. Members from southern counties rallied to defeat the proposal in 1868 and again in 1869.

Frustrated in their efforts to obtain financial help from the state, railroad promoters looked to local governments for assistance, as they had done during the earlier construction boom. Counties, towns, and cities along the older lines were still burdened with the debts they had incurred in the railroad enthusiasm of that time. Just as frenzied now as those places once had been, localities along the newly projected routes were ready to take the plunge into deep indebtedness. When asked in 1871 to vote on an exchange of $200,000 in county bonds for $200,000 in Wisconsin Central stock, the people of Ashland County were not deterred by the fact that the county had a population of only 300 and a revenue considerably smaller than the anticipated interest on the bonds. Nor were the people defeated by the opposition of Ezra Cornell and other absentee landowners, who were expected to pay the costs of the debt through an increase of taxes on their lands. To make doubly sure of a favorable vote on the bond issue, its advocates brought to the polls seventy Irishmen who were working at a local stone quarry but whose homes were in Chicago. In 1870, Neenah and Menasha voters both readily approved $50,000 bond issues in support of the railroad that would soon be named the Wisconsin Central. The company's president,

George Reed, a Menasha leader, also persuaded Boston capitalists to invest $2,000,000 in the company's stock. Even Milwaukee, though heavily in debt from previous loans to railroads, extended its credit again to newer projects—$105,000 to the Milwaukee and Northern for its line to Green Bay, $100,000 to the Northwestern Union for its line to Fond du Lac.[16]

Eastern financiers were more willing to assist in the consolidation than in the construction of Wisconsin railroads, and after the war the monopolistic trend accelerated, with considerable help from the wizardry of Wall Street. At the war's end, two companies already predominated among the railroads in the state—the Chicago and North Western and the Milwaukee and St. Paul. On the through haul across the state between Milwaukee and the Mississippi the only competitor of the M. & St. P. was the Milwaukee and Prairie du Chien, the successor of the original Wisconsin railroad, the old Milwaukee and Mississippi. Repeatedly the M. & St. P. had offered to buy the Prairie du Chien company, to consolidate with it, or to pool earnings with it. The most the Prairie du Chien managers would agree to was a pool, which was to go into effect in 1866. By that time, however, the company was to be taken from its managers and merged with the M. & St. P. as a result of stock manipulations in New York.

On the New York stock exchange a ring of speculators, prominent among them the brokerage firm of Henry Stimson & Company, had been quietly buying up the common stock of the Prairie du Chien railroad, and by November 1865 they had obtained all 29,880 shares of it. They then sprang the trap on what was to become notorious as the "Prairie Dog Corner." They suddenly called for delivery from other dealers who had been selling Prairie du Chien stock short. The price, which had been as low as $30 earlier in the year, now soared to $230 a share. Having made a killing on this transaction,

[16] Merk, *Economic History*, 277–278; Herbert W. Rice, "Early History of the Chicago, Milwaukee and St. Paul Railway Company" (doctoral dissertation, State University of Iowa, 1938), 256–257; Gates, *Wisconsin Pine Lands*, 192; Smith, *Millstone and Saw*, 56; Derby, "History of the Port of Milwaukee," 285–286. The quotation is from the *Chippewa Herald*, November 12, 1870.

Stimson and his associates expected to profit even more by arranging a merger with the M. & St. P.

The schemers discovered, however, that according to the fine print of the Prairie du Chien charter only the holders of preferred stock could vote—the common stock carried no voting rights. Though these men had a majority interest in the company, they had no control over its management. But they did not give up. Stimson hired a Madison lawyer, Benjamin F. Hopkins, to secure remedial legislation from the Wisconsin government. Hopkins earned his fee of $5,000. He prepared two bills, one in vague and general terms conferring on all stockholders the right to participate in corporate affairs, the other explicitly giving the holders of Prairie du Chien common stock the right to vote for the company's directors. In March 1866 the first bill was unobtrusively slipped into the assembly and the second was openly and frankly presented to the senate. Meeting furious denunciation from lobbyists for the Prairie du Chien management, the senate bill was promptly withdrawn. The assembly bill made its way unnoticed through both houses and was passed and signed in the rush of business at the end of the session. Acting under the authority of this law, the Wall Street owners of the common stock outvoted the holders of the preferred stock and elected their own board of directors for the Prairie du Chien company. The Wall Streeters then exchanged their Prairie du Chien shares for a larger number of M. & St. P. shares. Later the Prairie du Chien officials, having little choice, sold out to the victors.

In gaining possession of the Prairie du Chien, the M. & St. P. also succeeded to the Prairie du Chien's interests in Iowa and Minnesota railroads. After 1867 the M. & St. P. thereby controlled the entire route from Milwaukee by way of Prairie du Chien to McGregor, Iowa, and St. Paul and Minneapolis. In 1868 the M. & St. P. leased the West Wisconsin, then under construction from Tomah to Hudson, and a year later it bought a controlling interest in the Western Union, which operated a line from Racine by way of Beloit and Freeport to Savannah, Illinois. Thus by 1870 the one company got control of every through route from the Wisconsin shore of Lake Michigan to the Mississippi River.

By the end of 1873 the North Western's rails in Wisconsin comprised about a fourth of its total trackage in several midwestern states. The two major lines extended northward from the Illinois border, one to Marinette and the other to the Mississippi, across the river from Winona, Minnesota.

Between them the two largest railroad companies in Wisconsin, the M. & St. P. and the C. & N. W., owned or dominated every line of any importance in the state by 1868. That year the stockholders of the C. & N. W. elected to their board four directors of the M. & St. P., including the president, Alexander Mitchell, and the stockholders of the M. & St. P. elected the C. & N. W. president to theirs. For a time, in 1869 and 1870, Mitchell served as president of both corporations, which between them operated very nearly if not quite the greatest mileage of any railroad in the world. After 1870 he continued to direct the Milwaukee road and its subsidiaries. He also controlled, through ownership or lease, nearly all the grain elevators in Milwaukee.

Generally the two big Wisconsin railroad combinations avoided competing with one another, but from time to time the M. & St. P. engaged in rate wars with the Illinois Central, which offered competition across Illinois on the "long haul" between the Mississippi River and Lake Michigan. The Milwaukee road kept its rates high, however, on the "short haul" from interior points to the lake. Both the Milwaukee and the North Western discriminated in favor of certain large shippers. The two also arranged a pool, each retaining half of its freight receipts and dividing the rest with the other.[17]

Tremendous though the benefits were that the railroads brought, farmers and other shippers were more inclined to notice the evils—the seemingly extortionate and certainly dis-

[17] Merk, *Economic History*, 291–295, 298–299, 338–342; Rice, "Chicago, Milwaukee and St. Paul Railway," 179–189, 250–252; David B. Leonard, "A Biography of Alexander Mitchell, 1817–1887" (master's thesis, University of Wisconsin, 1951), 92–99; Kaysen, *Railroads of Wisconsin*, 8; Dale E. Treleven, "Railroads, Elevators, and Grain Dealers: The Genesis of Antimonopolism in Milwaukee," in *WMH*, 52 (Spring, 1969), 205–208, 213–214.

criminatory rates and the unconscionable influence of the "railroad lobby" over the people's representatives in the state legislature. As early as 1860 and again in 1864 a bill had been introduced to fix railroad rates, but the lobby defeated the first bill and emasculated the second. Despite the introduction of regulatory bills in every legislative session after 1864, not until 1874 did Wisconsin adopt a regulatory law, which proved to be utterly ineffectual.[18]

[4]

At one time Wisconsinites had expected the Great Lakes and the Mississippi River, together with their tributaries, to be the making of the state. After the war many of the people looked again to those waterways. In the absence of state regulation of railroads, the competition of river and lake traffic seemed the only means of keeping down transportation charges.

Some farmers of the upper Mississippi, confronted by a rising railroad rate and a falling wheat price, sent their 1865 crop downriver by boat. They hoped to revive the old route to New York by way of St. Louis and New Orleans. Milwaukee and Chicago grain dealers were temporarily concerned. "Can we afford to add to the natural attraction of the Mississippi," the Chicago *Tribune* asked, "the powerful repulsion of exorbitant railroad freights on all lines crossing that river or adjacent to it?" Cutting their charges somewhat, the railroads in 1865 held on to most of their wheat business. From 1866 to 1873 the rail lines drew more and more traffic away from the lower Mississippi. Wisconsin foes of the railroads joined in appeals to Congress to improve the river—especially to do something about the silt bars at its mouth and the rapids above Keokuk, Iowa—and Congress made appropriations, but the improvements failed to enable the river to compete with the rails in carrying such commodities as wheat.

Trains were taking business away from boats even on the upper Mississippi. After 1866 the railroad and steamboat

[18] Merk, *Economic History*, 338–342; George J. Kuehnl, *The Wisconsin Business Corporation* (Madison, 1959), 206–211.

interests there were separate, and the Northwestern Union
Packet Company dominated the river traffic between St. Paul
and St. Louis. At first this company operated thirty steamboats, eleven of them palatial side-wheelers, and 115 barges.
After 1867, when the Milwaukee and St. Paul extended its railroad to St. Paul, the number of vessels on the river began to
decline.[19]

Lake shipping also lost business to the railroads, though not
so drastically as river boating did. In the transport of goods to
and from the East, the railroads after 1865 gained an advantage
with the development of "through freight" or "fast freight"
companies, which owned their own cars and arranged with
interconnecting railroads to send the cars "through" from
shipper to consignee. One company guaranteed to deliver
Milwaukee shipments in New York in seven days. In 1866 more
than a third of the Milwaukee flour going east went by rail,
and by 1873 nearly two-thirds of it. Meanwhile a smaller
amount but increasing proportion of Wisconsin wheat also
went east by rail, and most of it by routes that avoided Milwaukee and other lake ports. More and more eastbound passengers
took the train, which was much faster and more convenient than
the lake steamer. In 1869 the Chicago and North Western was
running three trains a day from Milwaukee to Chicago, each
making the trip in less than four hours. A train left Chicago
at 3:15 in the afternoon and arrived in New York at 7:15 in
the morning of the second day, after forty hours en route. Sleeping cars went through without change, but there were as yet
no dining cars, and the train stopped from time to time for
meals.

To attract more freight to lake ports, businessmen in them
successfully brought about a reduction in transfer charges at
terminal facilities and in tolls on the Erie Canal. Shipping companies introduced steamboats of increased capacity and improved efficiency. While paddle-wheel passenger vessels continued gradually to disappear, screw-propeller freighters grew

[19] Merk, *Economic History,* 322–324, 355–362. Merk, on p. 324, quotes from
the Chicago *Tribune,* December 11, 1865. See also Rice, "Chicago, Milwaukee
and St. Paul Railway," 246–249.

in number as well as size. Sailing ships remained very active in local traffic on Lake Michigan, especially in the lumber trade, but the steamers dominated the long-distance transport through the lakes. As of 1873 the competition between the lakes and the railroads was approaching an equilibrium and was having some regulatory effect on long-haul railroad rates from Milwaukee to the East.

Milwaukee, as always more dependent on water routes than its great rival Chicago, was more interested in encouraging lake shipping. By 1869 the enlargement of Milwaukee harbor was long overdue. During the next few years the neglected stretch of the Milwaukee River near its mouth (south of the "straight cut" to Lake Michigan) was brought back into use, the narrow and shallow Kinnickinnic River was widened and deepened, and the Menomonee River was improved by the construction of canals. Already Milwaukee-based shipping lines were getting a good share of Lake Michigan commerce. Engelmann's East Shore Line operated six vessels back and forth from Milwaukee to Manistee and Grand Haven, Michigan. The Detroit and Milwaukee Line connected Milwaukee with eastern railroads by way of Grand Haven. The Goodrich Line, with six side-wheel steamers, provided regular passenger and freight service between Milwaukee and Chicago, Kenosha, Racine, Port Washington, Sheboygan, Manitowoc, and Two Rivers. This company continued to prosper even after the competing Milwaukee, Lake Shore and Western Railway had reached Sheboygan in 1872 and Manitowoc in 1873. By 1869 the tonnage of steamships registered at Milwaukee was greater than that at Chicago (12,453 to 11,175), though the tonnage of sailing vessels was much less (27,137 to 70,869). During the five years from 1869 to 1873, tonnage of ships built in each of the two ports totaled about the same.[20]

If the railroads were to have water competition on the Wisconsin transit itself, the old project of a water route across the state would have to be completed. The project had languished

[20] Merk, *Economic History*, 372–391; Bayrd Still, *Milwaukee: The History of a City* (Madison, 1965), 201n; Derby, "History of the Port of Milwaukee," 248–249, 255–261, 281–284, 312–333.

during the war, and by 1866 the Fox and Wisconsin Improvement Company was bankrupt. At a forced sale, in Appleton, a group of insiders that year bought its assets cheaply and reorganized it as the Green Bay and Mississippi Canal Company. The controlling group consisted mostly of New Yorkers, prominent among them Horatio Seymour, the wartime governor of New York. These financiers had investments in railroads, yet they sought federal aid for the waterway with the argument that the project, when finished, would serve as a restraint upon excessive railroad charges.

First the Green Bay and Mississippi Canal Company had to get from Congress an extension of time for the original land grant, which was due to expire in 1866. Then the company sought appropriations for making the Wisconsin River navigable from its mouth to Portage. After a new government survey, a report in 1868 recommended abandoning earlier plans to improve the river by means of wing dams. The report proposed, instead, that a canal be built alongside the river, crossing it at several points and passing through twenty-one locks. The estimated cost was $4,000,000. Congress never adopted this canal proposal but did appropriate money for wing dams from time to time. Finally, in 1872, the federal government purchased the company's interests in the waterway and took direct charge of the efforts to domesticate the Wisconsin. The company and its shrewd directors kept the rest of its assets—not only the water-power rights but also the land grant, which the federal government had given in the first place in order to finance the construction of the waterway.[21]

[5]

The iron horse by no means replaced the flesh-and-blood animal, though it did change some of the patterns of his use. As

[21] Joseph Schafer, *The Winnebago-Horicon Basin: A Type Study in Western History* (Madison, 1937), 126–131; Robert W. McCluggage, "The Fox-Wisconsin Waterway, 1836–1872: Land Speculation and Regional Rivalries, Politics and Private Enterprise" (doctoral dissertation, University of Wisconsin, 1954), 291–292, 315–350, 366–378.

of 1873, in fact, the period of his greatest service for draft purposes was yet to come, in Wisconsin as in other states. Wisconsin's count of horses in 1870 was 252,019, almost five times as large as the number of oxen, by then only 53,615. Many of the horses, like nearly all the oxen, were working in the fields, but more horses than ever before were pulling vehicles on the roads and streets.[22]

As railroads were built, they drove out of business the staging and freighting enterprises that had been operating coaches and wagons over the same routes. Yet the extension of tracks stimulated the opening of new stage and freight lines as feeders to the railroads. When, for example, the rails from Milwaukee reached Portage, in 1856, a stage began to run from there to Baraboo, and when they got to Kilbourn City another stage line was opened to Reedsburg. These stages carried passengers, mail, and express. When the railroad was completed from Madison to Baraboo and Reedsburg in 1872, the Madison-Baraboo stage line was discontinued. The trip had cost $2.50 and taken twelve hours by horse-drawn coach; it cost less than half as much and took only about an hour in the railroad cars. The Portage-Baraboo and Kilbourn-Reedsburg stages continued to operate, but only for local traffic. Where the later railroads extended into previously untapped territory, however, they were met at stops along the way, as the earlier railroads had been, by new stage and wagon lines that brought in passengers and freight.

The expansion of railroads delayed the development of good highways. Along the rail routes, existing wagon roads even deteriorated. Matt's Ferry, with its current-propelled boat attached to a rope across the Wisconsin River at Merrimac, was less efficiently run and less well kept up after the railroad had crossed the river nearby. (The ferry had already begun to suffer from a lack of maintenance, as a traveler from Madison found in 1871, when he had to drive his team through eighty yards of sandy shallows, in which he almost bogged down, be-

[22] *Ninth Census of the United States, 1870: Volume III,* p. 281.

fore reaching the boat.) The railroads had no interest in helping to facilitate wagon transport except in cases where they would directly benefit, as in the case of the bridge across the Wisconsin at the Dells. When this bridge was built in 1857, it was the most expensive and impressive in the state—a wooden truss structure 460 feet long with double tracks on top, eighty feet above the river, and a double carriageway thirty feet below the tracks. The carriageway was intended to give people on the opposite side of the river easy access to the railroad station at Kilbourn City. Still, for several years, the railroad company charged a toll for the use of its bridge. After the bridge's destruction by fire and reconstruction in 1866, the company opened it to public travel without charge. The company lost interest in maintaining a free bridge, however, once the rival North Western Railway had invaded the territory on the other side of the river by building to Baraboo and Reedsburg.[23]

The horse was as important for travel and transportation within cities as he was for getting from farm to town. Only Milwaukee had street railways with horsecars, the first of its lines, the River and Lake Shore, having opened in 1860. But other cities also depended on horse-drawn vehicles for the hauling of milk, bread, coal, and other necessities and for protection against fire. Like most of the rest of the country, Wisconsin could hardly get along without horses.

This fact was amply demonstrated when, in the fall and winter of 1872–1873, a plague of equine distemper hit the state. The epizooty was reported in Milwaukee on November 5 and in Beloit on the following day after moving westward from New York and, along the way, leaving horses incapacitated for periods of two or three weeks. In Milwaukee the disease

[23] Harry E. Cole, ed., *A Standard History of Sauk County, Wisconsin* . . . (2 vols., Chicago, 1918), 1: 314–319; Harry E. Cole, *Stagecoach and Tavern Days in the Baraboo Region* (Baraboo, Wisconsin, 1923), 32, 72; Gilson G. Glasier, ed., *Autobiography of Roujet D. Marshall, Justice of the Supreme Court of the State of Wisconsin, 1895–1918* (2 vols., Madison, 1923, 1931), 1: 228–230, 2: 289–299. In 1877 the Town of Newport and Columbia County began to pay the railway to maintain the bridge's pedestrian section.

spread rapidly through the livery stables, the city railway barns, and other horse-using establishments. The street railway stopped running. "The cars," a local paper observed, "have ceased to jolt." Deliveries were delayed. "Vast piles of goods cumber the sidewalks, and every available means of transportation is brought into requisition in delivering freight." Milkmen and bakers resorted to handcarts and draymen to ox teams, which they brought in from the countryside. The fire department was lucky enough to locate six yoke of oxen in Oconomowoc, but these were not enough to replace the stricken horses, and the mayor called upon citizens to help pull the engines and thus "save us from dire calamity." By the end of November the worst of the trouble was over in Milwaukee, but meanwhile the "horse epidemic" had pervaded Wisconsin. In January 1873 some areas of the state, from Monroe to the pineries above Eau Claire, were still recovering from the epizootic.[24]

The horseless carriage, as a practical device, lay a generation or more in the future, but already a forerunner had appeared in Wisconsin. This vehicle, the work of Dr. John W. Carhart, a preacher and physician recently arrived in Racine, had wagon wheels and a two-cylinder steam engine. It made a trial run on the Racine streets in 1873, but did not prove a practical success. Soon afterward the legislature offered a prize of $10,000 to any Wisconsin citizen who would develop a machine to take the place of the horse "on the highway and on the farm." Plank roads, railroads, waterways—all had been more or less disillusioning to Wisconsinites, yet the people remained eager for the improvement of transportation. They were ready to turn from the iron horse to the horseless carriage.[25]

[24] Still, *Milwaukee*, 248–249. Descriptions of the epidemic's effects are from the Milwaukee *Sentinel*, November 6, 11–13, 15, 26, December 2, 1872; January 10, 1873.

[25] Wisconsin State Highway Commission and United States Public Roads Administration, *A History of Wisconsin Highway Development, 1835–1945* (Madison, 1947), 19, quoting from *Laws of Wisconsin*, 1875, pp. 233–234; John W. Carhart in *DWB*. Though it is commonly held that Carhart built and tested his car in 1871, the Racine (weekly) *Journal*, May 7, 1873, confirms that the year was 1873.

13

The Halting Economy

W ITH the advent of peace, most of the states of the Northeast suffered a business decline, and uneasy Wisconsinites were
relieved when their state did not do the same. "There has been
apprehension among some that the closing up of the war and
the consequent fall of prices from war figures, would work widespread financial disaster," the Green Bay *Advocate* noted on
July 10, 1865. "But this has not proved true." The state's re-
spite was, however, brief. In 1867 Wisconsin and the rest of
the Northwest fell into a slump that lasted four years. Recovery
began in 1871, only to give way to the Panic of 1873, which
brought on the worst depression that the country had yet experienced.

During the postwar and predepression years, Wisconsin suffered from a shortage of money and credit. It was one of a number of states in the West and South that failed to get their
proportional share of the new national banks and national
banknotes. In 1865 it lost $2,300,000 in state banknotes when
a prohibitive federal tax wiped them out. At the same time it
gained less than $2,000,000 in note issues by its national banks.
It still lagged in 1870, when the census revealed that it had
less than 2.5 per cent as many national banknotes as the New
England states, though 12 per cent as much wealth. After 1870

the state banks in Wisconsin began to revive and to expand their loans, which they could do through the expanded use of checking accounts, since bank checks were more and more supplementing specie and currency as media of exchange. As yet, however, bank credit was not increasing fast enough to meet the needs of Wisconsin business. And the money supply would diminish if the federal government should retire the greenbacks, the inconvertible legal-tender treasury notes it had issued in the amount of over $400 million during the war. The effect would be deflationary even if the government did not eliminate the greenbacks but only provided for "specie payment," that is, for making them convertible into gold.[1]

Wisconsin businessmen continued to complain about the inadequacy of the available money and credit. In 1865 the "monetary facilities" fell short during the "busy season," according to a report of the Milwaukee Chamber of Commerce, and though the usual rate of interest was 10 per cent, "not infrequently money commanded 12 per cent and even higher rates in periods of great stringency in the market." In 1869 a Milwaukee delegate told the National Board of Trade that the West could not get sufficient money for "legitimate manufacturing purposes" at any reasonable rate, and in 1872 the Chamber of Commerce president said, "One thing that operates against a large increase of business is our deficiency in banking capital." Some local businessmen, conspicuous among them the large landowner Edward D. Holton, looked to gold as the only legitimate standard of value and called for making the greenbacks convertible into it. But others insisted that such a course would be disastrous for Wisconsin's economy, if not also for the nation's. "It would be for the general prosperity of this country," John Nazro, Milwaukee's "hardware king," declared in 1872, "if specie payments were not resumed

---

[1] Frederick Merk, *Economic History of Wisconsin During the Civil War Decade* (Madison, 1916), 228–229, quotes the Green Bay *Advocate*. See also Theodore A. Andersen, *A Century of Banking in Wisconsin* (Madison, 1954), 54–61.

for twenty years." (They were to be resumed in 1879, in accordance with an act that Congress passed in 1875, in the midst of the depression.) [2]

The idea of economic self-sufficiency for Wisconsin, or something approaching it, continued to have its advocates. "At present," the Milwaukee Chamber of Commerce lamented in 1871, "we are sending our hard lumber east to get it back as furniture and agricultural implements, we ship ores to St. Louis and New York, to pay the cost of bringing it back as shot, type, pipe, sheet lead, white lead, paint, etc., we ship away our wool crop and import cloths, carpets, blankets and other fabrics; we give rags for paper, and hides for boots and harness, and iron ore for stoves—and our consumers all the while are paying the double costs of this unnecessary transportation." In fact, the processing of raw materials within the state had advanced tremendously, even though Wisconsin did not yet approach self-sufficiency. By 1870, it was turning out manufactures that practically equaled in value all its farm productions.[3]

Between 1869 and 1872 the production and sale of Wisconsin wheat declined, yet wheat remained much the most valuable commodity among exports from the state. Then, in 1873, a good crop, over 26 million bushels in Wisconsin alone, resulted in shipments from Milwaukee that increased from about 14 million bushels in 1869 to nearly 25 million—the largest total ever. (By 1882 the total was to shrink to about

[2] Milwaukee Chamber of Commerce, *Annual Statement*, 1865, p. 56, complains of the tight-money market. The Milwaukee delegate who complains about the scarcity of capital is quoted in *Proceedings of the Second Annual Meeting of the National Board of Trade*, 1869, p. 194–197, 267–270. The Nazro quotation is from Milwaukee Chamber of Commerce, *Annual Report*, 1871, p. 143. See also *Proceedings of the Third Annual Meeting of the National Board of Trade*, 1870, pp. 191–193, 210–213; Milwaukee *Journal of Commerce*, November 13, 1872.

[3] Merk, *Economic History*, 124 (quotation); *Ninth Census of the United States, 1870: Volume III*, pp. 81, 582. For the year ending June 1, 1870, the value of all farm productions in Wisconsin was reported as $78,027,032; of all manufactured products, $77,214,326.

2 million bushels.) Other leading exports continued to be flour, lumber, and logs. Among the state's most significant imports were coal and salt in addition to manufactures of various kinds.[4]

[2]

There were signs of agricultural progress. Wild land continued to be converted into tillable fields, though not so rapidly during the war decade as during the 1850's, a gain of 2,153,176 acres in improved farms as compared with 2,700,668. Farmsteads in the older settled areas were looking better, with fewer log buildings and larger numbers of frame, brick, or stone. "Fewer of the old barns lie inaccessible and useless in the steaming, stenchy craters of surrounding manure heaps," the secretary of the State Agricultural Society observed in 1868; "and a less number of those newly built are found standing on the brow of a hill or on the brink of some stream, with a view to an easy riddance of such 'miserable offal' as, somehow, will accumulate in and about every stable and cow-yard!"

Whether or not stream pollution by manure was reduced, the water supply was improved in other ways. Windmills and pumps began to appear. In 1871 the youthful Roujet D. Marshall brought from Madison a new wind-powered "pumping rig," the first to be set up in his vicinity, to his father's farm in Delton township. No longer did he have to stand for hours at a stretch, shivering in the winter cold, to raise water for the livestock from the well—"a well consisting of a four-inch hole drilled in sand rock, eighty feet deep, equipped with a four by ninety-six inch tin bucket, with a valve in the bottom, attached to a rope and windlass by means of which a pail of

[4] John G. Thompson, *The Rise and Decline of the Wheat Growing Industry in Wisconsin* (Madison, 1909), 117–118; William E. Derby, "A History of the Port of Milwaukee, 1835–1910" (doctoral dissertation, University of Wisconsin, 1963), 288–314; *Ninth Census of the United States, 1870: Volume III,* pp. 583–584.

water at a time could be raised and discharged into the drinking trough."[5]

One measure of Wisconsin's advance beyond the pioneering stage of agriculture was the increase in the number of horses over the number of oxen. Much fewer than oxen in the state in 1850, horses had gone ahead by 1860 and, with a sharp decline in the ox count, were almost five times as numerous by 1870. The great majority of them were used as draft animals on the farms. Though horse breeding developed in Wisconsin, especially in Racine County, the breeders were mainly interested in the production of animals for riding and for pleasure driving, and they sold many of these for shipment to the western states. They gave little attention to improving the farm stock by crossing ordinary horses with thoroughbreds. As yet, Wisconsin had few heavy draft horses from abroad, few Percherons, Normans, Clydesdales, and the like. The common horses of the state, derived mostly from New York and Pennsylvania breeds, were rather small and light. They were not well suited for breaking virgin sod, and oxen continued to perform that slow, straining work.[6]

The mechanization of farms proceeded faster than ever. Wisconsin inventors contributed to it. Before the war, while working on his stepfather's farm in Iowa County, John F. Appleby at the age of eighteen had devised a knotting mechanism that was to become the basis for subsequent grain binders. After serving in the army he resumed his efforts to perfect the device, first on a farm near Mazomanie and later in Beloit.

[5] *Ibid.*, 81–91; Merk, *Economic History*, 44–45n, quotes the agricultural society official. See also Gilson G. Glasier, ed., *Autobiography of Roujet D. Marshall, Justice of the Supreme Court of the State of Wisconsin, 1895–1918* (2 vols., Madison, 1923, 1931), 1: 226–227.

[6] Joseph Schafer, *The Winnebago-Horicon Basin: A Type Study in Western History* (Madison, 1937), 192–201; Joseph Schafer, *A History of Agriculture in Wisconsin* (Madison, 1922), 117–120. The census counts in Wisconsin showed, for 1850, horses 30,179, oxen 42,801; for 1860, horses 116,180, oxen 93,652; and for 1870, horses 252,019, oxen 53,615. See *Ninth Census of the United States, 1870: Volume III*, pp. 82–91.

By 1872, Joseph Barta of Bangor (La Crosse County) had developed, patented, and sold to a manufacturer a binder of his own invention. Eventually Appleby was to win the competition after adapting his contrivance to the use of twine instead of wire. Meanwhile horsedrawn reapers, without the binding attachment, were becoming more and more numerous, as were horse-powered threshing machines. These threshers, with several teams of horses pulling the sweeps in a circle, were very hard on the animals. During the early 1870's, in Wisconsin as in other wheat-growing states and territories, movable steam engines began to drive threshers, and by the middle 1880's self-propelled steam engines, or tractors, were pulling some plows, reapers, and other equipment. Horse power had no sooner prevailed over ox power than it began to yield to steam power.[7]

The increase in wheat production from 1860 to 1869—and then the recovery and the new high in 1873 after a few years of decline—could also be taken as evidence of progress. By 1870 Dane, Dodge, and Columbia counties were the largest wheat producers, but the greatest proportional increases and highest yields per acre came from the comparatively fresh soils of St. Croix, Buffalo, and Trempealeau counties. As the center of wheat production shifted northwestward, the former leaders in the earlier settled southeast—Racine, Kenosha, Walworth, and Rock—had fallen far behind in both yield and total production. Overall, the quality of wheat shipped from Wisconsin was deteriorating. Of the 1865 crop, 71 per cent was graded "No. 1" and after 1868 the percentage fluctuated between 25 and 35. The average price per bushel remained high enough, until 1874, that most Wisconsin farmers were tempted to gamble on wheat

---

[7] John Francis Appleby in *DWB;* E. R. Jones, "A Bit of Twine Knotter History," in *WMH,* 12 (December, 1928), 225–227; Merle Curti, *The Making of an American Community: A Case Study of Democracy in a Frontier County* (Stanford, 1959), 162–175; Reynold M. Wik, *Steam Power on the American Farm* (Philadelphia, 1953), 60–81. For a vivid picture of threshing by horse power on a farm near Onalaska (La Crosse County) in the late 1860's, see Hamlin Garland, *A Son of the Middle Border* (New York, 1917), 50–57.

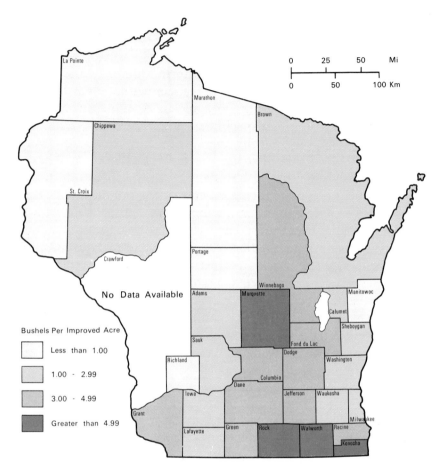

WHEAT YIELD, 1850

again and again, despite the risks of bad harvest weather, the effects of soil exhaustion, and the inroads of rust, smut, and finally the chinch bug.[8]

---

[8] Schafer, *Agriculture in Wisconsin*, 92–96; Merk, *Economic History*, 43–47; Derby, "History of the Port of Milwaukee," 288–290; Thompson, *Wheat Growing Industry*, 72. The percentages of "No. 1" refer to spring wheat received at Milwaukee. Spring wheat constituted much the larger part of the harvest; for Wisconsin, the census of 1870 reported 24,375,435 bushels of spring wheat and only 1,230,909 bushels of winter wheat for the preceding year. See *Ninth Census of the United States, 1870: Volume III*, p. 281.

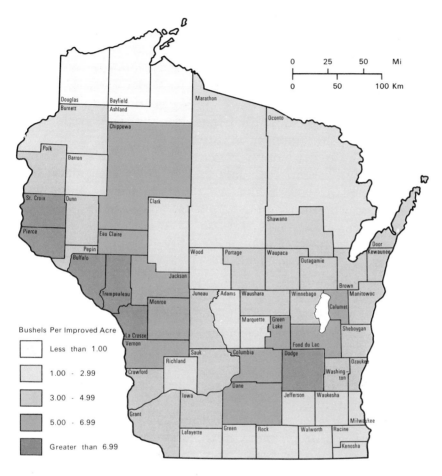

WHEAT YIELD, 1870

Diversification had been the watchword of Wisconsin's agricultural reformers since the beginning of statehood. Though the Civil War stimulated wheat production, it also encouraged experimentation with other farm products, such as sorghum and wool. After the war Wisconsin farmers experimented with still other things.

Many expected hops to make them rich, and many did profit handsomely for a time. Since the 1840's, hops had been grown in small quantities in Wisconsin. During the war the demand for them increased as the market for beer widened. Then, at the end of the war, the hop louse drastically cut the harvest in New York and other hop-producing states of the East. The price on the New York market rose from a high of 25 cents a pound in 1861 to as much as 70 cents in 1867. In response, more and more Wisconsin farmers turned to hop cultivation, and they enjoyed a bonanza as the state's yield went up from 135,587 pounds in 1861 to nearly 7 million in 1867. By then, Sauk County alone was said to be accounting for a fifth of the entire nation's crop, and the farmers of the county were realizing $1,500,000 on the one item. At harvest time boys, girls, and women assembled from far and near for a picking bee, at which they earned $1.50 to $2.00 and more a day. Suddenly, in 1868, disaster struck the Wisconsin growers when the Eastern crop recovered and the price dropped. Wisconsin hops, totaling almost 11 million pounds that year, brought to the grower an average of only 10 cents a pound, a price considerably less than the cost of production. The next year some farmers in the state made another try at hop growing but only added to their losses. Hops proved to be no lasting answer for farmers seeking an alternative to wheat.[9]

Another possibility was the sugar beet. The wartime scarcity of cane sugar had prompted Wisconsinites to experiment with beets as well as sorghum. Not till 1868, however, did the state's first sugar refinery appear, near Fond du Lac. This was the work of two German immigrants, one of them the former foreman of a refinery in Germany. Several other firms soon went into the business. One of the most successful, the First Sauk County Farmers' Association for the Fabrication of Beet Sugar, consisting of about fifty German farmers, relied on the services of another German sugar-refining expert. By 1870 the Milwaukee *Sentinel* could boast that Wisconsin's beet-sugar output exceeded the combined output of all the other states. So promising was the industry that, to encourage it, the legislature in

[9] Merk, *Economic History*, 37–43; Belle C. Bohn, "Hop Culture in Early Sauk County," in *WMH*, 18 (June, 1935), 389–394. For a contemporary account of the "hop craze," see the Milwaukee *Sentinel*, September 4, 1866.

1870 gave refining companies a ten-year exemption from taxes on their property and stock. Yet Wisconsin's beet sugar did not come close to equaling its maple sugar in value and failed to withstand the competition of Louisiana's returning cane sugar. Within a few years most of the Wisconsin refineries were out of business.[10]

Cranberries afforded a profitable enterprise for a few Wisconsin farmers and a rewarding sideline for others. Most of the cranberries grew wild, in sandy bogs with acidic water, and were gathered both for home consumption and for sale. The season for picking the berries was limited by state law. On a September day in 1866 a man and his three sons obtained thirteen bushels near New Lisbon, in an area where there were "a great many persons, some of whom were women and old men, and one was a soldier with but one leg, picking berries in the water about boot top deep." Already a few farmers were cultivating cranberries and producing them on a fairly large scale in the vicinity of Berlin.[11]

More important indications of the trend toward diversified farming were the increases in the acreage and production of corn, oats, and hay and in the numbers of livestock that they were used to feed—the horses, cows, pigs, and especially the sheep. Wisconsin's corn, oats, and hay acreage, which in the 1840's had been only slightly larger than that of wheat, by 1869 was producing a combined corn and oats harvest of 25 million bushels and a hay crop of 1,300,000 tons. During the 1870's the number of cattle was to grow at an accelerating rate, but during the 1860's the number of sheep grew much faster than the number of cows (sheep from 332,954 to 1,069,282; milk cows from 203,001 to 308,377). Wisconsin seemed on the way to becoming a wool-growing rather than a dairying state. Indeed, when the census takers made their rounds in 1870,

[10] Merk, *Economic History*, 33–34; Eric E. Lampard, *The Rise of the Dairy Industry in Wisconsin: A study in Agricultural Change, 1820–1920* (Madison, 1963), 51.

[11] Neil E. Stevens and Jean Nash, "The Development of Cranberry Growing in Wisconsin," in *WMH*, 27 (March, 1944), 276–294. The quotation is from the diary of Jabez Brown, August 27–September 8, 1866, in the Jabez Brown Papers.

only twenty-five Wisconsinites identified themselves as dairy-men or dairywomen. But in fact a much larger number of the 159,687 men and women engaged in agriculture were produc-ing butter and cheese, and fifty-four cheese factories were counted. These factories had sprung up recently in Wisconsin, the first one at Ladoga (Fond du Lac County) in 1864, the founder of which, Chester Hazen, was a recent arrival from New York state where the factory system of cheese making was already well established. The early development of cheese production in Wisconsin owed the most to New Yorkers, the descendants of English dairy farmers, who produced cheddar in the southeastern counties, but also to Germans in the east-central region and to Swiss settlers who produced Swiss and limburger in Green and neighboring counties. By 1870, slight-ly more than half of Wisconsin's cheese was factory made, and the whole output, of farm and factory, gave Wisconsin sixth place among the cheese-producing states, but Wisconsin still lagged far behind New York, the leader (3 million pounds to more than 100 million pounds). Wisconsin was eighth among the states in butter production.

Though countless men and women were to contribute to the rise of Wisconsin as a dairy state, no one was to make a bigger contribution than William D. Hoard. A New Yorker by birth and upbringing, Hoard lost money in the hop craze and then, in 1870, as publisher of the *Jefferson County Union*, turned to the promotion of dairying. He quickly perceived two obstacles to increasing the sales of Wisconsin butter and cheese. One was the bad reputation of the products, resulting from a lack of standards and the consequent poor quality in many cases. The other was the difficulty of reaching the mar-kets. Until 1872, almost all the Wisconsin cheese was sold to dealers in Chicago, New York, and Philadelphia, but this market was becoming glutted, and new outlets had to be found in the East and abroad. To deal with these problems, Hoard helped to organize the Wisconsin Dairymen's Association in 1872. This association undertook to improve the quality, uniformity, and packing of the state's cheese and butter, and it arranged for fast shipment in refrigerator cars, which were just coming into use, at reduced rates. By 1873 Wisconsin cheese was beginning to compete with New York cheese not only in the Eastern states but also in England.

As yet, however, the dairy revolution in Wisconsin was still in its earliest stages. To go into dairying, a farmer had to make a comparatively large expenditure for cows, shelter, and equipment. To succeed, he had to discipline himself to a rather difficult routine. So long as he could continue to get cash for wheat or wool, he hesitated to go heavily into debt in order to try something new. Wisconsin the dairyland—with its ubiquitous herds, its tremendous barns, and its towering silos— lay in the future.[12]

Whether or not they took up dairying, farmers continued to need money for clearing land, acquiring machinery, and expanding their production of wheat and other crops. They borrowed mainly from local lenders—from wealthier farmers or from bankers, mortgage brokers, or attorneys willing to extend credit with land as security—and to a much lesser extent from lenders in New York and other Eastern states. In Dane County more than half the farms were mortgaged by 1873, though this included only a few of the larger ones containing 160 acres or more. The typical debt ranged from $300 to $400, ran for a period between one and five years, and bore 10 per cent interest. The burden, already heavy for some farmers, became worse even before the onset of the depression. Foreclosures in the county increased from sixty-two in 1869 to seventy-seven in 1870 and ninety-seven in 1871, then fell to seventy-six in 1872 but jumped to 116 in 1873. In this panic year the record harvest of wheat failed to save the hard-pressed farmers, since the price suddenly collapsed, falling from $1.22

---

[12] Merk, *Economic History*, 22–30; Shafer, *Agriculture in Wisconsin*, 154–159; Lampard, *Rise of the Dairy Industry*, 23, 95–109, 112–113, 121–141; *Ninth Census of the United States, 1870: Volume I*, p. 764; *ibid.: Volume III*, pp. 81–91, 794; William Dempster Hoard in *DWB*.

to 90 cents in one month. Thus the panic and depression added its discouragement to the concentration on wheat as a cash crop.[13]

[3]

Next to the products of the farm, those of the forest were the most important for postwar Wisconsin. Already by 1860 the lumber industry, including wood manufactures of all kinds, produced more than one-fourth of the state's output. By 1870 it accounted for some 30 per cent of the industrial production, as measured by value, and for nearly 45 per cent of the industrial employment. During the decade, Wisconsin moved from sixth to fourth place among the lumbering states. Pennsylvania, New York, and Michigan led.

The Wisconsin pineries—mainly white pine—were being cut at a fast-accelerating rate. For the winter of 1860–1861 the harvest had been less than 400 million board feet, a considerable decline from the prewar high of about 475 million for 1856–1857. For the 1866–1867 season the timber cut totaled approximately 800 million board feet, more than twice as much as six years earlier. By 1871–1872 the yield had doubled again, amounting to some 1,600 million board feet. Not for nine years was this figure to be equaled. Lumber prices had been high and the business profitable during the period of greatest production, but prices and profits as well as output fell with the coming of the general depression.[14]

Preparations for the annual assault on the forest began in the summer with the construction of lumber camps and log-

[13] Alexander C. Kern, "Farm Loans and Mortgage Foreclosures in Dane County from 1867 to 1875" (master's thesis, University of Wisconsin, 1933), 37–45, 52, 64–66.

[14] Robert F. Fries, *Empire in Pine: The Story of Lumbering in Wisconsin, 1830–1900* (Madison, 1951), 108–111; *Ninth Census of the United States, 1870: Volume III*, pp. 583–584, 612–613; Merk, *Economic History*, 63–66. The figures on lumber harvests are from Merk, who bases his estimates on data from newspapers and other sources. Fries, p. 102, states that Eastern money provided the economic foundation of the Wisconsin lumber industry until the Civil War, after which businessmen in Chicago and Mississippi river towns invested heavily.

ging roads. In the autumn additional men were hired, oxen shod and other equipment readied, supplies gathered, and all sent upriver by boat or, in some cases, overland by wagon or train. During the winter the red-shirted lumberjacks, encamped in the woods, felled the pines with ax and saw, cut them into logs, and dragged or sledded these to frozen streams. With the coming of the spring thaw the logs floated down the flooding rivers, to be caught and stored in booms, or reservoirs, enclosed by strings of timbers. The log drive might be held up by a log jam, especially in times of low water. One of the worst jams occurred in 1869, when a boom above Chippewa Falls broke and the logs stranded in the rapids. More and more logs accumulated, until they backed up for fifteen miles and, in places, rose thirty feet into the air.

At a boom the logs were sorted in accordance with the log marks on them indicating ownership. The logs might go to mills in the immediate vicinity, or they might be consigned to mills farther downstream. In the latter case they might make the rest of the trip in the form of rafts. Log rafts originating on the Wisconsin tributaries of the Mississippi floated on down that river or, from 1865 on, were combined into larger rafts and were towed down the Mississippi by steamboats. Logs descending the Wolf River and fastened together at booms in Lake Poygan were pulled by steam tugs to Oshkosh and over Lake Winnebago to Fond du Lac. On the Menominee the logs were driven part of the way and rafted the rest of the way to Marinette.[15]

The location of sawmills depended in part on the ease of transporting logs. Along the Wisconsin River—whose shallows, narrows, and sinuosities made log-driving difficult—the mills were comparatively scattered, being placed as close as possible to the sites of lumbering operations. On the rest of the state's main logging rivers the mills clustered in certain areas. On the Chippewa, for example, they were mostly in the vicinity of

[15] Richard N. Current, *Pine Logs and Politics: A Life of Philetus Sawyer, 1816–1900* (Madison, 1950), 116–117; Fries, *Empire in Pine,* 16–33, 45–55; Merk, *Economic History,* 66–69, 95.

Chippewa Falls and Eau Claire, to which logs were brought from as far away as a hundred miles. On the Mississippi, near the mouth of the Black, was the sawmilling center of La Crosse. Elsewhere along the Mississippi, in the states of Minnesota, Iowa, Illinois, and Missouri, as well as Wisconsin, were still other mills that converted Wisconsin logs into lumber.

In both forest and mill the lumber industry depended upon the labor of immigrants, mainly Scandinavians, Germans, and Irish. By the end of the war loggers could earn as much as three to four dollars per day, with board, although wages fell far below that level during periods of depressed lumber prices. Women and children joined men in the sawmills and shingle mills, more so during periods of acute labor shortage.[16]

Improvements in machinery made the mills more and more productive. As late as 1870, waterwheels still outnumbered steam engines (427 to 377) in Wisconsin's sawmilling industry, but the steam engines were becoming larger and more efficient, and they already exceeded the waterwheels in total horsepower (16,119 to 11,668). The steam engines used sawdust for fuel, and a steam-powered device, developed in a Chippewa River mill in the late 1860's, carried the sawdust automatically from the saws to the boiler. Circular saws had recently come into general use; they were often supplemented by the gang saw, which consisted of several blades moving up and down together and could rip a log into several boards at once. As power and efficiency increased, so did the output per mill. In 1860 few plants could cut more than 50,000 board feet in a twelve-hour day. In 1867 one mill at Chippewa Falls produced 207,400 feet, and for a month in 1873 it produced an average daily cut of 325,000 feet. Meanwhile, during the decade of the 1860's, the number of sawmilling establishments in Wisconsin increased by less than 40 per cent, from 520 to 720, yet the state's total production of sawed lumber, as measured by value, increased by more than 225 per cent, from $4,616,430 to $15,130,719.[17]

[16] Fries, *Empire in Pine*, 13, 41–42, 55, 204–205; Merk, *Economic History*, 61.

[17] Fries, *Empire in Pine*, 41–42, 61; Merk, *Economic History*, 69–72; *Ninth Census of the United States, 1870: Volume III*, pp. 612–613.

From the mills along the watercourses emptying into Green Bay, ships carried the sawed lumber to yards in Milwaukee, Racine, and especially Chicago, which was much the largest single market for the Wisconsin product. From the mills along the tributaries of the Mississippi the lumber went to market in rafts, each of them consisting of several cribs and each of these consisting of twelve to twenty layers of boards. On the Mississippi the raft was perfected into larger rafts which, like the log rafts, were towed by steamboats (the towing of lumber rafts on the Mississippi had begun in 1864, one year before the towing of log rafts). The Mississippi lumber rafts grew larger and larger; by 1870, one of them might cover as much as three or four acres. All the way from Prairie du Chien to St. Louis, practically every river town was a marketing place for lumber. As railroads began to penetrate the pine regions, some rough lumber found its way to market by rail, but not a very large amount, since rail freight was much more expensive than water transport.[18]

It did pay, however, to ship finished lumber and millwork by rail. As soon as a mill owner gained access to a railroad, he had an opportunity to add to the value of his product by further processing it. "We should continually bear in mind . . . ," the Oshkosh *Journal* urged on November 6, 1869, "that the greater the quantity of skilled human labor which is added to a given quantity of raw material, the greater will be the wealth of the people." The editor called not only for mills to convert pine into sash, doors, and the like but also for factories to work up the hardwoods, which could not be floated down the

[18] Fries, *Empire in Pine,* 65–83; Merk, *Economic History,* 79–89. The rafting of both logs and lumber was a rather heroic enterprise. See J. M. Turner (a former raft pilot), "Rafting on the Mississippi," in *WMH,* 23–24 (December, 1939–September, 1940), 23: 163–176, 313–327, 430–438; 24: 56–65; W. H. Glover, "Lumber Rafting on the Wisconsin River," in *WMH,* 25 (December, 1941– March, 1942), 155–177, 308–324; and A. R. Reynolds, "Rafting Down the Chippewa and the Mississippi: Daniel Shaw Lumber Company, a Type Study," in *WMH,* 32 (December, 1948), 143–152. Log driving also had its heroes. Seventeen-year-old Edward Ankney, for one, astonished spectators on June 24, 1867, by standing on a log and riding it through the rapids of the Wisconsin Dells. See the Milwaukee *Sentinel,* June 27, 1867, which compared the feat to that of the famous contemporary tightrope walker Blondin in crossing over Niagara Falls.

rivers and therefore were being largely neglected. Already some hardwood as well as a considerable amount of pine was being used for wood manufactures in the state. By 1869 Wisconsin led all states in the production of shingles. Increasingly these were made by machinery, but they also continued to be turned out by hand, especially among the Germans and Belgians of the northeast, and Green Bay was the main center of the shingle trade. The more sophisticated woodworking plants were located principally at points around Lake Winnebago, in the lower Fox Valley, and along the Lake Michigan shore. From the many mills and factories came sash, doors, blinds, tubs, pails, churns, hubs, spokes, wagons, railroad cars, furniture (Sheboygan was already becoming noted for its chairs), and boats, not to mention lath, staves, and railroad ties. All together, the planed lumber, millwork, woodenware, and other wood manufactures by 1870 were bringing in more than half as much money as was the rough-sawed lumber.[19]

Sawmilling centers competed strenuously with one another, and no two of them more strenuously than Eau Claire and Chippewa Falls. The millmen of Eau Claire wished to erect at the Dells of the Chippewa a dam that would have contributed to the economic growth of Eau Claire at the expense of its neighbor and rival. In 1860 they had prevailed upon the legislature to pass the necessary bill, but a leading lumberman of Chippewa Falls had persuaded the governor to veto it. Repeatedly the advocates of the project lobbied for new legislation, and repeatedly the opponents managed to prevent it. In 1871 the legislature again passed a bill for the Chippewa Dells dam, and the governor again vetoed it, amid rumors of legislative bribes.

Meanwhile the Eau Claire and the Chippewa Falls millmen took the same side, at least for a time, in another conflict, known as the "Beef Slough war." This one pitted the upriver saw-

[19] Fries, *Empire in Pine*, 60–65; Merk, *Economic History*, 76–79, 146–148; Current, *Pine Logs and Politics*, 115–119 (quoting the Oshkosh *Journal*); Hjalmar R. Holand, *History of Door County, Wisconsin: The County Beautiful* (2 vols., Chicago, 1917), 1: 415; *Ninth Census of the United States, 1870: Volume III*, pp. 583–584.

milling interests, including those of both Chippewa Falls
and Eau Claire, against the downriver sawmilling interests,
such as those of La Crosse and of the Minnesota, Iowa, Illinois,
and Missouri lumber towns along the Mississippi. Allied with
the downriver sawmillers were timberland owners and loggers
and log drivers who supplied those sawmillers. Beef Slough,
the lesser of two channels of the Chippewa River near its
mouth, was a perfect place to sort logs and prepare them for
rafting to the downriver mills. To prevent its use for that purpose, the Chippewa River mill owners in 1866 bought land at
the entrance to the slough and secured from the legislature a
charter giving them the exclusive use of the channel.

Some Mississippi River mill owners then, in 1867, organized
the Beef Slough Manufacturing, Booming, Log Driving &
Transportation Company and began a campaign to obtain
rights to build and operate a boom there. In 1869 the company
got the rights by means of a legislative ruse and with the aid of
a Chippewa Falls lumberman who turned against the Eau Claire
lumbermen because of the Chippewa Dells controversy. Against
the continued resistance of most of the local mill owners and
their employees, who from time to time threatened a gun
battle, the Beef Slough company found it hard to carry on its
business and soon went bankrupt. In 1870 Frederick Weyerhaeuser, the German-born owner of a sawmill at Rock Island,
Illinois, and of timberland on the upper Chippewa, led a group
of Mississippi River lumbermen in leasing the Beef Slough
company's rights and in setting up a new firm, the Mississippi
River Logging Company. Eventually this syndicate was to
gain an almost complete monopoly of Chippewa Valley timber, and Weyerhaeuser was to emerge as the lumber king of
the Middle West and then of the Pacific Northwest.[20]

Though ultimately the largest, the Weyerhaueser combina-

[20] Paul W. Gates, *The Wisconsin Pine Lands of Cornell University: A Study
in Land Policy and Absentee Ownership* (Ithaca, 1943), 127–131; Daniel J.
Dykstra, "Law and the Lumber Industry, 1861–1881" (doctoral dissertation, University of Wisconsin, 1950), 213–286; Merk, *Economic History*, 90–95. See also
Ralph W. Hidy, Frank E. Hill, and Allan Nevins, *Timber and Men: The Weyerhaeuser Story* (New York, 1963), 45–51.

tion was only one of several large companies that developed as lumbering became more and more a big business, a highly integrated industry. Among the leading enterprisers were Knapp, Stout & Company, of Menomonie; the Union Lumber Company, headed by Thaddeus C. Pound, of Chippewa Falls; N. Ludington and Company, including Isaac Stephenson and Daniel Wells, Jr., of Marinette; the Eau Claire Lumber Company, under Joseph G. Thorp, and Daniel Shaw and Company, also of Eau Claire; and P. Sawyer & Son, of Oshkosh. In the early 1870's, Knapp, Stout & Company was reputed to be the largest lumber corporation in the world. The company carried integration to an extreme, not only operating sawmills but also owning pine lands, cutting and rafting logs, maintaining wholesale and retail lumberyards, manufacturing and repairing equipment, selling general merchandise to lumberjacks, and even farming and flour milling to provide food for the men and feed for the animals. The Union Lumber Company, having acquired comparatively little timberland of its own, suffered in consequence of rising stumpage costs and filed for bankruptcy following the Panic of 1873, occasioning tremendous hardship in Chippewa Falls. Other, less well capitalized companies also went under during the depression, and the monopolistic trend was hastened as surviving firms took over collapsing ones.

The lumber corporations along with the railroad corporations dominated the state legislature, and it did little or nothing to limit corporate size or activity. It assisted the lumbermen in their pursuit of profit, conferring special favors on them in their corporate charters. Thus, in 1866, it quickly passed a bill to incorporate the Eau Claire Lumber Company, a bill that Joseph G. Thorp had introduced, Thorp being both a state senator and the president of the firm. The act, which other lumbermen used as a model, gave few rights to stockholders and practically a free hand to the president and directors. Charters for boom companies bestowed even greater authority. For example, the charter of the Black River Improvement Company, which nineteen lumbermen of the Black

River Valley launched in 1864, granted the right of eminent domain and along with it the power to transform the landscape by constructing dams and rechanneling the river in Clark, Jackson, Trempealeau, and La Crosse counties. The 1871 act incorporating the Wausau Boom Company allowed this company to maintain virtual control over all Wisconsin River traffic in Marathon County.

These and other charters, including the one creating the Beef Slough company, encouraged monopolies by giving groups of lumbermen exclusive powers within certain districts. The lumbermen would have obtained fewer privileges if they had been compelled to incorporate under the general incorporation law of 1858 rather than being permitted to do so under special chartering acts. A constitutional amendment of 1871 and a new general law of 1872 tightened somewhat the requirements for incorporating, but the basis for the fabulous lumber fortunes of Wisconsin had already been laid in the era of loose incorporation laws.[21]

[4]

Lawmakers as well as lumbermen and farmers lacked interest in planning for the careful utilization of the Wisconsin forest. They concerned themselves, instead, with questions of "who could get the most the quickest" out of that fabulous resource, which once had been the property of the public. There resulted two disasters—one, the eventual deforestation of the state; the other, more immediate, one of the worst conflagrations in American history.

Before 1873 the legislature enacted a number of regulatory measures, but these were intended to protect lumbermen from each other, not to protect the trees. Laws forbade the altering of log marks, the unauthorized processing of logs other than

[21] Fries, *Empire in Pine*, 108, 122–160; Gates, *Wisconsin Pine Lands*, 124–125; Merk, *Economic History*, 72–75; Current, *Pine Logs and Politics*, 104–105; Dykstra, "Law and the Lumber Industry," 16–21, 35–39, 54–57, 69–70, 84–85, 96–97, 101. See also J. Willard Hurst, *Law and Economic Growth: The Legal History of the Lumber Industry in Wisconsin, 1836–1915* (Cambridge, 1964), 180–193.

one's own, or the obstructing of navigable streams. Other laws laid out lumber districts and put in each of them an inspector who was to facilitate log and timber transactions by authenticating the quantities involved. But no law provided for the protection of either the rivers or the woods. The state did not even take good care of its own timberlands, the school and university lands, upon which loggers continually and brazenly poached. In 1865 the commissioners of the school and university lands protested "this robbery of the children's inheritance." Rangers policed these lands during the logging season, but in 1871 the number of rangers was reduced from eight to four. Timber thieves, when caught on the state's lands, were merely required to buy the land they had stripped and to pay a penalty of 50 per cent of the price.[22]

"In a few years," a petition from Black River Falls millmen said in 1867, "the wealthiest portion of the pineries will present nothing but a vast and gloomy wilderness of pine stumps." The petition, however, was not asking the legislature to do anything effectively to conserve the forest. It was only calling for action against a log-driving association that was supplying downriver competitors. Few indeed were the real conservationists at that time, but there were some in the State Agricultural Society and in the State Horticultural Society. In response to the wishes of these two groups, the legislature in 1867 authorized a commission to look into the questions of forest depletion and what to do about it.

The three-member commission, with the self-made scientist Increase A. Lapham as its chairman, put together a hundred-page *Report on the Disastrous Effects of the Destruction of Forest Trees, Now Going on So Rapidly in the State of Wisconsin* (Madison, 1867). This report elaborated on the themes of Lapham's 1855 article, "The Forest Trees of Wisconsin," and incorporated the ideas of George Perkins Marsh, a Vermont lawyer, diplomat, and scholar whose 1864 book *Man and Nature; or, Physical Geography as Modified by Hu-*

---

[22] Merk, *Economic History,* 104–108 (quotation); Dykstra, "Law and the Lumber Industry," 26–27, 104, 286, 294–329, 355–356, 431–434, 486–488, 527.

man Action, was a pioneering conservationist work. Lapham and his fellow commissioners showed that "clearing the land of trees" not only threatened the wood supply but also harmed the natural environment, drying out the ground and diminishing the flow of springs while increasing the "suddenness and magnitude of floods and torrents" and permitting the soil to wash away. The commissioners found plenty of illustrations in Wisconsin, such as the case of the Milwaukee River and its tributaries, where mills had had to change over to steam because of declining waterpower and where spring floods had become "sufficient to carry away bridges and dams before deemed secure." In concluding, the commissioners urged that the state take action to conserve wood, as it was already doing to protect wildlife. "It would require no greater stretch of power to regulate the cutting of timber where it would obviously entail a public calamity, or to encourage its production where it is so much needed for the public good."

In response to the Lapham report, the legislature did nothing to regulate timber cutting and passed only an ineffectual measure to encourage timber production. This law of 1868 offered tax exemptions and cash bounties to landowners who would plant tree belts on their property along roads. Though the law remained in effect until 1905, apparently nobody ever took advantage of it. Meanwhile, a few voices continued to speak of the impending doom of Wisconsin and its forests. These would be exhausted in twenty-five years, predicted George Pinney, a Sturgeon Bay minister, in a paper he read before the State Horticultural Society in 1872. He denounced the lumbermen as an "army of vandals" who "like vampires" were "drawing the very life blood of our future prosperity, and rioting on the proceeds of pine boards and cedar posts." But the state was to take no effective steps toward forest conservation until there were practically no forests left to be conserved.[23]

[23] Merk, *Economic History,* 95, quoting from the petition. Vernon Carstensen, *Farms or Forests: Evolution of a State Land Policy for Northern Wisconsin, 1850–1932* (Madison, 1958), 7–15, quotes from the commission's report on the effects of clearing the land of trees, and quotes also from the remarks of George

In the absence of effective legal or other restraints, the lumber industry operated with enormous waste. Loggers cut the trees high and topped them low, leaving good wood behind in the stumps and trimmings. Log drivers and raftsmen lost countless logs that sank irretrievably in sloughs and other backwaters. According to a later estimate of the state forester, less than half of the usable timber of Wisconsin's great north woods ever reached the sawmill; the rest was left to rot or burn. At the sawmill the wastefulness continued. The circular saw cut a kerf a half inch wide, converting an excessive portion of the log into sawdust. While some of the larger and more up-to-date mills salvaged sawdust as fuel and used slabs to make lath, most of the other mills treated both sawdust and slabs as refuse, either dumping them in a stream or throwing them on a constantly burning pile.

Fire was an ever-present hazard throughout the forested area, and careless lumbering intensified the danger. The branches that loggers left in great heaps turned into tinder in dry weather, as did the timber trash that farmers put at the edges of their clearings and that railroad construction crews dragged to the sides of their rights of way. Almost everything else in the area was also combustible—the mounds of sawdust and other mill refuse, the roads corduroyed with brush and split logs over swampy ground, the streets filled and paved with sawdust, the sidewalks made of boards, the bridges consisting of planks upon timbers, the railroad ties, the houses built of logs or lumber and roofed with wooden shingles. Few were the sawmills that never burned down, and rare was the summer without a serious forest fire. Especially bad were the summers of 1863, 1864, and 1868. In 1863 flames swept the southwestern shore of Lake Superior, and smoke drifted for more than a hundred miles, darkening the sky as far away as

---

Pinney. The quotation about the spring floods is from Milo M. Quaife, "Increase Allen Lapham, Father of Forest Conservation," in *WMH*, 5 (September, 1921), 104–108. Graham P. Hawks, "Increase A. Lapham: Wisconsin's First Scientist" (doctoral dissertation, University of Wisconsin, 1960), 143–145, quotes from the report's conclusion that the state should take action to conserve wood. "The Forest Trees in Wisconsin" may be found in Wisconsin State Agricultural Society, *Transactions*, 1855, pp. 195–251.

La Crosse. The next year the fires were more widespread, threatening many settlements in heavily wooded areas, especially Wausau, Two Rivers, and Neillsville (Clark County). In 1868 the devastation was even more extensive, with bad fires along the Chippewa, Black, Wisconsin, and Wolf rivers and in Kewaunee and Door counties. But much the most terrible holocaust was yet to come. It struck northeastern Wisconsin, on both sides of the Green Bay, in the early fall of 1871.[24]

Since July 8, there had been no rain to speak of in that part of the state. By the summer's end, even the marshes were dry. Here and there small fires smoldered along the ground, further drying out the leaves of the trees and occasionally flaring up. "In the first week of October the air was so saturated with smoke that it pained the eyes," a resident of Little Chute wrote soon afterward, "and at night a reddish glow hung in the sky and struck fear in the heart of everyone." Much more vulnerable than the people of Little Chute were those of localities to the northeast, in Kewaunee and Door counties on the east side of the bay and in Oconto and Marinette counties on the other side.

There, in the evening of Sunday, October 8, a brisk wind suddenly came up, bringing thick clouds of smoke, showers of sparks, and long, leaping tongues of flame. On both sides of the bay these turned into veritable tornadoes of fire, with an unearthly roaring sound and the crash of falling trees. It seemed like the end of the world and, for many, it was. Only seventeen of about eighty inhabitants survived in the shingle-manufacturing settlement of Williamsonville, near Sturgeon Bay; thirty-five of the dead were huddled in a potato patch in the center of a clearing, hundreds of feet from the nearest woods. The catastrophe was worst at the village of Peshtigo, a few miles southwest of Marinette, where hundreds died and others saved themselves only by standing neck-deep in the Peshtigo River and dousing themselves to avoid the flames that billowed out over the water.

By the next morning the fires (to be remembered collectively

---

[24] Merk, *Economic History*, 70, 99–103; Bernhardt J. Kleven, "The Wisconsin Lumber Industry" (doctoral dissertation, University of Minnesota, 1941), 223–236.

as "the Peshtigo fire") had subsided, and before long a heavy rain began to fall. Reduced to ashes and charred ruins was a roughly fifteen-by-sixty-mile stretch of land west of the bay and a five-by-fifty-mile stretch on the Door peninsula. Within those areas, countless houses, barns, and other buildings had been destroyed, and fields as well as forests were now blackened wastes. Nobody knows how many persons lost their lives; estimates run as high as 1,500 but the actual number is probably between 1,200 and 1,300. Many others were injured, and several times as many lost their homes and all or nearly all their possessions.

On the very same night as the Wisconsin conflagrations—October 8, 1871—occurred the great Chicago fire. Though this destroyed many more buildings, it caused fewer deaths (about 250). Yet the Chicago disaster overshadowed the Wisconsin one, temporarily drawing away the attention even of Wisconsinites. Governor Lucius Fairchild, other state officials, and most of the legislators were in Chicago when they learned what had happened in their own state. They had got together a trainload of supplies for destitute Chicagoans and had gone along to oversee the distribution. By the time the governor could return to Madison, his twenty-five-year-old wife already had taken charge of Wisconsin relief, sending north from the capital a freight car that had been readied for Chicago, and arranging for other cars to be sent from Watertown, Fond du Lac, and Oshkosh. Governor Fairchild hurried to Green Bay to get a firsthand impression of the needs. The United States Army provided blankets, clothing, and rations of bacon, beans, and hardtack, but most of the assistance came from state funds and from private donations, especially from those of the Fairchild-led relief society. Afterward the governor reported that Wisconsin's "little children" had "emptied their long-hoarded savings-banks of pennies" in order to help the sufferers.[25]

[25] Robert W. Wells, *Fire at Peshtigo* (Englewood Cliffs, New Jersey, 1968), *passim*. See P. Pernin, "The Finger of God Is There,' in *WMH*, 2 (December, 1918–March, 1919), 158–180, 274–293, for an eyewitness account; and Arnold Verstegen to relatives in the Netherlands, October 20, 1871, in Henry S. Lucas, ed., *Dutch Immigrant Memoirs and Related Writings* (2 vols., Assen, Nether-

[5]

Wisconsin industry remained, on the whole, rather rudimentary during the immediate postwar years. More than two-thirds of its $77,000,000 output consisted of the primary processing of the yield from the forest, the field, and the mine. Yet the state already could boast some highly sophisticated manufacturing and even a capacity for mechanical innovation.

Manufacturing continued to be concentrated in Milwaukee County, which by 1870 had less than 9 per cent of the state's population but turned out about 23 per cent of its manufactured goods. Yet, during the 1860's, industrial production had been growing very little faster in Milwaukee County than in the state as a whole. Some other counties, foremost among them Winnebago and Fond du Lac, had been making much more rapid proportional gains, while still others, such as Dodge and Dane, had fallen far behind. Though Milwaukee produced nearly a quarter of the state's industrial output, the counties of Winnebago, Fond du Lac, Racine, Rock, and Jefferson together produced somewhat more than Milwaukee did, and the rest of the state accounted for the remaining production, almost half of the total.[26]

---

lands, 1955), 2: 172–174, for the quotation on the smoke-saturated air. See also Holand, *History of Door County*, 1: 421–428; Sam Ross, *The Empty Sleeve: A Biography of Lucius Fairchild* (Madison, 1964), 152–153; Joseph Schafer, "Great Fires of Seventy-One," in *WMH*, 11 (September, 1927), 104–106 (quotation about the children's donations).

[26] According to the *Eighth Census of the United States, 1860: Manufactures*, 656, and the *Ninth Census of the United States, 1870: Volume III*, p. 582, the leading counties in regard to value of manufactured products and the respective amounts in millions of dollars, were as follows:

1860	*1870*
1. Milwaukee (6.7)	1. Milwaukee (18.8)
2. Rock (2.0)	2. Winnebago (5.2)
3. Racine (1.3)	3. Fond du Lac (4.1)
4. Dodge (1.2)	4. Racine (3.8)
5. Fond du Lac (1.1)	5. Rock (3.5)
6. Dane (1.0)	6. Jefferson (2.5)
7. Winnebago (0.97)	7. Manitowoc (2.3)

Milwaukee's share of the state's total of $27,849,467 was 24.1 per cent in 1860 and 24.4 per cent of the $77,214,326 total for 1870. During the 1860's the state's industrial output increased 2.78 times; Milwaukee's increased 2.81 times.

Next to lumber, the most valuable product of Wisconsin industry was flour. But flour constituted only about one-fourth
of all manufactures (by value) in 1870, as compared with
two-fifths in 1860. This relative decline in the importance
of flour milling reflected the growing diversification of the
state's industry as a whole. In the immediate postwar years the
manufacture of flour for distant markets increased rapidly, and
milling became more and more concentrated, though small,
scattered mills continued to produce for local sale and to grind
the grain that farmers brought in for their own use.

By 1866 Milwaukee was already the largest flour-milling
center among all the western cities. Milwaukee millers benefited from the abrogation, in 1866, of a reciprocal trade treaty
with Canada and the consequent exclusion of Canadian millers
from the American market, at a time when poor wheat crops
in the middle and eastern states reduced the output of flour
in those states. At the same time, the Milwaukeeans began to
substitute steam for waterpower and greatly to enlarge the
capacity of their mills. Second only to Milwaukee, among
Wisconsin flour-milling centers, was Neenah-Menasha, which
aspired to be first. In 1866, however, the La Crosse business-
man-politician Cadwallader C. Washburn built, in Minneapolis, a flour mill that portended doom for the mills of Neenah-
Menasha and even those of Milwaukee. In 1870 Washburn
adopted a milling process developed by Hungarian millers,
which wasted less of the wheat and produced a finer and purer
flour. Three years later he erected a new roller mill, the largest flour mill in the United States. A technological revolution
was under way in the industry, a revolution that, together with
the opening of vast wheat lands west of the Mississippi, was to
make Minneapolis the milling capital of the West and of the
entire country.[27]

[27] Merk, *Economic History*, 129–140; Thompson, *Wheat Growing Industry*,
108–109; Margaret Walsh, "Transportation as a Factor in the Growth of Milwaukee Manufacturing, 1835–1870" (seminar paper, University of Wisconsin,
1968), 7–8; Charles N. Glaab and Lawrence H. Larsen, "Neenah-Menasha in
the 1870's: The Development of Flour Milling and Papermaking," in *WMH*,
52 (Autumn, 1968), 24, 29–30; Charles N. Glaab and Lawrence H. Larsen, *Fac-*

As both wheat growing and flour milling began to shift westward, some of the millers of Neenah-Menasha thought of papermaking as a promising new industry, one to which they might transfer at least a part of their attention and investment. In 1865–1866 the Neenah Paper Company, consisting of six of the leading businessmen and professional men of the community, set up one of the earliest paper mills in the Fox Valley. This was no offshoot of the lumber industry, since the raw material consisted of rags rather than wood pulp. The firm prospered and grew, setting an example for apprehensive flour millers such as John A. Kimberly and Havilah Babcock, who entered the papermaking business in 1872. Among the earliest investors in the business in the Fox Valley, several others also had been engaged in flour milling.[28]

Almost 40 per cent of Wisconsin's manufacturing as of 1870 consisted of the processing of agricultural products, besides milk, to make not only flour and meal but also tobacco goods, malt liquors, meat, leather, and shoes. The manufacture of cigars, snuff, and pipe tobacco was the fastest growing industry in the state, the value of the products increasing more than eightfold during the 1860's, from less than $150,000 to more than $1,220,000. This growth was not due to the increase in the Wisconsin tobacco crop, for the Wisconsin leaf was coarse and suitable mostly for cigar wrappers, but rather to the rising demand for tobacco products among the Germans of Milwaukee and to the presence of skilled cigar makers and other tobacco workers among them.

Brewing continued to develop in response to the increasing demand among non-Germans as well as Germans, both in Wisconsin and in other states. Observed the *Wisconsin Farmer* in

tories in the Valley: Neenah-Menasha, 1870–1915 (Madison, 1969), 54–55; Alice E. Smith, *Millstone and Saw: The Origins of Neenah-Menasha* (Madison, 1966), 71–72; Charles B. Kuhlmann, *The Development of the Flour-Milling Industry in the United States, With Special Reference to the Industry in Minneapolis* (Cambridge, 1929; reprinted, Clifton, New Jersey, 1973), 113–123.

[28] Glaab and Larsen, "Neenah-Menasha," in *WMH*, 52: 31, 34; Glaab and Larsen, *Factories in the Valley*, 86–89, 93–95; Smith, *Millstone and Saw*, 74; Maurice L. Branch, "The Paper Industry in the Lake States Region, 1834–1937" (doctoral dissertation, University of Wisconsin, 1954), 30–31.

1868: "The taste for beer and ale, and the custom and fashion making it 'respectable' to drink it, is largely growing. Statistics show the increase in consumption one year greater than its predecessor, to have been *thirty per centum*, for several years past—since war times." The Milwaukee breweries gained from the destruction of their Chicago competitors in the fire of 1871. By 1873 the Milwaukee breweries were producing 260,120 barrels a year, as compared with 36,000 in 1860 and 55,000 in 1865. From 30 to 50 per cent of the output of the three largest establishments (Best, Blatz, and Falk) was shipped to Chicago, St. Louis, New Orleans, Philadelphia, and other cities outside of Wisconsin. The Philip Best Company (Pabst), which operated the largest brewery in the United States, was exporting beer to Europe, even to Bavaria. As yet, the Milwaukee brewers shipped their beer only in kegs; none of them was to bottle it until Valentin Blatz began to do so in 1874.[29]

Meat packing in Milwaukee was five times as productive in 1871 as it had been in 1860. After rising rapidly during the war, in response to the army's large-scale purchases of rations, beef packing in the city had fallen off sharply but pork packing had gone on up in the postwar period. Profiting handsomely from wartime sales of mess pork, the Milwaukee grain-dealing and meat-packing firm of Plankinton & Armour, organized in 1863, was one of the largest meat processors in the country ten years later, with branches in Chicago and Kansas City and with a commission and exporting house in New York City. (A few years later Philip D. Armour was to take charge of the branch

---

[29] Merk, *Economic History*, 151–155, quoting from the *Wisconsin Farmer*, October 17, 1868; Walsh, "Growth of Milwaukee Manufacturing," 8–12, 27–28; Valentin Blatz in *DWB*. According to the *Eighth Census of the United States, 1860: Manufactures*, 657–658, and the *Ninth Census of the United States, 1870: Volume III*, pp. 583–584, the value of products for 1860 and 1870 was as follows, in millions of dollars:

	1860	1870
1. Flour and meal	$11.5	$20.4
2. Leather, boots, shoes	1.4	6.6
3. Malt liquor	0.7	1.8
4. Meat	0.6	0.1
5. Tobacco products	0.07	1.2

in Chicago, where he and several brothers already had set up their own packing and commission firms.) Slaughtering hogs from Minnesota and Iowa as well as Wisconsin, the Milwaukee packers sold their pork throughout the Eastern states and in England. By 1871 the city ranked fourth among American meat-packing centers.[30]

Tanning, though still fairly widely scattered throughout the state, was becoming more and more concentrated in a few lake-shore counties, especially Manitowoc, Racine, and, above all, Milwaukee. The war had stimulated the industry in Wisconsin, where it was already favored by the abundance of hemlock bark and animal hides and by the presence of experienced German tanners. During the war, government buyers had looked far and wide for leather, then in short supply. Afterwards the largest Wisconsin tanneries, such as the Pfister and Vogel Company, made harness leather of a quality so fine that they could sell it even in New York and Pennsylvania, states with a much bigger tanning industry than Wisconsin's. But the sales were mainly local. Milwaukee itself was a large and growing leather market because of the expansion of its shoemaking. This the wartime army demand had encouraged, as had the introduction of the McKay shoe machine, which was available on lease, so that newcomers needed no large capital in order to go into producing machine-made shoes.[31]

Growing at about the same speed as the state's boot and shoe industry was the manufacture of men's clothing, which also was located almost entirely in Milwaukee. Among the larger firms, as of 1870, there were five employing from forty to 300 workers each and producing ready-made clothes for men. Smaller firms, with fewer than ten employees apiece, did custom tailoring for a well-to-do male clientele, or they specialized in apparel, including millinery, for women and children. The largest of

[30] Merk, *Economic History*, 150–151; Bayrd Still, *Milwaukee: The History of a City* (Madison, 1965), 186–187; Rudolf A. Clemen, *The American Livestock and Meat Industry* (New York, 1923), 151–154.

[31] Charles E. Schefft, "The Tanning Industry in Wisconsin: A History of Its Frontier Origins and Its Development" (master's thesis, University of Wisconsin, 1938), 21–22, 34–43.

the Milwaukee clothing manufacturers were German Jews, though a majority of the city's clothing manufacturers were non-Jewish Germans. Few if any of the enterprisers, whatever their ethnic background, rose all the way from poverty to wealth. Like those in other industries, the great majority did well to rise a step or two on the economic ladder.[32]

For a time, in 1865–1866, many Wisconsinites thought petroleum would prove the most valuable resource ever to be extracted from the Wisconsin earth; they expected the Pennsylvania oil boom of 1864 to repeat itself in this state. To optimists, the oily scum on marsh waters (actually a product of decaying organic matter) seemed proof that underground were fabulous pools of the liquid gold. Dozens of oil companies were formed and hundreds of thousands of dollars were invested in oil stock, but no oil was found. Less extravagant were the expectations in regard to zinc, but these too were disappointed. During the 1860's the increase in zinc production was not enough to offset the decrease in lead production, and as of 1870 the value of the combined production ($556,000) was less than half as much as the state's tobacco products.[33]

Iron mining, however, was assuming an unwonted importance. The output of ore from the Dodge County and Sauk County mines—which a few years earlier had been less than 10,000 tons a year—jumped in 1870 to 100,000 tons. Especially valuable was Dodge County's hard Iron Ridge ore, which mixed well with soft Lake Superior ores from Michigan and found a market not only in Milwaukee but also in Cleveland, St. Louis, and Chicago. Vastly richer than the Iron Ridge deposits, the veins of the Gogebic Range, along the Wisconsin-

[32] Margaret Walsh, "Growth of Milwaukee Manufacturing," 18–19; Margaret Walsh, "Industrial Opportunity on the Urban Frontier: 'Rags to Riches' and Milwaukee Clothing Manufacturers, 1840–1880," in *WMH*, 57 (Spring, 1974), 175–194. According to the *Eighth Census of the United States, 1860: Manufactures*, 657–658, and the *Ninth Census of the United States, 1870: Volume III*, pp. 583–584, the value of Wisconsin-produced boots and shoes was $913,355 in 1860 and $2,271,425 in 1870; of men's clothing, $914,979 in 1860 and $2,260,004 in 1870.

[33] Merk, *Economic History*, 111–120; *Ninth Census of the United States, 1870: Volume III*, pp. 583–584.

Michigan border in the far north, were discovered in 1872 but were not to be exploited for several years.

Pig iron production went up considerably, the blast furnaces utilizing ores from both Wisconsin and Michigan mines. In 1865 only three Wisconsin furnaces were operating, but three years later there were eight: one at Green Bay, two at De Pere, two at Appleton, and three at Bay View, on the outskirts of Milwaukee. Between 1869 and 1871 the output increased nearly fivefold, from 6,516 tons to 31,897. This resulted mainly from the expansion of the works of the Milwaukee Iron Company, which a group of Chicago, Detroit, and Milwaukee capitalists had organized in 1866, which had opened one of the largest rolling mills in the country in 1868, and which two years later added what was reputedly the largest blast furnace in the northwest.

Foundries and machine shops multiplied, especially in Milwaukee, where the number of their employees grew from less than 200 in 1860 to approximately 1,000 in 1873. The most important of the foundrymen was Edward P. Allis, a New Yorker who had arrived in Milwaukee in 1846, had later gone into real estate and the leather business, and with two others had purchased the Reliance Iron Works in 1861. In 1865, in a swamp on Milwaukee's south side, Allis built the largest foundry in the northwest—300 feet long and three stories high. In 1869 he purchased the Bay State Iron Manufacturing Company. By 1872 he was responsible for a million-dollar annual output. His success was due not only to his command of capital and credit but also to his remarkable talent as an entrepreneur. He was quick to hire the ablest engineers and the most skilled workmen and to introduce the latest machinery and techniques. Among them, Allis and other Wisconsin foundrymen, large and small, were turning out products ranging from stoves, boilers, and ornamental ironwork to steam engines, locomotive parts, and flour-mill and sawmill machinery.

Shops and factories in various localities were producing farm implements of one kind and another. Not only was the J. I.

Case Company still expanding in Racine, with an output of 1,300 threshers in 1870 as compared with 500 in 1865 and 300 in 1860. Firms in Beloit, Delavan, Whitewater, Hartford, Columbus, Madison, La Crosse, and elsewhere were also manufacturing threshers, plows, hay mowers, reapers, sorghum mills, windmills and pumps, or other equipment for the farmer.[34]

Out of one of Wisconsin's many machine shops came the first practical writing machine, the direct ancestor of all the standard typewriters that would radically alter the efficiency and routine of business offices throughout the country. This invention resulted from a combination of Yankee ingenuity and acumen with German craftsmanship. The chief inventor, Christopher Latham Sholes, was descended from colonial New Englanders and had been a pioneer Wisconsin newspaperman. He got his first inspiration for the writing machine while spending his spare time in the Milwaukee machine shop of Charles F. Kleinsteuber. Kleinsteuber and one of his machinists, Mathias Schwalbach, not only embodied in metalwork the ideas of Sholes, but also contributed elements of their own devising.

Sholes' model differed from another "Type Writing Machine" that came to his attention in 1867 and that had all its types on a single plate. He put each of the types on a separate bar. On his first model the types struck upward against a sheet of paper—which was held flat in a moving frame—and knocked the paper against an inked ribbon. After trying in vain to find a capitalist who would either buy the invention or back its manufacture, he turned to an old friend, James Densmore, also a pioneer Wisconsin journalist, who bought an interest in the invention and took charge of the typewriter enterprise. "It

[34] Merk, *Economic History*, 115–116, 140–144; Ellis B. Usher, "Nelson Powell Hulst, 'The Greatest American Authority on Iron,'" in *WMH*, 7 (June, 1924), 385–405; Robert T. Hilton, "Men of Metal: A History of the Foundry Industry in Wisconsin" (master's thesis, University of Wisconsin, 1952), 27–53; Margaret Walsh, "Business Success and Capital Availability in the New West: Milwaukee Ironmasters in the Middle Nineteenth Century," in the *Old Northwest*, 1 (June, 1975), 160–163; Reynold M. Wik, "J. I. Case: Some Experiences of an Early Wisconsin Industrialist," in *WMH*, 35 (Autumn, 1951), 66–67; Stewart H. Holbrook, *Machines of Plenty: Pioneering in American Agriculture* (New York, 1955), 50–52, 55–58.

became a living soul only as and after you breathed the breath of life into it," Sholes afterward avowed to him. Densmore kept Sholes and his fellow inventors busy making improvements while he himself put one model after another in the hands of phonographers (stenographers) for testing. By the summer of 1872 the design was set essentially as it was to remain, except for the later addition of a shift and a front stroke. Even the keyboard arrangement was the familiar one: q w e r t y u i o p, and so forth.

That summer, Densmore rented an old stone building with a waterwheel, hired a few laborers and Schwalbach as their foreman, and undertook to manufacture typewriters. He did not have the equipment for mass production, and, largely handmade as they were, the typewriters were costing him more to make than he was selling them for. On March 1, 1873, Densmore and a new partner signed with E. Remington & Sons, manufacturers of guns and sewing machines, a contract according to which they would pay the Remingtons to manufacture typewriters and would themselves distribute them. There were still troubles ahead for Sholes, Densmore, and others associated with the invention, but at last the invention itself was successfully launched.[35]

[6]

Wages during the postwar period were said to be high in Wisconsin. The good pay was one of the attractions of the state, according to the pamphlet that the legislature published in 1867 in an effort to lure immigrants. Yet, according to the federal census of 1870, industrial workers' earnings in Wisconsin lagged well behind those in some other states. The year's average was only about $309 for Wisconsin; it was approximately $384 for

[35] Richard N. Current, "The Original Typewriter Enterprise, 1867–1873," in *WMH*, 32 (June, 1949), 391–407; Richard N. Current, *The Typewriter and the Men Who Made It* (Urbana, 1954), *passim*. At first the keyboard was arranged in alphabetical order. In 1872 it was changed to the standard keyboard for reasons of efficiency—to lessen the frequency of type-bar collisions and to increase the frequency of the alteration of the two hands.

the entire country, nearly $405 for New York, more than $426
for Massachusetts, $375 for Illinois, and $333 for Michigan.
The Wisconsin average was less than 12 per cent higher than
it had been a decade earlier; the national average was more
than 30 per cent higher than it had been. Since the cost of
living had risen more than workers' pay, real wages had fallen,
and they had fallen farther in Wisconsin than in the rest of
the country on the average. At the coming of the depression in
1873, money wages also dropped; by the winter of that year
they were as low for lumberjacks as they had been in 1861.[36]

Not yet did laborers look to either the state or the federal
government for direct wage support. But they did expect the
state to see that their wages were actually paid. Lien laws,
which as early as 1855 had given some protection to railroad
construction men, were extended in 1869, 1870, and 1871 to
cover other categories of workers, among them brick makers,
plumbers, electricians, and tinsmiths. Still lacking, however,
was a general law to assure wage payment for all workers by
giving them a claim on the assets of their employers. Also
lacking was legislation requiring employers to compensate
workers or their families for injury or death on the job. An
employee or his survivors could sue for damages on account
of loss of life or limb, but even if they could stand the expense, they had little chance of winning the case. The common law was on the employer's side.[37]

Under the influence of a national eight-hour movement,
many Wisconsin workers turned to the legislature for an act
to limit the work day, which in Wisconsin as in most of the
country was usually ten hours for six days each week. A Labor
Reform Association, was organized in Milwaukee in 1865,

[36] The average yearly wages have been calculated from data in the *Ninth
Census of the United States, 1870: Volume III*, pp. 392–393. A consumer price
index (1860=100, 1870=144) may be found in Clarence D. Long, *Wages and
Earnings in the United States, 1860–1890* (Princeton, 1960), 68. Information
on wages in the pineries, 1861 and 1873, is from Merk, *Economic History*, 110n.

[37] Frank N. Elliott, "The Causes and the Growth of Railroad Regulation in
Wisconsin, 1848–1876" (doctoral dissertation, University of Wisconsin, 1956),
249–250; Donald J. Berthrong, "Social Legislation in Wisconsin, 1836–1900"
(doctoral dissertation, University of Wisconsin, 1951), 155–156, 162–163, 183–184.

and soon developed into the General Eight Hour League of Wisconsin, with branches in several cities. Responding rather half-heartedly to pressure from the league, the legislature in 1867 passed a bill to make eight hours the legal work day—except when employees agreed to longer hours! At the Bay State Iron Manufacturing Company, outside of Milwaukee, the Machinists' and Blacksmiths' Union now demanded overtime pay of time and a half for hours above eight. Indignantly the president of the company replied that he had to compete with firms in New England and New York, where ten hours was still the rule, and where, he added, capital was more abundant and interest more reasonable than in Wisconsin. E. P. Allis offered to let his hands have eight hours of work for eight hours of pay, but none was willing to accept such a wage cut. Shipbuilders refused, however, to grant the same terms, and ship carpenters and caulkers struck for a while, then returned to work on the old basis of the ten-hour day. "Good-bye eight hour system," the Milwaukee *Sentinel* commented.[38]

Of the nation's many labor unions that appeared during the postwar decade, the largest originated in Wisconsin. This was the Knights of St. Crispin, a shoemakers' organization that was named for their patron saint. Skilled shoemakers were suffering from a decline in wages and job opportunities as a result of the introduction of machinery and the development of the factory system in shoe manufacture. To protect themselves, shoemakers needed an all-inclusive industrial union rather than the existing trade organizations of the skilled. Such, at least, was the conclusion of Newell Daniels, a Milwaukee boot treer, a recent arrival from Massachusetts, who in 1867 led in the formation of the first lodge of the Knights of St. Crispin, and who during the next few years served as "grand scribe" and organized other lodges in the East. By 1871 there were in the country, all told, a total of 50,000 or 60,000 members in some 400 lodges, including those in Racine, Waukesha, Janes-

[38] Merk, *Economic History*, 178–182; Thomas W. Gavett, *Development of the Labor Movement in Milwaukee* (Madison, 1965), 17–18; Milwaukee *Sentinel*, June 27, July 6, and July 15, 1867 (quotation).

ville, Kenosha, Watertown, Fond du Lac, Green Bay, Sheboygan, La Crosse, Portage, and Oshkosh, as well as Milwaukee. In principle the Knights opposed not the use of machinery but the hiring of green hands to run it. The Knights in Milwaukee owned and managed three co-operative shops. Then, in 1872, the national order began to collapse after some eastern lodges struck and were crushed by defeat. During the Depression of 1873 the Milwaukee lodges sold their co-operative shops and disbanded. Only the original Lodge Number 1 managed to survive and that only temporarily.[39]

Some other local unions also experimented unsuccessfully with producers' co-operatives, and these were endorsed by the National Labor Union, a Wisconsin branch of which was organized at Black River Falls in 1869. The so-called National Labor Union also favored political action and disapproved of strikes. Its Wisconsin branch invited all workers to join, regardless of their trade, and to exert the power of labor at the polls. The branch sponsored the formation of a Labor Reform party, which advocated such political reforms as the lengthening of voting hours from eight in the morning to eight at night. In 1870 the party claimed 5,000 members, but neither then nor later did it elect any candidates.[40]

Most of the Wisconsin unions, whether independent or affiliated with a national organization, were willing to strike, if they had to, in order to achieve their aim, which commonly was the maintenance or the increase of wage rates. "It is a notable fact," the Milwaukee *Sentinel* boasted in 1872, "that Milwaukee has not suffered in reputation through 'strikes' on the part of trades unions as have other cities." Yet, if fewer than in some other parts of the country, walkouts in Milwaukee and elsewhere in Wisconsin were much more numerous during the relatively prosperous year of 1872 than they had been dur-

[39] Merk, *Economic History*, 170–172; Gavett, *Labor Movement in Milwaukee*, 21–22; Don D. Lescohier, *The Knights of St. Crispin, 1867–1874: A Study in the Industrial Causes of Trade Unionism* (Madison, 1910), 1–37; Newell Daniels in *DWB*.

[40] Merk, *Economic History*, 182–185; Gavett, *Labor Movement in Milwaukee*, 18–21.

ing any of the preceding six years. During none of the years from 1866 to 1873, however, was the state without its striking laborers. Among those who quit work at one time or another were bellboys, masons' helpers, harvest hands, sailors, bridge builders, stonecutters, iron puddlers and iron heaters, common laborers, cigar makers, pipe layers, coal heavers, tailors, coopers, printers, brewery workers, stevedores, lithographers, and railroad construction men, some of whom rioted near Stevens Point in 1872, ripping up track and seizing a train.[41]

Very few if any of the strikes resulted in victory for the strikers. To some extent, no doubt, the workers were handicapped by their ethnic differences, but these certainly were not always insuperable. Thus the German Custom Shoemakers' Union of Milwaukee readily combined with the Yankee-led Knights of St. Crispin. The nine exhausted iron heaters who quit work and halted production at the Milwaukee Iron Company on an oppressively hot summer night in 1873 represented a variety of nationalities, as their names suggest—Clancy, Edmonds, Grimes, Ellis, Kneisler, Noblet, Ihling, Shannahan, and Ratka.

In any event, the employers usually had the greater bargaining power, political influence, mutual support, and journalistic backing. They could fire the strikers, hire replacements, and depend on the police to protect the strikebreakers. They cooperated closely with one another in emergencies, as in the case of the Milwaukee printers' strike of 1872. At that time several of the local newspaper-publishing and job-printing firms joined together in an employers' association to counter the typographical union. Publishers in Waukesha, Whitewater, and Janesville came to the rescue of those in Milwaukee by doing their printing for them, when they were shut down. The Milwaukee & St. Paul Railway Company added its support by offering free passes to nonunion printers heading for Milwaukee to fill jobs in the struck plants. Understandably the

---

[41] The quotation is from the Milwaukee *Sentinel,* August 23, 1872. The *Sentinel,* according to the card index of the newspaper in the Milwaukee Public Library, mentioned four strikes in the state in 1866, six in 1867, one in 1868, one in 1869, six in 1870, two in 1871, and thirteen in 1872. On the Stevens Point riot, see Merk, *Economic History,* 164–165n.

larger newspapers, with their own considerable payrolls to meet, were inclined to partiality in their reporting and editorializing on labor disputes. "In almost every instance," a coopers' strike in 1872 moved the Milwaukee *Sentinel* to remark, "strikes of trades' unions are inaugurated by the poor and shiftless members of the profession, who manage to get carried by the more skillful and industrious members of the craft."[42]

[42] These generalizations are based on numerous issues of the Milwaukee *Sentinel*. One apparently victorious strike is reported in the issue of November 12, 1873, which says the wages of lithographers were "fixed to the satisfaction of the employes." On the iron heaters, see the *Sentinel* for July 26, 27, and 29, 1873. For examples of strikebreaking, see the issues of August 9, 1867; July 28, 29, August 2, 1871; July 1, 2, 3, 17, 23, September 6, October 12, 1872; May 3, December 27, 1873. The quotation is from the issue of April 6, 1872.

14

Government and Welfare

To RAISE MONEY and men for winning the war and preserving the Union, the federal government briefly had intruded as never before upon the lives of the people of Wisconsin and the other states. Once the war was over, the federal government ceased its unprecedented interference, and the state and local authorities resumed their former sway. As in previous years, local government in Wisconsin impinged upon the people's life more frequently and more closely than state government did, though the difference between the two was narrowing. One measure of the difference still remained the amount of money that each raised and spent. For the fiscal year 1869–1870, the receipts from taxes and the expenditures of the local units—counties, towns, villages, and cities—were more than five times as large as those of the state.

Of the state's revenue, more than a third came from a property tax that the county authorities collected and turned over to the state treasury. About a fourth was derived from special taxes on railroad, express, and insurance companies. Another third, approximately, was the yield from the sale of state lands of various categories. The income from school and university lands would have been larger if the legislature, to help finance the war, had not directed in 1862 that the proceeds from those lands be invested in state bonds. In 1865 the legislature converted the bonds into certificates of indebtedness representing a perpetual loan of $1,500,000. Thus disappeared almost half of the school fund. What had been an asset was thenceforth a liability, on which the state had to keep paying interest.[1]

In assessing property and setting tax rates for a county, the board of county commissioners from 1861 to 1869 exercised a good deal of arbitrary authority. The commissioners in Wisconsin's northern counties often levied much the hardest upon the pine lands of absentee owners. If these men did not, like other property owners, appear promptly at the courthouse and make payment, they ran the risk of losing their lands at a tax sale. Rare was the resident taxpayer who objected to that kind of extortion when it was applied to nonresident land speculators, but not so rare the one who objected to his own assessment. The people of the town of Liberty Grove, in Door County, protested vehemently when, in 1867, the county board suddenly upped their town's valuation from $33,192 to $83,481 while lowering the town of Brussels' valuation from $27,736 to $24,200.

Liberty Grove was a Norwegian and Brussels a Belgian settlement. One of the three Door County commissioners in 1867 was Belgian, but none was Norwegian. The inhabitants of Liberty Grove saw a connection between their tax increase and their lack of representation on the county board.

The people of other towns throughout the state were also complaining about the unrepresentativeness of the commissioner system, under which every county, large or small, had only three board members, and these were elected from districts that were rather artificial (even in comparison with townships). In response to the widespread discontent, the legislature in 1869 provided for a return to the supervisor system, under which the chairman of each town board in a county served as a member of the county board of supervisors. As a

---

[1] *Ninth Census of the United States, 1870: Volume III*, pp. 66–67; Conrad E. Patzer, *Public Education in Wisconsin* (Madison, 1924), 114–115.

result, the Door County board in 1870 had fourteen members, including a Norwegian from Liberty Grove, and the tax assessments in that town were considerably reduced.[2]

Immigrants were taking a greater and greater part in local politics and were gaining an increasing share of government jobs, both local and state. For some time, Germans had been politically active in German communities, and the Irish both locally and in the state as a whole. But other groups—Norwegians, Belgians, Hollanders—had lagged somewhat. After the war, men of these nationalities began to hold a larger number of offices, especially in the towns and villages but also in the counties and even in the state government.

In the Trempealeau County town of Lincoln, for example, where Norwegians constituted a large minority, one of the three members of the town board was Norwegian in 1868, 1869, and 1870, and two of the three were in 1871 and 1872. A Norwegian appeared on the county board for the first time in 1870. From 1870 to 1874, however, the foreigners from non-English-speaking countries, a large majority of whom were from Norway, were less than proportionally represented on the county board (they made up about 24 per cent of the 1870 population but only 18.3 per cent of the 1870–1874 board membership). Proportionally represented were people of American birth (about 59 per cent of the population and 58.3 per cent of the board). But the Irish and other English-speaking foreigners were decidedly overrepresented (only 7 or 8 per cent of the population but 23.3 per cent of the board members).

In Door County the towns predominantly of one nationality came to have a town chairman of that nationality, and the mixed towns rotated the office among the different ethnic groups; but the Irish seem to have been more numerous among the incumbents than their numbers in the community would have war-

[2] Paul W. Gates, *The Wisconsin Pine Lands of Cornell University: A Study in Land Policy and Absentee Ownership* (Ithaca, 1943), 86–88; Hjalmar R. Holand, *History of Door County, Wisconsin: The County Beautiful* (2 vols., Chicago, 1917), 1: 98, 116, 374.

ranted. In the Brown County town of Green Bay the Belgians had marched together to the polls as early as 1858, and in Kewaunee and Door as well as Brown they were a political force to be reckoned with by 1866, when Kewaunee sent a Belgian, Constant Martin, to sit in the state legislature. In Brown and Outagamie counties the Dutch by 1873 could boast of having produced a district attorney, a superintendent of schools, a circuit court clerk, a register of deeds, and a state bank comptroller. Elsewhere in the state the Dutch were represented by three of their number in the assembly.

The growing participation of immigrants in government followed from an increasing political self-consciousness on their part. It led in the direction of cultural assimilation, since it gave immigrants an apprenticeship in American democracy and brought local leaders of foreign birth or parentage into co-operation with those of older American stock.[3]

In the city of Milwaukee the German and the Irish residents generally preferred to keep as much independence and power for the separate wards as they could. In 1868 they helped to defeat a new charter that would have taken from the ward councilors the supervision of public works within the respective wards and given an appointed board the management of such projects throughout the city. Reformers continued to complain of the "horde of greedy, unscrupulous contractors" who, in collusion with ward councilors, had "grown *fat*" on municipal business. In 1869 the question of a commission to have "general control of public buildings, streets, sewers, sidewalks, bridges, wharves, and the like in all parts of the city" came before the people as a separate proposition. This time it carried despite the majorities against it in the Irish third and the German sixth and ninth wards. The reform was in line

[3] Merle Curti, *The Making of an American Community: A Case Study of Democracy in a Frontier County* (Stanford, 1959), 296–297, 303, 339–340; Xavier Martin, "The Belgians of Northeast Wisconsin," in *Wis. Hist. Colls.*, 13: 381–384, 393; Henry S. Lucas, ed., *Dutch Immigrant Memoirs and Related Writings* (2 vols., Assen, Netherlands, 1955), 2: 132–133; Holand, *History of Door County*, 1: 102, 367–374; *Ninth Census of the United States, 1870: Volume I*, p. 377.

with a trend in American cities to seek economy and efficiency
in administration by setting up quasi-independent boards. Such
a board, the Public Debt Commission, had been laboring since
1861 to fund and reduce Milwaukee's formerly staggering indebtedness. By 1869 the dept commission had achieved notable
success, and the mayor declared that no other city in the United
States could show "so encouraging a financial exhibit" for
that year.[4]

Besides spending on public works, the governments of cities,
villages, towns, and counties also disbursed their revenues, as
in earlier years, on a variety of community services and, above
all, on the schooling of the young. The functions of the state
government were likewise reflected in its expenditures, which
included money for the operation of the prison, reform schools,
hospitals for the insane, institutes for the deaf and dumb and
the blind, a soldiers' orphans' home, and the historical society;
a larger sum for education; and an appropriation for the completion of the state capitol. This, the second of the Wisconsin
state capitols, had been under construction for a dozen years.
Completed by 1869 were the new dome and rotunda, the design of Stephen Vaughan Shipman, a Pennsylvania-born archi-
tect who had moved to Madison in 1855. The three-story building of yellow-brown Prairie du Chien stone had, on opposite
sides, wings with columned porticoes and, on the other two
sides, wings with corner turrets. In January 1872, the final
touches having at last been put on the interior, Governor Cadwallader C. Washburn proudly announced to the assembled
lawmakers: "The State Capitol is now finished at a total cost
of $550,000."[5]

---

[4] Bayrd Still, *Milwaukee: The History of a City* (Madison, 1965), 164–167. The
characterization of contractors is from the Milwaukee *Sentinel*, April 5, 1869.

[5] For a summary of state expenditures during the fiscal year 1869–1870, see the
Ninth Census of the United States, 1870: Volume III, p. 67. On the new capitol
and the complications that followed, see John O. Holzhueter, "The Capitol
Fence of 1872: A Footnote to Wisconsin Architectural History," in *WMH*,
53 (Summer, 1970), 243–255. The quotation is from p. 244. See also Stephen
Vaughan Shipman in the *DWB*.

[2]

After the war, public education in Wisconsin recovered from its recent setback and advanced falteringly in the direction of comprehensiveness and quality. An act of 1869, aiming to encourage the consolidation of school systems, authorized the voters at a town meeting to combine local districts into a single district co-extensive with the town. But the law was merely permissive, and voters distrusted it, fearing it would curtail their rights and might increase their taxes. During the first year after it was passed, only four towns took advantage of it, and during the next year one of the four returned to the old arrangement, with multiple, independent districts.

The number of schoolhouses kept on increasing—in Winnebago County, for example, from eighty-one in 1855 to 120 in 1873. Some of the new ones, especially in the cities, were up-to-date and handsome buildings, like Racine's New Third Ward School, which, when it opened in 1869, impressed one arriving boy as "the finest in the world." Out in the country, however, old and dilapidated structures remained in use. More than a third of the schoolhouses in Winnebago County, the state superintendent reported in 1873, were in poor condition. Three years earlier the county superintendent had reported that parents sent their children to schools they would consider "unfit to shelter their cattle," with rooms "blackened wtih smoke and dirt," unhealthful, and oppressive in their "cheerless monotony." A majority of the rural schools in the county lacked wall maps, blackboards, and libraries, except perhaps for a copy of *Webster's Unabridged Dictionary,* which a law of 1855 had intended to supply to every school in the state. Teachers, more than two-thirds of them women by 1870, continued to be, for the most part, poorly paid and poorly trained. A top graduate of an ungraded common school could still take a school of his or her own after passing the teacher's examination, without normal, collegiate, or even secondary training. In district schools the janitorial duties of the teacher persisted.

"I expected to commence school but had to work all day helping fix up stoves and seats," Jabez Brown noted in his diary at
the start of the winter term, 1869–1870, in Hillsborough (Vernon County).[6]

An act of 1866 extended the school year from a minimum of
three to a minimum of five months throughout the state. Probably most districts, even in rural areas, met the new require-
ment, since by law they could receive their share of the proceeds
of the state school fund only if they did so. Some city schools,
like those of Oshkosh, were holding classes for ten months by
1868. But no law yet required children to attend for five
months or for any length of time. On an average day the proportion of children of school age (between five and twenty
years old) actually in school was about 65 per cent—no higher
in 1870 than it had been in 1860. Forty or fifty thousand
children were not going to school at all. Attendance, at least
in Trempealeau County, was especially low among the poor,
and lowest among the poor of other than an English-speaking
background. For the state as a whole, the proportion of illiterate
adults remained fairly high, about 17 per cent, and for some of
the immigrant groups the proportion was considerably higher.
Concerned friends of education lobbied in Madison, and in
1873 the assembly directed the state superintendent of public
instruction to investigate and report on truancy and compul-
sory-attendance laws in the United States and abroad. In his

[6] Patzer, *Public Education in Wisconsin,* 63–64; Helen F. Patton, "Public
School Architecture in Racine, Wisconsin, and Vicinity from the Time of
Settlement to 1900" (doctoral dissertation, University of Wisconsin, 1965), 375;
Robert C. Robertson, "The Social History of Winnebago County, Wisconsin,
1850–1870" (master's thesis, University of Chicago, 1939), 70–71, quoting the
county superintendent in the Oshkosh *Journal,* December 3, 1870; Belle Cush-
man Bohn, "Early Wisconsin School Teachers," in *WMH,* 23 (September, 1939),
58–61; diary of Jabez Brown, December 13, 1869, in the Jabez Brown Papers. For
data on schoolhouses and supplies in other counties, see Wisconsin Superintendent
of Public Instruction, *Annual Report,* 1873, pp. 77–82 and 104–105 of the appendix. On the sex ratio of teachers and their salaries, see *Ninth Census of the
United States, 1870: Volume I,* p. 452, and U.S. Commissioner of Education,
Annual Report, 1871, pp. 371–372, reproducing the 1870 report of the Wisconsin
superintendent of public instruction.

report the superintendent recommended compulsory attendance for Wisconsin, but the legislature took no further action for the time being.[7]

The vast majority of Wisconsin's public schools—4,450 of 4,859, according to the census of 1870—still belonged to the category "ungraded common." Public secondary education was slowly recovering from the effects of the prewar depression and the war. As of 1865, high schools were to be found in Kenosha, Racine, Janesville, Sheboygan, Oshkosh, Green Bay, La Crosse, Fond du Lac, Madison, Watertown, and Prairie du Chien. In 1868 a high school again opened in Milwaukee, which had been without one for several years. Advocates of public high schools kept on complaining that too many community leaders gave their support and sent their children to private academies. Local boosters considered an academy, like a college, to be a community asset. For want of one, the *Island City Times* lamented in 1866, Neenah and Menasha had "lost the citizenship of many men" who would have been "honor to the towns" but who had moved elsewhere because rival communities "possessed superior educational facilities." Private and parochial schools, elementary as well as secondary, were gaining in certain localities, as in Milwaukee, where in 1868 they had more than a third of the total enrollment. In the state as a whole,

[8] Patzer, *Public Education in Wisconsin*, 74–76; Robertson, "Social History of Winnebago County," 64–66, 82; Wisconsin Superintendent of Public Instruction, *Annual Report*, 1873, pp. 35, 72. Curti, *Making of an American Community*, 397–401, finds that, among families with less than $2,000 worth of property in Trempealeau County, school attendance of Norwegians was relatively low, but among families with more than $2,000 it was the same or better as for the American-born. He also finds that, in the case of families with less than $1,000, the attendance, while lowest among the non-English-speaking immigrants, was highest among the immigrants from Great Britain, British North America, and Ireland—higher among those groups than among the American-born. According to the *Ninth Census of the United States, 1870: Volume I*, pp. 396–397, Wisconsin at that time contained 35,031 persons over ten years of age who could not read and 55,441 who could not write. Of the 55,441, there were 14,113 native Americans and 41,328 foreigners by birth. For the per cent of children in school, see *ibid.: Volume I*, p. 394, and *ibid.: Volume II*, pp. 563 and 565; and *Eighth Census of the United States, 1860: Population*, 526, and *ibid.: Mortality and Miscellaneous Statistics*, 507.

however, the public schools continued to enroll all except a tiny fraction of the entire number of pupils.[8]

Leaders of the Norwegian Lutheran clergy had never reconciled themselves to the predominance of public education in Wisconsin. After the war the president of the Norwegian Synod, H. A. Preus, revived a plan that had been dormant since 1859, a plan to set up a state-wide system of parochial schools, on the model of the Missouri Synod system, as the church's substitute for public education. Already most of the Wisconsin congregations operated parochial schools, but these were a supplement and not a substitute; they usually ran for only one to three months and could not hold their students when the common schools were in session. Preus and other clergymen wished to expand and improve the church schools.

Prominent laymen, however, strongly objected. Among them, in 1869, were Knud Langeland, former editor of Wisconsin's and the nation's first Norwegian-language newspaper, *Nordlyset,* and then editor of the Chicago *Skandinaven,* and Rasmus B. Anderson, a twenty-three-year-old instructor at Albion Academy. Langeland and Anderson proposed, as an alternative plan, that the congregations exert their influence on the public schools. At a Madison meeting in 1869, Anderson led in organizing the Scandinavian Lutheran Education Society, to encour-

[8] *Ninth Census of the United States, 1870: Volume I,* p. 470; Patzer, *Public Education in Wisconsin,* 80–82; Still, *Milwaukee,* 216, 220; Robertson, "Social History of Winnebago County," 80–82; Joseph Schafer, "Genesis of Wisconsin's Free High School System," in *WMH,* 10 (December, 1926), 123–149; Neenah-Menasha *Island City Times,* October 2, December 11, 1866. According to the 1870 federal census, *Volume I,* p. 470, Wisconsin had thirty-five public high schools, but Schafer (pp. 141–142) estimates only ten for 1870, while those listed by Patzer for 1865, plus the Milwaukee high school that opened in 1868, come to a total of twelve. The census recorded 337,008 pupils in public schools and only 3,857 in other nontechnical schools (451 in academies, 1,319 in "day and boarding," and 2,087 in "parochial and charity"). But Still gives 6,409 as the 1868 enrollment of the private and parochial schools in Milwaukee alone. And according to the 1870 report of the state superintendent of public instruction there were 267,891 pupils attending public schools and 15,618 (plus another estimated 7,000) attending private schools. See U.S. Commissioner of Education, *Annual Report,* 1871, pp. 371–376, reproducing the 1870 report of the Wisconsin superintendent of public instruction.

age the training of Scandinavian Lutherans as teachers and professors and the teaching of Norwegian history and literature. For himself, Anderson got an appointment as instructor in modern languages at the University of Wisconsin; soon he included Norwegian in the program, and in 1875 he was to be given the first regular chair in Scandinavian studies in the United States. Meanwhile, in some districts where the Norwegian Lutherans controlled the school boards, the parochial-school teachers served also as the common-school teachers. So great was the opposition within the Norwegian community (not to mention the prohibitive cost), however, that no Norwegian Lutheran parochial system arose to compete with the public system.[9]

The Roman Catholic hierarchy also renewed its efforts to extend its parochial education. In 1866 Bishop John Martin Henni impressed upon parents the need for religious instruction and urged priests to start schools in all the parishes. In 1868 Bishop Michael Heiss called for the establishment of a church-controlled normal school. "The sisters are not in sufficient number and cannot always give satisfaction," Heiss maintained, "and the school-brothers do not succeed." Some of the priests opposed the idea, yet with the aid of a $1,200 donation from King Ludwig of Bavaria the first Catholic normal school in the United States opened near Milwaukee in 1871. More serious than the shortage of teachers was the shortage of money, and church spokesmen became more insistent than ever in demanding a share of the public money for parochial schools. The "very air" of the public schools seemed to have in it something "repulsive to christianity" (that is, to Catholicism), the Wisconsin Catholic monthly *Star of Bethlehem* insisted in 1870. The public schools, this paper contended, were really denominational schools. "Protestants are welcome to them." But let the Catholics, too, have their state-supported

[9] Theodore C. Blegen, *Norwegian Migration to America: The American Transition* (Northfield, Minnesota, 1940), 252–269, 274; Arlow W. Andersen, "Knud Langeland: Pioneer Editor," in *Norwegian-American Studies and Records,* 14 (1944), 129–131; Lloyd Hustvedt, *Rasmus Bjørn Anderson, Pioneer Scholar* (Northfield, Minnesota, 1966), 51–60, 65–72, 89–122.

educational system in Wisconsin, as they did in Prussia, Austria, and France. When Governor Lucius Fairchild rebuked the Catholics for their demand, the *Star of Bethlehem* responded, "Is he wiser than the statesmen of Europe?"[10]

This implication—that the European way was better than the American way—was not likely to sit well with the old-stock, Protestant, nativistic residents of Wisconsin. Yet many of them were willing to concede, even to boast, that there was, in fact, a close affinity between Yankee Protestantism and public education. "The common-school system is the offspring of the religion of the Bible," the Wisconsin Methodists resolved at their 1870 conference in Janesville; "Nowhere except among Evangelical Protestants has a plan of instruction, embracing all the children of the community, ever been adopted." The Methodists took pride in the election of one of their ministers, the Reverend Samuel Fallows, as state superintendent of public instruction in 1870. Several of his predecessors in office had been prominent lay or clerical Protestant figures. So had been, and still were, most of the other leaders of public education in Wisconsin. And a disproportionate number of teachers, in the 1870's as in previous decades, were men and women of old American, Protestant backgrounds.[11]

German as well as Norwegian leaders kept up their efforts to control the public schools in their own communities, though

---

[10] Peter Leo Johnson, *Crosier on the Frontier: A Life of John Martin Henni, Archbishop of Milwaukee* (Madison, 1959), 118, 121–122; Heiss to Kilian, June 22, 1868, in the *Salesianum*, 12 (October, 1916), 4 (for the Heiss quotation); *Star of Bethlehem* (a monthly published by the St. Louis Brothers in Milwaukee), October, 1869; January, February, March, October, 1870. The quotations are from the March, January, and February, 1870, issues respectively. The agitation in Wisconsin for Catholic parochial schools and for state support was largely a phenomenon led by the German hierarchy of the church. Wisconsin's Irish Catholics, who had not known a parochial school system in Ireland and who were not bothered by the language question, were generally more satisfied with the public schools, especially when—as was true in many Irish neighborhoods and rural settlements—the public school teachers were often Irish-Catholic. See M. Justille McDonald, *History of the Irish in Wisconsin in the Nineteenth Century* (Washington, D.C., 1954), 216–221.

[11] P. S. Bennett and James Lawson, *History of Methodism in Wisconsin* (Cincinnati, 1890), 236; Alan W. Brownsword, "Educational Ideas in Early Wisconsin, 1848–1870" (master's thesis, University of Wisconsin, 1958), 65–69.

the mass of the people, German as well as Norwegian, appeared
to remain indifferent. The Milwaukee German-language newspaper *Herold* complained in 1867 that the city's eighth ward,
though having a German majority in its population, had not
a single German teacher in its public schools. The reason for
this, the *Herold* explained, was simply that the Germans in
the ward had "left the administration of the public schools to
the fashion-setting [*tonangebenden*] Americans." In two other
predominantly German Milwaukee wards, the sixth and ninth,
the school commissioners were German, but they felt themselves on the defensive when, in 1870, the executive committee
of the school board recommended a pay cut for assistant prin-
cipals who were also teachers, and one of the non-German commissioners suggested that, "if male teachers would not find it
profitable to teach at the proposed salaries, capable ladies
could be found to step into their places." Citizens of the ninth
ward gathered at a protest meeting, at which the German principal of the ward school played a prominent role. Unanimous
resolutions of the meeting declared male teachers better quali-
fied than female because "better able to maintain a proper
degree of discipline," called for a restoration of the former
salary scale, objected to the "effort towards the centralization
of our school system," and demanded that teachers in the ninth
and tenth grades be appointed only upon the recommendation
of the commissioners of the various wards. Teachers in the
German-controlled districts continued to be almost exclusively
men.[12]

For the time being, the issue of Bible reading in the public
schools, so hotly controversial in the 1850's, remained quiescent.
The question of the use of foreign languages, however, flared
up anew. Amendments to the school code in 1867 specified
that, in the public schools, "no branch of study" should be
taught in "any other than the English language" and that no
person should receive a teaching certificate who did not

<hr>

[12] The quotations are from the Milwaukee *Herold,* June 20, 1867, and the
Milwaukee *Sentinel,* August 8, 1870. See also Lloyd P. Jorgenson, *The Founding
of Public Education in Wisconsin* (Madison, 1956), 149.

"write and speak the English language with facility and correctness." Both Norwegians and Germans expressed a sense of outrage, and two years later they persuaded the legislature to permit the teaching of a foreign tongue, though for only one hour a day. As a teacher in a Norwegian district in Pierce County, Nils P. Haugen convinced his school board that the children needed English most of all and that he ought to forgo the permissible hour of Norwegian. Despite the law, however, some public schools went on using a foreign language for all instruction, especially in German communities.[13]

A new emphasis on Americanism in the curriculum resulted from the Civil War. At the first postwar meeting of the state teachers' association, returning veterans urged the teaching of citizenship, and the delegates adopted the following resolution: "It is the serious duty of every true teacher to instruct his pupils in the political history and civil government of our state and nation, so that the people may preserve their own rights and liberties and have a just regard for those of others, and make the state in fact, as it is in theory, an organization for the highest good of the people." In 1871 the legislature gave a delayed and incomplete response when it made the United States Constitution and the Wisconsin constitution required subjects in the common schools. Several years later it was to add American history to the list of requirements.[14]

[3]

Milton Academy, which had been under the direction of the pastor of the local Seventh Day Baptist Church, became Milton College with an 1867 charter prohibiting religious tests for trustees, administrators, faculty members, or students. The College of Our Lady of the Sacred Heart opened in Watertown in 1872 under the supervision of Holy Cross Fathers whom

---

[13] *Ibid.*, 145–148; Patzer, *Public Education in Wisconsin*, 65–68, 446; Nils P. Haugen, *Pioneer and Political Reminiscences* (Madison, n.d.), 18–19. The English-language provision, published in the revised school code of 1867, was approved by the legislature of the previous year; see *Laws of Wisconsin*, 1866, chapter 111.

[14] Patzer, *Public Education in Wisconsin*, 69–70.

Archbishop Henni had invited from Notre Dame, Indiana. Older private or church-related colleges gradually gained prestige with the passing years. Most significant for the long-run future of higher education in Wisconsin, however, were developments in the state institutions—both the university and the normal schools—from which was to grow the University of Wisconsin system of a century later.[15]

For the institution at Madison, a new era began soon after the war, an era of progress toward the status of a true university. A legislative act of 1866 reorganized the university administration by allowing the governor rather than the legislature to appoint the regents and by increasing their authority. The new board immediately adopted bylaws providing that it should elect the president and the professors at each annual meeting and thus implying that none of them was to have more than a year-to-year tenure. In 1867 the regents ended a long interregnum when they attracted the theologian and naturalist Paul Chadbourne from a Williams College professorship to the Wisconsin presidency. With a talent for academic leadership he pleased the regents while guiding them and choosing his own faculty; but after three years he resigned, preferring to become president of Williams College. His successor at Wisconsin, John Twombly, a Methodist minister, proved to be more a churchman than an educator or administrator. After holding the office from 1871 to 1874, Twombly resigned under pressure from the regents.[16]

Included in the 1866 reorganization of the university was a provision for the establishment of an agricultural college as a part of the institution. The aim was to entitle the university to the 240,000 acres of land that the federal government, under the Morrill Act of 1862, had offered the state for the endowment of a college of agriculture and mechanical arts. Ripon College

[15] On Milton College, see William F. Allen and David E. Spencer, *Higher Education in Wisconsin* (Washington, D.C., 1889), 62–65. On Sacred Heart College, see Johnson, *Crosier on the Frontier*, 121.

[16] Merle Curti and Vernon Carstensen, *The University of Wisconsin: A History, 1848–1925* (2 vols., Madison, 1949), 1: 207–245.

and Lawrence University sent lobbyists to Madison in 1866 to try and get the agricultural college and the endowment. At first, the senate voted in favor of Ripon, then reversed itself and concurred with the assembly in deciding for the state university, on the condition that Dane County provide $40,000 in county bonds for the purchase of an experimental farm. The legislature set a minimum price of only $1.25 an acre for the Morrill grant, hoping for quick sales and immediate cash rather than delaying in an effort to maximize the long-run gain. In doing so, the legislature had little choice, since holding the lands and making the state a land speculator would have been very unpopular.[17]

Yet friends of the university were able to accuse the legislature of neglecting the university's interests in disposing too cheaply of both the new land scrip and the older university lands, and they were thus able to open the way for state support of higher education with tax money. In 1866, proceeds from the Morrill grant were still to come in, and the university had too little income for its regular departments, to say nothing of the added burden of an agricultural college. The first president of the board of regents under the reorganization—Edward Salomon, the former governor—contended that the university was suffering from the mismanagement of its lands and of the fund derived from them. In particular, he charged that the legislature in 1862 had diverted $100,000 from the fund for war purposes and thus had deprived the university of the annual interest on that amount. To make up for the income that was being lost, the legislature in 1867 passed a bill to appropriate to the university $7,303.76 a year for eleven years. After turning down, three years in a row, appeals for an appropriation for an additional building, the legislature in 1870 provided $50,000 for the construction of what was to be known as Ladies' Hall (later Chadbourne Hall). Then, in 1872, the

[17] Wilbur H. Glover, "The Agricultural College Lands in Wisconsin," in *WMH*, 30 (March, 1947), 261–272; Curti and Carstensen, *University of Wisconsin*, 1: 296–301.

legislature initiated an annual tax to raise $10,000 as a supplement to the income of the university fund. At last, Wisconsin was firmly committed to the principle of direct financial aid to the university.[18]

The reorganization act of 1866 specified that "the university in all of its departments and colleges" should be "open alike to male and female students." But Chadbourne accepted the presidency on the condition that women be confined to a separate "Female Department," and the law was amended so that they would be. So long as he remained, students of opposite sexes saw one another only while on their way to and from segregated classes or at infrequent social gatherings. The building that became Ladies' Hall was originally intended for a Female College. With the departure of Chadbourne, however, the university turned again in the direction of complete co-education. "And now, regardless of sex," Governor Lucius Fairchild said in 1871, "may the best scholar win."

By 1873, the university had not yet become what its first head had envisaged a quarter of a century earlier—the apex of an educational pyramid covering the state. Each high school still set up its own curriculum, without regard to the university's program, and the university still maintained its own preparatory department. When in that year President Twombly proposed that all the high schools serve as preparatory departments for the university, he provoked criticism on the part of representatives of both the high schools and the private colleges. The high schools, some said, were intended to fit young people for the world, not for the university. The private colleges, some feared, would lose out to the university in the competition for high-school graduates. Premature was the unification plan that Twombly and his fellow members of a committee drew up for the Wisconsin teachers' association. This plan would have

[18] Irvin G. Wyllie, "Land and Learning," in *WMH*, 30 (December, 1946), 170–173. Wyllie maintains that the Wisconsin university lands, both those from prewar grants and those from the Morrill grant, were in fact well managed. Patzer, *Public Education in Wisconsin*, 265–266, disagrees. See also Curti and Carstensen, *University of Wisconsin*, 1: 302–310.

required the high schools to make their courses "correspond with the standard for admission to the University," and it would also have geared the normal-school curriculum to the university curriculum, so that students completing the two-year program at one of the normal schools could easily go on for the final two years at the university.[19]

The three normal schools in operation by 1873 had resulted from an act of 1865, which authorized the state to set up its own separate institutions for training teachers and not continue to subsidize private academies and colleges for doing so. According to the new law, the regents of normal schools were to establish these institutions and maintain them with the income from a fund into which was to go one-half of the proceeds from the sale of the state's swamp and overflowed lands, the other half going into a fund for drainage projects. Before locating the first of the normal schools, the regents followed the example of similar authorities in Massachusetts and other states and advertised for bids from communities that would be willing to offer land, money, and buildings. Proposals and promises quickly came from villages and cities— including Baraboo, Berlin, Fond du Lac, Geneva (Lake Geneva), Milwaukee, Neenah-Menasha, Omro, Oshkosh, Platteville, Prairie du Chien, Racine, Sheboygan, Stoughton, Trempealeau, Waupun, and Whitewater—where local leaders were especially convinced that a normal school would bring in business if not also culture.

Visiting several of the proffered sites and looking at normal schools in other states, the regents narrowed their selection to Platteville and Whitewater. They wished to open at least one of the institutions as soon as possible. Platteville was bidding only $5,000 in cash (as compared with several other places bidding $30,000 or more), but was also offering the buildings

---

[19] Patzer, *Public Education in Wisconsin,* 255–256, 261–264, quoting the 1866 law and Governor Fairchild; Curti and Carstensen, *University of Wisconsin,* 1: 369–376, 480–490 (quotation from p. 489); Mrs. William F. Allen, "The University of Wisconsin Soon After the Civil War," in *WMH,* 7 (September, 1923), 20–29.

and grounds of the Platteville Academy, a going concern, available for immediate use. In October 1866 the metamorphosed academy began its career as Wisconsin's first normal school. Whitewater, the second choice, did not yet have the money ($25,000) or even the land it had promised. Citizens raised enough by private subscription to buy a ten-acre site and voted a tax to raise most of the construction money, which proved inadequate and had to be supplemented from the state normal-school fund. Three stories high, more than a hundred feet long, faced with cream brick, the Whitewater building seemed worthy of its distinction as the first specifically designed for a normal school in Wisconsin. It was dedicated in April 1868, and classes began immediately.

Whitewater was in the first congressional district, and Platteville in the third. At first the board of regents intended eventually to place a normal school in each of the six districts, choosing Stoughton in the second, Sheboygan in the fourth, and Oshkosh in the fifth, but with the understanding that the institutions in these places should not be developed until the state's educational needs should warrant. The Oshkosh State Normal School opened in September 1871. Having established three of the schools in the southern part of their state, the regents changed their priorities and decided to locate the next one in the north, in the sixth district, as soon as the income from the normal-school fund would justify another institution. The winning candidate was River Falls, whose campus site received the board's approval in 1873.

From the beginning, the mission of Wisconsin's state normal schools was somewhat ambiguous. A debate arose on the question whether they ought to emphasize pedagogical training or general education. In actual practice they tried to accomplish a bit of each. Their influence did not reach as far as it might have done, to help in the development of a teaching profession, since prospective teachers did not have to possess credentials from any normal school. The great majority continued to get their certificates simply by taking an examination administered by local superintendents and after 1868 by a state board of examiners.[20]

[4]

Once the war was over, local governments could resume and extend community services that, for four years, they had been compelled to neglect to some degree. They could give increased attention to fire protection, water supply, waste disposal, and other provisions for the well-being of the public. As among the various municipalities, however, the advance was quite uneven. Milwaukee, being much the largest of them, faced much the most serious problems and also went much the farthest in assuming public responsibilities.

Despite the danger of conflagrations, especially in the lumbering areas, some villages still provided little or no fire protection. Eau Claire, for example, had no fire-safety ordinances and no fire-fighting equipment. Sawmill owners there issued their own regulations and furnished their own apparatus. Forehanded householders kept a supply of sand and a full rain barrel for emergencies, and when a blaze occurred the people converted themselves into a fire brigade, forming a chain to pass buckets of water up from the river. Menasha acquired a volunteer fire company in 1863 after a disastrous blaze at a pail factory, and between 1865 and 1868 Neenah replaced its bucket brigade and homemade apparatus with newer equipment. Even earlier was Milwaukee, which by 1861 had its first modern steam fire engine and had semiprofessional firemen, who served half time for half pay. In the early 1870's the city

[20] William H. Herrmann, "The Rise of the Public Normal School System in Wisconsin" (doctoral dissertation, University of Wisconsin, 1953), 150, 155–184, 228–229, 260–261; Walker D. Wyman et al., *History of the Wisconsin State Universities*, ed. Walker D. Wyman (River Falls, Wisconsin, 1968), 7–12, 22–26, 57–60, 96–99, 134–138; Richard D. Gamble, *From Academy to University, 1866–1966: A History of Wisconsin State University, Platteville, Wisconsin* (Platteville, 1966), 95–105; John Lankford, "'Culture and Business': The Founding of the Fourth State Normal School at River Falls," in *WMH*, 47 (Autumn, 1963), 26–34.

completed the transition to professionalism, with a well-trained, full-time force.[21]

Until then, no village or city did more about supplying water than to maintain public pumps and cisterns. At the public pumps in Milwaukee, water-fetching citizens often had to wait until thirsty horses had drunk their fill from their owners' pails—or from any pail that was handy. The Milwaukee *Sentinel* advised: "The remedy is to be found in every well-regulated city: a capacious trough, whose contents will be free to every horse. Aldermen and Councilmen, attention!" In Milwaukee, as everywhere else in the state, the vast majority of people still depended on their own wells, springs, or other sources of water. Whether wells were public or private, they were likely to be contaminated by sewage, especially in the city. Many Milwaukee families therefore relied on rain water that they captured in cisterns and filtered before using. There had long been talk of piping water from Lake Michigan, and in 1871 a municipal board of water commissioners, headed by Alexander Mitchell, ordered the work to begin, in accordance with plans that the city engineer of Chicago had drawn up. Before the end of 1873, Milwaukee had its municipal water system.[22]

In dealing with sewage and other wastes, Milwaukee again led other municipalities in the state, yet its facilities remained inadequate. As of 1865, the city had some older wooden sewers and some more recent tile ones, but not for several years after the creation of the board of public works, in 1869, did the authorities begin to develop a city-wide sewerage system. Meanwhile fastidious Milwaukeeans complained of stinking streams in the downtown gutters and other revolting instances of air and water pollution, some of which the sewerage system, even when it was completed, could hardly be expected to eliminate. In the spring of 1866 the people of the west side feared they were threatened with cholera as a result of the "sickening

---

[21] Willard F. Miller, "A History of Eau Claire County During the Civil War" (master's thesis, University of Wisconsin, 1954), 106–108; Alice E. Smith, *Millstone and Saw: The Origins of Neenah–Menasha* (Madison, 1966), 162; Still, *Milwaukee*, 235. See also S. F. Shattuck, comp., *A History of Neenah* (Neenah, Wisconsin, 1958), 215.

[22] Milwaukee *Sentinel*, August 8, 1870; Still, *Milwaukee*, 247–248.

effluvia," the "stench and miasmatic odors," that the southwest wind frequently brought from slaughterhouses and lard-rendering plants on the marsh, where blood and entrails were floating "by the cord." At the instigation of the fourth ward's leading businessmen, the common council directed the offenders to clean up their premises. But polluters continued to pollute, and the authorities had to take repeated action to enforce the ordinances against it. "Under the direction of the Mayor," the *Sentinel* reported in the summer of 1872, "the police have commenced notifying property owners who have used alleys adjoining their premises, for depositing garbage, ashes and filth generally, that they must have the nuisance removed." The municipal authorities themselves, however, assumed no responsibility for removing and disposing of such wastes.[23]

Another persisting nuisance to be abated, in large and small communities alike, was that of animals whose owners failed to look after them properly. Having earlier set a penalty for a man letting his hog run loose, the Trempealeau town meeting resolved in 1866: "Any person having a Bull in his possession and allowing him to run at large shall be liable to a fine of Fifteen Dollars." In 1867 the city of Milwaukee threatened to exterminate stray dogs. When the governing board of the newly incorporated village of Stoughton met in 1868, the first official action was to keep animals from running at large (the second action to restrain drunkards; the third, to provide sidewalks). Back of the demand for confining or controlling animals, there was of course a concern for private property and personal safety, but at times there was also an interest in the preservation of the natural environment. Thus the *Sentinel*, in 1872, called for a much larger fine than the five dollars customarily imposed on those arrested for hitching their horses to trees on the Milwaukee streets. "The idea of allowing a horse to tear the bark off from a tree and ruin in a few moments what nature has been years in producing!"[24]

One Milwaukeean suffered, in 1872, from a nuisance that

[23] *Ibid.*, 239, 241–242; Milwaukee *Sentinel*, April 10, 1866, June 1, 1872.
[24] Curti, *Making of an American Community*, 300–301; *Wisconsin State Journal*, December 16, 1928; Milwaukee *Sentinel*, April 29, 1867, April 5, 1872.

he blamed on the common council, or rather on a particular member of it, Valentin Blatz. The complaining resident and property owner lived near Blatz's brewery, which used "steam signals" to communicate with its employees. The "fearful, diabolical shrieks and screams of that devilish machine of human torture" kept many people in the neighborhood awake during much of the night and early morning, the resident said in a letter to the editor of the *Sentinel*. If anyone else would make such "hellish noises" and at such hours, he would be arrested. Therefore why should a council member, who was "responsible for the peace, comfort, health and general welfare of his constituents," be allowed to get away with such "infernal disturbances"?

As yet, few people in Wisconsin or elsewhere expected local governments to do much to provide recreational facilities. Though, as early as 1848, some Milwaukeeans had suggested the creation of a city park, the majority long remained content with vacant lots as playgrounds and the commercial public gardens as places of amusement. In the late 1860's, however, Milwaukeeans were inspired by the example of New York City, Cleveland, and Detroit to reconsider the matter. Proposed for Milwaukee was a park along the lake front, one that would be accessible to people who could not "afford to go into the country for their recreation." Such a park, extending from Division Street to Biddle Street, was opened in 1869.[25]

[5]

By the early 1870's, Wisconsin was making some progress toward centralization and rationalization in the care of dependents, but the care remained barely adequate at best. Even in the minds of humanitarians, the poor themselves were responsible for their poverty. It was due to their innate moral defects, their laziness, improvidence, and intemperance. Indiscriminate charity would only reward such traits and encourage pauper-

[25] Milwaukee *Sentinel*, September 7, 1872; Still, *Milwaukee*, 242, quoting the *Sentinel*, July 26, 1867.

ism. Yet the public must provide some relief, for otherwise the community would be "liable to imposition, theft, disease, crime, and its attendant evils and taxations."[26]

Seemingly, a disproportionate number of the dependents were foreign-born. Immigrants made up less than 35 per cent of the state's population, yet figures represented them as constituting about 65 per cent of the paupers and the insane and about half the prisoners. "It is a striking fact, calling for our earnest consideration," Dr. Joseph Hobbins commented, "that the Germans, Irish and Scandinavians *import* and *transmit* more insanity—three to one—than the American-born population produce." Dr. Hobbins, himself an immigrant, born and trained in England, argued that mental illness was "largely heriditary." But he also agreed with the superintendent of the Wisconsin State Hospital for the Insane that it could result from the living conditions of the "large poor class" in Wisconsin, especially in the northern part of the state, who knew little except "hard work, exposure to a severe climate, bad and insufficient diet, cheerless homes." In any event, the incidence of insanity as well as poverty and criminality among the immigrants was not so dramatically high as it appeared to be. Of the adult population, the foreign-born made up not around 35 per cent but nearly 60 per cent, as compared with 50 to 65 per cent of the inhabitants of jails, asylums, and poorhouses (assuming these percentages to be more or less accurate).[27]

The number of poor needing and receiving public aid varied, of course, with the condition of the economy, and the number was considerably smaller in 1870 than it had been in 1860,

[26] Donald J. Berthrong, "Social Legislation in Wisconsin, 1836–1900" (doctoral dissertation, University of Wisconsin, 1951), 16, 236–238. The quotation is from the Wisconsin Board of Charities and Reform, *Annual Report*, 1873, p. 253.

[27] For statistics on foreign-born dependents and on the adult population in 1870, see the *Ninth Census of the United States, 1870: Volume I*, p. 568, and *ibid.: Volume II*, pp. 473–484, 580, 585, 596, 599. For 1871 and 1872 statistics, see Virgil E. Long, "State Supervision and Control of Welfare Agencies and Institutions in Wisconsin: Processes and Structures" (doctoral dissertation, University of Wisconsin, 1944), 22, and Wisconsin Board of Charities and Reform, *Annual Report*, 1872, pp. 225, 268–269, 272–273. Dr. Hobbins is quoted from Joseph Hobbins, "Health of Wisconsin," in Western Historical Company, *The History of Sauk County, Wisconsin* . . . (Chicago, 1880), 242–243. See also Joseph Hobbins in *DWB*.

when Wisconsin and the nation had not yet recovered from the Depression of 1857. Even so, the burden in 1870 was too great for governmental units to bear alone, and private organizations had to help. In Oshkosh, for example, the Ladies' Aid Society supplemented the "temporary relief" that the county afforded, the Amateur Dramatic Association contributing $235 to "alleviate the want and suffering" of more than fifty families who appealed for assistance during the winter months. In various communities, Germans, Scandinavians, and other ethnic groups continued to maintain and expand their own relief societies. By 1871, eleven private institutions for the dependent were operating in the state, nine of them in Milwaukee—two hospitals (the Catholic St. Mary's founded in 1859, and the Lutheran Passavant founded in 1863), six orphanages, one home for seamen, another for the friendless, and a school. Seven of the eleven were Catholic, two were Protestant, and two were nonsectarian. All received some money from the state, but they depended mainly on voluntary contributions.[28]

By 1870, twenty-two of Wisconsin's fifty-eight counties were maintaining poorhouses. These then contained a total of 1,240 inmates, of whom 197 were classified as insane (108 female, eighty-nine male), forty as epileptic, thirty as feebleminded, twenty as blind, and eight as deaf and dumb. More than 200 were children, and fifteen to twenty babies were born in the poorhouses each year. Conditions in most of these places were as bad as ever, with dark, damp basement rooms, pallets of dirty straw on the floor, and swarms of lice and bedbugs. Outside the poorhouses were 2,560 other indigents subsisting at least in part on public funds. Each town was responsible for the maintenance of its own paupers, whether or not they were institutionalized, and the town taxpayer turned a deaf ear to pleas that he make better provision for them. "Is it reasonable,"

[28] *Eighth Census of the United States, 1860: Mortality and Miscellaneous Statistics,* 512; *Ninth Census of the United States, 1870: Volume I,* p. 568; Robertson, "Social History of Winnebago County," 22–23; Long, "Welfare Agencies and Institutions in Wisconsin," 27–28; Roy A. Suelflow, *A Plan for Survival* (New York, 1965), 185–186; Smith, *Millstone and Saw,* 91–93, 191–192.

he would respond, "that we should be asked to provide better accommodations for the poor, many of whom are reduced to poverty by their own evil conduct, than we provide for ourselves and families?"[29]

By 1871, forty-eight of the fifty-eight counties had jails. Milwaukee County, in the previous year demolished its old jail and held its prisoners in a modern "house of correction." Most of the other jails were jerrybuilt, insecure, and unsanitary, with no facilities for bathing and with interior privies that left an "atmosphere so foul and offensive as to be intolerable to a person coming into it from the outer world." These institutions were schools of vice into which were promiscuously herded the old and young, male and female, sane and insane, innocent and guilty (witnesses and persons awaiting trial along with the convicted). "A minute and careful examination of the jails of Illinois Wisconsin and Michigan, by kindred commissions specially appointed for this purpose, reveals the fact that as proper places of punishment, they fail to accomplish the object of their creation," an 1872 report declared. "They are an absurd attempt to cure crime, the offspring of idleness, by making idleness compulsory."[30]

At the end of the war the state had taken steps to provide some care for one class of dependents—those whom the war itself had produced. When, in 1865, the former governor's widow, Cordelia A. P. Harvey, returned to Madison from her Samaritan labors in the South, she brought with her several war orphans. Of such orphans, there were several thousand more in Wisconsin. Mrs. Harvey determined to do something for them. She persuaded the federal government to donate the use of Harvey Hospital (the Madison army hospital, con-

[29] Long, "Welfare Agencies and Institutions in Wisconsin," 28–33, 47; Curti, *Making of an American Community*, 111–112; Berthrong, "Social Legislation in Wisconsin," 17–20, citing the Wisconsin Board of Charities and Reform, *Annual Report*, 1871, pp. 33–43, 65, 70–71; the quotation is from p. 87.

[30] Long, "Welfare Agencies and Institutions in Wisconsin," 28, 32–35, 57, quoting from the Wisconsin Board of Charities and Reform, *Annual Report*, 1871, p. 124, and from the declaration of a conference of the state boards of Illinois, Wisconsin, and Michigan, meeting in Chicago in 1872, as printed in *ibid.*, 1872, pp. 17–18.

sisting of the Farwell house and three added wings) and then persuaded the state government to purchase and support it as the Soldiers' Orphans' Home. She served as its first superintendent. From 1866 to 1874, when the state discontinued it (most of the orphans having reached their teens), the home sheltered between 200 and 300 children at a time. Meanwhile, in 1867, the legislature passed an act "to provide for destitute soldiers and their families." The law merely authorized towns to raise and disburse money (not to exceed $150 per person) for that purpose.[31]

The orphanage in Madison was the sixth of the state welfare or reform institutions to be set up, the others being the institute for the blind in Janesville, the prison in Waupun, the institute for the deaf and dumb in Delavan, the hospital for the insane in Madison, and the industrial school for boys in Waukesha. Reformers insisted that there ought to be still more institutions—for orphans, for delinquent girls, for "idiotic and imbecile youth"—but the thrifty legislature refused to sanction any of these. It did provide, in 1870, for a second mental hospital, Oshkosh winning over Milwaukee, Watertown, La Crosse, and Fond du Lac in the competition for a site. The new hospital, opened in 1873, and the older one, with successive enlargements, could accommodate a combined total of fewer than 600 patients, or fewer than half as many as needed care and treatment. Hundreds continued to be confined in poorhouses or jails.[32]

The state prison came in for a great deal of criticism, much of it from Democrats seeking to discredit one Republican state administration after another. Governors exposed themselves to the charge of partiality when they pardoned convicts. With the pardoning power Governor Lucius Fairchild freed "Sleeky

[31] Ethel A. Hurn, *Wisconsin Women in the War Between the States* (Madison, 1911), 144–147; Berthrong, "Social Legislation in Wisconsin," 29–32. See also Wisconsin Soldiers' Orphans' Home Board of Trustees, *Final Report*, 1894.

[32] Long, "Welfare Agencies and Institutions in Wisconsin," 19–20, 25–26, 29, 49–55; Berthrong, "Social Legislation in Wisconsin," 60–65, 210–212, 223–224, 228–231, quoting on p. 229 from a legislative bill introduced in 1868 by the Committee on Charitable and Benevolent Institutions.

John," a notorious figure in Milwaukee vice and crime, and then, in 1868, Michael Gamble, who was serving a term for second-degree murder. Democrats said that Gamble had bought his pardon with a $1,000 contribution to the Republican party. Democrats also accused the prison commissioner of spending as much to maintain convicts in Waupun as he would have to pay to put them up at one of the leading Milwaukee hotels. (The yearly cost of keeping the approximately 200 prisoners averaged $255.33, which was indeed a larger sum than the annual income of many a common laborer in Wisconsin.) Chair manufacturers objected to the use of prison labor, from 1867 on, to make chairs that the prison sold in competition with private enterprise.[33]

The prison was administered by a commissioner, who was popularly elected for a two-year term. Each of the other state institutions was under the management of an executive who owed his position to a separate board of trustees, who in turn received their appointments from the governor. The governor could remove trustees, and the legislature could investigate and withhold appropriations from any of the various institutions. Until 1871, however, there was no regular, continuous agency for planning, co-ordinating, and supervising the operations of those institutions, not to mention the dozens of county jails and poorhouses. Some of the institutional boards had become virtually autonomous and self-perpetuating local cliques that aroused suspicion of gross favoritism.

Having dismissed an Episcopalian as superintendent, the Congregational and Presbyterian trustees of the Delavan institute for the deaf were in the thick of a controversy in 1868 over alleged discrimination on religious grounds. Governor Fairchild was beset with appeals to intervene, and he began to call for a supervisory agency—which, if it accomplished nothing else, might at least shield the governor from direct involve-

---

[33] Miriam Z. Langsam, "The Nineteenth Century Wisconsin Criminal: Ideologies and Institutions" (doctoral dissertation, University of Wisconsin, 1967), 112–118; Long, "Welfare Agencies and Institutions in Wisconsin," 24, 40–45; Berthrong, "Social Legislation in Wisconsin," 72, 253–254.

ment in such embarrassing disputes. In 1870 a legislative committee investigating the Delavan affair also recommended that Wisconsin set up a central body to check the various boards, as six other states had recently done. Some people endorsed the proposal on the assumption that it would lessen the rate of increase in public spending. "If we keep on a few years," the Madison *Democrat* warned in rather far-fetched alarm, "is it not more than probable that the whole machinery of the state will merge into a mere machine to raise revenues to support the criminal and the afflicted?"[34]

An act of 1871 created the State Board of Charities and Reform, to consist of five part-time unpaid members, whom the governor was to appoint for staggered five-year terms, and a full-time salaried secretary whom the board was to hire. Its duties were to "investigate and supervise the whole system of the charitable and correctional institutions supported by the state or receiving aid from the state treasury," to investigate poorhouses and other provisions for the poor, jails, and "all places of confinement," and to make recommendations for the improvement of all the foregoing. Thus the mandate was broad, including as it did the county jails and poorhouses and such private institutions as received state aid; yet the mandate was thin, since it gave no power to initiate actual changes.

Once in operation, the State Board of Charities and Reform received from the institutional boards their budget requests, approved or modified these, and transmitted them to the legislature. During the early years the state board recommended a smaller appropriation than the total the various boards had asked for. The legislature granted more than the recommendations but less than the original requests. Thus the new agency exerted little influence on the institutional budgets. For awhile the prison commissioner remained rather independent of the board. In 1873, however, the state board proposed and the legislature approved a reorganization, in

---

[34] Langsam, "Nineteenth Century Wisconsin Criminal," 118–125; Berthrong, "Social Legislation in Wisconsin," 44–52, 77–80; Long, "Welfare Agencies and Institutions in Wisconsin," 30–31, 37, 61–76; Madison *Democrat,* January 28, 1871.

which the commissioner, or warden, was selected by three directors whom the governor appointed.

The state board had less success in its efforts to reform the local procedures in caring for the poor. It sent questionnaires to local officials but got few replies. It investigated jails and poorhouses and drew up reports on the atrocious conditions, only to find its work ignored. So it turned to private groups for help—to the Christian women of Kenosha, to the Ladies' Bible and Benevolent Association of Milwaukee, and other organizations of the kind. These groups brought pressure on the officials and made some headway toward cleaning up the poorhouses and jails. But there was no dramatic change.[35]

[6]

As a law-enforcement agency, the Wisconsin state militia was even less effective in the postwar than in the prewar years. Indeed, the militia system hardly recovered from its wartime collapse. Friends of the system tried to revive it, and by the end of 1870 they had organized twenty-four volunteer companies. These were hard to maintain, however, for they had to buy their own uniforms and pay all their other expenses except for arms, the only thing the state provided until 1873. In that year the state began a modest cash subsidy ($100 per company at first, $300 from 1875 on). This stimulated the recruiting of additional units, but they too were short-lived. "At present," the state's adjutant general reported after a year's experience with the subsidy, "companies will organize and, stimulated by the novelty of parade and glitter of uniform, the organization [will] survive just long enough to involve the members in an expense which they cannot bear, then [will] disband, entailing upon the state the cost of transporting and re-transporting arms and accoutrements, etc." The militia was

[35] Langsam, "Nineteenth Century Wisconsin Criminal," 125–130; Long, "Welfare Agencies and Institutions in Wisconsin," 106–109, 290–313; Berthrong, "Social Legislation in Wisconsin," 80–81, 198–200; *Laws of Wisconsin,* 1871, pp. 197–201.

yet to develop, under the name of the National Guard, into a strong force capable of breaking strikes and putting down mob violence.[36]

In some Wisconsin communities, at the war's end, the police departments had not yet recovered from budget cuts following the Panic of 1857. In Milwaukee, the *Sentinel* complained in 1865, there was but one patrolman for every 3,000 inhabitants, while "in nearly every other city in the Union" there was one for every 1,000. Soon Milwaukee doubled police salaries and nearly doubled the number of policemen, enlarging the force to forty-two. Though the ratio, even so, was only one patrolman for every 1,700 people, the mayor boasted in 1869 that Milwaukee was the "most orderly city on the continent." Election day in 1872, the *Journal of Commerce* was pleased to report, "passed with the orderliness peculiar to Milwaukee" and without the "noise, and rows, and brick-bats, and bowie knives with which the free-born American in other cities" was "wont to emphasize his sense of freedom."[37]

Elsewhere in Wisconsin, however, people were in no such self-congratulatory mood. In Trempealeau County the papers contained a disturbing quantity of crime news—burglaries of stores and shops, the stealing of wood from a woodpile, the theft of a cow, public drunkenness, fights, incest, adultery, attempted rape—and editorials deploring the lawless trend of the times. Galesville was getting worse and worse during the 1870's, it seemed to one of the local pioneers. "Have we no civil laws and civil forces?" this man finally asked in despair. Many others throughout the state shared his feeling that the legal and judicial system was failing to protect law-abiding citizens from the criminal element. In some places this fear rose at times to a hysterical pitch.[38]

[36] Jerry M. Cooper, "The Wisconsin Militia, 1832–1900" (master's thesis, University of Wisconsin, 1968), 187–196, quoting the adjutant general on p. 196; Ralph J. Olson, "The Wisconsin National Guard," in *WMH*, 39 (Summer, 1956), 231–233.

[37] Still, *Milwaukee*, 233, quoting the Milwaukee *Sentinel*, November 17, 1865, and the mayor from *ibid.*, April 21, 1869; Milwaukee *Journal of Commerce*, November 6, 1872.

[38] On crime and attitudes toward it in Trempealeau County, see Curti, *Making of an American Community*, 118–121.

Fearful and frustrated, some Wisconsinites were ready to take the law into their own hands, or to applaud those who did so. Even in Milwaukee, which took such pride in its orderliness, mobs still appeared occasionally, though in the postwar years there was nothing comparable to the bank riot or the lynching of 1861 or the antidraft demonstrations of 1862. Some Milwaukeeans objected to the way the police dealt with prostitutes, periodically arresting and fining and then letting them go, thus "practically making them pay a license to the city and thus making the city a party to the iniquity." On a June evening in 1869 the irate neighbors of Big Mollie suddenly gathered outside her bawdyhouse and "completely riddled [it] with stones." The police arrived in time to rescue Big Mollie and to arrest four of her girls.[39]

To deal with "epidemics" of horse stealing, which were especially frequent from 1867 on, farmers and others organized "vigilance committees." Reporting a gang of Crawford County horse thieves, "very adroit in their operations," the Prairie du Chien *Union* advised the people to use "summary measures" on any of the thieves they might catch. But even officers of the law sometimes found it difficult to capture such criminals. In 1869 some members of the Dell Moon gang defied the sheriff, who, with a ten-man posse, had tracked them to a hide-out in Eau Claire County, and the sheriff and his men failed to bring in either the thieves or the stolen horses.[40]

"We are asked why we did not notice a row in one of our saloons last week, wherein a person was nearly killed by a blow on the head with an axe," the *Island City Times* of Neenah and Menasha commented one day in 1866. "We usually prefer to pass such 'trifling affairs' over lightly, not wishing to create an impression abroad that we have here all the vices of a city without the corresponding benefits of a metropolitan population and government." A few years later a group of Menashans tarred and feathered a man for what must have

[39] Milwaukee *Sentinel*, September 17, 1867, and June 28, 1869.
[40] Joseph Schafer, *The Winnebago-Horicon Basin: A Type Study in Western History* (Madison, 1937), 253–254; Milwaukee *Sentinel*, November 13, 1867, and July 26, 1869.

seemed to them like more than merely trifling affairs. If half the stories about the man were true, the Oshkosh *Journal* opined, he had not "got half his just deserts." Concern about crime reached a new height in the community when, in 1871, a prisoner escaped from the Winnebago County jail in Oshkosh, killed his wife in Neenah, and then committed suicide. A committee of Neenah business leaders denounced the attorney who earlier had defended the man, as well as the law officers who had allowed him to escape. The resulting Citizens League launched a campaign against liquor as a presumed cause of crime and in favor of city government as a presumed means of controlling it. Neenah received its city charter in 1873.[41]

After going seven years without a lynching, Wisconsin was the scene of five mob murders in three years, from 1868 to 1871, in addition to several near-lynchings. One of the latter occurred early in 1869 in Monroe, when a hotel servant girl, Angeline Shroyer, shot and killed her seducer, a well-to-do Irish farmer by the name of Patrick Crotty, and a crowd of Crotty's friends followed Angeline menacingly to jail but decided not to brave the sheriff's pointed revolver. Another threatened lynching of an accused murderer was averted that same week in Prairie du Chien, when the sheriff, with an armed force that he quickly increased from eight to forty men, held off a mob of several hundred while he sneaked his prisoner off to Milwaukee on a freight train.

But no one interfered with the raging multitude that came to the Richland Center jail in September 1868 for the fifteen-year-old Neville boy, the alleged robber-murderer of a young Irish housewife. Men dragged the boy out with a rope, breaking his neck instantly, and women stoned him along the way to the appointed tree, though he was already dead. Any attempt to rescue him, the *Wisconsin State Journal* said, "would have been useless, as the mob was composed principally of Irishmen, who were determined to avenge the death of their country woman." A year later lynchers also made short work of an Indian who, according to the Kilbourn City *Mirror*, had murdered a Frenchman in the cranberry marsh north of Necedah and had been jailed in New Lisbon. "On Sunday a masked mob came down from Necedah, forcibly entered the jail, and, taking the Indian out, hung him to the nearest tree." When in 1871, at a German ball in Oconto, a butcher went berserk and fired into the crowd of revelers, fatally wounding one of them, the crowd turned immediately into a lynch mob. On this occasion the law officers temporarily saved the intended victim, putting him in the Oconto jail, a flimsy wooden structure. The next day, after the wounded man died, the mob "overpowered the officers, and, with a big beam, smashed the jail down," seized the mad butcher, and hanged him "right in the village."[42]

The law-and-order hysteria went to its greatest extremes in the central Wisconsin River valley, and particularly in Portage, where two lynchings occurred in less than forty-eight hours. Already, in September 1869, a "portion of our community," as the Portage *State Register* observed, had been in a "state of feverish excitement—and bolts and bars, guns, pistols, big knives, clubs and broomsticks" had been "the order of the day, or rather of the *night*," in consequence of a series of burglaries. Then, to add to the excitement and touch off the events leading to the violence, local police arrested, for attempted robbery, an ex-convict who was feared and hated throughout the area as a desperado, one who thus far had managed to avoid punishment for the most heinous of his alleged crimes.[43]

The man was Pat Wildrick, of Kilbourn City. More than a year earlier, after serving a two-year term in the prison at

[42] Milwaukee *Sentinel*, September 30, 1868 (quoting the *Wisconsin State Journal*, September 28, 1868); January 20, January 23 (quoting the Monroe *Sentinel*, January 20), October 2, 1869 (citing the Kilbourn City *Mirror*, September 29, 1869); June 1, 1871.

[43] Portage *State Register*, September 18, 1869. For a brief account of the two lynchings, see Western Historical Company, *The History of Columbia County, Wisconsin* (Chicago, 1880), 494–495.

Waupun for highway robbery, Wildrick had recommenced his evil ways, according to the charges brought against him. His elderly fellow townsman, Schuyler S. Gates, had departed from the Dells with about $2,400 and a youthful wife, going down river in two rowboats lashed together, his ultimate destination presumed to be Kansas. The first night out, while Mr. and Mrs. Gates were camping on the bank near Sauk City, a pair of masked men fell upon them, beating him, taking his money, and leaving him for dead after one of them had raped her. Suspecting Wildrick, who had disappeared from Kilbourn City shortly after the Gates's departure, the sheriff of Columbia County tracked him to a bawdyhouse near McGregor, Iowa, and took him to Baraboo, where he was lodged in the Sauk County jail. The judge set bail at $5,000, too much for Wildrick to raise, so the prisoner broke out, but was recaptured. Then, accusing the judge of prejudice and demanding a change of venue, he was transferred to Juneau County, where the new judge reduced the bail to $2,000. Wildrick was out on bail, after repeated postponements of his trial, when he was caught in the act of robbing, on a Portage street, a young Norwegian with whom he had been drinking and playing cards.

That was on a Friday night, September 10. The next Monday, Wildrick's previous victim Schuyler S. Gates (who had recovered from the beating) was found dead near the Sauk County end of the bridge at the Dells. He had been murdered, but not robbed, by an assailant or assailants whose identity and motive were unknown. Many who heard the news jumped to the conclusion that the murderers were confederates of Wildrick and that they had undertaken, on his orders, to eliminate the witness most threatening to him.

While the news was going the rounds in Portage, the examination of Wildrick on the recent charge of attempted robbery got under way there. On this occasion his attorney was William H. Spain, an Irishman, a Civil War veteran, a bitter and unpopular man whose difficult personality might have been both cause and result of his lack of success at the Portage bar. Spain now further antagonized many of his fellow citizens by abusing them while defending his robber-client. He was quoted as saying that, "if Wildrick was a bad man, he was better than they." To them, however, Spain seemed like one more of many delayers of justice in the Wildrick case.

On Thursday afternoon Spain encountered Barney Britt, a farmer and the courthouse janitor, on the street in Portage. Also Irish, Britt had served as a private in the Nineteenth Wisconsin, Company D, of which Spain had been captain. "The war for the Union created many feuds among those who had previously been neighbors and friends," the Neenah-Menasha *Island City Times* was afterward to comment, "and the peace following sees many a vow of vengeance, for real or fancied wrongs, being fulfilled." Certainly former Captain Spain and former Private Britt quarreled every time they met. This time, Spain shot and killed Britt. Having given himself up, Spain was being escorted down the sidewalk by a marshal and a deputy sheriff when a rapidly gathering crowd of several hundred, largely Irish, overpowered the officers, dragged Spain to the nearest tree, and suspended him from it. He was dead less than an hour after he had killed Britt. The one man left a wife and four children, the other a wife and eight.

On the night of the next day, Friday, one week after the re-arrest of Wildrick, dozens of men took the train from Kilbourn City to Portage, and many others arrived by crossing the Wisconsin River bridge on foot, on horseback, or in wagons. About one o'clock on Saturday morning, September 18, three of the men, by a ruse, induced the sheriff and a deputy to open the jail door, and others then seized and tied up the officers. Quickly and quietly the mob took Pat Wildrick out and strung him up. On Saturday night, back in Kilbourn City, men again showed their righteousness by driving the madam and girls out of the "hell-hole of Kilbourn" and tearing the place down. Meanwhile Wildrick's father had brought home his son's body in the expectation that the local Catholic church would provide funeral services for it. "We hear," the Kilbourn City *Mirror* reported, "that on Sunday the Catholics refused to let it be buried in their ground, and that it was taken to Lyndon for burial."

The Portage *State Register* regretted the recent "tragic

scenes"—"which not infrequently occur in far Western towns, but are happily less frequent in communities where law and order are the established order of things"—yet the paper defended the "action of the people in executing" Wildrick. It maintained that, like the vigilantes of early California, the "law-abiding" people of Wisconsin were fully justified in taking upon themselves the punishment of criminals who otherwise would go unpunished. The small-town weeklies of the state's interior sided with the Portage paper, the Mauston *Star* saying the *Register* "expressed only the sentiment of every respectable citizen in the Wisconsin River Valley," and the Columbus *Republican* asking, "after all, what is this twofold tragedy but an appeal of the outraged instincts of a community, from the notorious inefficiency of our criminal machinery, and the disgusting results of the 'law's delay'?" The Madison *Democrat* suggested that mob justice was to be expected in view of Governor Fairchild's proclivity for pardoning convicts. But the big-city dailies, Republican and Democratic alike, deplored the Portage events. "Another stain has been added to the reputation of our state by these lawless proceedings," declared the Milwaukee *News*, adding that the Portage editor was as guilty of murder as were the two mobs, since he had incited the second one by approving the first. The Portage editor retorted: "The *News* indirectly espouses the cause of the worst criminals in the land—we are content to receive its denunciations, and hope it will be happy in receiving the plaudits of every villain in the State for its *noble stand in behalf of law and order.*"[44]

About three months afterward, in December 1869, a grand jury looked into the Portage lynchings. The presiding judge, in his charge to the jurors, gave them the impression that the lynchers were not to blame. At fault, instead, were those Wis-

---

[44] Portage *State Register*, September 18, 25, October 2, 1869. In its issues of September 25 and October 2 the *State Register* quoted the following papers: Chicago *Tribune*, Whitewater *Register*, Baraboo *Republic*, Milwaukee *Wisconsin*, Fond du Lac *Commonwealth*, Columbus *Republican*, St. Paul *Pioneer*, Milwaukee *News*, Mauston *Star*, Neillsville *Clark County Republican*, Milwaukee *Sentinel*, and Neenah-Menasha *Island City Times*. See also the Milwaukee *Sentinel*, September 17, 18, 21, 27, 1869, quoting and disputing the Portage *State Register;* and the Madison *Democrat*, October 4, 1869.

consinites who had a "weak and misplaced sympathy for murderers." In his native county and the surrounding counties in central New York, the judge related, there had been only one murder during all the years when he was growing up there. In the four counties of his judicial circuit in Wisconsin, however, there had been twelve indictments for murder in less than five years, but only one conviction for murder, plus four for third-degree or fourth-degree manslaughter. If Wisconsin were to keep people from taking the law into their own hands, he argued, the state must reform its trial procedures so as to make convictions more certain. Despite this long and tendentious charge from the bench, the grand jury indicted eleven men for the lynching of William H. Spain.

"But why indict only eleven?" the *State Register* demanded. The furious editor insisted that at least four times as many were involved and that most of them were at least as respectable as the jurors who indicted them. Indeed, he contended, at least a third of the jurors were aliens and hence ineligible for jury duty. He went into a tirade against the whole "grand (humbug) jury" system. To his relief, the judge quashed the indictments.[45]

This editor, who so commended the violent ways of the Wild West to his fellow citizens of Portage, was the father of Frederick Jackson Turner, who was later to be famous and influential as a historian, the author of the frontier interpretation of American history. In 1869 the boy was in his eighth year. He was never to forget: "I have seen a lynched man hanging from a tree when I came home from school. . . ." Yet, as one of the youthful orators at his high-school commencement in 1878, this son of the Portage publisher was to describe the press as "one of the greatest of civilizers and public teachers. . . ."[46]

[45] Portage *State Register*, December 11, 18, 25, 1869; Milwaukee *Sentinel*, December 18, 21, 1869. The remarks of the judge were printed in the Portage *State Register*, December 11, 1869; the editorial position in the issue of December 18, 1869.

[46] Ray A. Billington, "Young Fred Turner," in *WMH*, 46 (Autumn, 1962), 40, 43–44, quoting Turner to Carl Becker, December 16, 1925, and Turner's 1878 high-school oration.

15

A Society
Still in Formation

[1]

Woman's PLACE, as most Wisconsinites of whatever ethnic background viewed it, continued to be in the home. Though the Civil War had added to women's job opportunities, there was little or no lasting effect. Indeed, female employees constituted only about 5 per cent of the total labor force engaged in "mechanical and manufacturing industries" in 1870—roughly the same percentage as in 1860. Most employed women held jobs of the same sort as had long been considered women's work. They constituted substantially 100 per cent of the milliners and dressmakers and more than 95 per cent of those engaged in laundering. On the other hand, they made up less than 3 per cent of clerks, salespersons, and bookkeepers. Among the professions, the only one as yet freely open to women was schoolteaching, and they held over 76 per cent of the teaching jobs (their salaries averaged less than two-thirds as much as those of male teachers). A woman still found it difficult to gain acceptance in the medical profession. In 1869, when Laura J. Ross was proposed for membership in the Milwaukee Medical Society, a "bitter contest" developed which dragged on for several weeks before "Miss Dr. Ross" was finally admitted by a vote of ten to three.[1]

As household managers, however, most wives and mothers were fully occupied, especially those who had little or no support from a helpmate. One of those was Hamlin Garland's grandmother McClintock, whose husband was "weirdly unworldly," lacking in the work ethic that supposedly characterized his Yankee kind, and uninterested in the cultivation of the family farm in the coulee country near La Crosse. "Only the splendid abundance of the soil and the manual skill of his sons, united to the good management of his wife, kept his family fed and clothed." Another capable wife of a ne'er-do-well, Letitia Wall, a "gentlewoman" from North Carolina, made a living in Grant County by weaving carpets from rags, while Alpheus Wall fished and drank. The Norwegian wife of a hard-working and hard-drinking Swede knitted and sold or bartered mittens, scarves, and stockings to help the family develop a farm near Sparta. War widows and other widows, if they had no farm to manage, took what jobs they could find in order to keep themselves and their children alive until a possible second marriage. A widower looked for another wife. When a well-to-do Dutch farmer returned from Holland to Little Chute with his new bride, he ran into some criticism on account of his remarriage. "I was left with five children, the oldest one fourteen, the youngest a year and a half old," he protested. "Someone was needed to take care of them and to manage the household."[2]

[1] *Eighth Census of the United States, 1860: Manufactures,* 657–658; *Ninth Census of the United States, 1870: Volume III,* p. 583; *ibid.: Volume I,* p. 764. For the academic year 1869–1870, in Wisconsin's public schools, female teachers received an average monthly salary of $28, male teachers $43. See the U.S. Commissioner of Education, *Annual Report,* 1871, p. 371. The Milwaukee *Sentinel,* January 23, 1869, carries the item on Dr. Ross.

[2] Hamlin Garland, *A Son of the Middle Border* (New York, 1917), 20–21; Joseph Schafer, "Letitia Wall, A Wisconsin Pioneer Type," in *WMH,* 8 (December, 1924), 193–198; Oluf Erickson, "Olaf Erickson, Scandinavian Frontiersman," in *WMH,* 31 (September, 1947–March, 1948), 13–14, 17–18; Angie Kumlien Main, "Annals of a Wisconsin Thresherman" (the thresherman's Norwegian mother was a widow), in *WMH,* 11 (March, 1928), 301–308; Arnold Verstegen writes of his remarriage to relatives in Holland, November 17, 1870, in Henry S. Lucas, ed., *Dutch Immigrant Memoirs and Related Writings* (2 vols., Assen, Netherlands, 1955), 2: 171.

The household remained a center of industrial activity, especially on the farm. There was usually a definite division of labor, though it varied some from family to family and, still more, from one ethnic group to another. In families of old American stock the womenfolk, with the passing of the war, returned to doing only the work in and around the house. In many German families, younger women still milked the cows and even labored in the fields. The German father might rule his wife and children like a *Herr*, with strict notions regarding the kinds of work that were beneath a man's dignity. Yet both men and women knitted in some German households, and among the Norwegians there were entire families that specialized in weaving.[3]

The home continued to serve as a medical center also. For the vast majority of the people, no hospital was accessible. The mother treated minor ailments with familiar remedies, such as sulphur and molasses, or with something that she looked up in a "doctor book." In serious cases she provided emergency care until the arrival of a physician. The diseases most prevalent, in the experience of a practitioner who covered a circuit from Merrimac to Mazomanie in the 1870's, were pneumonia, bronchitis, tonsillitis, mastoiditis, pleurisy, and tuberculosis, though there were also cases of more terrifying maladies such as smallpox, cholera, and typhoid fever. This doctor, like most others of the time, invariably visited his patients in their homes.[4]

Houses of frame, brick, or stone had almost completely replaced crude log cabins except on the farthest reaches of settlement in the north. Typically, houses were heated by wood-

[3] Regarding an English family near Dodgeville, see Oscar Hallam, "Bloomfield and Number Five: The American Way of Life in a Wisconsin Rural Community in the 70s, as seen by a Small Boy," 8–9, 13, 16–17, 34–36, 90, 110–111, 115–116, an unpublished typescript [1944] in the SHSW; regarding a German family, Rose Schuster Taylor, "Peter Schuster, Dane County Farmer," in *WMH*, 28–29 (March–September, 1945), 28: 277–289, 431–454; 29: 72–84; regarding German, Norwegian, and Bohemian families, J. F. Wojta, "Town of Two Creeks: From Forest to Dairy Farms," in *WMH*, 27 (June, 1944), 420–435; regarding an American family in Sauk County, Melissa Brown, "The Jabez Brown Twins: A Family Portrait," in *WMH*, 30 (September–December, 1946), 39–58, 198–224.

[4] Hallam, "Bloomfield and Number Five," 326–328; J. V. Stevens, "Getting Down to Cases," in *WMH*, 20 (June, 1937), 390–403.

burning stoves, few except the best city residences having furnaces. Not even the richest dwellings were, as yet, equipped with flush toilets, which were not to be available in a truly sanitary and odor-free form until the 1880's. Window screens were still rare. One new convenience, however, had begun to come into use in the 1860's—the kerosene lamp, a great improvement upon the candle and upon oil or camphene lamps —extending the hours for more or less comfortable work, study, or play.

On dark, cold winter evenings the family members, especially the youthful ones, might sit around the kitchen range or the dining-room table and entertain themselves with stories or games, though among devout Methodists and many Lutherans card playing was taboo, as was dancing. Long confinement in a crowded house in the country often led to irritability, however, and the strain was especially severe for the materfamilias, who had fewer opportunities to get out during the day. In warmer seasons there was the company of neighbors who came to assist with picking hops, husking corn, or harvesting or threshing wheat. But to the mother of the family, with extra mouths to feed, these occasions generally meant more work than recreation.[5]

As late as 1867, few men and still fewer women in Wisconsin were seriously concerned about inequality, political or other, between the sexes, and these few were almost all of Yankee descent. One of them was John T. Dow, a thirty-five-year-old farmer of Rock County. As an assemblyman, Dow introduced a resolution for a constitutional amendment to extend the suffrage to "every person of the age of twenty-one or upwards." After an eloquent speech by Dow, the assembly passed the measure quickly and by a margin of more than two to one. A senate committee, endorsing the resolution, reported that God, in giving women brains and a soul, presum-

[5] Hallam, "Bloomfield and Number Five," 10–14, 240–241; Mary D. Bradford, *Memoirs of Mary D. Bradford: Autobiographical and Historical Reminiscences of Education in Wisconsin, Through Progressive Service From Rural School Teaching to City Superintendent* (Evansville, Wisconsin, 1932), 93–94; Garland, *Son of the Middle Border,* 31–32, 35–36.

ably did not intend them to be limited to nursing babies and baking bread. The senate approved, eighteen to nine. But by law the next legislature would also have to act favorably if the amendment were to be ratified. To keep up the pressure, Dow called a convention in Janesville, which chose an executive committee that included his wife. Nevertheless, when the new legislature met in 1868, he was no longer one of the lawmakers, and the legislative mood had changed. The resolution was rejected by the assembly, forty-six to thirty-six. Most women did not want the ballot anyhow, the *Wisconsin State Journal* commented. It was theirs by right, Dow replied. If only one woman in the whole state desired to vote, she should be allowed to.

Undaunted, Dow started over by arranging another convention, this one in Fond du Lac. One of the speakers related the cause of suffrage to that of morality. "Have you no sympathy for those who have gone down to the gates of Hell for the sake of a few crumbs to save their children from starvation?" Paulina Roberts demanded. "Mother, has your worn heart never [gone] out in sympathy for those sons who have been lured by temptation into gambling hells and drinking saloons, and from there into houses of prostitution, all of which men have licensed?" The convention set up and put John T. Dow at the head of the Equal Rights Association of Wisconsin.

The next year, 1869, some of the same people attended yet another gathering, in Milwaukee. Also present were the nation's two outstanding woman suffragists, Susan B. Anthony and Elizabeth Cady Stanton, who were making their first tour of the West, to organize their own societies in Indiana, Illinois, Missouri, and Wisconsin. There emerged the Wisconsin Woman's Suffrage Association, with the following officers: president, Dr. Laura J. Ross, the same woman whom the male physicians of Milwaukee had just admitted, grudgingly, to their professional club; secretary, Augusta Chapin, pastor of the Universalist Church in Milwaukee; corresponding secretary, Lila Peckham, a graduate of Antioch College; treasurer, her brother George W. Peckham. Officers and members immediately took a train for Madison to lobby for a newly introduced woman-suffrage resolution, but it too lost in the senate. During the next three years, other suffrage measures failed to pass, even a modest one proposing merely that taxpaying women be allowed to vote in local elections on matters affecting schools. After 1872, no such measures at all were offered in the legislature for several years. The movement suffered from the fact that Dr. Ross and others among the small number of professional women were too busy with their professions to give much attention to it.

My 1873, advocates of female suffrage in Wisconsin were understandably discouraged. They had about the same social standing, one of them in Racine remarked in a letter to the *Woman's Journal,* as advocates of arson. Still, she believed that woman's sphere was expanding in the state. She noted, as signs of the times, that Wisconsin women were lecturing on temperance and one was even holding Methodist revival meetings.[6]

Women remained disadvantaged, however, in small ways as well as large. When they went on horseback, custom required them to ride sidesaddle, which was more difficult and dangerous than sitting the horse straight, though presumably more modest. "Considerable excitement was created on one of our principal streets yesterday," the Stevens Point *Pinery* once reported, "by the appearance of a dashing young lady, riding astride a magnificent horse." Teen-age girls of a poor Sauk County family hated their ugly dresses, homemade of unbleached muslin dyed a "dirty gray-black," but they had no choice except to wear them. And wives of rich men in Mil-

[6] Lawrence L. Graves, "The Wisconsin Woman Suffrage Movement, 1846–1920" (doctoral dissertation, University of Wisconsin, 1954), 20–37, quotes the committee report from the *Wisconsin Senate Journal,* 1867, p. 1009, Dow's response to the *Wisconsin State Journal* in the issue of March 7, 1868, Paulina Roberts' speech as reported in the Fond du Lac *Commonwealth,* September 23, 1868, and the letter from Racine in the *Woman's Journal,* 4 (August 16, 1873), 258. See also Donald J. Berthrong, "Social Legislation in Wisconsin, 1836–1900" (doctoral dissertation, University of Wisconsin, 1951), 105–107; and Theodora W. Youmans, "How Wisconsin Women Won the Ballot," in *WMH,* 5 (September, 1921), 3–32.

waukee felt compelled to obey the dictates of fashion, however disagreeable the consequences. Longer skirts than for many a year were decreed in 1872, and so, the Milwaukee *Sentinel* observed that spring, the city could abandon the notion, if it had ever entertained it, of hiring sweepers to clean the filthy sidewalks, since the "fashionable ladies" were going to do it for nothing. "Not with ignoble brooms will the work be done, but with rich silks, satins and velvets trailed after them as they promenade."[7]

[2]

In the use of leisure outside the home, some Wisconsinites depended more and more on organizations, on scheduled events, on commercial or professional entertainment. Others continued to rely largely on casual get-togethers. Differences in social life persisted and even increased among economic classes, nationality groups, and farm, village, and city dwellers. The gap widened between the fashionable world of Milwaukee, at one extreme, and the humble universe of a factory or farm laborer at the other.

Yet each community came to have its own elite, even in such a remote and rural county as Trempealeau. There the same names appeared over and over again in newspaper accounts of charitable works, betterment projects, and social occasions. The leaders of Trempealeau society were the men who were also prominent in business, the professions, farming, and politics—or the wives of such men. Seldom if ever were the county's Norwegians, Germans, or Poles, even the wealthiest of them, mentioned in connection with social gatherings except for those of their own ethnic groups.[8]

[7] On the Sauk County girls, see Brown, "Jabez Brown Twins," in *WMH*, 30: 54. The Stevens Point *Pinery* is quoted in the Milwaukee *Sentinel*, November 21, 1863. The *Sentinel*, June 9, 1868, has a burlesque discussion of equestrian etiquette for ladies and gentlemen. The comment on skirts is in *ibid.*, April 5, 1872.

[8] Merle Curti, *The Making of an American Community: A Case Study of Democracy in a Frontier County* (Stanford, 1959), 107–110.

Throughout the state, in villages or cities of a few thousand or more people, organizations like the Young Folks of Neenah arranged for "socials" regularly during the winter months. Various associations sponsored dances. Fire companies held festivals or grand balls to raise money. Labor unions gave parties for members and their families, as did mutual-benefit societies like the Hibernian Benevolent Society of Milwaukee. Freemasons and other orders, among them the Nora Lodge which Madison Norwegians formed in 1871, met for their secret rites. In small as well as large communities, church groups and other groups were responsible for summer picnics.[9]

If some social organizations engaged in rather frivolous activities, others rationalized their existence on the basis of self-improvement. During the war a few of the "leading women" of Baraboo, at their head the Unitarian minister's wife, formed a reading circle, "believing that they had a right to, and should pay attention to what was going on in the world of science, the arts, and philosophy, as well as to the duties of housekeeping." The husbands referred to the reading circle as the "Goose Club," and the members adopted that as its name. The Young Men's Library Association of Neenah, after its founding in November 1865, devoted itself to discussions of contemporary issues, taking as its first topic: "Is it policy to extend suffrage to the negroes in the South?" The Young Men's Literary Society of Menasha, meeting in the Methodist vestry to organize in September 1866, also carried on debates, its first subject being "Resolved, That the maxim 'Our Country right or wrong,' is unjustifiable."[10]

Private associations continued to sponsor the only lending libraries in the state. As late as 1873 Wisconsin still lacked

[9] See, for example, Bayrd Still, *Milwaukee: The History of a City* (Madison, 1965), 209–210; Jacob O. Stampen, "The Norwegian Element of Madison, Wisconsin, 1850–1900" (master's thesis, University of Wisconsin, 1965), 50; and the Neenah-Menasha *Island City Times*, March 20, December 18, 1866, January 1, 15, 1867.

[10] The Baraboo women's club is described in Western Historical Company, *The History of Sauk County, Wisconsin . . .* (Chicago, 1880), 545. The Neenah-Menasha *Island City Times*, November 28, 1865, and September 11, 1866, has items on the young men's societies.

public libraries (in the sense of tax-supported ones) except for the library of the state historical society in Madison. Few families or individuals yet owned many books. William Plocker of Fond du Lac County was a remarkable exception. London-born, once the skipper of a Great Lakes steamer, Plocker interested himself not only in scientific agriculture and in government, music, and architecture but also in book collecting. He willed his collection, including his 1610 Nuremberg Bible, to the state historical society. The library association of Gilmanton, in Buffalo County, also was the beneficiary of a will. It started in 1866 with an endowment of only $500, however, and so, as in the case of other library associations, the members had to pay for the privilege of belonging—$5 to join, $1 a year to stay in. The members met quarterly to return old books and draw new ones, and if two or more members wanted the same item, they had to bid for it, paying a rental fee. The plan was based on a Vermont model, which had originated in Massachusetts. Among the Wisconsin circulating libraries, the largest was that of the Milwaukee Young Men's Association, which by 1867 owned 10,000 volumes (and which in 1878 was to donate them to the city for a public library).[11]

Milwaukee, though quite provincial in comparison with New York or even Chicago, had an abundance of excellent theatrical and musical entertainment, both professional and amateur, as well as commercial productions of broad appeal. Within a four-month period in 1869, traveling companies presented, among other things, four concerts in Music Hall and four performances of an opera in the Grand Opera House. The local Musical Society also gave concerts and operas such as Aubert's *Fra Diavolo*, and both the Philharmonic Society and the Re-

[11] On Plocker, see Joseph Schafer, *The Winnebago-Horicon Basin: A Type Study in Western History* (Madison, 1937), 255–256. Garland, *Son of the Middle Border*, 35, says: "We had few books in our house." On the Gilmanton library, see Mrs. L. R. Jones, "The Howard Library Association," in *WMH*, 23 (March, 1940), 304–307; and on the Milwaukee Library, Still, *Milwaukee*, 215–216. For a recent survey history of Wisconsin libraries, see John C. Colson, "The Public Library Movement in Wisconsin, 1836–1900" (doctoral dissertation, University of Chicago, 1973).

becca Lodge staged operas. All these were patronized by the well-fed, well-clothed, and well-to-do, who made a startling contrast with some of their fellow townspeople. "Crowds of little ragamuffins congregate about the entrance of the Grand Opera House," the *Sentinel* once observed, "to the annoyance of visitors to that favorite place of amusement." From time to time, Shakespearean troupes visited the city, Edwin Booth appearing there on at least one occasion. Companies also arrived with the most up-to-date and realistic plays, such as *Under the Gaslight*, which a Chicago company promised to produce with "full scenic effect, a train of cars running across the stage at a terrible rate, a man tied on the track, and everything else necessary to a regular sensational drama." Circuses appeared, among them P. T. Barnum's. This circus disappointed one out-of-town family who came early to see the morning procession as well as the evening performance, but found in the parade "a large camel team (7 span) and that was about all," and considered the show itself "a humbug."[12]

Some of the lesser cities of the state could boast of at least occasional musical and dramatic performances by true artists. The internationally famous Ole Bull spent a good deal of his time in Madison, where in 1870 he married a Wisconsin girl (Sarah Thorp, daughter of J. G. Thorp, a millionaire lumberman), and where he frequently delighted the people, especially his fellow Norwegians, with the "heavenly strains" of his violin. Edwin Booth performed in Madison, drawing theatergoers from as far away as Dodgeville. Neither in Dodgeville nor in Mineral Point nor anywhere else in Iowa County was there a theater. Many farm and village folk believed theaters to be houses of the devil. Small-town performers, however, could put on plays with a moral message, such as *Ten Nights in a Bar-Room*, which Stoughton actors presented on a Friday and a Saturday in 1868, to "full houses" both nights. "Dont you think Stoughton is coming up in the world," a local Norwe-

---

[12] Milwaukee *Sentinel*, April 5, 1872, on the ragamuffins; Still, *Milwaukee*, 206–210, quoting the *Sentinel*, June 14, 1869, on *Under the Gaslight*; Diary of Anson Buttles, October 3, 1872, on Barnum.

gian youth wrote, in English, to his American girl-friend, "boasting a dramatic troup." Circuses made the rounds, some of them originating in the state (though the Ringling Brothers' circus was not to appear until the 1880's). Many good church members thought circuses also wicked, what with the men and women in tights, though even the most pious were willing to view the menageries. Some Protestants got their greatest entertainment from the drama of itinerant revivalists and the music of traveling gospel singers.[13]

As urbanization and leisure increased, sport took a larger and larger place in the life of Wisconsinites, especially those of the middle and upper classes in the larger villages and the cities. Farm youths often turned work into play. "Buoyant, vital, confident, these sons of the border bent to the work of breaking sod and building fence quite in the spirit of sportsmen," Hamlin Garland was to recall in regard to his native American neighbors. "With them reaping was a game, husking corn a test of endurance and skill, threshing a 'bee.' " Such young men rejoiced in the county fair, since it offered not only sociability and spectator sports such as horse racing but also an opportunity for competition, a chance to win a prize for an exhibit. To farmers, however, horseback riding was less of a sport than it was becoming for city people, such as the party of twenty or thirty gentlemen and ladies who made an "equestrian excursion" from Milwaukee to Whitefish Bay on a fine October morning in 1865. The riding horse seemed about to be superseded as a means of urban recreation when, early in 1869, the velocipede craze reached Milwaukee. The velocipede—a crude bicycle with wood-spoked, iron-rimmed wheels and pedals on the front axle—promised to be a boon for businessmen and professional men who got too little exercise.

[13] Albert O. Barton, "Ole Bull and His Wisconsin Contacts," in *WMH,* 7 (June, 1924), 417–444; Stampen, "Norwegian Element of Madison," 52–53; John Lindas to Betsy Williams, January 31, March 15, 1868, in Beulah Folkedahl, ed. and trans., "Norwegians Become Americans," in *Norwegian-American Studies,* 21 (1962), 121–122. See also Hallam, "Bloomfield and Number Five," 17–19; and Ayres Davies, "Wisconsin, Incubator of the American Circus," in *WMH,* 25 (March, 1942), 283–296.

But the fad quickly passed, not to be revived until several years later with the advent of the lighter and more efficient high-wheel machine. While both rural and urban men and boys hunted and fished, the well-to-do of the cities were developing sophisticated water sports as they formed boat clubs and acquired racing shells and even yachts.[14]

A new pastime, croquet, gained favor in the late 1860's, especially among the genteel. It appealed to Protestant clergymen, among others, and so many Methodist preachers took it up that it became an issue at their annual conference in 1871. "How about croquet?" was a question presumed to be in the minds of many of the laity. "If you ministers play this for amusement, and become all absorbed in it, as some of you seem to, may we not play at other games for the same purpose?" The conference restated the church's familiar position—"that such amusements as dancing, playing at cards, circus and theater-going, are inconsistent with Christian character"—but refrained from denouncing croquet. Other denominations also exempted the new pastime from their usual scruples, and the Oshkosh *Journal* referred to it as "Presbyterian billiards."[15]

Another new game, baseball, attracted a much wider range of enthusiasts. Though men and boys had played cricket and other bat-and-ball games earlier in Milwaukee and elsewhere in the state, the city's first baseball club appeared in the spring of 1860. By 1870, practically every village had at least one team, and Milwaukee had three, one of which consisted entirely of Germans. Another, the Cream City Club, was the state champion in 1868 and went on to defeat the Cincinnati Red Stockings two years later. At this level the game was already thoroughly professional, with bids as high as $10,000

[14] Garland, *Son of the Middle Border*, 20–21; Hallam, "Bloomfield and Number Five," 339; Milwaukee *Sentinel*, October 16, 1865; Still, *Milwaukee*, 227; Robert C. Robertson, "The Social History of Winnebago County, Wisconsin, 1850–1870" (master's thesis, University of Chicago, 1939), 100.

[15] The account of Methodists and croquet is in P. S. Bennett and James Lawson, *History of Methodism in Wisconsin* (Cincinnati, 1890), 239–240; Robertson, "Social History of Winnebago County," 104–105, quoting the Oshkosh *Journal*, June 11, 1870.

for star players. A Milwaukee team was to join the National League in 1878.

Intercollegiate athletics lagged somewhat. At the University of Wisconsin the gymnasium was seldom open in the early 1870's. Women students played croquet, and some of the men opposed one another in rather disorganized baseball and football contests. Football, the student newspaper reported in 1871, had "reached its zenith at the University. What a scientific game! One man kicks the ball, falls down, and 40 or more, yell at the top of their voices." On June 3, 1873, the faculty allowed a group of students to visit Beloit College "for the purpose of playing a game of baseball"—apparently the university's first intercollegiate game of any kind.[16]

Tourism was just beginning in Wisconsin, though some of its scenic spots had attracted occasional visitors for years. At the end of the war the capital itself had become something of a summer resort, and in the spring of 1867 the *Wisconsin State Journal* predicted that, this season, the city would be crowded "in greater numbers than ever" with vacationers from St. Louis, Memphis, and other places in the hot and humid South. Geneva was drawing more and more visitors from Chicago. But the most famous of the Wisconsin spas during these early years was Waukesha, which owed its sudden rise largely to a New York businessman, Richard Dunbar, who stopped there in 1868 and 1869, drank from the local springs, and convinced himself that the water ameliorated his diabetes. Acquiring rights to the springs, Dunbar undertook to convince the rest of the world that the water had curative powers. By 1873 an imposing resort hotel, the Fountain Spring House, the project of a Chicago millionaire, was under construction at Waukesha.

Sightseeing was becoming a regular business in the Devils Lake and Wisconsin Dells areas. On Devils Lake a small steamboat began to make the rounds with tourists in 1868. After the railroad from Madison arrived in 1872—the tracks passing right

[16] Still, *Milwaukee*, 227; Robertson, "Social History of Winnebago County," 104. The quotations are from Merle Curti and Vernon Carstensen, *The University of Wisconsin: A History, 1848–1925* (2 vols., Madison, 1949), 1: 387–390.

along the lakeshore with utter (but unnoticed) disregard for scenic and ecological damage—summer visitors had easy access from Chicago. Soon a hotel, the Cliff House, and a row of cottages sprang up along the edge of the lake. The Dells gained publicity from Henry H. Bennett, who acquired a photographic shop in Kilbourn City in 1865 and began to take pictures of the nearby scenery. When an occasional stranger or two arrived to see the Dells, Bennett took them through in a rowboat. By 1873 the crowds were too large for him to accommodate, and Captain A. Wood began to operate a sightseeing steamboat of his own construction.[17]

[3]

Religion remained a dominant influence in the lives of many if not most Wisconsinites, as the churches in general continued to concern themselves very much with worldly as well as otherworldly affairs. For countless people, church attendance was in itself a means of satisfying a gregarious urge, as it no doubt was for the Cottage Grove woman whose only diversion from her household cares, except for brief visits with neighbors, was participation in prayer meetings. On a May night in 1866 she arrived at such a gathering "very tired" but soon felt that "the fire of Gods love began to burn" and that she "could have shouted aloud the praise of God." Many of the parties and picnics and other social activities of church members still revolved around their particular churches. Thus religion brought people together, on weekdays as well as Sundays.

It also kept people apart. Its separating effect is seen in the example of Roujet D. Marshall's father, who, having converted

---

[17] Milwaukee *Sentinel,* May 1, 1867; *Wisconsin State Journal,* April 29, 1867. For references to Madison as a summer place, see James S. Ritchie, *Wisconsin and Its Resources* . . . (3d revised edition, Philadelphia, 1858), 104–106; and Daniel S. Durrie, *A History of Madison* . . . (Madison, 1874), 241. See also Lillian Krueger, "Waukesha: 'The Saratoga of the West,'" in *WMH,* 24 (June, 1941), 394–424; Western Historical Company, *History of Sauk County,* 399–400; A. C. Bennett, "A Wisconsin Pioneer in Photography," in *WMH,* 22 (March, 1939), 268–279.

from Congregationalism to Seventh Day Adventism, preoccupied himself with signs of Christ's second coming and insisted upon observing the Sabbath on Saturday. This, as Marshall was later to remark, "was reflected in a measure upon the whole family, tending to isolate them" from other people in the town of Delton. Persisting as Wisconsin's deepest religious division by far, however, was the one between Protestants as a whole, especially the most evangelistic among them, and Roman Catholics. Competition between the two groups, for the control of lives and the capture of souls, went on unabated.[18]

Already larger, before the war, than any of the Protestant churches except the Methodist, the Catholic Church in Wisconsin made a determined effort to maintain and increase its membership during the war and after. Zealous and able missionaries, among them the Jesuit Arnold Damen, journeyed about the state to restore the faith of backsliders and to convert the unconverted. Preaching in German, French, Dutch, and English, the missionaries aspired to win the hearts of not only immigrants but also natives, including those of evangelical Protestant background. "Many of the prejudices of Appleton have been removed," Father Damen reported after a campaign there in 1864, "and many are investigating the truths of our holy religion, particularly many of the students of the methodist college [Lawrence], who attended in great numbers." To accommodate the church's growth, Bishop John Martin Henni urged the Roman authorities to divide his diocese, which they did in 1868, creating the new sees of Green Bay and La Crosse. Bishop Henni also sponsored the *Star of Bethlehem*, a Catholic family magazine that took an assertive line from its founding in 1869. It contended that the prosperity and freedom of the United States was "not due to the principles of Protestantism, but to Catholicity," and proclaimed: "The

[18] An entry in the Jane B. Kelly Diaries, May 17, 1866, describes her feelings at prayer meeting. Marshall's remark is in Gilson G. Glasier, ed., *Autobiography of Roujet D. Marshall, Justice of the Supreme Court of the State of Wisconsin, 1895–1918* (2 vols., Madison, 1923, 1931), 1: 90–93, 135–137. Social differences between two neighboring Methodist churches are described in Oscar Hallam, "Bloomfield and Laxey Methodism," in *WMH*, 30 (March, 1947), 292–310.

Republic is becoming Catholic." Wisconsin itself, however, was not becoming Catholic very fast. The proportion of Catholics in the state's population does not appear to have been much higher in 1870 than it had been in 1860—not more than 25 per cent. Yet by 1870 they had overtaken the Methodists and had become the largest religious group.[19]

Eager as he was to expand the church in Wisconsin, Bishop Henni confronted a dilemma while attending, along with Bishop Michael Heiss of the new La Crosse diocese, the Vatican council that met in Rome in 1869–1870. At this council arose the question of papal infallibility. Both Henni and Heiss believed firmly in the principle, but Henni agreed with other American delegates who feared that its formal adoption would be inexpedient for them, living as they did in a country of heretics, for the dogma could be expected to antagonize non-Catholics and hinder the work of conversion among them. At first, Henni therefore joined with eighteen bishops from the United States in petitioning to put off consideration of the question. Later, however, he came out, with Heiss, in favor of defining the church's infallibility as an attribute of the pope. The Vatican council promulgated the controversial doctrine, and on Henni's return to Milwaukee he received a gala welcome from local Catholics, including the mayor.

The Wisconsin hierarchy, however, continued to be under some strain, not because of doctrinal differences but because of ethnic jealousies. Irish and other English-speaking priests still resented the dominance of Germans, whose numbers and influence in the Wisconsin church organization were as disproportionate as ever, if not more so, by the 1870's. There was not a prelate or a vicar-general in the entire state, and at St.

[19] A. Damen to Henni, March 7, 1864, typescript in the St. Francis Seminary archives, Milwaukee; Peter Leo Johnson, *Crosier on the Frontier: A Life of John Martin Henni, Archbishop of Milwaukee* (Madison, 1959), 180–181; *Star of Bethlehem*, October 1869, June 1870; John Martin Henni in *DWB*. A rough estimate of the number of Catholics in the state may be taken from the rounded figures given in diocesan reports in *Sadlers' Catholic Directory, Almanac, and Ordo for the Year of Our Lord 1872: With a Full Report of the Various Dioceses in the United States and British North America* (New York, 1872). The total for Wisconsin's three dioceses was approximately 245,000.

Francis Seminary there were only two of thirteen professors whose native tongue was English, as non-German clergymen pointed out. There were far fewer English-speaking priests than there were English-speaking parishes, many of these being in the care of German pastors. The Irish accused the German clergy of conspiring to maintain a monopoly of church offices.[20]

Much less numerous in Wisconsin than the Catholics—and much less unified—were the Lutherans, whose various synods kept to their independent ways, and whose congregations still seemed prone to squabbling with one another. The two largest of the German synods, the Missouri and the Buffalo, held a colloquy in 1866 and agreed to co-operate, but some of the local members were less willing to do so. In one Wisconsin town, where churches of the two synods stood almost side by side, the majority of the Buffalo congregation voted to merge with the Missouri congregation, but the minority stood pat, and a part of it broke off and joined a third synod, the Wisconsin. Other local groups seceded from either the Missouri or the Buffalo Synod because of their dislike for private confession and aligned themselves with the Wisconsin Synod, the only one of the three to disapprove the practice. Two years after its rapprochement with the Buffalo organization, the Missouri Synod came to an understanding with the Wisconsin Synod, when representatives of the two met in Milwaukee. According to the agreement, these synods were to recognize each other as orthodox and were to co-operate in such matters as the founding of new churches, neither one encroaching on territory that the other was already serving.[21]

Separate from the German Lutherans were the Norwegian Lutherans, and they too had frequent differences among themselves. Racking the Norwegian Synod, after slavery had already been abolished in the United States, was a strange and unreal dispute over the question whether slavery in all times and places, including those of the Bible, was necessarily a sin. Finally, in 1869, the synod condemned the "sins and ungodli-

[20] Johnson, *Crosier on the Frontier*, 182–187, 192–193.
[21] Roy A. Suelflow, *A Plan for Survival* (New York, 1965), 120–121, 129, 138–139.

ness" of the American brand of bondage, and the divisive debate quieted down. A smaller fragment of the Lutheran Church, the Scandinavian Augustana Synod, became itself fragmented when its leaders disagreed about the administration of a church school, Marshall Academy, in Dane County. In 1869 the synod divided into a Norwegian and a Swedish branch, and the next year the Norwegian branch divided into the Norwegian-Danish Augustana Synod and the Conference of the Norwegian-Danish Evangelical Lutheran Church in America.[22]

Among Wisconsinites, much the most numerous of the Protestants, almost as numerous as the Catholics, were the Methodists. They moved toward consolidation rather than fragmentation. The three Methodist conferences in the state were reduced to two when, in 1868, the West Wisconsin Conference and the Northwest Wisconsin Conference were merged in what was claimed to be "the first instance of the kind in the history of Methodism." Of the eight districts in the combined conference, a small one with six preachers and 317 members was Norwegian, and the American clergymen congratulated their "dear [Scandinavian] brethren" on their "remarkable success in planting Methodism among their people." American revivalists had less success in planting it among other foreigners. After a series of camp meetings at Monroe and Mazomanie, in 1868, the pioneer Methodist missionary Alfred Brunson, then seventy-five years of age, complained that old settlers, including many of his faith, were selling out to German immigrants and moving westward, and the resulting loss of Methodists was so great that the net gain in membership was small. "We had, also, infidels, Adventists, Spiritualists, and Catholics to contend with, so that true godliness made but little progress."

Brunson looked to his "German Methodist brethren" for mission work among their fellow countrymen, and missionaries of the Evangelical Association, the German counterpart of the Methodist Church, were active and successful, though they

---

[22] Theodore C. Blegen, *Norwegian Migration to America: The American Transition* (Northfield, Minnesota, 1940), 448–453; Beulah Folkedahl, "Marshall Academy: A History," in *WMH*, 47 (Spring, 1964), 249–260.

ran into some resistance. Catholics frequently opposed the use of school buildings by Protestants for religious purposes, and in 1868, when the Reverend Adam Kemmerer, preaching in German, started a series of revival meetings in a log schoolhouse near Green Bay, the Irish in the community objected so strongly that he transferred the meetings to the house of a friendly German farmer. This revival led to the founding of Zion Evangelical Church and the building of an edifice of its own. The Reverend Louis von Ragué, an Evangelical missionary in Sheboygan County, believed that if the Evangelicals had proselyted with sufficient zeal, they would soon have outnumbered the Lutherans in Wisconsin. As it was, by 1870 they could claim churches with two-thirds as much seating capacity as the Lutherans, and they had twice as many congregations as they had buildings.[23]

Thus Wisconsin was still a missionary field, and for some denominations it was quite a fresh one. Until 1868 the Disciples of Christ, or Campbellites, had no organized churches in the state. Then Henry Howe arrived as an itinerant minister, to travel about by horse and buggy and hold services in town halls, schoolhouses, private homes, and even clearings and groves, while he and his family subsisted on a temporary stipend from the Disciples' missionary board and then on donations from converts. Other denominations, however, were becoming secure and prosperous enough to help support missions abroad. In 1872–1873, during its first year of operation in Wisconsin, the Woman's Foreign Missionary Society raised $2,128 among the state's Methodists for carrying the gospel to

[23] The remark about Scandinavian brethren is in Bennett and Lawson, *Methodism in Wisconsin*, 396–397. The other quotations are in Alfred Brunson, *A Western Pioneer* . . . (2 vols., Cincinnati, 1872, 1879), 2: 350, 354–355. See also "Observe 60th Church Year," in the Green Bay *Press-Gazette*, October 20, 1930; and J. H. A. Lacher, ed., "Rev. Louis von Ragué's Experiences in Sheboygan County," in *WMH*, 10 (June, 1927), 435–452. In the absence of reliable statistics on church membership at the time, the seating capacity of church buildings, as shown by the number of "sittings" recorded in the federal census, may be taken as a very rough indicator for purposes of comparison. The *Ninth Census of the United States, 1870: Volume I*, pp. 506–525, gives the following figures: for the Evangelicals, 179 "organizations," 88 "edifices," and 24,175 "sittings"; for the Lutherans, 171 "organizations," 156 "edifices," and 36,780 "sittings."

heathen women, particularly in India. This—the outflow of missionary funds—was a sign of Wisconsin's advance toward ecclesiastical maturity.

In Wisconsin the federal census takers in 1870 counted, or estimated, a grand total of 1,466 religious edifices, with "sittings" for 423,015 worshipers. According to the tallies, or the guesses, the Catholics (with 104,000) and the Methodists (with 103,240) each had more than twice as many church accommodations as their nearest competitors, the Congregationalists (44,960), the Baptists (42,980), or the Lutherans (36,780). Next in line were the Evangelicals (24,173), the Presbyterians (23,930), and the Episcopalians (21,200). Far behind were the United Brethren (5,650), the German Reformed (3,260), the Universalists (3,150), the Moravians (2,500), the Unitarians (1,900), the Christians (1,450), and the Dutch Reformed (1,015). Numerically the least significant were the Swedenborgians (800), the Jews (750), the Seventh Day Adventists (650), and the Friends (375). In Milwaukee there were two synagogues after 1869, the second one belonging to a reform congregation, but total synagogue membership had not increased since 1857. Some persons of Jewish background, like some of Christian backgrounds, were indifferent to religion, a few had converted to Christianity, and still others had joined freethinking groups.[24]

There were signs that free thought was gaining. In January 1867 the Baraboo admirers of Thomas Paine wished to celebrate his birthday in the Free Congregational Church (Unitarian) but, because of the opposition of church members, had to meet in a private hall instead. The next year they observed the day in the church without objection and with a full attendance, and they "lost nothing of their social standing or re-

[24] Jessie H. Nebelthau, *The Diary of a Circuit Rider: Excerpts from the Notes of Henry Howe, Made While Traveling in Southern Wisconsin Between the years 1864 and 1868 as a Missionary of the Disciples of Christ* (Minneapolis, 1933), viii, 4, 11, and *passim;* Bennett and Lawson, *Methodism in Wisconsin*, 251; Louis J. Swichkow and Lloyd P. Gartner, *The History of the Jews of Milwaukee* (Philadelphia, 1963), 46–51; *Ninth Census of the United States, 1870: Volume I*, pp. 506–525.

spectability." This presumably showed the "intellectual development" of Baraboo. When Harvard's John Fiske, the foremost American popularizer of the Darwinian theory of evolution, lectured on the subject in Milwaukee in 1872, the *Journal of Commerce* defended his right to be heard, though acknowledging that some citizens would consider his views "atheistic and materialistic." One Milwaukee German freethinker was pessimistic, however, after making a trip through the state to seek subscribers for a free-thought periodical he published. Apparently he sold few subscriptions, for he concluded that Wisconsin's so-called free men and free congregations no longer cared about "intellectual enlightenment." The liberal cause, he thought, was languishing even in Milwaukee, which had ceased to be the German Athens and, with the "rampant growth of Catholicism," had become *"das deutsche Rom."*[25]

Most clergymen, Protestant as well as Catholic, were unrelenting in their hostility toward agnosticism and atheism. Yet Protestants continued to share much of the freethinkers' attitude toward Catholicism, and Catholics continued to entertain much the same feeling toward Protestantism as toward free thought. Protestant ministers, particularly Lutheran ones, took occasion in their sermons to criticize Catholic beliefs and practices. Denouncing the Vatican council's assertion of papal infallibility, a Congregational pastor told his flock: "The great effort of that council was to anchor the nineteenth century back to the ninth; to send the world backward, not after God, but after man, to the devices which he happened to think of God." A Norwegian Lutheran preacher informed his congregation that Catholics were taught an erroneous view of marriage, since they were led to believe that monkish celibacy was a "holy and perfect state." But many German Lutherans, as they had done

[25] Western Historical Company, *History of Sauk County,* 539–540, describes the Unitarians' celebration of Paine's birthday. See also the Milwaukee *Journal of Commerce,* October 2, 1872. M. Hedwigis Overmoehle, "The Anti-Clerical Activities of the Forty-Eighters in Wisconsin, 1848–1860: A Study in German-American Liberalism" (doctoral dissertation, St. Louis University, 1941), 263, quotes Samuel Ludvigh in *Fackel,* 18 (1866), 198.

before the war, disagreed with other Protestants when, in the postwar years, the issues of drink and Sunday observances were revived.[26]

The Protestant churches varied in their stands on temperance. Some, though disapproving alcoholic beverages, refused to support the leading temperance organization, the Good Templars, since it was a secret society. Most zealous on the question were the Methodists, whose state convention in 1867 resolved to discountenance the raising of hops or the production of anything else that would "probably be used in the manufacture of malt or spirituous liquors." Baptists, Congregationalists, and Presbyterians also adopted resolutions favoring temperance; but the Episcopalians and the Lutherans, like the Catholics, took no official position on the subject.

Catholics, too, differed among themselves. To some extent, Bishop Henni himself was willing to co-operate with Protestant temperance advocates. When, in 1867, the pastor of the Plymouth Congregational Church in Milwaukee called on Henni with a group of reformers, the bishop promised to assist their effort to bring about the Sunday closing of the city's taverns. Henni also approved the work of the Catholic Total Abstinence Union, and by 1872 the state contained about twenty Catholic temperance societies, whose members were almost all Irish. Yet there remained a gulf between the Protestant and the Catholic temperance workers. The Protestants, once again, were demanding laws to make people abstain from drink. The Catholics, as always, insisted on persuasion and voluntary measures but no legal compulsion. Some Catholic leaders welcomed the controversy. "The Germans will not allow their Sunday glass of beer to be taken away from them," the rector of St. Francis Seminary wrote in 1867 to his mission headquarters in Munich. "At any rate the Catholic Church gains in public estimation

[26] John L. Dudley, *The Method of Revelation: Sermon Preached at Plymouth [Congregational] Church [Milwaukee] by Rev. J. L. Dudley, Pastor, Sunday Morning, September 25, 1870*, p. 5, a pamphlet in the SHSW; Herman A. Preus, "Second Sunday After Holy Three Kings Day, Muskego, 1874," manuscript sermon in Luther College Library, Decorah, Iowa.

and influence, though not in the degree claimed by the exaggerated reports in the . . . newspapers."[27]

[4]

It might seem that, in Wisconsin and in other Northern states with large numbers of immigrants, the Civil War ought to have set the melting pot to bubbling and speeded up the assimilation process. No doubt the mingling of the native and the foreign-born in the camp and on the battlefield did have something of an assimilating effect. Yet it must be borne in mind that, of Wisconsin's foreign-born troops, a great many were segregated in companies and even regiments consisting entirely or almost entirely of men of a single nationality. It must be remembered, too, that some elements of the state's population were much more reluctant to serve than others, indeed so reluctant that they rioted against the draft. The quite different and conflicting responses could only have heightened already existing tensions. Thus, in Wisconsin at least, the war seems to have had a negative as well as a positive effect on assimilation.[28]

Prewar ethnic conflicts were afterward revived, such as the controversy about sumptuary laws against such things as drinking and Sabbath-breaking. And wartime estrangements per-

[27] Joanne J. Brownsword, "Good Templars in Wisconsin, 1854–1880" (master's thesis, University of Wisconsin, 1960), 62–69; Bennett and Lawson, *Methodism in Wisconsin,* 223–224, on raising hops; Johnson, *Crosier on the Frontier,* 171; M. Justille McDonald, *History of the Irish in Wisconsin in the Nineteenth Century* (Washington, D.C., 1954), 225–228; Peter Leo Johnson, ed., Joseph Salzmann to Ludwig Ignatz Lebling, July 31, 1867, in the *Salesianum,* 42 (April, 1947), 68.

[28] Authorities agree that the war did, in fact, overcome ethnic antagonisms and bring about assimilation. "The Clash that alienated sections reconciled their component nationalities." John Higham, *Strangers in the Land: Patterns of American Nativism, 1860–1925* (New Brunswick, 1955), 12–14. " 'Americanization' . . . is exactly what happened. . . ." Ella Lonn, *Foreigners in the Union Army and Navy* (Baton Rouge, 1951), 659–661. "The four years of bloody strife destroyed not only the old South but also . . . the varied immigrant America of the North." Marcus Lee Hansen, *The Atlantic Migration, 1607–1860: A History of the Continuing Settlement of the United States* (Cambridge, 1941), 306. These generalizations are dubious when applied to Wisconsin, whatever their merit when applied to other Northern states.

sisted. Doubtless there were other antiwar immigrants who underwent an experience comparable to that of Dutch-born Chrysostom A. Verwyst. During the war, while studying for the priesthood at St. Francis Seminary, he was compelled to pay the $300 commutation fee in order to escape the draft, because his father had voted, though he himself had never done so. When, after paying the fee, young Verwyst did go to the polls, he was rejected as an alien. Long afterward he recalled: "I was so deeply disgusted at this manifest humbug and conceived so great a dislike for Uncle Sam that I did not take out my citizenship papers until about fifteen years later."

Among veterans, if any were left with a lessened sense of ethnic identity as a result of service in segregated units, certainly the Irish were not. In the case of the "Irish Regiment," the Seventeenth, the war experience had the effect of greatly stimulating group consciousness and assertiveness. Before the war, the Irish in Wisconsin had been widely scattered and had seldom co-operated among themselves. The Seventeenth brought hundreds of them together, bound them with ties of comradeship, and developed their *esprit de corps*. During and after the war many of them joined the Fenian movement and took up its rather quixotic mission of liberating the Irish fatherland by striking at British power near at hand, in North America. In 1866, some 150 Fenians left Milwaukee and another sixty-four left Fond du Lac to take part, along with their fellows from other states, in a hoped-for conquest of Canada. Wisconsin's Irish voters, with a new awareness of their power in state politics, generally cheered the Fenians on and threatened to punish at the polls any politician who stood in their way.[29]

In the 1870's the physical and social separateness of the various groups, native and foreign-born, was on the whole as great as, or even greater than, it had been in the preceding decades. Generally the immigrants, except for the British, continued to

[29] "C. A. Verwyst's Reminiscences of a Pioneer Missionary," in Lucas, ed., *Dutch Immigrant Memoirs*, 2: 185–186; McDonald, *Irish in Wisconsin*, 142; Johnson, *Crosier on the Frontier*, 135. Johnson relates that Bishop Henni, like the bishops of Ireland, disapproved the Fenian movement and used his persuasive powers to discourage it in Milwaukee.

live apart from the American-born, each group in its own rural community or urban neighborhood. Everyone was quite conscious of ethnic differences. "There was an Irish ward," the Yankee-descended Frederick Jackson Turner was to reminisce about his native Portage, "into which we boys entered only in companies." Even while welcoming immigrants and giving friendly reports of their activities, old-stock American editors of English-language newspapers (meaning the vast majority of journalists and journals) treated the foreign-born as distinct categories with peculiar characteristics and interests. Editors, like people in general, did not refer to "German-Americans," "Irish-Americans," and so forth, but spoke of "Americans" on the one hand and "Germans," "Irish," "Norwegians," and the like on the other. Typical of news reporting was the account of a Fourth-of-July brawl in a Manitowoc County saloon, a brawl "in which stones, knives, and pistols were freely used. Germans, Irishmen, Bohemians and Americans participated. Two Bohemians were seriously injured." Also typical was the report of a "melee between a few of the young Irish and Germans" in Waumandee, Buffalo County, where an American bystander was accidentally shot and killed.[30]

Ethnic stereotypes commanded as wide a belief as ever. Not only the American-born but also the foreign-born took for granted the existence of a distinctive personality for each group, though members of a particular group did not necessarily accept all the traits that others assigned to it. According to widely held beliefs, the Irishman was light-hearted, witty, improvident, but also gloomy, superstitious, and vengeful, as ready to fight as he was to sing or laugh. The German was hardworking, plodding, dull, beery, yet clever, artistic, musical. The Norwegian was reliable, thorough, thrifty, though stubborn and contentious, and so naïve that he was quite vulnerable to exploitation by unscrupulous strangers. As for the

[30] Turner to Carl Becker, December 16, 1925, in Ray A. Billington, "Young Fred Turner," in *WMH*, 46 (Autumn, 1962), 41; Curti, *Making of an American Community*, 97–102. Descriptions of the brawls are in the Milwaukee *Sentinel*, July 14, September 27, 1869.

American, he was, in the eyes of immigrants, a true descendant of the Puritan: industrious and intelligent but cold, cautious, narrow-minded, hypocritical, and all too willing to cheat in his over-eager pursuit of the dollar.[31]

When Wisconsinites of old stock talked of "Americanizing" the immigrant, they usually had in mind the idea of imposing upon him, or at least upon his children, the traditional characteristics of New Yorkers and New Englanders. Many, though by no means all of the newcomers, for their part, wished to retain their national identities and their familiar ways. "They change their sky and not their mind who cross the sea," a poetry-quoting priest told the St. Patrick's Benevolent Society of La Crosse. At the conclusion of the Franco-Prussian War in 1871, Milwaukee Germans celebrated the fatherland's victory with three days of festivities, during which they displayed the red, white, and black of the new empire—alongside the red, white, and blue of the United States. Whether considered as individuals or as groups, Wisconsin's immigrants varied considerably in the rates at which they took on American habits and American views. To some degree, people of native stock adopted European customs. Thus acculturation was a two-way process, and the result was a mixture, by no means a mere reproduction of the imagined Yankee type.

Down to the 1870's the mixing, both cultural and physical, still proceeded rather slowly. The language difference delayed it, causing many Germans and Norwegians to keep to themselves. Churchmen kept on striving to maintain the language along with the religion of the Old Country, Lutherans continuing to worship in German or Norwegian, and many of the Catholics in German, French, or Dutch. Schools furthered assimilation to any great extent only when they brought together children of foreign-born and native families. Education therefore had more of an assimilating effect in Racine and

[31] Curti, *Making of an American Community,* 91–97; McDonald, *Irish in Wisconsin,* 250; Dorothy B. Skardal, "Double Heritage: Scandinavian Immigrant Experience Through Literary Sources" (doctoral dissertation, Radcliffe College, 1962), 149–157, 304, 307; Joseph Schafer, *The Wisconsin Lead Region* (Madison, 1932), 232–233.

Kenosha counties, where the sons and daughters of Germans and Yankees often mingled in the classroom and on the playground, than in Milwaukee and Ozaukee counties, where most of the German children saw only others of their kind and were taught largely or entirely in the German language, whether they attended public or parochial schools.[32]

Poverty embarrassed the poorest immigrants in the presence of the American-born and hindered assimilation. As the poor emerged from their poverty, they were more readily accepted by Americans and as Americans. The prosperity of the Irish settlers of Erin Prairie, in St. Croix County, the St. Paul *Northwestern Chronicle* declared in 1867, thoroughly refuted the "ignorant and too frequently malicious slanderers" who, "taking some barroom loafer as a model," judged all Irish people accordingly. Six years after arriving in Waupaca County with her desperately poor parents from Norway, a pretty teen-age girl had done well as a milliner and a dress designer. When, at a dance in the village of Waupaca, a would-be partner addressed her in Norwegian, she scornfully stared at him and said: "Aye don't speak Norvejan, aye bane American." As the Belgians on the Door Peninsula prospered they began to farm more and more as the Americans did, using a larger and larger number of machines; and some of the young people quit wearing wooden shoes.[33]

Assimilation preceded amalgamation. That is, a couple learned to share a common culture, at least to the extent of understanding the same language, before beginning to share a married life. In the four southern lakeshore counties there

[32] *Ibid.*, 233–249; Joseph Schafer, *Four Wisconsin Counties: Prairie and Forest* (Madison, 1927), 183–184; McDonald, *Irish in Wisconsin*, 250, quotes the Reverend C. F. X. Goldsmith in a St. Patrick's Day speech given to the La Crosse St. Patrick's Benevolent Society, March 17, 1872. See also Still, *Milwaukee*, 130.

[33] Curti, *Making of an American Community*, 185–186; McDonald, *Irish in Wisconsin*, 106–107, quotes an "editorial correspondent" in the St. Paul *Northwestern Chronicle*, December 21, 1867. See also Alfred O. Erickson, "Scandinavia, Wisconsin," in *Norwegian-American Studies and Records*, 15 (1949), 197; Xavier Martin, "The Belgians of Northeast Wisconsin," in *Wis. Hist. Colls.*, 13: 392.

was an increase in the proportion—from about 7 per cent in 1860 to more than 10 per cent in 1870—of Wisconsin families in which the husband and the wife were born in different countries. Marriage very seldom occurred between persons of German and Norwegian birth, or between either a German or a Norwegian, on the one hand, and someone of Irish or British birth on the other. Most intermarrying was between the foreign-born and the American-born, and in more than half these cases the American-born partner had parents of the same ethnic background as his or her spouse.

More often than not, the American-born partner was a woman, since there was among immigrants an excess of men of marriageable age. Within an ethnic community there was sometimes resistance even to intermarriage of this kind. "Remember that you are born and brought up in this country and have absorbed the ideas habits and tastes peculiar to this country from babyhood," a member of the Stoughton Norwegian community, in 1872, advised his sister-in-law, who was wondering whether she should wed an upper-class young man from Norway. "In the society which you as [an] american woman (I mean american in ideas) will feel most at home, he will be a stranger."[34]

Despite the actual slowness of amalgamation, some Wisconsinites were impressed by what seemed to them the rapid "intermingling of blood," and they worried about its possible consequences. The apprehensive expressed fears, for example, "concerning the influence of Celtic blood upon the American temperament, already too nervous." There was no danger, the English-born physician Joseph Hobbins concluded. England herself, the doctor said, illustrated the good that could result from a blending of nationalities. What was going on in Wisconsin, he was confident, would "tend to preserve the

[34] Schafer, *Wisconsin Lead Region*, 240–249; Schafer, *Four Wisconsin Counties*, 173–178; Curti, *Making of an American Community*, 104–106; John Lindas to his sister-in-law Bella, May 26, 1872, in Folkedahl, ed., "Norwegians Become Americans," *Norwegian-American Studies*, 21: 131–132.

good old Anglo-Saxon character, rather than to create any
new character for our people." Others continued to predict,
however, that the future would "give us a *new type,* distinct
from all other peoples."[35]

[5]

After the Civil War the white people of the state seemed to
remember more vividly the negative role of the Indians—the
1862 Sioux uprising in Minnesota and the imagined threat of
other uprisings in Wisconsin—than the positive role, the willing
service of men from most of the Wisconsin tribes, especially
from the Menominee, in the Union army. Certainly the war
record of the red volunteers caused no visible improvement
in the white folks' treatment of the Indians.

True, the federal government undertook certain reforms of
its Indian policy. At the persuasion of humanitarians, President Ulysses S. Grant with the approval of Congress set up, in
1869, a Board of Indian Commissioners, appointing to it ten
men "eminent for their intelligence and philanthropy" whom
he charged with overseeing the government's Indian affairs.
Grant, in his "peace policy," also looked to religious organizations to recommend Indian agents, and he directed federal sub-
sidies to church groups for operating religious schools—to the
Catholics, for example, for taking charge of education among
Wisconsin's Menominee. These mission schools tried to give
a practical education. After 1871 the government ceased to
pretend that it was dealing with sovereign nations when it dealt
with Indian tribes, and it adjusted its relations with them not
by treaties but by congressional acts. The new policy of treat-
ing the Indians as "wards of the nation" was well-meant, but it
further weakened their tribal character without preparing them
for self-dependent citizenship. Shifting again, the government
in 1873 began to spend less on mission-operated schools and
more on government-operated ones. In these the instruction

[35] Joseph Hobbins, "Health of Wisconsin," in Western Historical Company,
History of Sauk County, 237.

was in English and was so formal and regimented that it aroused little desire to learn the white man's ways.[36]

Meanwhile, in disposing of pine on Wisconsin reservations, the federal government showed itself more responsive to the desires of white lumbermen than to the needs of the reservation dwellers. From time to time the secretary of the interior issued permits allowing the Menominee to sell "dead and down" timber and even some of the standing trees on their reservation. Certain lumbermen, with the connivance of Indian agents, took advantage of the Indians by paying them less than the market price for logs. Eager for larger quantities, local lumbermen demanded that the government dispose of reservation timber and timberland. In 1870 Congressman Philetus Sawyer obtained an act for the sale of part of the pine lands of the Menominee. With the pineries that remained to them, these Indians managed to develop something of a sawmilling business, but the neighboring Stockbridge were less fortunate. Most of their pine lands were also sold under the act, without the consent or even the knowledge of the tribe, to a lumber corporation. The Stockbridge, to eke out their thirty-dollar annuities, were left with the sorry alternatives of trying to raise crops on their sandy, barren soil, leaving the reservation and renting farms from whites, doing seasonal work for them, hunting and trapping game, and picking wild berries.[37]

With no reservation at all in Wisconsin, the Winnebago had still greater difficulties in subsisting. Some of the chiefs, how-

[36] Clyde A. Morley, "A General Survey of the Schooling Provided for the American Indian Throughout Our Country's History with a Special Study of Conditions in Wisconsin" (master's thesis, University of Wisconsin, 1927), 50–54; Martha E. Layman, "A History of Indian Education in the United States" (doctoral dissertation, University of Minnesota, 1942), 349–365.

[37] Richard N. Current, *Pine Logs and Politics: A Life of Philetus Sawyer, 1816–1900* (Madison, 1950), 72–74, 115; Schafer, *Winnebago-Horicon Basin*, 73–76. An account of the Menominee timberland is in Patricia K. Ourada, "The Menominee Indians: A History" (doctoral dissertation, University of Oklahoma, 1973), 214–228. For a contemporary white man's impressions of the Menominee, see Willard H. Titus, "Observations on the Menominee Indians," in *WMH*, 14 (September–December, 1930), 93–105, 121–132. Titus wrote these observations in 1875, after a few years of ministering to the Indians as a medical doctor. His feelings constituted a strange mixture of admiration and contempt.

ever, demonstrated at least a little economic enterprise. In the late 1860's one of them held a medicine dance and feast, near Tomah, and admitted whites as guests and spectators for twenty-five cents apiece. Another chief put up printed posters inviting whites to attend his show, near Trempealeau. He was thought to have cleared several hundred dollars from the paid attendance.[38]

A few Winnebago, those who owned land and lived on it in more or less the manner of the whites, were well accepted and even highly respected by their white neighbors. Outstanding among these few was Chief Yellow Thunder. Along with the rest of his tribe he had been forcibly removed to the west of the Mississippi River in 1840, and like many of his fellow tribesmen he had returned as soon as he could, he and his wife walking nearly 500 miles. On his return he bought forty acres in northeastern Sauk County, built a log house on his land, and settled there with his wife. After his wife's death in 1868 he seldom stayed in the log house, but lived most of the time in a tent that he pitched near the Wisconsin River. Tall, stately, he dressed much like a white man except for the inconspicuous black ribbon ornament in his hair and the blanket he wore in place of a coat. A devout Catholic, he showed no bitterness or resentment on account of the dispossession of his people. In the fall of 1873 a knee injury led to blood poisoning for Yellow Thunder, and his white neighbors helped to care for him in his final illness. Before he died the federal government made another attempt to remove the Winnebago from Wisconsin.

Ever since the Indian troubles of 1862, whites in Wisconsin had been demanding the removal of the Winnebago. Finally, a regiment of infantry was sent from Fort Snelling, in Minnesota, to round up the stray bands and take them to Nebraska. A few days before Christmas, 1873, about 150 of the Indians were encamped along the Baraboo River, between Baraboo and Portage, for a powwow. A company of troops broke up

---

[38] Brunson, *Western Pioneer*, 2: 356–357. For mention of other Winnebago feasts and dances, to which whites were invited, see Curti, *Making of an American Community*, 85–86.

the party, herded the people to Portage, and put them aboard a train. Yellow Thunder and other landowners were exempted from the removal drive. All together, about 860 Winnebago were transferred, with much hardship, to the Nebraska reservation, where they were not welcome and where they did not want to be. Within a few months, more than half of them were in Wisconsin again, and thereafter others kept trickling back.[39]

[6]

For some of the recently freed slaves, Wisconsin seemed a land of opportunity after the war, though the state by no means became a haven for blacks. They rapidly took over as deck hands on the Mississippi River steamboats after being brought in to break a strike of Irish roustabouts in 1866. The wages, however, declined. Blacks continued to arrive in Fond du Lac, to augment the already sizable Negro colony there, with the encouragement of a friendly white man, who helped them find jobs. Freedmen from the South joined other black communities in Wisconsin, particularly the one in Milwaukee. The result, at least in that city, was to lower the black community's economic and social status. Relatively fewer of the Milwaukee blacks than before the war were now literate, skilled or semi-skilled, self-employed, or propertied. Residential segregation increased as the blacks crowded together more and more in the central city, on the lowlands adjoining the Milwaukee River.[40]

[39] George W. Thatcher, "The Winnebago Indians, 1827–1932" (master's thesis, University of Wisconsin, 1935), 179–180; Harry E. Cole, ed., *A Standard History of Sauk County, Wisconsin* (2 vols., Chicago, 1918), 1: 172–173, 177–184; Milwaukee *Sentinel*, December 27, 1873; U.S. Commissioner of Indian Affairs, *Annual Report*, 1874, p. 37; Nancy O. Lurie, "The Winnebago Indians: A Study in Cultural Change" (doctoral dissertation, Northwestern University, 1952), 167–169.

[40] Frederick Merk, *Economic History of Wisconsin During the Civil War Decade* (Madison, 1916), 169; Bill Hooker, "Fond du Lac, Its Sawmills and Freedmen—A Sketch," in *WMH*, 16 (June, 1933), 423–427; William J. Vollmar, "The Negro in a Midwest Frontier City: Milwaukee, 1835–1870" (master's thesis, Marquette University, 1968), 82–88. The *Ninth Census of the United States, 1870: Volume I*, p. 292, shows 161 of Milwaukee's 176 blacks living in the adjacent third, fourth, and seventh wards.

Wisconsin blacks revealed an urge for self-improvement, and individuals here and there made considerable progress, as random newspaper reports suggested. In Oshkosh three "full grown colored men" attended the First Ward School to gain the literacy they had been deprived of. In Racine "nearly all the colored young men" took part in a debating society of their own. In Kilbourn City a "colored gentleman, formerly from Georgia," gained admittance to the bar and opened a law office. "Another evidence of the downfall of cast[e]," one editor commented.[41]

Other evidence indicated, however, that the spirit of caste remained strong in the state. The great majority of whites had little or nothing to do with blacks and, indeed, seldom even saw them. A few showed a curiosity that was friendly enough. Professor William Francis Allen of the University of Wisconsin published *Slave Songs of the United States* (1873), a collection and a discussion of words and melodies he had gathered while on a wartime educational mission among the freed people of the South Carolina Sea Islands. On a dare, two white girls reportedly kissed a black manservant at a party in the village of Green Lake. The two gained instant notoriety, even beyond the state boundaries, for being "depraved in taste and vulgar in habits." The very sight of a Negro could be startling in some parts of Wisconsin, as it was in Plymouth, Sheboygan County. "Plymouth," ran an 1870 report, "has been agitated by the appearance of a 'nigger' in its midst."[42]

There were no more widely reported lynchings—if any—of Wisconsin blacks after the Milwaukee lynching of Marshall Clark in 1861, but there were occasional incidents of prejudice and outright violence. Some of these were reported in the press. In Beaver Dam, for example, a group of whites assaulted a Negro in 1865, and he sued one of them for damages. In

---

[41] Milwaukee *Sentinel*, February 22, 1866, January 15, 1870, and March 20, 1871.

[42] Curti, *Making of an American Community*, 88–91. The two girls were denounced in the Detroit *Free Press*, February 16, 1868, quoted in Forrest G. Wood, *Black Scare: The Racist Response to Emancipation and Reconstruction* (Berkeley, 1968), 144–145. The Milwaukee *Sentinel*, December 21, 1870, published the report of Plymouth's Negro; and the October 15, 1873, issue mentioned Allen's book.

Madison a "slight fracas" occurred between blacks and whites in 1867. "The whites were the aggressors," the Milwaukee *Sentinel* reported, "and, it is gratifying to learn, got badly worsted." In Racine, in 1868, a mob threatened a house that two "gentlemen of color," recent arrivals from Indiana, occupied with their white wives. The black men threw stones at the menacing crowd, then fled with their wives, taking a train to Milwaukee. "They were followed by the Marshal of Racine, who arrested them on a warrant for assault and battery." In Milwaukee a Negro complained in 1869 of "ill-treatment towards colored passengers" on the Waukesha train. He said the conductor refused to seat black women in the "ladies' car" and "compelled them to go into the gentlemen's or smoking-car," where there were not even seats available. In La Crosse, after spending thirty days in jail, two Negroes had to promise to leave town in order to get out.[43]

Blacks, most of them Methodists, shared religious beliefs with whites but preferred to worship in their own congregations. Even very small black communities organized churches and, as soon as possible, constructed church buildings. Whites often assisted. The Wisconsin Conference of the Methodists, for example, contributed in 1867 to the building fund of the "colored people" of Janesville. The African M. E. Church of Milwaukee, burdened with debt in 1873, looked to the people of the city, white as well as black, for financial aid. Some black Methodists rivaled their white coreligionists in temperance zeal. The Wisconsin Order of the Good Templars, the secret temperance society, defied the anti-Negro rule of the national office and welcomed black members. There is no evidence that any of these belonged to predominantly white lodges in Wisconsin, but the Trumbull Lodge in Madison consisted entirely of Negroes, thirty-five of them in 1867, and they were "regularly in attendance" at its meetings.[44]

The blacks of Wisconsin continued, as they had done before

[43] Milwaukee *Sentinel*, July 3, 1865, June 19, 1867, October 6, 1868, June 28, 1869, and November 9, 1871.

[44] Bennett and Lawson, *Methodism in Wisconsin*, 223; Brownsword, "Good Templars in Wisconsin," 29–30; Milwaukee *Sentinel*, December 20, 1867, December 18, 1872, and January 11, 1873.

the war, to celebrate on August 1 the anniversary of emancipation in the British West Indies. Now they usually added, on the same day, a commemoration of the "newly acquired freedom of the colored race in the United States," as the Prescott *Journal* put it in announcing the Pierce County celebration in 1866. Blacks also observed January 1, the anniversary of Lincoln's final proclamation, as Emancipation Day. And they still took special interest in celebrating the Fourth of July, with its reaffirmation of human equality. They observed the occasion in their own way. Members of the large Fond du Lac Negro community held annually a "regular old-fashioned barbecue" near their church.[45]

With aspirations still lively, Wisconsin's blacks generally expected fulfillment in the state. Seldom did they look to Africa as the land of their dreams. When, in 1869, "a colored man by the name of Alonzo De Leon" appeared in Wisconsin, on a lecture tour to raise money for planting a colony in the Niger Valley, he attracted audiences of whites as well as blacks, but converted few if any of the blacks into African colonists. Recently the Negroes of Wisconsin had made a tremendous advance toward equality when they received the right to vote. How they did so is part of the political story of the time.[46]

[45] Milwaukee *Sentinel,* July 18, 1866 (quoting an item from the Prescott *Journal*), December 20, 1867, July 14, 1869, June 27, 1871, June 13, July 9, 1872, and August 13, 1873.

[46] On De Leon's lecture in Dodgeville, see the Jabez Brown diary, July 20, 1869, in the Jabez Brown Papers.

16

The Politics
of Reconstruction

[1]

A T THE END of the Civil War the Republican or "Union" party dominated Wisconsin politics. Republicans held the governorship and all the other state administrative posts, the three positions on the state supreme court, a large majority of the places in each house of the legislature, five of the six congressional seats, and both of the United States senatorships. For eight years more the party continued to keep itself in power, though with a fluctuating share of the total vote. Then, in 1873, the Republicans faltered, losing the control of the state government that they had held since 1857.

The Republicans' almost unbroken record of success during the reconstruction years was by no means automatic. It depended on the care with which the leaders maximized the party's strengths and minimized its weaknesses. Its greatest strengths were its appeals to patriotism (or sectionalism), idealism, and materialism. The leaders could identify the party with noble causes, with the war aims of union and freedom, and so long as their fellow partisans controlled Congress and the Presidency they could also promise the more solid benefits of the federal patronage and the federal pork barrel. To some extent, the party's weaknesses derived from its very strengths. Antislavery idealism, insofar as it carried over to the postwar movement for Negro rights, ran against the much stronger force of racism. The reform spirit, which animated the anti-slavery drive, also gave rise to demands for sumptuary laws against drinking and Sabbath-breaking, laws that would turn away foreign-born voters, who looked upon such legislation as a product of continuing nativism. Moreover, the reforming impulse directed itself against monopolies, against corporations in general and railroads in particular, and as a result of the Republicans' effectiveness in promoting federal aid to private enterprise, especially through the financing of "internal improvements," the party exposed itself to charges of favoritism toward big business.

The leaders had to deal carefully, then, with the shifting crosscurrents of sectionalism, idealism, materialism, racism, nativism, and antimonopolism. Only by so doing could the politicians hold the party together and keep it on top. Holding it together required some effort, since the party was and had been from the beginning a congeries of rather disparate elements. It had originated in 1854 as a coalition consisting mainly of Whigs but containing also Free Soilers and other dissident Democrats. As it grew it incorporated all except a few of the Know Nothings and at the same time, by disavowing Know Nothing aims and muting temperance and Sabbatarian cries, it managed to attract a number of immigrants, at least among some of the Protestant groups. Before the war it overcame centrifugal tendencies by emphasizing the one principle that all its various followers held in common, the principle of free soil, or opposition to the extension of slavery into the territories. During the war the party drew the support of additional Democrats, some as converts, others as fellow travelers, and it made use of a centripetal force even stronger than free-soilism, the force of a shared determination to win the war. Once the war had been won and slavery had been abolished, however, the leaders, if they were to remain in power, needed to find new issues that would unite the party, while continuing to avoid those that might divide it.

[2]

One possibility was to keep the war memories alive and thus maintain the identification of the Republican party with patriotism and the opposition with treason. This could be done, in part, by making an issue of the veterans, backing them in peace as in war, and thus cultivating their support along with the support of their relatives and friends and of self-consciously loyal citizens in general.

Lucius Fairchild, the first three-term governor of Wisconsin (1866–1872), early saw the possibility. Himself a veteran, one who had lost his left arm at Gettysburg, Fairchild campaigned in 1865 as the Soldier's Friend. He got endorsements from his old comrades and promised generous benefits, including preference in political appointments, to all Wisconsin soldiers and especially to the disabled. In his first inaugural the governor, his empty sleeve conspicuous, spoke of the nobility of sacrifice in the nation's cause. He referred to secession as treason and called for the hanging of Jefferson Davis as a traitor. In 1866 the Grand Army of the Republic's Madison department, a veterans' organization that Fairchild had helped to form, demanded that all leaders of the late Confederacy be condignly punished and that they be completely debarred from politics.

Once a colonel, now governor, Fairchild continued to view himself as still, at least potentially, a commander of troops against the traitorous foe. Again and again he referred to the veterans' "fears of another civil war" in case of a Democratic victory. "I confess to some little feeling of this kind," he wrote confidentially, in 1866, "and to a strong wish to prepare, so far as I am able as the governor of this state, to meet all enemies on their own terms." Publicly he insisted that only the maintenance of the Republicans in power would prevent a renewal of rebellion. Year after year he and his followers continued to identify the Republican party with the Union army, as they did at an 1866 rally in Madison, where youthful party workers flaunted banners reading "We vote as we fought, against traitors," and "Where the traitor's bullet failed his ballot shall not conquer."[1]

If most of the men who had served the Union in war could be counted upon to support the Republican party in peace, most of those who had evaded service could be expected to assist the Democrats. So, while encouraging the veterans to vote, the Republicans could further help themselves by taking the ballot away from men who, when drafted, had failed to report or who, after induction, had deserted. This would be as constitutional as it would be just, the state attorney general advised the legislature in 1866, confirming the opinion his predecessor had given the previous year. Accordingly, laws of 1866 and 1867 disfranchised draft dodgers and deserters, provided for the publication of a list of their names, and required the posting of three copies of the list at every polling place. A "blue pamphlet" containing some 12,000 names was printed. Inclusion of a man's name was to be taken as *prima facie* evidence of his guilt and hence of his ineligibility to vote. Democrats protested that the laws violated the ancient Anglo-Saxon principle of no punishment without prior conviction, and the critics were by no means appeased when, in 1868, an amendment made it possible for a listed man to get his name removed by proving his innocence to the satisfaction of the attorney general. Even before the official pamphlet had been published, Governor Fairchild was already preparing partial lists to be used against Democrats in the Congressional elections of 1866. For a few years the pamphlet was of some value to the Republicans. Despite the zeal of Fairchild and certain of his fellow partisans, however, the disfranchising laws soon became dead letters.[2]

[1] Sam Ross, *The Empty Sleeve: A Biography of Lucius Fairchild* (Madison, 1964), v, 66–76, 79–94; Mary R. Dearing, *Veterans in Politics: The Story of the G. A. R.* (Baton Rouge, 1952), 94, 104–105, 140–141, 147, 180, quoting Fairchild (p. 105) in a letter to Timothy O. Howe, July 24, 1866, in the Lucius Fairchild Papers. See also Karen J. Wise, "Wisconsin and the Fourteenth Amendment, 1865–1867" (master's thesis, University of Wisconsin, 1966), 69–70; *Wisconsin State Journal,* October 19, 1866.

[2] Chicago *Tribune,* January 19, 1866; *List of Persons, Residents of the State of Wisconsin, Reported as Deserters from the Military and Naval Service of*

For Republicans, the question of taking the vote away from deserters was much less controversial than the question of giving it to blacks, whatever their war records. At the end of the war the issue of suffrage for Wisconsin Negroes was touchy indeed, despite their infinitesimal number and their willing service in the Union cause. Wisconsin's blacks had done their part and, understandably, they thought this entitled them to the ballot. "The record of the last four years is still before us," a convention of the "colored citizens" of Wisconsin resolved on October 9, 1865; "white men and colored have fought side by side. . . . Our deeds upon the battle fields have been sealed in blood, and render us worthy all the privileges that we ask of the voters."[3]

The next month the voters could decide on Negro suffrage in a referendum—the third such referendum to be held in accordance with the constitution of 1848. In the 1849 election a suffrage bill had been favored by 5,265 ballots and opposed by only 4,075, but a total of more than 31,000 votes were polled in the election itself. Fewer than a third of the voters had bothered to express themselves on the bill. Though it had received more affirmative than negative votes, it had not received in its favor a majority of all the votes cast at the election, and even its proponents therefore considered it as lost. In 1857 another suffrage bill was voted down by 41,345 to 28,235. Then, in 1865, the legislature passed yet another bill, in response to a petition from 102 blacks.[4]

At their state convention that September in Madison the Republicans faced the question whether to endorse the suffrage proposal and make it a party issue in the fall election. A leading party organ, the *Wisconsin State Journal* of Madison, was

the United States (Madison, 1868), 3–6 and *passim,* bound in *Wisconsin Miscellaneous Pamphlets,* vol. 17; Alfons J. Beitzinger, *Edward G. Ryan, Lion of the Law* (Madison, 1960), 82–83; Ross, *Empty Sleeve,* 93–94. The "blue pamphlet" law was repealed in 1869; see *Laws of Wisconsin,* 1869, p. 141.

[3] Milwaukee *Sentinel,* October 10, 1865; Edward Noyes, "The Negro in Wisconsin's Civil War Effort," in the *Lincoln Herald,* 69 (Summer, 1967), 70.

[4] Milwaukee *Sentinel,* March 29, November 8, 21, December 24, 1849; *Wisconsin Blue Book, 1940,* p. 225; Leslie H. Fishel, Jr., "Wisconsin and Negro Suffrage," in *WMH,* 46 (Spring, 1963), 184, 190.

urging the adoption of a platform of principles around which the "genuine and earnest Union men" could rally, was reporting that a large majority approved the suffrage bill, and was citing in its favor the highest party authority, that of President Andrew Johnson, who had said that "each State should be left to regulate the question of suffrage for itself." Yet, in fact, Johnson was unwilling for Wisconsin or other Northern states to be left to regulate the question in favor of the blacks. His agent in Wisconsin was Senator James R. Doolittle, a former Democrat, the Senate's foremost wartime advocate of the "colonization" abroad of freed slaves, and an unctuous but effective orator. "All attempts to make this new issue of Negro suffrage a plank in the platform of the party," Doolittle told Fairchild, "is simply suicide." Presiding at the Madison convention, Doolittle managed to exclude from the platform any reference to Negro suffrage in Wisconsin.

Some of the Republicans, the former antislavery radicals, now the "friends of equal rights," denounced the "pernicious influence" of Doolittle and threatened to break away from the "Union" party. They called a second convention, to meet in Janesville and represent the "liberty-loving" people of the state. In Janesville the radicals found themselves a decided minority of the Union party, however, and they concluded their rump session by endorsing the candidates who had been nominated in Madison.[5]

During the 1865 campaign the Democrats, who had an explicit antisuffrage plank in their platform, called upon Fairchild to debate the question with their gubernatorial candidate, Harrison C. Hobart. Some of the Republican newspapers frankly advocated equal voting rights, and so did the radical politicians, prominent among them Sherman Booth and Byron Paine, the one the hero of the Joshua Glover slave rescue of 1854 and the other the attorney who had defended Booth and

[5] Wise, "Wisconsin and the Fourteenth Amendment," 4–10; Fishel, "Wisconsin and Negro Suffrage," in *WMH*, 46: 190–192; *Wisconsin State Journal*, September 5, 1865. The Doolittle quotation is from a letter to Fairchild, September 3, 1865, in the Fairchild Papers.

persuaded the state supreme court to defy federal authority and declare the fugitive-slave act of 1850 unconstitutional. But Fairchild hid behind his party's noncommital platform and refused to speak out. His advisers cautioned him that Negro suffrage was distasteful to many party members and particularly to war veterans. "Nothing would please the copperheads more than to induce or compel you in some way to define your position in writing," one of his friends counseled. "The 'Nigger' is the only card they have left." By his silence, however, Fairchild risked losing the support of radical voters. So, late in the campaign, he wrote letters to Booth and other radical politicians telling them he personally favored Negro suffrage and wished them to quote him whenever they met with like-minded Republicans.[6]

When the returns were in, the strategy of Fairchild seemed to have worked. He won by 10,000 votes and Negro suffrage lost by almost 9,000. The suffrage bill did much better in the Republican than in the Democratic counties, but nowhere did it do so well as Fairchild himself. Of the thirty-eight counties he carried, only twenty-four had a majority for the bill. Of the remaining nineteen counties, which his opponent carried, not one gave a majority for it. His fears regarding the veterans' antipathy to it appear to have been justified, if the separately counted soldier vote is taken as an indicator. By November 1865 only about 1,500 Wisconsin soldiers were still voting in the field. They went more than three to one, 1,169 to 330, against the bill while going for Fairchild in about the same proportion. The "suffrage question, if made an issue, would have carried us under," Doolittle assured him after the election.[7]

Despite the suffrage proposition's defeat, the radical Repub-

---

[6] Wise, "Wisconsin and the Fourteenth Amendment," 9–13, quoting a letter from William E. Smith to Fairchild, October 18, 1865, in the Fairchild Papers; Ross, *Empty Sleeve,* 72–74; Dearing, *Veterans in Politics,* 66.

[7] Fishel, "Wisconsin and Negro Suffrage," in *WMH,* 46: 193; Ross, *Empty Sleeve,* 73–75; Wise, "Wisconsin and the Fourteenth Amendment," 14. Returns by counties are in Returns, 1865, Election Return Statements of the State Board of Canvassers, 1848–, Series 214, Records of the Secretary of State, WSA. Doolittle's letter to Fairchild, dated November 13, 1865, is in the Fairchild Papers.

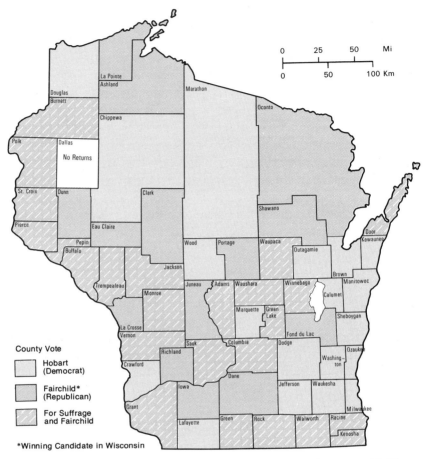

County Vote

▨ Hobart
   (Democrat)

▨ Fairchild*
   (Republican)

▨ For Suffrage
   and Fairchild

*Winning Candidate in Wisconsin

GUBERNATORIAL ELECTION AND SUFFRAGE VOTE, 1865

licans were soon to have their way, and blacks were to be voting at the next election in Wisconsin. At the recent election a Milwaukeean named Ezekiel Gillespie had gone to the polls, along with Sherman Booth, and had offered his ballot even though he was unregistered, the board of registry having turned him away as a person of "mixed African blood." The election inspectors refused his ballot. Gillespie, with the aid of his lawyer, Byron Paine, then sued the inspectors, who offered a demurrer before the county court which promptly moved the case on appeal to the state supreme court.

In *Gillespie v. Palmer et al.* (1866) Paine undertook to prove that Gillespie already had the right to vote in 1865 because the Negro suffrage measure had actually been approved at the 1849 election, in the very first referendum under the state constitution. The constitutional phrase "a majority of all votes cast at such election," Paine argued, must mean simply a majority of the votes cast on the specific issue. Otherwise, the measure could never be passed—even if all the voters should mark their ballots in its favor. These ballots could not add up to a "majority of all votes cast" at the election, for "all votes" would be the sum of those cast for the proposition plus those cast on both sides for governor plus those for lieutenant governor and so on. Surely the framers of the constitution had not intended any such thing, nor had they meant to require more votes for passing a suffrage bill than for ratifying a suffrage amendment, which would require approval by merely "a majority of the voters voting thereon."

The three judges, all Republicans, accepted Paine's reasoning, literal and strained though much of it was. They ruled that, despite the consensus to the contrary, which had prevailed for nearly seventeen years, Negroes had had the right to vote in Wisconsin since 1849, when a majority of voters casting ballots on the proposition—but only one-sixth of those voting in the election—had assented to a suffrage bill.[8]

The court's decision created "quite a commotion" in Milwaukee. Some Democrats threatened that any Negro attempting to vote in the upcoming local election would be mobbed. The blacks were not intimidated, and though there was the "rare sight of negroes voting," the election on April 3, 1866, was one of the quietest the city had ever experienced. "Not a single fight occurred at any of the polls." Some of the black voters were immediately summoned, for the first time, for jury duty. In the Madison election the Negro turnout was

[8] William J. Vollmar, "The Negro in a Midwest Frontier City: Milwaukee, 1835–1870" (master's thesis, Marquette University, 1968), 76–82; Fishel, "Wisconsin and Negro Suffrage," in *WMH,* 46: 194–196; Wisconsin Supreme Court, *Reports,* vol. 20, pp. 544–562.

large. There was even a black candidate for mayor, William Ḥ. Noland, and he received 306 votes to 691 for his opponent, Elisha Keyes. But Noland, a leader of the Madison black community, got no votes from his fellow blacks. All his votes came from Democrats, who had announced his candidacy against his will and as a joke. In a dignified election-day statement he declared he was a "Union man," that is, a Republican, and was himself voting the "straight Union ticket." "If any Democrat wishes to compliment me let him go and do likewise." In both Madison and Milwaukee nearly all the Negroes apparently voted straight Republican except in some Milwaukee wards where the Republicans put up no slates.

For Wisconsin Republicans, the Negro vote proved an asset only in marginal instances. It made the difference between defeat and victory, for example, in one of the closely contested Madison wards in 1866. But the Negro vote was too small to affect the outcome of most elections. Calculating the consequences of the possible defection of Johnson adherents, Republican politicians concluded, in May 1866, that the loss would be "more than balanced by the enfranchised colored vote." This conclusion depended, however, more on the smallness of the anticipated loss than on the largeness of the anticipated gain. After all, there were only a few hundred black adult males in the state.[9]

On balance, Negro suffrage at home was more a liability than an asset to Wisconsin Republicans. Their black support confirmed the charge of "niggerism" and helped the Democrats turn the widespread Negrophobia to their account. Democratic newspapers never tired of recalling supposed Negro "outrages" and describing Republican candidates as "Negro lovers." The Oshkosh *City Times* implied that Congressman Philetus Sawyer, for one, would stoop to almost anything for the "vote of a

[9] Milwaukee *Sentinel*, March 31, April 4, 5, 7, 10, May 28, 1866; the Noland quotation is from the issue of April 10. David Montgomery, *Beyond Equality: Labor and the Radical Republicans, 1862–1872* (New York, 1967), states, p. 83: "During the elections of 1866, Negro candidates were elected for the first time to state offices in both Wisconsin and Massachusetts." In fact, no Negro was elected to state office in Wisconsin in 1866 or for many years after that.

nigger" and accused him of neglecting whites to patronize blacks. If the party division had been closer, if the Republicans had been weaker, the added burden of race prejudice might have been too much for the party to bear.[10]

[3]

While bearing that burden, the party leaders also had to deal with the potentially disruptive issue of the postwar reconstruction of the South. In Wisconsin, as in other states, the party had adopted the name "Union" so as to encourage the affiliation of Democrats who backed the war effort. At the national convention of 1864 the Republicans had sealed the coalition by choosing the War Democrat Johnson as Lincoln's running mate. After Lincoln's assassination and Johnson's accession, the coalition could remain intact only so long as the Democrat in the White House could keep the loyalty of the Republicans in Congress and throughout the country.

At the outset Johnson seemed to be in a position to exert an especially strong hold on the Union party in Wisconsin. His assistant postmaster general—whom he was to elevate to the head of the Post Office Department in July 1866—was Alexander W. Randall, a two-term governor of the state. Randall's friend Elisha W. Keyes was postmaster as well as mayor of Madison. Through his friendship with Randall he had a large share in the disposal of jobs in the more than 1,000 Wisconsin post offices. Associated with Keyes was Horace Rublee, chairman of the Republican (Union) state committee and co-owner and co-editor of the *Wisconsin State Journal*. Together, Keyes and Rublee ran the Madison Regency, the most powerful Republican machine in the state. When Johnson took over, Keyes urged the people to "rally around" the new President as he tried to reunite the nation.

Johnson soon had on his side not only the Republican bosses

---

[10] Richard N. Current, *Pine Logs and Politics: A Life of Philetus Sawyer, 1816–1900* (Madison, 1950), 58, quoting from the Oshkosh *City Times,* October 13, 1868.

of Wisconsin but also the state's senior senator, James R. Doolittle. At the time of Lincoln's death Doolittle had been cooperating with Lincoln in his effort to reconstruct and readmit Louisiana on fairly quick and easy terms. Doolittle differed with his Senate colleague from Wisconsin, Timothy O. Howe, who was dissatisfied with Lincoln's policy and wished Lincoln "w'd tell the rebels" that the President could "only grant pardons" and that Congress alone could admit states. At first Doolittle feared that Johnson, as President, would deal too harshly with the defeated Southerners, but Doolittle soon convinced himself that Johnson's policy would be essentially the same as Lincoln's. Before long he felt that he and Johnson, along with Senator Preston King of New York, constituted a "trio whose hearts & heads" sympathized "more closely and more deeply than any other trio in America" (and King was shortly to commit suicide, leaving Doolittle and Johnson as twin spirits).[11]

The Wisconsin party's first big postwar test of unity and of support for the Johnson administration occurred at the September 1865 state convention. As chairman of the platform committee, Doolittle was ready with a set of resolutions applauding Johnson's program for speedily restoring the Southern states. He got his resolutions adopted after seeing the delegates turn down, by an overwhelming voice vote, an amendment calling for Negro suffrage in the South—a plank he thought would have driven "thousands of War Democrats" out of the party. To Johnson he boasted of his success, and the *Wisconsin State Journal* gave its approval to his stand on restoration, but other party organs dissented, as did Senator Howe, and some of the radicals condemned Doolittle as a rebel sympathizer. Thus, despite the seeming consensus he had contrived, the party already was developing strains.

[11] Richard W. Hantke, "Elisha W. Keyes and the Radical Republicans," in *WMH*, 35 (Spring, 1952), 203–208; Biagino M. Marone, "Senator James Rood Doolittle and the Struggle Against Radicalism, 1857–1866" (master's thesis, Marquette University, 1955), 33–35; Howard K. Beale, *The Critical Year: A Study of Andrew Johnson and Reconstruction* (New York, 1930), 36; John T. Morse, Jr., ed., *Diary of Gideon Welles, Secretary of the Navy Under Lincoln and Johnson* (3 vols., Boston, 1911), 2: 385–386. The quotations are from Howe to Doolittle, April 13, 1865, in the James R. Doolittle Papers; and Doolittle to his wife, April 26, 1865, in *SHSW Proceedings*, 1909, p. 291.

After the 1865 election Johnson's assistant postmaster general, Randall, predicted to a Wisconsin correspondent, "There is coming a 'big row' shortly which will and is clearing out the whole radical portion of our party and probably leading the Democratic element of the party to 'seek new alliances.'" A "big row" was indeed on the way, and some former Democrats were to desert the Wisconsin organization, but the radicals were by no means to be cleared out. The party itself was to be radicalized. Randall and the rest of Johnson's friends, not his opponents, would have to look for new alliances.[12]

When, during the winter of 1865–1866, Johnson and the congressional Republicans quarreled over reconstruction policy, only two members of the Wisconsin delegation took the side of the President. These two were Senator Doolittle and Congressman Charles A. Eldredge, the lone Democrat from the state. Senator Howe and the other five congressmen supported the Republican program to postpone the seating of senators and representatives from the South, to extend the life and powers of the Freedmen's Bureau, and to confer civil rights upon Southern blacks.

At first the Madison Regency tried to stay out of the fight. Keyes kept still and occupied himself with his duties as mayor of Madison. Rublee's *Wisconsin State Journal*, without taking a stand, gave equal space to the opposing speeches of Doolittle and Howe. But neutrality was no longer possible for Wisconsin Republicans after Johnson vetoed the Freedmen's Bureau bill and then the civil rights bill, thus ending all hopes for a compromise. The Republicans in the legislature, thoroughly aroused, telegraphed instructions to the state's senators in Washington to vote for overriding the second veto. When Doolittle disregarded the instructions, the legislature formally requested him to resign. Now even the Madison Regency split. Keyes, after failing to "squelch" or even "tone down" the resignation demand, assured Doolittle the country would "yet see the folly" of pursuing a course different from Doo-

[12] Marone, "Senator James Rood Doolittle," 35–44; Wise, "Wisconsin and the Fourteenth Amendment," 14–15. The Randall quotation is from a letter to Horace A. Tenney, November 21, 1865, in the Horace A. Tenney Papers.

little's. Keyes called a "Union meeting" and there spoke out
in favor of Johnson's policy. Rublee, however, warned Doolittle that the great majority of Wisconsin Republicans were
deeply alarmed by the President's course. The *Wisconsin
State Journal* criticized the vetoes and endorsed Howe's position.[13]

Wisconsin politicians brought about something of a party
realignment as they prepared for a trial of strength between
Johnson's adherents and his opponents in the campaign of
1866. As two of his top lieutenants in the land, Senator Doolittle and Postmaster General Randall played leading roles in
the National Union movement, through which its sponsors
intended to bring together a great middle grouping of Republican and Democratic voters and thus elect to Congress a
majority favorable to the President. But Randall and Doolittle
failed to rouse much Republican support for the movement
even in their home state. Keyes himself lay low for the time
being. Co-operating with the two Johnson leaders was Alexander Mitchell, banker, railroad magnate, and one of Milwaukee's
richest men, who had acted with the Republicans during the
war but was now about to leave them and join the Democrats.
"It requires no sacrifice from Democrats to support Johnson,"
another Republican-for-Johnson heard from a man in Appleton, "but, with Repub's, they must brace against [the] bulk
of previous political associations." Indeed, Democrats flocked
to the President's standard with an enthusiasm that to Doolittle
was gratifying and yet embarrassing, especially when he was
flattered by Marcus M. Pomeroy, editor of the La Crosse *Democrat* and lately the most viciously anti-Lincoln Copperhead
in the state if not in the entire country. For a time there were
two parties claiming the magic name of "Union"—the National
Union and the Republican Union. Soon the former became
practically indistinguishable from the regular Democratic organization, and the latter reconstituted and retitled itself as
simply the good old Republican party.

[13] Hantke, "Elisha W. Keyes," in *WMH,* 35: 204–205; Wise, "Wisconsin and the
Fourteenth Amendment," 19–22. The Keyes quotation is from a letter to Doolittle, February 27, 1866, in the Doolittle Papers.

During the 1866 campaign, however, party lines and party loyalties remained uncertain and confusing enough that Randall and Doolittle found it hard to make effective use of presidential patronage. Randall was quoted as saying that only those sustaining the President should eat his bread and butter —which led Johnson's foes to dub his followers the Bread and Butter party. The problem was to know who could be depended upon to sustain the President. Alexander Mitchell advised Doolittle that their side would "gain little additional political strength by removing A. & appointing B." unless B. should actually prove a better Johnson man. "I do not see that the new appointees . . . are likely to be any better administration men than the old—if as good." Another difficulty lay in the jealousy between Republican and Democratic friends of the President. Democratic leaders feared that Doolittle and Randall, "because of old party associations," were "more likely to bestow the patronage at their disposal" upon Republicans than upon Democrats. Nevertheless, the patronage dispensers made a number of changes in Wisconsin. What effect these had, other than to exacerbate the anti-Johnson feeling of many Republicans, it would be hard to say.

The bitterness of the campaign solidified the Republican party, bringing tightly together all its factions except the tiny group of die-hard Johnsonites. The proposed Fourteenth Amendment became a test not only of Republicanism but also of patriotism, of true Unionism. According to the Milwaukee *Sentinel,* which had lost its government printing contract because of its anti-Johnson stand, the "Rebels" were giving no sign that they had ceased to be "deadly enemies of the Union." They were refusing to ratify the amendment and they were adopting black codes which, for "atrocity," found "no equal in the annals of Russian serfdom." Condoning and encouraging the recalcitrant Southerners were Johnson and Doolittle. From one voter, who signed himself "Four Fifths of Wisconsin," Doolittle received this bit of advice: "You have turned *Traitor* to your State and gone over to Johnson and the *rebels*. . . . Come home and put a *ball* through your *rotten* head."

Such bitterness made for a sizable Republican turnout on

election day. As the 1866 returns showed, the party had gained more from conversions than it had lost from defections. The five Republican congressmen were re-elected, along with the one Democrat, and the Republican majority in the state legislature was increased from forty-seven to fifty-nine. Addressing the legislature early in 1867, Governor Fairchild took the result as a mandate for ratification of the Fourteenth Amendment: "Most of you are here to-day, because your constituents knew that you deemed this amendment just and necessary." Both houses promptly ratified it.[14]

Wisconsin Republicans maintained their unity in supporting the passage of the reconstruction acts of 1867, the impeachment of Johnson, the presidential candidacy of Ulysses S. Grant, and the ratification of the Fifteenth Amendment. They ceased to consider Johnson's friend Doolittle even nominally a party member, and they did not count him among the seven Republican senators who broke ranks at the impeachment trial, though they blamed him, along with each of the seven, for the one not-guilty vote that proved decisive in bringing about the acquittal. When his senatorial term ended in 1869, they replaced him with Matthew H. Carpenter, a postwar convert from the Democratic faith who had confirmed his Republicanism with his oratorical attacks on Doolittle during the 1866 campaign. Keyes having come out, after a two-year silence, for Grant and then for Carpenter, the new senator used his influence with the new President to get Keyes continued as Madison postmaster. Soon Keyes became the state Republican

[14] Hantke, "Elisha W. Keyes," in *WMH*, 35: 205–206; Marone, "Senator James Rood Doolittle," 63–66, 91, 100, 136; Wise, "Wisconsin and the Fourteenth Amendment," 38–43, 52–53, 72, 84–85; James R. Sellers, "James R. Doolittle," in *WMH*, 17–18 (December, 1933–December, 1934), 18: 27–28; *Wisconsin Blue Book, 1866*, pp. 84, 98–100; *Wisconsin Blue Book, 1867*, pp. 166, 170–172, 254–277. The Republican-for-Johnson quotation is from a letter from Sam Ryan to Horace A. Tenney, May 21, 1866, in the Tenney Papers. The Mitchell quotation is from a letter to Doolittle, May 14, 1866, in the Doolittle Papers. The quotation of a Democratic leader is from a letter from Sylvanus Cadwallader to George H. Paul, May 7, 1866, in the George H. Paul Papers. The Milwaukee *Sentinel* quotes are from the issue of July 30, 1866. The letter from "Four Fifths of Wisconsin," dated July 3, 1866, is in the Doolittle Papers. Fairchild's remark is from his address of January 10, 1867, a copy of which is in the Fairchild Papers.

boss. With such a skillful organizer in command, with Carpenter and Howe co-operating in the Senate, with a harmonious delegation in the House, and with a sympathetic and obliging occupant of the Presidency, the Wisconsin party operated as a highly efficient and fairly cohesive organization, despite the continued tension of personal rivalries within it.[15]

A number of Wisconsinites, or ex-Wisconsinites, were also active as Republican politicians in one or another of the Southern states. These men were mostly former Wisconsin soldiers who had remained in or returned to the South, viewing it as a land of economic opportunity, a new frontier. Some of the newcomers from Wisconsin, like some of those from other Northern states, went into politics when the reconstruction acts gave the vote to the freedmen and made possible the rise of the Republican party in the South. The Republicans from the North soon came to be denounced as "carpetbaggers."

Among the carpetbaggers from Wisconsin, the most prominent was Harrison Reed, once a newspaper publisher in Milwaukee and in Madison and one of the founders of Neenah. Reed served as governor of Florida (1868–1872), a fellow Wisconsinite as lieutenant governor, and still another, a brother of Alexander W. Randall, as chief justice of the Florida supreme court. John S. Harris, a former Milwaukee businessman, was elected to the United States Senate from Louisiana. At least two men from Wisconsin represented Southern constituencies in the national House of Representatives, the one being sent from Alabama, the other from Tennessee. Wisconsinites also held office as lieutenant governor of Alabama, state treasurer of Texas, and public land and immigration commissioner of Arkansas. Wisconsin men were mayors of Nashville, Chattanooga, and other Southern cities. They filled jobs as local of-

---

[15] Hantke, "Elisha W. Keyes," in *WMH*, 35: 207–208; Alexander M. Thomson, *A Political History of Wisconsin* (Milwaukee, 1900), 166–173, 185; E. Bruce Thompson, *Matthew Hale Carpenter: Webster of the West* (Madison, 1954), 106–118; William Gillette, *The Right to Vote: Politics and the Passage of the Fifteenth Amendment* (Baltimore, 1965), 145. See also Claude Albright, "Dixon, Doolittle, and Norton: The Forgotten Republican Votes," in *WMH*, 59 (Winter, 1975–1976), 91–100.

ficials and sat in state legislatures throughout the South. Among the lesser jobholders the most conspicuous Wisconsinite was Albert T. Morgan, once a farm boy in the vicinity of Fox Lake, who, in Mississippi, became a delegate to the state constitutional convention, a member of the state senate, and the sheriff of Yazoo County. Morgan outraged conservative white Mississippians by marrying a mulatto woman and by shooting to death a political rival who tried to take over the sheriff's office.[16]

[4]

Though doing handsomely for Grant in the presidential election of 1868, the Republicans did much less well for their gubernatorial and legislative candidates in the state elections of 1867 and 1869. The party's majorities in the legislature shrank to ten in the assembly and only one in the senate. From the returns some of the Republican leaders drew the lesson that the bloody shirt and radical reconstruction no longer were adequate as campaign appeals. "Reconstruction is gone," Governor Fairchild opined. He thought the party ought to put less emphasis on abstract principles and more emphasis on material interests. "A material programme founded on proposed advantages to the people," a friend had advised, would be "ten times as strong as any other, and would set all other parties aside and make a new party for itself, if necessary."

There was a material program that had long been immensely popular in Wisconsin, so popular that none of the state's politicians had ever dared oppose it, though they might disagree as to how and where it ought to be applied. That was, of course, the old Whig program of federal aid for internal improvements. As successors of the Whigs, the Republicans had endorsed such aid in their national platforms. Hence in Wisconsin the Re-

[16] David H. Overy, Jr., "The Wisconsin Carpetbagger: A Group Portrait," in *WMH,* 44 (Autumn, 1960), 22–23, 32–35, 38–39, 44–47. For a sketch of Reed's career in Florida, see Richard N. Current, *Three Carpetbag Governors* (Baton Rouge, 1967), 3–35. Morgan tells his own story in *Yazoo; or, On the Picket Line of Freedom in the South* (Washington, D.C., 1884).

publicans had a more persuasive claim than the Democrats to being true devotees of the policy.

Much along that line remained to be done for the state after the war. There were harbors to be dredged and deepened at all the lake ports. There were canals to be dug and, most important, the ambitious Fox–Wisconsin waterway, connecting Lake Michigan and the Mississippi River, to be completed. Though the southern part of the state was already crisscrossed by rail lines, there were still railroads to be built in the north. Wisconsinites were practically unanimous in believing they must have better and cheaper transportation, by land and water, if they were to market profitably their two most valuable products—wheat and lumber—and if they were to develop the state's economy as a whole. Few doubted that they must have federal assistance if they were to achieve these aims.

Wisconsin Republicans used the state's need for internal improvements to justify their demands for a radical reconstruction of the South. If the Southern states should be restored quickly and with little change, Senator Howe warned in 1866, the Southern representatives could join with Northern Democrats to block the kind of economic legislation that Wisconsinites desired. The *Wisconsin State Journal* presented figures to show that, under Johnson's plan of restoration, the South would offset the Northwest in congressional power. As a matter of fact, the Northwest often ran into conflict with the Northeast, whose representatives generally had much less enthusiasm for improvement expenditures than for tariff protection. Whatever their differences on economic policy, however, the Northwestern and Northeastern Republicans had a common interest in opposing the early readmission of Southern Democrats, who could be expected to resist the appropriations and the tariffs alike.

From 1865 on, Wisconsin's Republican congressmen kept busy introducing and pressing requests for surveys, land grants, and construction money in furtherance of plans for building railroads and canals and improving rivers and harbors. In the annual pork barrel, the river and harbor appropriation bill, the Wisconsin delegates usually got most of what they wanted, in exchange for their support of tariff measures. In the 1868 bill, however, they received only enough for the repair and maintenance of works already under way, the Northeastern Republicans taking the position that extravagance would be politically unwise in an election year. The Wisconsin Democrats then tried to claim for themselves the improvements cause. They contended that, once their party was in power in Washington, Congress would spend less on reconstructing the South and more on improving the North. They made the most of the fact that their presidential candidate, Horatio Seymour of New York, was a director of the Green Bay and Mississippi Canal Company, the company that had charge of the Fox–Wisconsin waterway. Seymour's election, they said, would mean a President who would take a personal interest in the development of the state.[17]

All along, Governor Fairchild had advocated internal improvements in addition to veteran benefits. In 1869, when he was seeking a third term without the backing of the state machine, he made improvements the paramount issue and himself their foremost champion. He hoped to attract the support of railroad promoters, pine-land speculators, and others in northwestern Wisconsin by keeping alive the St. Croix land grant, which was intended for the construction of a line from the Mississippi River to Lake Superior, and which was about to expire. At the same time he expected to win over the farmers along the Fox–Wisconsin route by providing a new stimulus to that project. "Give 'em *hell* on *Improvements,* and you're all right in this section," a well-wisher advised him. He met with the governors of Iowa and Minnesota to arrange for bringing their combined pressure upon Congress, obtained a promise

---

[17] Helen J. Williams and Harry Williams, "Wisconsin Republicans and Reconstruction, 1865–70," in *WMH,* 23 (September, 1939), 17–39. That article is based on Helen Jenson's more descriptively titled "Internal Improvements and Wisconsin Republicanism, 1865–1873" (master's thesis, University of Wisconsin, 1937). The quotations are from Fairchild to Zachariah Chandler, May 6, 1869, and Lorenzo Sherwood to Fairchild, December 27, 1867, in the Fairchild Papers.

of $5,000 from his own legislature to pay for lobbying, visited Washington to use his persuasive powers on congressmen, addressed a Portage gathering of enthusiasts from Wisconsin and neighboring states, and indeed talked about improvements at every opportunity. That year Wisconsin again got a fairly generous share of the river and harbor appropriations, and Fairchild secured his re-election without the assistance of Boss Keyes.[18]

By 1870 the advocates of a Fox–Wisconsin canal were convinced it would never be completed unless the federal government not only provided much more money but also assumed responsibility for the project. The twofold task of securing federal funds and arranging for a government purchase fell mainly upon Congressman Philetus Sawyer, of Oshkosh. His fellow townsmen long had dreamed of converting Oshkosh into a great inland seaport through the completion of the canal, and he himself had worked hard to get appropriations for that and for other Wisconsin improvements ever since going to Congress in 1865. As an influential member of the House committee on commerce, Sawyer took personal charge of the 1870 river and harbor bill, and he also helped in the passage of a measure authorizing the government to buy the Fox–Wisconsin works and rights from the Green Bay and Mississippi Canal Company. Oshkosh Democrats asserted that, as a friend of the Chicago and North Western Railway, Sawyer secretly aimed to thwart the canal enterprise and, in the purchase bill, had consented to terms he knew the company would reject. Late in the campaign, by pre-arrangement, the company itself refuted the Democrats by announcing its acceptance of the government's terms. On election day the voters returned Sawyer to Congress with his largest majority yet.

"I am as usual getting up the River & Harbor bill, and that dont damage our prospects any," Sawyer wrote to Fairchild in

[18] Ross, *Empty Sleeve*, 103–122. On Fairchild's influence with the state press on improvements, see John O. Holzhueter, "The Wisconsin Editors and Publishers Association, 1853–1877" (master's thesis, University of Wisconsin, 1966), 157, 164–165, 168, 173–174, 180–206. The advice of the well-wisher is in a letter from Leslie J. Perry to Fairchild, September 3, 1869, in the Fairchild Papers.

1872. So long as Sawyer remained in the House of Representatives, until 1875, he continued to see that his state and district got an undue share of federal largess. To what extent this contributed to Wisconsin's economic growth, it is hard to say. Much of the government's money seemed simply to disappear in the shifting sands of the rivers to be "improved," and the dream of a great ship canal was never to be realized. There can be no doubt, however, that the expenditures contributed mightily to the success of Wisconsin's Republican party.[19]

[5]

By 1872 the party had recovered most of its former strength. After a setback in 1870 it had made gains in 1871, increasing its majorities in both houses of the legislature and bringing to the governorship another Republican, the wealthy businessman and former congressman Cadwallader C. Washburn, who won the office over Doolittle, by 1871 an out-and-out Democrat once more. The Wisconsin Democracy, despite its acquisition of Doolittle and Mitchell and other one-time Johnson Republican leaders, seemingly remained an almost hopeless minority party. As a contemporary observed, it was "like an ox in a blizzard turning his tail to the storm"; it "kept up its organization, fought on the defensive as well as it could and faced the inevitable," that is, defeat. Yet it possessed one tremendous potential advantage, one that could transform defeat into victory if the circumstances were right. In the past the Democratic party had been the favorite with most of the immigrants. It now needed only to regain its previous share of the ethnic vote.[20]

To both parties in Wisconsin, this vote was crucial, since the state contained such a large foreign-born population. The Roman Catholics—German, Irish, Dutch, Belgian, French–Canadian—remained with few exceptions faithful to the Democratic party, but the Republican party had attracted most of the British and the Norwegians and some of the Protestant

[19] Current, *Pine Logs and Politics*, 50–54, 64–85, quoting Sawyer to Fairchild, February 15, 1872, in the Fairchild Papers.
[20] The quotation is from Thomson, *Political History*, 286.

Germans. To keep its supremacy after the war, the party had to maintain if not increase its proportion of the foreign vote.[21]

In 1866 the Republicans tried to curry favor with the Irish by cheering them on in the Fenian movement. The Fenians claimed more than 6,000 Wisconsin members, who contributed money and men for a proposed invasion of Canada. President Johnson, enforcing the neutrality laws, sent troops to stop the invasion and arrest its leaders. Wisconsin Republicans denounced Johnson for his interference, and Democratic newspapers ridiculed his critics for their pretended "love for the Irish." To show the Republicans' insincerity, the Democratic Appleton *Crescent* raised the pointed question: "Why did not the Howe-Sawyerites repeal the damnable *Neutrality laws* before they adjourned?" Apparently the Republicans beguiled few Irishmen for very long. Irish precincts, such as the townships of Erin in Washington County and Erin Prairie in St. Croix County, continued to give the Republicans at most eight or ten votes out of 200 or more.[22]

To the extent that they were associated with Negro suffrage in Wisconsin and radical reconstruction in the South, the Republicans repelled rather than attracted Catholic immigrants, Germans in particular. The most overwhelming majorities against the 1865 suffrage proposal came from the heavily German counties north and northwest of Milwaukee, while the largest majorities in its favor came from southeastern counties with the highest proportion of settlers with a New York or New England background. The semiofficial organ of the Wisconsin hierarchy, the German-language Milwaukee *Seebote*, continually deplored the congressional program of reconstruction. The procurator of the Milwaukee seminary for priests, writing to a missionary and funding society in Munich, said

---

[21] On Wisconsin's ethnic vote as of 1860, see Joseph Schafer, "Who Elected Lincoln?" in the *American Historical Review*, 47 (October, 1941), 51–63. On the importance of the German Lutheran vote to the Republicans after the war, see Paul Kleppner, *The Cross of Culture: A Social Analysis of Midwestern Politics, 1850–1900* (New York, 1970), 110–112.

[22] M. Justille McDonald, *History of the Irish in Wisconsin in the Nineteenth Century* (Washington, D.C., 1954), 142–149, 152–158, quoting the Appleton *Crescent*, November 3, 1866.

the Republican congressmen, "perhaps the most depraved" in
the country's history, were beginning to be "ashamed of their
constant attacks on President Johnson," but they still were proceeding to "torment the South in an unnatural manner." Native Protestant spokesmen, however, endorsed the radicals and
their policy. The Presbyterian and Congregational Conference
of 1866 approved of granting civil rights to freedmen. The
Methodist Conference of 1868 declared that the same moral
issues were involved in reconstruction as in the rebellion.[23]

While antagonizing German Catholics, the Republicans could
continue to hold the support of many German Protestants—
freethinkers, evangelicals, and some Lutherans—so long as the
party refrained from taking up the causes of Sabbatarianism or
temperance. Most of the German immigrants, whatever their
religion, continued to enjoy and to insist upon their traditional "German Sunday" with its after-church drinking, dancing, and general *Gemütlichkeit*. But pious sectarians of old
American stock viewed such merrymaking as a profanation of
the Sabbath. The same Puritan ethic that prescribed emancipation and equal rights prescribed also temperance and a quiet
Sunday—to be enforced by the government if necessary. During the war and immediately after it, the puritanical reformers
concentrated their attention on saving the Union and freeing and elevating the slaves. For the time being the state's
strict liquor-control act, repealed in the early 1850's, was not
revived. The prewar Sunday-closing law remained on the
books but went unenforced.[24]

[23] The quotation is from Peter Leo Johnson, ed., Joseph Salzman to Ludwig
Ignatz Lebling, July 31, 1867, in the *Salesianum*, 42 (April, 1947), 68; *Minutes
of the Annual Meeting of the Presbyterian & Congregational Convention of
Wisconsin. Held at Fort Atkinson, Oct. 3d.–7th, 1866* (Fond du Lac, 1866), 25–
26; P. S. Bennett and James Lawson, *History of Methodism in Wisconsin* (Cincinnati, 1890), 228–229; Tabular Statement of Votes Polled in the Several Counties,
1865, Certificates of the State Board of Canvassers, 1848——, Series 213, Records
of the Secretary of State, WSA.

[24] On the clash of cultures, see Joseph Schafer, "The Yankee and the Teuton
in Wisconsin," in *WMH*, 6–7 (December, 1922–December, 1923), 7: 148–171, and
Joseph Schafer, "Prohibition in Early Wisconsin," in *WMH*, 8 (March, 1925),
281–299; Herman J. Deutsch, "Yankee-Teuton Rivalry in Wisconsin Politics
of the Seventies," in *WMH*, 14 (March–June, 1931), 266–267, 403–406.

Before long, however, the voices of moral reform began to be heard again, and risky though the drink issue was, the Republicans eventually took it up. In 1872 Governor Washburn recommended that the legislature consider the subject of liquor-control, and in response a Rock County representative, Alexander Graham, introduced a thoroughgoing bill. This would require a $2,000 bond from liquor licensees, would make them liable for damages caused directly or indirectly by the intoxication of customers, and would impose heavy penalties on those convicted of drunkenness. When the legislature passed and the governor signed the Graham law, Germans understandably blamed the Republican party. German leaders, among them the brewers Valentin Blatz and Joseph Schlitz, formed the Wisconsin Association for the Protection of Personal Liberty, accused the Republicans of having converted Wisconsin into a police state, and called upon liberty-loving citizens to vote for candidates pledging to repeal the liquor act.[25]

The party loyalty of German Republicans, already strained by the Graham law, was further weakened as a result of the party split that developed from the Liberal Republican opposition to President Grant. Previously, in 1870, Wisconsin party leaders had turned the Franco-Prussian War to their own advantage; they had taken care that German voters should be "led to see that in the Franco-German War the Republicans have stood by the Germans & Fatherland while the Democrats have gone almost body & soul for the French." Now, in 1872, the anti-Grant Republicans were trying to deflect the German vote to the Liberal cause by showing that the Grant administration had, in fact, helped the French and hurt the Prussians. In the Senate, Carl Schurz of Missouri joined Charles Sumner of Massachusetts in charging that the administration, in a flagrant breach of neutrality, had sold government arms to E. Remington & Sons for resale to France. Schurz, formerly a Wisconsinite, still had a following among Wisconsin Germans. Senator

---

[25] Bennett and Lawson, *Methodism in Wisconsin,* 239; Joanne J. Brownsword, "Good Templars in Wisconsin, 1854–1880" (master's thesis, University of Wisconsin, 1960), 87–91.

Carpenter did his best to refute the charge. As a leading member of an investigating committee, he wrote what Sumner called a "whitewashing report."[26]

In Wisconsin the Liberal Republican movement was largely a Teutonic phenomenon. Milwaukee Germans organized on March 19, 1872, the first Liberal Republican club in the state. Germans rallied to the cause in such numbers that some leaders were a little embarrassed, and one spokesman made a point of denying that it was essentially a German affair. The most influential German-language paper of the Republicans, the Milwaukee *Herold*, switched from the regular party to the Liberal faction. To counter the Liberal appeal, the Grant Republicans subsidized a previously neutral German-language paper in Madison and another in Milwaukee, and they nominated German candidates for Congress in the two districts (out of the new total of eight) where the Democrats presented the greatest threat.

In the 1872 election the Liberal Republicans and the Democrats faced one serious handicap. Their presidential candidate, Horace Greeley, had a long record as a radical Republican and a moral reformer. Personally, he was a teetotaler, a contemptible "water-bibber," as Wisconsin Germans saw him. He had little charm for either disaffected Republicans or regular Democrats—like the one in Dane County who found it hard to "digest the Greeley dose, which with all its sugar coating" was "very nauseous" to him. On election day thousands of apathetic Liberals and Democrats stayed at home. Grant carried the state, 104,992 to 86,477, though with a smaller majority than in 1868. Six of the eight Republicans running for Congress were victorious, as were a majority of those running for the state legislature. The party had staved off the disaster that had threatened as a consequence of the liquor law and the German defections.[27]

---

[26] Current, *Pine Logs and Politics*, 67; Thompson, *Carpenter*, 166–175.

[27] Herman J. Deutsch, "Disintegrating Forces in Wisconsin Politics of the Early Seventies," in *WMH*, 15 (December, 1931–June, 1932), 169–172, 174–181; Graham A. Cosmas, "The Democracy in Search of Issues: The Wisconsin Reform Party, 1873–1877," in *WMH*, 46 (Winter, 1962–1963), 93–97, quoting the Dane

But temperance remained an explosive issue, and the Republicans did nothing to defuse it. In the 1873 legislature they tightened instead of relaxing or repealing the Graham law. As if this were not enough, the acting mayor of Madison began to enforce the old law against selling or giving away liquor on Sundays. To protest the "abridgment of their natural freedom," antitemperance leaders called a convention in Milwaukee and sought the support of all liberty-loving citizens, "without discrimination as to birth-place, party, or religious belief." Most of the delegates were Germans (they argued over the question whether the proceedings should be in German or in English), and prominent among them were saloonkeepers, brewers, and distillers. These interests would be able, as Governor Washburn feared, to provide the Republicans' opponents with ample finances, with all the "sinews of war," in the state election of 1873.

When putting together the ticket for that election, the Republicans gave German voters additional reason for taking offense. The Republican leaders had intended, as usual, to name a German for the important position of state treasurer and a Norwegian for the much less prestigious job of immigration commissioner. But the Norwegians vehemently objected, insisting on the treasurer's post for one of their own, Ole C. Johnson. To appease the Norwegians, the bosses put Johnson in the place of Henry Baetz, the incumbent treasurer and the party's most influential German politician. They left Baetz off the ticket altogether and placed a comparatively obscure German at the tail end of it.[28]

[6]

Thus, as the fateful election of 1873 approached, the Republicans confronted the prospect of losing the votes of Germans who

---

County Democrat; William H. Fox to E. M. Hunter, August 27, 1872, in the Paul Papers. See also Kleppner, *Cross of Culture*, 110–112.

[28] Deutsch, "Yankee-Teuton Rivalry in Wisconsin Politics," in *WMH*, 14: 267–270, 272–277, 412, quoting on p. 275 from the Milwaukee *Sentinel*, August 7, 1873; Brownsword, "Good Templars in Wisconsin," 92.

considered themselves the victims of discrimination on ethnic grounds. But the Republicans also faced the danger of a much more massive defection on the part of farmers and businessmen, of whatever nationality, who were discontented for economic reasons. Resentment against big corporations, monopolies, and especially railroads had been festering for several years, and now the resentment was coming to a head.

The railroad companies were becoming the biggest and most monopolistic of corporations, the Chicago and North Western and the Milwaukee and St. Paul acquiring ownership or domination of every line of any importance in the state. Alexander Mitchell, president of the M. & St. P., also controlled, through ownership or lease, nearly all the grain elevators in Milwaukee. Thus the one man held in his grasp the entire Milwaukee wheat trade. On September 15, 1873, just as the political campaign was getting under way, both of the big railroad combinations raised their rates. Three days later the Panic of 1873 began.[29]

Antimonopoly and antirailroad agitation in Wisconsin had first reached a peak in 1865–1866. In those two years a total of twenty-one railroad regulation bills were introduced in the legislature, and in every year thereafter to 1873 one or more regulatory measures were proposed. Only two were passed. An 1867 law prohibited forever the consolidation of the Chicago and North Western with the Milwaukee and St. Paul, but the law did nothing to prevent the interlocking directorate or the pooling arrangement that the two companies soon set up. An 1871 amendment to the state constitution restricted the legislature's power to pass special chartering acts, of the kind which previously had conferred excessive privileges on railroad companies. The amendment required the legislature to frame a new general incorporation law, and the legislature

---

[29] Frederick Merk, *Economic History of Wisconsin During the Civil War Decade* (Madison, 1916), 292–299; Milwaukee *Sentinel,* September 19, 1873; Dale E. Treleven, "Railroads, Elevators, and Grain Dealers: The Genesis of Antimonopolism in Milwaukee," in *WMH,* 52 (Spring, 1969), 205–208, 213–214.

did so, but this left the existing companies with all the privileges they had obtained earlier in their special charters.[30]

The antirailroad agitation that was to reach a new peak in 1873–1874 came from businessmen as well as farmers, from wheat dealers as well as wheat growers. Exorbitant charges for transportation and storage cut into the profits of commission merchants who bought the grain from farmers and shipped it to Milwaukee and stored it in elevators for later forwarding to eastern markets. One of these merchants, Francis H. West, as president of the Milwaukee Chamber of Commerce from 1871 to 1873, made himself the outstanding critic of Alexander Mitchell, the railroads, and their monopolistic practices. Meanwhile the distressed farmers were joining the Patrons of Husbandry and discussing their common grievances at the meetings of their local Granges. In Wisconsin, where the first Grange was organized in 1871, the order grew very slowly until 1873. Then the number of Granges suddenly increased from less than three dozen to about 300.[31]

Throughout the years of agitation, each of the major parties had occupied a rather equivocal position in regard to big business and its alleged abuses. From 1866 on, the Republican governors, Fairchild and then Washburn, had repeatedly warned of the dangers of monopoly and called for state regulation of railroads. In his 1873 message Governor Washburn told the lawmakers and the people once again that the "many vast and overshadowing corporations" were "justly a source of alarm." But Washburn himself was a very rich businessman, rapidly growing richer from flour milling and other enterprises. Some other prominent Republicans also were wealthy, among

[30] Merk, *Economic History,* 306, 325–328, 342; Herbert W. Rice, "Early History of the Chicago, Milwaukee and St. Paul Railway Company" (doctoral dissertation, State University of Iowa, 1938), 268–269; Chester C. Brown, "A Comparative Study of Constitutional Development in the Old Northwest, 1847–1875" (master's thesis, University of Wisconsin, 1937), 152–154.

[31] Treleven, "Genesis of Antimonopolism in Milwaukee," in *WMH,* 52: 209–211; Solon J. Buck, *The Granger Movement: A Study of Agricultural Organization and Its Political, Economic and Social Manifestations, 1870–1880* (Cambridge, 1913), 50, 54, and unpaged table between pp. 58 and 59.

them the millionaire lumberman Philetus Sawyer. "In every instance, and at all times," the Oshkosh *City Times* contended in 1870, reviving the language of Jacksonian Democracy, "the votes cast by Mr. Sawyer have been against the productive interests of the country, and in favor of the capital which is continually aggregating and combining to depress and control Labor, and establish a supremacy which will soon be seen in lines dividing the people into castes—making the poor dependent upon and subservient to the rich."[32]

Yet the Democrats could hardly make convincing their boast of being the party of the common man when their leadership included the greatest plutocrat of all, Alexander Mitchell, who was elected to Congress in 1870. He and other so-called "Bourbons" ran the Wisconsin Democracy. "You are represented as being the favorite candidate of the monied monopolies and corporations," the Bourbon James R. Doolittle heard from a party strategist while running for governor in 1871. "I know there is a deeper & wider feeling on this subject in the state than you are aware of." The "anti-monopolist mob" had much greater voting strength than the monopolists. Could not the Democratic candidate be as much of a "people's" man as the Republican?

In addition to the stigma of Bourbonism, the taint of treason still handicapped the Democratic party. As late as 1871, one politician observed, many Wisconsinites continued to fear that, if the party should regain power in the state and nation, the Thirteenth, Fourteenth, and Fifteenth amendments would "be abrogated if possible, the rights of the Negro be ignored and the public debt be repudiated." At the beginning of 1872 the Madison *Democrat* asked, "Shall the Democratic party abandon its name" and form a new party? For the election of 1873, they were to do just that.[33]

In 1873 the Grangers laid down a challenge to both of the

[32] Brown, "Constitutional Development in the Old Northwest," 137–140; C. W. Butterfield, "History of Wisconsin," in Western Historical Company, *The History of Sauk County, Wisconsin . . .* (Chicago, 1880), 98; Current, *Pine Logs and Politics,* 71; *Governor's Message and Accompanying Documents,* 1872, vol. 1, p. 28; Oshkosh *City Times,* October 26, 1870.
[33] Horace S. Merrill, *Bourbon Democracy of the Middle West, 1865–1896*

major parties in Wisconsin. At a Watertown convention, in August, they denounced corruption in government and demanded state regulation of the railroads. Some delegates urged the formation of a third party. This was not done; indeed, the rules of the Patrons of Husbandry forbade the Grange, as such, to take part in political activity. But there was nothing to prevent the members from throwing their support to one set of candidates or another.

When the Republicans met for their regular convention in August, they tried to identify their party with the farmers' cause. They renominated Washburn, the well-known advocate of railroad regulation. Keeping silent on temperance, they declared themselves in favor of honest government, the establishment of a state commission to regulate railroads, and the outlawing of the common railroad practice of awarding free passes to public officials.

Shrewdly the Democrats and the Liberal Republicans, who had maintained their coalition since the 1872 campaign, avoided giving any party name to their 1873 convention. They labeled it a "People's Reform Convention," and they invited the attendance of "all Democrats, Liberal Republicans, and other electors of Wisconsin friendly to genuine reform." Many Grangers responded. The emerging platform condemned temperance legislation and committed the new party to enacting laws "for the restriction of the power of chartered corporations, for the regulation of railway tariffs, and for the protection of the people against systematic plunder and legalized robbery." The candidate for governor was William R. Taylor, an organizer of the Grange in Wisconsin, president of the State Agricultural Society, and, incidentally, a member of a temperance society, the Good Templars. The rest of the ticket included a German, an Irishman, and a Norwegian. Some of the candidates were Democrats and others Liberal Republicans, but only one, a former congressman now running for attorney

(Baton Rouge, 1953), 69–71; Madison *Democrat,* January 4, 1872. The advice from a party strategist is in a letter from J. A. Noonan to Doolittle, September 25, 1871, in the Doolittle Papers. The concern about the return of the Democrats to power was expressed in a letter from Cyrus Woodman to E. W. Farley, September 22, 1871, in the Cyrus Woodman Papers.

general, was a prominent politician. Supposedly the candidates were men of the people, not professional office seekers. The new organization came to be known as the Reform party.[34]

Urging on Republican campaigners, Boss Keyes cautioned them that their opponents had gotten up "a plausible programme and ticket"—even though in fact the "old Bourbon Democrats" were the "main spirit of the effort," the Reform convention had been "run and controlled in the interests of railroads," and the candidates were "wholly under the influence of these corporations." True enough, the Reformers had the financial support not only of the beer and liquor interests but also of Mitchell's and other railroad companies. The railroad men feared manufacturer Washburn more than they did farmer Taylor, but many of the farmers apparently could see little choice between the two as antimonopolists. On election day a good many farmers, most of them probably Republicans, refrained from voting. Washburn, who had previously won by 10,000 votes, now lost by 15,000, as the Reformers elected their entire state ticket and fifty-nine assemblymen to forty-one for the Republicans, though only sixteen senators to seventeen. "You have been the victim of a situation created by the follies or worse than follies of the party," a sympathizer wrote to Washburn. "Moreover with a Granger who had the support of the railways, & a Good Templar who had the confidence of the whiskey & beer ring for an opponent, queer results might be looked for."[35]

[34] Earle D. Ross, *The Liberal Republican Movement* (Ithaca, 1919), 207–209; Cosmas, "Democracy in Search of Issues," in *WMH,* 46: 97–99; Brownsword, "Good Templars in Wisconsin," 94. The invitation to the convention and the platform are in the Milwaukee *Sentinel,* August 31, September 25, 1873.

[35] Merrill, *Bourbon Democracy,* 85–88; Cosmas, "Democracy in Search of Issues," in *WMH,* 46: 101; Deutsch, "Disintegrating Forces in Wisconsin Politics," in *WMH,* 15: 294–296; Frank N. Elliott, "The Causes and the Growth of Railroad Regulation in Wisconsin, 1848–1876" (doctoral dissertation, University of Wisconsin, 1956), 286–293. Keyes's analysis is in the draft of a letter to "Republican friends," October 7, 1873, in the Elisha W. Keyes Papers. The sympathizer's analysis of the defeat is in a letter from Horace Rublee to Washburn, December 4, 1873, in the Cadwallader C. Washburn Papers. In 1873 the Wisconsin Republicans also bore some of the odium of national corruption, since the scandals of the Grant administration were coming to light, and Senator Carpenter brazenly defended the Credit Mobilier and the Salary Grab. See Thompson, *Carpenter,* 192–205.

[7]

The year 1873 marked a dividing line in the history of Wisconsin. Not only did it complete the first quarter-century, roughly the first generation, in the life of the state; it also brought cataclysmic changes—the onset of economic depression for Wisconsin and the rest of the country, the crescendo of a popular demand for reform in the relations between business and the state government, and the overthrow of the party that had dominated state politics since before the war. The depression was to last for several years and was to prove the worst that Wisconsinites and other Americans had yet experienced. The reform effort was to bring forth only an ineffectual railroad-regulation law, which was soon to be repealed. Within a few years the Wisconsin Republicans were to be as securely in control of state politics as they had ever been, and not till 1890, with ethnic and economic discontent again peaking simultaneously, were they to suffer another overturn comparable to the one of 1873.

Even before the Panic of 1873, some Wisconsinites had begun to take a pessimistic view of the state's future. One of these was Edward G. Ryan, long a leader of Wisconsin Democrats, then somewhat discredited as a wartime Copperhead, recently the Milwaukee city attorney and recovering political influence as a crusader against railroad abuses, and soon (1874) to become the state's chief justice. In June 1873 Ryan addressed the graduating class of the university at Madison, whose members gathered in the assembly chamber of the capitol to hear him. "There is looming up a new and dark power," he warned. This was the power of "vast corporate combinations of unexampled capital." Two of these combinations, the big railroad companies of Wisconsin, were already threatening the very sovereignty of the state. "The question will arise and arise in your day, though perhaps not fully in mine," the aging lawyer told the youthful graduates, "which shall rule—wealth or man; which shall lead—money or intellect; who shall fill public stations—educated and patriotic freemen, or the feudal serfs of corporate capital." Among those listening to Ryan on that occasion was an eighteen-year-old who was yet to enter the university. This young man was never to forget the judge's "prophetic words" and was to repeat them many a time in speeches of his own. His name was Robert M. La Follette.[36]

Yet, as the state approached its twenty-fifth anniversary, the prevailing mood seemed to be one of optimism. Surviving pioneers, many of them members of recently formed old settlers' clubs, not only looked back with a feeling for history but also looked ahead with a sense of destiny. Milwaukeeans were reminded of the remarkable growth of their city—only a few decades ago a "small, unimportant village, situated on two bluffs and divided by a sluggish river and an almost impenetrable tamarack swamp"; now the "home of an hundred thousand busy people." What might they "not expect in the coming thirty years?"[37]

The people of towns still small and unimportant had grounds for similar self-congratulatory amazement. "I have lived in this country now twenty years," Arnold Verstegen wrote in 1870, "and the progress that I have seen in that short space of time is like a dream." When Verstegen had first appeared in Little Chute, in 1850, there was only one store in the forest-hidden hamlet, news of the outside world was weeks old when it got there, and traveling any distance was difficult, dangerous, and slow. "Now passengers arrive here in the afternoon, who in the morning were still in Chicago," he bragged to his Dutch relatives in the Old Country. "Daily papers gather news by telegraph from distant parts of the country, and it reaches the readers when it is still fresh." In addition to stores, office buildings, and factories, there were fine schools and churches,

---

[36] "Addresses by Hon. Edward G. Ryan, Late Chief Justice of Wisconsin, Delivered before the Wisconsin Law School, 1873, and Hon. Matt. H. Carpenter, Late United States Senator, Delivered before the Columbia Law School, 1870" (Madison, 1887), 31–32, a bound pamphlet in the SHSW; Robert M. La Follette, *La Follette's Autobiography: A Personal Narrative of Political Experiences* (Madison, 1913), 22–24; Beitzinger, *Ryan*, 100–110.

[37] On old settlers' and pioneers' clubs, see, for example, Western Historical Company, *History of Sauk County*, 443, and Bayrd Still, *Milwaukee: The History of a City* (Madison, 1965), 250–251. The comment on Milwaukee's growth was made by a correspondent of the Columbus *Ohio State Journal*, reprinted in the Milwaukee *Sentinel*, February 3, 1869, and quoted by Still, p. 255.

for there had been advancement in spiritual as well as material things. "The Catholic Church too has made great progress," and an imposing new brick edifice was under construction in Little Chute.[38]

When the Reverend Alfred Brunson went from Prairie du Chien to New York City, to attend a Methodist conference in 1872, he could not help thinking how things had changed since he first made his way to Wisconsin, nearly forty years before. The trip then, by wagon, required six weeks. The same trip now, by train, took two days and two hours. But Brunson, too, was most impressed by the great strides that religion appeared to be making. At the Baraboo conference of the Methodists in 1873, one hundred years after the first Methodist conference in America, he preached the centennial sermon. Taking into account "all branches of the Christian Church, and their advancing Christian efforts," he said, "in another century the millennium must be near at hand."[39]

Even after the financial panic had struck, the faith in progress remained alive and comforting, as in the sermon that William H. Brisbane, a Baptist minister originally from South Carolina, delivered in the Congregational Church of Arena (Iowa County) on Thanksgiving Day, 1873. "Twenty years ago when I first came among you our neighborhood was comparatively a wilderness," the Reverend Mr. Brisbane recalled. "But see what a change"—nicely cultivated farms and beautiful farmhouses, all kinds of agricultural machinery, a railroad with passenger trains four times a day and freight trains at all hours of the day and night, a village with "comfortable if not elegant" residences, numerous stores and shops, "some devout Christians," and three meeting houses for the worship of God. "Surely for all these things we should 'offer unto God thanksgiving.' "[40]

[38] Verstegen to his brothers and sister-in-law, November 17, 1870, in Henry S. Lucas, ed., *Dutch Immigrant Memoirs and Related Writings* (2 vols., Assen, Netherlands, 1955), 2: 151, 171–172.

[39] Alfred Brunson, *A Western Pioneer . . .* (2 vols., Cincinnati, 1872, 1879), 2: 371, 383–384.

[40] William H. Brisbane, Thanksgiving sermon preached on November 27, 1873, in the William H. Brisbane Papers.

APPENDIX

THE GOVERNORS OF WISCONSIN, 1848–1873

Name	Birthplace	Party	Term in Office	Birth/ Death
NELSON DEWEY	Connecticut	Dem.	June 7, 1848–Jan. 5, 1852	1813–1889
LEONARD J. FARWELL	New York	Whig	Jan. 5, 1852–Jan. 2, 1854	1819–1889
WILLIAM A. BARSTOW	Connecticut	Dem.	Jan. 2, 1854–Mar. 21, 1856	1813–1865
ARTHUR MCARTHUR	Scotland	Dem.	Mar. 21, 1856–Mar. 25, 1856	1815–1896
COLES BASHFORD	New York	Rep.	Mar. 25, 1856–Jan. 4, 1858	1816–1878
ALEXANDER W. RANDALL	New York	Rep.	Jan. 4, 1858–Jan. 6, 1862	1819–1872
LOUIS P. HARVEY	Connecticut	Rep.	Jan. 6, 1862–Apr. 19, 1862	1820–1862
EDWARD SALOMON	Prussia	Rep.	Apr. 19, 1862–Jan. 4, 1864	1828–1909
JAMES T. LEWIS	New York	Rep.	Jan. 4, 1864–Jan. 1, 1866	1819–1904
LUCIUS FAIRCHILD	Ohio	Rep.	Jan. 1, 1866–Jan. 1, 1872	1831–1896
CADWALLADER C. WASHBURN	Maine	Rep.	Jan. 1, 1872–Jan. 5, 1874	1818–1882

ESSAY ON SOURCES

DIRECTLY OR INDIRECTLY the manuscript collections of the State Historical Society of Wisconsin have served as the main sources for this volume. They have provided material for the book itself and, still more, for the monographs upon which it is largely based. All manuscripts cited in the footnotes of the present work are in the Society's collections, except in rare cases where a different location is indicated. Indispensable aids in the use of the collections are the following: Alice E. Smith, ed., *Guide to the Manuscripts of the Wisconsin Historical Society* (Madison, 1944); Josephine L. Harper and Sharon C. Smith, eds., *Guide to the Manuscripts of the State Historical Society of Wisconsin: Supplement Number One* (Madison, 1957); and Josephine L. Harper, ed., *Guide to the Manuscripts of the State Historical Society of Wisconsin: Supplement Number Two* (Madison, 1966). The state archival holdings of the Society are described in David J. Delgado, ed. and comp., *Guide to the Wisconsin State Archives* (Madison, 1966).

Newspapers also have served, directly or indirectly, as an important source. Still of some value for locating these is Ada Tyng Griswold, comp., *Annotated Catalogue of Newspaper Files in the Library of the State Historical Society of Wisconsin* (Madison, 1911 edition). More recent and broader in scope is Donald E. Oehlerts, comp., *Guide to Wisconsin Newspapers, 1833–1957* (Madison, 1958), which describes and locates the files wherever held. The Oehlerts volume would have been easier to use if it had been provided with running heads. In the Milwaukee Public Library is a card index to the Milwaukee *Sentinel* for the years 1837 through 1879, and a supplement in progress for the years through 1890. This newspaper is extensively cited and quoted not only because of the convenience of the index but also because of the completeness of the coverage of Wisconsin news at a time when the *Sentinel* was far and away the most informative paper in the state.

Footnotes in the present work indicate the extent to which it has made use of unpublished theses and dissertations. These vary tre-

mendously in their value. Some, lacking in synthesis and generaliza-
tion, do little more than provide guides to and quotations of newspaper and manuscript material. Others, better thought out and
better organized, present ideas as well as information. Theses and
dissertations are listed, though not evaluated, in Robert C. Nesbit
and William Fletcher Thompson, eds., *A Guide to Theses on Wisconsin Subjects* (Madison, 1964), and *A Guide to Theses on Wisconsin Subjects: A Supplement* (Madison, 1966). Many of the
best theses and dissertations have been published, in whole or in
part, in the quarterly *Wisconsin Magazine of History,* which, of
course, includes material of other origins also. An index to the
magazine appears annually, and cumulative indexes have appeared
in 1934, 1946, 1955, 1964, and 1973. Another repository of important
writings consists of the twenty volumes of *Collections of the State
Historical Society of Wisconsin,* which are indexed in volume 21
(Madison, 1915). Brief sketches of many figures of the era can be
found in the *Dictionary of Wisconsin Biography* (Madison, 1960).

This book owes so much to so many authors, whose names appear
on the ensuing pages and in the footnotes, that it would be invidious
to single out any of them for special notice. Nevertheless, several
of the writers have contributed so much to Wisconsin history of
the period 1848–1873 and have put this writer so deeply in their
debt that they merit mention here. The honor roll consists of the
following: Vernon Carstensen, Merle Curti, William B. Hesseltine,
Frank L. Klement, Frederick Merk, Joseph Schafer, and Alice E.
Smith.

LOCAL HISTORIES

Local histories published in or soon after the period under dis-
cussion have to some extent the quality of primary sources. Exam-
ples of such histories, nearly contemporaneous, include Daniel S.
Durrie, *A History of Madison. . .* (Madison, 1874); C. E. Jones,
*Madison: Its Origins, Institutions and Attractions. Persons, Places
and Events Graphically Delineated. A Reliable Guide-Book for
Tourists* (Madison, 1876); William J. Park, ed., *Madison, Dane
County and Surrounding Towns; Being a History and Guide to
Places of Scenic Beauty and Historical Note Found in the Towns
of Dane County and Surroundings, including the Organization of
the Towns, and Early Intercourse of the Settlers with the Indians,
Their Camps, Trails, Mounds, etc. with a Complete List of County
Supervisors and Officers, and Legislative Members, Madison Village
and City Council* (Madison, 1877); and James S. Buck, *Pioneer His-*

tory of Milwaukee (4 vols., Milwaukee, 1876–1886). Between 1879 and 1882 the Western Historical Company of Chicago published a series of county histories, one for almost every county of southern Wisconsin, and a single volume dealing with all the counties to the north of a line drawn, roughly, from Prairie du Chien to Green Bay, *History of Northern Wisconsin, Containing an Account of Its Settlement, Growth, Development and Resources; An Extensive Sketch of Its Counties, Cities, Towns and Villages, Their Improvements, Industries, Manufactories, Biographical Sketches, Portraits of Prominent Men and Early Settlers; Views of County Seats, Etc.* (Chicago, 1881). These volumes include a good deal of reminiscence by early settlers. Each of the volumes also contains a summary account of the state's history, by C. W. Butterfield.

From the 1900's to the 1930's a number of other county and area histories of a more or less traditional type appeared. Representative of these are the following: Publius V. Lawson, ed., *History of Winnebago County, Wisconsin: Its Cities, Towns, Resources, People* (2 vols., Chicago, 1908); Augustus B. Easton, ed., *History of the Saint Croix Valley* (Chicago, 1909); Carl Zillier, ed., *History of Sheboygan County, Wisconsin, Past and Present* (2 vols., Chicago, 1912); Deborah B. Martin, *History of Brown County, Wisconsin, Past and Present* (2 vols., Chicago, 1912); James E. Jones, ed., *A History of Columbia County, Wisconsin: A Narrative Account of Its Historical Progress, Its People, and Its Principal Interests* (2 vols., Chicago, 1914); Thomas H. Ryan, ed., *History of Outagamie County, Wisconsin: Being a General Survey of Outagamie County History including a History of the Cities, Towns and Villages throughout the County, from the Earliest Settlement to the Present Time* (Chicago, [1911]); John M. Ware, ed., *A Standard History of Waupaca County, Wisconsin. . .* (2 vols., Chicago, 1917); Hjalmar R. Holand, *History of Door County, Wisconsin: The County Beautiful* (2 vols., Chicago, 1917); Harry E. Cole, ed., *A Standard History of Sauk County, Wisconsin: An Authentic Narrative of the Past, with Particular Attention to the Modern Era in the Commercial, Industrial, Educational, Civic and Social Development* (2 vols., Chicago, 1918); Royal B. Way, ed., *The Rock River Valley: Its History, Traditions, Legends and Charms. . .* (3 vols., Chicago, 1926), dealing with the history of Jefferson, Dodge, Dane, and Rock counties; and William A. Titus, ed., *History of the Fox River Valley, Lake Winnebago, and the Green Bay Region* (3 vols., Chicago, 1930). John G. Gregory wrote a *History of Milwaukee, Wisconsin* (4 vols., Chicago, 1931). He also edited *Southeastern Wisconsin: A History of Old Milwaukee County* (4 vols., Chicago, 1932); *South-*

western Wisconsin: A History of Old Crawford County (4 vols., Chicago, 1932); and, with Thomas J. Cunningham, *West Central Wisconsin: A History* (4 vols., Indianapolis, 1933).

Since the 1920's several Wisconsin regions and localities have become the subjects of scholarly studies. Joseph Schafer, undertaking a "domesday book" survey of the state, produced three interesting if rather unsystematic volumes. His *Four Wisconsin Counties: Prairie and Forest* (Madison, 1927) compares Kenosha and Racine counties with Milwaukee and Ozaukee. The *Wisconsin Lead Region* (Madison, 1932) is an interpretative account of Grant, Iowa, and Lafayette counties. *The Winnebago-Horicon Basin: A Type Study in Western History* (Madison, 1937) investigates aspects of life in the counties of Winnebago, Calumet, Fond du Lac, and Dodge. Merle Curti and his associates attempt to test the validity of the Turner thesis, regarding the democratizing effects of the frontier, through an intensive investigation of the early years of Trempealeau County. Whatever the cogency of their argument on that point, they certainly present a good deal of valuable data and insight in *The Making of an American Community: A Case Study of Democracy in a Frontier County* (Stanford, 1959). "We do not claim, nor do we believe," the authors say, "that our conclusions with regard to Trempealeau hold for frontier areas in general." Nevertheless, many of their generalizations can be applied to other Wisconsin localities. Useful studies of a lesser scope are Willard F. Miller, "A History of Eau Claire County During the Civil War" (master's thesis, University of Wisconsin, 1954); Robert C. Robertson, "The Social History of Winnebago County, Wisconsin, 1850–1870" (master's thesis, University of Chicago, 1939); Helen M. Wolner, "The History of Superior, Wisconsin to 1900" (master's thesis, University of Wisconsin, 1939); and J. F. Wojta, "Town of Two Creeks: From Forest to Dairy Farms," in *WMH*, 27 (June, 1944), 420–435. Urban histories of high quality are Bayrd Still, *Milwaukee: The History of a City* (Madison, 1965); Albert H. Sanford, H. J. Hirshheimer, and Robert F. Fries, *A History of La Crosse, Wisconsin, 1841–1900* (La Crosse, 1951); Alice E. Smith, *Millstone and Saw: The Origins of Neenah-Menasha* (Madison, 1966); and Charles N. Glaab and Lawrence H. Larsen, *Factories in the Valley: Neenah-Menasha, 1870–1915* (Madison, 1969). John O. Holzhueter's *Madeline Island & the Chequamegon Region* (Madison, 1974) is popular history based on sound scholarship.

Wisconsin may be viewed in the setting of its neighbors in Henry C. Hubbart, *The Older Middle West, 1840–1880: Its Social, Economic and Political Life and Sectional Tendencies Before, During, and After the Civil War* (New York, 1936).

Land and Population

The natural environment, together with its progressive revelation and analysis, is well treated in Lawrence Martin, *The Physical Geography of Wisconsin* (Madison, 1965). Phases of the subject find treatment in Leonard S. Smith, *The Water Powers of Wisconsin* (Madison, 1908); John T. Curtis, *The Vegetation of Wisconsin: An Ordination of Plant Communities* (Madison, 1959); Hartley H. T. Jackson, *Mammals of Wisconsin* (Madison, 1961); and Owen J. Gromme, *Birds of Wisconsin* (Madison, 1963). Other aspects of the state's natural history are treated in Angie Kumlien Main, "Thure Kumlien, Koshkonong Naturalist," in *WMH,* 27 (September, 1943–March, 1944), 17–39, 194–220, 321–343; and A. W. Schorger, "The Wisconsin Natural History Association," in *WMH,* 31 (December, 1947), 168–177.

For general accounts of the disposal of the public domain, see Benjamin H. Hibbard, *A History of the Public Land Policies* (Madison, 1965); and Paul W. Gates, *History of Public Land Law Development* (Washington, D.C., 1968). Among important special studies are the following: Duane D. Fischer, "The Disposal of Federal Lands in the Eau Claire Land District of Wisconsin, 1848–1925" (master's thesis, University of Wisconsin, 1961); Wilbur H. Glover, "The Agricultural College Lands in Wisconsin," in *WMH,* 30 (December, 1947), 261–272; Gordon O. Greiner, "Wisconsin National Railroad Land Grants" (master's thesis, University of Wisconsin, 1935); Thomas H. Patterson, "The Disposal of Wisconsin's Common School Lands, 1849–1863" (master's thesis, University of Wisconsin, 1961); Malcolm J. Rohrbough, "The Acquisition and Administration of the Wisconsin Swamp Land Grant, 1850–1865" (master's thesis, University of Wisconsin, 1958); and Irvin C. Wyllie, "Land and Learning," in *WMH,* 30 (December, 1946), 154–173.

Indispensable for information on the relations of red men and white are the successive volumes of the *Annual Report* of the U.S. Commissioner of Indian Affairs. Frederick W. Hodge, ed., *Handbook of American Indians North of Mexico* (2 vols., Washington, D.C., 1907, 1910), is also a basic tool. A valuable introduction to Wisconsin's aborigines is Nancy O. Lurie, "Wisconsin: A Natural Laboratory for North American Indian Studies," in *WMH,* 53 (Autumn, 1969), 3–20. Based mainly on the annual reports of the Indian commissioner is Georgia M. Shattuck, "Indian Cessions, Removals and Reservations in Wisconsin" (bachelor's thesis, University of Wisconsin, 1904). Broader in scope than their titles imply are Martha E. Layman, "A History of Indian Education in the

United States" (doctoral dissertation, University of Minnesota, 1942); and Clyde A. Morley, "A General Survey of the Schooling Provided for the American Indian Throughout Our Country's History, with a Special Study of Conditions in Wisconsin" (master's thesis, University of Wisconsin, 1927). Particular tribes receive attention in Richard F. Morse, "The Chippewas of Lake Superior," in *Wis. Hist. Colls.*, 3: 338–369; Benjamin G. Armstrong, "Reminiscences of Life Among the Chippewa," in *WMH*, 55–56 (Spring, 1972–Winter, 1972–1973), 55: 175–196, 287–309; 56: 37–58, 140–161; Patricia Ourada, "The Menominee Indians: A History" (doctoral dissertation, University of Oklahoma, 1973); Felix M. Keesing, *The Menomoni Indians of Wisconsin: A Study of Three Centuries of Cultural Contact and Change* (Philadelphia, 1939); Janet Riesberry, "A History of the Menominee Nation, 1816–1856" (master's thesis, University of Wisconsin, 1939); "A Mission to the Menominee: Alfred Cope's Green Bay Diary," in *WMH*, 49–50 (Summer, 1966–Spring, 1967), 49: 302–323; 50: 18–42, 120–144, 211–241; J. N. Davidson, *Muh-he-ka-ne-ok: A History of the Stockbridge Nation* (Milwaukee, 1893); John O. Holzhueter, "Negro Admixture Among the Brotherton, Stockbridge, and Oneida Indians of Wisconsin" (1966), a seminar paper in the SHSW; Nancy O. Lurie, "The Winnebago Indians: A Study in Cultural Change" (doctoral dissertation, Northwestern University, 1952); and George W. Thatcher, "The Winnebago Indians, 1827–1932" (master's thesis, University of Wisconsin, 1935).

Immigration from Europe is given an overview in Marcus Lee Hansen, *The Atlantic Migration, 1607–1860: A History of the Continuing Settlement of the United States* (Cambridge, 1941). On German migration and its backgrounds, see Mack Walker, *Germany and the Emigration, 1816–1885* (Cambridge, 1964); Kate Everest Levi, "Geographical Origin of German Immigration to Wisconsin," in *Wis. Hist. Colls.*, 14: 341–393; Kate A. Everest, "How Wisconsin Came By Its Large German Element," in *Wis. Hist. Colls.*, 12: 299–334; Ira J. Kligora, "The German Element in Wisconsin, 1840–1880" (master's thesis, University of Wisconsin, 1937), which, despite its title, deals mainly with the travel of Germans to Wisconsin and the location of their original settlements; and Frank S. Beck, "Christian Communists in America: A History of the Colony of Saint Nazianz, Wisconsin, During the Pastorate of Its Founder, Father Ambrose Oschwald, 1854–1873" (master's thesis, St. Paul Seminary, St. Paul, Minnesota, 1959). John A. Hoffman discusses "The Dutch Settlements of Sheboygan County," in *WMH*, 2 (June, 1919), 464–466. On the immigration of Scandinavians, and especially Norwegians, see Theodore C. Blegen, *Norwegian Migration to America, 1825–1860* (Northfield, Minnesota, 1931), and its sequel *Norwegian Migration to America: The American Transition* (Northfield, Minnesota, 1940); Carlton C. Qualey, *Norwegian Settlement in the United States* (Northfield, Minnesota, 1938); Henrietta Larson, ed. and trans., "An Immigration Journey to America in 1854," in *Norwegian-American Studies and Records*, 3 (1928), 58–64; and Thomas P. Christensen, "Danish Settlement in Wisconsin," in *WMH*, 12 (September, 1928), 19–40. On the immigration of other groups, see Henry S. Lucas, *Netherlanders in America: Dutch Immigration to the United States and Canada, 1789–1950* (Ann Arbor, 1955); Antoine de Smet, "L'émigration belge aux Etats-Unis pendent le XIXe siècle jusqu'a la guerre civile," in *Album Antoine de Smet* (Brussels: Centre National d'Histoire des Sciences, 1974), 443–460; Antoine de Smet, "La communauté belge du nord-est du Wisconsin: Ses Origines. Son Evolution jusque vers 1900," *ibid.*, 461–506; Hjalmar R. Holand, *Wisconsin's Belgian Community: An Account of the Early Events in the Belgian Settlement in Northeastern Wisconsin, With Particular Reference to the Belgians in Door County* (Sturgeon Bay, Wisconsin, 1933); Xavier Martin, "The Belgians of Northeast Wisconsin," in *Wis. Hist. Colls.*, 13: 375–396; Charlotte Erickson, *Invisible Immigrants: The Adaptation of English and Scottish Immigrants in Nineteenth-Century America* (Coral Gables, Florida, 1972); Grant Foreman, "Settlement of English Potters in Wisconsin," in *WMH*, 21 (June, 1938), 375–396; Louis A. Copeland, "The Cornish in Southwest Wisconsin," in *Wis. Hist. Colls.*, 14: 301–334; and Marcus Lee Hansen, *The Mingling of the Canadian and American Peoples* (New York, 1970).

Efforts to attract settlers from abroad are recounted by Theodore C. Blegen in "The Competition of the Northwestern States for Immigrants," in *WMH*, 3 (March, 1919), 3–29. An important mapmaker and author of promotional pamphlets receives attention in Graham P. Hawks, "Increase A. Lapham: Wisconsin's First Scientist" (doctoral dissertation, University of Wisconsin, 1960); and Milo M. Quaife, "Increase Allen Lapham, First Scholar of Wisconsin," in *WMH*, 1 (September, 1917), 3–15. John H. Lathrop wrote a sixteen-page pamphlet entitled *Wisconsin* for the Wisconsin State Emigration Agency; it was later reprinted as "Wisconsin and the Growth of the Northwest," in *De Bow's Review*, 14 (March, 1853), 230–238. Among the printed works intended to bring in immigrants, the following are representative: Carl de Haas, *North America, Wisconsin: Hints for Immigrants*, translated by F. J.

Rueping from the original published in Germany in 1848 (Fond du Lac, Wisconsin, 1943); Joseph Schafer, ed. and trans., "Christian Traugott Ficker's Advice to Emigrants," in *WMH*, 25 (December, 1941–June, 1942), 217–236, 331–355, 456–475; Samuel Freeman, *The Emigrant's Hand Book and Guide to Wisconsin, Comprising Information Respecting Agricultural and Manufacturing Employment, Wages, Climate, Population &c.; Sketch of Milwaukee, The Queen of the Lakes; Its Rise and Progress; Business and Population; List of Public Officers; With a Full and Accurate Table of Statistical Information of That and Other Ports on Lake Michigan; Also Table of Routes from New-York, Boston, &c., to Milwaukee, Racine, and Kenosha; and Other General Information to Emigrants* (Milwaukee, 1851); John Gregory, *Industrial Resources of Wisconsin* (Milwaukee, 1855); and James S. Ritchie, *Wisconsin and Its Resources; With Lake Superior, Its Commerce and Navigation, Including a Trip Up the Mississippi, and a Canoe Voyage on the St. Croix and Brule Rivers to Lake Superior, To Which are Appended, The Constitution of the State, With the Routes of the Principal Railroads, List of Post-Offices, etc.* (3d revised edition, Philadelphia, 1858). Examples of "America letters" can be found in Emil Baensch, trans., "Letters and Diary of Joh. Fr. Diederichs," in *WMH*, 7 (December, 1923–March, 1924), 218–237, 350–368; Theodore C. Blegen, ed., *Land of Their Choice: The Immigrants Write Home* (Minneapolis, 1955); John A. Houkam, ed., "Pioneer Kjaerkebon Writes from Coon Prairie," in *WMH*, 27 (June, 1944), 439–445; "Norwegian Immigrant Letters," in *WMH*, 15 (March, 1932), 356–359; Lillian Krueger, "Introductory Note to the History of St. Nazianz," in *WMH*, 31 (September, 1947), 84–91; and Lowell J. Ragatz, ed. and trans., "A Swiss Family in the New World: Letters of Jakob and Ulrich Buhler, 1847–1877," in *WMH*, 6 (March, 1923), 317–333.

Settlement and resettlement are the themes of Mary J. Read, "A Population Study of the Driftless Hill Land During the Pioneer Period, 1832–1860" (doctoral dissertation, University of Wisconsin, 1941); Michael P. Conzen, *Frontier Farming in an Urban Shadow: The Influence of Madison's Proximity on the Agricultural Development of Blooming Grove, Wisconsin* (Madison, 1971); Daniel E. Schob, "Sodbusting on the Upper Midwestern Frontier, 1820–1860," in *Agricultural History*, 47 (January, 1973), 47–56; Peter J. Coleman, "The Woodhouse Family: Grant County Pioneers," in *WMH*, 42 (Summer, 1959), 267–274, and "Restless Grant County: Americans on the Move," in *WMH*, 46 (Autumn, 1962), 16–20; Josie G. Croft, ed., "A Mazomanie Pioneer of 1847," in

WMH, 26 (December, 1942), 208–218; Mary J. Atwood, "John Wilson, a Sauk County Pioneer," in *WMH*, 8 (September, 1924), 67–70; and Oluf Erickson, "Olaf Erickson, Scandinavian Frontiersman," in *WMH*, 31 (September, 1947–March, 1948), 7–28, 186–207, 326–338. The following deal in one way or another with the population movement to California: William H. Herrmann, "Wisconsin and the California Gold Rush" (master's thesis, University of Wisconsin, 1940); Larry Gara, "Gold Fever in Wisconsin," in *WMH*, 38 (Winter, 1954–1955), 106–108; John O. Holzhueter, ed., "From Waupun to Sacramento in 1849: The Gold Rush Journal of Edwin Hillyer," in *WMH*, 49 (Spring, 1966), 210–244; and Joseph Schafer, ed., *California Letters of Lucius Fairchild* (Madison, 1951).

Population statistics are found in a broadside compiled by Horace A. Tenney, "Census of Wisconsin from the Year 1836 to August 1860, Inclusive," bound together with other broadsides and pamphlets collected by the SHSW library, in a volume with the binder's title, *Census of Wisconsin, 1836–1880*; and in the first volumes of the *Seventh Census of the United States, 1850*; the *Eighth Census of the United States, 1860*; and the *Ninth Census of the United States, 1870*.

THE ECONOMY

The most useful statistics on manufacturing for 1850 are printed in *Senate Executive Documents*, 35 Cong., 2 sess., no. 39 (serial 984), while the third volumes of the census reports for 1860 and 1870 contain statistics on wealth and industry. Agricultural data are contained in the 1850 census report, in the second volume of the 1860 census, and in the third volume of the 1870 report. Lee Soltow, *Patterns of Wealthholding in Wisconsin since 1850* (Madison, 1971), throws some light on the distribution of wealth and income in the state. Frederick Merk, *Economic History of Wisconsin During the Civil War Decade* (Madison, 1916), is a pioneering study of enduring worth. All subsequent writers on almost any phase of the subject must acknowledge a tremendous debt to Merk.

Travel and transportation by horse-drawn vehicles needs further study. Wisconsin State Highway Commission and United States Public Roads Administration, *A History of Wisconsin Highway Development, 1835–1945* (Madison, 1947), provides an introduction to the subject. Edward D. Karn, "Roadmaking in Wisconsin Territory" (master's thesis, University of Wisconsin, 1959), describes practices that continued into the period of statehood. Patricia J. Pommer, "Plank Roads: A Chapter in the Early History of

Wisconsin Transportation (1846–1871)" (master's thesis, University of Wisconsin, 1950), is informative, though poorly organized. Harry E. Cole helps fill the gap in knowledge of stagecoaching with his *Stagecoach and Tavern Days in the Baraboo Region* (Baraboo, Wisconsin, 1923), and his *Stagecoach and Tavern Tales of the Old Northwest,* ed. Louise Phelps Kellogg (Cleveland, 1930). Joseph Schafer fills another gap with "Ferries and Ferryboats," in *WMH,* 21 (June, 1938), 432–456.

On railroads, an excellent general account, much more comprehensive than its title indicates, is Frank N. Elliott, "The Causes and the Growth of Railroad Regulation in Wisconsin, 1848–1876" (doctoral dissertation, University of Wisconsin, 1956). The authoritative summary of railroad construction is James P. Kaysen, "The Railroads of Wisconsin, 1827–1937" (master's thesis, University of Wisconsin, 1938), which was published with the same title by The Railway and Locomotive Historical Society, Inc., Boston, in 1937. Balthasar H. Meyer, "A History of Early Railroad Legislation in Wisconsin," in *Wis. Hist. Colls.,* 14: 206–300, summarizes the first railroad proposals and charters. Herbert W. Rice traces the development of one of the two great Wisconsin railroad combinations in his "Early History of the Chicago, Milwaukee and St. Paul Railway Company" (doctoral dissertation, State University of Iowa, 1938). Philip A. Schilling gives an original and thoughtful interpretation in "Farmers and Railroads: A Case Study of Farmer Attitudes in the Promotion of the Milwaukee and Mississippi Railroad Company" (master's thesis, University of Wisconsin, 1964). Robert S. Hunt also takes a new and revealing approach in *Law and Locomotives: The Impact of the Railroads on Wisconsin Law in the Nineteenth Century* (Madison, 1958). Albert Fishlow explores *American Railroads and the Transformation of the Ante-Bellum Economy* (Cambridge, 1965).

On waterways, Samuel Mermin examines *The Fox–Wisconsin Rivers Improvement: An Historical Study in Legal Institutions and Political Economy* (Madison, 1968). Robert W. McCluggage, "The Fox–Wisconsin Waterway, 1836–1872: Land Speculation and Regional Rivalries, Politics and Private Enterprise" (doctoral dissertation, University of Wisconsin, 1954), is a massive and detailed account, dealing, as the title suggests, more with land speculation than with water transportation. For additional treatments of land selling, see the references above under Land and Population having to do with the disposal of the public domain. See also the following: Larry Gara, *Westernized Yankee: The Story of Cyrus Woodman* (Madison, 1956); Paul W. Gates, "Frontier Land Business in Wisconsin," in *WMH*, 52 (Summer, 1969), 306–327; Paul W. Gates, *The Wisconsin Pine Lands of Cornell University: A Study in Land Policy and Absentee Ownership* (Ithaca, 1943); Irene D. Neu, "Land Credit in Frontier Wisconsin" (master's thesis, Cornell University, 1945); Clare L. Marquette, "The Business Activities of C. C. Washburn" (doctoral dissertation, University of Wisconsin, 1940); and James W. Whitaker, "Wisconsin Land Speculation, 1830–1860: Case Studies of Small Scale Speculators" (master's thesis, University of Wisconsin, 1962). Paul W. Gates also assesses "The Role of the Land Speculator in Western Development," in the *Pennsylvania Magazine of History and Biography,* 66 (July, 1942), 314–333.

Joseph Schafer intends to give only a "sketch" of the subject—to serve as a background for his "domesday" series—in *A History of Agriculture in Wisconsin* (Madison, 1922), and he therefore devotes a large part of the book to settlement and pioneering. The agricultural statisticians Walter Ebling, Clarence D. Caparoon, Emery C. Wilcox, and Cecil W. Estes present a factual survey in Wisconsin Crop and Livestock Reporting Service, *A Century of Wisconsin Agriculture, 1848–1948* (Madison, [1948]). Important monographs and special studies include the following: Vernon Carstensen, *Farms or Forests: Evolution of a State Land Policy for Northern Wisconsin, 1850–1932* (Madison, 1958); Benjamin H. Hibbard, *The History of Agriculture in Dane County, Wisconsin* (Madison, 1904); Alexander C. Kern, "Farm Loans and Mortgage Foreclosures in Dane County from 1867 to 1875" (master's thesis, University of Wisconsin, 1933); Eric E. Lampard, *The Rise of the Dairy Industry in Wisconsin: A Study in Agricultural Change, 1820–1920* (Madison, 1963); Neil E. Stevens and Jean Nash, "The Development of Cranberry Growing in Wisconsin," in *WMH*, 27 (March, 1944), 276–294; John G. Thompson, *The Rise and Decline of the Wheat Growing Industry in Wisconsin* (Madison, 1909); and Reynold M. Wik, *Steam Power on the American Farm* (Philadelphia, 1953). Advancements in agriculture are summarized in Paul W. Gates, *The Farmer's Age: Agriculture, 1815–1860* (New York, 1960); and Clarence Danhof, *Change in Agriculture: The Northern United States, 1820–1870* (Cambridge, 1969).

On the lumber industry in the state, the best single book is Robert F. Fries, *Empire in Pine: The Story of Lumbering in Wisconsin, 1830–1900* (Madison, 1951). Other general accounts having some value are Bernhardt J. Kleven, "Wisconsin Lumber Industry" (doctoral dissertation, University of Minnesota, 1941); and George W. Hotchkiss, *History of the Lumber and Forest Industry of the North-*

west (Chicago, 1898). There is much information on lumbering in Thomas E. Randall, *History of the Chippewa Valley, A Faithful Record of all Important Events, Incidents and Circumstances That Have Transpired in the Valley of the Chippewa From its Earliest Settlement by White People, Indian Treaties, Organization of the Territory and State; Also of the Counties Embracing the Valley, Senatorial, Assembly and Congressional Districts, &c.* (Eau Claire, Wisconsin, 1875). W. H. Glover describes "Lumber Rafting on the Wisconsin River," in *WMH*, 25 (December, 1941–March, 1942), 155–177, 308–324. Other accounts of rafting are A. R. Reynolds, "Rafting Down the Chippewa and Mississippi: Daniel Shaw Lumber Company, a Type Study," in *WMH*, 32 (December, 1948), 143–152; and J. M. Turner, "Rafting on the Mississippi," in *WMH*, 23–24 (December, 1939–September, 1940), 23: 163–176, 313–327, 430–438; 24: 56–65. The following deal with particular lumbermen or companies: Ralph W. Hidy, Frank E. Hill, and Allan Nevins, *Timber and Men: The Weyerhaeuser Story* (New York, 1963); William G. Rector, "The Birth of the St. Croix Octopus," in *WMH*, 40 (Spring, 1957), 171–177; Arthur R. Reynolds, *The Daniel Shaw Lumber Company: A Case Study of the Wisconsin Lumbering Frontier* (New York, 1957); and Isaac Stephenson, *Recollections of a Long Life, 1829–1915* (Chicago, 1915). Legal aspects of the lumber industry are treated in Daniel J. Dykstra, "Law and the Lumber Industry, 1861–1881" (doctoral dissertation, University of Wisconsin, 1950); J. Willard Hurst, *Law and Economic Growth: The Legal History of the Lumber Industry in Wisconsin, 1836–1915* (Cambridge, 1964); and A. Allan Schmid, "Water and the Law in Wisconsin," in *WMH*, 45 (Spring, 1962), 203–215. A fine narrative of the conflagration of 1871 is Robert W. Wells's *Fire at Peshtigo* (Englewood Cliffs, New Jersey, 1968). On this subject, see also Joseph Schafer, "Great Fires of Seventy-One," in *WMH*, 11 (September, 1927), 96–106; Stewart H. Holbrook, *Burning an Empire: The Story of American Forest Fires* (New York, 1943); P. Pernin, "The Finger of God is There," in *WMH*, 2 (December, 1918–March, 1919), 158–180, 274–293, a vivid firsthand version; and Frank Tilton, *Sketch of the Great Fires in Wisconsin at Peshtigo, the Sugar Bush, Menekaune, Williamsonville, and Generally on the Shores of Green Bay; With Thrilling and Truthful Incidents by Eye Witnesses* (Green Bay, 1871), which is based on newspaper reports and personal narratives and letters. Concerns about conservation are included in Milo M. Quaife, "Increase Allen Lapham, Father of Forest Conservation," in *WMH*, 5 (September, 1921), 104–108.

Margaret Walsh, *The Manufacturing Frontier: Pioneer Industry in Antebellum Wisconsin, 1830–1860* (Madison, 1972), the basis of which is her more detailed doctoral dissertation (University of Wisconsin, 1969), provides an interpretive over-all view. On the manufacture of farm implements, see Stewart H. Holbrook, *Machines of Plenty: Pioneering in American Agriculture* (New York, 1955); Reynold M. Wik, "J. I. Case: Some Experiences of an Early Wisconsin Industrialist," in *WMH*, 35 (September, 1951), 3–6, 64–67; and F. B. Swingle, "The Invention of the Twine Binder," in *WMH*, 10 (September, 1926), 35–41. A distinguished work in business history is Thomas C. Cochran, *The Pabst Brewing Company: The History of an American Business* (New York, 1948). Two works pertinent to Wisconsin are Charles B. Kuhlmann, *The Development of the Flour-Milling Industry in the United States, With Special Reference to the Industry in Minneapolis* (Clifton, New Jersey, 1973); and Rudolf A. Clemen, *The American Livestock and Meat Industry* (New York, 1923). Particular industries are treated in Robert T. Hilton, "Men of Metal: A History of the Foundry Industry in Wisconsin" (master's thesis, University of Wisconsin, 1952); Charles E. Schefft, "The Tanning Industry in Wisconsin: A History of Its Frontier Origins and Its Development" (master's thesis, University of Wisconsin, 1938); Genivera E. Loft, "The Evolution of the Wood-Working Industries of Wisconsin" (master's thesis, University of Wisconsin, 1916); Mowry Smith, Jr. and Giles Clark, *One Third Crew, One Third Boat, One Third Luck: The Menasha Corporation (Menasha Wooden Ware Company) Story, 1848–1974* (Neenah, Wisconsin, 1974); Charles N. Glaab and Lawrence H. Larsen, "Neenah-Menasha in the 1870's: The Development of Flour Milling and Papermaking," in *WMH*, 52 (Autumn, 1968), 19–34; Publius V. Lawson, "Papermaking in Wisconsin," in *SHSW Proceedings*, 1909, pp. 273–280; Maurice L. Branch, "The Paper Industry in the Lake States Region, 1834–1947" (doctoral dissertation, University of Wisconsin, 1954); Margaret Walsh, "Industrial Opportunity on the Urban Frontier: 'Rags to Riches' and Milwaukee Clothing Manufacturers, 1840–1880," in *WMH*, 57 (Spring, 1974), 175–194; Bernhard C. Korn, "Eber Brock Ward, Pathfinder of American Industry" (doctoral dissertation, Marquette University, 1942), an account of a pioneer industrialist interested in iron and steel and other manufactures; Margaret Walsh, "Business Success and Capital Availability in the New West: Milwaukee Ironmasters in the Middle Nineteenth Century," in the *Old Northwest*, 1 (June, 1975), 159–175; and Orin G. Libby, "Chronicle of the Helena Shot Tower," in *Wis.*

Hist. Colls., 13: 335–374. A Milwaukee invention is recounted in Richard N. Current, "The Original Typewriter Enterprise, 1867–1873," in *WMH*, 32 (June, 1949), 391–407, and at greater length in the same author's *The Typewriter and the Men Who Made It* (Urbana, 1954). The following deal with industrial labor: Thomas W. Gavett, *Development of the Labor Movement in Milwaukee* (Madison, 1965); Don D. Lescohier, *The Knights of St. Crispin, 1867–1874: A Study in the Industrial Causes of Trade Unionism* (Madison, 1910); and Gertrude Schmidt, "History of Labor Legislation in Wisconsin" (doctoral dissertation, University of Wisconsin, 1933).

Banking and related businesses form the subject of several studies: Theodore A. Andersen, *A Century of Banking in Wisconsin* (Madison, 1954); Leonard B. Krueger, *History of Commercial Banking in Wisconsin* (Madison, 1933); David B. Leonard, "A Biography of Alexander Mitchell, 1817–1887" (master's thesis, University of Wisconsin, 1951); Alice E. Smith, "Banking Without Banks: George Smith and the Wisconsin Marine and Fire Insurance Company," in *WMH*, 48 (Summer, 1965), 268–281, and *George Smith's Money: A Scottish Investor in America* (Madison, 1966); and Harold F. Williamson and Orange A. Smalley, *Northwestern Mutual Life: A Century of Trusteeship* (Evanston, Illinois, 1957).

Indispensable for a year-to-year summary of trade and commerce in Milwaukee and across the state are the *Annual Statements* and *Reports* of the Milwaukee Chamber of Commerce. The annual *Proceedings of the National Board of Trade* help put Wisconsin's postwar economic issues into a national context. Commerce, especially in wheat, is treated in John G. Clark, *The Grain Trade in the Old Northwest* (Urbana, 1966); William E. Derby, "A History of the Port of Milwaukee, 1835–1910" (doctoral dissertation, University of Wisconsin, 1963); and Henrietta M. Larson, *The Wheat Market and the Farmer in Minnesota, 1858–1900* (New York, 1926), which deals with grain trading through Wisconsin. Business organization is discussed in Daniel J. Dykstra, "Corporations in the Day of the Special Charter," in the *Wisconsin Law Review*, 1949 (March–May), 310–335, 469–493; and George J. Kuehnl, *The Wisconsin Business Corporation* (Madison, 1959).

THE SOCIETY

Religion in Wisconsin has been the subject of comparatively little scholarly study, and that little has had to do with particular religious groups rather than with the subject as a whole. The Roman Catholics have been especially fortunate in their historians, above all Peter Leo Johnson. His *Crosier on the Frontier: A Life of John Martin Henni, Archbishop of Milwaukee* (Madison, 1959), is practically a history of the church in the state from the 1840's to the 1880's. Other rewarding books of his are *Daughters of Charity in Milwaukee, 1846–1946* (Milwaukee, 1946); *Halcyon Days: The Story of St. Francis Seminary, Milwaukee, 1856–1956* (Milwaukee, 1956); and *Stuffed Saddlebags: The Life of Martin Kundig, Priest, 1805–1879* (Milwaukee, 1942). Useful biographies by other authors are *The Seed and the Glory: The Career of Samuel Charles Mazzuchelli, O. P., on the Mid-American Frontier* (New York, 1950), by Mary E. Evans; and *Right-Hand Glove Uplifted: A Biography of Archbishop Michael Heiss* (New York, 1968), by M. Mileta Ludwig. Unfriendly relations between Catholics and non-Catholics are treated in M. Hedwigis Overmoehle, "The Anti-Clerical Activities of the Forty-Eighters in Wisconsin, 1848–1860: A Study in German-American Liberalism" (doctoral dissertation, St. Louis University, 1941); and Leonard G. Koerber, "Anti-Catholic Agitation in Milwaukee, 1843–1860" (master's thesis, Marquette University, 1960). These two works are especially valuable for their translated quotations from German-language newspapers such as the Milwaukee *Seebote*.

On the Lutherans in Wisconsin, the best general account is Roy A. Suelflow, *A Plan for Survival* (New York, 1965). Also useful are John P. Koehler, *The History of the Wisconsin Synod*, ed. Leigh D. Jordahl (St. Cloud, Minnesota, 1970); and Henry E. Jacobs, *A History of the Evangelical Lutheran Church in the United States* (New York, 1899). On the Norwegian Lutherans, see E. Clifford Nelson and Eugene L. Fevold, *The Lutheran Church Among Norwegian-Americans: A History of the Evangelical Lutheran Church* (2 vols., Minneapolis, 1960). Einar Haugen, "Pastor Dietrichson of Old Koshkonong," in *WMH*, 29 (March, 1946), 301–318, uses church records in recounting the pastor's career from 1844 to 1850. Apostate Lutherans figure in Joseph Schafer, "Scandinavian Moravians in Wisconsin," in *WMH*, 24 (September, 1940), 25–38.

The native Protestant groups vary in the quantity and quality of their written history. Regarding the largest of the groups, P. S. Bennett's and James Lawson's *History of Methodism in Wisconsin* (Cincinnati, 1890) contains a good deal of primary material, including quotations and summaries of conference reports. An interesting primary source is the autobiography of the onetime circuit rider Alfred Brunson, *A Western Pioneer: or, Incidents of the Life and Times of Rev. Alfred Brunson, Embracing a Period of Over Seventy Years* (2 vols., Cincinnati, 1872, 1879). Much has been written on the Presbyterians and Congregationalists. Having in part the character of primary sources are Stephen Peet's *History of the Presbyterian and Congregational Churches and Ministers in Wisconsin: Including an Account of the Organization of the Convention and the Plan of Union* (Milwaukee, 1851); and Dexter Clary's *History of the Churches and Ministers Connected with the Presbyterian and Congregational Convention of Wisconsin, and of the Operations of the American Home Missionary Society in the State for the Past Ten Years* (Beloit, Wisconsin, 1861). More recent studies include William F. Brown, *Past Made Present: The First Fifty Years of the First Presbyterian Church and Congregation of Beloit, Wisconsin . . . together with A History of Presbyterianism In our State up to the Year 1900* (Chicago, 1900); Frank N. Dexter, ed., *A Hundred Years of Congregational History in Wisconsin* (Fond du Lac, Wisconsin, 1933); and Charles J. Kennedy, "The Congregationalists and the Presbyterians on the Wisconsin Frontier" (doctoral dissertation, University of Wisconsin, 1940), which was published under the title "The Presbyterian Church on the Wisconsin Frontier," in the *Journal of the Department of History: The Presbyterian Historical Society*, 18–19 (December, 1938–March, 1940), 18: 139–166, 186–210, 243–274, 289–321, 323–358; 19: 1–40.

Other native Protestants are treated in Harold E. Wagner, *The Episcopal Church in Wisconsin, 1847–1947: A History of the Diocese of Milwaukee* (Waterloo, Wisconsin, 1947); Edgar L. Killam, *Centennial History of the Wisconsin Baptist State Convention* (Oconomowoc, Wisconsin, 1944); and Jessie H. Nebelthau, *The Diary of a Circuit Rider: Excerpts from the Notes of Henry Howe, Made While Traveling in Southern Wisconsin Between the years 1864 and 1868 as a Missionary of the Disciples of Christ* (Minneapolis, 1933). J. J. Schlicher writes of the German Reformed and of German freethinkers in "The Beginning and Early Years of the Mission House," in *WMH*, 25 (September, 1941), 51–72, and "Eduard Schroeter the Humanist," in *WMH*, 28 (December, 1944–March, 1945), 169–183, 307–324. Berenice Cooper has a brief article on "Die Freien Gemeinden in Wisconsin," in *Transactions of the Wisconsin Academy of Sciences, Arts and Letters*, 53 (1964), 53–65.

On Wisconsin's Jewish congregations, see Louis J. Swichkow, "The Jewish Community of Milwaukee, Wisconsin, 1860–1870," in the *Publication of the American Jewish Historical Society*, 47

(September, 1957), 34–58; Louis J. Swichkow and Lloyd P. Gartner, *The History of the Jews of Milwaukee* (Philadelphia, 1963); and Manfred Swarsensky, *From Generation to Generation: The Story of the Madison Jewish Community, 1851–1955* (Madison, 1955).

Ethnicity is treated in most of the works referred to above in connection with immigration. For accounts of particular immigrant groups and cultures, see also Albert B. Faust, *The German Element in the United States, with Special Reference to Its Political, Moral, Social, and Educational Influence* (2 vols., Boston, 1909); M. Justille McDonald, *History of the Irish in Wisconsin in the Nineteenth Century* (Washington, D.C., 1954); Arnold Mulder, *Americans from Holland* (Philadelphia, 1947); Lee W. Metzner, "The First Kirmess," in *WMH*, 14 (June, 1931), 339–353; Edward G. Hartmann, *Americans from Wales* (Boston, 1967); Dorothy B. Skårdal, "Double Heritage: Scandinavian Immigrant Experience through Literary Sources" (doctoral dissertation, Radcliffe College, 1962), and *The Divided Heart: Scandinavian Immigrant Experience through Literary Sources* (Lincoln, Nebraska, 1974). Relations among immigrant groups or between them and the American-born are discussed in Joseph Schafer, "The Yankee and the Teuton in Wisconsin," in *WMH*, 6–7 (December, 1922–December, 1923), 6: 125–145, 261–279, 386–402; 7: 3–19, 149–171; Peter N. Laugesen, "The Immigrants of Madison, Wisconsin, 1860–1890" (master's thesis, University of Wisconsin, 1966); Kathleen N. Conzen, " 'The German Athens': Milwaukee and the Accommodation of Its Immigrants, 1836–1860" (doctoral dissertation, University of Wisconsin, 1972); and John D. Beck, "Acculturation and Religious Institutions: A Case Study of Acculturation in Sauk County, Wisconsin, by Special Reference to Religious Institutions" (master's thesis, University of Wisconsin, 1940). Much more needs to be done in the study of Wisconsin's ethnic groups in the period, especially with respect to inter-group relations, acculturation, and the persistence of cultural pluralism.

Wisconsin's tiny black minority receives attention in Edward Noyes, "A Negro in Mid-Nineteenth Century Wisconsin Life and Politics," a biographical sketch of William H. Noland, of Madison, in the *Wisconsin Academy Review*, 15 (Fall, 1968), 2–6, 21; and William J. Vollmar, "The Negro in a Midwest Frontier City: Milwaukee, 1835–1870" (master's thesis, Marquette University, 1968).

Physical conditions and hazards of living in early Wisconsin are detailed in several works by Peter T. Harstad: "Sickness and Disease on the Wisconsin Frontier" (master's thesis, University of

Wisconsin, 1959); "Health in the Upper Mississippi River Valley, 1820 to 1861" (doctoral dissertation, University of Wisconsin, 1963); and a series of articles on "Disease and Sickness on the Wisconsin Frontier," dealing with malaria, cholera, smallpox, and other diseases, in *WMH*, 43 (Winter, 1959–1960–Summer, 1960), 83–96, 203–220, 253–263. Reform movements are presented in Joanne J. Brownsword, "Good Templars in Wisconsin, 1854–1880" (master's thesis, University of Wisconsin, 1960); Frank L. Byrne, "Cold Water Crusade: The Ante-Bellum Wisconsin Temperance Movement" (master's thesis, University of Wisconsin, 1951); and Lawrence L. Graves, "The Wisconsin Woman Suffrage Movement, 1846–1920" (doctoral dissertation, University of Wisconsin, 1954).

Various uses of leisure are described in Lillian Krueger, "Social Life in Wisconsin: Pre-Territorial through the Mid-Sixties," in *WMH*, 22 (December, 1938–June, 1939), 156–175, 312–328, 396–426. Art in one form or another figures in Richard W. E. Perrin, "Greek Revival Moves Westward: The Classic Mold in Wisconsin," in *WMH*, 45 (Spring, 1962), 199–202, and his book, *The Architecture of Wisconsin* (Madison, 1967); John O. Holzhueter, "The Capitol Fence of 1872: A Footnote to Wisconsin Architectural History," in *WMH*, 53 (Summer, 1970), 243–255; Alice E. Smith, "The Fox River Valley in Paintings," in *WMH*, 51 (Winter, 1967–1968), 139–154; J. J. Schlicher, "Hans Balatka and the Milwaukee Musical Society," in *WMH*, 27 (September, 1943), 40–55, and "The Milwaukee Musical Society in Time of Stress," in *WMH*, 27 (December, 1943), 176–193; and A. C. Bennett, "A Wisconsin Pioneer in Photography," in *WMH*, 22 (March, 1939), 268–279. John C. Colson discusses "The Public Library Movement in Wisconsin, 1836–1900" (doctoral dissertation, University of Chicago, 1973).

Aspects of social life are revealed in a number of biographical and autobiographical writings. Among the more interesting of these are the *Life Story of Rasmus B. Anderson, Written by Himself*, assisted by Albert O. Barton (Madison, 1915); Lloyd Hustvedt, *Rasmus Bjørn Anderson, Pioneer Scholar* (Northfield, Minnesota, 1966); Fredrika Bremer, *The Homes of the New World: Impressions of America* (2 vols., New York, 1864, 1868), an account of her travels, which took her to Wisconsin in 1850; Albert O. Barton, "Ole Bull and His Wisconsin Contacts," in *WMH*, 7 (June, 1924), 417–444; George Esser, *Memoirs of My Life: An Autobiography*, translated from the German by Hermann Eisner (n.p., [1953]), a pamphlet in the SHSW; Hamlin Garland, *A Son of the Middle Border* (New York, 1917); Theodore C. Blegen, "Colonel Hans

Christian Heg," in *WMH*, 4 (December, 1920), 140–165; *Autobiography of Roujet D. Marshall, Justice of the Supreme Court of the State of Wisconsin, 1895–1918,* edited by Gilson D. Glasier (2 vols., Madison, 1923, 1931); John Muir, *The Story of My Boyhood and Youth* (Madison, 1965); Melissa Brown, "The Jabez Brown Twins: A Family Portrait," in *WMH*, 30 (September–December, 1946), 39–58, 198–224; Rose Schuster Taylor, "Peter Schuster, Dane County Farmer," in *WMH*, 28–29 (March–September, 1945), 28: 277–289, 431–454; 29: 72–84; Oscar Hallam, "Bloomfield and Number Five: The American Way of Life in a Wisconsin Rural Community in the 70s, as Seen by a Small Boy" [1944], an unpublished manuscript in the SHSW; *A Pioneer in Northwest America, 1841– 1858: The Memoirs of Gustaf Unonius,* edited by Nils Olsson and translated by Jonas O. Backlund (2 vols., Minneapolis, [1950, 1960]); and *America in the Forties: The Letters of Ole Munch Raeder,* reports of his travels, 1847–1848, edited and translated by Gunnar J. Malmin (Minneapolis, 1929). Other correspondence bearing on social life is to be found in *An English Settler in Pioneer Wisconsin: The Letters of Edwin Bottomley, 1842–1850,* edited by Milo M. Quaife (Madison, 1918); Alfred O. Erickson, "Scandinavia, Wisconsin," in *Norwegian-American Studies and Records,* 15 (1949), 185–209; *The Strange American Way: Letters of Caja Munch from Wiota, Wisconsin, 1855–1859, with an American Adventure, Excerpts from "Vita Mea" an Autobiography Written in 1903 for His Children by Johan Storm Munch, and with an essay, Social Class and Acculturation by Peter A. Munch,* translated by Helene Munch and Peter A. Munch (Carbondale, Illinois, [1970]); *Intimate Letters of Carl Schurz, 1841–1869,* edited and translated by Joseph Schafer (Madison, 1928); *Dutch Immigrant Memoirs and Related Writings,* edited by Henry S. Lucas (2 vols., Assen, Netherlands, 1955); and "Norwegians Become Americans," edited and translated by Beulah Folkedahl, in *Norwegian-American Studies,* 21 (1962), 95–135. An interesting collection of anecdotes and descriptions is Lillian Krueger's small volume, *Motherhood on the Wisconsin Frontier* (Madison, 1951).

The federal census reports offer various social statistics on such things as nativity, age, literacy, occupations, churches, libraries, and mortality and its causes. See the *Seventh Census of the United States, 1850,* and the additional volume for that year on *Mortality Statistics; the Eighth Census of the United States: Population;* and the *Ninth Census of the United States: Volume I, Volume II,* and *Volume IV.*

GOVERNMENT AND ITS FUNCTIONS

State and local government receive considerable attention, of course, in local histories and in other general works. Monographs dealing with specific aspects of the subject include the following: Chester C. Brown, "A Comparative Study of Constitutional Development in the Old Northwest, 1847–1875" (master's thesis, University of Wisconsin, 1937); Hollis W. Barber, "Development of Some of the Administrative Departments of the Government of Wisconsin from 1850 to 1930" (doctoral dissertation, University of Wisconsin, 1935); Oliver D. Weeks, "The Development of County Government in Wisconsin" (doctoral dissertation, University of Wisconsin, 1924); Wisconsin Historical Records Survey of the Work Projects Administration, *Origin and Legislative History of County Boundaries in Wisconsin* (mimeographed, Madison, 1942); and George S. Wehrwein, "County Government in Wisconsin," in the *Wisconsin Blue Book, 1933*, pp. 85–101. Donald A. De Bats, "The Political Sieve: A Study of Green Bay, Wisconsin, 1854–1880" (master's thesis, University of Wisconsin, 1967), analyzes the governing elites of that city.

Education, the most expensive function of state and local government, is recorded in all its aspects, public and private, scholastic and collegiate, in a massive tome, *The Columbian History of Education in Wisconsin,* edited by John W. Stearns (Milwaukee, 1893). William F. Allen and David E. Spencer furnish a brief, overall treatment in *Higher Education in Wisconsin* (Washington, D.C., 1889). Merle Curti and Vernon Carstensen are authors of the standard account of the university at Madison, *The University of Wisconsin: A History, 1848–1925* (2 vols., Madison, 1949). Wilbur H. Glover recounts the development of an important unit of the university in *Farm and College: The College of Agriculture of the University of Wisconsin: A History* (Madison, 1952). Mrs. William F. Allen, widow of a distinguished professor, reminisces about "The University of Wisconsin Soon After the Civil War," in *WMH*, 7 (September, 1923), 20–29. An institution that came to share the campus of the university is the dominant theme of William B. Hesseltine's "Lyman Copeland Draper, 1815–1891," in *WMH*, 35 (Spring, 1952), 163–166, 231–234, and his *Pioneer's Mission: The Story of Lyman Copeland Draper* (Madison, 1954); and the same institution is the subject of Clifford L. Lord and Carl Ubbelohde, *Clio's Servant: The State Historical Society of Wisconsin, 1846–1954* (Madison, 1967). In "The Rise of the Public Normal School System in Wisconsin" (doctoral dissertation,

University of Wisconsin, 1953), William H. Herrmann relates the beginnings of a system that was eventually to be merged with the University of Wisconsin. John Lankford discusses the origin of the college at River Falls in " 'Culture and Business': The Founding of the Fourth State Normal School at River Falls," in *WMH*, 47 (Autumn, 1963), 26–34. Recent institutional histories include Walker D. Wyman *et al., History of the Wisconsin State Universities,* ed. Walker D. Wyman (River Falls, Wisconsin, 1968); Richard D. Gamble, *From Academy to University, 1866–1966: A History of Wisconsin State University, Platteville, Wisconsin* (Platteville, 1966); and James T. King and Walker D. Wyman, *Centennial History: The University of Wisconsin—River Falls, 1874–1974* (River Falls, Wisconsin, 1975).

Leading private institutions of higher learning are sketched in Dorothy Ganfield Fowler, "Wisconsin's Carroll College," in *WMH*, 29 (December, 1945), 137–156; Louise P. Kellogg, "The Origins of Milwaukee College," in *WMH*, 9 (July, 1926), 386–408; Samuel M. Pedrick, "Early History of Ripon College, 1850–1864," in *WMH*, 8 (September, 1924), 22–37; Samuel Plantz, "Lawrence College," in *WMH*, 6 (December, 1922), 146–164; Robert K. Richardson, "The Mindedness of the Early Faculty of Beloit College," in *WMH*, 19 (September, 1935), 32–70, and " 'Yale of the West'—A Study of Academic Sectionalism," in *WMH*, 36 (Summer, 1953), 258–261, 280–283; and Grace N. Kieckhefer, *The History of Milwaukee–Downer College, 1851–1951* (Milwaukee, [1950]), and "Milwaukee–Downer College Rediscovers Its Past," in *WMH*, 34 (Summer, 1951), 210–214, 241–242.

With respect to the early public schools, the best general account is Lloyd P. Jorgenson, *The Founding of Public Education in Wisconsin* (Madison, 1956), summarized in "The Origins of Public Education in Wisconsin," in *WMH*, 33 (September, 1949), 15–27. But also still useful is Conrad E. Patzer, *Public Education in Wisconsin* (Madison, 1924), which deals with higher as well as primary and secondary education. The *Annual Reports* of the Wisconsin Superintendent of Public Instruction contain useful statistical information as well as reports from county superintendents. Alan W. Brownsword relates education to religion and morality in "Educational Ideas in Early Wisconsin, 1848–1870" (master's thesis, University of Wisconsin, 1958); and William W. Updegrove discusses the issue of Bible-reading in the public schools in "Bibles and Brickbats: Religious Conflict in Wisconsin's Public School System during the Nineteenth Century" (master's thesis, University of Wisconsin, 1970). Helen F. Patton concerns herself not only

with schoolhouses but with practically every aspect of school life
except the curriculum in "Public School Architecture in Racine,
Wisconsin, and Vicinity from the Time of Settlement to 1900"
(doctoral dissertation, University of Wisconsin, 1965). Joseph Schafer explains the "Genesis of Wisconsin's Free High School System,"
in *WMH*, 10 (December, 1926), 123–149. Jabez Brown's diaries,
in the Jabez Brown Papers, record his experiences as a teacher
and principal in Juneau, Sauk, and Vernon counties. A Kenosha
woman recalls life both as a pupil and as a teacher in the "Memoirs
of Mary D. Bradford," in *WMH*, 14–16 (September, 1930–September, 1932), 14: 3–47, 133–181, 283–313, 354–402; 15: 47–68, 182–218,
297–349, 446–494; and 16: 47–84, and reprinted with an additional
three chapters and an appendix as the *Memoirs of Mary D. Bradford: Autobiographical and Historical Reminiscences of Education In Wisconsin, Through Progressive Service From Rural School
Teaching to City Superintendent* (Evansville, Wisconsin, 1932).

Private and parochial schools receive attention in the following:
J. Q. Emery, "Albion Academy," in *WMH*, 7 (March, 1924), 301–
321; Beulah Folkedahl, "Marshall Academy: A History," in *WMH*,
47 (Spring, 1964), 249–260; Josiah L. Pickard, "Experiences of a
Wisconsin Educator," the reminiscences of a former principal of
Platteville Academy, in *WMH*, 7 (December, 1923), 125–147; Elizabeth Jenkins, "How the Kindergarten Found Its Way to America,"
in *WMH*, 14 (September, 1930), 48–62; Mary Josine Prindaville,
"History of Catholic Education in [the] Diocese of Green Bay"
(master's thesis, Catholic University of America, 1952); Arlow W.
Andersen, "Knud Langeland: Pioneer Editor," in *Norwegian-
American Studies and Records*, 14 (1944), 122–138, concerning a
controversy over Lutheran parochial schools; and Arthur C. Paul-
son and Kenneth Bjørk, eds. and trans., "A School and Language
Controversy in 1858: A Documentary Study," *ibid.*, 10 (1938), 76–
106.

On welfare and correctional institutions, see Donald J. Berthrong, "Social Legislation in Wisconsin, 1836–1900" (doctoral
dissertation, University of Wisconsin, 1951); Virgil E. Long, "State
Supervision and Control of Welfare Agencies and Institutions in
Wisconsin: Processes and Structures" (doctoral dissertation, University of Wisconsin, 1944); and Miriam Z. Langsam, "The Nineteenth Century Wisconsin Criminal: Ideologies and Institutions"
(doctoral dissertation, University of Wisconsin, 1967). Much useful information can be found in the *Annual Reports* of the Wisconsin Board of Charities and Reform. The best history of the
Wisconsin Soldiers' Orphans' Home is in the Board of Trustees'

Final Report, 1894. Jerry M. Cooper, "The Wisconsin Militia, 1832–1900" (master's thesis, University of Wisconsin, 1968), describes what was in part a law-enforcement agency. Carrie Cropley, "The Case of John McCaffary," in *WMH*, 35 (Summer, 1952), 281–288, tells of the murder and execution that led eventually to the abolition of capital punishment. Ira C. Jenks, *Trial of David F. Mayberry, for the Murder of Andrew Alger, Before the Rock Co. Circuit Court, Judge Doolittle Presiding, July 10th and 11th, 1855, Containing the Arguments of the Attorneys, and a Full and Correct Account of His Death by a Mob* (Janesville, Wisconsin, 1855), is a full contemporary account of the Mayberry lynching.

PARTY POLITICS

The SHSW has the manuscript papers of a number of persons involved in the politics of the era. The richest collections are the papers of James R. Doolittle, Lucius Fairchild, Elisha Keyes, and George H. Paul, a Kenosha-Milwaukee newspaperman and Democratic politician. Also useful are the papers of Cadwallader C. Washburn; Washburn's one-time business partner, Cyrus Woodman; Timothy O. Howe; Horace A. Tenney, a Madison Republican; John H. Tweedy, a Milwaukee Whig-Republican; and Charles D. Robinson, a Green Bay newspaperman. County-level election totals may be found in the *Wisconsin Blue Books*; in James R. Donoghue, *How Wisconsin Voted, 1848–1972* (Madison, 1974); in Series 140, 211, 213, and 214 in the WSA, as cited in the Note on the Maps; and in the tabular statements of the State Board of Canvassers as published in such newspapers as the *Wisconsin State Journal* and the Milwaukee *Sentinel*.

Alexander M. Thomson was active in politics during the period 1848–1873, and he included many of his personal reminiscences in *A Political History of Wisconsin* (Milwaukee, 1900), which is especially interesting for its gossipy details. Parker M. Reed's *The Bench and Bar of Wisconsin: History and Biography* (Milwaukee, 1882), contains a good deal of political as well as judicial and legal history.

Politicians, along with other important figures of the time, may be traced in the *Dictionary of Wisconsin Biography*. Relevant biographical studies include the following: E. Bruce Thompson, *Matthew Hale Carpenter: Webster of the West* (Madison, 1954); Herman J. Deutsch, "Matt Carpenter: A Senator of the Seventies," in the *Proceedings of the Pacific Coast Branch, American Historical Association*, 1929, pp. 187–199; Biagino M. Marone, "Senator

James Rood Doolittle and the Struggle Against Radicalism, 1857–1866" (master's thesis, Marquette University, 1955); James L. Sellers, "James R. Doolittle," in *WMH*, 17–18 (December, 1933–December, 1934), 17: 168–178, 277–306, 393–401; 18: 20–41, 178–187; Sam Ross, *The Empty Sleeve: A Biography of Lucius Fairchild* (Madison, 1964); Nils P. Haugen, "Pioneer and Political Reminiscences," originally published in the *WMH*, 11–13 (December, 1927–December, 1929), 11: 121–152, 269–300, 395–436; 12: 41–57, 176–191, 271–293, 379–402; 13: 121–130, and as a book bearing the same title (Madison, n.d.); Albert Erlebacher, "Senator Timothy Otis Howe and His Influence on Reconstruction, 1861–1877" (master's thesis, Marquette University, 1956); William H. Russell, "Timothy O. Howe, Stalwart Republican," in *WMH*, 35 (Winter, 1951), 90–99; Richard W. Hantke, "The Life of Elisha Williams Keyes" (doctoral dissertation, University of Wisconsin, 1942), and two articles, "Elisha W. Keyes, the Bismarck of Western Politics," in *WMH*, 31 (September, 1947), 29–41, and "Elisha W. Keyes and the Radical Republicans," in *WMH*, 35 (Spring, 1952), 203–208; Alfons J. Beitzinger, *Edward G. Ryan: Lion of the Law* (Madison, 1960), and "The Father of Copperheadism in Wisconsin," in *WMH*, 39 (Autumn, 1955), 17–25; Richard N. Current, *Pine Logs and Politics: A Life of Philetus Sawyer, 1816–1900* (Madison, 1950); Chester V. Easum, *The Americanization of Carl Schurz* (Chicago, 1929); Joseph Schafer, *Carl Schurz, Militant Liberal* (Evansville, Wisconsin, 1930), and Schafer, ed., *Intimate Letters of Carl Schurz*; Horace S. Merrill, *William Freeman Vilas: Doctrinaire Democrat* (Madison, 1954); and Merle Curti, "Isaac P. Walker: Reformer in Mid-Century Politics," in *WMH*, 34 (Autumn, 1950), 3–6, 58–62.

Political journalism is the subject of Donald E. Rasmussen, "Wisconsin Editors and the Civil War: A Study of the Reaction of Wisconsin Editors to the Major Controversial Issues of the Civil War" (master's thesis, University of Wisconsin, 1952). Particular journalists are treated in the following: Joseph C. Cover, "Memoirs of a Pioneer County Editor," in *WMH*, 11 (March, 1928), 247–268; Richard N. Current, "The First Newspaperman in Oshkosh [James Densmore]," in *WMH*, 30 (June, 1947), 408–422; four articles by Frank Klement, " 'Brick' Pomeroy: Copperhead and Curmudgeon," in *WMH*, 35 (Winter, 1951), 106–113, 156–157, "Deuster as a Democratic Dissenter During the Civil War: A Case Study of a Copperhead," in the *Transactions of the Wisconsin Academy of Sciences, Arts and Letters*, 55 (1966), 21–38, "Milwaukee Critics of Lincoln," in the *Historical Messenger*, 16 (September, 1960), 2–7, and "A Small-Town Editor Criticizes Lincoln: A Study in Editorial

Abuse," in the *Lincoln Herald,* 54 (Summer, 1952), 27–32, 60; Curtis W. Miller, "Rufus King and the Problems of His Era" (master's thesis, Marquette University, 1963); and J. J. Schlicher, "Bernhard Domschçke," in *WMH,* 29 (March–June, 1946), 319–332, 435–456. Business and political aspects of journalism are revealed in John O. Holzhueter, "The Wisconsin Editors and Publishers Association, 1853–1877" (master's thesis, University of Wisconsin, 1966).

Journalism is discussed in relation to the political participation of an ethnic group in the following: Olaf H. Spetland, "The Americanizing Aspects of the Norwegian Language Press in Wisconsin, 1847–1865, with Particular Reference to Its Role in Local, State, and National Politics" (master's thesis, University of Wisconsin, 1960); Theodore C. Blegen, "The Early Norwegian Press in America," in the *Minnesota History Bulletin,* 3 (November, 1920), 506–518; Arlow W. Andersen, "Venturing into Politics: The Norwegian-American Press of the 1850's," in *WMH,* 32 (September, 1948), 58–79, and "Knud Langeland: Pioneer Editor," in *Norwegian-American Studies and Records,* 14 (1944), 122–138; and Carl F. Solberg, "Reminiscences of a Pioneer Editor," ed. Albert O. Barton, *ibid.,* 1 (1926), 134–144. Participation by another group is the subject of Ernest Bruncken, "The Political Activity of Wisconsin Germans, 1854–1860," in the *SHSW Proceedings,* 1901, pp. 190–211; Joseph Schafer, "Who Elected Lincoln?" in the *American Historical Review,* 47 (October, 1941), 51–63; and Andreas Dorpalen, "The German Element and the Issues of the Civil War," in the *Mississippi Valley Historical Review,* 29 (June, 1942), 55–76. Paul Kleppner provides useful insights for the study of ethnicity and politics in *The Cross of Culture: A Social Analysis of Midwestern Politics, 1850–1900* (New York, 1970). Kleppner includes the politics of Wisconsin, Michigan, and Ohio. Despite the dates in his title, he is concerned almost exclusively with the period after 1880, but his basic generalizations presumably apply to the earlier years also.

Among period studies, a remarkable piece of work is Robert R. Flatley's "The Wisconsin Congressional Delegation from Statehood to Secession, 1848–1861," a bachelor's thesis (University of Wisconsin, 1951) that puts to shame many a master's thesis and compares well with some doctoral dissertations. The following deal with the emergence of slavery as an issue: Clinton M. Fair, "Internal Improvements and the Sectional Controversy" (master's thesis, University of Wisconsin, 1937); William J. Maher, "The Antislavery Movement in Milwaukee and Vicinity, 1842–1860" (master's thesis, Marquette University, 1954); Theodore C. Smith, "The

Free Soil Party in Wisconsin," in the *SHSW Proceedings*, 1894, pp. 97–162, and *The Liberty and Free Soil Parties in the Northwest* (New York, 1897); and Frederick J. Blue, "The Free Soil Party and the Election of 1848 in Wisconsin" (master's thesis, University of Wisconsin, 1962), and *The Free Soilers: Third Party Politics, 1848–54* (Urbana, 1973).

The rise of the Republican party and the problems of the new organization get attention in Aaron M. Boom, "The Development of Sectional Attitudes in Wisconsin, 1848–1861" (doctoral dissertation, University of Chicago, 1948); Richard L. Hanneman, "The First Republican Campaign in Wisconsin, 1854" (master's thesis, University of Wisconsin, 1966); Joseph Schafer, "Know-Nothingism in Wisconsin," in *WMH*, 8 (September, 1924), 3–21, and "Prohibition in Early Wisconsin," in *WMH*, 8 (March, 1925), 281–299; and Frank L. Byrne, "Maine Law Versus Lager Beer: A Dilemma of Wisconsin's Young Republican Party," in *WMH*, 42 (Winter, 1958–1959), 115–120. Difficulties of the Democrats are treated in John B. Sanborn, "The Impeachment of Levi Hubbell," in the *SHSW Proceedings*, 1905, pp. 194–213; *The Trial in the Supreme Court, of the Information in the Nature of a Quo Warranto Filed by the Attorney General, on the Relation of Coles Bashford vs. Wm. A. Barstow, Contesting the Right to the Office of Governor of Wisconsin* (Madison, 1856), the official report of the disputed gubernatorial election of 1855 and the litigation arising from it; and Kenneth W. Duckett, "Politics, Brown Bread, and Bologna," in *WMH*, 36 (Spring, 1953), 178–181, 202, 215–217, concerning the railroad land-grant scandal of 1856. The intensification of sectionalism in the prewar years is the theme of Robert N. Kroncke, "Race and Politics in Wisconsin, 1854–1865" (master's thesis, University of Wisconsin, 1968); James L. Sellers, "Republicanism and State Rights in Wisconsin," in the *Mississippi Valley Historical Review*, 17 (September, 1930), 213–229; Alfons J. Beitzinger, "Federal Law Enforcement and the Booth Cases," in the *Marquette Law Review*, 41 (Summer, 1957), 7–32; and Joseph Schafer, "Stormy Days in Court—The Booth Case," in *WMH*, 20 (September, 1936), 89–110. On another Booth case, see *The Trial of Sherman M. Booth for Seduction: Evidence and Summing up of Counsel in the Case of the State versus S. M. Booth, for Seducing Caroline N. Cook* (Milwaukee, 1859). The approach of secession and war is reflected in William B. Hesseltine, "The Pryor-Potter Duel," in *WMH*, 27 (June, 1944), 400–409; and Robert L. Schwab, "Wisconsin and Compromise Efforts on the Eve of the Civil War" (master's thesis, Marquette University, 1957).

On wartime politics, see William B. Hesseltine, *Lincoln and the War Governors* (New York, 1948), and "Lincoln's Problems in Wisconsin," in *WMH*, 48 (Spring, 1965), 187–195; Jacque Voegeli, "The Northwest and the Race Issue, 1861–1862," in the *Mississippi Valley Historical Review*, 50 (September, 1963), 235–251, and *Free But Not Equal: The Midwest and the Negro During the Civil War* (Chicago, 1967); and the following works by Frank Klement: "The Soldier Vote in Wisconsin During the Civil War," in *WMH*, 28 (September, 1944), 37–47; "Copperheads and Copperheadism in Wisconsin: Democratic Opposition to the Lincoln Administration," in *WMH*, 42 (Spring, 1959), 182–188; *The Copperheads in the Middle West* (Chicago, 1960); and "Wisconsin and the Re-Election of Lincoln in 1864: A Chapter of Civil War History," in the *Historical Messenger*, 22 (March, 1966), 20–42.

Reconstruction politics is the subject of Joseph R. Conlin, "The Politics of Reconstruction in Wisconsin, 1865–1866" (master's thesis, University of Wisconsin, 1962); Leslie H. Fishel, Jr., "Wisconsin and Negro Suffrage," in *WMH*, 46 (Spring, 1963), 180–196; Karen J. Wise, "Wisconsin and the Fourteenth Amendment, 1865–1867" (master's thesis, University of Wisconsin, 1966); Helen Jenson, "Internal Improvements and Wisconsin Republicanism, 1865–1873" (master's thesis, University of Wisconsin, 1937); Helen J. Williams and Harry Williams, "Wisconsin Republicans and Reconstruction, 1865–70," in *WMH, 23* (September, 1939), 17–39; Claude Albright, "Dixon, Doolittle, and Norton: The Forgotten Republican Votes," in *WMH*, 59 (Winter, 1975–1976), 91–100; Louise P. Kellogg, "The Senatorial Election of 1869," in *WMH*, 1 (June, 1918), 418–420; David H. Overy, Jr., "The Wisconsin Carpetbagger: A Group Portrait," in *WMH*, 44 (Autumn, 1960), 15–49; and Richard N. Current, *Three Carpetbag Governors* (Baton Rouge, 1967). The overthrow of the Republicans in 1873 and the events leading up to it are ably discussed in two series of articles by Herman J. Deutsch: "Yankee-Teuton Rivalry in Wisconsin Politics of the Seventies," in *WMH*, 14 (March–June, 1931), 262–282, 403–418; and "Disintegrating Forces in Wisconsin Politics of the Early Seventies," in *WMH*, 15 (December, 1931–June, 1932), 168–181, 391–411. Dale E. Treleven shows political discontent arising from business interests as well as agricultural interests in "Railroads, Elevators, and Grain Dealers: The Genesis of Anti-monopolism in Milwaukee," in *WMH*, 52 (Spring, 1969), 205–222. Graham A. Cosmas examines the opposition to the Republicans in "The Democracy in Search of Issues: The Wisconsin Reform Party, 1873–1877," in *WMH*, 46 (Winter, 1962–1963), 93–108. Railroad

regulation in Wisconsin is placed in the nationwide setting in
George H. Miller, *Railroads and the Granger Laws* (Madison,
1971). Aspects of reconstruction politics are touched upon in Horace
S. Merrill, *Bourbon Democracy of the Middle West, 1865–1896*
(Baton Rouge, 1953); and Mary R. Dearing, *Veterans in Politics:
The Story of the G.A.R.* (Baton Rouge, 1952).

The Civil War

The starting point for any study of the Civil War is the collection commonly cited as the *Official Records* and bearing the full
title *The War of the Rebellion: A Compilation of the Official
Records of the Union and Confederate Armies* (128 vols., Washington, D.C., 1880–1901). William G. Paul, comp., *Wisconsin's Civil
War Archives* (Madison, 1965), is a guide to manuscript sources
on Wisconsin's role. Of particular value is the manuscript Muster
and Descriptive Roll for Wisconsin regiments, Series 1144, Records
of the Adjutant General, in the WSA. Published sources are in
Reuben G. Thwaites, ed., *Civil War Messages and Proclamations
of Wisconsin War Governors* (Madison, 1912); and Wisconsin Commission on Civil War Records, *Records and Sketches of Military
Organizations, Population, Legislation, Election and Other Statistics Relating to Wisconsin in the Period of the Civil War* (Madison, 1914). A reference work also sponsored by the Commission
on Civil War Records is *Wisconsin Losses in the Civil War: A
List of the Names of Wisconsin Soldiers Killed in Action, Mortally
Wounded or Dying From Other Causes in the Civil War, Arranged
According to Organization, and Also in a Separate Alphabetical
List* (Madison, 1915). Another listing is *List of Persons, Residents
of the State of Wisconsin, Reported as Deserters from the Military
and Naval Service of the United States* (Madison, 1868), bound at
the SHSW in *Wisconsin Miscellaneous Pamphlets*, vol. 17. Two
fairly full and detailed over-all accounts are William D. Love,
*Wisconsin in the War of the Rebellion; A History of All Regiments
and Batteries the State Has Sent to the Field, And deeds of her
Citizens, Governors and other Military Officers, and State and
National Legislators to suppress the Rebellion* (Chicago, 1866);
and Edwin B. Quiner, *The Military History of Wisconsin: A Record of the Civil and Military Patriotism of the State in the War
for the Union, With a History of the Campaigns in which Wisconsin Soldiers have been Conspicuous—Regimental Histories—
Sketches of Distinguished Officers—the Roll of the Illustrious Dead
—Movements of the Legislature and State Officers, etc.* (Chicago,

1866). A much briefer but very useful survey is Frank L. Klement, *Wisconsin and the Civil War* (Madison, 1963).

The first response is told in Walter S. Glazer, "Wisconsin Goes to War, April, 1861" (master's thesis, University of Wisconsin, 1963); and in Carl R. Fish, "The Raising of the Wisconsin Volunteers, 1861," in *Military Historian and Economist*, 1 (1916), 258–273. The problems of the governors in raising men and money are shown in Robert H. Jacobi, "Wisconsin Civil War Governors" (master's thesis, University of Wisconsin, 1948); P. Marcus Schmidt, "The Dependence of the Lincoln Administration on the Northwestern Governors" (master's thesis, University of Wisconsin, 1936); Spencer C. Scott, "The Financial Effects of the Civil War on the State of Wisconsin" (master's thesis, University of Wisconsin, 1939); James W. Shannon, "State Aid to Wisconsin Soldiers and Their Families: Financial and Humanitarian" (master's thesis, University of Wisconsin, 1915); and Carl R. Fish, "Social Relief in the Northwest During the Civil War," in the *American Historical Review*, 22 (January, 1917), 309–324. Carolyn J. Mattern portrays soldier training and camp life in "Soldiers When They Go: The Story of Camp Randall, 1861–1865" (master's thesis, University of Wisconsin, 1968). Ethel A. Hurn recounts the role of *Wisconsin Women in the War Between the States* (Madison, 1911); while a personal account is Mary A. Livermore's *My Story of the War: A Woman's Narrative of Four Years Personal Experience as Nurse in the Union Army, and in Relief Work at Home, in Hospitals, Camps, and at the Front, During the War of the Rebellion, With Anecdotes, Pathetic Incidents, and Thrilling Reminiscenses Portraying the Lights and Shadows of Hospital Life and the Sanitary Service of the War* (Hartford, Connecticut, 1889). The following throw light on the draft and the resistance to it: Fred A. Shannon, *The Organization and Administration of the Union Army, 1861–1865* (2 vols., Cleveland, 1928); Peter T. Harstad, ed., "A Civil War Medical Examiner: The Report of Dr. Horace O. Crane," in *WMH*, 48 (Spring, 1965), 222–231; Linn I. Schoonover, "A History of the Civil War Draft in Wisconsin" (master's thesis, University of Wisconsin, 1915); Lawrence H. Larsen, "Draft Riot in Wisconsin, 1862," in *Civil War History*, 7 (December, 1961), 421–427; Peter Leo Johnson, "Port Washington Draft Riot of 1862," in *Mid-America*, new series, 1 (January, 1930), 212–222; William W. Winterbotham, "Memoirs of a Civil War Sleuth," in *WMH*, 19 (December, 1935–March, 1936), 131–160, 276–293; Mary D. Meyer, "The Germans in Wisconsin and the Civil War: Their Attitude Toward the Union, the Republicans, Slavery, and Lincoln" (master's thesis, Catholic University of America, 1937); and Ella Lonn, *Foreigners in the Union Army and Navy* (Baton Rouge, 1951). Milo M. Quaife relates the Indian scare in "The Panic of 1862 in Wisconsin," in *WMH*, 4 (December, 1920), 166–195. Charles M. Oehler recounts *The Great Sioux Uprising* (New York, 1959). Edward Noyes shows the role of "The Negro in Wisconsin's Civil War Effort," in the *Lincoln Herald*, 69 (Summer, 1967), 70–82. Jackson R. Horton brings the boys home in "The Demobilization of Wisconsin Troops after the Civil War" (master's thesis, University of Wisconsin, 1952).

Campaigns and battles are recounted in regimental and company histories, among them the following: Edwin E. Bryant, *History of the Third Regiment of Wisconsin Veteran Volunteer Infantry, 1861–1865* (Madison, 1891); Julian W. Hinkley, *A Narrative of Service with the Third Wisconsin Infantry* (Madison, 1912); Evan R. Jones, *Four Years in the Army of the Potomac: A Soldier's Recollections* (London, 1882), an account of the Fifth Regiment; Rufus R. Dawes, *Service with the Sixth Wisconsin Volunteers*, ed. Alan T. Nolan (Madison, 1962); Philip Cheek and Mair Pointon, *History of the Sauk County Riflemen, Known as Company "A," Sixth Wisconsin Veteran Volunteer Infantry, 1861–1865* (Madison, 1909); [John M. Williams], *"The Eagle Regiment," 8th Wis. Inf'ty Vols., A Sketch of Its Marches, Battles and Campaigns, From 1861 to 1865, With a Complete Regimental and Company Roster, And a Few Portraits and Sketches of Its Officers and Commanders, By a "Non-Vet" of Co. "H."* (Belleville, Wisconsin, 1890); David McLain, "The Story of Old Abe," in *WMH*, 8 (June, 1925), 407–414, regarding Company C of the Eighth and the company's mascot; Frank A. Flower, *Old Abe, the Eighth Wisconsin War Eagle, A Full Account of his Capture and Enlistment, Exploits in War and Honorable as well as Useful Career in Peace* (Madison, 1885); [Hosea W. Rood], *Story of the Service of Company E, and of the Twelfth Wisconsin Regiment, Veteran Volunteer Infantry, in the War of the Rebellion* (Milwaukee, 1893); James M. Aubery, *The Thirty-Sixth Wisconsin Volunteer Infantry, 1st Brigade, 2d Division, 2d Army Corps, Army of the Potomac* [Milwaukee, 1900]; and Robert C. Eden, *The Sword and the Gun, A History of the 37th Wis. Volunteer Infantry, From Its First Organization to Its Final Muster Out* (Madison, 1865).

A famous unit that included three Wisconsin regiments is the subject of Alan T. Nolan's well-researched and well-written book, *The Iron Brigade: A Military History* (New York, 1961). Stanley E. Lathrop analyzes the personnel of a cavalry regiment in "Vital

Statistics of the First Wisconsin Cavalry in the Civil War," in *WMH,* 5 (March, 1922), 296–300. Michael H. Fitch retells *The Chattanooga Campaign, With Especial Reference to Wisconsin's Participation Therein* (Madison, 1911). C. George Extrom presents the career of a Wisconsin war hero in "General Joseph Bailey and the Red River Dam" (an unpublished paper, a sound recording of which is at the SHSW, which Extrom read before the Madison Civil War Round Table in 1965, and of which he kindly lent the present author a copy). The following are personal accounts of war experiences: George S. Bradley, *The Star Corps; Or, Notes of an Army Chaplain, During Sherman's Famous "March to the Sea"* (Milwaukee, 1865); John A. Kellogg, *Capture and Escape: A Narrative of Army and Prison Life* (Madison, 1908); Jenkin L. Jones, *An Artilleryman's Diary* (Madison, 1914); Adelia C. Lyon, comp., *Reminiscences of the Civil War* (San Jose, California, 1907); and Henry E. Whipple, *The Diary of a Private Soldier* (Waterloo, Wisconsin, 1906).

Soldier life is best revealed in letters home. Edwin B. Quiner collected clippings from newspapers printing soldier letters; these are arranged by regiments and are indexed in ten scrapbook volumes under the title "Correspondence of Wisconsin Volunteers, 1861–1865," in the SHSW library. Elizabeth A. Bascom used manuscript collections in writing "Why They Fought: A Comparative View of the Impact of the Civil War on Five Wisconsin Soldiers, with Selections from Their War Letters" (master's thesis, University of Wisconsin, 1941). Bell I. Wiley quotes from many Wisconsin soldier letters in *The Life of Billy Yank: The Common Soldier of the Union* (Indianapolis, 1952). Wisconsin soldier letters have also been published in the following: Stephen E. Ambrose, ed., *A Wisconsin Boy in Dixie: The Selected Letters of James K. Newton* (Madison, 1961); Theodore C. Blegen, ed., *The Civil War Letters of Colonel Hans Christian Heg* (Northfield, Minnesota, 1936); Frank L. Byrne, ed., *The View from Headquarters: Civil War Letters of Harvey Reid* (Madison, 1965); Frank L. Byrne and Andrew T. Weaver, eds., *Haskell of Gettysburg: His Life and Civil War Papers* (Madison, 1970); Elizabeth Eaton Hincks, *Undismayed: The Story of a Yankee Chaplain's Family in the Civil War* ([Chicago], 1952); Luther M. Kuhns, ed., "An Army Surgeon's Letters to His Wife," in the *Proceedings of the Mississippi Valley Historical Association,* 1913–1914, pp. 306–320; Daniel R. Porter, "The Colonel and the Private Go to War," in *WMH,* 42 (Winter, 1958–1959), 124–127; "Letters of a Badger Boy in Blue," in *WMH,* 4–5 (September, 1920–September, 1921), 4: 75–100, 208–217, 322–344,

431–456; 5: 63–98; Leo M. Kaiser, ed., "Civil War Letters of Charles W. Carr of the 21st Wisconsin Volunteers," in *WMH*, 43 (Summer, 1960), 264–272; R. G. Plumb, ed., "Letters of a Fifth Wisconsin Volunteer," in *WMH*, 3 (September, 1919), 52–83; Margaret Brobst Roth, ed., *Well, Mary: Civil War Letters of a Wisconsin Volunteer* (Madison, 1960); Henry L. Swint, ed., "With the First Wisconsin Cavalry, 1862–1865: The Letters of Peter J. Williamson," in *WMH*, 26 (March–June, 1943), 333–345, 433–448; and John O. Holzhueter, ed., "William Wallace's Civil War Letters: The Atlanta Campaign," in *WMH*, 57 (Autumn, 1973–Winter, 1973–1974), 28–59, 91–116.

INDEX

ABOUT THE AUTHOR

RICHARD N. CURRENT is University Distinguished Professor of History in the University of North Carolina at Greensboro. A native of Colorado, he was educated in the public schools of Colorado Springs and at Oberlin College, Tufts University, and the University of Wisconsin. As a student at the Madison campus and as a faculty member both there and at Lawrence University in Appleton, he has spent a good part of his life in Wisconsin. He has written two other books about Wisconsin's past, and is author of the Wisconsin volume in the Bicentennial State History series.

ABOUT THE BOOK

THE text was composed on the Linotype in Baskerville, a face designed by the English letter founder and printer John Baskerville (1706–1775). The book was printed by offset lithography on acid-free, all-sulphite book paper with a laid finish, specially manufactured for the *History of Wisconsin* by the Whiting-Plover Paper Company of Stevens Point, Wisconsin, a Division of the Nekoosa-Edwards Paper Company. It was bound in pyroxylin-impregnated Holliston Roxite linen.